MW00640517

This Book is Dedicated to
Rudolph Valentino's Godson

Robert Warren Ullman

1923-2005

Published by:
Viale Industria Pubblicazioni
Torino, Italy
viplibri@libero.it

First Edition Published in The United States of America by
The Rudolph Valentino Society, LLC., 2011.

Second Edition Published in 2013 by Vivace Edizioni, an imprint of
Viale Industria Pubblicazioni.

Special Edition Published in 2015 by Viale Industria Pubblicazioni.
Copyright 2015
by Evelyn Zumaya

The Moral Right of the Author has been Asserted

All rights reserved under international copyright conventions. No part
of this book may be reproduced or utilized in any form or by any
means, electronic or mechanical, including photocopying, recording,
or by any information storage and retrieval system, without
permission in writing from the author.

Opera protetta dalla legge del 22 Aprile 1941 n. 633 ("Protezione del
diritto d'autore e di altri diritti connessi al suo esercizio") e successive
modificazioni, e dal Titolo IX del Libro Quinto del Codice Civile
Italiano.
In deposito presso il SBN http://www.sbn.it/opacsbn/opac/iccu/free.jsp

ISBN: 9788890706394

Cover Design by Sepsispod@gmail.com

Author's Note

While writing *Affairs Valentino* in a narrative non-fiction style, I added minimal dialogue to construct the story line. Whenever possible, the dialogues cited are direct quotes. All court testimony is taken verbatim from court transcripts, which are on file with the State of California. Although I have excerpted some of these passages, I have not altered them in any way. As financial records are an important element of this story, I wish to add that dollar amounts should be multiplied by ten, an approximate monetary conversion, in order to understand their relevancy today.

I used two aliases to protect the identity of key characters, William Pelf and the Evanston Collector. I wish to clarify that Mr. Pelf never refused my request for interviews, but add that the Valentino family, through their family spokeswoman, did refuse my request to be interviewed for this publication.

With regard to the court records, one important point must be made. As Mr. Pelf expressed to me, anyone referencing those specific court documents missing from the L.A. County Hall of Records, incriminates themselves as having had them in their possession. I offer this as a warning, for this constitutes a felony in the State of California.

The Ullman family holds the exclusive copyright to the George Ullman memoir. Any unauthorized use of the Ullman memoir is strictly prohibited as it is protected by U.S. copyright laws which will be enforced.

I also wish to add that since the first publication of *Affairs Valentino* in 2011, several authors, bloggers and online sources have reported upon elements of this book which misrepresent my research with false statements. The issuing of lengthy passages and references from this book without proper attribution constitutes plagiarism. I ask readers to reference only this publication. I reissue *Affairs Valentino* to share the results of further research I have conducted. This new addition to this story is included exclusively in the *Postscript*.

Evelyn Zumaya
Turin
January 2015

"...A feature writer for *The Los Angeles Times* labeled Valentino as nothing more than the product of Hollywood creation. This, of course, is pure nonsense, because there really was something extraordinary that happened when Rudy was photographed in any role. He had magnetism in person, of course, but the camera revealed something deep and mysterious..... It might have been the reflection of his soul...."

George Ullman, *"The S. George Ullman Memoir"*

"He whom the Gods love, dies young."

Menander

... *Born Guglielmi !*

An Introduction
by
Chicca Guglielmi Morone

When I met Evelyn Zumaya, the author of this exceptional book, I confess I held all the reservations that the topic of Rudolph Valentino has brought into my life. I was not convinced of the necessity of a new publication regarding my distant relative, who more than eighty years after his death is still now, as he was, a target of useless gossip and monstrous lies which have resulted in an overall complete misunderstanding of his true essence.

I began reading this book with a certain detachment, but after a while I became involved on many levels by the lively narration, the broad panorama - even if romanticized - of the life of this actor in all its splendor and miseries. All the narration has been documented by evidence, researched and discovered, with an incredible meticulousness and patience by the author during fifteen years. This work deserves all our respect and, on my behalf, a sincere gratitude because she explained something to me that I have questioned since I was a young girl.

For in the Guglielmi family, the name "Rudolph Valentino" often provoked murmurs of disapproval by my two aunts – both born near him within a few kilometers distance. This was the same reaction of my father, who frequently visited Maria and Gabriella Strada, (respectively sister and niece of Rudolph) here in Turin. I remember very well the irritation when we, as children, were obliged to go visit them at least one Saturday afternoon a month!

My two aunts (both graduated with scientific degrees) remembered the embarrassment of their father when their young American relative, Rodolfo, arrived in Turin to say hello on his way to Milan to visit his sister, Maria. When he asked to tour the city, he was instead kept in the house (at Vittorio Emanuele II, 82) in order to avoid the social scandal of having such a relative.

During the 1990's, I knew Jean Valentino, "the nephew" of the actor and his beloved wife Maria. They were a very cordial and fascinating couple who graciously hosted me in their home knowing the close relationship of my family with Gabriella. (Maria passed away in 1962). On that occasion, Jean shared a letter with me which Rudolph Valentino sent to his mother from aboard the Cleveland during his trip between Italy and America. While reading this letter, I felt a strong emotion which I will never forget.

As I started reading *Affairs Valentino* by Evelyn Zumaya, I began to understand the importance of this story and the deep meaning of the life and death of Rudolph Valentino.

His name still resonates after more than a century (and I add this is so despite many people) because he possessed a soul that was truly special, a burning spirit, one made more intense through the sensitivities of his esoteric studies and his relationship with Natacha Rambova and her connections to Madame Blavatsky.

The ease with which he passed from one screen character to another, the ability to immerse himself into his disparate acting personalities, was always dominated by an absolute love. His successes, which were often followed by serious practical problems, gave him a life of highs and lows rendering it difficult for him to ever maintain a total equilibrium.

I am convinced that it was the profound melancholy resulting from his divorce from his beloved Natacha Rambova, the feeling that he was loved not for his own intimate essence but for the screen roles he was playing, and because he was not granted the opportunity to adopt his dearly loved "nephew", that contributed to his being a most conflicted man even if he looked apparently satisfied. The advanced state of gangrene, diagnosed by the surgeon during the operation of the abdomen was not the result of simple indigestion, but the consequence of a degenerative situation which started some time before August, 1926.

To Evelyn Zumaya, goes all the merit for having brought to light Rudolph Valentino and his unknown family relationships, which are now understandable due to her documentation and the testimony of witnesses she discovered, the most important of which are those of the children of George Ullman, his most faithful friend and executor.

Chicca Guglielmi Morone

From Myth to Truth

A Commentary by Antonio Miredi

My interest in Valentino happened by chance. In regards to the generational and cultural backgrounds of film personalities that captured my most immediate interest, were those seemingly, "cursed" of Marilyn Monroe and James Dean. Yet, in the crowded pantheon of faces and characters born from the eye of the wonderfully illusory Tenth Muse, the ghost of Valentino stood out as ultimate myth invisible, suffocated by a lazy cultural criticism which has diminished his artistic force and denigrated his human story.

However, in the early nineties, at a Biennial of Photography in Turin, dedicated to America and the Emigrants, I was projected onto the path of a great Valentino adventure.

Among the photographs on display at this event, a significant few concerned the Italian emigrant who came to be remembered as the first true superstar of the cinema: Rodolfo Guglielmi, a.k.a. Rudy Valentino. These photographs were not displayed specifically to inspire new curiosity. However, while the eyes of the attending journalists and spectators were concentrated upon the entire exhibition, I was already captivated by something unusual and evocative: a sort of tabernacle, a book of simple, yet arcane poems titled, "Day Dreams". The author was Rudolph Valentino! At that time, this book had never been translated into Italian and was almost completely unknown.

An epiphany hit me which generated a desire to research and study, especially when I discovered the beauty of a coincidence. Valentino's birth and death was a semantic parable, occurring coincidentally with the very years of the birth and death of silent film.

Thus began my journey, at first solely the intellectual perusing of bookstores and libraries; then geographically as I traveled from Castellaneta to Paris. I was always on the trail of this incurable dreamer who revolutionized film. I experienced many emotions throughout my research and discoveries as my thoughts were soon confronted by the inevitable obstacles, adversity and resistance.

Just when I was ready to surrender my work, another "chance" occurred; and I am not hesitant to define this "chance" as an "inevitability". I was at last able to abandon my frustrating and sterile scholarly pursuit of knowledge about Valentino.

This occurred after a meeting in 1994, with the writer Chicca Guglielmi Morone. Meeting Chicca Morrone was the true beginning of my flight into this adventure as the merging of our interests and energies presented many possibilities for new sources of information and new documents to analyze. Valentino's poems woke from their long slumber of words unexplored and silenced. Chicca's revelation of her trunk full of photographs, images, spreadsheets, as well as a precious family album unreleased was an event to be celebrated.

At last, the poems titled, "Daydreams", could be admired; page by page, letter by letter, without the constraints of a limited time frame. This study was made possible thanks to a camaraderie I now share with Chicca Morone; both of us devoted to Valentino's words. I was at last able to restore more of an essence of dignity to his work.

I never abandoned my vigilant attention to every detail of the Daydreams poems, even if I did in many ways turn away from the "scientific" analysis typical of a certain cultural snobbery.

I found in the book, *Affairs Valentino*, by Evelyn Zumaya this same passion and vigilance I share with Chicca Morone. Ms. Zumaya's book is a wealth of news, new information, new documented materials full of new details which for the most part are quite unexpected.

I discovered more truth, through those documents concerning Valentino's rebellion against his employers – about his subsequent triumph as a great movie star. I learned through documents that Rudy was indeed a victim of the cynical Hollywood machine that attempted to cage him within the stereotype of the Eternal Lover (obscuring the genuine romantic feeling that nurtured his marriage to Natacha Rambova).

In the last few years, there have been occasions and publications which have restored some measure of Valentino's human dignity and his art so often obscured. The precious, "Affairs Valentino" is now poised to be a new and important stone thrown into the waters of the literature about Rudy – assuredly provoking strong reactions and controversy – but those waters should never remain in danger of returning stagnant.

Long life, then, to the books and the people who help to restore knowledge to Rudolph Valentino's natural and true life story.

Antonio Miredi

Table of Contents

Affairs Valentino

A Prologue

The Vanishing Act

The French Riviera, Friday evening, August 20, 1926 -

A few miles west of Nice, in the coastal village of Juan les Pins, the residents of the palatial Hudnut chateau are preparing for the evening's seance. Gathering in a darkened room in the opulent manse, are American cosmetics tycoon Richard Hudnut, his wife Muzzie, her daughter Natacha Rambova and her friend from New York City, George Wehner.

A dreary portrait of Russian spiritualist Helena Petrovna Blavatsky hanging high above the fireplace and one low wooden table are the room's only appointments. Helena Blavatsky's portrait is barely discernible in the pitch darkness, but the austere woman's eyes appear to gaze down upon the room named in her honor with an unsettling intensity. Designated solely for seances, the "H.P.B." room is sealed from the Mediterranean sunlight out of respect for the dearly departed. For without vigilant attention to the blinds and heavy draperies, the room would grant little sanctuary to any souls wandering about in their afterlife.

The Hudnut family has just endured a harrowing week, after receiving a cablegram from New York the previous Monday with news of Rudolph Valentino's sudden hospitalization. Natacha's high anxiety over her ex-husband's illness is no surprise to her mother. Muzzie remains convinced that her daughter and "Rudy" are still deeply in love despite their bitter divorce some eight months earlier.

With no telephone service at the Hudnut chateau, Rudolph Valentino's closest friend and business manager, George Ullman, provided Natacha with updates on his condition throughout the week via frequent cablegrams from New York. Confident that Rudy was young and healthy, Natacha and her family responded by wiring their prayers and best wishes for his speedy recovery.

On this Friday morning the news from New York was heartening.

1

George Ullman dutifully reported that Rudy was recuperating and even demanding he be allowed to smoke one of his black tobacco cigarettes. Relieved by this encouraging cablegram, the Hudnut household responded with breezy optimism throughout the afternoon.

It was during this trying week that Natacha's friend George Wehner paid a visit to the Hudnut chateau. Wehner was a man of many talents and claimed at various times in his career he'd worked as an actor, a musician and a composer. But on this occasion he performs in one of his favorite roles by conducting seances as a psychic and medium. During each of his seances in the H.P.B. room that week, his dear friend Natacha reverently awaited news, via the spirits, of Rudy's condition. Despite her unwavering faith in Wehner's psychic abilities, each of the week's seances ended with her tearful sobbing.

On this Friday night the good news from George Ullman has considerably calmed Natacha. As she enters the darkened H.P.B. room, she nods silently to her mother, her stepfather, who she affectionately calls Uncle Dickie, and her doting medium George Wehner. She kneels at the low table and closes her eyes to summon the spirits for more encouraging news from Rudy's bedside thousands of miles away.

❧

Beverly Hills, Friday morning PST, August 20, 1926 -

High in the hills above the busy streets of Los Angeles, the morning sun dries any hint of moisture from the manicured gardens along Bella Drive. This particular morning is no different than any other day on the prestigious hilltop. The predictable sun, predictable heat and predictable quiet are precisely why Rudolph Valentino makes this neighborhood his exclusive address. By most standards, his majestic aerie Falcon Lair is considered a modest residence. But like other homeowners in the neighborhood he spared no expense in the purchase of as much shade from the California sun as possible. Because his estate is home to a menagerie of pedigreed pets, he thoughtfully provided more than the usual lavish landscaping as their comfortable shelter.

Whenever Rudolph Valentino and his manager George Ullman are traveling, Falcon Lair is left in the care of the estate's handyman

Luther H. Mahoney, nicknamed "Lou". When these frequent occasions arise, Lou revels in his complete authority over the Bella Drive domain. For he despises taking orders, especially when they are issued by "Mr. Valentino's" manager, George Ullman.

When Lou is left in charge of Falcon's Lair, the first order of his usual day is to check in with the groomsman to ensure Mr. Valentino's dogs and horses are set for the day. On this Friday morning, Lou's trek from the main house down to the kennel is delayed by a few telephone calls. He first answers George Ullman's regular morning call from New York to learn that Mr. Valentino is improving. Lou then answers a call from movie star Pola Negri's secretary, Florence Hein. Miss Hein's nagging curiosity about Rudy's condition annoys Lou as he feels nothing but resentment and anger towards Pola Negri. Lou remains fiercely loyal to Natacha and as far as he is concerned Mr. Valentino's Polish mistress, Pola Negri will always be an unwelcome guest at Falcon Lair. Nevertheless, he shares a few details from George Ullman's optimistic report with Florence Hein.

George Ullman's morning telephone call lifts Lou's flagging spirits and as he begins his routine inspection of the kennels, he is convinced Mr. Valentino will be home soon. The Irish wolfhound and the good-natured bull dog are Lou's particular favorites and even the kennel's most recent arrival, a black water spaniel, appears to be adjusting to his new home. With his once over of the kennels complete, Lou tromps back up the steep slope to check on the construction underway on Falcon Lair's driveway. He shrugs off the nagging memory of George Ullman's final words to him before leaving on this last journey east with Mr. Valentino; "Look for another job, Lou!" But Lou has no intention of relinquishing his control over Falcon Lair. Any anxiety over his abrupt firing and impending dismissal does little more than sour his already prickly disposition.

That Friday morning two gardeners have just arrived at Falcon Lair with a delivery of several cypress trees. Lou has the men in a sweat in no time as he snaps his orders.

"I want these trees planted and watered before noon," he demands. "I want 'em looking like they've been here twenty years by the time Mr. Valentino gets home."

❧❧

Hollywood, Friday morning PST, August 20, 1926 –

A few miles south of Falcon Lair, Florence Hein hurries across the Famous Players-Lasky studio lot. It is only a brief walk to the sound stage where Pola Negri is filming that morning, but the secretary's quick steps can barely get her there fast enough. She is quite aware that Pola is furious at George Ullman for not having called her all week and can't wait to share the good news she just heard from Lou Mahoney.

Florence is so beside herself with her fresh bulletin on Rudy that by the time she bursts onto the set of Pola's latest film, *Hotel Imperial* she is nearly sprinting. When she spots Pola on the far side of the sound stage, she notices she is absorbed in a heated discussion with the film's director, Mauritz Stiller. Florence begins waving frantically to grab her attention but Pola eyes her secretary's flailing arm, flashes a disapproving glare her way and returns to her argument with Stiller.

Florence Hein has no other option but to park her prim self in a chair on the sidelines and wait. Yawning cameramen lean on their equipment, the blazing Kleig lights are switched off and everyone sits tight as Pola Negri storms back and forth across the set delivering a lengthy tirade in her heavy Polish accent. The issue is not resolved quickly but eventually Pola winds down and filming resumes. While the cameras roll, Florence Hein sits patiently by until the troublesome scene is wrapped. It is an exasperating wait before she is finally able to give Pola every last detail of Lou Mahoney's reassuring news about Rudy.

New York City, Friday noon EST, August 20, 1926 -

George Ullman's wife, Beatrice, who prefers to be called Bee, has just telephoned The Ambassador Hotel's room service placing an order for lunch to be delivered to their suite. She looks forward to the meal and a few iced drinks as a sorely needed moment of calm before her husband returns to Rudy's bedside at The Polyclinic Hospital. George and Bee Ullman are both physically spent from the past week's events and New York's unrelenting heat wave is only adding to their distress. This welcome meal will be the first quiet time they have spent together in days.

Before sitting down to eat, Bee places a telephone call to their childrens' nurse in Los Angeles to ensure that all is well with their two little boys. For one brief moment, life for Bee Ullman seems to return to normal and the horror of the past week appears to be over. Her husband, however, is not as relieved. Even the optimistic messages Bee wired that morning to Rudy's brother, Alberto and ex-wife, Natacha have not shaken George's profound anxiety over Rudy's condition.

"Let me get this straight, Bee," George looks up from his lunch, "They said it would take thirty-six hours?"

Bee reads the strain on her husband's face.

"That's exactly what they said George. The lab in Detroit couldn't possibly deliver Metaphen here in New York for thirty-six hours. Dr. Rawls believes the only way a delivery could be made any sooner would be to send an airplane. Even then there's no guarantee that the medication would have any effect on Rudy."

George has to agree with his wife's assessment that treating Rudy with injections of Metaphen was a desperate and dangerous measure. The mercury-based antiseptic was not readily available and was often toxic, even deadly, if used under the wrong circumstances. Even so, George is trying to negotiate a fast delivery.

"Rudy's on the mend," Bee says, "Forget about the Metaphen, George. It's too risky."

Her calming voice has no effect upon her husband and he is up from the table, pacing about the hotel suite. It gnaws at him; why were the doctors not more relieved when their gravely ill patient appeared to rally? If Rudy's condition was still not a question of life and death why did they continue to even discuss the use of Metaphen?

The several whirring electric fans strategically positioned around the hotel suite are having no effect on George and he is sweating profusely. The robust thirty-three year old, who was usually not so susceptible to the heat, turns to his wife.

"I'm going back to the hospital."

Juan les Pins, Friday night, August 20, 1926 -

George Wehner's dulcet voice fills the H.P.B. room as he summons the spirits to guide him through the evening's murmurings. Natacha closes her eyes and takes comfort in the familiar ritual and her memories of the many seances she shared with Rudy over the past four years.

Within a few minutes, Wehner's voice changes pitch and he begins speaking directly to Natacha as Rudy's American Indian spirit guide, Black Feather. In the guise of the ancient warrior, Wehner relates he is unable to speak with her for long because he cannot leave Rudy's bedside. Black Feather's few words are followed by Wehner's delivery of a lengthier message from Rudy's other spirit guide, an Egyptian he calls Mesolope.

As Mesolope, Wehner narrates an involved overview of Rudy's earthly life which ends in the startling revelation that within the next few days Rudy will pass on to a higher level of consciousness; his time on this earthly plane is complete. In light of George Ullman's positive cablegram that very day, Mesolope's ominous prediction makes no sense to Natacha. She is stricken by Wehner's words and rushes out of the H.P.B. room and up the stairs to the bedroom sanctuary she once shared with Rudy.

There she retreats for the remainder of the night with nothing to do but wait for another cheering cable from New York the following morning. With complete faith in Wehner's psychic abilities, Natacha feels she has little alternative but to prepare herself for the inevitably dire news.

Not long after Natacha left the seance, her mother Muzzie checked in on her distraught daughter. She finds Natacha seated by her bedroom window smoking a cigarette, her hair unbound from its signature coils and turban. Knowing she can not coax Natacha from her seclusion, Muzzie makes no effort to do so. Instead, she leaves her anxious daughter alone to await the words she knows to be on their way.

❧

Rudy's condition takes a grim turn for the worse on Sunday afternoon and this makes it impossible for George to leave the hospital for very long. He knows Rudy sleeps soundly for at least an hour after each of his regular injections of morphine and it is after one of these doses that George seizes the opportunity to rush to The Ambassador Hotel for a quick shower and shave.

His wife Bee wastes no time trying to convince her exhausted husband to crawl into bed and sleep for a few hours. He dismisses her by saying he has only a few minutes to shower before Rudy wakes from his last morphine injection. Any relief George feels from his hurried shower is fleeting and within a half an hour he is trudging again down the eighth floor hospital corridor and wiping sweat from his forehead. He finds Rudy still sleeping and gives the medical charts clipped to the foot of the bed a quick scan. George turns to the nurse on duty.

"Call my wife at The Ambassador Hotel. Tell her to call Frank Mennillo and have them both get over here right away."

Within the hour Bee and Rudy's godfather, Frank Mennillo arrive at The Polyclinic Hospital. With the imposing Italian businessman Frank now sharing the vigil at Rudy's bedside, George and Bee are able to sit in a nearby hospital office to dispatch more cablegrams. While Bee sits at a desk filling out the message forms, George takes a few steps across the room to gaze out a cheerless window at the city below. He is suddenly overwhelmed by a desire to be home in Los Angeles, in his den, playing his violin. For one moment it is not the middle of the night and he is not listening to an office clock ticking away in Rudy's death chamber. For George, it is a peaceful Sunday afternoon and he is a virtuoso soaring through a Brahms concerto.

"George. What about Alberto?" Bee pauses for her husband's direction.

George sighs at the very mention of Rudy's brother, Alberto. It is like sticking his hand into a flame to summon that man back in his direction. While Bee waits for his response, George grasps the awful irony of Alberto's recent departure from New York. He recalls the day only a few weeks earlier when he accompanied Rudy to the pier to see Alberto and his family off on their return trip home to Italy.

7

George is absolutely certain of one thing at that moment. Alberto is as difficult as Rudy is handsome and the brothers Valentino are like night and day, black and white. During Alberto's most recent visit to Falcon Lair, he and Rudy quarreled, sniped and seldom agreed on anything. By the time they said their goodbyes at the ship's pier, George knew their sibling relationship had deteriorated to an all-time low.

George stares out the eighth floor hospital window and watches the rank and file of Rudy's faithful fans on the street below. He tries to shake his dread at Alberto's impending return, but with the clock ticking away he turns to Bee.

"Wire Alberto, let's get it over with."

ം

Juan les Pins, Monday 11:30 a.m., August 23, 1926 -

Breakfast preparations are well under way in the chateau's kitchen as the Hudnut chef busies himself with the final touches of another expertly executed meal. Outside, a gardener trims meticulously at the shrubbery's barely perceptible stray growth. High above his pruning, Muzzie stands before an oversized window surveying her gardener's morning ritual. Despite the chateau's radiant formal gardens and the enticing aroma of the chef's breakfast emanating from the kitchen below, there is nothing beautiful about this morning. Muzzie is deeply concerned about her daughter who has not eaten in two days and who has just refused another meal.

Natacha was devastated by her psychic's message during the Friday night seance and instead of waiting for George's cablegram the following day, she wired him on Saturday and again on Sunday demanding more updates on Rudy's condition. She then resigned herself to the tedium of waiting for the next hand-delivered cablegram. When none arrived, her desperation set in. Furious at George for not having cabled her for two long days, there is little else she can do but chain-smoke one cigarette after another and wonder just what was going on in Rudy's hospital room.

ം

Aboard the USS Homeric, Monday, 3 p.m., August 23, 1926 -

The White Star Line's ocean liner, *The Homeric* steams across the Atlantic towards New York City. On the first day of the great ship's August crossing, Alberto Guglielmi Valentino sits on a deck chair smoking a cigarette. He was facing the specter of a third week at sea. He had just returned to Italy from New York, when he received George Ullman's wire with news of his brother Rodolfo's sudden illness.

George's last cablegram advised Alberto to return to New York at once because his brother had taken a turn for the worse. As Alberto once again plodded up the gang plank, he could scarcely believe that his younger brother could be so gravely ill. When he left him in New York only a few weeks earlier he seemed to be in perfect health.

Alberto suffered from seasickness and he knew he would spend most of his time in oceanic transit feeling nauseous and weak. The thought of spending the next ten days on another ocean voyage has him wallowing in a foul mood.

"Nove più giorni di questo! " (*Nine more days of this.*)

This thought has him up from his deck chair and heading across the deck towards his cabin. Stumbling to keep his footing on the swaying ship, he flicks his cigarette out to sea and decides that he might just try sleeping all the way back to New York.

Beverly Hills, Monday 9 a.m. PST, August 23, 1926 -

A few whiptail lizards skitter up onto the warming boulders near Falcon Lair's chain link fence. On this morning their sunbathing will be brief as the most prized resident of Rudolph Valentino's kennel, the Doberman Pincer, Kabar, is on the prowl.

When the dog begins pawing on the metal fencing at the end of the run, the lizards zip off the rocks and back into hiding. The other dogs in the kennel pant to attention as Kabar leaps up onto his muscular hind legs and slams the fence full force before dropping his weight back down to the dry earth. Looking up towards the main house, the great dog throws his head back and begins wailing up at the morning sun as if it were a full moon. Kabar's howling echoes throughout the canyon below Bella Drive.

Inside Falcon Lair, Lou Mahoney hears Kabar's cries and reacts much the same as the other dogs in the kennel. The gruff handyman's heart skips a beat and the hair on the back of his neck bristles. With no idea just what could be upsetting his boss' most cherished pet, Lou lumbers through the house and heads down to the kennel to investigate the mournful sound.

Under ordinary circumstances the persistent barking of Falcon Lair's dogs would have merited nothing more than a call down to the groomsman in the stables. But Kabar's distress demands urgent attention. Lou knows he is the only dog to ever travel with Mr. Valentino and the only dog permitted inside the main house. Whenever Mr. Valentino is at home, Kabar sleeps faithfully by his bedside in the master bedroom. Lou feels anxious as he hurries towards the kennels. He knows enough about dogs to recognize the cry of an animal in a sure state of agony.

While Lou makes his way to the kennel, comedienne Beatrice Lillie is driving home and passing by the Valentino property on Bella Drive. When she hears Kabar's howling, she becomes so distracted she loses control of her car, bounces off the narrow road and lands in a ditch.

As Beatrice Lillie assesses her predicament, back in the kennel Lou is shouting commands at the frantic Kabar. He knows Mr. Valentino trained the dog in Italian, but unfortunately Italian is beyond Lou's understanding. So Kabar registers no reaction to Lou's commands and continues to howl. It is as if the dog wants the world to know that Rudolph Valentino, his loving master, has just died in a hospital bed some three thousand miles away.

New York City, Monday 1 p.m. EST, August 23, 1926 -

Within minutes of Rudolph Valentino's death, George Ullman delivers the news to reporters gathered in the hospital press room. He then returns quickly to the eighth floor of the Polyclinic Hospital to devote his full attention to the safe and swift removal of

Rudy's body from the premises. He is acutely aware that crowds are pressing dangerously in on the hospital's every entrance and he knows he can not waste a second of precious time to react to his own profound loss. The shocking news is hitting the street hard and George can hear the hell breaking loose.

As the clamor of Rudy's fans in the street intensifies, the muggy air in the hospital corridors grows more stifling for George. As expected, his announcement of Rudy's death ignited the solemn encampments of fans outside the hospital into a full scale riot. Reporters began sprinting over each other in a desperate effort to claim the front line. By one o'clock that afternoon, only a half an hour after Rudy's death, George has managed to avoid the fracas and is standing with his arm around his wife in a narrow hallway by the hospital morgue's side entrance.

They stare in disbelief as two workmen struggle by them towards the door carrying a large wicker laundry hamper draped with heavy gold fabric. The workmen heft their load into the back of a waiting truck strategically parked in a back alley. Alongside this truck sits a New York City cab with the meter running. As the delivery truck pulls slowly out of the alley to head towards Campbell's Funeral Home on Broadway, Bee and George slide into the back seat of the taxi to make their own escape. As the cab speeds away, George glances back over his shoulder. The crowds swarming on the street in front of the hospital have no idea that Rudolph Valentino has just made his last successful getaway.

Juan les Pins, Monday evening, August 23, 1926-

Natacha has fixated on the view from her bedroom for so long that at one point she actually thinks she sees Rudy on the manicured gardens below her window. There, on the Court of Palms, he is playfully teasing Kabar by turning to hold a stick higher from the leaping dog's reach. The cablegram with the news of Rudy's death will not arrive at the Hudnut Chateau for another twenty-four hours. But on Monday evening, as Natacha's vision of the luminous dog and his master fades all too quickly, she realizes at that very moment that Rudy is gone.

North Atlantic, the USS Homeric, Monday evening -

Alberto Guglielmi is sleeping so soundly that it takes the cabin boy a few minutes of furious pounding on his cabin door to rouse him. When Alberto finally does stumble to the door, he opens it with a gruff,

"What you want?"

Sensing the man's irritation at his intrusion, the youngster shoves the cablegram in his hand, turns and leaves. Alberto closes the cabin door and shuffles back to his narrow bed. Even though Bee Ullman sent the wire in Italian, in his drowsy state Alberto still struggles to comprehend the words. As the great ship dips into another rolling wave, he reads the cable once again and flips it onto the nightstand.

"*È morto! È morto! Rodolfo!* " he murmurs. (He's dead, He's dead.)

Beverly Hills, Monday, 10:00 a.m. PST, August 23, 1926 -

When Kabar refuses to respond to Lou Mahoney's commands, the handyman throws his arms in the air and surrenders the stressful situation to the groomsman. He then plods back up to the main house where he enters to the sound of a ringing telephone. It is George, telephoning from New York. Lou listens for a few seconds and then sets the receiver back on the phone cradle without saying a word.

Kabar's plaintive howling grows louder and Lou gives a shout down to the kennels for the groomsman to bring the dog up to the house. As soon as Lou opens the door, the black Doberman streaks past him, running through the front hallway and towards the master bedroom. Lou follows the dog into Mr. Valentino's bedroom and locks the door behind him. As he sits his heavy frame onto the end of the bed, Kabar is already wide-eyed and panting in his familiar position on the floor.

Lou stares at the colorful room which he always maintains in perfect order for Mr. Valentino's return. The bed's low, rounded blue enamel head-board glistens in the morning sun and its gilded ball feet are freshly polished. The two orange enameled night tables flanking the head-board and the room's black satin overstuffed chairs were all cleaned that very morning. Lou catches himself in mid gaze, rises from the mighty bed and moves into action. There are, after all, a few important things demanding his immediate attention.

His beefy hands swing open the two heavy closet doors and he paws through the clothing inside until he finds exactly what he is looking for; Pola Negri's silk negligees. Lou hates how she spent night after night in Mr. Valentino's bed and despises the fact that she left such intimate items in this closet. He yanks the lacy nightgowns from their hangers and hurls them towards the bed.

"Son of a bitch," Lou mumbles, "Son of a bitch."

At that moment he resolves that no one will ever know that Pola Negri was sleeping with Mr. Valentino. With Kabar panting in approval, Lou's chapped hands snag at more finery and the pile of sensuous fabric on the bed grows. With Lou's raid on the closet complete, he then rummages through a few dresser drawers and flips the last of Pola's delicates onto the bed. He returns to the closet to grab a leather satchel embossed with the letters RVG, crams it full of the provocative evidence and latches the case shut.

New York City, Monday afternoon EST, August 23, 1926 -

While Rudy's body is en-route to Campbell's Funeral Home, George and Bee manage a few minutes of privacy in their taxi cab as it speeds towards The Ambassador Hotel. George dreads the impending confrontation with the army of press that will surely be waiting for him there and braces for the onslaught.

As the cab turns down Park Avenue and wedges its way through traffic and oblivious pedestrians, George dabs his eyes with his handkerchief and adjusts his glasses. Just as he expects, when the press outside The Ambassador Hotel see his cab pulling up to the curb, they surround the vehicle. George pays the cabbie, runs his hand over his hair, straightens his tie and prepares to meet the press.

Beverly Hills, Monday 10:30 a.m. PST, August 23, 1926 -

Lou hefts the satchel of Pola Negri's lingerie from the master bedroom to Falcon Lair's foyer and slides it across the polished floor towards the front door. He then turns his attention to a small doorway located behind a nearby flight of stairs. Removing a wad of keys from his pocket, he tries a few before he finds the key that swings the door wide open. He gropes in the musty hiding place until he locates a small tin box. With another rifle through his keys, he is able to snap the box's padlock open. Even in the darkness Lou is relieved that the contents of the box are still safely inside.

He ensures that Mr. Valentino's watches, rings and cufflinks are all in order, clicks the lid shut and steps out of the closet. In complete command, he places the small tin box of jewelry next to the leather satchel by the front door and continues his sweep of Falcon Lair.

❧

New York City, Monday afternoon EST, August 23, 1926 -

George paces back and forth in the sitting room of his Ambassador Hotel suite while engaged in a heated telephone conversation with Rudy's attorney in Los Angeles, W. I. Gilbert.

"Find the will, damn it! I need to know what is required of me at this point!"

As the hotel's telephone connection crackles, George waits for the line to clear and turns to ask Bee,

"Have the cables been sent to Alberto and Natacha?"

"Yes," Bee replies,"and I just received one from Alberto with news that he's due here the first of September."

George is only beginning to comprehend the magnitude of the day's horrific events. He has no doubt that as soon as Alberto arrives in New York he will attempt to assume control over his brother's affairs. Alberto never held the slightest authority over Rudy's business affairs, but suddenly his position looms large for George. Bee pours her husband a shot of bourbon from his flask as he resumes his conversation with Attorney Gilbert.

"Find a copy of the will and as soon as you do, call me!" George shouts, "Find it, God damn it!"

14

Beverly Hills, Monday 11 a.m. PST, August 23, 1926 -

With the conviction of an armed crusader, Lou moves in on Falcon Lair's office safe. He kneels before the lock and after a few fumbles, the tumblers fall into place and the heavy metal door creaks open. Lou knows he is alone in the house but still catches a quick glance over his shoulder. He rifles through the safe's jumble of loose papers and documents and it is a few minutes before he finds what he is looking for; a two page document labeled - "The Last Will and Testament of Rudolph Guglielmi Valentino." He scans the first page of the will, then flips to the document's second page and pauses to read carefully.

Lou's single word breaks the room's hallowed silence, "Never!"

Chapter One

Skeletons in the Closet

Nine years earlier, Long Island, New York -

Some people believe in fate. Taxi cab driver James Donner did not. Consequently, he would later attribute the events of August 5, 1917, to nothing more than his own rotten luck. During the summer of 1917, Donner was employed by the James Hamilton Garage in Roslyn, New York. It was just after eight o'clock on that fateful Friday night, when the garage dispatcher answered the telephone call from Mrs. Blanca Elena DeSaulles. Despite the woman's heavy Spanish accent, the dispatcher managed to jot down her information; the Crossways on the Roslyn Estates would be the pick up. Mrs. DeSaulles requested that she be driven to her ex-husband's summer home on Whaleneck Avenue, located in the Meadowbrook section of Westbury. The dispatcher handed the information on to driver James Donner. Mistakenly believing this call to be nothing out of the ordinary, the unsuspecting cabbie drove off into the night towards the Roslyn Estates.

Upon his arrival at the prestigious Crossways, Donner was surprised to see his two passengers waiting for him by the estate's gatehouse. A striking young woman wearing a long, thin white sweater, Mrs. Blanca DeSaulles and her maid Suzanne Moreau rushed towards his cab and wasted no time sliding into the back seat. Mrs. DeSaulles leaned forward to give Donner his instructions, "Drive as fast as possible because I must arrive before my ex-husband returns from the Meadowbrook Club." Donner would later recall in his statement to the police that Mrs. DeSaulles was in a highly agitated state and chattered incessantly throughout the entire drive.

He nodded politely as she continued with her far too much information. She went on how she had just spoken with her ex-husband's cook and how he assured her that the master of the house would not return for some time. She told Donner several times how the cook explained that her little son Jackie was already sound asleep for the night. The cabbie's feigned interest prompted Blanca to launch into lengthier explanation of how her ex-husband was violating a court order which required him to return the child to her days earlier. Maid Suzanne Moreau attempted to calm the distraught mother while Donner responded by pressing on the gas pedal. As Blanca laid out every last detail of her plot to snatch her child before her ex-husband returned from his club, her captive audience remained unaware just how determined she truly was. They had no idea she was armed and dangerous.

The moment James Donner rolled the cab to a stop in front of Jack DeSaulles' Whaleneck Avenue home, he realized his frantic passenger's grand plan had already failed. Despite Blanca's fierce belief that her ex-husband would not be home until later that evening, the six foot tall, athletically built Jack DeSaulles stood on his front porch glaring at the arriving cab. The specter of a contentious face-to-face confrontation did nothing to dampen Blanca's resolve to rescue her baby boy. She ordered her maid Suzanne to accompany her, stepped out of the cab and began marching straight down the walkway. Jack DeSaulles greeted his ex-wife's sudden appearance by crossing his arms over his chest. Blanca had barely reached the porch steps when she made her demand that he immediately surrender little Jacky.

"You have told me again and again you would return my boy! I will not leave without him!"

Maid Suzanne was clearly intimidated by Jack DeSaulles' unexpected presence and ignored her mistress' order to stay close. While she hovered a few feet from the cab, James Donner eyed the scenario unfolding on the porch and fidgeted with the steering wheel.

Jack DeSaulles' diminutive ex-wife stepped up onto the porch as he bellowed down at her, "You will never see Little Jacky again!" When he repeated his threat in an even louder voice, Blanca DeSaulles' world went red. Before cabbie Donner or maid Suzanne could make the slightest move to intervene, she pulled a revolver from the pocket of her white cashmere sweater and took aim. Jack DeSaulles had exactly one split second to register a reaction before Blanca lunged forward shouting, "There is *nothing* left for me to do!" She then pulled the trigger five times in rapid succession.

Her first two shots tore into Jack DeSaulles' right bicep and a third ripped deep into his chest. As he turned to grasp for the screen door, Blanca fired two final bullets into the small of his back. He lurched forward and managed a few faltering steps before toppling face first and unconscious onto an old and faded couch. As maid Suzanne and cabbie Donner began to comprehend what they had just witnessed, Blanca made a fast move to retrieve her son.

But as soon as she opened the screen door, she heard the voice of Jack DeSaulles' cook telephoning the police. She set the revolver down on the foyer floor next to a hat rack, shut the screen door and pulled her sweater tightly across her chest. Flashing a quick glance at her ex-husband's bloodied body, she hurried down the front walkway, grabbed her dumbstruck maid by the arm and pulled her into the darkness of the yard while muttering over and over,

"I will *not* leave without my Little Jacky. I will *not* leave without my little Jacky."

Cabbie James Donner bolted from his cab and rushed to Jack DeSaulles' side, while a few miles away at the Nassau County police station the front desk officer answered the cook's hysterical telephone call. Upon hearing the news that Jack DeSaulles had just been shot, he dispatched two police officers and a crime scene photographer to the residence. They arrived just in time to see the blood-soaked and unconscious victim of the crime being lifted by stretcher into a waiting ambulance.

While the police officers converged onto the crime scene, Blanca and Suzanne cowered in a row of hedges on the rear of the property. The two women peered through the branches and watched the cops recover the revolver from the foyer and the police photographer heft his heavy Autograflex camera just high enough to capture a shot of the entire length of the bloody couch. Blanca crouched lower into the shrubbery as Deputy Sheriff Thorne prowled the yard in search of a perpetrator. It was only a few heart-stopping minutes before he came upon the two women and to his surprise one of them confessed to the crime immediately.

"I killed him and I'm glad I did! He refused to give me my child although he was ordered by the court to do so on the first of July. He refused again and again since then to let me have my boy."

Upon hearing Blanca's confession, Deputy Thorn latched a pair of handcuffs on her delicate wrists and thought it odd she seemed so resigned to her fate. The maid, on the other hand, sobbed uncontrollably when she was taken into custody as a material witness to the crime.

The two women were then whisked by squad car to the Nassau County police station where less than an hour after the shooting, Jack DeSaulles' ex-wife was informed that he had just died from his injuries. The police officers on duty that balmy summer night found it difficult to believe that this winsome and sophisticated young beauty had just murdered the father of her only child in full view of several eye witnesses. Even Sheriff Phineas Seaman found it impossible to reconcile the grisly crime scene with the alluring woman in the white cashmere sweater being booked on murder one.

Blanca DeSaulles had been in lock up for less than an hour when she summoned Sheriff Seaman, demanding she be allowed to make a personal phone call. He obliged and permitted her to place a single call. She was overheard speaking for a few minutes with an unidentified man saying, "I have just shot Jack! I am in jail in Mineola! It was over the child!" Sheriff Seaman could hear Blanca's mystery man on the other end of the phone line repeating, "Oh my God! My God!"

Jack DeSaulles' murder inspired sensational headlines and every local newspaper carried the story front and center the following morning. New Yorkers seeking refuge from the city's humidity in the comfort of their Long Island summer homes awoke to the shocking news that one of their high society neighbors had been gunned down in his own home the previous night. While they read every last juicy detail, Blanca DeSaulles sobbed in the arms of her Defense Attorney, Henry Uterhart as she related her version of the past evening's horrific events.

She recalled the details of the taxi cab ride with her maid from her home to her ex-husband's summer home and wept hysterically as she told the attorney how she and Jack DeSaulles fought continually over his visitation violations.

"Mr. Uterhart," she said, "I only took the gun last night as protection on the dark road!" She continued with her explanation saying her sole intention had been to retrieve her four year old son, John Jr., "Little Jacky". She insisted that she urged the cab driver to hurry because she wanted to arrive at her ex-husband's residence before he returned from the Meadowbrook Club later that night. She tearfully continued by saying that by the time the cab arrived a little before ten in the evening, Jack was already home. Blanca dabbed her eyes as she recounted the gory details of the confrontation on the porch.

"He told me I would never see my son again, not now, not ever!"

It was then, she said, that she reached for the revolver hidden in the pocket of her sweater. The rest was a matter of police record.

At this point Blanca informed her attorney that she was too ill to continue and that she could think of nothing else but the last time she saw her baby boy as he played happily with his toy boats in his bath. Attorney Uterhart could clearly see that his client was distraught over the whereabouts of her son. He consoled her with assurances that he would immediately look into the matter and began gathering his notes. Sliding the papers into his briefcase, he nodded to the guard at the cell door letting him know he was ready to leave.

Blanca was so emotionally distraught that Henry Uterhart decided it was not in her best interest to inform her that the probability of building a winning defense for her would be nearly impossible. Instead, he concluded his interview that morning knowing full well that her very life depended upon his ability to portray her as an innocent and victimized mother. To do so, it would be imperative that he shield any sordid details of her divorce the previous summer from the prying eyes of the local press.

Henry Uterhart's legal mind raced as he stepped out of Blanca's cell and strode down the long corridors of the Nassau County Courthouse. He knew that Jack and Blanca DeSaulles' divorce had been last summer's high profile scandal and that most of the furor involved the couple's extramarital affairs. Truthfully, Henry Uterhart had no idea how he would prevent the reports of Blanca's own love affair from resurfacing. The fact that her alleged lover had been an Italian cabaret dancer made the task before him all the more daunting.

Henry Uterhart's legal predicament could scarcely have occurred at a worse time. Cabaret dancers, especially Italian cabaret dancers, were being perceived by most New Yorkers as unsavory characters. An outspoken segment of the city's population were specifically targeting the dancers' lifestyles and ethic origins and newspapers regularly printed such headlines as, "Afternoon Dances Develop a New Kind of Parasite Whose Victims are the Unguarded Daughters of the Rich," and "Cabaret Dancers - The New Villains on Broadway". Exacerbating an already volatile situation, New York's District Attorney publicly alleged that the tools of cabaret dancer's trade were cocaine and heroin. Vice squads were busy raiding even the more reputable tango clubs and along the streets of New York, cabaret dancers were fair game for many an irate boyfriend, father, husband or brother.

Ardent critics of these cabaret dancers were horrified to discover their own wives and daughters sliding across the dance floors of New York's tango parlors in the arms of dancers who were primarily dark-skinned foreigners. They considered even minimal contact between the flirtatious dancers, most often Mexican, Argentine and Italian and their predominately wealthy, white female clientele to be nothing short of scandalous behavior.

Unfortunately for attorney Henry Uterhart, Blanca DeSaulles engaged in a blatant extramarital affair the previous summer with one of these Italian cabaret jockeys. This particular jockey was noted for his skill dancing the tango; a dance perceived as so outrageous that young women were warned that the "backward bending" and "quick dips to the side" might even be physically harmful. Uterhart also knew that Jack DeSaulles successfully prevented his ex-wife from protesting his violations of visitation rights by threatening to file a counter suit naming her dancing partner as co-respondent.

Uterhart knew only too well that if Blanca's Italian, tango-dancing lover could be subpoenaed during her murder trial, his appearance in the courtroom would seal her fate. With this in mind, the attorney resolved to make his first order of business on Blanca's behalf to have a word with her favorite dancer. Feeling the weight of the dire task before him, Henry Uterhart took a deep breath and stepped through the front doors of the Nassau County Courthouse. There, he was mobbed by reporters shouting in his direction,

"Was Blanca DeSaulles being threatened by a counter divorce suit naming Rodolfo Guglielmi as co-respondent? Will the Italian cabaret dancer be subpoenaed in the murder trial?"

The attorney lowered his head, braced himself and issued a terse "No comment!"

❧

By the time Blanca DeSaulles murdered her ex-husband in the summer of 1917, she had known the tango dancing "Rodolfo" for two years. They first met at a benefit supporting French invalids of the First World War. The benefit was organized by Blanca's sister-in-law,

Caroline DeSaulles. Caroline spared no expense, hired a full orchestra and festooned a ballroom with French and American flags. On the night of the gala event, the ballroom was teeming with wealthy dowagers and token war victims, all hobbling about as Caroline DeSaulles' guests of honor. The orchestra inspired sufficient patriotic sentiment by playing stirring ditties, while local celebrities mingled among the esteemed guests to flatter them into writing hefty checks. One of these local celebrities was a popular, strikingly handsome twenty-year-old tango dancer from the cabaret Club Maxim; Count Rodolfo Guglielmi de Valentina.

Fortunately for Count Rodolfo, Caroline DeSaulles was not one of those New Yorkers who perceived tango clubs as a blight upon society. She wholeheartedly rejected the pervasive rhetoric extolling the evils of cabaret dancers and happily included Count Rodolfo on her benefit's invitation list. Just as she predicted, the young Italian attracted more than his fair share of women and easily beguiled his fawning admirers into giving generously to the worthy cause. None of the benefit's attendees were sure Count Rodolfo was in fact a Count, or a Marquis as he was sometimes referred to, but as Club Maxim's most sought after dance instructor he was unquestionably the most popular guest at Caroline's war benefit.

His every word and slightest gesture had women blushing, tittering and commenting upon such things as his perfect white teeth and irresistible fiery gaze. They pointed to a profound scar on his cheek and wondered if the deep wound was inflicted in a gallant duel in the defense of a beloved. While Rodolfo worked the benefit dance floor in a wake of coy smiles, Caroline's sister-in-law, Blanca Elena, was not quite as fickle. She did not immediately succumb to the cabaret dancer's charm and exotic good looks.

That evening she was dressed, as she always was, in the latest Parisian fashion. Blanca purchased all of her designer clothing and expensive perfumery in Europe and consequently when she made her benefit entrance that night she was dripping in style and social position. There were no tawdry ribbons wound around Blanca's chapeau, for she wore nothing but fur trim, ermine or chinchilla. These details made an instant, yet fateful impression upon Count Rodolfo.

Blanca's reaction to his initial overture was appropriate aloofness. Nevertheless, the dashing Count persisted in his efforts and before long he and the young South American beauty were engaged in casual small talk. He learned she was Chilean and spoke not only

Spanish, but English and French as well. Rodolfo spoke passable English, some Spanish and perfect Italian and French. His French mother had instructed him and his siblings well in her native tongue. During Rodolfo and Blanca's first exchange, he was most grateful to her for having done so.

During this conversation, Blanca and Rodolfo discussed art, the opera and ballet. Although they did not spend a great deal of time together that evening, apparently the popular tango dancer made a reasonable impression upon Jack DeSaulles' wife. For over the course of the next few weeks, she frequently left her little son Jacky with her maid Suzanne to head straight for Club Maxim's for more intimate conversation with the Count.

Maxim's tea dances became the perfect opportunity for Blanca to languish in Rodolfo's arms on the dance floor and before many of these afternoons slipped by they fell deeply in love. There was one unfortunate hitch to their nascent love affair; Blanca was married to a husband fourteen years her senior with a social standing of great renown.

Husband Jack was once the captain of his Yale football team which was considered a notable achievement in New York society at the time. While his wife was carrying on at the Club Maxim, he was working as a partner in his family's prestigious Park Avenue real estate firm of Heckscher & DeSaulles. This influential position garnered Jack DeSaulles powerful allies, including President Woodrow Wilson. Despite these impressive achievements and well-placed friends, Jack's unhappy and wayward wife managed to scheme ample quality time with her Italian lover.

As Blanca swayed back and forth across Club Maxim's dance floor in Count Rodolfo's arms, she whispered tearful accounts of her husband's own infidelities to an ever-sympathetic ear. She claimed that on one occasion she discovered Jack in their apartment in a compromising position with a Broadway showgirl. As Rodolfo listened to Blanca's heartrending tales, he resolved to free the young mother and her little son from this louse of a husband. It would not be long before he devised an ill-fated plan to do so.

Carrying on a love affair with Blanca promptly compromised Rodolfo's position as a favorite cabaret dancer at Club Maxim's. His other dancing partners bristled at Blanca's excessive time with their dancer and Blanca in turn resented every second he spent with anyone else. To remedy the dicey situation, Rodolfo sought some form of employment that did not involve accommodating the attention of a bevy of regular, possessive dancing partners. It was not long before he secured a position dancing with acclaimed vaudeville performer, Bonnie Glass. This was a respectable promotion for Rodolfo and he was thrilled to be appearing on stage in her nightclub act at Chez Fysher on Forty-Fifth Street. As soon as he began his new job, Bonnie Glass married and announced to her new dancing partner that she was quitting the vaudeville circuit. Rodolfo was suddenly unemployed.

He remained adamant not to return to the problematic drama of the cabaret dance floor and instead auditioned with another popular danseuse in New York, Joan Sawyer. Sawyer was a well-known dancer who waltzed and fox-trotted her way to such professional acclaim that she once performed for the President at the White House. It was with no hesitation that she gave the handsome Rodolfo the nod and invited him to join her on an upcoming tour of the East Coast vaudeville circuit.

Despite the prolonged absences necessitated by his touring with Joan Sawyer, Rodolfo and Blanca continued to nurture their dream that she would one day divorce Jack DeSaulles. However, the young lovers were well aware that New York state law stipulated a single cause for divorce; adultery. Fortunately for Blanca and Rodolfo, Jack DeSaulles commanded an impressive reputation as a philanderer and they knew it would not be too difficult to catch him in the act.

It was then Rodolfo hatched a plan to do just that by ensuring his attractive new employer, Joan Sawyer was introduced to Jack DeSaulles. True to form, Jack wasted no time luring the dancing diva into bed. In doing so he was unaware that his new mistress' fresh young dancing partner, Rodolfo was in fact spending a great deal of quality time with his wife Blanca. Joan Sawyer was equally as clueless to her predicament and on several occasions she naively relied upon Rodolfo to act as her cover while she and Jack met for their afternoon trysts.

In remarkably short time, Blanca and Rodolfo gathered sufficient evidence of her husband's wayward ways and she was able to sue him for divorce naming Joan Sawyer as co-respondent. Because Rodolfo eye-witnessed Jack DeSaulles' illicit liaisons, he eagerly awaited his subpoena and the opportunity to deliver blistering testimony on Blanca's behalf in divorce court. In a noble but woefully short-sighted act of chivalry, he prepared to share the necessary evidence to guarantee Blanca's divorce. However, he did not foresee that his testimony would all but destroy his reputation, end his career as a tango dancer in New York and land him in jail.

≪୨ఞ≫

Contrary to the abject poverty to riches life story that Rudolph Valentino's employers later crafted at the height of his fame for fan magazine publication, the true story of his earliest days in New York City was not quite as incredible. In his widely circulated autobiography, published many years later, he detailed a desperate search for employment, food and shelter and related how he spent a few nights shivering on a bench in Central Park. As this version of the story goes, he arrived in America as an immigrant of humble origins where he was beset by destitution and hard luck. It was only by virtue of his hardy self-reliance, grit and pluck that he eventually triumphed over his overwhelming and dire circumstances. Presenting his story in this Horatio Alger format was a wise move on Valentino's behalf, for the truth might not have elicited quite as much sympathy from his adoring public.

When the eighteen-year-old Rodolfo first arrived in America the end of December 1913, he did not wander the streets, live as a tramp nor suffer too frightfully long on a park bench in Central Park. Although these familiar anecdotes had a little basis in fact, when he first docked in New York City he was greeted by his sponsor and wealthy benefactor, Frank Mennillo. Mennillo awaited his arrival and acted as faithful "Padrino" or godfather from the day Rudolph Valentino first set foot in America until his dying breath.

At the time it was a common practice for Italian families to arrange for a sponsor or "Padrino" to meet their relatives upon their arrival in New York. This person was typically financially well-established in America. Although the term literally translates as godfather, at the turn of the century the word "Padrino" meant simply a sponsor who acted as benefactor, protector and mentor.

When Rodolfo arrived from Italy, Frank Mennillo and his brother Ciro were wealthy Italian businessmen who amassed their good fortunes furnishing New York's Italian community with familiar goods shipped directly from the homeland. The Mennillo brothers were both graduates of the University of Naples and immigrated to America in 1904, where they opened automobile dealerships in New York as well as in Boston and imported Italian "ceci" or chickpeas, olive oil and other Italian products. Frank Mennillo achieved national recognition when he introduced one particular Italian relish, the olive, to East Coast dinner tables. This distinction would earn him the life-long moniker of "The Olive King." Frank Mennillo founded the American Olive Company and not only imported and distributed ripe olives throughout the U.S., he also personally designed some of the first machinery used in the relatively new process known as canning.

Frank and Ciro Mennillo had known Rodolfo Guglielmi di Valentina's family in Italy for many years. Consequently, they were briefed on the subject of Rodolfo's arrival well in advance. The brothers were not entirely surprised by the circumstances surrounding young Rodolfo's hasty mid-winter departure for America. The cablegram from the Guglielmi family arrived in New York as a formal request, petitioning the Mennillo brothers to sponsor Rodolfo upon his arrival and intervene if immigration officials questioned why he was arriving in America instead of the family's first born son, Alberto. Although the honor of immigrating to America was usually bestowed upon the eldest son, the Guglielmi family apparently made an exception.

As Frank Mennillo read the cablegram, he felt particular empathy with Rodolfo's plight. For Frank's position of social respectability in New York City in 1913, belied his many tumultuous years as a youth in Italy where he caused his well-to-do family no small amount of grief. One of his notorious teenage disappearances triggered a frantic, international search by relatives and Mennillo family friends. Fortunately, the runaway Frank left a warm trail and his family was stunned to learn just how fast and far the teenager had traveled; across the Mediterranean Sea to Africa. They finally found Frank in a remote village where he had taken up housekeeping with a devoted concubine. He was promptly hauled home to Italy where he then followed the straight and narrow by heading for America with his brother Ciro.

By the time Rodolfo arrived in New York, his still youthful godfather, Frank Mennillo, was fourteen years his senior. Frank was a married man and he and his wife Zelinda were the proud parents of a three-year-old son, Arnold. It would be Frank Mennillo who first escorted the wide-eyed Rodolfo on a tour of New York, which included a visit to the Mennillo brothers' personal tailor to order a new suit, complete with top hat and spats. The fastidious Frank Mennillo instructed Rodolfo in the latest styles of mens' fashion and impressed upon him that no gentleman would ever be seen in public without a pair of spotless white spats. Despite the physical hardships and those alleged nights spent on benches in Central Park, Frank Mennillo was a generous presence in Rudolph Valentino's life from his first day in America.

While Rodolfo was carrying on his illicit love affair with Mrs. Blanca DeSaulles in 1915, padrino Frank was preparing to leave New York City and relocate all of his business holdings to California. There, he would continue in his position as the majority stockholder in his American Olive Company and purchase a theater, a seafood cannery on Terminal Island in Los Angeles and establish eleven olive canneries as well as an Italian plum tomato cannery in California's central valley. He planned to receive additional financing for most of these businesses by securing generous loans from the influential president of The Bank of Italy, Amadeo Pietro Giannini, better known as A. P. Giannini.

In the days just prior to his departure for the west coast, Frank was concerned that the twenty-year-old Rodolfo would not fare well in his absence. Despite his own youthful indiscretions, Frank was a staunch Catholic and wholeheartedly disapproved of his young friend's infatuation with Jack DeSaulles' wife. He repeatedly implored Rodolfo to terminate all relations with the married woman and reminded him that such an involvement would only bring more shame upon his good family's name. Frank emphasized his point by reminding Rodolfo of the circumstances surrounding his abrupt departure from Italy. But blinded by his love for Blanca, Rodolfo continued to ignore the sage advice when Frank left for California.

It was one year after Frank's departure, when Rodolfo and Blanca were anxiously anticipating her day in divorce court. Their attempts at discretion became increasingly feeble and Blanca often checked into a suite at The Hotel Majestic on Central Park West and Seventy-Second Street under the name of Mrs. John Smythe. On August 17, 1916, Mrs. John Smythe again reserved a suite at the Hotel Majestic where she planned an intimate celebration with her dear Rodolfo later that evening. That very afternoon he would at last be taking the witness stand to deliver his testimony on her behalf.

Rodolfo was not the only witness to deliver damning testimony against Jack DeSaulles in divorce court that day; Jack's valet provided his own share of tattling on his boss. But it was the sight of the dashing Italian tango dancer, ensconced on the witness stand, that sent Jack DeSaulles into a homicidal rage. The brash Count Rodolfo blatantly risked everything, including his job, to publicly incriminate his boss

Joan Sawyer and Blanca's husband. The apparent extent of his devotion to Blanca DeSaulles left little to anyone's imagination. When he was asked if he ever witnessed any liaisons between his employer Joan Sawyer and Jack DeSaulles, Rodolfo had his answer.

"Yes, while Joan and I were appearing at Keith's in Washington, she left to travel to New York to see Jack DeSaulles. I accompanied her as far as Times Square the next morning. When I called for her at his apartment he was standing there in his pajamas waving to her."

When Jack DeSaulles' attorney asked, "Mister Guglielmi, doesn't it strike you that you are doing your employer rather a bad turn to come here and give this testimony this way?" Rodolfo responded, "No sir, because I have a special reason."

His open declaration of a "special reason" was then entered into court record and officially went public. News of Count Rodolfo's revelation flew out of the courtroom and inspired new rumors that whipped up a frenzy of renewed interest in the DeSaulles' divorce proceedings. The press responded to the ruckus by cramming the morning editions with lengthy articles about the courtroom's entire cast of colorful characters. The public soon learned that Blanca Elena DeSaulles was the niece of a former president of Chile and the daughter of Senora Blanca Erazzuriz-Vergara, one of the wealthiest women in Chile. After a privileged childhood in a suburb of Valparaiso on her mother's estate in Vina del Mar, the teenage Blanca fell in love with a much older man, American businessman John Longer DeSaulles.

These news reports revealed one more shocking disclosure; at the time Blanca married Jack DeSaulles he was thirty-three and she was a mere sixteen. The news reports did not disclose that after their marriage Blanca and Jack moved to New York City where she promptly discovered he was an incorrigible philanderer. For this reason, it was not long after the birth of their son Jack, Jr. that the couple separated. Despite the DeSaulles' marital woes, until their day in divorce court, Jack DeSaulles incorrectly assumed that his beautiful wife Blanca was oblivious to his many indiscretions. He also believed she was his faithful wife.

Consequently, it was not until Count Rodolfo took the witness stand that Jack DeSaulles realized he had been duped. While he had been carrying on with every beauty on Broadway, including Joan Sawyer, his wife was not only aware of his dalliances but she was spending long afternoons in the arms of her beloved Italian tango dancer. Although Blanca's divorce was all but guaranteed by Rodolfo's powerful testimony, they were both about to pay a steep price for his courtroom bravado.

❧

Rodolfo's euphoric victory lap with "Mrs. Smythe" in her Hotel Majestic suite was clipped short, when a furious Joan Sawyer tossed her dance partner on the nearest curb the day after his appearance on the witness stand. Any pride Rodolfo felt while delivering his testimony quickly dissolved into public disgrace and immediate unemployment. In his desire to free Blanca from her abusive husband, he had sorely underestimated the wrath of Jack DeSaulles, who exacted his swift retaliation.

The precise details of how Rodolfo landed in a holding cell in Manhattan's infamous jail, known as the Tombs, would vanish over the years. The surviving facts of his three day incarceration reveal a sketchy tale of likely entrapment set in motion by Jack DeSaulles and his powerful cronies in New York; a New York where cabaret dancers, even ex-cabaret dancers, were always fair game.

On September fifth, Rodolfo visited acquaintances in an apartment on Seventh Avenue near Carnegie Hall and answered a knock at the door. Three suited men identified themselves as an Assistant District Attorney and two police detectives. They arrested Rodolfo on the spot and also took into custody a middle-aged woman, Georgia Thym, who happened to be in the apartment at the time. Although neither Rodolfo nor Georgia Thym were officially charged with any crime, they were both held as material witnesses in the operation of an alleged house of ill repute. Ironically, the District Attorney claimed the apartment where their arrest took place was being used to frame unsuspecting visitors.

Rodolfo's bail was fixed at an exorbitant ten thousand dollars. How and why he came to be visiting this address at that precise moment remains unclear. But the following day local newspapers carried a cryptic statement revealing that Rodolfo Guglielmi de Valentina was arrested after a certain well-known New York businessman notified the police of his whereabouts.

Rodolfo's only recourse to raise the ten thousand dollar bail was to contact Frank Mennillo, who was by then three thousand miles away in California. Convinced that Jack DeSaulles had masterminded his arrest, Rodolfo could do little else but wait out the situation while locked in a holding tank in Manhattan's Tombs.

❧❧❧

At the time of his arrest, the holding tank in Manhattan's Tombs was thick with thieves and wedged with men in every stage of social decrepitude. Rodolfo sat lost in the lot, perspiring heavily and rapidly losing his battle to maintain the press of his white dress shirt. One hooligan eyed his futile efforts and curled his mouth in an exaggerated effort at pronunciation,

"What kind of name is Rudolfoo?"

Obliging the confrontation, Rodolfo responded with an explanation.

"It is Rodolfo, Rodolfo Alfonzo Rafaello Pierre Filibert Guglielmi Valentina D'Antonguollo. I am the son of a Calvary officer, Giovanni and my mother Maria Gabrielle is the educated daughter of a French engineer."

By then the troll of a man had lost his fleeting interest in his cellmate's name and was shuffling to the opposite side of the holding tank. Rodolfo, proud son of a Calvary officer was left alone with his thoughts. For a few minutes he left the rancid cell by recollecting his childhood in the small town of his birth, Castellaneta. In this daydream, he was again a little boy scampering over the sunny hillside olive orchards and playing in the great ravine. He remembered clearly his challenging his playmates with a crudely thrown together wooden sword and hiding from the villains of his make-believe.

Before returning to the bleak reality of the Tombs holding tank, he savored one more memory of another incarceration that took place many years earlier when the King of Italy paraded past his grammar school. He recalled how his teachers were fearful he would pull one of his usual pranks and how they confiscated his clothing and locked him in a room high above the street for the duration of King's visit. This had only fueled his youthful determination to see the King. Sliding down a rain gutter and ducking into a nearby stable, he salvaged a ragged pair of pants and a jacket used to muck out the horse stalls. After rolling up the pant legs and tying a rope around his waist, he slipped into the crowds in the street just in time to see the King ride by.

The bars of Manhattan's Tombs would not be so easily breached. With no rain gutters to slither down and no nearby ravine in which to find easy shelter, Rodolfo was forced to spend three long days watching drunks, thieves and rats come and go. He was wracked with guilt and worried that his mother would learn of his predicament. He did not sleep a wink. Consumed with dread, he became increasingly resolved to the sure and impending indignity of deportation and steerage passage on the next ship bound for Italy.

On the third day of his imprisonment, Rodolfo was informed that his bail had been reduced to fifteen hundred dollars and that it had been paid in full. Whether news finally reached Frank Mennillo in California or whether Blanca secretly dispatched an envoy with the cash, Rodolfo was again a free man. For a twenty-one year old dancer who lived and worked dressed in tails, a top hat and spats, Rodolfo's three days in the Tombs levied grievous injury not only to his pride but to his spiffy wardrobe. If Jack DeSaulles had happened along Center Street in lower Manhattan on the morning Rodolfo was released from The Tombs, he would have had his Yale quarterback reputation taken down a notch by one disheveled and wild-eyed tango dancer.

Despite Rodolfo's incarceration, the court granted Blanca her divorce and she and her ex-husband were awarded joint custody of their son Jacky. Over the course of the next year, the notoriety of her scandalous love affair eventually waned, but during this time Jack waged an unrelenting campaign to eliminate Blanca from his son's life. He threatened again to file a counter divorce suit against her publicly naming Rodolfo as co-respondent. As Jack continued to violate his court ordered five months per year custody of his son, the tensions between the two parents mounted. Consequently, Blanca could scarcely risk engaging in any behavior which might cost her custody of Little Jacky and she was forced to choose between her son and her lover.

By the spring of 1917, Jack DeSaulles was exploiting every opportunity to buy favor with his four-year-old son Jacky. He plied the child with candy and expensive toys while continually making derogatory remarks about his mother. Embroiled in this daily strife,

Blanca's feelings for Rodolfo diminished and it was not long before he realized the unwelcome and painful turn of events.

Although the DeSaulles divorce was no longer news, this did not alter the fact that in a socially conscious New York City, Rodolfo Guglielmi di Valentina had worn out his welcome. He'd narrowly escaped deportation and his association with the DeSaulles divorce and subsequent arrest left him drifting dangerously towards the status of social pariah.

In his generous padrino Frank Mennillo's absence, he scrounged part time work as a five dollar a day extra in a few movies and as a diversion he paid for a few flying lessons at an airfield in Mineola, Long Island. Perhaps the location of the flying school was more of a motivation than any sincere love of aviation. Blanca DeSaulles' summer home on the Roslyn Estates was located only a few miles from the Long Island air field.

It was about this time that Rodolfo befriended an aspiring actor, Norman Kerry. Handsome, dashing and athletic, Norman Kerry had just recently moved to New York City from his hometown of Rochester in upstate New York. Kerry was born into affluence which ensured that his every endeavor would be supported by his well-to-do family. Rodolfo was not quite as fortunate and with the exception of asking Frank Mennillo for support, he was financially on his own. Jobs were scarce and he was growing impatient for his successful career in America to manifest. Adding to his frustration, Blanca grew increasingly distant. With godfather Frank Mennillo sending glowing reports of the golden opportunities in California to his troubled godson, it was not long before Rodolfo assessed his impossible situation, said his good-byes and headed west.

After becoming the movie star known as Rudolph Valentino, all hints of his past indiscretions were meticulously eradicated from his life story. Consequently, the details of his life from the time of his incarceration in the Tombs in the fall of 1916, to his sudden departure from New York and appearance on the west coast are a jumble of conflicting dates, flimsy alibis and studio whitewash.

It has been reported he auditioned for the traveling road show *The Masked Model* and that he left New York employed by this vaudeville review. Although a photograph was taken in New York where he appears to be included in the cast, his actual departure via *The Masked Model* is hard to verify. For by the time the show opened in San Francisco, Rodolfo Valentina was not listed as a member of the cast. A draft registration form confirms he was in San Francisco by June 1, 1917. Whatever the actual date of his arrival one fact is certain; Rodolfo Valentina was never as much headed towards California as he was far away from New York. One fact is certain. Because Frank Mennillo happened to be living in San Francisco, Rodolfo made that city his first destination.

Blanca DeSaulles did not fare well mentally in the wake of his departure that summer and his leaving may have contributed in some measure to her breakdown. On August fifth, the unthinkable occurred when she shot and killed Jack DeSaulles. It was not long after hearing the news, that Rodolfo received the request from her attorney Henry Uterhart imploring him to keep as many miles between himself and Blanca's impending murder trial as possible.

Rodolfo realized he had no alternative but to heed the attorney's words. He understood Uterhart's concerns and knew if the prosecution were able to subpoena him into court his testimony could literally kill Blanca by impugning her reputation as a devoted mother. Uterhart emphatically made his point.

"You will *not* contact Blanca or make any attempt to do so or you will condemn her to the electric chair."

෴

Despite the undisputed fact that Blanca murdered Jack DeSaulles in full view of several eye-witnesses, on December 5, 1917, she was granted an acquittal, found innocent on all charges and granted full custody of her son. Blanca rejoiced at the good news with her mother who sailed from Chile to be by her daughter's side. Blanca's defense was justifiable homicide as a result of Jack DeSaulles' outrageous insult; the insult being his refusal to return her child and his statement that she would never be allowed to see her child again.

Two contrary portraits of Blanca were presented in the courtroom during her trial. The prosecution detailed accounts of her regularly "dancing her heels off," of her "snobbishness," and alleged that she was a frivolous, spoiled young woman with a penchant for gay parties, expensive clothes and the company of one notorious Italian cabaret dancer. The prosecution's inability to subpoena the cabaret dancer was a severe blow to their case as his presence in the courtroom would have cast Blanca in a much less innocent light.

For en lieu of her preferred ermine trim, chinchilla collars and chamois gloves, attorney Henry Uterhart orchestrated Blanca's courtroom appearances by ensuring she arrived in sweetly bowed gingham dresses with wide, white starched collars. The jury was effectively swayed by her image as a wronged and vulnerable young mother. As they filed into the courtroom to hand down their verdict, the foreman gave Blanca a wink and a thumbs-up. When the verdict of innocent was read, several jurors rushed from the jury box to hug Blanca with one juror gushing,

"We're your friends little girl."

Blanca's loyal jury was careful not to acquit her by reason of insanity and thereby guaranteed her legal right to retain custody of little Jacky.

While Blanca's acquittal was being handed down in New York, America's sweetheart, movie star Mary Pickford was filming her seventh movie that year, *The Little Princess*. In this film, she played the part of a young girl reared in India and then sent to London to attend an exclusive boarding school. With much of the story's action taking place in London, the film's director Marshall Neilan gave careful consideration to the selection of an appropriate location to recreate these scenes. He decided upon the streets of San Francisco and recruited several local policemen to appear in the film dressed as English Bobbies. The filming of *The Little Princess'* San Francisco location scenes drew crowds of spectators. Consequently, when the "English Bobbies" were not working in front to the camera, they were marshaling onlookers away from the busy set. On one afternoon production was delayed as director Neilan positioned the costumed police officers into position for the next scene. While Neilan took his time, the star of the film, Mary Pickford and her leading man, Norman Kerry sat nearby studying their scripts.

It was not uncommon for visitors to meander onto the set and on most occasions these guests presented no more than a moment's distraction from the actor's daily grind. However, on that day one visitor appeared who captured everyone's eager attention and women especially widened their eyes for a better view. The young man was such a flash of debonair, everyone wondered if the film's screenwriter,

Francis Marion had just written the part of some urbane aristocrat into her screenplay.

Rodolfo Valentina's demeanor made quite the impression that day until he spotted his friend, Norman Kerry. At that moment his brilliantly executed illusion of being much older and self-important shattered, and his faultless wardrobe did little to contain his childlike exuberance. He waved in Norman's direction which prompted Norman to leap from his chair yelling,

"Rodolfo! Old man it's good to see you!"

Director Neilan's next shot was again delayed while Norman Kerry gave his friend a tour of the set. He introduced him to everyone and did not miss an opportunity to explain the mechanical workings of the cameras, the lights and the type of film being threaded into the cameras. Rodolfo had worked on a few movie sets in New York, but the cameras on the set of *The Little Princess* were state-of-the-art and he was mesmerized by the latest technology. When shooting finally resumed, he sat by and watched attentively as the cameramen began cranking their cameras. The long stares from Rodolfo's spellbound audience of women on the set did not go unnoticed by Norman Kerry and he made a point of telling his friend,

"Rodolfo, you should get into pictures yourself. Meet me for a drink tonight and we'll talk about it."

Elated at Norman's suggestion, Rodolfo accepted the invitation. He was eager to leave San Francisco and had no single valid reason to remain in the city one more day. Since his arrival on the west coast, he had pursued several business undertakings but was still in search of a steady income. Frank Mennillo often covered his daily expenses and that standing offer to work in one of Frank's many canneries or his tractor dealership always loomed in the back of Rodolfo's mind.

It was upon Frank's introduction, that Rodolfo met with the President of The Bank of Italy, A. P. Giannini to solicit financial backing for the purchase of a vineyard. Despite Giannini's reputation as an aggressive lender to Italian immigrants, he was not impressed by the proposal and refused Rodolfo's request for the loan. With his fleeting dream of owning his own vineyard dashed, Rodolfo registered for the draft and attempted to enlist in the war effort. Due to his poor vision he was refused at every turn. While he floundered for direction, he resorted to teaching dance at a small dance studio and secured a few weeks work as chorister in the musical *Nobody Home*. He considered none of these ventures to be career milestones.

His visit to the set of *The Little Princess* and Norman Kerry's suggestion that he have a go at a career in the movies sparked renewed enthusiasm for a future in America. So by the time he met Norman Kerry for that drink, Rodolfo needed no further convincing that a career in the movies and a trip south to Hollywood might be the perfect solution to his professional impasse. Norman Kerry kept his promise to assist his friend by telephoning Frank Carter, the road manager for Al Jolson's traveling show *The Passing Show*. Kerry knew that Jolson's production was in its final days of preparation before leaving San Francisco for a run down the California coast to Los Angeles. He persuaded Carter to give his friend from New York a shot and after a brief audition as a chorister, Rodolfo Valentina joined *The Passing Show's* cast. With another loan from Frank Mennillo in his pocket, Rodolfo boarded the train for Los Angeles.

His shiny new dream of a career in the movies was far from a unique idea at the time, as the lure of instant riches in Hollywood was inspiring hope in even the most world-weary of souls. Americans were heading for Los Angeles in droves and studio entrances were teeming with starving actors and actresses all equally confident that fame and fortune awaited them on the daily call lines for extras. As the train carrying the cast of Al Jolson's *Passing Show* steamed south along the California coastline past Ventura, past Oxnard, nearing Los Angeles, one more bit player was about to hit town. Before he would achieve any more significance than his fellow aspirants jockeying for position in those daily call lines, a few more tumultuous years would pass.

Chapter Two

Opportunity Knocks on Room A4

Hollywood, two years later, November 6th, 1919 -

It was just after four in the morning when guests of the Hollywood Hotel began grumbling in their broken sleep. The sound of a man's angry shouting in one of the hotel's hallways was shattering all hope of any peaceful night's rest. A few pajama clad heroes stumbled out of bed and headed in the direction of the commotion to issue a perfunctory, "Hey! Pipe down!" But their demands were ignored, as the source of the ruckus continued slamming his fist on the door of his new bride's hotel suite.

Rudolph Valentino found himself in this frustrating predicament only a few hours after his marriage to actress Jean Acker. Just as she and her new husband were about to enter their hotel bridal suite, she panicked and slammed the door in his face. While he protested, Mrs. Rudolph Valentino refused to crack the door in the slightest fearing that "Rudy" as she called him, would burst through any opening and consummate his wedding night then and there. To the exasperation of nearby hotel guests, it didn't appear the bride was about to have a change of heart. It was only after the hotel's night manager threatened the irate bridegroom with a call to the police, that anyone on the floor was able to doze off again.

Abandoning his strong armed seduction of his bride, Rudy slumped down to the hallway floor to sit with his back pressed against Jean's door. He had not doubted her sincerity when she agreed to marry him a few days earlier and had no idea what prompted her to suddenly slam on the brakes. To make matters worse, their wedding took place only a few short hours earlier before a roomful of friends and Metro Pictures executives. In the wee hours of the following morning, fledgling actor Rudy Valentino struggled to comprehend the awful turn of events.

At the time of his engagement, Metro Pictures issued an official press release announcing the marriage of their contract actress Miss Jean Acker to an unknown bit-player, Rudolph Valentino, previously known as Rudolfo Valentina. The studio's treasurer, Joseph Engels hosted the ceremony in his home and Metro's General Manager Maxwell Karger witnessed the ceremony from the groom's side and signed the marriage certificate. After the brief ceremony, the entire wedding party celebrated at the Hollywood Hotel where Metro Pictures spared no expense on a raucous party. The wedding guests devoured an extravagant buffet and danced until dawn to the strains of a full orchestra.

At some point during the evening, the happy couple slipped away from the festivities and headed for their suite. But instead of leaping into her husband's arms to be carried over the threshold, Jean jilted her hubby with all the finesse of a swift kick in the pants. For a few minutes, Rudy attributed his wife's disturbing behavior to a simple case of wedding night jitters. But like any other warm-blooded bridegroom, he'd made his own plans for the night and they did not include standing alone in a hotel hallway. When his bellowing failed, he'd resorted to pounding on the door. Before surrendering to his ignoble situation, bridegroom Rudy issued one last appeal, only to hear Jean's tired voice call out,

"Please, Rudy, I have to work tomorrow, I'll call you."

Accepting what he hoped to be only a temporary rejection, Rudy began a slow march home towards his own modest apartment. Jean's reaction was not the only wound to his dignity that morning; he had no car in which to make a speedy getaway and he was wearing brand new patent leather shoes which were about to scuff and grind on a long walk home. Instead of spending his first morning as a married man languishing in his wife's arms, he was about to trudge home alone with ample time to reflect upon the most recent events in his life.

It seemed he had been searching for the perfect wife to provide him with a home and children for far too long. He knew it had become common knowledge among Hollywood's single movie starlets that he never refused an invitation for a home cooked meal. The Gish sisters, Dorothy and Lillian invited him to their home for lavish meals in order to vie for his attention. Actress Pauline Frederick and her mother countered those efforts with even more mouth-watering enticements and doting female companionship. On the previous Christmas Eve, screen star Viola Dana invited Rudy to join in her family's holiday celebration. He was so deeply moved by their hospitality, he agreed to appear as Santa Claus by gluing cotton on his chin and squeezing into a threadbare Santa suit. So by the time Jean Acker came into his life, he had long since decided it was high time he had his own cozy home.

Rudy met Jean shortly after receiving the devastating news of his mother's death and he gratefully succumbed to Jean's comforting smile and hand holding abilities during this sorrowful time. His response to her kindhearted sympathy was an impromptu marriage proposal. In his highly vulnerable state it made little difference that within the time frame of rational prenuptials, he'd known Jean only for a moment.

During the weeks prior to his hasty marriage proposal, Rudy found work in the film *Once to Every Woman* and completed a small appearance in a single scene in another movie titled, *The Eyes of Youth*. Despite securing these roles, he was deep in debt to everyone; his friends, his landlord, his dry-cleaner as well as tailors in Los Angeles and New York. Nevertheless, when he awoke on his wedding day he was elated and definitely not worrying about his many unpaid bills.

He was well aware Metro Picture's top brass would all be attending his wedding and remained overly-confident that he was about to at last experience his passage from obscurity in the motion picture industry to stardom and financial reward. But as fate did not have it, only a few hours after the wedding ceremony he found himself rejected, slogging his way home while watching the sun rise over the City of Angels.

He consoled himself with the prospect of stopping by a garage on Sunset Boulevard later in the day to do a little mechanical work in exchange for a loaner vehicle. Perhaps, he thought, he would then drive to the beach in Santa Monica to wile away the day until Jean finished her work at the studio. He reminded himself that Jean was in fact his lawfully wedded wife, but this did little to alter his increasingly sullen mood. He did not spend his first morning as a married man dwelling upon the positive and he was extremely short of patience as he reviewed his latest misfortunes.

There was the sore subject of the recent repossession of his first car, his Mercer Raceabout. The monthly loan payment of fifty dollars a month seemed like a fair price when he purchased the vehicle, but acting jobs were few and too many payments slipped by unpaid. Remembering how meticulously he maintained the Mercer's engine and how the vehicle cruised along the highway at one hundred miles an hour only added to his depressing state. As he neared the end of his morning's trek, he tried to shake off any lingering torment of his repossessed car and Jean's brutal rejection. By the time he realized he was a few blocks from his apartment, he was thinking only of sleep.

He stumbled into the stark rooms he called home and began his ritual of undressing. His suit coat was hung on its wooden hanger, the hard collars and cuffs were removed from his dress shirt and his patent leather shoes were buffed to a brilliant shine and slipped into their felt bags. Before going to bed that morning, he sat for a few minutes at a small table to scratch out a poem in honor of his new bride.

The young poet, sitting in his underwear, had no way of knowing he would never sleep with his wife Jean. And as he carefully selected each word and phrase, he had no way of knowing she would tell a friend many years later that she never slept with him on their wedding night because he told her he had gonorrhea. He also had no way of knowing then that it would be rumored Jean a lesbian or that a file of documents would one day be discovered in his lawyer's archives revealing her claim of a medical condition which prevented her from ever having sexual intercourse. And on that early morning as the forlorn bridegroom perused his finished poem, he had no way of knowing that Jean Acker would one day, in the not too distant future, be the last woman to see him alive.

By the time Rudy married Jean Acker, he had been living in Hollywood for almost two years and appeared in a dozen mediocre movies. It is doubtful that any of these films would have received the slightest footnote in cinema history if his name had not appeared in the cast of characters. In most of these early screen roles, he was cast as the stereotypical villainous parlor cad. He knew his dark skin was a liability in the motion picture industry and for this reason he was typecast from his day one in Hollywood.

In his earliest films his characters were most often smarmy foreign villains such as Count di Fraccini in *The Married Virgin* and Jose Dalmarez in *Stolen Moments*. Whenever he did find work in a sympathetic role, his characters were typically anglicized and given names such as Richard Bradley in *Society's Sensation* and Dick Thayer in *All Night*.

When Rudolph Valentino first auditioned for work in front of a movie camera, Italian immigrants were being subjected to widespread discrimination and xenophobic rhetoric. As hundreds of thousands of Italian immigrants flooded into New York's Ellis Island every year, many social movements of the day began adding to the furor by exploiting the public's resentment of the immigrants to further their own causes. Temperance organizations portrayed Italians as violent, excessive drinkers and fundamentalist Protestants sought to inspire anti-Catholic sentiment by labeling them as "agents of the Pope". Valentino appeared in his first movies at the height of this national immigration crisis and consequently there was little opportunity for him to be cast in the role of a screen hero.

Motion picture executives adamantly believed American audiences would never tolerate the effrontery of an Italian leading man and were not willing to risk a box-office flop to prove otherwise. With many hopelessly prejudiced Americans perceiving Italian immigrants as dirty, aggressive folks who reeked of garlic, Hollywood producers exploited these ready stereotypes as models for perfect film villainy. Prompted to stay in step with the times, they hired a young Italian actor who looked the part. Eager for the work, a young Rudy Valentino did his best to please his employers with sufficiently menacing scoundrel appearances. But unlike his foreign predecessors and counterparts, he added a new twist to the predictable theme of screen skullduggery. This variation seemed unavoidable, as Rudy was also disarmingly handsome, sexy and slick.

The fact that most of his early screen roles were denigrating to him personally made little difference to most of the women in his audiences. His physical attractiveness was duly noted, despite his meager performances. On the other hand, men in his audiences shifted in their theater seats and squirmed at the obvious unsettling female response and not-so-hidden smiles on their date's glowing faces. For Rudy was hard at work in these insignificant screen roles and deftly and elegantly redeeming every wicked character he played.

Despite securing consistent work in the movies, by the end of 1919 he was thoroughly discouraged with his being typecast as the scheming villain. Nevertheless, debt collectors still loitered outside his door and he was forced to swallow his pride and accept any work in the movies no matter how demeaning the assignment.

By eking out a meager income from his work onscreen, he successfully avoided accepting day labor in Frank Mennillo's multitude of California businesses. But by the fall of 1919, as Rudy prepared to marry Jean Acker, he was left with no other option but to succeed financially in the movies. Just as his love for Jean Acker was grabbing the attention of some of Hollywood's most influential moguls, Rudy's financial situation took a precarious turn for the worse. His trusty godfather Frank Mennillo was no longer anyone's wealthy benefactor and had, in fact, gone bankrupt.

Frank's catastrophic financial descent in the fall of 1919, resulted from an olive poisoning in the Midwest which caused the death of several people. This olive poisoning did not involve any of Frank's products or his canning processes, but the panic generated by the devastating episode prompted his financial backer, A. P. Giannini, to call in all of the loans he held on Frank's many businesses.

In a desperate effort to raise the capital to repay Giannini, Frank purchased a Packard touring car and hired a chauffeur to ferry him between Los Angeles and San Francisco in order to liquidate all of his business holdings. He closed eleven of his olive canneries, his fish cannery on Terminal Island, his truck and tractor dealership and a theater in Los Angeles. Ultimately, Frank was unable to raise all of the money he owed Giannini. "The best loved and best hated banker in California", accepted Frank's partial payment by issuing a vendetta; he would personally see that Frank Mennillo never worked another day in California. With a roll of bills totaling a mere five hundred dollars in his pocket, the Olive King packed his remaining possessions in several trunks and headed for New York City.

With his reliable padrino Frank Mennillo flat broke, Rudy's financial independence in Hollywood suddenly became a critical necessity. He knew it was imperative he apply himself as an actor or face the dreaded possibility of a return to economically impoverished southern Italy. Determined to remain in America, he pounded the pavement in search of any screen roles and dove recklessly into a hasty marriage to Jean Acker. It was just as his wedding gained the attention of Metro's top executives, that a casual introduction set the ultimate gambit of his wild success into motion.

In his position as press secretary with the Famous Players-Lasky studio, Harry Reichenbach was certainly someone to know in Hollywood. Reichenbach was a pioneer in the field of public relations and credited with creating some of the first and most outrageous publicity stunts. In 1918, he orchestrated one of his infamous pranks when he maneuvered a lion, hidden in a piano case, into a four star hotel suite. After fifty pounds of raw meat was ordered by the occupant of the suite, a guest registered as Mr. T. R. Zan, the hotel manager was dispatched to investigate. After Mr. T. R. Zan failed to answer his door, the manager entered the hotel room to find the lion lolling on the bed. As the terrified hotel manager retreated to sound the alarm that a wild beast was on the premises, Harry Reichenbach held a press conference in the hotel lobby to promote the new movie, *Tarzan*, starring Elmo Lincoln.

It would be Harry Reichenbach, who first suggested to Rudolph Valentino that he contact movie star Clara Kimball Young's manager, Herbert K. Somborn. He told him Somborn was auditioning actors for a small role as a cabaret dancer in her next movie. Rudy acted on Harry Reichenbach's tip and telephoned Somborn to set up an audition.

Somborn agreed with Reichenbach's assessment and deemed Rudy a perfect fit for a part in Clara Kimball Young's movie *The Eyes of Youth*. The upcoming film's storyline revolved around Young's role as a woman who is shown three paths for her future in a crystal ball. The script was divided into three vignettes and the particular scene Somborn offered to Rudy was in the third and last segment of the film.

Unfortunately, in this particular assignment Rudy would again portray his most dreaded stereotype of the cabaret parasite. But with his padrino unable to be of any financial assistance, Rudy was in no position to refuse income and happily accepted the small part. A paycheck from *The Eyes of Youth* would keep his landlord at bay for a little while. His fear that he might have to go further into debt or rely upon ballroom dancing in order to make ends meet were powerful incentives to accept the lamentable part.

It was just as Rudy completed his one scene in *The Eyes of Youth* that he received news of his mother's death and met Jean Acker. And it was soon after his whirl-wind and bitterly disappointing marriage that the film opened in Los Angeles. But by the time *The Eyes of Youth* was released, Rudy's attention was focused less on his latest small part and more on his ever evasive new bride. For the entire first month of their married life, Jean had been a frustrating tease and they had yet to spend a single night together.

On December fifth, an unexpected invitation from Jean caught Rudy off guard. Excited by the enticing prospect that she might at last become his wife in every sense of the word, he shared the good news with his friends. However, this much anticipated night with Jean only resulted in more exasperation as absolutely nothing happened. Jean complained she didn't feel well, said she was simply exhausted and left her husband in an even more debilitating state of frustration.

As his aggravation over the situation intensified, Metro Pictures loaned the professional services of their contract actress Jean Acker to the Famous Players-Lasky studio. Jean was sent off to Lone Pine in the Sierra Mountains to film location shots for *The Roundup* starring Fatty Arbuckle. She neglected to pass news of her trip along to her frantic husband before leaving town. As soon as Rudy learned of her departure, he wired his wife to inform her that he was utterly miserable. He closed his first missive by imploring they at least spend Christmas together. Jean's wire in return was infuriating in its simplicity stating,

"I cannot promise to visit Christmas. Heartbroken, but work before pleasure. Be a good boy. Remember me every second. Jean"

Rudy fired off his next wire to his wife in Lone Pine informing her that he was on his way to join her on location. Adamant he would at least spend Christmas with Jean, he boarded a train at The Southern Pacific Arcade Depot and headed north to Inyo County and Bishop, California, the train station located nearest to the Lone Pine set.

By the time the train arrived late that afternoon, a recent snow squall had transformed Bishop into a winter wonderland. As Rudy stepped off the train and eyed the pine trees drooping under the weight of the fresh snow, he realized he was woefully under-dressed. He quickly made his way to the Famous Players-Lasky commissary and as he stomped the snow from his street shoes he inquired which cabin belonged to his wife, Jean Acker. The answer to his question cut through him with a sub-zero chill as cold as the banks of snow outside. Jean Acker was not there.

He learned that as soon as his wife finished reading his last telegram, she skipped out of camp and boarded the next train headed for Los Angeles. Rudy refused to believe a word and shouted for all to hear that she must still be there. He crashed about opening doors in a boisterous search for his wife. But Jean had indeed given him the slip. Evidently, by the time Rudy arrived, the oater's character of Miss Polly Hope rushed through her final scene and left.

Round-Up's extras, cast and crew sympathized with Rudy's rage at his wife's hasty departure. The film's director, George Melford offered him some sage advice by saying, "Hey kid, calm down and have something to eat." But with the next train not scheduled to leave for Los Angeles until the following morning, Rudy had no choice but to sit out the night sipping hot coffee and eating ham and egg sandwiches. By dawn he stood shivering at the Bishop train station, reeling from yet another fresh wound of humiliation suffered at the delicate hands of his illusory wife.

The return trip down through the mountain passes was a tedious ride which did nothing to calm his agitated state of mind. By the time the train slowed into the Los Angeles Arcade Depot, the sandwiches he'd stuffed in his pockets and his patience were long gone. He had once again worked himself into a seething fury.

Indeed at some point during the train's chugging across the interminable miles, he abandoned any illusion that he was actually a married man. And before the train could come to its screeching halt in Los Angeles, Rudy was sprinting across the station platform, hell-bent on finding Jean. He knew exactly where to find her; at her friend Grace Darmond's home. Grace was also a Metro actress who lived with her mother in Hollywood and Rudy knew Jean was a permanent guest in their home.

On that fateful afternoon, Grace Darmond's mother answered a loud rapping on the front door to find a furious Rudolph Valentino standing before her. With no explanation for his sudden appearance, he rushed past the startled woman and stomped up the hall stairs towards Grace's second floor apartment. Before Grace's mother could call out to alert her daughter, Rudy burst through the door and stormed into the parlor. At the sight of the rumpled and unshaven Rudy, Grace let out a shriek,

"Jean! It's Rudy!"

Grace attempted to stand her ground and ordered Rudy to sit down.

"She's in the bath, Rudy. I'll tell her you're here."

Hearing her husband's thunderous entrance, Jean called out to him from the bathroom. The moment Rudy heard her voice he charged across the parlor and began slamming his fist on the bathroom door. This time Jean made the mistake of opening it.

She was in the process of tying a robe around her dripping self when he burst through the door. Before she could say another word or raise a finger in self defense, he leveled a fierce backhand across the side of her face which sent her sprawling onto the bathroom's tiled floor. Jean cowered by the bath tub anticipating her husband's next strike. To her surprise he dissolved into instant remorse, helped her to her feet and began pleading for her forgiveness. While the side of her face grew swollen and beet red, he explained how he had been traveling for two days and was so distraught that she had left Lone Pine.

His attempt to plead his case ended abruptly when Grace rushed to Jean's defense and Grace's mother grabbed Rudy by the back of his coat. As she began yanking him out of the bathroom, he yelled over his shoulder to Jean, "Its Christmas time, you are my wife and I only wanted to spend the holidays with you!" Grace's mother responded for Jean by saying,

"Young man if you do not leave immediately I will call the police."

Despite Rudy's protests, she tugged away, hauling him through the parlor, down the stairs and out the front door which slammed loudly behind him.

Metro Pictures soon issued a formal press release announcing the separation of Jean Acker and Rudolph Valentino and dated the couple's separation December sixth. No mention was made of the botched attempt at a reunion in Lone Pine.

Rudy wasted no time mourning his fiasco of a marriage and occupied his time with an urgent search for work on screen and the enjoyment of his burgeoning social life. During the first few weeks after his separation from Jean, he traveled with friends to Palm Springs where he met another aspirant in the motion picture industry, cameraman Paul Ivanochevitch. Ivanochevitch would soon to change his name to Paul Ivano and become one of Rudy's closest friends.

Despite his growing list of influential friends, consistent and lucrative work for Rudy in Hollywood continued to be elusive. With his godfather Frank Mennillo sending news that he was stabilizing himself financially in New York, Rudy decided to follow suit in the hopes of securing better roles in movies being produced on the east coast.

On the train ride east he wiled away the long hours perusing the popular novel by Vincente Ibanez, *The Four Horsemen of the Apocalypse.* Along with every other actor in Hollywood, he knew that Metro Pictures was about to convert the best-selling book into a major motion picture and he was determined to audition for any possible role in the highly-publicized production.

Although Rudy was still legally a married man, by the time he reached New York City he felt absolutely no allegiance to his marriage vows and enjoyed the company of female friends as an exhilarating escape from the disappointments of the past few months. Pining for Jean Acker had taken up enough of his precious time.

❧

The Eyes of Youth had been playing in theaters for a few weeks before Metro Pictures' head screenwriter June Mathis attended an afternoon showing. She hoped to review the film and report her professional opinion to her boss, Metro President Richard Rowland. As the theater orchestra played the closing strains of their opening overture and *The Eyes of Youth* finally flickered into focus, June Mathis relaxed in her seat and paid close attention.

About two-thirds of the way through the movie, one bit actor caught her eye; Rudolph Valentino. He played the character of Clarence Morgan, a handsome, yet nefarious, cabaret dancer. According to the script, Clarence Morgan was paid a substantial amount of cash by the film heroine's husband to engage her in an incriminating situation which would provide him with grounds for divorce.

The plot thickens when Clarence Morgan lays his trap for the heroine after arriving at a roadside inn and checking into room number A4. There, he telephones the heroine, "Gina", to inform her that her husband has been seriously injured in a car accident. He concludes the brief call by adding that he is the doctor attending to her injured husband.

Gina wastes no time speeding to her husband's side. Meanwhile, in room A4, Clarence Morgan prepares for his victim's arrival by removing his tie and pouring himself a stiff drink. When the panicky Gina arrives, Morgan greets her at the door and without her knowledge locks the door behind her back. When she does not immediately see her husband, he explains he is being examined by another physician in an adjoining room. Gina gets her first whiff of the rat when Morgan offers her a drink and stands far too close for her comfort. When she turns to escape, she discovers the door is locked. At this point Morgan assaults the poor woman.

While Gina struggles valiantly against her assailant, her husband, accompanied by the inn's manager, hears the fracas and takes his cue. He pounds on the door as she calls out desperately for her husband. This is Clarence Morgan's cue to lean in with even more force upon the traumatized woman and tear her dress from her shoulder. The fabric rips and Gina is left screaming, fully exposed and fumbling to cover her breasts. Unfazed, Morgan presses his hand over her mouth and calls out, "Darling, I know you love me, but what of your husband?" Hearing the woman's screams, the inn's manager batters down the door to discover the half-nude and horrified Gina. And this was the end of the steamy little scene and the extent of Rudy's six minutes of work in *The Eyes of Youth*.

The producers of *The Eyes of Youth* hoped their audiences would react to the character of Clarence Morgan with horror and repugnance. To their astonishment, Rudolph Valentino's portrayal of the character generated the opposite effect. His six minutes of lechery consistently inspired a collective gasp from theater audiences and even more surprisingly, women were paying to watch the torrid scene over and over.

June Mathis may have had much the same reaction. But unlike other women in the audience she had an eye for undeveloped talent and noticed something in Rudolph Valentino's brief performance. She also wielded considerable influence at Metro Pictures, had the power to act upon her reaction and promptly did so.

At the time she was negotiating her way through the early production stages of Metro's *The Four Horsemen of the Apocalypse*; the story of an Argentine playboy who through a series of political and domestic twists and turns ends up living in Paris and dying on the battlefield during World War One. The saga of the story's main character, Julio Desnoyers, is set against a backdrop of the war and his family's struggle as he and his relatives find themselves fighting on both sides of the conflict.

When June Mathis presented Metro Pictures' President Richard Rowland with her screenplay for the film version of the Ibanez novel, he was so impressed he granted her complete authority to hire cast, crew and director. True to form, most of June's selections for *Four Horsemen's* cast and crew were as controversial as the book itself. She selected an unknown, Rex Ingram as director and it was only after much debate that Richard Rowland finally approved this nomination. Immediately after watching Rudy's six minutes in *The Eyes of Youth*,

June telephoned Metro's offices with more alarming news for Richard Rowland,

"Richard, I've found my Julio."

As was the case with her choice of director, June was forced to argue for her choice for the film's leading actor. Richard Rowland recalled Rudolph Valentino as Jean Acker's scorned husband and knew only a little about his unimpressive work in a string of minor films. He thought June was off the mark and told her in no uncertain terms that he didn't feel Valentino had enough screen experience to handle such a complex and challenging role. June stood her ground and told Rowland she would personally coach young Valentino through every scene if necessary. With this assurance Rowland relented and granted his approval.

While June Mathis was arguing her case, her new discovery was completing his scenes in the film *Stolen Moments* and about to begin work in *The Wonderful Chance* with director George Archainbaud. Rudy had no idea why he was suddenly called off the set and summoned to meet with Metro President Richard Rowland. He was only informed that all of his impending scenes were to be filmed as soon as possible as the studio needed him in Los Angeles as soon as possible.

When Rudy arrived at Metro Pictures' New York executive offices, the receptionist had no idea who he was and blithely asked if he had an appointment. He replied that Mr. Rowland sent for him and took a seat as the woman shuffled off to announce his arrival. She soon returned and motioned for Rudy to follow her through a pair of imposing office doors. Richard Rowland stepped out from behind his desk to shake Rudy's hand.

"Rudolph, Miss June Mathis wants to cast you in the role of Julio in *The Four Horsemen*."

Still clutching the executive's hand, Rudy stumbled forward a step to ask Richard Rowland if he could please repeat what he had just said. Rowland thought he detected tears welling in the actor's dark eyes. He had. Overcome by the news, Rudy lowered his head and let out an audible sob. At this point Rowland felt their handshake continuing just a bit too long and pulled back. From a safe distance behind his desk he made an effort to restore some sense of decorum.

"You will be returning to California as soon as you conclude your current obligations here on the east coast. There will be a car and driver waiting for you when you arrive at the train station in Los Angeles and a suite will be leased in your name at the Hollywood Hotel. And Rudolph, buy a new suit."

Rudy purchased more than Richard Rowland's recommended new suit before he left New York. He went directly to Manhattan's lower west side garment district where he ensconced himself in the shop of one of New York's finest certified master tailors. He proceeded to sort through bolts of wool flannel, Scotch and Harris tweeds and order an entire wardrobe of custom-made suits and jackets. Severely trying the tailor's patience, he nit-picked his way through the minutiae of cuff details, lapel design and trouser length and paid far too much attention to the infinitesimal workings of the perfect fit.

The tailor was accustomed to accommodating a demanding clientele but had never met anyone as seriously invested in the creation of his apparel as Rudy. Despite his obsessive weighing of each and every decision, progress was eventually made and after hours of grueling measuring Rudy's order was at last complete. It was at that point that he made several last minute purchases; sweaters, silk ties, bow ties, shirts of every color in putty, peach, blue gray and cedar, in addition to an alpaca overcoat, a silk top hat and a Borsolino fedora of beaver fur. Rudy's eclectic taste astonished the tailor as he usually catered to a more conservative clientele.

The tailor surmised correctly that when it came to the subject of personal attire Rudy was no stuffed shirt. After all he came from Southern Italy where men wore brightly colored shirts and jewelry as a sign of personal style and success. However, this was not the accepted practice in America at the time and Rudy's predilection for loud shirts and uncommon accessories was about to challenge the staid male establishment's imperative that mens' fashions be distinguished and appropriately conformist.

As Rudy selected his colorful shirts that day, he was indeed naive to the fact that beauty had but one gender in American society. A well-tailored suit was one thing but garish shirts, wristwatches and jewelry were another issue entirely. Nevertheless, Rudy ordered a few more earsplitting ties while the exasperated tailor turned his attention to the task of preparing an invoice for this wardrobe extraordinaire. As he tallied, Rudy informed him that he was charging all of these purchases on credit and that the entire order should be delivered to his suite at the Hollywood Hotel in Hollywood, California. By the tailor's long face and silent response, Rudy could see he would have to sell this proposition and he started talking.

"If you would telephone Mr. Richard Rowland at Metro Pictures, he will guarantee my payment. All of these suits and shirts will be worn by me in the motion picture, *The Four Horsemen of the Apocalypse.*"

Before the tailor put his pen back to paper he raised an eyebrow and inquired,

"You will be appearing in this picture?"

"Yes, I will play Julio." Rudy answered," Do you know the book?"

The tailor had indeed read the Ibanez novel and did not answer. He was already scribbling down the delivery information and closing his mighty sale. "Julio" then grabbed the receipt, shook the tailor's hand and left. Rudy's transformation into the character of the macho, vainglorious Argentine, Julio Desnoyers was already well under way. The role of the handsome, young hero who tragically dies young had been perfectly cast.

Chapter Three

Calling the Shots

Seven years later, November 26, 1926 - George Ullman's office in Los Angeles

Bee Ullman read *The Los Angeles Times* front page article titled "Sheik's Shade Waits Cue" to her husband as he sorted his way through a towering stack of papers on his desk.

"Miss Hudnut, known on the stage as Natacha Rambova, arrived on the Homeric with George B. Wehner, who said he is a medium associated with the American Society for Physical Research. The gist of the screen star, Rudolph Valentino's revelations concerning his activities since his death last August as confided to Miss Rambova, through the mediumship of Wehner at her chateau near Paris follows. The medium said that while he was at Miss Rambova's chateau he received a psychic message that Valentino was going to die. He also said that Valentino and Miss Rambova at one time conducted many seances."

Bee paused in her morning read to say, "You really should call her George." He mumbled a few unintelligible words in her direction and continued with the work at hand. Ignoring his lack of response, Bee returned to the article.

"Natacha Rambova alleges that the dead star has 'talked' to her and that through the mediumship of Wehner, Valentino revealed that he is a citizen of the astral plane.

There, Valentino met Enrico Caruso and has heard the late tenor sing. He has also visited theaters (on the worldly plane) where his pictures were being shown and has been pleased at the 'flattery' he sensed in the minds of the audiences. He wishes that his will (which left nothing to Miss Rambova) be carried out as executed and believed this will be done."

George was not surprised to hear Natacha had publicly acknowledged she and Rudy participated in seances or that she made her admission with her trusty psychic by her side. He knew he should

52

call Natacha while she was in New York but also knew he was unlikely to do so anytime in the near future. In the two months since Rudy's death, he and Natacha had not exchanged a single word of communication.

"I'll call her after the auction," George assured his wife, "I just don't have time right now."

This was an accurate assessment on his part. For by the end of November 1926, George Ullman was in deep over his head managing Rudy's business and his work days were only growing longer. A great deal of his time was spent processing a surging paper trail. Prior to Rudy's death, all of his correspondence both business and personal was directed to the attention of his last employer, United Artists Studios where it was processed by an efficient mail room staff. Following his death, the thousands of letters addressed to Rudolph Valentino, Rudy, *The Sheik*, Rudolph Valentino Productions and Mr. George Ullman were all delivered directly to George's office.

Morning sacks of mail, crammed with letters from Rudy's grieving fans, were heaved against George's office door. He was acutely aware these letters represented the foundation of his success or failure as the executor of Rudy's estate and with this in mind he gave each one careful consideration. He accomplished this monumental task with the assistance of Bee and his secretary Clara Trask. The letters, letters and more letters contained every conceivable enclosure from mass cards and tear-stained pages of poetry to photographs, locks of hair and intensely personal revelations.

"Dear Rudolph, I have been wicked! And I shall never go to heaven if you do not pray for me. Pray for me, Rudolph dear, Rudolph dear saint, for you and I know there was no love like ours, and when my husband takes me, in silence I cry your name. It is your heart beating against my full breasts that I feel, not his."

A few of the letters even contained disturbing threats of suicide.

"Rudy, My life is an empty void, send me a sign that you want me in heaven and I will join you there."

Along with such desperate pleas, George was receiving legitimate requests to rename colleges, mountains, rivers and state parks in Rudy's honor. Sculptor Alessandro Gabelleri petitioned George for a commission to create an official Rudolph Valentino memorial statue. The letters and requests followed no stock format and ran the gamut from eloquently composed messages on expensive stationary to scrawled misspellings on scraps of paper. One missive asked George to grant his personal endorsement of a "Home Valentino Shrine" which included a small framed photo of Rudy, a candle, a stick of incense and a thin liturgical pamphlet.

Whether the letters were from Rudy's fans in England or America, their individual presentation held little relevance as the message was always the same; love for Rudolph Valentino and despair over his passing. Some of the most unsettling letters were those from women claiming they had given birth to Rudy's love children. In the few months since Rudy's death, George had opened more than a dozen announcements of various Valentino offspring with some of the letters even including a photo of the tot in question.

The additional business correspondence relating to the settlement of Rudy's estate added considerably to the volume of mail being processed. The official appraisal of the Valentino estate had just been completed and on November twelfth the public notice of his death was issued to his creditors. The race to demand payment began and invoices and requests for immediate remittance began pouring into George's office.

On the same morning that Bee read news of Natacha's return from France, George opened over thirty requests for payment from Rudy's creditors. Included in the morning mail that day were invoices from The Excel Electric Company, Western Hay and Grain, The Sun Lumber Company, The California Yacht Club, The Los Angeles Marble and Tile Company, Standard Oil and Murphy Motors. The not-so-pretty picture of Rudy's dire financial situation at the precise moment of his death lay strewn on George's desk; a story told by a great deal of money owed.

Despite this grim reality, George remained optimistic. He had scheduled the first estate auction to take place on December tenth at The Hall of Art Studios in Hollywood and was confident this single event would generate ample funds for the estate reserves. But as George ripped into invoice after invoice, he could not shake a sense of dread that this growing heap of unpaid bills might just be the tiniest tip of an iceberg. Perhaps the true extent of Rudy's indebtedness still loomed well beneath the surface.

And on this busy morning, George's check-writing, accounting and correspondence perusal was interrupted by a call from the manager of the Ambassador Hotel on Wilshire Boulevard. It seemed that Rudy's brother, Alberto was on the premises and requesting the lease of a luxury bungalow. The hotel manager explained he was telephoning George for a guarantee that Mr. Alberto Guglielmi Valentino would be able to pay the steep monthly rent of seven hundred and fifty dollars.

Without a second of hesitation George replied curtly, "I'm not vouching for any such thing right now!"

Suspecting that Alberto's attorney Milton Cohen had accompanied him to the Ambassador Hotel, George asked the hotel manager to put Mr. Guglielmi's representative on the line. Sure enough, Milton Cohen answered.

"Milton," George asked," why don't you and Alberto meet me at Hollywood Jack's in a half an hour and we'll work this out. I've got another idea I want to run by you anyway."

George hung up the telephone and relayed Alberto's request to his wife. She seemed less surprised than her husband to hear of Alberto's desire to secure a prestigious Ambassador Hotel address and reminded George that Pola Negri maintained her own bungalow on the Ambassador's grounds. Perhaps, Bee mused, Pola was about to ensconce Alberto in a bungalow next door. George agreed this might be the case and added that he was fast reaching the end of his long rope where Alberto was concerned. He was not looking forward to his next face-to-face with the man at Hollywood Jack's. In anticipation of the conversation, he placed a quick telephone call to his own attorney, Leonard Wilson and asked him to attend the meeting. With the potentially contentious exchange with Alberto Valentino only a few hours away, George returned to the endless processing of the morning mail.

Although reading through the daily mail was time-consuming, this was the only aspect of George's role as Rudy's executor that was not crawling with legal complications. The fulfillment of the promise George made to Rudy assuring him he would settle his estate grew exponentially more daunting with each passing day. And there was scarcely a moment when George's profound grief at the tragic loss of his closest friend did not threaten the necessary professional focus required to accomplish the job before him. As he slogged through the overwhelming logistics, his personal sadness was compounded by one disturbing realization; the situation before him was only worsening because one critical piece of paper had simply vanished.

♌

When George initially assumed his role as Rudy's estate executor, he believed the appointment would be a fairly straightforward assignment. He would simply liquidate all estate assets, pay all outstanding debts and follow the terms of Rudy's, "Last Will and Testament" to the letter. Unfortunately for George and everyone concerned, Rudy's will generated nothing but confusion and discord from the moment the document was retrieved from his office safe at Falcon Lair.

Rudy signed his "Last Will and Testament" on September 1, 1925, one year before his death. He executed this particular will a few weeks after his bitter separation from his second wife Natacha and the terms of the document reflected his emotional state of mind. In a blind rage, he instructed his attorney Raymond Stewart to draw up a new will to replace a previous will in which he bequeathed his entire estate to Natacha. In this new will, Rudy specified her inheritance as one thin dollar bill.

Ignoring both his attorney and his manager's advice, Rudy proceeded to have the new will drawn up. It was also at this time he informed George that he planned to attach a sheet of instructions to the new will to further detail the execution of his final wishes. He then proceeded to relate verbally a few of these instructions to George. At the time George perceived the new will as a vindictive and rash act and believed Rudy would have another will drawn up as soon as his fury at Natacha subsided.

Only one year later, George found himself in the throes of settling Rudy's estate and sorely regretting that he never insisted upon reading a copy of the spiteful will or the attached sheet of specific instructions. His role as executor was seriously complicated when no such sheet of instructions could be located. George was confused as he studied the existing single page of the document and found no mention of Rudy's sheet of instructions other than a cryptic reference stating that his executor should dispense any estate income, "as I have this day instructed him." Consequently, during George's first days as executor he spent considerable time rifling through Rudy's office files in a desperate search for the missing sheet of instructions. Determined

56

to locate the document, he contacted the attorney who executed the will, Raymond Stewart to see if he could shed some light upon the baffling situation.

Attorney Stewart recalled drawing up a sheet of instructions at the same time Rudy executed his September 1925, "Last Will and Testament." He also told George that he had no copy of said instructions in his files and in fact had little recollection of the specific terms of the document. He claimed the last he ever saw of the document in question was on the day he delivered the will to Rudy at Falcon Lair. At that time, he said, neither the will nor the attached sheet of instructions had been signed by Rudy or any witnesses.

George grew frustrated when he could not locate what he believed to be a valid portion of Rudy's will. This left him no other option but to file the existing, single paged document with the court. He also guaranteed his performance as executor by posting a personal $100,000.00 bond issued by The Independence Indemnity Company. Despite the fact that his authority as executor was considerably weakened by the vague terms of Rudy's will, George proceeded as best he could to carry out the business of settling the estate.

The most immediate ramification of George's dilemma concerned the future of Rudy's production company, Rudolph Valentino Productions. As Rudy's business manager, George was the sole administrator of the production company and consequently the only person with any understanding of the inner workings of the complex business. In the initial weeks following Rudy's death, George was adamant that the production company remain operational as a potential means to generate future income for the estate. But as Rudy's one page will made no mention of his production company and did not specify that his executor continue to act as its administrator in the event of his death, George was left grappling with too many unanswered questions.

Had Rudy intended to authorize him to act as both executor of his estate and administrator of Rudolph Valentino Productions? Was George legally bound as executor to act upon his clear recollection of Rudy's oral instructions to him specifying this dual authority or should he simply comply with the terms of the existing one page will and act only as executor? Only after a thorough examination of the situation did George decide it would be in the best interest of the estate to act as estate executor and simultaneously continue in his role as head of Rudolph Valentino Productions.

During this time, George faced one other troubling dynamic contributing to the escalating tensions surrounding the settlement of Rudy's estate. Within a few weeks of Rudy's death, Alberto Valentino settled in Los Angeles and his daily presence in executor George's life rapidly deteriorated from irksome nuisance to intolerable aggravation. The terms of Rudy's vague will became the flash points of the disintegrating relationship between the two men. If George found the one page will confusing, brother Alberto would never have been able to interpret a single line of the document had it not been for Pola Negri's immediate intervention.

In sharp contrast to Alberto and George's increasingly hostile relationship, Alberto and Pola Negri were becoming fast friends. Pola Negri had taken her recently deceased lover's brother under her high profile wing. She offered to assist him in any way possible and instructed her personal attorneys to facilitate Alberto's understanding of the fuzzy terms of Rudy's will. Alberto was relieved to learn his brother bequeathed Natacha the sum of one dollar, but was outraged at the news that George Ullman was named executor of the estate. Alberto was further peeved when he learned his brother designated a financial interest in the estate to two other people; his sister Maria Strada and Natacha's aunt, Teresa Werner. There was one other clause in the will that Alberto did not apparently grasp. This was a provision stating that anyone contesting the will risked the reinstatement of the previous will which bequeathed Rudy's entire estate to Natacha Rambova.

Despite Pola Negri's attorney's best advice, Alberto promptly contested Teresa Werner's claim to any share in Rudy's estate. Perhaps he was unaware that his brother did not name Teresa Werner in his will solely as a gesture of gratitude for the motherly role she played in his life. He included her in his will to ensure continued financial support for the beloved "Auntie" in the event of his death. For during the last years of his life, Rudy instructed George to pay the monthly mortgage on Teresa Werner's Los Angeles home. Nevertheless, Alberto petitioned the court to strike Teresa Werner's name from the will and requested that he be appointed as estate executor. It was his wish, he informed the court, that George Ullman be removed from any administrative position over his brother's production company. Furthermore, he requested that the production company be immediately dissolved and all assets liquidated.

The same day George received notification of Alberto's legal action, he dispatched a cable to Teresa Werner in France imploring her to return to Los Angeles at once to defend her interests in the will. Teresa Werner heeded George's advice and sailed for the U.S., arriving in Los Angeles on November eighth.

The court denied every one of Alberto's requests and stung him with a painful reminder. By contesting his brother's will, he risked losing everything if Rudy's previous will was reinstated. Alberto could do little but accept the court's decision. In sore need of income he began petitioning executor George for cash advances against what he presumed to be his future share of Rudy's estate. George accommodated Alberto's requests by issuing checks drawn upon the Rudolph Valentino Production Company bank account. With each check, George reiterated to Alberto that one of those oral instructions Rudy shared with him, directed him, as executor, to dispense only weekly stipends of estate funds to the three people mentioned in the will. Alberto vehemently replied that no such sheet of instructions ever existed and pressed George for more cash advances. With no hard evidence to prove his claim, George continued to disperse estate funds as lump sums to not only to Alberto but to the other two other individuals mentioned in Rudy's existing will, his sister Maria Strada and Teresa Werner.

These cash advances were not Alberto's only source of income. George became aware that he was removing items from his brother's property, Falcon Lair and liquidating them into ready cash. This situation undermined George's efforts to conduct a comprehensive inventory of Rudy's personal belongings in advance of the estate auctions. One week earlier, on November twelfth, he forwarded official legal notification to Alberto demanding the return of two items he removed from Falcon Lair; Rudy's dog, Kabar and Rudy's Franklin Coupe automobile. The fact that neither dog nor car had yet to be returned became just more fuel for the next volatile confrontation between Rudy's brother and one perturbed executor.

Hollywood Jack's Steakhouse was located across the street from George's office on Santa Monica Boulevard. Every noon hour the establishment's front doors were in constant motion as the daily power lunch crowd filed in. George considered the popular eatery his second office, with its high leather booths providing adequate privacy and the food being predictable fare. As he stepped through the swinging doors, he spotted his attorney Leonard Wilson already seated in his regular booth. Wilson looked up and greeted his client with a, "What's up?"

George slid into the seat and gave him his answer, "Alberto is about to lease a bungalow at the Ambassador and wants another five thousand dollar advance."

A waiter paused to pour George a cup of coffee.

"Tell him no," Wilson replied.

Before George could respond, Alberto and his attorney Milton Cohen made their entrance. Their arrival silenced Hollywood Jack's customers as all heads turned towards the door in a collective stare. It wasn't that the steakhouse clientele recognized Alberto as Rudolph Valentino's brother. The freeze frame was in response to the formidable appearance of Rudy's prized Doberman, Kabar. The impressive animal stepped past waiters and onlookers and as soon as he recognized George, he edged towards him for a pat.

Alberto appeared oblivious to the stir generated by the mighty dog's arrival and tossed the leash on the floor to take a seat next to his attorney. While Kabar flopped in a heap under the table, George wasted no time getting down to business by explaining to Alberto and Milton Cohen how Rudy's assets had not yet been liquidated and that cash was still in short supply. He then itemized a few of the latest invoices he'd just received for payment.

"I opened invoices this morning for forty suits Rudy ordered in London and bills are still arriving from Paris and New York."

As George raised his voice to be heard over the din of the lunch crowd, attorney Milton Cohen interrupted him.

"We wish to know by what authority you are continuing to run Rudolph Valentino Productions, George. There is not a single reference in the will charging you in this respect. And where is this reference to your assertion that Rudy instructed you to dispense only a weekly stipend to Alberto? In fact we find the existing will so vague we plan to have it stricken."

George expected Cohen's offensive and leaned back in his seat to watch Alberto light one of Rudy's black tobacco cigarettes. Forging ahead with his own agenda, George continued to outline his plan to generate income for Rudy's production company by promoting his last two movies, *The Son of the Sheik* and *The Eagle*. He explained that he was in the process of mailing form letters to thousands of Rudy's fans who had written him a credible letter within the past year. This letter, he said, directed fans to form local groups, or memorial guilds, in Rudy's honor with the specific purpose of demanding that his last two movies be shown in local theaters.

When George paused his explanation, Milton Cohen continued to expound upon the subject of Rudy's will. He repeated that there was no written evidence that Rudy ever charged George with the authority to manage his production company in the event of his death. He then threatened George by saying that if he did proceed to do so, he would object in court to all of his transactions in this capacity.

George fought to control his temper and reminded Alberto and Milton Cohen that Rudy personally instructed him to continue managing Rudolph Valentino Productions. He said Rudy assured him he disclosed this provision on a second page of the will which should have been attached to the original document. Throughout George's explanation, Alberto sat fuming and puffing away at his cigarette. Although he was still relatively unclear as to the daily operations of Rudolph Valentino Productions, he was well aware of one point; he despised George Ullman and his role in his brother's estate. When he reached his breaking point he leaned across the table towards George. Ignoring his attorney's gesture to remain silent Alberto demanded,

"You show me the instructions!"

Leonard Wilson cut him off.

"We have been unable to locate a copy of the instructions, Alberto. But the fact remains, if George does not continue to operate Rudolph Valentino Productions, you sir, will soon have no further income to draw upon from the estate."

Alberto reacted to this challenge by demanding that George write him a check for the five thousand dollars and guarantee his Ambassador Hotel bungalow. His booming voice prompted Kabar to reposition himself under the table. George glowered into his cup of coffee and wondered if Rudy's passion for living far beyond his means might possibly have been genetic. He could not fathom how Alberto spent so much money in the few weeks since his arrival in Los Angeles. George looked up, returned Alberto's dirty look and told him that all he could offer was a review of the production company's ledgers to see what reasonable amount he could advance. Alberto reacted to this news with an unexpected burst of fluency in English.

"I will be in charge of my brother's business now!"

At this point the scene went public and Alberto resorted to speaking in Italian by levying more charges which neither the two attorneys nor George could understand. Milton Cohen took his cue and decided it was time to escort his client towards the door. George reacted to the sight of Kabar trotting along behind the two men with his leash dragging on the floor by muttering,

"That bastard!"

The noon crowd at Hollywood Jack's was not unaccustomed to an occasional fracas. After all it was over these very tables that careers were made and destroyed and some of the sweetest deals in lotus land were negotiated. So it was only a minute or two before Hollywood Jack's patrons lost all interest in the commotion.

But George was steaming mad. "How the hell can Alberto afford to pay a top notch lawyer like Milton Cohen?"

Leonard Wilson reminded him that the highly-paid celebrity attorney, Milton Cohen also represented Pola Negri. George agreed her influence was not only apparent by Milton Cohen's presence but in Alberto's request for the bungalow and requests for cash advances. George knew first hand what little respect Pola had for money, especially when this lack of respect involved other people's money. He also knew the Valentino brothers were particularly vulnerable to her penchant for extravagance.

George threw back the last of his coffee and told his attorney he didn't intend to devote another minute of his day to Alberto Valentino. With this said, he slapped the tab on the table and stormed out of Hollywood Jack's. It was a short walk across the street to his office and Leonard Wilson kept pace as he tried to explain just how he would counter Alberto's objections in court. But George was distracted and barely listening to his attorney's suggestions. He could not shake the unsettling image of Kabar, lumbering after Alberto with his leash rattling along on the floor.

Two months later, January, 1927 -

Malibu Colony is a narrow strip of coveted land wedged as a domino formation of premium beachfront properties. The decks of these lavish homes face west in order to afford homeowners a perfect view of each evening's blazing sunset. Although one or two storms occasionally blew in off the Pacific to challenge the precarious structures, these were rare occasions. One would be hard-pressed to find a more idyllic spot in which to languish in a sea breeze and bask in the salt air.

The deck of Pola Negri's Malibu beach house was the one place she could find solace and sit obscured from the view of casual passers-by on the beach below. During the winter months, she often sat cloaked in a flannel blanket to take refuge on a deck chair and gaze at the horizon. On one chilly day, she returned from her work at the studio to again keep watch from her deck and lose herself in contemplation. Southern Californians never spent such cold days outdoors, but Pola Negri grew up on the streets of Warsaw and she found the brisk air downright balmy.

Pola was a woman with only a passing acquaintance with emotional restraint and on that day she again anguished, feeling misunderstood by the press and Rudy's fans. On January seventh, she submitted a claim of fifteen thousand dollars against his estate. At the time, she informed the press she loaned Rudy this amount of money some time before his death and claimed her request for payment was only to give every cent to his brother, Alberto. She explained her generosity by stating that Alberto assured her he intended to use the fifteen thousand dollars to bring his wife and twelve year old son, Jean, from Italy so they might live with him in Los Angeles. But despite Pola's best attempt at clarification, the public's response to her request from Rudy's estate was less than favorable.

As soon as she received George's check for the amount in full, she passed the money along to Alberto. To Pola's distress he made no move to bring his family to Los Angeles. Meanwhile, the press had a field day at her expense with their negative implications. If she really loved Rudy, they alleged, she would never have demanded his estate reimburse her for a personal loan. In the wake of this publicity, she began to grasp the larger picture of just where she stood with Rudy's fans. Most of them hated her and not only disapproved of her claim against his estate but believed she was exploiting his death to gain publicity.

As the foghorns droned on across the Pacific Ocean, Pola sank further into her torment and on that gray, winter day she lost her struggle to ignore the public's opinion of her actions. She watched the surf break and recede, tucked the blanket around her legs and tended to her brooding.

63

At some point she heard her secretary Florence Hein speaking with Alberto Valentino as he arrived at the beach house. They exchanged a few words before he stepped out onto the deck to greet Pola in his heavy Italian accent.

"I'm going to be a movie star. They tell me I will take Rudolfo's place in movies!"

Pola responded with a blank stare, "Doing exactly what Alberto?"

"I have spoken with Silvano Balboni, June Mathis' husband. He told me the public idolizes your brother. It would receive you with open arms in pictures. You look like him all but your nose. I ask him what must be done? I have my nose. I have no other. Perhaps you tell me how to change it. I ask him and he told me plastic surgery!"

Despite Alberto's visible excitement, Pola tried to think of a fast and tactful way to tell him that the whole idea of plastic surgery was crazy.

"Have you told Ullman about this?" She asked. "And when is Jean coming from Italy? Have you made any arrangements?"

Alberto ignored the first question, "Jean is in school in Turin. He will stay there."

❧

During the weeks prior to Rudy's two estate auctions, one held in December in Los Angeles and a second in January in San Francisco, George conducted an extensive inventory of Rudy's estate, published an expensive, slickly-produced catalog and made every effort to maximize every sale. He held high expectations that the public auctioning of Rudy's homes, his custom-built automobiles, his horses, pedigreed dogs and hundreds of personal belongings would fetch a handsome return which could promptly be deposited in the bank.

During this busy time, George retained Falcon Lair's handyman, Lou Mahoney on the Rudolph Valentino Production Company payroll and assigned him the task of organizing the auction's inventory both at Falcon Lair and at the production company's prop house on Santa Monica Boulevard. As George endeavored to increase the value of some of the items on the auction block, he instructed Lou to bring Rudy's yacht into dry-dock for a fresh coat of paint and even resorted to stamping Rudy's signature inside a few of his rare books to increase their value by a few dollars. In order to ensure further top dollar returns, George also invested estate funds in the restoration of Rudy's antique collections.

Despite all of his and Lou's efforts, bids at the first auction in Los Angeles were far below reasonable asking prices and the event was a thoroughly depressing experience for George. Even a substantial bid made on Falcon Lair failed to result in the final sale of the property as the prospective owner did not provide a satisfactory cash deposit. At the time, the motion picture industry was only decades old and collecting celebrity memorabilia was still a new concept. Whether Rudolph Valentino owned an item or not often held little sway over a prospective buyer's decision.

The sale of Rudy's personal belongings was not only professionally discouraging for George but privately heart wrenching. He had been present during those happier days when Rudy, the avid collector, enthusiastically filled his home with antique armor, tapestries, furniture and art. Initially, George hoped all of the collections would find appreciative owners, but he was barely able to give some of the valuable items away at any price.

His frustration with the modest success of the Los Angeles auction was further compounded by Alberto's intense interest in the speedy liquidation of his brother's belongings. As estate executor, George realized all of Rudy's possessions, no matter how insignificant their value, were legally the property of his estate. But his efforts as executor to enforce this technicality were at best sporadic and for a while sentiment prevailed over the legal protocols of estate settlement.

When Rudy's sister Maria Strada arrived from Italy in January, George drove her to Falcon Lair and stood by as she sorted through her brother's remaining personal effects. Among the other items she selected were Rudy's emerald and platinum cuff links, an emerald ring, a sapphire ring, his white gold cigarette case and an amber and sapphire cigarette holder appraised at $3,428.00. Legally, George never should have permitted her to remove a single sock from the premises, but motivated by sympathy he said nothing as Maria selected many more valuable items from her brother's last home. It was not long before George realized this gesture set precedence for an escalation in the removal of item after item by everyone concerned.

Even George kept items he considered of insignificant market value; Rudy's personal and business address books, a small oil landscape painted by Rudy, stacks of photographs and letters and other artifacts as well as random pieces of furniture. With Lou

Mahoney's assistance, Maria shipped her estate items to her home in Italy. And on one occasion George watched as Alberto slipped a small tin box full of Rudy's jewelry into his coat pocket. George was not sure how many pieces of jewelry were in this container, but he did know it was a sizable cache of some fifty items including Rudy's favorite platinum wristwatch. Alberto also boxed up and carted away all of Rudy's clothing, including his suits, riding boots and hats. Even Lou Mahoney had a hand in removing property, including lace and Pola Negri's lingerie which his wife later stitched into fancy dresses for their daughter.

This haphazard disbursement of Rudy's personal effects only served to widen the feud between George and Alberto. With the inevitable questions being bandied about as to who took what, when and where, accusations were soon flying and a profound and irrevocable distrust between the two men set in. By the end of January 1927, as Rudy's second estate auction was held at the Curtis Studios in San Francisco, George and Alberto were no longer meeting face-to-face and were communicating only through their attorneys.

In the hopes of selling a few more items remaining on the auction block, George extended the San Francisco estate auction for several days. When sales continued to be unremarkable, he made the decision to call an end to the peddling of Rudy's wares. On the final day of the San Francisco sale, he informed the auction house that the public auctioning would terminate at the close of that business day. With the total sales from both auctions at barely one hundred thousand dollars, George faced the grim reality of exploring other options to pay Rudy's enormous debt while somehow continuing to generate future income for his estate.

As George concluded his last day of business in the Curtis Studios, the considerable weight of his situation left him exhausted and discouraged. Clearing Rudy's debt was not his only immediate concern. Rudy's sister Maria had decided to remain in Los Angeles for a few weeks and was hiring her own attorneys. George also knew that Alberto had recently retained several new lawyers who were already flooding his office in Los Angeles with more legal documents.

Brushing aside these stressful thoughts of the Guglielmi's proliferating legal muscle, George prepared for his return trip home to Los Angeles. He was set to board the next southbound train out of San Francisco and would soon be spending time in the back yard of his Foothill Drive home in Beverly Hills with his nine year-old son, Danny, and four year old son, Bobby. As George handed the auctioneer's clerk his shipping instructions, he realized the disheartening business of auctioning Rudy's estate was officially over.

"That's it," he told the clerk, "Have all of this shipped to the prop house in Los Angeles."

As soon as the clerk stamped a final seal on the day's receipts, George chucked the fistful of papers into his briefcase and stepped out onto Sutter Street to hail the first passing cab. The cabby was a burly fellow puffing away on a stump of a cigar; George settled back in his seat,

"Third and Townsand, the Southern Pacific station."

The taxi cab careened through traffic with a few harrowing near misses, but George was so lost in thought he barely noticed. There were too many bills to pay, too many mouths to feed and Alberto and Maria were mobilizing more attorneys in Los Angeles. At that prospect, George removed his flask from his overcoat pocket and swallowed a long swig of warm bourbon.

"Old story," he mused aloud.

The cabby turned his head and uttered a guttural, "Huh?"

"Old story," George repeated, "It's the same old story that took place in Italy some one hundred years ago after a man named Guglielmi got into a row with a fellow by the name of Colonna. Their beef turned violent and Guglielmi ended up killing his arch enemy Colonna."

The cabby motored on as George related the rest of his tale. "The way I was told, it was after Colonna's murder, sometime around the year 1850, when brigands raided the Guglielmi - Valentino family's hideaway and forced them to move to a village in southern Italy called Castellaneta."

The cabby chomped on his cigar and glanced into his rear view mirror, "Valentino?" he asked, "*The Sheik*?"

"Yeah," George sighed, "one and the same."

For the remainder of the ride George sat in silence. Between sips of bourbon, he strategized just how he would clear Rudy's enormous debt which by then had reached a staggering total of $300,000.00. Despite this overwhelming prospect, the bootleg spirits strengthened his resolve to arrive in Los Angeles, spend a day with his boys and then renew his drive to turn the balance sheet of Rudy's estate right side up. As the cabbie wended his way south on Third Street, George stared out the window. He could not help but notice more down-trodden "have-nots" loitering in the streets instead of the well-dressed "haves" of San Francisco's financial district.

This visible specter of poverty and failure threatened his bourbon inspired confidence and as the cab pulled up to the Southern Pacific Station he removed the flask from his coat pocket and threw back a few more gulps. By the time he boarded the Southern Pacific that afternoon he was sufficiently lit and feeling invincible. And as he settled into his seat for the long ride home, he savored thoughts of his impending success as Rudy's executor and of that long-overdue telephone call to Natacha.

Chapter Four

Babykins

The hills above Hollywood, five years earlier in the spring of 1921 -

Natacha Rambova gripped the steering wheel of her Buick Roadster as the car bounced along the rutted road. She scanned the shadows for potholes while narrowly avoiding a few nocturnal creatures as they skittered towards the safety of the dark brush. The Buick rolled along and Natacha made every effort to prevent her precariously perched passenger from flying off the back of the vehicle.

Rudy straddled the Buick's lowered canvas roof, with one leg in the back seat and the other draped across the trunk. Across his lap he held a loaded Winchester hunting rifle. Decked out in a woolen jacket, a pair of plus-four knickers, a beret and a cartridge belt, he was fit to kill. He and Natacha were poaching quail and rabbit on the Robertson Cole Ranch in the Santa Ynez Canyon just north of Santa Monica. They often hunted in the canyon and always set their limit for each hunt at eight birds and four rabbits. As Natacha maneuvered the Buick along the dirt road, Rudy prepared to bag his last bird of the night. He was a straight shot and seven unlucky birds had already been tossed on the back seat. With a final blast, another plump quail was headed for the garlic and olive oil.

Having met their quota in quail, Natacha parked the roadster in the bushes so Rudy could track the rabbits on foot. With his rifle tucked under his arm, he set out to clear a path through the dry brush and quickly fired a few more shots. Before long, he bagged his four rabbits and headed back towards the Buick. By then, morning light threatened their cover of darkness and it was time to hurry down through the canyon towards their little home on Sunset Boulevard. With the rifle and quarry hidden safely in the trunk, Rudy took the wheel of the Buick to speed towards Hollywood. Within a half a mile, he spotted a police officer standing in the road motioning him to pull over.

Rudy slammed on the brakes and pulled the Buick onto the road's gravel shoulder. The officer strolled over to the car and asked if either of them had heard any gunshots or seen anyone with a gun.

With their kill still warm in the baggage compartment, both Rudy and Natacha sat frozen in their seats. The actor took his cue.

"Why, yes sir we did." Rudy offered. "We did just pass a man with a rifle a way back."

He looked to Natacha for acknowledgment of the fact, "Right?"

She feigned disinterest in the conversation and gave a half-hearted shrug. The officer bought their bluff, thanked them both and Rudy hit the accelerator. For a moment the two poachers stared straight ahead, as if the warden could still see their guilty faces. When Natacha felt it was safe to do so, she caught a quick glance over her shoulder to make sure the officer was indeed fading into the distance.

"Rudy, this was the last time!" She vowed.

He reached to give her a playful pat.

"What a performance, Babykins!"

The car swerved, Natacha screamed and Rudy recovered the steering wheel just in the nick of time.

From the moment Rudolph Valentino laid his infamous sloe-eyes on Natacha Rambova, his friends all knew she was "always Rudy's girl." The two were introduced on the Metro Pictures' studio lot where she worked as an art director and he as an actor. Although Rudy never spent a single night in bed with his wife Jean Acker, when he met Natacha he was still a married man. In the eyes of the law and Jean Acker, he was not at liberty to be carrying on with anyone, let alone the talented and beautiful Natacha Rambova.

Most formal photographs of Rudy and Natacha give the impression they were sedate, middle-aged and erudite. However, first-hand accounts from their friends and family reveal the opposite and portray them as openly passionate about each other and as fun-loving and thrill-seeking as any of their peers. Stylistically, Natacha Rambova could not be described as a flapper, as she wore her hair wound into a bun and preferred long dresses. But her outward appearance belied her free-spirit and both she and Rudy lived their private lives as avant garde artists with little allegiance to any dogma or social convention. Consequently, his marital status at the time of their introduction did nothing to restrain either of them from engaging in a public love affair.

"Natacha, I want you to meet Rudolph Valentino. Rudolph, this is Miss Rambova, my art director."

With these words, producer and actress, Alla Nazimova presented her next candidate for the lead role in her production of *Camille* to the film's art director, Natacha Rambova. Natacha was surprised to see Rudolph Valentino standing at her office door and astonished he would consider auditioning for the role. It was common knowledge in the Hollywood community that Alla Nazimova once publicly accused Rudolph Valentino of being a home-wrecking Lothario. Nazimova lived in New York City during the DeSaulles divorce hearing as well as Jack DeSaulles' murder trial. During a dinner party at the Ship's Café in Santa Monica, she chided Rudy about his role in the DeSaulles' scandals. In the presence of several Metro executives and actress Dagmar Godowsky, Nazimova referred to Rudy as a pimp and put the blame for Jack DeSaulles' murder squarely upon his illicit affair with Mrs. DeSaulles.

So when Natacha first shook Rudy's hand, she assumed he had forgotten the incident at the Ship's Cafe. Natacha had just rejected several actors for *Camille's* lead male role and her initial reaction to Rudy was much the same as it had been for every other candidate; he hardly looked the part. It did not help matters that Nazimova escorted Rudy to meet Natacha directly from the set of the *Uncharted Seas*, where he had just completed a scene requiring a dousing with a studio-generated snowstorm of mica used as artificial snow. By the time Nazimova left Rudy alone with Natacha, the Los Angeles heat was not helping his faux Yukon appeal and he was glistening with sweat, melting stage make-up and white shiny flecks.

Natacha eyed Rudy for a few moments before asking if he would submit to a make-up test. He agreed, but asked if in return she might please put in a good word for him with Madame Nazimova. If Rudy hadn't smiled with this request Natacha might never have handed him the part. She would never be sure whether it was his straight white teeth or the flecks of white mica on his face, but she was dazzled. With a click of his heels and a slight bow, Rudy grinned and turned to leave. The role was his and before long so was the heart of the film's art director.

It was not surprising that Rudy and Natacha were immediately attracted to each other. She bore a resemblance to Blanca DeSaulles and he fit Natacha's profile of beau ideal as he was foreign, handsome and physically well-built. Being the more reserved of the two, Natacha gave a brief impression she was not easily wooed and co-workers on the set of *Camille* remembered her initial annoyance at Rudy's

71

flirtations. They also recalled that when Natacha did return his affections, it was obvious to everyone they were a steamy item. On a few occasions, filming was delayed while everyone on the set waited for the two rumpled lovers to emerge from Rudy's dressing room. The fact that Rudy was still married to Jean Acker was a minor glitch on their cloud nine. During the filming of *Camille*, Jean Acker's husband and Natacha Rambova fell madly in love.

They dismissed the concerns of their nay-saying friends by explaining they were merely friends working overtime to ensure *Camille's* success. But they fooled no one. Making their romance even more of a poorly-guarded secret, Rudy did not hide the fact he found Natacha's Sunset Boulevard bungalow a far more entertaining place to sleep than his own apartment. Within the first few weeks of their affair, his clothes began a gradual sift into Natacha's closet and every time he arrived at the door of her tiny home he carried another armload of belongings.

Natacha and Rudy made their first public appearance in December of 1920 when they arrived, dressed in tango outfits, to attend a costume ball at the Alexandria Hotel. Word of their brazen debut shot back to Jean Acker and one month later on January eighteenth, she filed a suit of separate maintenance against her husband, naming Natacha Rambova as co-respondent. Despite the fact that Jean Acker had never shown the slightest interest in being Rudy's wife, at least in the biblical sense, she launched an ambitious campaign to secure her title and his financial support. By the time her day in divorce court finally arrived, she hoped to have ample evidence that she deserved substantial alimony. Eager to tip the scales of justice in her favor, she hired a private detective to shadow her husband and ordered him to case out Natacha's Sunset Boulevard bungalow.

In light of the consistent roles Rudy was securing in respectable movies at the time, it may be difficult to believe he would risk jail time by poaching for his dinner in the hills above Hollywood. Nevertheless, his wee hour raids into the ravines were not the result of any excess imbibing of prohibition liquor. The truth was; he was out of work, flat broke and hungry for those quail dinners.

The public had yet to view his first major screen performance in *The Four Horsemen of the Apocalypse* as the film's release was delayed until March of 1921. Metro Pictures made this decision in order to time the opening of the film with the convening of the assembly of the League of Nations and the dedication of the Tomb of the Unknown Soldier. This marketing strategy left Rudy's performance as Julio Desnoyers sitting in film cans all winter long while he completed work in three more films for Metro, *Uncharted Seas*, Nazimova's *Camille* and *The Conquering Power*.

Nearing the end of production on *The Conquering Power*, Rudy approached Metro Pictures requesting they grant him a raise. He was earning a salary of three hundred and fifty dollars a week and at the time both he and Natacha felt four hundred and fifty dollars would be fairer compensation.

Rudy's mentor at Metro Pictures, screenwriter June Mathis, assured him that his performance dominated *The Four Horsemen* and on the eve of the film's debut she encouraged him to press Metro for the modest raise in pay. June Mathis reminded him how she and director Rex Ingram previewed the early footage of the film and found his work so impressive, they rewrote the script to showcase his character.

Metro Pictures invested nearly a million dollars in the production of the anti-war film and on the eve of the film's international release studio executives were not about to reward it's young and untested lead actor. Metro's response to Rudy's request for the raise and final offer was an extra fifty dollars a week. Offended by their decision, Rudy informed his employers he would complete work on *The Conquering Power* under protest. He was hardly surprised when his Metro Pictures' paychecks ceased and he was informed there was no further work scheduled for him in any future Metro films.

Meanwhile *The Four Horsemen of the Apocalypse* premiered and was hailed as a cinematic masterpiece with Rudy's performance as Julio receiving glowing praise. But while critics were raving over his performance, the rising star was again out of work and slipping deeper into debt. He and Natacha were living on a cash advance she received for work on another Alla Nazimova production, *Salome*. It was only through Rudy and Natacha's resourcefulness that they managed to keep the Sunset Boulevard bungalow larder full and their two newly-acquired Great Dane puppies fed. Friend and cameraman Paul Ivano moved into the bungalow to share expenses and Natacha pawned her jewelry and refurbished used furniture to make do.

At low tide, the three friends drove to the Santa Monica pier in Natacha's Buick roadster to gather mussels for dinner and Rudy and Natacha executed midnight poaching raids into the Hollywood hills with military precision. Together with Paul Ivano, they launched a small business venture by placing an offer in movie fan magazines; anyone forwarding a quarter would receive a photograph of Rudolph Valentino as Julio Desnoyers. Even as the bags of letters, with quarters enclosed, arrived at the bungalow, Paul Ivano secured little work as a cameraman, Rudy still had no work and Natacha resorted to taking in design students.

It was then, with all the common sense of two artists giddy with love, that Rudy and Natacha added yet another mouth to their household. When Universal Studio's animal trainer, Curly Stecker showed them a six week old lion cub, they begged him to allow them to keep the cat as a pet. Curly explained it was impossible, if not dangerous, to domesticate a lion, but Natacha and Rudy argued to the contrary. Curly knew better and told them so, but "Zela" the lion cub soon joined the bungalow household.

Not long after Zela's arrival, Rudy announced to Natacha and roommate Paul Ivano that he had just signed a one picture contract with the Famous Players-Lasky Company. He said the offer came about after he received a note from Famous Players-Lasky executive, Jesse Lasky and the studio's president, Adolph Zukor. He explained that the note congratulated him for his fine work in *Four Horsemen* and this prompted him to stop by Jesse Lasky's office to thank him for the kind wishes.

It was during the ensuing one hour meeting with Lasky, that he signed a contract stipulating he would be cast in the lead role in one film. More importantly, Rudy told Natacha and Paul, that he walked away from the meeting with a week's paycheck in his pocket as a signing bonus. Thrilled with the work and the fast cash, he said he hurried straight back to the bungalow to share his good news. Natacha and Paul were not as overjoyed as he had hoped. They both wondered how Rudy could have been so impulsive to sign rashly on the bottom line.

Rudy paid no attention to their lukewarm reaction. After all he was supporting a substantial debt and still owed his tailor in New York a great deal of money. He reminded them there were many mouths to feed at the bungalow, even if they were several dogs, a lion cub and a new addition to their zoo; a green moss monkey. He also informed

Natacha and Paul that he was about to receive a paycheck of five hundred dollars a week to play the lead role in the film version of the popular novel, *The Sheik*. He added, that if the film turned out to be a box-office success, Jesse Lasky guaranteed him a longer, even more lucrative contract.

The three friends celebrated Rudy's news by scrounging some bootleg wine and inviting June Mathis and her mother to crowd around a table in the bungalow's living room for a spaghetti dinner. Rudy was elated and eagerly anticipating his impending work in *The Sheik*. Within the next few weeks he would be able to clear a few tabs around town and make many surprised tailors, barbers, automotive shop owners and grocers very happy.

❧

In 1921, there was probably no more effective guarantee for an author's success than to have their work branded sadomasochistic, misogynistic pornography fit for censorship and banishment. E.M. Hull's graphic tale of a Sheik's abduction and rape of a proper English lady met all of this criteria. Despite an organized campaign to condemn her work, when the controversial book first appeared in English bookstores it became an instant bestseller and sparked a firestorm of popular obsession.

It was not long after the book's release, that the public learned the E.M. in E.M. Hull stood for Edith Maude; Edith Maude Winstanley was the author's full name. The revelation that the torrid action novel was written by a woman from the Derbyshire countryside stunned the book's mostly female readership and its ardent critics. Even Edith Winstanley's neighbors found this impossible to believe for they knew her as the shy, retiring wife of a gentleman farmer who bred prize pigs.

This news piqued the interest of a young executive at the Famous Players-Lasky Company's London office. Twenty-six year old Walter Wanger, the studio's general manager in charge of production, paid close attention to *The Sheik's* popular appeal. He knew the book was about to make its way across the Atlantic and was confidant Mrs. Winstanley's novel would hit a vein of frenzied response in America.

Wanger contacted Famous Players-Lasky's Vice President in charge of production, Jesse Lasky to alert him to the book's arrival. Lasky relied heavily upon Wanger's critical analysis of all prospective stories the studio targeted for production and listened attentively to his assessment of E.M. Hull's bestseller. In advance of *The Sheik's* arrival in the U.S., Wanger returned from the studio's London office and passed his copy of the sensational book on to Jesse Lasky's secretary, Jeanne Cohen. Wanger had little doubt Edith Hull's, Sheik Ahmed would elicit the same reaction from Miss Cohen as he had from a legion of palpitating women in England. When Lasky's secretary finished her speed read, she was smitten and Walter Wanger needed no further convincing.

He handed the book on to one of Famous Players-Lasky's readers for interpretation, in synopsis form, before Jesse Lasky and other studio executives. The first dramatic presentation of *The Sheik*, as rendered by Miss Julia Herne, was so effectively executed that Lasky was immediately sold on the project. He summoned Walter Wanger to his office and uttered three words that would forever change Rudolph Valentino's life; "Buy the book."

While other Hollywood studio executives were scratching their heads and accessing the feasibility of adapting the racy book into a motion picture, Walter Wanger wasted no time and closed the deal by purchasing the rights to Edith Hull's, *Sheik* for $12,500.00. His prediction that the book would be successful in America proved to be on target, as *The Sheik* quickly achieved bestseller status. Due to Wanger's foresight, within three months from the time the book first reached its American audience, the film version was in full production on the desert sands near Yuma, Arizona.

The star of the film wanted desperately for *The Sheik* to be a success and thereby guarantee a more substantial contract for himself with Famous Players-Lasky. When Edith Hull learned Rudolph Valentino would be playing her Sheik Ahmed, she sent him an inscribed copy of the book. Rudy kept her signed edition on his nightstand and studied the book as he labored over his latest role. He found the contradictions in the Sheik's character difficult to interpret and struggled with Ahmed's disparate traits of savage tribesman and European, educated gentleman. By the first day of shooting he was so riddled with anxiety that Adolphe Menjou, the actor portraying the Sheik's friend, Doctor St. Hubert, made a point of befriending his jittery co-star.

While Rudy worked diligently on his performance, women across America had no idea the screen version of *The Sheik* and the actor playing the lead role were about to hit them full-force. As *The Sheik* was being filmed on the sands of Buttercup Valley in Arizona, life for most of these unsuspecting American women was nothing short of wretched. One year earlier, on August 26, 1920, they were finally granted the right to vote, although this historic victory had yet to translate into any real womens' liberation. It was still a man's world and the majority of women spent their daily lives well-restricted within the mental and physical confines of their homes as they toiled over laundry, cooking, cleaning and caretaking.

Most homes still lacked the simple conveniences that would eventually free women from such arduous domestic servitude. In 1921, many housewives hand pumped water, cooked over hot coal stoves and labored from dawn to dusk in the service of their family. It was profoundly disturbing to the controlling males of these households when many of these housewives began demonstrating a few sure signs of rebellion. But womens' rising hemlines, bobbed hair and make-up were not their only budding guerrilla activities.

Copies of subversive literature, such as E.M. Hull's *The Sheik* were discovered wedged under mattresses and womens' audible sighs were not going unnoticed as they caught a quick read between their rug beating and floor scrubbing. Men grew increasingly worried and they were not about to allow the slightest crack in their status quo. Every effort was made to stifle the troubling trend.

In 1921, a bill was pending in the state of Utah which, if passed, would provide for a fine and imprisonment for any woman daring to wear her skirt higher than three inches above her ankle. And any women participating in local bathing beauty contests were hauled off to the pokey and charged with indecent exposure. But the effects of these and a range of other repressive campaigns were about to be undone by one lone rider.

Just over the humdrum horizon of a nation of disempowered women, a nervous actor, cast in the role of Sheik Ahmed, was adjusting his desert robes and rehearsing his sprints across the Arizona sand dunes on his Arabian stallion. Rudolph Valentino was about to ride to the rescue.

☙❧

Rudy's paychecks from *The Sheik* were a godsend for the Sunset Boulevard household. Bills were stamped paid, leftovers filled the icebox and the Great Danes, the moss monkey and the lion cub Zela were all fat and sassy. Even Natacha and Paul Ivano threw themselves into the excitement of the production of *The Sheik* by appearing as extras along with a little girl by the name of Loretta Young. In August, when Rudy returned from shooting the final retakes on the sand dunes in Oxnard, California, he arrived with a gopher snake and a new German Shepard he called, Sheik. While filming was completed on the studio lot in Hollywood, Rudy was able to drive home every day for lunch. His motivation for these hurried lunch hours at the bungalow was an extensive restoration of a 1914 Cadillac.

For months he complained to Natacha saying her Buick roadster had no pick-up as it puttered around Los Angeles. When she finally gave the nod to use the Buick as a trade-in, he was off in search of a vehicle upgrade. Natacha hoped he would find something reasonable in exchange, but when he pulled up in front of the bungalow honking the horn of a 1914 Cadillac in desperate need of body work, she could only stare in amazement.

Rudy's renovation of the vehicle bordered on obsession as he installed a cigarette lighter, added new spot headlights, mirrors, applied a new coat of black paint and meticulously hand-painted the custom trim. Every lunch hour during the final days of filming *The Sheik*, he headed home to eat as fast as possible in order to devote as much time as possible to the Cadillac.

From a sly vantage point across the street, his wife Jean Acker's detective caught an eyeful during those backyard, bungalow lunch hours. For a few days the detective watched Rudy as he sat draped in his Sheik costume while Natacha sketched his portrait. While she drew, Rudy ate sandwiches and tossed bits of bread to the several dogs sitting before him anticipating every morsel. To the detective's astonishment a monkey, tied to a tree in the backyard, shrieked and pulled at its leash. And as soon as Rudy finished eating his lunch, he removed his desert robes, tossed them on a nearby table, threw on a pair of greasy coveralls and headed straight for the Cadillac.

"His love was as hot as the desert sands!"

With this sizzling declaration, full page advertisements in the *Los Angeles Times* assured movie goers in the largest possible flowing letters that *The Sheik* would surpass all of their expectations. On November 1, 1921, the film premiered at Grauman's Million Dollar

Theater in Hollywood and crowds strained against the barricades near Broadway and Third Street. Traffic snarled and policemen waved their arms and shouted at several valiant attempts to break through the flimsy wooden restraints. A few arrests were made, but for the most part the crowd anticipating the first glimpse of *The Sheik* kept their enthusiasm in check.

To accommodate the crush of moviegoers, Grauman's scheduled *The Sheik* to play continuously from eleven in the morning to eleven at night. They fixed their matinee ticket price at thirty-five cents and all evening performance seats at an unheard of fifty-five cents. Grauman's management took full advantage of the movie's hype and booked no less than eight prologue stage attractions with every performance accompanied by the theater's full orchestra, the Wurlizter organ and a piano.

Additional musical numbers including Liszt's Second Hungarian Rhapsody and a vocal offering by Mr. Darrell Cole were added to the already lengthy program. During the last stage act before the actual showing of *The Sheik*, a bevy of desert harem dancers, billed as Grauman's "Far Dance Interpretations," swarmed the stage with swirling gauze skirts and tinkling bells. Throughout the night's pageantry, the star of the show sat nervously in his box seat. He was utterly clueless that he was about to be broadsided by his own transcendent performance and life as he knew it would never be the same.

Rudy and Natacha were seldom early risers and on one fall morning they were sleeping in once again. Daylight failed to cause the slightest stir in the bungalow and they lay sprawled across their bed in a room vaguely resembling a mortuary chapel. The bedroom furniture was painted enamel jet black, a pitch black carpet covered the floor and the windows were shrouded in mauve taffeta. Rudy and Natacha rested in their peace in yards of black satin bedding while curled at their feet, half hidden in the rumpled covers, lay Zela the lion cub.

Even as the lion cub slept, she grew faster than her owners cared to acknowledge. Her tiny snarls which they found so irresistible three months earlier, were becoming more threatening by the day. Denying the reality of the cat's inevitable metamorphosis into a deadly beast, Rudy and Natacha continued to allow her to sleep on their bed.

It was Zela who first heard the whack against the outside of the bedroom wall that morning. She snarled to her feet and before Rudy or Natacha could make a move, the cat pounced from the end of the bed up onto the sill of a small screened window. Her sudden weight against the screen caused it to topple out onto the yard and to her owner's horror, Zela disappeared through the opening.

Natacha grabbed a robe and ran out the front door, while a dazed Rudy, with his hair on end, followed a few steps behind. Half a block from the open window, they found Zela with her prey. She was tearing at the tattered pant leg of a suited man who was hopping towards a parked car. When Zela heard Natacha's voice, she turned long enough to release her catch.

Rudy arrived just in time to sweep the heavy animal into his arms while Natacha caught a long look at the man speeding away in his car. It was no mystery to her why this suit was hovering by their bedroom window. Jean Acker's detective had finally been successful and witnessed exactly what he was hired to uncover; Rudy and Natacha without cover.

With her day in divorce court fast approaching, Jean Acker was gathering an arsenal of evidence in a bid for financial support from the man she summarily rejected. But just as she and her lawyer were putting the finishing touches on her case, they were forced to recalculate all of her requests for monetary compensation. *The Sheik* was opening in theaters across the country and any figures they had previously tallied had to be promptly inflated.

If cautious mothers and fathers were anxious about the effects motion pictures were having on their children before *The Sheik*, after the movie premiered they broke into a full sweat. Despite all their protests, teenagers filled each showing to capacity and gasped in the dark as Rudolph Valentino's Sheik Ahmed rode his horse at full speed across the desert, kidnapped a refined English lady and raped her for a seemingly interminable time in some dusky tent.

It may be hard to fathom today, but in 1921, Rudy's onscreen behavior as *The Sheik* was considered such revolutionary, hardcore lovemaking that he instigated a national sensation. His performance generated instant box office heat and caused women to faint in their theater seats, besotted teenagers to emulate his every move and inspired parents, as well as conservative organizations across the heartland to collectively wince. Flashing what quickly became his signature menacing glare, Rudy had swaggered onto the screen to crease a few new wrinkles in the neatly-pressed, puritanical ways of love making.

On a twenty foot high screen, before an audience of predominately women and impressionable teenagers, Rudy violated every rule of proper parlor courtship. Not satisfied to grant the damsel a tidy peck on the cheek, he pressed his mouth in the palm of her hand, along the inside of her arm, the side of her neck and planted his hands anywhere he wished in full view of the camera. Reaction to a few of *The Sheik*'s more passionate kisses was so overwrought that theater owners resorted to hiring uniformed nurses to stand poised in the aisles with smelling salts, their eyes glued to the screen in anticipation of their cues.

And if Rudy's behavior as *The Sheik* did not sufficiently outrage, the fact that he was Italian made obsessing on him even more illicit. The same year *The Sheik* premiered, Congress passed the Emergency Quota Act restricting the number of Italian immigrants arriving in the U.S. each year. Anti-Italian sentiment was rampant in 1921, and contributed in great measure to the uproar over *The Sheik*'s popularity. With wives, daughters and girlfriends finding the film's Italian leading man so appealing, xenophobes sharpened their tongues and pencils in an all out assault on Rudolph Valentino. Most of this hostile rhetoric fell on deaf ears and the campaign to deter youth from the lure of the foreigner known as, Sheik Rudolph Valentino, by and large failed miserably.

Undeterred, local newspapers published anti-Sheik editorials and ministers grew red-faced as they pounded their pulpits, imploring their parishioners to avoid the temptation of the corner picture show's box office sensation, *The Sheik*. Children were duly warned that by failing to resist any temptation to emulate the Sheik they would taint their family's respectable names forever. Rudy's audiences were intoxicated by his exhilarating new way of making love and embraced his sensational performance as a titillating education in unheard of displays of passion.

In the eyes of his female fans, Rudy quickly assumed the stature of pioneer, champion, and five-star shaman of sexual liberation. They were adamant that when it came to romance and love making, he outplayed anyone on screen and deserved the moniker; The Great

Lover. Beaus and husbands, on the other hand, with few references in their world for such displays of love, could only sigh in frustration. Their only recourse was to pay the price, sit through *The Sheik* and watch the master at work. With so many people up in arms, wilting and wondering, *The Sheik's* box-office revenues were fat. Rudy had scored one major hit.

Jesse Lasky was more than pleased with Rudy's performance and offered him a second contract stipulating his appearance in one more movie with Famous Players-Lasky. Rudy would be paid seven hundred dollars a week to star in the lead role of the screen version of Frank Norris' seafaring adventure novel, *Moran of the Lady Letty*, scheduled to be filmed in San Francisco. Paul Ivano was hired as a cameraman and he and Rudy made the trip to San Francisco together a few days before shooting began.

After their long days filming on the docks of San Francisco, Rudy and Paul returned to their suite at the St. Francis Hotel where they ate an early dinner, napped until midnight and then hit the Barbary Coast to paint San Francisco a serious red.

With Natacha's work on Nazimova's production of *Salome* intensifying, she opted to remain in Los Angeles. One morning as she sat with her coffee and a fresh copy of the *Los Angeles Times*, she happened to scan a daily gossip column. There in black and white was the detailed report; the star of *The Sheik*, Rudolph Valentino and cameraman, Paul Ivano had been spotted in San Francisco the past several nights in the company of the beautiful actress, Miss Aileen Pringle.

Natacha steamed at the kick-in-the-teeth item, packed a suitcase and boarded the next train up the California coast to San Francisco. With her mother, Muzzie and step-father Uncle Dickie traveling in Europe, she planned to stay in their San Francisco home on Nob Hill. Determined to get to the truth of the matter and find out whether her lover was having too much fun without her, she arrived in San Francisco later that evening.

Across the city by the bay, just as the two drinking buddies were showered, shaved and natty, their hotel room telephone rang. Paul Ivano answered the call to hear Natacha's voice and listened for a few seconds before asking, "Where are you darling?"

Natacha shot back, "Don't call me darling!"

Paul scribbled down an address, mumbled an "okay" and turned to Rudy, "Natacha wants you to come to this address at once."

Rudy was puzzled as to why Natacha had suddenly surfaced in San Francisco, but nevertheless followed her directions to an impressive residence near the Fairmont Hotel. When a stone faced butler opened the door and motioned him into the foyer, Rudy was not slightly bowled over. He paused to absorb what he thought must surely be a figment of his imagination; gold-leafed Louis XV furniture, gold inlaid floors, gold framed art work and gliding down a winding staircase, a gold-gilt Natacha. Rudy stood transfixed as she made her grand entrance wrapped tightly in a gold silk evening dress. In the rush of his enthusiastic embrace, all of Natacha's suspicions about Aileen Pringle vanished as quickly as the press of her silky gold gown.

That night Natacha explained her palatial San Francisco home to Rudy by filling him in on key details about her and her family. He listened attentively and tried to reconcile the Natacha he knew with such opulence. For most of the previous year they had shared a cramped bungalow furnished with orange crates and second hand furniture which they painted themselves in the back yard on Sunday afternoons. At times they had barely been able to scrounge their evening meals and keep their pets fed. He never imagined Natacha's family to be so wealthy and wondered why he never bothered to investigate.

Natacha explained that her real name was Winifred Kimball Shaughnessy Hudnut and that she was born to an Irish father and a Mormon mother. The Nob Hill mansion belonged to her mother's fourth husband, Richard Hudnut, who was her stepfather "Dickie". He was the founder of a cosmetics empire and creator of the popular DuBarry cosmetics line. Uncle Dickie had legally adopted her. Rudy listened to Natacha's revelations and slowly realized the bohemian artist he'd fallen in love with, was in fact an heiress.

Natacha's cathartic confession had an exhilarating effect upon her and her euphoria inspired a spontaneous plan the following morning. She convinced Rudy he should act as her mannequin in a photo shoot with Hudnut family friend, photographer Helen MacGregor. Spent from a night of heady revelation and lovemaking, Rudy was game for anything. Consequently, in Helen MacGregor's studio on Post Street, he submitted readily to Natacha's whimsical design. His willingness to play along may have had more to do with the fact that his only role was to stand naked and allow Natacha to slather him with grease paint and Vaseline while he struck a few poses.

That afternoon, Natacha dressed Rudy as the ballet dancer Nijinsky in *Prelude a l'Apres-Midi d'Une Faune*. She parted his hair, wound it into impish curls and spread black and white grease paint over his body in large swaths. After a fig leaf and a few clusters of grapes were strategically secured, photographer Helen MacGregor went to work. The grease paint photos of Rudolph Valentino were French postcard racy by 1921 standards and Natacha was satisfied with her work of art. When she and Rudy returned to Hollywood, she passed a few copies along to their friends. Neither Natacha nor Rudy could foresee that Jean Acker would get her dainty hands on a few of the more revealing shots. With her divorce hearing close at hand, Jean passed them along to her attorney and felt confident she finally had Rudy by the fig leaf.

On November twenty-third, divorce court convened and Jean's lawyer summoned a nervous Rudolph Valentino to the witness stand to testify. While a courtroom of reporters scribbled on their notepads and a crush of flappers packed the gallery, Jean's lawyer removed two of Helen MacGregor's photographs from his briefcase and paraded around the courtroom holding Valentino "d'une faune" high enough for all to see.

The satyric get-up worked well for Nijinsky, but did little for the young man then appearing coast to coast as *The Sheik*. *The Sheik* had only been in theaters for a few weeks, but in that short time the public had effectively melded the character of Sheik Ahmed with the young actor playing the role. The shock of the risque photos of the Sheik in a state of complete undress and debauchery reverberated throughout the courtroom.

Rudy took a deep breath and explained to the court how the photos were nothing more than a study for a proposed movie role. Jean's attorney raised his voice to press his point further with dramatic accusations that this, your honor, was precisely what Mr. Valentino was up to with his mistress while he was not supporting his lawfully wedded wife, Jean Acker. When Rudy's lawyer, W.I. Gilbert rose to object, the judge dismissed the entire matter.

The photos of the naked Sheik Ahmed, as he had submitted to his mistress for dress-up were soon forgotten. For when Jean Acker took the stand to testify how her husband beat down Grace Darmond's bathroom door and slugged her square in the face, the crowd gasped and tittered. The court then proceeded to hear further testimony from Rudy's friends and from Metro executive, Maxwell Karger and his wife.

Mrs. Karger took the stand to testify, saying it was only six hours after her wedding that a sobbing Jean Acker confided in her how her marriage to Rudy had been a terrible mistake. She said Jean was devastated and sorely regretted her actions. Testimony ended with Jean tearfully telling the court she was too ill to work because of the stress of the divorce. This prompted the judge to order an inquiry into Jean's actual physical condition and necessitated a postponement of the proceedings until December sixteenth.

During the break in the court's proceedings, box office returns from *The Sheik* proved beyond a shadow of a doubt that Rudy had succeeded in creating a blockbuster for Famous Players-Lasky. To his great relief, Jesse Lasky followed through on his promise by offering him a long term, lucrative contract. Upon Lasky's advice, Rudy engaged the Robertson and Webb Agency to negotiate a three year deal which guaranteed him a salary of twelve hundred and fifty dollars a week during the first year of the contract, two thousand dollars a week the second year and three thousand dollars a week for the third year. With his second film for Famous Players-Lasky, *Moran of the Lady Letty*, set for immediate release, Rudy was scheduled to begin work on the first film under his newly inked contract; a screen interpretation of Elinor Glyn's popular novel, *Beyond the Rocks* co-starring Hollywood legend Gloria Swanson.

When divorce proceedings resumed on December sixteenth, Rudy testified Jean refused to grant their marriage any actual existence and this statement was reinforced when Jean admitted under oath that the marriage was never consummated. Love letters from Rudy begging Jean as his "dear little wife," to allow him to "furnish her with a home" were submitted to the court. Jean sobbed throughout her testimony as she claimed she was still in poor health and desperately in need of her husband's financial assistance.

When the Judge called an end to the testimony, Rudy was confidant his interminable wait for his divorce was nearly over. Unfortunately, the Judge announced he would not render his decision until January tenth.

❧❧

Universal Studios' animal trainer, Curly Stecker was correct when he warned Natacha and Rudy that their lion cub would eventually grow into a wild animal. In the days preceding this painful realization, Rudy was the only person able to physically handle the cat. After he suffered several savage rakes, he and Natacha made the painful decision, loaded Zela into the Cadillac and headed off to her new home at animal trainer Felix "Doc" Graff's ranch in nearby Azusa. All of the animals on Doc Graff's ranch belonged to actress, writer, animal right's activist and independent movie producer, Nell Shipman. And all of the creatures in Graff's private zoo, both tame and wild, appeared with Nell Shipman in her wildlife adventure films.

If Natacha and Rudy had not been able to consult with Doc Graff and Nell Shipman, their Sunset Boulevard bungalow zoo might not have fared nearly as well. They frequently drove to Azusa in the San Gabriel Valley to visit Doc Graff's compound. Rudy especially loved to perch atop the many habitats' wire mesh runways in order to watch the animals below and was particularly fond of one East Indian honey bear. Zela could scarcely have found a more suitable home than Doc Graff's Azusa estate. However, this provided little consolation to either Rudy or Natacha and as Zela was locked into her own enclosure, they both wept.

They took solace in the fact that Rudy's paychecks had quickly created sufficient funds to make a sizable down payment on a home at 6770 Wedgwood Place in the Whitley Heights neighborhood of Los Angeles. Recovery from Zela's loss would be eased by the excitement of the purchase of this spacious new home overlooking Highland Avenue and Cahuenga. Until Rudy's divorce was declared final in January, he would keep a few personal possessions and a legal address at Paul Ivano's new apartment which was located a convenient ten minute walking distance away.

Rudy and Natacha moved into their Whitley Heights home the week before Christmas. Although their few belongings from the bungalow barely filled a single room and the heat and electrical service had not yet been connected, they ignored the inconvenience and proceeded to deck the empty halls for the holidays. On Christmas Eve, a crackling fire warmed the living room and they trimmed a towering tree with candles and red ribbons. Absorbed in their plans to renovate the new home, they discussed the construction of kennels, stables and garden pathways while hoping that on January tenth the judge would grant Rudy his divorce and they would be free to marry. Sometime around midnight, Rudy had a strange request for Natacha.

"Wait upstairs until I return. And don't come downstairs until I call you."

He seemed excited with his subterfuge, so Natacha played along. After fifteen frosty minutes shivering in a cold bedroom, she finally heard him call out, "Babykins, come on down!"

Just as Natacha reached the light of the flickering Christmas tree and the welcome warmth of the fireplace, she heard a tiny yelp. There, in front of the tree, Rudy stood grinning with all the pride of a new parent. Peeping from the cuff of a Christmas stocking tacked precariously to the mantel was the furry face of a Pekingese puppy. It was love at first sight for Natacha and she named her baby Peke, Little Chuckie.

Natacha and Rudy spent the remainder of their first Christmas Eve in their new home as Little Chuckie's rapt audience and they both later remembered that night as being one of the happiest of their lives. They laughed, talked for hours and nearly froze to death. As the fire burned into embers and bed-covers seemed the only solution to the chill, Rudy removed an envelope which he'd tucked in the boughs of the Christmas tree and handed it to Natacha. While he awaited her reaction, she unfolded the single sheet of white paper and read a poem written for her which he titled, "You."

"You are the history of love and its justification.
The symbol of devotion.
The blessedness of womanhood.
The incentive of chivalry.
The reality of ideals.
The verity of joy.
Idolatry's defense.
The proof of goodness.
The power of gentleness.
Beauty's acknowledgment.
Vanity's excuse.
The promise of truth.
The melody of life.
The caress of romance.
The dream of desire
The sympathy of understanding

87

My heart's home
The proof of faith.
Sanctuary of my soul.
My belief in heaven.
Eternity of all happiness.
My prayers.
You. "

Chapter Five

Best Friend and Manager

Falcon Lair, ten years later in the spring of 1930 -

Lily May wiped her hands on her apron as she listened to the stranger's every word. He seemed to be a well-meaning fellow, but she could hardly believe a word he was saying. He said he stopped by to tell her all about those green and blue lights he saw flying through the house the night before. Lily May was terrified at the development and could only utter a quiet, "Aw, gwan."

As the stranger continued to explain how everyone in the neighborhood knew Rudolph Valentino's ghost haunted his last home, Lily May shuddered and felt a cold shiver run up the back of her neck. Although she was her employer's loyal, hardworking cook, she was a most timid woman. Having said all he came to say, the stranger abruptly turned and left. As soon as he was out of sight, Lily May untied her apron, plopped it on the kitchen table and was off to inform her boss, Hollywood cowboy hero Harry Carey, that she would not spend another minute in Falcon Lair.

The stranger at the kitchen door was well informed when he told Lily May she was the last to know. By March of 1930, so many people had seen the eerie lights in Rudolph Valentino's home on Bella Drive that rumors the place was haunted were old, old hat. Harry Carey, however, had ignored the stories when he leased Falcon Lair after returning from filming his latest movie, *Trader Horn* in Africa.

Falcon Lair had been vacant for most of the time since Rudolph Valentino's death. Even promising offers for the infamous residence failed to result in a final sale when cash deposits were not large enough to satisfy the court. Estate executor George Ullman still held the mortgage on the property at the time Harry Carey signed the lease in March of 1930. Harry agreed to the monthly rent of one hundred and fifty dollars and moved in with his wife Olive and their two small children, son Dobe and daughter Cappy. He felt sure Falcon Lair would be a perfect home and the stables a fine spot to park his famous movie star pony, Sonny.

Harry and Olive Carey considered the persistent and hair-raising reports of Rudolph Valentino's ghost drifting by the windows of their new home, utter nonsense. But when a trembling Lily May threw in her apron, Harry decided it was time to telephone his landlord, George Ullman. A torrential rain was flooding the streets of Los Angeles the night George answered Harry's telephone call requesting he come at once to Falcon Lair. George dreaded the short drive and didn't believe in ghosts, but he had to remind himself of that fact as duty once again forced him back to Falcon Lair.

He turned his car up the steep driveway of 2 Bella Drive and parked directly in front of the home's main entrance. Cursing the sheets of driving rain, he flipped the collar of his suit coat up around his neck and made a dash for it. It was only a few minutes before the front door swung open and George stepped into the warmth of the familiar foyer. Harry Carey wasted no time complaining how rumors of Valentino's ghost had just cost him the family's beloved cook. George assured him there was probably a logical explanation, handed him his dripping hat and headed through the house to a side room near the kitchen. There, he walked straight to a bookcase and pushed it aside to reveal a small hidden door.

He leaned his shoulder into the door saying, "Rudy had a tunnel built to connect the main house with the servant's quarters."

After some effort, the door creaked open, revealing a dark passageway beyond. George brushed aside the few cobwebs blocking the doorway and walked into the tunnel with a bewildered Harry Carey picking his way close behind. A few bats fluttered over the two men before vanishing into the darkness of the musty corridor. Some fifteen feet into the passageway, George paused and pointed to several long strands of electrical wiring dangling loosely down one side of a chimney. As he and Harry approached the chimney, they could see the wiring was connected to a small metal terminal box on the floor.

"There's your answer," George said to Harry.

Clenching his cigarette in the corner of his mouth, George knelt down, grabbed the metal box and gave it a quick yank. With a loud pop, a few sparks and a plume of smoke, the box was torn from its tether. Harry Carey was speechless at the discovery of the tunnel and by his landlord's apparent disregard for the threat of electrocution.

Leaving the smoldering wiring to the bats, George headed back towards the light of the house as he gave Harry an explanation.

"A while back we had a caretaker here who thought he'd make a few bucks holding seances in Rudy's bedroom. My wife and I attended one of his events because he was convinced if I showed up Rudy would materialize. He hired some local woman to act as a medium and we all sat around a table in the pitch dark. Before long we heard all sorts of noises and some character wound up in gauze appeared, mumbled a word or two and then disappeared. Every few minutes another figure, about the same height and build as the previous ones, made an appearance. Before long the same character, this time dressed as the Sheik, appeared and started moaning, 'I am here George. I am Rudy.' I guessed at that point I had served my purpose as far as the caretaker was concerned, so I handed the medium a five dollar bill for her trouble and my wife and I left. I found out later the caretaker strung his electrical wiring for his bogus seance effects down that chimney. Maybe the wind or the bats caused the rig to flicker on and off."

As the two men returned to the foyer, Harry handed George his hat and thanked him for removing the caretaker's wiring to the not-so-netherworld. George then headed out into the stormy Los Angeles night to hurry home. For by March of 1930, he was almost always in a hurry and reports of Rudolph Valentino's ghost were the least of his worries.

As he drove back down the winding muddy road from Falcon Lair that night, his mind was absorbed in an incongruent agenda; the plunging stock market, failing banks, unpaid legal bills, the medical details of tuberculosis and the business of canning tomato juice. The windshield wipers slapped back and forth in the driving rain, aggravating his overwrought mind.

Over the past three and a half years he felt he'd done an admirable job as Rudy's executor and he was proud of his successful promotion of Rudy's last two films, *The Eagle* and *The Son of the Sheik*. He had collected sufficient royalties from these two movies to clear Rudy's $300,000.00 debt and still managed to retain everyone on the Rudolph Valentino Production Company payroll in addition to regularly issuing cash advances to Rudy's three apparent heirs. George turned his car into another sharp bend on his slippery ride home and realized that despite these successes, the hard truth was that the business of settling Rudy's estate had become nothing more than legal quicksand for him.

The driving rain confused his train of thought. How, he asked himself, how had it all come to this? He tried to recollect. Perhaps his sure sink into this logistical morass began some seven years earlier in 1923, when Rudy met two scientists named Albert Lambert and Jean Gauthier.

༄༅

During the last years of his life, Rudolph Valentino owned and operated Cosmic Arts Incorporated, a scientific research laboratory in New York City. He funded all of the laboratory's expenses including rent, utilities, office supplies, laboratory equipment and the salaries of two scientists, Albert Lambert from Brussels and Jean Gauthier. As owner of the laboratory, Rudy not only paid Gauthier and Lambert's salaries, but also the salary of Richard Ingalls, a sales representative who promoted the two scientist's work. Whenever the need arose, Rudy loaned the two scientists and Richard Ingalls the services of his New York secretary, Estelle Dick.

Albert Lambert and Jean Gauthier discovered a mineral which they registered with the U.S. Patent Office as Lambertite. Their scientific research involved experimentation with Lambertite and the development of a chemical process utilizing this mineral in a revolutionary technology of film processing. Rudolph Valentino not only owned the laboratory, he held the patent on the chemical process called, The Lambert Process. Rudy purchased The Lambert Process patent in May of 1923 and hoped to resell the patent and pocket a substantial profit if Lambert and Gauthier were ever successful in their experimentation. The prospect of a scientific breakthrough in his laboratory was not the only motivation for Rudy's purchase. For several years the laboratory served as his corporate identity, or legal alter ego, and a safe shelter for all of his financial transactions.

After purchasing Cosmic Arts, all of Rudy's studio contracts were assigned to the laboratory's ownership and the laboratory, in turn, paid his salary. This business practice was widely used and legal. It would be two years after assuming ownership of the laboratory when George reorganized all of Rudy's financial holdings, including Cosmic Arts, under the ownership of a newly-created corporate identity, Rudolph Valentino Productions.

By March of 1930, George was still acting as both the executor of Rudy's estate and head of Rudolph Valentino Productions. In this capacity, he was underwriting Cosmic Arts Incorporated as a subsidiary of Rudolph Valentino Productions. He nearly sold The Lambert Process patent for a quarter of a million dollars in June of 1927, but before a final sale could be transacted the deal fell through. Determined to recuperate some of Rudy's years of investment, George continued to issue checks to scientists Lambert and Gauthier in New York and record all of their Cosmic Arts' expenditures in his Rudolph Valentino Productions' accounting ledgers.

During the first three and a half years after Rudy's death, George bankrolled Cosmic Arts, Inc. to the sum of just over $18,000.00 dollars. Unfortunately for George, every item he recorded in his ledgers under the heading of "Cosmic Arts Expenditures" was being added to a lengthy list of transactions coming under scrutiny by Alberto Valentino and his fleet of attorneys. They challenged George's underwriting of Cosmic Arts, Inc. and believed the laboratory to be an illegitimate expenditure of the estate. They maintained that George, as executor, had no authority to continue financing the laboratory as a subsidiary of Rudolph Valentino Productions.

Alberto did not deny that his brother's executor had done an admirable job spinning straw into gold. He also did not dispute the fact that by March of 1930, George had cleared all of Rudy's $300,000.00 debt and increased the estate's worth to nearly $300,000.00. Alberto's objections to George's executorship did not concern the value of the estate but the interpretation of George's authority over Rudolph Valentino Productions and the continued existence of Rudy's production company.

Alberto challenged George's claim that Rudy personally granted him the dual authority to act as executor and head of Rudolph Valentino Productions. He also rejected George's assertion that Rudy charged him with this dual role on a sheet of instructions which should have been attached to his will. Alberto repeatedly petitioned the court to order George to cease and desist in his role as head of Rudolph Valentino Productions and requested the production company be declared an asset of the estate and immediately liquidated into cash. The court had yet to issue a final ruling in response to his request. Meanwhile, George remained resolute saying it was only through his efforts as head of Rudy's production company that he had been able to generate funds for the estate and thereby disperse cash advances to not only Alberto but to the other two people mentioned in Rudy's will, Alberto's sister Maria Strada and Teresa Werner.

Nevertheless, Alberto was determined to oust George from any role in Rudy's estate and instructed his lawyers to delve deeper into George's "Executor's Accounts" for any just cause to do so. During the three years following Rudy's death, Alberto's attorneys objected to George's "Executor's Accounts" on some forty occasions. They objected to his ability to draw a salary as executor, to the various bank accounts he held in several banks in Los Angeles on behalf of Rudolph Valentino Productions and even to the format of his book-keeping.

During the second week of April 1930, George's "Executor's Accounts" were scheduled to be reviewed by the court once again. But unlike George's previous court appearances, on this occasion he would not merely be endeavoring to have his accounts approved by the court, he would be taking the witness stand to defend his personal integrity and professional performance as well. For Alberto had just filed a lawsuit charging him with fraud and mismanagement of the Valentino estate. When George was notified of Alberto's lawsuit he issued a terse statement to the press saying,

"The filing of the suit against me is ill-advised, especially in view of the fact that there was no estate when Valentino died and all of the value has been created since that time."

Alberto filed his lawsuit against his brother's executor only five months after the stock market crashed on Black Tuesday in October of 1929. The increasingly bleak economic situation made the lawsuit an even more devastating turn of events for the Ullman household. With a family to support and legal fees mounting, George's pursuit of the almighty dollar was as much of a grim reality as it was for every other American that spring. In an effort to secure his future income, he established his own talent agency, the S. George Ullman Agency at 8979 Sunset Boulevard. Despite his most optimistic projections, by the spring of 1930 his income from his agency was doing little to relieve his dire financial situation. In light of his shrinking salary, he wondered how much longer he would be able to afford the services of his attorney, Leonard Wilson.

George did not wonder how Alberto afforded his crack team of Hollywood's finest legal minds, as he believed he was still receiving substantial financial backing. He knew Alberto's relationship with Pola Negri had recently soured after she loaned him another seven thousand dollars. As Alberto had yet to make good on the loan, Pola terminated their friendship. In light of their estrangement, George doubted Pola was still bankrolling Alberto's legal team.

Unfortunately, during the course of transacting the business of Rudy's estate, George knew he had made a powerful enemy of the one person he did suspect to be Alberto's new underwriter; Joe Schenck. Schenck was Rudy's last employer and during the weeks immediately following Rudy's death, George's relationship with him had been amicable. On a handshake, Schenck even assured George there would be a position waiting for him with his United Artists as soon as he settled Rudy's affairs. But by the spring of 1930, George Ullman and Joe Schenck openly hated each other. Three ugly altercations provoked their bad blood; the buy-out, the life insurance policy and the bum's rush.

∝ᘓᔫ∝

As the president of United Artists Studios, Joe Schenck was a two-fisted Hollywood mogul who never tolerated the slightest threat to his bottom line. He earned his position of dominance in the motion picture industry as a ruthless power player and notorious heavy weight. Joe Schenck's business was always priority over the interests of any friend, foe or family. For example, one of his many diverse business holdings was his brother-in-law, Buster Keaton's production company, Buster Keaton Productions. When Keaton's film, *Steamboat Bill, Jr.* faltered at the box-office, Schenck sold his production company to MGM studios. Schenck told his brother-in-law nothing about the sale until it was a done deal and Keaton consequently lost all artistic control over his films, turned to alcohol and faded away. Joe Schenck was not one to tread lightly. And those who happened to get in his way, whether a brother-in-law or George Ullman were doomed to feel the impact of his heavy stride.

During the last two years of Rudy's life, George negotiated two impressive contracts on his behalf with Joe Schenck's United Artists Studios. The two movies Rudy made under the first of these two United Artists' contracts were his last two films, *The Eagle*, which opened in the fall of 1925 and *The Son of the Sheik* which opened shortly before his death. It was only a few months before Rudy's death, when George negotiated the second contract with Joe Schenck. Under the terms of this second contract, Rudy was scheduled to appear in *The Firebrand*, a film depicting the life of Italian Renaissance sculptor,

Benvenuto Cellini. Pre-production on this film began shortly before Rudy's death.

At the time the second contract with United Artists was signed, Schenck purchased a life insurance policy on Rudy in order to protect his studio's investment in the film. Schenck had no idea that the then apparently healthy thirty-one year old star of his upcoming feature, *The Firebrand*, would die before a single scene of the movie could ever be filmed.

A few weeks after Rudy's death, Schenck telephoned George with what he believed to be a generous offer; he would buy out Rudy's percentage in the profits of his last two films, *The Eagle* and *The Son of the Sheik* for one lump sum and Rudy's financial interests in both films would then terminate. Schenck told George he would be wise to accept the offer as no dead man's films had yet to make a dime. What would be the point, he asked, of holding out for a percentage in two films that were sure to flop. George flatly declined the offer.

He responded by informing Schenck that he was confidant *The Eagle* and *The Son of the Sheik* would make a great deal of money for United Artists as well as for Rudolph Valentino Productions. Schenck shot back by telling George he was ill informed and Rudy's percentage from the films would amount to little. George refused to discuss the subject further. He soon proved Schenck's dire projections to be wrong by successfully promoting Rudy's last two films. Joe Schenck wrote many hefty royalty checks to Rudolph Valentino Productions which eventually totaled $321,326.60. It was not long after nixing Schenck's buyout offer that George made another appointment with the fuming executive.

In Schenck's United Artists' office, George held him accountable for every term of Rudy's second contract. He told Schenck that as executor of Rudy's estate he had personally reimbursed United Artists every dime Rudy received as cash advanced for his work in *The Firebrand*; the film he never lived to complete. George also reminded Schenck that the life insurance policy held by United Artists on Rudy more than covered all pre-production expenses for *Firebrand* and resulted in a substantial surplus of cash for the studio.

George elaborated by saying he considered this surplus of cash from the life insurance policy a profit for United Artists which was generated by Rudy. As Rudy's second contract assured him 25% of all profits generated by his films, George told Schenck he was there to collect Rudy's twenty-five percent on the life insurance surplus.

Schenck was livid when George demanded he pay up and write him a check then and there to Rudy's estate for another forty thousand dollars.

George was promptly shown the office door, but remained undeterred by Schenck's ire and continued to press the sore subject for weeks. Joe Schenck finally relented and cut a check for the forty thousand dollars made out to Rudolph Valentino Productions. George was satisfied he scored another substantial financial victory for the estate but he had yet to realize just who he had crossed in the process.

Soon after receiving the forty thousand dollars, George telephoned Schenck's office once again; this time to discuss the position Schenck offered him with United Artists. Joe Schenck's secretary informed George that Mr. Schenck was in his New York office and said he should meet with him there to discuss any future employment. George purchased his fare to New York by eking the cash out of the slim Ullman household budget and boarded an eastbound train.

When George met with Schenck in United Artists' New York offices, he reminded the mogul he had promised him a job. Schenck was dumbstruck by George's audacity and replied he had no memory of ever having said any such thing. He gruffly told George there would never be a position for him with United Artists and gave him the transcontinental bum's rush towards the door. Angry words were exchanged before George's ignoble exit and before the office door officially slammed shut behind his back. From that moment on there were no further communications between Joe Schenck and George Ullman.

By the spring of 1930, as George faced Alberto's lawsuit on charges of fraud and mismanagement, the indomitable Joe Schenck had become an even bigger fish in the big pond. As one of Hollywood's most illustrious power brokers, he'd changed rank at United Artists from President of the studio to Chairman of the Board. He'd also earned a prestigious seat on the board of directors of The Bank of America; a position granted to him by the bank's president, A. P. Giannini. As an influential Hollywood money man, Giannini owned both The Bank of America and The Bank of Italy and would eventually merge his two financial houses into the Bank of America.

In 1919, Giannini financially ruined Rudy's benefactor Frank Mennillo and vowed Frank would never work another day in California. Many years later, Giannini's cohort, Joe Schenck made a similar vow to another of Rudy's close friends; his manager, George Ullman. Crossing men as powerful as A. P. Giannini and Joe Schenck was always bad business as Frank Mennillo knew well and as George Ullman was about to discover. The vendettas these men issued were never taken lightly and never forgotten.

The fact that Alberto's cadre of Hollywood celebrity lawyers all happened to be affiliated in some capacity with Schenck's United Artists was not lost on George. He was well-aware that as his status with Joe Schenck sank to persona-non-grata, Alberto Valentino's a-list of attorneys grew. Alberto's attorney Milton Cohen not only represented Pola Negri but Joe Schenck's wife Norma Talmadge, the United Artists' star Charlie Chaplain and other Hollywood elite such as Gloria Swanson, Fatty Arbuckle, and John Gilbert.

Alberto's attorney James C. Scarborough represented several other United Artists' stars including cowboy hero William S. Hart. And attorney Morton E. Feiler was an executive with Joe Schenck's Theater Circuit Company. As Alberto's United Artists attorneys prepared their case of Guglielmi v. Ullman, they recognized a bounty of billable hours and settled in for the long haul of filing petitions, objections and affidavits with the court. With Schenck's legal arsenal at his disposal, victory seemed almost guaranteed for Alberto. But despite being armed for the battle before him, Alberto was fraying from a few difficult years struggling to strike it rich in Hollywood. Throughout the four years since his famous brother's death, he had been relentlessly blaming George Ullman for every rough edge.

On October 20th 1927, a headline in *The Los Angeles Times* read, "Valentino II Sports New Face". The accompanying article included both before and after profile shots of Alberto as well as an account of how he spent the previous afternoon strolling Hollywood Boulevard showcasing his newly-improved profile for reporters. He informed them he was seeking a career in the movies and his wife would soon be doing the same. He then continued to divulge the details of his recent plastic surgery which altered his nose in order to appear more photogenic. Alberto's satisfaction with his new nose would be fleeting as the procedure soon failed. He would explain his troubling nasal predicament to one interviewer,

"The days of the bandages were long. Then what happens? Horrible! My nose sticks up. It is too short. I return to the doctor to say something must be done. I told him this nose is more unpleasant than before. I said to him,' I ask that you give me a nose that will photograph. I do not demand pure Grecian nose just the one the camera will like. It is not as good as before.' "

With his nose in ruins, screen roles failed to materialize for Alberto and by September of 1928 he had secured work in only one film, *Tropic Madness* with Leatrice Joy. He appeared to be conflicted about portraying his quest for a movie career to the public and in one interview he stated he "never intended to go into pictures". He claimed that his lust for a film career was all a misconception as it was "other people" who pushed him to replace his brother. In this same interview, he claimed he had refused all film offers that came his way. After stating he would not "dream of imitating" his brother, he said when an appropriate time passed since Rudy's death, he would make a bid for his own movie success just to "keep his brother's name alive."

Nevertheless, he did not receive immediate offers from the motion picture industry. Instead, Alberto resigned to awaiting his windfall from Rudy's estate, all the while collecting cash advances from executor George and a modest paycheck from an office job at MGM studios. Alberto Valentino was no ordinary office worker at MGM, especially in regards to legal representation as he consistently had access to a ready team of overly-qualified attorneys.

When further complications from the plastic surgery on his nose required subsequent surgical procedures, his attorneys sued his surgeon, Dr. William Balsinger. His suit against Dr. Balsinger whet Alberto's appetite for litigation and he instructed his attorneys to file another lawsuit in June of 1929. On this occasion he sued for damages incurred upon his vehicle after an accident that occurred on Las Palmas Avenue. His attorneys filed their petitions with the L.A. municipal court and Alberto won his case and an award for the total amount of all damages; nine dollars.

A few months later he gave the nod to his lawyers to file another lawsuit. This suit charging his nemesis George Ullman with fraud and mismanagement of his brother's estate. Although George was outraged by Alberto's actions, he was not surprised by the timing of the lawsuit. He knew his stormy relationship with Alberto had recently taken a drastic turn for the worse after he ceased advancing lump sums of cash to Rudy's beneficiaries. In an effort to bring fiscal order to the haphazard petitioning and issuing of cash advances, George initiated the dispensation of cash in regular weekly amounts according to his own recollection of Rudy's oral instructions.

Alberto was irate at this change in policy, but George reiterated that Rudy personally instructed him to do so many years before. According to George's memory, Rudy instructed him to dispense one hundred dollars a week to Alberto and fifty dollars a week each to Rudy's sister Maria Strada and Teresa Werner. Teresa Werner did not object to George's decision to dispense regular weekly checks. Over the years she never questioned his integrity, his professional performance, his decision to act upon his recollection of Rudy's oral instructions and never filed a single objection to his executor's accounts. Rudy's sister, Maria, who left Los Angeles to return to Italy in March of 1927, also filed no complaint in regards to George's stipends or to his adjustment in procedure.

Alberto's reaction was stridently opposite. For years George had accommodated his requests for substantial amounts of estate funds and the instigation of a one hundred dollar a week allowance put a serious crimp in his comfortable lifestyle. Since his younger brother's death Alberto had ensconced himself in Hollywood in true star fashion. Initially, the Hollywood press embraced his bid for stardom as he was, after all, a Valentino by blood and this might have guaranteed his ascendancy as America's next Sheik. Although Alberto was portrayed by the press as the older, more mature and studious member of the Guglielmi family, during his first days in Hollywood, George paid Alberto's bills and knew a stridently different man.

The "Alberto", George knew enjoyed epicurean tastes and a lifestyle that included a bungalow at the Ambassador Hotel, cases of the finest bootleg wines, gourmet meals served in his bungalow from the Ambassador's kitchen and a parade of female companionship. George was scarcely surprised to learn Alberto's reaction upon hearing he would be living on his salary from MGM and a one hundred dollar a week stipend.

Alberto levied his protest through his lawyers, but George remained resolute in his decision. He believed he owed his allegiance to the financial order of Rudy's estate and not to the continued support of Alberto's comfortable lifestyle. He felt he'd been generous with Alberto by permitting him to periodically live rent free in both Rudy's Whitley Heights' home and in Falcon Lair. He had offered little resistance to Alberto's requests for cash advances and in the first year after Rudy's death he issued several bank drafts to Alberto including two checks for $10,000.00; one in December of 1926 and a second one issued in June of 1927.

George's ledgers revealed Alberto spent money as recklessly as his deceased brother Rudy. Alberto's annual income for the calendar year February 1926 to February of 1927 was just over $50,000.00; a hefty income in 1927 by any standard. In January of that same year Pola Negri reported she gave Alberto an additional $15,00.00 and during the months previous to Rudy's death, entries in Falcon Lair's household ledgers itemize checks issued to Alberto totaling another $7,000.00. Although George complied with Alberto's requests and successfully bankrolled his lifestyle for years, Alberto vigorously objected to the initiation of the weekly stipend of one hundred dollars. In a sure course of self-annihilating legal action, he continued to snap at the very hand that was feeding him by filing the lawsuit against George. This expected turn of events came in the wake of another highly-publicized event, also orchestrated by Alberto, which took place on a platform at the train station in Pasadena.

❧

Alberto personally notified the Los Angeles press to share the news that his son, Jean was at last arriving from Italy. He told them the fifteen year old was traveling in the company of opera star, Tito Schipa who happened to be traveling to Hollywood to sign a contract with Metro-Goldwyn-Mayer studios. As reporters gathered on the train station platform in anticipation of Jean's arrival, Alberto delivered his statement,

"Jean really resembles his dead uncle. Of course he is young and at the age when boys change in appearance, but I can see a real likeness."

He then explained how he had just enrolled the boy in a private school where he would receive dramatic training. When the Santa Fe Chief came into view, the reporters began to shove for their best vantage point. The engine steamed to a halt and Alberto led the pack of men as they rushed towards the car bearing the famous teenager. The moment Jean stepped from the train he was caught in the full glare of his dead uncle's limelight.

While Alberto bustled about positioning the confused youth for another statement to the press, every reporter present stood agape.

They could all see the striking resemblance in the young man's eyes; those signature eyes of his uncle Rudolph Valentino. Jean's hair was slicked straight back and he flashed a look of intense anger towards the crowd of men staring at him as he blurted only one comment:

"My ambition is to be a sound engineer! Don't say I want to be an actor! I don't!"

✌✊

In advance of the impending proceedings of Guglielmi v. Ullman, the court ordered an audit of George's books and ledgers. He complied with the court order and surrendered his Rudolph Valentino Productions' ledgers along with boxes of office receipts, invoices and check registers dating as far back as February of 1926 to Harry H. Baskerville at the Baskerville Audit Company.

Accountant Harry Baskerville also requested to review Rudolph Valentino's personal financial paper trail for the last seven months of his life. George regretted the invasion of Rudy's privacy, but boxed up Falcon Lair's household ledgers, Rudy's payroll records and statements from his various bank accounts and delivered the entire lot to Harry Baskerville. George was also asked to submit Rudy's first contract with Joe Schenck and all legal documents and contracts pertaining to the operation of the laboratory in New York City, Cosmic Arts Incorporated.

George was determined to challenge Alberto's charges of fraud and mismanagement by standing proudly behind his years of hard work as Rudy's executor. After all, the numbers did not lie and he had cleared Rudy's staggering debt, successfully promoted his last two films and accumulated a surplus of money for the estate in the process. Accomplishing this during the early days of the great depression was an astounding feat by any economic measure. While George was reaping these profits, the stock market crashed and the country was thrown into a crippling economic crisis. Banks across the country were failing by the hundreds and bread lines of the unemployed wrapped around city blocks. Despite George's successes during hard times, Alberto's lawsuit loomed before him and he could do little else but work feverishly to generate a viable and steady income from his S. George Ullman Agency.

Although he signed a few minor actors and actresses with his agency and represented several Hollywood notables such as Theda

102

Bara, her husband Charles Brabin, Peggy-Jean "Baby Peggy" Montgomery and Erich Von Stroheim, by 1930 none of these actors generated sufficient work for George to earn much from his percentage. Supporting his family from these less than mighty stars' earnings made for a tough go.

Nevertheless, George was confident he could prove to the court that he had acted honestly and in accordance with Rudy's wishes. In order to do so, he desperately needed to locate any existing copy of the missing page of Rudy's instructions. If Rudy had actually signed this document, thus rendering it a legal portion of his will, it was critical to George's defense that he enter the courtroom with the document in hand.

Alberto's lawyers were prepared to assert that since no copy of those instructions had been located they alleged the document never existed. Without evidence that Rudy charged George with the dual role as head of his production company and executor of his estate, they planned to argue George was only appointed to act as executor. In this sole capacity they alleged he should have received authorization from the court for every single business transaction, no matter how trivial, made on behalf of Rudolph Valentino Productions. They also alleged that without proof of this dual role, Rudolph Valentino Productions and all of it's subsidiaries should be declared assets of the estate and liquidated.

If Alberto's attorney's were successful in convincing the court to rule in his favor, George would be held personally responsible to reimburse the estate for every cent he had earned, spent or invested during the course of operating Rudolph Valentino Productions, as well as being held liable for the reimbursement of all of the money he advanced to the heirs since Rudy's death.

George maintained that it would have been logistically impossible for him to obtain the court's permission for every daily transaction he made in the course of running the corporation, Rudolph Valentino Productions. He claimed in doing so his work would have come to a standstill, terminating the employment and salaries of everyone involved and ending his ability to advance cash to the three heirs. With many mouths to feed, from his own children to every employee of Rudolph Valentino Productions, George felt he had no other option but to run the company the same as he had during Rudy's life.

In the days prior to the commencement of court proceedings, George continued to attend to the business of his executorship by working long hours poring over the Rudolph Valentino Production company ledgers. He fielded a myriad of estate issues which included everything from processing Rudy's fan mail to the removal of faulty wiring at Falcon Lair to quiet reports of his restless ghost. He was also occupied with the upcoming dedication of the first official memorial to Rudy scheduled to take place on what would have been his thirty-fifth birthday.

Noted sculptor Roger Noble Burnham completed his commission of a four foot bronze male nude statue titled, "Aspirations" which would be installed in the center of a lily pond in Hollywood's DeLongpre Park. Burnham was paid handsomely for his artistry and the same year he completed "Aspirations" he was commissioned to create the impressive Trojan Warrior statue for the University of Southern California for a $10,000.00 fee. George funded the commission of Burnham's memorial statue through donations made to the Valentino Memorial Guild primarily by a New York widow, Mrs. Zunilda Mancini. Mancini's late husband was Italian and she was eager to fund the Rudy tribute as she believed "all Italians were good men."

But George's attentions were not solely focused upon the May sixth dedication of the Burnham statue, as he was deeply involved in the planning of his defense with his attorney, Leonard Wilson. Wilson informed his nervous client that Alberto's attorneys would open their case against him by specifically targeting his investment of Valentino estate funds in two failed loans.

The subject of failed investments was an all too familiar news story during the spring of 1930. But the fact these two particular financial fiascoes involved movie star Rudolph Valentino's money made them front page headlines. The public was about to eagerly follow all the juicy details of the courtroom proceedings and learn all about *The Sheik's* association with two failed businesses; a busy bank on the corner of Eighth and Broadway in Los Angeles and a cannery, churning out cans of tomato juice, on K Street in Merced, California.

❧

The crux of Alberto's lawsuit would be his ability to convince the court that his brother's executor acted irresponsibly and fraudulently when he loaned estate money to The Pan American Bank and "padrino" Frank Mennillo. Leonard Wilson and Alberto's attorneys spent considerable time preparing their cases by scrutinizing these two loans.

They learned that when the value of Rudy's estate reached $287,000.00, with $125,000.00 of this amount in liquid cash, George made three investments. The first of these investments was a $22,000.00 loan to movie star, Mae Murray. Within a few months, she repaid the loan plus interest which George promptly deposited in the bank. Heartened by the modest success of this first loan, George negotiated two more investments. Rather than enter the speculative equity market, he took a more conservative approach and over a period of two years he made two secured loans. The first of these two loans was to Vab, Frank Mennillo's tomato juice cannery then under construction in Merced, California.

After Frank was forced to close his many Californian businesses in 1919, he left the cannery business, moved to the east coast and lived in New York and Washington D.C. where he accepted a position with the Italo-American League or Italian American League. Through his connections with this organization, Frank was appointed Vice-Chairman of the Italian-American National Campaign Committee for the election of Warren G. Harding. He then began barnstorming with Harding rallying crowds in Italian neighborhoods and delivering translations of his speeches. A few months before Rudy's death, Frank decided to return to the canning business in California he helped to pioneer and he purchased five acres of land in Northern California, near Merced, where he began the construction of a tomato juice cannery.

By January of 1927, he was busy raising capital for his new California venture when he received a letter from the Valentino family in Italy requesting he sponsor Rudy's sister Maria and her husband when they arrived in New York that January. While Frank was squiring them about New York City, his name was appearing prominently in local headlines. Apparently an ambassador from Salvador, Count Robert Ramon De Clairmont, left a teenage daughter of one of Frank's close friends in a family way and Frank challenged him to a duel.

While the gallant Frank Mennillo was embroiled in the defense of the young woman's honor, he was also escorting Maria Strada to meet with his New York attorney. In addition to other business transacted at that meeting, it was then Maria granted Frank power of attorney. Over the next several days, Frank assisted Maria and her husband as they prepared to travel west for California to visit her brother Alberto.

Frank left New York for California the following December, and arrived in Los Angeles shortly before Christmas. George met "The Olive King" at the train station. Whenever Frank visited Los Angeles he always stayed at The Jonathan Club and it was there he and George held their first business meeting. Over dinner and a cigar in the private club's Italian Renaissance Room, Frank shared the details of his plans for his new cannery and asked George for a loan from Rudy's estate to complete the construction of the plant. With Frank's years of experience in the canning business, the deal seemed sound to George.

He'd also known Frank since 1923, and knew the true extent of his financial generosity towards Rudy. To close the deal, Frank presented George with a personal letter of guarantee written by Maria Strada. She addressed the letter to George and requested that upon Frank's return to Los Angeles, he was to charge his expenses against her future share of Rudy's estate and "give him directly on account of me, how much he will ask for."

Upon Maria's written request, George granted a loan to Frank in the form of six checks totaling $40,000.00 dollars, which he issued over a period of a few months. As collateral on the five-year loan, Frank gave Rudolph Valentino Productions five thousand shares of stock in his company, Vab. The loan's contract was signed, George was granted a position as qualifying director on Vab's Board of Directors in order to oversee the investment and Frank then headed north to the San Joaquin Valley.

There he met with an officer of the local branch of The Bank of Italy and requested a line of credit for his new business. In response, the banker presented Frank with a teletype he'd just received from the bank's president, A. P. Giannini stating that Mr. Frank Mennillo's credit was no good in that or any other bank. It was painfully clear to Frank that Giannini had not forgotten his vow to prevent him from ever doing business in California. Construction on Frank's cannery was completed solely upon his Rudolph Valentino Production Company's loan of $40,000.00 and the business was then operated on a cash only basis.

Four hundred miles to the south, George was already negotiating his second investment and by March of 1928, he loaned

$50,000.00 to The Pan American Holding Company; the controlling interest in The Pan American Bank at Eighth and Broadway in Los Angeles. When the bank opened with great fanfare in December of 1926, their advertisement read, "Bring your problems and your deposits here." For George the key word in this ad would be "problems." He accepted six hundred and eighty shares of capital stock from the bank as collateral on the three month loan. At the time the stock was valued at one hundred dollars a share.

Unfortunately, during this three month period the west coast stock market experienced a wild fluctuation. On June eleventh, "Blue Monday," investors rushed into San Francisco's Montgomery Street brokerage houses to sell, sell, sell. The plunge was so drastic and devastating that within a few days, A. P. Giannini's Bank of Italy and Bank of America stock dropped twenty points and lost some twenty million dollars. It would be two weeks before the situation stabilized and during those two weeks many banks in California failed.

The Pan American Bank at Eighth and Broadway was one of the ill-fated banks that collapsed during the frenzied trading. George reacted to the crisis by granting the bank a ninety day extension on their loan. When he demanded full payment at the end of this extension he learned that the California State Banking Department had ordered The Pan American Bank to close its doors and Rudolph Valentino Productions' six hundred and eighty shares of stock were declared worthless pieces of paper. As a partial payment on the loan, George accepted $25,000.00 and a parcel of real estate from The Pan American Bank. Unfortunately for George there was even more distressing news coming from Merced; Frank Mennillo's tomato juice cannery wasn't faring much better than The Pan American Bank.

A. P. Giannini had continued to block Frank Mennillo's return to the San Joaquin Valley by sending word to all of his branches of the Banks of Italy and Banks of America informing them to have nothing to do with the New York businessman. While Frank fought to stay solvent, the value of his cannery's stock plummeted and unable to repay Rudolph Valentino Productions he asked George to refinance his loan.

As George made both of these loans from profits he generated for Rudy's estate, his failed investments in The Pan American Bank and Mennillo's cannery did not financially cripple Rudolph Valentino Productions. But Alberto Valentino had been poised for years to capitalize upon any stumbling on George's behalf and leapt upon the news of The Pan American Bank's closure and Frank Mennillo's faltering tomato juice plant.

❧❧

On the eve of The Pan American Bank's failure, George and Bee Ullman welcomed the arrival of their third child, a baby girl. Upon the advice of their neighbor across the street, silent film vamp, Theda Bara, George and Bee named their baby, Brenda. At the time of the baby's birth, Theda Bara was immersed in the occult and it was only after lengthy sessions over her crystal ball that she divined Brenda to be the perfect name for her friend's child. However, the spiritual authority of Theda Bara was no match for baby Brenda's five-year-old brother, Bobby. He took one quick look at his new baby sister and since it happened to be Easter time, he renamed her Bunny. The moniker held fast and Brenda would always be known as Bunny.

Shortly after giving birth to baby Bunny, Bee Ullman contracted tuberculosis. At that time, tuberculosis was no minor infliction as antibiotics had yet to be discovered. The tuberculosis spread rapidly throughout both of Bee's lungs. Her physicians initiated a course of drastic treatment which involved several radical surgeries and eventually the surgical removal of one lung and several ribs. Her recovery would be measured in years, not days and caused unending worry for all of her loved ones. Her husband George was profoundly affected by her grave illness.

Bee's survival from these surgeries required retreats to the healing dry air of Palm Springs during the damp winter months in Los Angeles and lengthy stints of bed rest and recuperation. George spent many sleepless nights by his wife's side and did his best in his role of doting caretaker and father. He took great pride in his expertly prepared roast beef Sunday dinners and found the time and financial resource to ferry his children to the Hollywood Bowl for evening concerts. During the darkest days of Bee's illness, the Ullman's little boys and baby Bunny were often left in the care of a nurse as George worked long hours resolving the legal issues of Rudy's estate while wresting a living as a talent agent.

By March of 1930, his loyalty to his friend Rudy had reached epic proportions and he drove himself relentlessly. He juggled his stressful personal life, the demands of his talent agency and the continuing business of Rudolph Valentino Productions. Torn between his desire to honor the wishes of his deceased friend and settle the

108

affairs of his estate and the very real possibility that this course of action posed a serious threat to his family's financial security, George was often short-tempered, stretched to his limit, smoking far too many cigarettes and losing a great deal of sleep.

As the bright and scholarly son of Anna and Joseph Ullman, "Samuel" George was raised as a classically trained violinist. Joseph and Anna Ullman were both immigrants, Joseph a tailor from Hungary and Anna from Germany. Their son, preferring to be called George, spent his childhood at 1606 Avenue B in New York City and dreamed of one day making his parents proud by becoming the conductor of a symphonic orchestra. As a teenager he was driven to this goal and practiced his violin day and night while poring over orchestral musical scores. But these studious pursuits ultimately did little to prepare him for the direction his life would take.

Instead of standing poised before a symphonic orchestra with baton in hand, he would find himself a desperate man, huddled over a desk in his lawyer's office facing charges of fraud and mismanagement. After years of obsessively searching for a missing sheet of paper that might vindicate him, he was about to walk into a courtroom vulnerable, empty handed. Nearly consumed with dread over this prospect and the unwelcome publicity the impending proceedings would generate, he took heart in his attorney's assurance that the court would rule in his favor and clear his good name.

While George plotted his defense with his attorney, Leonard Wilson, he knew Alberto Valentino was busy putting the finishing touches on his offensive with attorneys James C. Scarborough, Scarborough's associates Bowen, McGee, Mann and Sumner and celebrity attorneys, J.D. Knickerbocker and Milton Cohen. Unfortunately, maestro George Ullman knew full well that court battles were won and lost according to the attorney's price tags and he saw it coming.

Chapter Six

The Third Degree

May 1922, Eight years before George Ullman's day in court -

The City of Palm Springs is located in the Coachella Valley about one hundred miles southeast of Los Angeles. Back in 1922, movie stars in search of some peace and quiet found Palm Spring's mountain vistas and three hundred and fifty sunny days a year, comfortably far from the limelight. But on Monday, May fifteenth, this cherished seclusion was being violated in the lobby of the Desert Inn and some bad news was traveling fast.

Los Angeles Detective Sergeant Jess Winn stood at the Desert Inn's front desk grinding his cigarette into a heavy glass ashtray, listening intently to the voice on the phone. Sergeant Winn and his partner Sergeant King had been waiting for over an hour in the desert heat for their call to go through to L.A. County District Attorney Thomas Woolwine. By the time Sergeant Winn got his word in edgeways, there were beads of sweat on his forehead.

"That's right Mr. Woolwine, we've got five witnesses saying Valentino spent his wedding night here in Palm Springs."

With a guttural "yup", Sergeant Winn set the heavy receiver back on the phone cradle and turned to his partner saying, "Looks like we nailed him. Valentino is going down."

Sergeant King mopped his forehead with a handkerchief and stuffed it back into his suit coat pocket. "A smoke screen," he said, "between you and me, that's all it is. As soon as this Valentino story breaks, nobody will be reading squat about D.A. Woolwine's problems."

The two gumshoes had just tailed the Valentino wedding party all the way from Mexicali, Mexico and were ready to call it a day. They'd hoped to file their report with the D.A. and then head out of Palm Springs. But the cooler air of Los Angeles would have to wait, as the D.A. had just ordered them to skulk about for a little more dirt on the movie star's wedding night.

Unaware they were being followed by detectives, Rudy and Natacha were settling into what they thought would be their blissful honeymoon. Rudy's long awaited divorce from Jean Acker was finally granted in January and the decree was filed with the court on March fourth. Despite Rudy and Natacha's rush to marry, they waited until May for a break in their workloads and a few uninterrupted weeks for a honeymoon. Their marriage plans were complicated by one not so minor snag; Rudy was only granted an interlocutory decree of divorce from Jean Acker.

Under California law, an interlocutory decree required both parties in a divorce to remain unmarried for a period of one year before the divorce was considered final. But in Hollywood in 1922, there was a generous and well-known loop hole in this unpopular statute. The frustrating year's wait was routinely circumvented by a quick drive south to Mexico where couples exchanged their "I dos" before a Mexican judge. Since California law had no jurisdiction in a foreign country, authorities were powerless to prevent this practice.

Before leaving for their marriage in Mexicali, Rudy and Natacha informed attorney, W.I. Gilbert of their impending south of the border marriage. Despite Gilbert's opposition, Rudy set the necessary paper work in motion. On Friday night, May twelfth, a small wedding party including Rudy, Natacha and their friends, Paul Ivano, Alla Nazimova and actor, Doug Gerrard left Palm Springs for the drive to Mexicali, Mexico. They spent the night in El Centro, California. No one in the wedding party noticed that a car had been following them all the way from Palm Springs or that two men lurked in the lobby of El Centro's Golden Hotel.

The following morning the Valentino wedding party arrived at the home of Mexicali's mayor and news of the movie star's arrival threw the citizens of Mexicali into a flurry of preparation. Women bustled about a long table in the mayor's yard and tended to a spread of tamales, enchiladas and stacks of steaming tortillas. While the mayor perused the marriage license and positioned the wedding party for the ceremony, a mariachi band struck up a rendition of "La Paloma" on the veranda. Since May thirteenth also happened to be Paul Ivano's birthday, there was much to celebrate.

As the sounds and aromas of a true fiesta filled the air, a dozen onlookers crowded into the mayor's office. With Doug Gerrard, "Gerry" acting as best man, Rudy and Natacha exchanged their wedding vows and were at last pronounced husband and wife. The groom gave his bride a kiss, a few champagne toasts were tipped and Mexicali erupted in celebration. Early that evening the newlyweds thanked their hosts, waved to the cheering crowd and began their drive north back to Palm Springs.

Despite all of Rudy's meticulous attention to the details of his wedding, he'd overlooked one critical detail. In order to have completely circumvented California's law of interlocutory divorce, at some point before leaving Mexico he should have pulled the car over and consummated his marriage. Unfortunately, he was unaware just how important the exact location of this consummation would prove to be.

By marrying Natacha in Mexico and neglecting to spend at least one night with her there before crossing the U.S. border, he risked having his actions interpreted as a willful intent to circumvent California law. But Rudy and Natacha were in such a celebratory mood, they headed straight back to Palm Springs. They were completely oblivious that two detectives continued to track their every move and skulk just out of view hoping to pinpoint the exact location of their wedding night.

The Valentino's marriage was consummated in Palm Springs, in Riverside County and this technicality constituted Rudy's violation of the terms of his interlocutory divorce decree. But until Rudy and Natacha Valentino crawled into bed on their wedding night, no one had ever been questioned or prosecuted on this point.

So when the newlyweds arrived in Palm Springs, the detectives followed them to their accommodations on the old Palm Springs Hotel property. And it was from the lobby of the nearby Desert Inn that the two detectives filed their report with District Attorney Thomas Woolwine. Woolwine believed he had enough evidence to charge Rudy with a violation of the terms of his interlocutory divorce decree. This would be the first time a case built upon the technicality of the location of the consummation of the marriage would be tested in any California court.

It wasn't that D.A. Woolwine was eager to set a legal precedent, he was just an increasingly desperate man with motivations of a more personal and nefarious nature. On the same day as Rudolph Valentino's Mexican wedding, a commission convened in Los Angeles to investigate allegations that D.A. Woolwine had sexually harassed and illegally fired an employee, Ida Wright Jones. To complicate matters, D.A. Woolwine was up for election that year and he needed to hatch some plan to divert the public's attention away from the grim headlines being printed in his honor.

Learning through his studio snitches that Rudolph Valentino was planning to marry in Mexicali, D.A. Woolwine armed two detectives with cameras and dispatched the two men to follow the wedding party. He hoped to light up the front pages of every newspaper in Los Angeles with some flashy headlines as evidence he was hard at work upholding the law and defending public morality.

He also knew the public couldn't read enough news about Rudolph Valentino and reports of his bedroom activities with his beautiful bride would be eaten up by his fans. While the public was devouring every titillating detail, D.A. Woolwine surmised that the reports of the commission investigating the charges against him would come and go before anyone realized it had even happened.

≈≈≈

About the same time Woolwine received Detectives Winn and King's telephone call from Palm Springs, the Valentino's were saddling up a couple of horses to head into the canyons for a morning ride. Miles from the bright lights of tinsel town, Rudy and Natacha were taking to the hills in their chaps and ten gallon hats and happy to be far from the rabid attention of Rudy's growing legions of fans. During the six months since *The Sheik's* opening in Hollywood, the temptation for Rudy's fans to press in on him was seldom repressed and he was under constant pursuit.

Rudy sightings had women fainting into heaps on sidewalks and hotel carpets, grasping hysterically at his clothing and yanking clumps of hair from his head. On his honeymoon in Palm Springs, he would be safe from harm's way while he and his new bride rode their horses along the dry creek beds to head up through the hidden canyons high in the San Jacinto Mountains.

Whenever Rudy and Natacha visited Palm Springs, they stayed at the old Palm Springs Hotel which was owned by two sisters, Florilla and Cornelia White. The sisters rented their rooms and bungalows, furnished but without meals, to handle the overflow from the Desert Inn. Florilla White was a beloved resident of Palm Springs and a doctor of homeopathic medicine. The philanthropic doctor held great affection for Rudy and Natacha and awarded them both with honorary memberships in her Desert Rider's Club. As full members, the honeymooners had their choice of any of the club's finest horses.

On Wednesday, May seventeenth, Rudy and Natacha returned from their ride in the high country to learn that attorney W.I. Gilbert had just called. He left a message with Dr. White, saying that Rudy should phone him immediately. Sensing urgency in his lawyer's message, Rudy quickly had him on the line. Within the first minute of their conversation any hope for an idyllic honeymoon evaporated into the hot desert air. Rudy's face paled and he turned to his wife.

"We have to return to Los Angeles tonight. They're threatening to charge me with bigamy."

Natacha listened quietly while Rudy finished his conversation with Gilbert. Confused and stung by the development, on this occasion they did exactly as the attorney ordered and packed their bags. Around seven in the evening, they pulled out onto the highway to drive across the desert towards Los Angeles.

In the privacy of the car, Natacha made no attempt to hold back her emotions. She was distraught, sobbing and unable to fathom why they had been singled out when so many others had done the same thing. Rudy consoled her as best he could and fought to keep his attention on the dark highway stretching on before him.

By nine o'clock they spotted the lights of Los Angeles. The dismal ride home had exhausted both of them and even an enthusiastic reception from their German Shepherds barely lifted their flagging spirits. They'd begun that day in their desert hideaway as newlyweds with only weeks of honeymoon in their thoughts. They fell into bed that night dreading what the next twenty-four hours might bring.

The next day was an unnerving one for Rudy and Natacha. They spent the afternoon in attorney Gilbert's office being duly informed of Rudy's precarious legal situation and learning the details of the possible charges against him. Gilbert explained how Rudy would plead not guilty to felonious bigamy. He then revealed the penal code fixing the punishment for the crime as a fine not to exceed five thousand dollars and imprisonment not to exceed ten years in a state penitentiary.

He told them he'd spoken with Rudy's employer, Famous Players-Lasky's attorneys and they were all in agreement on one point. Natacha's immediate departure from Los Angeles was imperative. Gilbert emphasized that for the time being she could not be far enough away, even suggesting she might seize the opportunity to travel to Europe until the entire bigamy issue was resolved.

Natacha debated the attorney at length and insisted she had no intention of leaving her work in Hollywood and abandoning her husband when he needed her most. Gilbert countered that Natacha's own reputation was at risk if she did not leave at once. Unable to dispute the logic of his argument, Rudy nodded in agreement. Natacha then resigned herself to her inevitable departure by insisting it would only be a brief retreat. At this point, Gilbert informed the pair that Jesse Lasky had already made her travel arrangements and a ticket would be waiting for her at the Pomona train station that evening. They rushed home from Gilbert's office with barely enough time for Natacha to pack and drive to Pomona for her hurried departure.

The conductor on that Thursday evening run of the Eastbound Union Pacific hollered out his, "All Aboarr-rr-d!" to a few stragglers and punched a final ticket or two before the train could begin its slow roll out of the Pomona station. A peanut vendor chucked the goobers in his roaster and busied himself with his brown paper bags while two teenage girls, gawking blankly at nothing in particular, slumped out of the train's open windows. At that moment the usual evening scene became extraordinary, when Natacha dashed onto the station platform and rushed towards the train. She carried a cardboard hat box and in her arms she clutched a Pekinese puppy. No sooner did she reach the train's steps, than Rudy appeared with a ticket in hand. The girls lolling out the train window sprang to life and began waving their arms and shouting, "Oh, It's Rudolph! Oh, It's Rudolph! Ain't he grand?"

When the object of their chorus ignored their racket, they struck up the familiar chant, "Rudy! Rudy! Rudy!"

He handed the conductor the ticket just as the train began to roll. Natacha paused for a moment on the car's narrow steps and Rudy jogged along for a few feet to lean in and give her a quick peck. The Union Pacific picked up speed and headed east, leaving Rudy staring down the tracks at the flailing arms of his braying teenage fans.

Aboard that eastbound train, Natacha quickly realized what Jesse Lasky thought of her. Despite the publicity surrounding her

115

marriage to Rudy, he'd arranged for only coach passage and before the Eastern Union Pacific left Pomona she'd been squarely recognized by passengers and the railroad's crew. Sizing up her situation, she launched a futile search for seclusion away from prying eyes, rude remarks and after the train's first stop, aggressive reporters. Mapping out all possibilities, she found a dismal few.

Meanwhile, Rudy returned to W.I. Gilbert's office where he listened to more of his attorney's explanations of how a deal with the D.A. could be struck in order to have all of the charges dropped. Gilbert told his client he would take the case all the way to the Supreme Court if necessary and explained how the charges could be considered unconstitutional because a state had no authority to prosecute an offense committed outside its jurisdiction, in this case in a foreign country. Rudy nodded dutifully to Gilbert's words but his thoughts were drifting off to that Eastbound Union Pacific.

As it turned out he had reason to be worried. At every stop, Natacha was hounded by the press who seized the opportunity to write long, inaccurate articles about her. It seemed false news reports about the Sheik's enigmatic lover made for great copy. But the more Natacha was pressed for information, the more she dug in her heels and refused to respond to the reporter's questions. They ignored her defensive silence and at each stop across the country she was hounded by hoards of inquisitive reporters shouting in her direction.

On Saturday, May twentieth, the Eastbound Union slowed into the Chicago rail yard and Natacha dreaded the predictable impasse of reporters at the station. Unable to bear another onslaught, she took refuge in a baggage car and hoped to make her escape from the train unnoticed. When a conductor discovered her perched on a large sack of mail, he tried to convince her to make her move.

"Come on Miss, You've got to change trains."

Just as Natacha feared, her path was blocked by yet another wall of reporters shouting in her direction. As she lowered her head and wedged her way through the crowd she heard one reporter call out, "Have you heard they threw Rudolph in jail today?"

She ignored the question and with tears welling in her eyes, she dashed towards the station. Another reporter shouted, "Will you stick by him Natacha? Do you still love him?"

With this she turned around, looked the reporter straight in the eye and gave him a single word of response, "Forever!"

The L.A. County Jail was no comfortable place to spend a Sunday afternoon. The slab benches and broken toilets were a long contrast to the aesthetic beauty of Rudy's home in Whitley Heights. Absolutely no attorney on earth could have calmed such a rage as his that day and even W.I. Gilbert thought it wise to keep a neat distance from the steel bars of Rudy's cell. Gilbert explained to his furious client that his bail was being paid at that very moment by his friends June Mathis and Doug Gerrard. But Rudy had been awake all night and let loose with an angry outburst in Italian. He did not care who heard him or if anyone could understand his tirade of invectives. When he paused momentarily to drag on his cigarette, Gilbert broke in, "As soon as your bail is processed you'll be out of here, Rudy. Think about your statement to the press. They're waiting outside and are loaded for bear."

Only twenty-four hours earlier, upon the advice of Famous Players-Lasky's attorneys, Rudy had surrendered to the District Attorney. As soon as he stepped foot in D.A. Woolwine's office, he was arrested and charged with two counts of bigamy. He was then handcuffed and escorted to the county jail where his bail was set at ten thousand dollars. With every bank in Los Angeles closed on Saturday afternoon, he'd resigned himself to waiting for the arrival of Famous Players-Lasky's emissary to post his bail.

After a few hours it was evident no envoy from his employers would arrive in time to spring him. Doug Gerrard and June Mathis began calling in a few favors in a frantic effort to raise their friend's bail. Gerry telephoned his friend, Dan O'Brian, the San Francisco Chief of Police, who he knew was visiting in Los Angeles. Although Chief O'Brian was unable to raise the money, the actor Thomas Meighan, who happened to be with O'Brian at the time of the call, overheard the conversation. Without asking the identity of the actor in trouble, Meighan offered to help post his bond. None of these transactions happened in time to prevent Rudy from spending the night suffering in the company of a motley crowd of petty thieves and vagrants.

When Rudy's fans read news of his arrest that weekend, they not only stood by their screen idol but subjected District Attorney Woolwine to considerable pressure. No matter where he went, he was bombarded with questions concerning his plans to prosecute Rudolph Valentino. The public demanded to know why he would charge one person with a crime and not indict others who had blatantly done the same thing. They reminded Woolwine that in October of 1921, the actress Dagmar Godowsky received her interlocutory divorce decree and promptly departed for Mexico to marry screen actor Frank Mayo. Why, they asked, were no charges being brought against her?

Woolwine explained that Rudolph Valentino's case was of an international nature and because there had been no legal precedence he would wait until the courts decided the outcome to decide whether he would charge others. It sounded like double talk to Rudy's fans, the Hollywood press and to Rudy's lawyer.

Newspapers gave so much play to Rudy's marital plight, that many couples poised to make the easy drive to Mexico thought better of their scheme. After reading the reports of D.A. Woolwine's charges against Valentino, those lovebirds already on their way south hit the brakes, turned their cars around and headed home.

On Sunday morning, newspapers announced the news with sensational headlines such as, "Valentino Arrested on Bigamy!" "Investigation of Valentino Wedding Opens!" and "Inquiry Begun by Woolwine". But by Sunday afternoon, Rudy's bail was posted and as he walked out of the Los Angeles County jail with June Mathis and W.I. Gilbert, he made no attempt to dodge the waiting press. He paused to give them his statement as to why he married Natacha.

"...I, of course, regret deeply that I should have done anything that would lower me in the estimation of the American people, who have been so kind to me and have accepted me at every turn for more than I conceive to be my real worth, and who have graciously called me 'the lover of the screen'. I will say that the love that made me do what I have done was prompted by the noblest intention that a man could have. I loved deeply, but in loving I may have erred."

The press shouted more questions his way, but he nodded graciously and said he had no further statement. He was headed home to prepare a defense for his preliminary hearing which was scheduled for June first. Newspapers across the country carried his statement in its entirety and whether the public was sympathetic or not to his predicament, it made front page news. The *Los Angeles Times* carried a composite photograph of Natacha, Jean Acker and Rudy with a headline, "Now He's Wondering Which One is his Wife." There was no uncertainty in Rudy's mind. He would defend his Mexican marriage in court, let the truth be known and soon reunite with Natacha.

The District Attorney's charges of bigamy only added to Rudy's already stressful situation. His arrest came shortly after three shaky months on the set of his latest film, *Blood and Sand*. When Rudy signed his new contract with Famous Players-Lasky months earlier, he'd envisioned a successful working relationship with the studio. But by May of 1922, any cordial relations between Rudy and his bosses, Jesse Lasky and Adolph Zukor had ceased. Lasky and Zukor's refusal to post Rudy's bail was the culmination of months of ugly dispute which had Rudy inching towards a breaking point.

It was on the previous January seventeenth, that Rudy signed his new contract obligating him to complete six movies with Famous Players-Lasky and their newly acquired distributing company, Paramount. After first filming *Beyond the Rocks* with Gloria Swanson, Rudy began work in *Blood and Sand*. Being cast in the lead role in this production turned out to be a mixed blessing for Rudy.

Initially, he was thrilled to be cast as another Vicente Blasco Ibanez character and threw himself into his character of the bullfighter, Juan Gallardo. He researched all aspects of life in the ring, grew stiletto sideburns and at his own expense hired a matador as his personal adviser. Both Rudy and Natacha were committed to ensuring that the quality of *Blood and Sand* meet the same high standards of the finest art films being produced in Europe. With this in mind, they submitted a long list of requests to Jesse Lasky.

They asked that George Fitzmaurice, the French-born director of romantic dramas be hired and demanded *Blood and Sand* be filmed on location in Spain. Lasky's prompt and brusque dismissal of all of their requests rankled both Rudy and Natacha. He informed them that in an effort to curb production costs, *Blood and Sand* would be filmed on a studio back lot and on his own ranch with footage of any bullfighting scenes being shot in Spain and spliced into the final release. He also rejected Rudy's choice of George Fitzmaurice as director by stating that Fred Niblo, fresh from his successes with the Douglas Fairbanks films, *The Three Musketeers* and *The Mark of Zorro*, had already been hired.

Rudy fumed and felt he had been set in his place in no uncertain terms. He refused to accept the studio's policy that all actors, no matter how valuable, were merely expected to show up for work, follow the director's orders and keep quiet. Tensions ran high before production on *Blood and Sand* ever got underway. Each contentious exchange between Rudy, Lasky and Zukor chipped away at their deteriorating relationship.

The daily flare-ups plaguing the set of *Blood and Sand* were trivial matters compared to Rudy's reaction after viewing the final cut of the movie. When Lasky edited out a critical segment of the plot line, this set off another fire fight between artist and producer. Rudy lobbied and protested, but his campaign to have the footage reinserted into the film failed. By the time *Blood and Sand* was being readied for release, Rudy was completely frustrated. He reminded Lasky how he had verbally guaranteed him artistic input in his films. He argued that despite being the star of *Blood and Sand*, he carried no more weight in the production of his films than a five dollar a day extra. His words of protest fell on deaf ears.

By mid May, the publicity campaign for *Blood and Sand* was in high gear and Famous Players-Lasky was submitting reams of copy about the film and its star to fan magazines and news services. This glut of news about Rudolph Valentino only intensified his detractors and the timing of his Mexican nuptials could scarcely have been clumsier.

By the time Rudy married on May thirteenth, District Attorney Woolwine wasn't the only person taking direct aim at Rudy. Just as he was preparing for his marriage in Mexicali, conservative religious and social organizations were once again accusing him of being a threat to the values they held dear. They blamed his influence on a wide range of social problems and were convinced his movies and their childrens' unhealthy obsession with *The Sheik* were turning all youth into lazy, sex-obsessed vagrants.

Famous Players-Lasky deemed additional publicity necessary and issued more slick, sanitized articles about Rudy to appease his detractors. In Hollywood during May of 1922, the air was so thick with conservative moral indignation most motion picture industry executives were choking on it. Some townsfolk worked themselves into a real lather and no matter how flowery the studio prose about *Blood and Sand*'s star, the mere mention of Rudolph Valentino's name added fuel to the torches in the heady campaign to clean up Hollywood.

Only a few months earlier, several high profile scandals had rocked the motion picture industry; the manslaughter trial of Roscoe "Fatty" Arbuckle, the murder of director William Desmond Taylor and the drug related death of actor Wallace Reid. In an effort to protect their box office revenues and present a positive image of the movie industry, studio executives formed the Motion Picture Producers and Directors Association (MPPDA) and appointed Will H. Hays, a prudish Presbyterian elder and former U.S. Postmaster General, to head the association. They hoped Will Hays' squeaky clean, high-profile presence would create an impression that the motion picture industry was putting movie stars, such as the controversial Rudolph Valentino, on notice.

While Will Hays was enjoying his first days on the beat as the movie industry's "czar" and being scuttled about Hollywood for photo op sessions with studio moguls, Rudy was being released from the county jail and facing a hearing on bigamy charges. If Will Hays believed the headlines in the Los Angeles papers, it appeared that District Attorney Woolwine was just as eager as he was to clean up moral decay in Hollywood. It also appeared matinee idol Rudolph Valentino was about to make a fine example of what could happen to any movie star participating in immoral behavior.

The buzz in Los Angeles focused upon one key point; would Jesse Lasky allow Rudolph Valentino to trade in his Sheik's burnoose for pinstripes and a ball and chain and actually serve time in a California State penitentiary? The press did their best to explain the legal ramifications of Rudy's situation and sought out prominent divorce court judges to provide legal explanations of the finer points of an interlocutory decree of divorce.

Meanwhile, the man at the center of the brouhaha retreated to his home on Wedgwood Place to deal with the most disturbing aspect of the charges against him; his separation from Natacha. He was miserable without her. Rudy and Natacha were not typical newlyweds of their day who married to set up housekeeping and spend their life together after a proper honeymoon. Even though Rudy continued to maintain his residence for appearances sake as Paul Ivano's apartment on Fairfield Avenue, he and Natacha had already been living together for months as husband and wife. They shared in the daily routine of their Whitley Heights home and their enforced estrangement left Rudy to face the burden of managing his life and the household alone.

When they moved into their Wedgwood Place love nest at Christmas time in 1921, the house was more than a decade old and in need of repair. With the exterior stucco starting to crack, they'd initiated extensive structural renovations and within a few months, two full-time workers were conducting the restoration. The cost of these renovations made little impression on either Rudy or Natacha as they spent well beyond his healthy paychecks and charged many purchases, including their contractor's services, on credit. Rudy spent a king's ransom equipping a garage with the latest in automotive tools and hired a valet, a cook and a stable groomsman to care for their menagerie.

For a little while Rudy and Natacha's bright future in the motion picture industry had been enough inspiration for them to dispose of their income with the fiscal abandon of crowned heads of state. By the time they began planning their Mexican marriage, the rooms that were barren the previous Christmas Eve were furnished with a burgeoning collection of antiques and artifacts. Natacha purchased tapestries, draperies and period furniture, while Rudy indulged himself in antique armor and weaponry.

But like a scene from one of his melodramatic movies, the enjoyment of their happy home came to a screeching halt with his arrest on charges of bigamy. In a matter of a few days, a bereft Rudy found himself rattling about the house, sinking into a fine melancholy while Natacha was being transported from her elegant Hollywood home to the woods of upstate New York.

At the same time Rudy was delivering his statement to the press upon his release from the L.A. County jail, the eastbound Union Pacific with Natacha on board arrived in New York City. In anticipation of her arrival, her stepfather, Uncle Dickie and mother, Muzzie closed their suite in the Biltmore Hotel and prepared to whisk her away to their chateau on the French Riviera. But when they laid eyes on the exhausted Natacha, they found her in such a fragile emotional state they postponed any trip abroad. They sent word instead to Foxlair, their country estate in the Adirondacks, saying they were on their way with their daughter to spend some time in the wooded retreat. They hoped some mountain air and guaranteed privacy would mend Natacha's broken heart.

Uncle Dickie Hudnut created his estate, Foxlair over a twenty year period, ensuring that the twelve hundred acre Shangri-La was well hidden high in a secluded valley in the Adirondack Mountains. With the nearest town a few miles away, Natacha would be sheltered from the notoriety surrounding her husband's arrest and her controversial Mexican marriage.

Despite being tucked away, Natacha was inconsolable over her marriage interruptus and the wilds of upstate New York could not have felt further away from Rudy if she had been parked on the dark side of the moon. She was devastated by his impending trial and his possible conviction on the charge of bigamy which might result in ten years in prison and the end of his career. Unable to waver from her state of high apprehension, Natacha feared the worst.

On June first, tittering onlookers packed the courtroom as Rudolph Valentino's preliminary hearing on the charges of bigamy convened. Despite the confusing legal technicalities, his fans grasped the most important element of the case. His freedom depended upon the exact location of his wedding night. This provocative image was sufficient motivation for a mob of reporters and assorted flappers to converge upon the courthouse.

The privileged few who arrived early enough to secure a seat in the courtroom kept their eyes glued on the courtroom's swinging double doors and suffered through their wait for Rudy's arrival. When he finally strode in accompanied by his attorney, the audible wave of suspiration in his honor did nothing to lighten his disheartened shuffle to his seat. He slumped back in his chair, oblivious to the fracas in the back of the courtroom as one overwrought flapper yelling "Rudy! Rudy! Rudy!" was removed by a security guard.

The judge demanded more order in the court as he began hearing the evidence. District Attorney Woolwine's case hinged upon his ability to prove the Valentinos consummated their marriage within the geographical boundaries of California. In this effort, he ordered elaborate floor plans of the Valentino's bedroom at Dr. White's to be drawn up and requested two pairs of pajamas, allegedly worn by the honeymooning couple, be tagged for submission as evidence. He then called his parade of witnesses to verify the precise location where sex had, in fact, taken place between the Sheik and his wife. While the flappers snickered at every tantalizing detail, their Sheik was barely tolerating the macabre scene and was visibly stressed. He sat in somber silence looking like the cornered animal he was.

In order to avoid a stint in a state penitentiary, it was imperative Rudy's attorney prove he never slept with Natacha on their wedding night in Palm Springs. It hadn't been that long since Rudy appeared in another Los Angeles' courtroom to hear his first wife, Jean Acker testify her marriage to him had never been consummated. Nevertheless, Attorney Gilbert took a deep breath and presented his lamentable line of defense by stating that his client Rudolph Valentino, the great lover of the silver screen, had not yet consummated his second marriage. No matter how it appeared to his public, Rudy's only concern was that he avoid those ten years of hard time.

Attorney Gilbert summoned the Valentinos' entire wedding party to testify on Rudy's behalf. Both Alla Nazimova and Paul Ivano took to the witness stand, but as neither were U.S. citizens they both risked deportation if their testimony were proven to be false. As they would intimate long after the fact, it just happened to be. They testified Natacha was ill on her wedding night and as a result of her condition the newlyweds were unable to sleep together. Ivano testified Rudy slept on the porch that night and said a neighbor of Dr. White's had walked by to witness the fact.

The neighbor he referred to was summoned to the witness stand by Rudy's defense. He was an elderly Cahuilla Indian who wandered by Dr. Florilla White's late on the Valentino's wedding night. He delivered his testimony by saying he spoke with a man who was sleeping on the porch. It would be the Cahuilla Indian's moment of mistaken identity that would clinch the case for Rudy. The critical testimony, as admitted into court records, read that Valentino spent his wedding night sleeping alone on the porch. Unknown to the Cahuilla Indian, it was not Rudolph Valentino but his best man Doug Gerrard who slept on the porch. At the time of the Cahuilla Indian's brief conversation with Doug Gerrard, Rudy was sound asleep with Natacha.

On June fifth, the judge dismissed the charges of bigamy against Rudolph Valentino on grounds of insufficient evidence. Rudy's elation at having escaped a lengthy prison stay was tempered by the realization that his marriage to Natacha was declared null and void and he and his bride were ordered by the court to maintain separate residences for the remainder of the year.

A few days after the charges were dismissed, Jesse Lasky released his own statement to the press. He assured the public that District Attorney Woolwine could still convene a grand jury and reopen Valentino's bigamy case. He made it clear Famous Players-Lasky was committed to ensuring Valentino and Natacha Rambova maintained separate domiciles for the entire year. This public hand slapping did not please Rudy. If Jesse Lasky thought this pronouncement would improve working relations with his top box office star, he was woefully in error.

Further aggravating the situation, Lasky ordered studio detectives to tail the couple and report back to him if Rudy and Natacha were ever caught in bed together or in any other incriminating situation. It was obvious to Rudy his employers could keep him in line by threatening to pass along any of the detective's revelations to the District Attorney. Knowing he held no cards, Rudy bowed at least for a little while to the studio's authority.

❧❧

By mid-June Rudy was completing work on his next film, *The Young Rajah* and had worked himself into a black-hearted mood. He argued, brooded and exhibited a very thin skin. Without Natacha he was unmanageable and made little attempt to hide the fact. As filming on *The Young Rajah* wrapped, Jesse Lasky presented his indignant star with another legal document to sign. This paper stated that by affixing his signature he would effectively waive any artistic input in all phases of the production of his future movies with Famous Players-Lasky. Rudy was incensed, refused to sign and flipped the document back at Lasky.

Making matters worse, Lasky proceeded to inform Rudy that all of the studio's legal fees incurred from his bigamy hearing would be deducted from his future paychecks. Reaching his boiling point, Rudy hurried through his scenes in *The Young Rajah* and headed home to Whitley Heights.

He took solace in the company of his friends, Paul Ivano, Doug "Gerry" Gerrard, Robert Florey, Mario Carillo and the French actor, Jean de Limur. They rallied to distract Rudy from his stressful situation by ferrying him around Los Angeles for dinners and clubbing, including trips to the Ocean Park Pier and the speakeasy, the Plantation in Culver City. But Rudy's heart was seldom along for the ride and most evenings he opted to stay at home and compose long love letters to Natacha.

The logistics of running his household that summer became increasingly the concern of his valet, cook and groomsman who stood helplessly by and watched while the young master of the house nursed his depression with rash expenditures. As Rudy incurred exorbitant phone bills and telegram charges and instigated more costly renovations on his home, the household staff was not always sure there would be enough money to cover their weekly paychecks.

The summer wore on and Rudy spent most of his time at home with his dogs, writing poetry and puttering about his garage. He took fencing lessons and to the distress of his friends began refusing their invitations. At some point he also began contemplating a decision to break his contract with Famous Players-Lasky. He vowed never again to allow any employer to assume such control over his life. The more he agonized over his situation, the easier a solution became; he would simply run away.

During his final days in his Whitley Heights home that summer, Rosa Rosanova, the actress who played the role of his mother in *Blood and Sand*, came to Rudy's aid as mother confessor. Rosa, who was then fifty-three years old, took the despondent Rudy under her maternal wing. She was fond of him and he called her "Madre". It broke Rosa's heart to hear co-workers on the set of *Blood and Sand* referring to Rudy behind his back as "that wop dishwasher." So Rosa made a point of checking in on her friend and some evenings she would stop by the Italian grocery store and arrive at Wedgwood Place with all the ingredients for his favorite dinner, spaghetti.

While Rudy tended to the pot of boiling spaghetti, he bent her sympathetic ear. And whenever Rosa found an opportunity to do so, she tried to persuade him to pay more attention to his household finances and to the stacks of unopened mail littering the house.

"Rudy," she asked, knowing his answer to her question, "Are you happy?"

"How shall I answer you?" he sighed," I am happy but my heart is heavy with regret. I am a success, but beyond there is something that I dare never speak of, Rosa. I can not work for Mr. Lasky another day and I am leaving Los Angeles very soon. I am going to New York for the opening of *Blood and Sand* and then I will go to see Natacha at Foxlair."

"Rudy," Rosa replied, "You have no choice but to stay here. You have a contract and the court has forbidden you to stay with Natacha."

Rudy was adamant. "Nothing you say will change my mind."

It was clear to Rosa that Rudy had already made his decision. "How will you leave New York City without being discovered by Lasky's detectives, your fans, the press?" she asked.

Rudy smiled and fixed his gaze on some sure and distant scenario. "Travestimento, Rosa... in disguise."

Chapter Seven

About Face

A few weeks later, deep in the Adirondack Mountains -

During the summer of 1922, North Creek, New York was the only place residents of the Sacandaga Valley could hop on a train, use a telephone or send a telegram. Occasionally, New Yorkers from the "city of" made their way to North Creek to hunt or fish. But by and large the not-so-bustling hub was an outpost well off the beaten path and any effort to venture further into the sticks would have required an ax.

Lazy summer afternoons in North Creek offered little in the way of amusing diversion. But during the summer of 1922, there was plenty of excitement whipping about town and several of the train station's clerks became local celebrities. The clerks enjoyed their brush with limelight when telegrams flew back and forth between one North Creek summer resident, Natacha Rambova and one Hollywood, California resident, movie star Rudolph Valentino. Despite the station clerk's best attempts at feigned disinterest, those telegrams always left them agog.

As the pie-eyed clerks glued their thin paper message strips onto the Western Union forms, they marveled at the length of Rudolph Valentino's telegrams. On a few occasions, Natacha Rambova's arrival at the station interrupted their furtive perusals and in a flurry of shuffling paper the telegrams were slipped back into their envelopes. Before Natacha could suspect that anything was amiss, the clerks managed to resume their usual nonchalance.

Natacha drove down the single lane road from her stepfather's hilltop estate, Foxlair, several times each week to mail her letters, send telegrams, collect those waiting there for her and use the only telephone in town. While a station clerk placed her regular call to Rudy in Los Angeles, she would wait in her car with the Peke, Little Chucky. As soon as her call to Los Angeles went through, she was waved back into the station.

Natacha Rambova's presence caused no small stir in North Creek that summer. Even the few people who somehow missed all of the newspaper accounts of her Mexican marriage to the Sheik found it difficult not to stare. Her haute couture was unlike anything they'd ever seen. If her hair wasn't wound into a shimmering silk turban, it was tucked under a hat so dramatic, it would have stopped traffic if it had been perched on a chair let alone the head of such a glamorous woman. If there had been much traffic on North Creek's droll and dusty streets, Natacha would have brought it all to a halt.

It didn't take long for the station clerks to share every detail they read in the telegrams exchanged between Natacha Rambova and Rudolph Valentino with the entire town. Consequently, everyone knew Rudy called her "Babykins" and in light of her overly reserved demeanor they found this hilarious. That summer it was common knowledge among the population of North Creek, just how much the famous couple missed each other and that their home in Los Angeles was a lonely place for Rudy. All of the latest news straight from the set of Valentino's latest movie, *The Young Rajah,* was scuttled out of the train station to be whispered ear to ear over backyard fences.

Everyone made a valiant effort to keep their faces straight and Natacha had no idea her correspondence with Rudy was being passed around town like new currency. One could well imagine the townsfolk's pained restraint when news came across the wire that Rudolph was making his way towards Foxlair. Rocking chairs on North Creek's porches picked up a little speed, a few more glasses of lemonade were tossed back and long afternoons were wiled away second guessing the precise moment of his arrival.

The station clerks surmised Rudolph Valentino would be arriving by car from Albany and traveling with a friend, another Hollywood actor, Douglas Gerrard. Apparently "Gerry" and Rudolph Valentino planned to surprise Natacha and the Hudnut household because no one was able to glean a single clue from his telegrams as to the precise time of their arrival. The usual summertime complaints about the heat and the humidity soon gave way to the rumors about Rudolph Valentino. Even though North Creek had no picture show, a movie star was still a movie star.

As the fields and ditches in the Adirondack forests grew thick with goldenrod and baked in the summer's stifling heat, the air in North Creek was rife with anticipation about the Sheik's impending arrival. And on one sultry afternoon as the tiny tree frogs, or peepers as they were referred to by the locals, began their annual chirping, the station clerks noticed Natacha placed her regular phone call to Los Angeles to a number in New York City; surely Rudolph Valentino was on his way to North Creek.

The object of Rudy's quest had just passed her dreary summer crossing the days and weeks off a sentence she never expected to serve. While he was completing his work on *The Young Rajah* in Hollywood, on the other side of the continent, Foxlair's household staff grew weary of the morose Natacha. They may not have known all the particulars of her situation, but they were well informed on one point; she was inconsolable. From the moment she stepped foot on the estate late in May, she secluded herself in her bedroom and word went out among the estate's staff to leave her undisturbed.

Natacha's stay in Foxlair's main house, the "Big House", presented the estate's staff with ample fodder for gossip about the household's elusive mistress. The maid would whisper to the laundress that Miss Natacha did nothing more than sleep, read and draw. They both guessed she did little else but sit and stare for interminable stretches of time at the long view out her bedroom window. The other members of Foxlair's staff were aware of Natacha's activities, for they had all seen the beautiful young woman seated at her window with her eyes fixed on a distant point across the rolling hills. Some days they noticed she sat there motionless for hours apparently hypnotized by the view of the Sacandaga River as it drifted east to join the Hudson a few miles down stream.

Natacha cloistered herself in a blue bedroom which like the rest of the interior of Foxlair's Big House offered as much rustic, woodsy charm as a Park Avenue penthouse. For in striking contrast to the dense forest outdoors, Foxlair's Big House was as finely appointed as Richard Hudnut's chateau on the French Riviera. The Big House was lavishly furnished with twinkling Italian chandeliers and French furniture upholstered in silk and draped with linen and lace antimacassars.

Despite the fact that the prestigious home lacked electricity and telephone service, Richard Hudnut guaranteed the Foxlair experience rivaled any extravagant resort. He retained a retinue of overly qualified maids and butlers, a Swedish masseuse and a personal

French chef. While the raccoons, woodchucks, porcupines, squirrels and an occasional bear carried on the outdoor business of Foxlair's wild acres, the indoor residents on the hill enjoyed luxuries unheard of in that neck of the woods. In Natacha's blue bedroom, a glass vanity glittered with Richard Hudnut's crystal blue and white DuBarry perfume bottles and on chilly nights, a Limoge-tiled wood stove burned exclusively birch and precisely cut logs. Natacha could scarcely have settled into a more perfect place in which to pine.

Except for her brief forays to the North Creek train station, she maintained her isolation in the blue room and this prompted her mother and stepfather to despair in their efforts to lighten their daughter's heavy heart. But behind her closed door Natacha was not wasting her time. Defying the thousands of miles that separated her from Rudy and her life in Los Angeles, she stayed on the job and continued her work from high above the Sacandaga River. There was plenty for her to do and even more for her to worry about.

༄༅

The July issue of *Photoplay* magazine included the following piece written by Dick Dorgan. It was titled, "A Song of Hate."

"I hate Valentino! All men hate Valentino! I hate his oriental optics; I hate his classic nose; I hate his Roman face; I hate his smile; I hate his glistening teeth; I hate his patent leather hair; I hate his Svengali glare; I hate him because he dances too well; I hate him because he's a slicker; I hate him because he's the great-lover of the screen; I hate him because he's an embezzler of hearts; I hate him because he's too apt in the art of osculation; I hate him because he's leading man for Gloria Swanson; I hate him because he's too good looking.

Ever since he came galloping in with The Four Horsemen he has been the cause of more home cooked battle royals than they can print in the papers. The women are all dizzy over him. The men have formed a secret order (of which I am running for president and chief executioner as you may notice) to loathe, hate and despise him for obvious reasons.

What! Me jealous?--Oh, no, I just hate him."

This was not Dick Dorgan's first swipe at Rudy. In his review of *The Sheik* he referred to his character of Sheik Ahmed as "a wop or something." This racial slur sent Rudy storming into his boss Jesse

Lasky's office demanding Dorgan be banned from ever stepping foot on the Famous Players-Lasky lot. But by the time Dorgan's "Song of Hate" was released in 1922, relations between Rudy and Jesse Lasky were so irreparably broken, Rudy did not bother to issue much of a protest.

Nearly one year after *The Sheik* opened at Grauman's Million Dollar Theater, his box office success in the wildly popular film had failed to translate into the slightest elevation of professional stature in the eyes of Famous Players-Lasky management. Rudy's strained relationship with the studio further deteriorated on the set of *The Young Rajah* as his objections were received as just more insubordination. Both Jesse Lasky and Adolph Zukor upheld the studio dictum that actors were meant to be seen and quite literally never to be heard.

In addition to refusing Rudy the slightest artistic voice in his films, they did little to protect him from an onslaught of hysterical female fans. Rudy became especially infuriated after learning the studio's publicity departments were releasing copy to fan magazines implying he allowed female fans into his dressing room.

Rudy was not alone in his objections to the policies of Famous Players-Lasky. The U.S. government's Federal Trade Commission filed an anti-trust suit against Lasky and Zukor's organization and declared their system of block-booking illegal. Block-booking was the term used to describe the practice of forcing theaters to show all of the movies a studio produced in order to show a single one. Forcing many inferior "cheater films" on theaters was a sore subject with Rudy.

Lasky underestimated his star's sincere artistic integrity as well as his fierce loyalty to his paying audiences. Consequently, by the time Dorgan's "Song of Hate" hit news stands in the summer of 1922, Rudy's exasperation over the treatment he was receiving from his employers and his lack of power to do a thing about it sent him spiraling into despair. There were many people who supported Dick Dorgan's, "I Hate Valentino!" position and it seemed to Rudy that the more their ilk failed to impugn him in the eyes of his ardent fans, the more bilious and denigrating their rhetoric became. As Sheik fanaticism reached the peak of mania, hating Sheik Rudolph was fast becoming as pandemic as idolizing him.

Despite the finger wagging and disapproving clucks from *The Sheik*'s ardent opposition, Rudy's young male fans enjoyed being called "Sheiks" and their girlfriends delighted in being called, "Shebas." But as these young men could scarcely be seen parading about town in desert robes, they resorted to mimicking Rudy's personal hair style and manner of dress. As parents protested this outrageous behavior, the label "Sheik" came to imply more than a Valentino emulator, but an adept, too ardent lover. The word was increasingly used to describe almost any socially unacceptable behavior or attire as well as participants in juvenile delinquency. Terms such as, "sub-sheik," and "sheiktess" fine tuned the broader definition of "Sheik-like" behavior and became assimilated into the public vernacular.

With such awesome authority over his fans, whenever Rudy changed his hair style, wore a new shirt color or grew stiletto sideburns so did thousands of young "Sheiks". Even with this tremendous sway over popular culture, he continued to have no influence upon Famous Players-Lasky executives. No matter how inferior a script, director, sets or costumes, he was powerless to alter the situation in the slightest way.

With Natacha three thousand miles away at Foxlair, Rudy grew increasingly frustrated and lonely and acted distant and cold to his co-workers. His temper flared on the set of *The Young Rajah* as he railed openly against the rushed shooting schedules and slipshod production. So when Jesse Lasky informed him that he would be attending the opening of *Blood and Sand* in New York during the first week of August, Rudy initially told him to forget it. Another heated exchange broke out between the two men before Rudy finally agreed to travel to New York and promote the film.

Towards the end of July, he boarded the train for New York with his friend Gerry. Jesse Lasky believed he finally had his despondent star in line. But Lasky was about to be reminded of one sobering fact about Rudolph Valentino. He had married, legally or otherwise, a shrewd ally and fierce defender in Natacha Rambova and she was not about to tolerate any further disrespect directed at Rudy from anyone at any level in the motion picture industry.

For while Rudy completed his work on the set of *The Young Rajah*, Hollywood's most promising young art director, Natacha Rambova devoted her summer of exile to plotting a strategy of victory over Famous Players-Lasky. While Foxlair's residents assumed she was moping idly in her room, quite the opposite was true. She crammed every nook and cranny of her small blue bedroom with books and papers and pored through the stacks in search of plum roles for Rudy. She drew inspiration for his future film projects from European studios and aspired only to their high standards of artistic excellence. She knew European actors were seldom subjected to the hack production methods of Hollywood producers whose focus was on a film's length, its number of reels and profit margins.

With the tactical application of a battlefield general, Natacha immersed herself that summer in a mythical vision of her future with Rudy. Her goal was their complete artistic control over all films in which they invested their artistic efforts and upon which they staked their reputations. It made little difference to Natacha that no artist had ever wielded such power over a studio or that her visionary tour de force was decades before its time. She entertained no thoughts of failure or compromise.

She was, after all, in love with America's top box office star and committed to defending his illustrious position. She was driven in her efforts not only out of artistic integrity but out of love. Unfortunately for Natacha, it was because of her passion for Rudy that she sat in seclusion in her blue bedroom at Foxlair. In her brief twenty-five years of life she had not been so lucky in love and that summer she was still nursing one tangible battle scar as proof of this fact.

As she plotted Rudy's future from the solitude of her bedroom, a profound scar, inflicted by a previous lover, was still tender enough to threaten her peace of mind. With ample time on her hands, she reflected upon her grievous injury inflicted one fateful afternoon soon after her arrival in Hollywood as a member of the Imperial Russian Ballet.

When the athletically handsome founder of the Imperial Russian Ballet, Theodore Kosloff opened his school of ballet in New York City, one of his first pupils was a seventeen-year old Winifred Shaughnessy. Ignoring a substantial and illegal age difference, Kosloff and young Winifred were soon lovers. When their affair was exposed, Kosloff slipped Winifred out of New York and into hiding in rural England. Winifred's mother, Muzzie was frantic and paid Pinkerton Detectives' salaries for nearly a year before they finally located her wayward daughter. By then Winifred had assumed her Russian stage name of Natacha Rambova and celebrated a critical birthday; she'd reached the age of legal adulthood at eighteen.

With Muzzie now powerless over her daughter's rash decisions, Natacha began touring the U.S. with Kosloff and settled in Hollywood with his dance troupe while he made his bid for a screen career. But Kosloff was as unfaithful as he was domineering and his mistress' patience soon wore thin. However, his explosive temper made the mere thought of any escape from his tyranny, risky business. Natacha eventually timed her brave flight to freedom to coincide with one of Kosloff's weekend hunting trips with director, Cecil B. DeMille. As soon as her possessive lover left that tragic afternoon, Natacha packed her bags, hefted them to the front porch and parked herself in a chair to await a taxi cab.

A few cigarettes into her wait, she was horrified to see Kosloff returning with his shotgun in hand. Upon spotting Natacha's hat boxes, satchels and trunks stacked on the front porch, he leveled an immediate response to her mutiny. He hefted the shotgun waist high and blasted away. The lead shot shredded the front of her skirt and ground deep into her thigh. With blood streaming down her leg, Natacha turned to run into the house to make an escape through a rear entrance. As she scrambled to safety through a kitchen window, Kosloff fired another shot in her direction. By then Natacha was making her way around to the front of the house, just in time to hail her cab.

Theodore Kosloff's homicidal temper cost him his talented dancer and lover and effectively ended Natacha's professional dancing career. According to her friends, she shed few tears over the entire episode and instead focused her attention upon the handsome Italian actor, Rudolph Valentino. Any life lessons she might have learned from the still healing injury to her leg did nothing to diminish her love for Rudy during her summer days at Foxlair estate. She did her best to fend off those vexing memories of her brutal lover, Kosloff by reading and re-reading Rudy's tender love letters and dreaming for hours on end about their bright and idealistic future.

꧁꧂

On August sixth, Rudy and Gerry arrived in New York City to attend the opening of *Blood and Sand* at the Rivoli Theater on Broadway. The star of the film had only one thought in mind and it was not his appearance at the Rivoli. With his beloved Natacha only a few short hours away, he made immediate plans to skip town. On the

135

day of his desertion, he assumed his incognito by donning a thread-bare tweed suit, a pair of dark glasses and a scruffy, fake beard. He and Gerry then headed across Manhattan to board a train north to Albany. As the train began its slow roll northward, towards the remote destination, Rudy and Gerry believed mistakenly they would be far from harm's way.

❧

Fletcher Dunkley's farmhouse and chicken farm was located on the single lane dirt road connecting Foxlair estate with the North Creek station. The winding gravel road passed only thirty feet from the front porch of the Dunkley's run-down clapboard home. Fletcher's chickens furnished the eggs for Foxlair and after one morning's delivery, he returned home with incredible news for his wife and two teenage daughters. While they listened in disbelief, he explained how Richard Hudnut's laundress informed him movie star Rudolph Valentino was traveling all the way from California to visit Foxlair. Since Fletcher Dunkley lived on the only access road to the estate, he assumed Valentino would have to drive right past the house.

The Dunkley daughters were weak-kneed at the prospect and begged their father to allow them to wait on the porch to see the Sheik pass by. Fletcher was horrified at the prospect and assured them they would not be seen gawking from the porch. He informed his daughters, the Hudnut's maid was sure she heard that Valentino would be traveling in disguise, so if they did see him they were to act as if they had seen nothing at all. There would be no waving, yelling, nothing of the sort from the Dunkley residence.

The older of the two Dunkley daughters, Sophronia or "Phrony" for short, took it upon herself to negotiate the details of the impending Valentino sighting with her father. Even in the wilds of upstate New York, teenage girls knew all about Rudy Valentino and Phrony Dunkley was beside herself with anticipation. Bravely ignoring all threats of reprimand, she glued a small newspaper photo of Valentino dressed as the Sheik to the faded floral wallpaper in her bedroom. She'd never seen the movie *The Sheik*, but she had seen plenty photographs of Rudolph Valentino.

It was during Fletcher's next egg delivery that he heard the latest scuttlebutt about Valentino's arrival in North Creek. He hurried home to alert his two anxious daughters; the movie star would be

136

arriving later that day. It was a long afternoon for the two girls fidgeting from their vantage point in an upstairs bedroom window, their eyes fixated on the road below. It was an unbearable wait but they were finally rewarded.

Just at sundown a large touring car roared up the road and in a cloud of dust and gravel the great vehicle passed right beneath the Dunkley girls' open mouths. They could plainly see two men in the back seat; one bearded man was wearing a hat and dark glasses and another passenger looked nothing like Rudolph Valentino. For a moment Phrony and her little sister weren't sure what they'd seen. But when they remembered their father said Valentino would be traveling in disguise the thrill sank in. At that moment Phrony and her sister joined the many folks in the Sacandaga Valley who would forever refer to the summer of 1922, as their Valentino summer.

ন্থেড়ী

The touring car's bearded passenger sprinted across Foxlair's stone veranda and rapped loudly on the door of the Big House. A stunned Muzzie Hudnut took a moment to recognize her semi son-in-law before she was brushed aside by her daughter rushing into Rudy's arms. The sight of Rudy's failed hayseed vogue set Natacha into peels of laughter which echoed throughout a greatly relieved household. And as Rudy removed his driving goggles, he was unaware they'd left rings of dirt around his eyes and this struck Natacha as even more side-splitting.

The sound of laughter filled the front room of the Big House and Rudy and Gerry were welcomed to Foxlair as chivalrous heroes for having rescued the damsel in distress. Their luggage was carried up the front stairs and Rudy's bags were delivered to a room furnished especially for him with a wide double bed covered with a brocade bedspread. From the day he flipped that heavy spread off his bed, Natacha's little blue room gathered dust.

With Rudy and Gerry at her side, Natacha at last abandoned her summer hermitage and began exploring Foxlair's wooded grounds. The three friends trekked the Hudnut acres investigating each building, the garage, the several barns and the chicken coop. There was no doubt that having famous people in their midst was a rare occurrence for the folks servicing the Hudnut estate, but any reticence to welcome movie stars into their provincial world soon dissipated. Before a single day passed, Famous Players-Lasky's top box office star had inspired an instant loyalty and he felt safely hidden in the Adirondacks, far from powerful studio heads and a menacing District Attorney in Los Angeles.

On his ride up the mountain to Foxlair, a curtain lowered on all things Hollywood and the Adirondack woods enveloped Rudolph Valentino. A long way from the bustling streets of Los Angeles, he took to life in the outback with an enthusiasm he hadn't experienced since he was a little boy. He tinkered under an old truck, swam with Gerry and Natacha in the trout pond, stayed up all hours playing poker and befriended the estate's many pets, a fox kept in a man-made den, a flock of sheep, beagles, Irish setters, donkeys and swans. The Foxlair estate made such an impression on Rudy that he vowed one day he would create a similar home for himself and Natacha.

Early every morning the rooster crowed his morning's alarm from the hen house and the crows cawed high in the pines. Meanwhile, the bleary-eyed residents of Foxlair were served a sumptuous breakfast on an elegant table set with linens, crystal and a china pitcher of fresh milk. But even in the midst of this idyllic routine everyone was keenly aware Rudy was not only visiting Foxlair to spend time with Natacha. He had walked off his job. During his first few days at Foxlair he refused to discuss the thorny subject and appeared to have forgotten all about his angry bosses and the many bill collectors he'd just left far behind in Los Angeles. But Natacha knew it would not be long before Jesse Lasky and Adolph Zukor made a move.

She pressed Rudy into conversation about the future of his career and reasoned with him that he at least owed it to his fans to return to work. She wanted to know just how long he planned to stay in the woods, puttering on old trucks and patting dogs. Her attempts to motivate him into taking any action where his career was concerned, inevitably dissolved into playful embraces and another round at one of Foxlair's many diversions. For at Foxlair they were free to live as husband and wife and share the double bed in Rudy's room. That alone became a most compelling argument to linger in the woods just a few days longer.

Except for a few brief jaunts into North Creek, Rudy and Natacha spent their time together on Foxlair's grounds. They enjoyed their summer evenings with Gerry in the front room of the Big House, often playing cards by oil lamp and always talking late into the night.

Some nights Rudy would crank the Victrola record player, roll back the French rugs and pull Natacha into his arms for a tango or a waltz. Gerry would sit out as official third wheel and audience.

As the dog days of summer wore on, Rudy's physical appearance began to resemble more of a rugged woodsman than the actor who had cut and run from New York a few weeks earlier. This had Natacha growing increasingly wary and she intensified her efforts to convince him to return to his film career. She followed him reading passages from books she'd earmarked for prospective films and tempted him with the assurance that all of his future films would be produced in Europe. Rudy made an effort to listen attentively but his daily hikes up the mountain paths with a dog at his side were far more enticing propositions. He knew he was still under contract with Famous Players-Lasky and that Natacha was justified in nudging him in the direction of more practical matters. As days turned into weeks and the inevitable showdown with his employers loomed, it was with grim resignation Rudy agreed he'd probably been lost in the woods long enough.

Late on the afternoon of Sunday, August twenty-seventh, the clerks at the North Creek station peered over their spectacles to watch an unfamiliar car pulling into town. They greeted the arrival of the two men driving the Ford sedan with the long stares reserved for all out-of-towners. The local populace of North Creek had been keeping their ears to the ground where strangers were concerned and immediately suspected these two men might have a possible connection to the movie star hiding at Foxlair.

Meanwhile, the two strangers parked their Ford on a side street and believed they'd slipped into town unnoticed. It was not long before they had their mark in their sights; Rudolph Valentino just happened to make a rare appearance in North Creek. He was headed for the station to wire instructions to his attorney in New York to accept no further pay checks from Famous Players-Lasky.

While word of Rudolph Valentino's walk-out was being tapped by wire towards New York, dark clouds settled in over North Creek and a rumble of distant thunder promised some relief from the late August heat. As the first few raindrops plopped onto the dusty street, Rudy walked out of the North Creek station and paused for a moment to pull the canvas roof up on the Hudnut's touring car. Just then the cloudburst cut loose and he hopped into the car to drive back up the mountain.

As the townsfolk peered from behind their curtains, they watched the mysterious Ford sedan roll slowly past the station and follow a wary distance behind Rudy. Perhaps some local turncoat succumbed to the temptation of a roll of fresh Hollywood bills and had reported the whereabouts of Rudolph Valentino. Whatever the case, it was obvious to even the dullest minds in North Creek, that a thinly-veiled bit of treachery was underfoot.

∾૭∾

The thunderstorms rolled by and lightening cracked late into the night. They were the kind of late summer rain showers that only made the air stickier and they did little to cool the three poker players seated around the table in the front room of Foxlair's Big House. Between downpours, the evening's silence was broken only by the sound of the three friend's laughter, rain dripping from the eaves and the deep croaks of a few bullfrogs down by the trout pond. Uncle Dickie had gone into New York for a few days, Muzzie was already tucked in her bed and Rudy, Natacha and Gerry were absorbed in another round of penny ante.

As the cards were being shuffled for another hand, Natacha caught the slight movement of the screen door and spotted the shadow of a man standing on the veranda. Continuing to sort through her cards she whispered,

"Someone's out there. There's a gun in Uncle Dickie's dresser drawer, Gerry. Go and get it."

Gerry stood and made the announcement, "My turn to get the drinks," and then he quickly disappeared.

Rudy and Natacha continued their cover by chatting about the cards they'd just been dealt. Upstairs, Gerry retrieved a pistol from Uncle Dickie's dresser drawer. Instead of returning to his friends in the front room, he headed down a flight of stairs towards the rear of the residence. He exited through a back door and eased his way around the side of the house and across the dark veranda. With the pistol drawn, he stood on the slick flagstone and yelled at the shadowy figure lurking behind the screen door.

"Damn you! Hold up your hands or I'll shoot!"

The startled man turned and lunged at Gerry. The two men struggled for a few moments before the intruder managed to heave Gerry off the veranda and onto the ground some twelve feet below. After slipping in the mud, Gerry regained his footing just in time to fire three rapid shots in the general direction of the fleeing prowler. He hit his mark. The sound of the gunfire and the wounded man's expletives alerted Rudy and Natacha to Gerry's skirmish outside. Rudy threw back his chair and ran up the stairs to Muzzie's room to retrieve a shotgun he knew she kept by her bed. In his rush, he sent priceless vases and furniture crashing to the floor. Natacha made a valiant effort to scramble along pleading,

"No! No, Rudy! You'll be killed!"

Natacha's voice startled her mother, who woke just in time to see Rudy grabbing the weapon from the corner of her bedroom. Before she could understand what was going on, he was sprinting back down the staircase calling out, "Gerry's been killed!"

Rudy burst through the screen door, giving the shotgun a quick pump to make sure the chamber was loaded. But by then the intruder had made his escape and Gerry was making his way through a rear entrance. He reappeared in the front room covered in mud and for one awful moment a bleary-eyed Muzzie thought Gerry was the intruder. When all confusion was resolved, Rudy, Natacha and Gerry set off to tromp through the mud and drizzle in a futile effort to find the wounded spy.

It was only in the light of day that they were able to locate the man's tracks and find a cigar butt he'd tossed off the veranda. Later that morning Rudy and Natacha drove down to the North Creek train station to make a few inquiries. There, the clerks reported they had seen two men in town the day before and these same two men returned to the station earlier that morning. They also witnessed one of the men purchasing a ticket for New York as he limped with the assistance of two canes. The second man drove off in the Ford Sedan.

Natacha and Rudy saw through the previous evening's subterfuge. They agreed the two strangers in North Creek were no doubt private detectives dispatched by Jesse Lasky or D.A. Thomas Woolwine. Either man could have hired the private eyes to work the woods on their behalf; Lasky in search of information about his star's disappearance and Woolwine still threatening to reopen Rudy's bigamy case if he was ever discovered in bed with Natacha.

Whatever Lasky and Woolwine's possible motives, the entire episode shattered any illusion Rudy was safely hidden away at Foxlair. Before he and Natacha left the train station that morning, Rudy studied the plain faces of the townsfolk as they peered in his direction. The good citizens of North Creek no longer seemed as welcoming as they had a few weeks earlier and Rudy was seized by an acute paranoia. Every burning issue he had successfully ignored for weeks suddenly demanded his immediate attention. On the drive back up the mountain to Foxlair, he and Natacha made hurried plans to return to New York City and within a few hours they were packed and ready to leave.

Muzzie said goodbye to Gerry and hugged Natacha and Rudy assuring them she would see them soon in New York. Rudy jotted down his new address in New York for her; that of his friend Frank Mennillo at the Hotel des Artistes on 67th Street. With Natacha seated in the touring car's front seat and Little Chuckie panting on her lap, Gerry and Rudy wedged the last of the luggage into the baggage compartment. Rudy and Natacha then began a solemn return trip to civilization to book separate passage on separate trains and resume their separate lives in separate homes.

With Rudy at the wheel, he sped the touring car at break neck speed down the winding dirt road. The car careened around the corner and Foxlair's Big House quickly disappeared behind the trees. On that afternoon as the car zipped passed the Dunkley farm, Phrony missed seeing her idol Rudolph. But if she had been looking out her bedroom window, she would have noticed a certain glint in his eyes. Rudy was outraged that he'd been stalked by detectives all the way to Foxlair where weapons had been fired, a man wounded and poor Muzzie terrified. The previous night's events left him shaken and struggling to comprehend the disturbing fact that his very presence at Foxlair put his loved ones in mortal danger. With no hesitation he decided it was time to remove them from harm's way, return to New York to draw his battle lines at a safe distance and face his enemy head on.

Chapter Eight

The Whole Truth

Los Angeles, eight years later, in the spring of 1930 -

Unlike his famous namesake, Rudolph Valentino Coppola did not live a single day. Upon his death, the stillborn Rudolph Coppola's grief-stricken parents filed a malpractice suit against their obstetrician. During the opening day of the court's proceedings, baby Rudolph's mother, Angelina Coppola took the witness stand to deliver her heart-rending replies to a line of questioning from the obstetrician's defense attorney. Angelina Coppola was overcome with emotion at several points during her testimony and this prompted the judge to halt the proceedings to give the woman time to dab her eyes and take a sip of water. It was during one of these pauses that a young woman seated in the courtroom jumped to her feet. Before a stunned courtroom she yelled out,

"I have been sent to protect you, Angelina Coppola! I have been sent to protect you, Angelina Coppola!"

The woman then rushed forward towards the witness stand. The judge demanded order while a bailiff restrained the shrieking woman. Despite the bailiff's heroic efforts as he wrestled the woman out of the courtroom, she railed on for all to hear.

"Last Christmas day I was guided by the spirit of Rudolph Valentino and I found Mrs. Coppola weeping at her son's grave! Rudolph sent me here today under the spell of his master guide Black Feather!"

As the bailiff dragged the woman towards the courtroom doors, his captive dug in her heels, rolled her eyes and ranted in a language no one understood. The only intelligible words in her tirade, which she repeated again and again, were "Rudolph Valentino."

The woman was later identified as spiritualist and medium, Shelly Roane Vier. Although Miss Vier was never heard from again, many people present in courtroom that day later admitted her claims caused some degree of spine tingling. Even the most skeptical found it difficult to dismiss the unsettling notion that the spirit of Rudolph

Valentino guided the medium to find Rudolph Valentino Coppola's mother at her tiny son's grave on Christmas Day.

❧◦❧

News of the infant Rudolph Valentino Coppola's death did not merit front page coverage in *The L.A. Times* in the spring of 1930. Instead, the headlines announced Babe Ruth's freshly-inked contract with the New York Yankees, details of outlaw Clyde Chestnut Barrow's extradition from Ohio to Texas and the courtroom proceedings of Rudolph Valentino's manager George Ullman. By May sixteenth, George Ullman's hearing on charges of fraud and mismanagement brought against him by Alberto Valentino was finally underway and the press was hot on the story. Their early coverage reported how the court ordered George temporarily removed as executor pending the outcome of the hearing. In his absence, A. P. Giannini's Bank of Italy was appointed administrator of the Valentino estate.

George anticipated his temporary dismissal and Giannini's appointment, but Frank Mennillo was livid hearing that his arch enemy was assuming authority over Rudy's estate. Frank and George were not the only people impacted by the court's initial orders. The judge also specified the suspension of all disbursement of estate funds, including Alberto's weekly stipend of one hundred dollars, until a verdict was issued. This was not welcome news for Alberto as he had grown accustomed to receiving George's regular, weekly payments. With estate funds frozen for the duration of the court proceedings, Alberto would be forced to live solely on his modest salary from his office job at MGM studios. With the exception of the attorneys, his lawsuit against George was about to become a financial strain on everyone involved.

Just prior to the first day of court testimony, George was notified that court appointed accountant Harry Baskerville's audit found no errors or discrepancies in his estate ledgers. When Alberto's attorneys received the results of Baskerville's report, they shifted the focus of their lawsuit from the examination of George's books to the legal definition of his authority. If Alberto could not prove George mismanaged the estate, he would attempt to prove he managed it without the proper authority.

144

As court proceedings got underway, George resigned himself to making the daily trek across Los Angeles to the County Courthouse to defend his actions. On the morning of May fifteenth, he was sworn to tell the whole truth and nothing but and settled in to spend the remainder of the day on the witness stand. The courtroom was filled to capacity with reporters and spectators waiting for George's attorney Leonard Wilson to cease in his pacing and get down to the business of the day.

From his seat on the witness stand, George eyed Alberto's lawyers across the courtroom. He reminded himself that the slick team of Scarborough, Mann and Sumner were not his real adversaries, for these men were just the latest hired guns of Alberto Valentino and his behind-the-scenes financial backer, Joe Schenck. When attorney Wilson finally approached the witness stand, he took a deep breath and began his line of questioning.

"Mr. Ullman, what was your capacity in connection with your employment, if there was any employment, between yourself and Rudolph Valentino at the time of his death?"

George cleared his throat, "I was Mr. Valentino's personal representative and business manager. At the time of Mr. Valentino's death, I knew the exact condition of the affairs, and his finances, so far as he was concerned, as far as the productions were concerned. I was the only one that did know."

"Now, Mr. Ullman," Wilson continued, "What did you do in connection with the showing or causing to be shown, and any other activities in connection with the disposition, the distribution and later the showing of Valentino's two pictures, *The Son of the Sheik* and *The Eagle* after the death of Rudolph Valentino?"

George hesitated for a moment before responding.

"It was my job to exploit these films and pay off the indebtedness. I also had the task of disposing of my friend's personal effects. He had about $16,000.00 worth of hardware which he collected as souvenirs; swords, armor and the like. It cost me $35,000.00 to fix up the legends and publicize this stuff but I sold it for $97,000.00 and I was criticized for spending this $35,000.00 too."

He paused again to collect his thoughts before he continued.

"In the first place, I began the memorial associations and corresponded with, oh, I would estimate between 35,000 and 40,000 people over a period of two years. I answered every inquiry and maintained contact with all fans, with all the admirers of Valentino just exactly as I did before his death. In fact, I laid more stress, gave these letters more personal attention than I did before his death. Before his death we were accustomed to sending out form letters with fan pictures. After his death, I sent out personal letters and pictures. I had motion picture slides made which I distributed throughout the world to the picture theater owners. I addressed all picture theater owners of this country, asking them to secure members of the Valentino Memorial Association."

George glanced up at the courtroom clock and proceeded to elaborate.

"I am trying to group the things that I did in as orderly a way as I can in order not to make my statement too long. My only purpose after Rudy's death was to perpetuate his name, first, because, as I stated before, of my friendship for him, my love for him; and second of all, because I wanted his pictures to be shown, because, prior to this time, no pictures had ever been shown beyond a time after a man's death. I knew of the difficulties which lay in the way of public opinion. The public's mind forgets people that have been great celebrities; they are forgotten except in retrospective. I may say I proceeded to operate exactly as I had before his death, with the one exception of not attempting to obtain further employment for him. I kept his pictures alive, and exploited and promoted interests of the pictures just exactly as if he had been alive."

Leonard Wilson's direct examination of his client then shifted to the situation George faced in New York City following Rudy's death. George replied,

"I had to overcome the argument of the church as to the mode of burial. I had to engage policemen to keep order in the mob that congregated everywhere. I had between thirty-five and forty newspaper reporters constantly around me and kept them supplied with stories and things to keep them going."

Reacting to a ripple of interest in the courtroom, Wilson raised his voice to ask, "The body lay in state back there for a while?"

"Yes, sir."

"How long?"

"The body lay in state, open to the public for about two days, and then we held the body for six days more, contrary to the law of New York, in order to give Rudy's brother an opportunity to see the body before it was buried."

Wilson turned to face the court before he asked his next question. "What was the first thing the brother said to you upon his arrival?"

George's answer inspired another buzz throughout the courtroom.

"He wanted to know how much the estate would amount to."

Alberto's attorney, James C. Scarborough, was on his feet demanding at top volume that George's last answer be stricken from the record.

∽≪✞≫∽

George's days on the witness stand left him little time to devote to his S. George Ullman Agency. He did his best, however, to spend as many early morning hours in his office as possible before his daily court appearances. Despite a bleak national economic situation, he managed to secure steady work for the actors he represented which, by 1930, included John Carradine and Frank Orth. He even found a few roles for his three children as extras in Eddie Cantor's *Kid Millions* and cast his six-year old son, Bobby in Herbert Brenon's first talking film, *Lummox*.

On one of those early mornings, George sat at his desk wrapping up the day's business before the drive downtown to the courthouse. He plopped his fedora on his head, leaned back in his chair and pulled open the desk drawer to slip a few files off his desk. He paused for a moment and fumbled through the drawer's narrow space until he found a small packet of letters tied with a piece of string.

George had salvaged these letters in a sentimental moment while conducting the inventory of Rudy's estate. He untied the string, flipped it on the desk and opened one of the envelopes. In measured handwriting, Rudy had written this particular love letter to Natacha in French. George held the letter for a few minutes before realizing time was running short. He would soon be summoned back to the witness stand. Facing another full day in court, he re-folded the precious correspondence and slid it into its envelope. He then tucked the letters safely in the back of his desk drawer.

That day Rudy's sister Maria Strada was scheduled to testify and her appearance would provide George with a break in his lengthy testimony. Maria returned to Los Angeles from Italy on April twenty-third with the sole purpose of testifying on her brother Alberto's

147

behalf. She traveled from Turin to dispute George's claim that she had authorized the loan of estate funds to Frank Mennillo. George and Maria held opposing views of what transpired between them during her previous visit to Los Angeles in 1927. They both agreed they held a meeting at the Rudolph Valentino Production prop house on Santa Monica Boulevard. But George claimed during this meeting she granted him permission to financially assist Frank Mennillo; Maria alleged the opposite.

George maintained he loaned Frank the $40,00.00 upon Maria Strada's personal directive. He also claimed that as head of Rudolph Valentino Productions he was authorized to invest estate profits to generate future income for the estate. In his defense, George presented as evidence to the court the original letter, handwritten by Maria, in which she requested he assist Frank Mennillo upon his return to Los Angeles. The letter, dated December 1, 1927 read in part,

"As it is natural that his expenses shall not be supported by him, I would be very grateful to you if you would give him directly on account of me, how much he will ask you for."

George believed her request was outlined clearly in this letter; Maria and her brother Alberto thought differently. Alberto maintained that despite what his sister expressed in her note, George, as executor, should have obtained the court's permission for the loan. According to Alberto, because George lacked the authority to make the loan, he, not Frank Mennillo should be held responsible to reimburse the estate for the full amount.

Consequently, when George took the witness stand, Alberto's attorney James Scarborough questioned him at length about the details of the Mennillo loan and challenged the authenticity of Frank's receipts for George's checks. Scarborough also informed the judge that Frank Mennillo was to have been subpoenaed to appear in court that day but could not be located. It would be up to George to explain the situation from the witness stand.

"There were several elements that entered into my loaning Frank Mennillo this money. In the first place, I relied a great deal upon the knowledge I had of his previous friendship for Valentino. In the second place, I thought that the business venture was extremely good, would turn out to be a profitable one, which I still think it will be. In the third place, I always presumed that I was conducting the corporation and, therefore, had the power to loan out funds that had accumulated. I wanted to make money for the corporation so that I could make pictures. In the fourth place, I relied a great deal upon the representations of the fact that he was here in Maria's stead. I believed that he was. He had her power of attorney; at least I was told so."

Maria Strada was summoned to the witness stand to respond to James Scarborough's questions.

"After your first arrival in Los Angeles in 1927, Mrs. Strada, did you meet George Ullman?"

"Yes, on January 13, 1927."

"Did you have a talk with him at that meeting?"

"Yes, sir."

"Do you recall during your visit of meeting Mr. Ullman at a house here in Los Angeles where some of your brother's property was stored?"

"Yes, I remember."

"Did you have a conversation with Mr. Ullman at that time? Did you talk with Mr. Ullman?"

"I talked, yes, about the property, about the souvenirs, the swords, the personal property of my brother, and I chose some personal property."

"Did you also meet George Ullman at his house during that visit, at his residence?"

"Yes."

"Mrs. Strada, during your visit to Los Angeles in 1927, did you and Mr. Ullman ever have a conversation about Frank Mennillo?"

"Yes."

"Did Mr. Ullman have anything to say in that conversation about Mr. Mennillo?"

"Yes. He said he was a fine man, a very good friend of my brother, that Mr. Ullman expressed all his highly estimation and affection for Mr. Mennillo."

Leonard Wilson then began his cross examination.

"I will ask you, Mrs. Strada, if you do not remember at that property house, in the presence of S. George Ullman and one other witness whose name you can now not recall, if you did not state that you had appointed Mr. Mennillo to represent you and that he would come out here and straighten out the trouble that your brother Alberto was causing?"

149

Maria shot a furtive glance across the courtroom at James Scarborough. He nodded and she continued,

"I never say anything of the kind to Mr. Ullman."

George was then summoned back to the witness stand, reminded that he was still under oath and asked for more details about the meeting in question.

"Who all was present?"

"Nobody was there but Lou Mahoney, Maria Strada and I."

"State what was said in reference to Frank Mennillo."

"Maria Strada told me at the time that she met Frank Mennillo in New York, he had taken her to an attorney whose name was William Grossman, that she wanted Frank Mennillo to come here and represent her interests, whatever they may be in the estate. She stated she had implicit faith in Mennillo and that he would be here at her expense; that I was to give him whatever he may ask for in connection with her share of the estate."

Under re-direct by James Scarborough, Maria acknowledged she guessed this conversation took place and she was then asked about her receipt of the many cash advances issued by George Ullman.

"Now will you state to the court what money you have received from the estate?

"I received on March 21, 1927 a draft on The Wilshire National Bank for $5000.00 when I was myself in Los Angeles and from personal property at the same time for $3,428.00 and when I was back in Italy I received four cashier's checks from Mr. Ullman for $1000.00 each on the Pan-American Bank."

"At what point did you receive the $4000.00?"

"I received May 4, 1928 being myself in Italy."

"You were in Italy then?"

"Yes, sir."

"You got the checks from George Ullman through the mail then?"

"Yes."

If there was one subject that rankled Alberto Valentino, it was the fact that George Ullman continued to draw a regular paycheck of $400.00 a week from Rudolph Valentino Productions during his first two years as executor. Under George's original contract, signed in 1923,

150

Rudy agreed to pay George $1400.00 a week. But Rudolph Valentino Productions' ledgers reveal Rudy's manager was seldom paid more than $400.00 a week. It was for this reason that after Rudy's death George continued to draw his $400.00 a week paycheck. At this rate of pay, his salary for his first two years as executor would have totaled just over $40,000.00. When he submitted a claim to the court for half of this at $22,300.00, his authority to do so came under heavy fire from Alberto's attorney, James Scarborough who opened his line of questioning concerning George's paychecks by asking,

"You state on page six of your account, Mr. Ullman, that from the date of the death of the deceased, Rudolph Valentino, until, on, or about the 13th day of November 1928, you advanced to yourself the sum of $22,300.00; is that correct?"

George nodded and replied, "...Yes, when I first took over the estate and the corporation and attempted to make something out of it, I went to Rudy's attorney, Mr. W. I. Gilbert and I asked him point blank...I told him, rather, that this would take all of my time, that I would have to work harder than I ever did before...I asked Mr. Gilbert whether he thought it would be correct for me to draw a salary. He said he did not see any reason why I should not...He told me that other attorney's acting for the heirs did not object to the payment to me of $30,000.00 for my services up to that date, and thereafter I would receive ten percent of all other moneys that would be brought into the estate by my efforts."

Scarborough turned to address the judge. "If the court please, we ask that this witness' statement be stricken as purely hearsay."

The judge denied his request by saying, "You asked him why he did so, why he took the salary. We do not need any argument. He stated his reason for doing so."

After muttering, "All right, I have no further questions." James Scarborough returned to his seat.

To corroborate George's statement that he drew his salary upon the advice of Rudy's attorney, W.I. Gilbert was called to the witness stand to recall his conversation with George. He testified;

"Well, Mr. Ullman outlined in a general way some things that he had been doing for the estate to build up its value and inquired of me as to compensation for himself. He stated he was doing a great many things that as executor he did not think he was supposed to do and asked me if the court would allow him compensation for that. I told him that unquestionably the court would allow him additional compensation. He asked me then if the court would allow him the same amount of pay that he had drawn from Mr. Valentino in his lifetime. I told him I couldn't say to that, but I thought if the services were the same as in Mr. Valentino's lifetime that this would be very persuasive to the court..."

Gilbert continued with his testimony, "I don't know whether I should make this statement or not but I am going to make it and they can strike it out. It has been generally known that the death of a star practically destroyed the value of any existing pictures."

James Scarborough shouted another objection,

"We move to strike that answer out!"

George's attorney Leonard Wilson interrupted Scarborough to address the judge.

"Your Honor, We think Mr. Gilbert ought to be allowed to finish his statement."

The judge asked Gilbert if his statement would have a conclusion.

"Yes, your honor." Gilbert testified, "Well at any rate, I know that Mr. Ullman put in a very large effort in merchandising the Valentino productions after his death, both in correspondence, advertising and boosting so as to keep the value of those screens up in spite of his death."

W. I. Gilbert had represented Rudolph Valentino in one capacity or another for nearly a decade and his appearance in the courtroom and his testimony carried substantial weight. As he stepped down from the witness stand, he gave a slight nod to George. Whether his words of support would have any sway over the court and spare George's neck remained to be seen.

❧

In 1930, most twelve year old boys knew plenty about the good guys and the bad guys after reading "cops and robbers" adventure stories in popular pulp magazines such as "The Black Mask" and "Dragnet". Authors of these magazine's articles did a remarkable job of defining good from evil for their adolescent audience. Unfortunately for George Ullman's eldest son Dan, when it came to the subjects of unauthorized loans and disbursements of estate funds, differentiating good from evil was not quite so black and white.

Dan Ullman was a typical twelve-year old, and his simplistic definitions of hero and villain made it difficult for him to comprehend his father's legal problems. His parents assured him he had nothing to worry about, but Dan suffered from an active imagination and feared his Dad might be headed for jail. Unlike his little brother Bobby and his baby sister Bunny, Dan remembered his favorite "Uncle Rudy". His young mind raced as he read the front page headlines being printed about his father, "Kin Accuse Executor for Valentino," "Valentino Estate Fraud Charges Oust Executor" and "Ballyhoo for Valentino Funeral Told in Court".

Dan struggled to understand just what the trouble was between his father and Uncle Rudy's brother. His Dad endeavored to explain the situation point by point by telling his son that what the press called "ballyhoo" was a reference to his efforts to promote Uncle Rudy's films and keep his name profitable for his estate. But Dan needed more of an explanation and quizzed his parents at length. No matter what answers they gave him, he remained focused on one thought; his Dad went to court everyday to prove to the world that he was not a crook.

The lengthy court proceedings were not the only thing exacting an emotional toll on the Ullman family. Facing the steep price of his legal representation, George was forced to sell his Foothill Road home and move his family into a rented home on Linden Drive. He also decided he would not wait for the court to reinstate him as executor upon the conclusion of the hearing and on July seventh, he tendered his formal resignation. He believed he would soon be exonerated on every charge brought against him by Alberto, his executor's accounts would finally be approved by the court and he would then be free to move on with his life and career. George told the press he resigned as executor to prevent "discord from clouding the memory of my dear friend."

This was well-intended but wishful thinking on George's behalf. The memory of his dear friend was already rife with discord and George Ullman's resignation as executor did not prevent him from facing considerable more time on the witness stand.

"When did you start west with the body of Rudolph Valentino?"

"I believe it was nine days later," George testified, "I think it was the first of September."

"You brought the body directly to Los Angeles?" his attorney asked.

"Yes, sir."

"What sort of accommodations did you provide?"

"We had a private car. In fact we had two private cars for which we did not pay anything except at the regular rate of passenger service. I had previously arranged by wire all the details of the funeral here."

"And the body was brought here?"

"Yes," George shifted in his seat, "The body was brought here and taken off at an outlying station and services were held at Beverly Hills. Subsequently the body was placed in a crypt in the Hollywood Cemetery, the crypt not being the property of the estate. It was a borrowed crypt from a friend of Valentino."

Wilson paused in his pacing and turned to ask George,

"Now, why did you conduct this ceremony, I will call it, for want of anything better to think of now; why did you conduct this ceremony in the manner that you did in the city of New York?"

"I did that in order to obtain international publicity for the name of Valentino, and further the sales of his pictures which I knew he had, well the corporation had an interest in."

"What corporation do you mean?"

"Rudolph Valentino Productions."

"After your return to Los Angeles and this funeral that was conducted in the manner that you just testified, what did you do in reference to the formation and organization of The Rudolph Valentino Memorial Association?"

"I wrote to people whose names I had from previous correspondence in fan mail asking their cooperation in keeping Rudy's name alive even though he had passed away and instructed them that the only way to keep the name alive was to apply to see his pictures at various theaters wherever they may be. The result was the formation of Valentino Memorial Clubs throughout the world. I estimate there must have been sixty-five or seventy of them, the majority of which I am president of. They have conducted services annually and during

154

the year, have gone to theaters insisting on seeing Valentino's pictures, especially the last two. That was a thing I asked them to do."

"What were these last pictures?" Wilson asked.

"*The Eagle* and *The Son of the Sheik*."

Wilson pressed on by asking for details of George's efforts to promote Rudy's name in the days following his death.

"Immediately upon the conclusion of the services for Valentino," George testified, "I had an expert make a catalog for the purpose of holding an auction, a public auction, and advertised this auction in the same manner as a performance, as a show would be advertised, in order to get the interested people of Los Angeles to come to the sale."

"Did you build a stage there?" Wilson asked.

"I built a stage and had spotlights. I had various other things, such as a number of policemen guarding the property, and for the effect it would produce."

The judge then interrupted attorney Wilson saying he wished to ask George a question.

"Mr. Ullman," the judge inquired, "as long as you have described, in a word, the affair in New York as having been staged for the benefit of publicity, it may be personal curiosity on my part but I would like to know if the performance here was also staged, his burial and funeral?"

George turned to face the judge, "In a manner it was, yes, sir, because I arranged all of these things that happened by wire, by telegram from New York. I had people here working with me all the time."

"You mean for its effect on sentimental people?"

George answered the judge by facing the spectators in the courtroom, "It was not only that. It was natural because I wanted to give Valentino, who was not only a business associate but a very dear personal friend of mine; I wanted to give him the finest funeral I knew how to give."

❧❧

In November, Falcon Lair's ex-handyman, Lou Mahoney was subpoenaed to testify on George's behalf. At the time of his impending testimony, Lou was operating a dry-cleaning business on Highland Avenue. This was the same business previously owned by Rudy and known as Ritz Cleaners. Because the business was an asset of Rudy's estate at the time of his death, the Ritz Cleaner's financial accounts, as well as the details of the transference of its ownership to Lou Mahoney received a thorough going over by the court during the court proceedings of Guglielmi v. Ullman.

When George delivered his testimony regarding the cleaning business, he stated it was sometime after the San Francisco estate auction in January 1927, that he cleared the dry cleaner's nearly $3000.00 of debt and appointed Lou in charge. By March of that same year, George said he officially signed ownership of the business over to Lou. He then sold the business to Lou for $250.00. Despite this testimony, Lou would later claim George gave him the business along with a company truck on the agreement that he reimburse the estate the $250.00 whenever he could afford to do so. Lou apparently ran the business for a few years, for in 1930, when a census taker knocked on his front door, he reported his occupation as "dry-cleaner".

In the days prior to Lou's November courtroom appearance, he was following every detail of George Ullman's legal travails as covered in the local papers. At the same time, Lou was also perusing news reports of another court room drama involving another of his past employers; Inspector Thomas J. Kelly. Before Lou moved to Los Angeles from New York City, he served seven years on the New York City police force with Inspector Kelly's Twelfth Inspection Division in Queens. Described as one public official who "could not be touched," Inspector Thomas J. Kelly was no stranger to courtroom showdowns.

While Lou was a member of the infamous precinct, Inspector Kelly and several of his officers were charged on multiple occasions with lax enforcement of Prohibition laws, covert relationships with local bootleggers and speakeasies, evidence tampering and the stashing of ill-gotten gains in small tin boxes. In November of 1930, Lou was reading all about it; Inspector Kelly and his gang were once again in trouble with the law. It seemed retired Judge Samuel Seabury's investigation of the New York City police involved many of Lou's old precinct buddies. On this occasion, Inspector Kelly and Lou's cohorts were accused of incarcerating women and extorting money from them on trumped up charges. As Lou was reading the latest testimony from his fellow officers in New York, he faced his own imminent day in court where he would deliver testimony in Alberto's lawsuit against George Ullman.

When Lou took the witness stand he was asked to elaborate upon the events immediately following his famous employer's sudden death.

"State what you saw at this time..."

"I seen the big staff working in the office all the time up at the house inventorying the estate."

"Were you present at any of these sales?"

"They handled them all."

"What did Mr. Ullman do at these sales?"

"Supervised the entire work of the sale."

"Was he the one that built the stage out there?"

"No, sir."

"Did he order it built?"

"He ordered every thing pertaining to the sale handled."

Lou continued his testimony by stating that he first met Rudolph Valentino in November of 1925. Whether this was a slip of the gruff young Irishman's tongue or perjury, Lou actually met Valentino one year earlier in the fall of 1924. Nevertheless, he informed the courtroom that "Mr. Ullman" worked hard and after Mr. Valentino's death he ensured that everyone working for Rudolph Valentino Productions "was fed and paid". Attorney Wilson closed his line of questioning by asking Lou precisely what Mr. Alberto Valentino was doing during this same time frame. Lou replied,

"Nothing."

His answer prompted another objection from Attorney James Scarborough.

∼◦∼

Late on the afternoon of November 12th, courtroom reporters clock-watched, slumped in their seats and scribbled halfheartedly on their notepads. Leonard Wilson seemed to sense they needed something to pique their interest and produced two blank checks signed by Rudolph Valentino. Everyone in the courtroom had witnessed Rudolph Valentino's signature on many documents during the prolonged hearing but they still craned their necks for a better look. The judge gave each check a closer scrutiny and then asked Wilson why he wished these two particular documents to be tagged as evidence.

Leonard Wilson explained; these checks were in George Ullman's possession and if he had intended to loot the Valentino estate he could have easily done so by simply filling out Valentino's blank notes for any amount the estate could pay. Wilson then described how Valentino gave the blank checks to George in February of 1926.

"George Ullman kept these signed note forms all these four years he was working to build up the estate for the heirs who are now attacking his reputation."

The judge denied the admission of the bank notes by stating,

"Mr. Ullman has already demonstrated to the court that he is a very competent man with figures and accounts. As an appointee of the court he comes before the court with all the presumption of integrity."

The court proceedings continued to drag on into December, when the judge made the announcement to adjourn until January. Before leaving the courtroom for the holiday break, George made a startling revelation to the court from the witness stand when he alleged that "a document of the utmost importance was stolen from Valentino's safe." He explained his claim by saying this document should have been attached to the original copy of Valentino's will.

George went on to state how this paper supported his claim Valentino directed him to act both as executor and as head of the production company. He added that prior to Valentino's death, his will was kept in his Falcon Lair office safe and only three people knew the combination to that safe; Rudolph Valentino, his brother Alberto and Lou Mahoney. Reporters smelled a juicy headline and the next morning the public read all about the document's "mysterious disappearance" and the "rifling" of Valentino's safe.

There was not much the court could do to resolve the issue of the missing portion of the will and on the day before the holiday recess, testimony was focused instead upon the subject of the transference of Cosmic Arts Inc. stock at the time of Rudy and Natacha's divorce. But with everyone's minds on Christmas and the New Year, the judge decided to postpone this line of questioning until after the holidays. His last order of business was to order the lawyer who handled the Valentino's divorce, Raymond Stewart, to submit a copy of the Valentino's property settlement for his review when court reconvened at the end of January.

It was only a few days after court adjourned, that George answered his office telephone to hear attorney Raymond Stewart's voice on the line. Stewart asked George if he was sitting down.

"What the hell's going on Ray?" George asked.

Stewart sounded out of breath. "You'll never guess what I just found in Rudy's divorce file."

"Go on." George replied.

"A beat up carbon copy of those instructions Rudy left for you." Stewart said with a snort of disbelief.

George was already reaching for his hat.

"I'll be right over."

༒

Within a half an hour, George was standing in Raymond Stewart's office holding a tattered and smudged sheet of onion skin paper which read,

> *"To S. George Ullman,*
>
> *I have this day named you as executor in my last will and testament; it is my desire that you perpetuate my name in the picture industry by continuing Rudolph Valentino Productions, Inc., until my nephew Jean shall have reached the age of 25 years; in the meantime to make motion pictures, using your own judgment as to numbers and kind, keeping control of any pictures made, if possible.*
>
> *Whenever there are profits from pictures made by the Rudolph Valentino Productions, Inc., it is my wish that you will pay to my brother Alberto the sum of $400.00 monthly, to my sister Maria the sum of $200.00 monthly and to my dear friend Mrs. Werner the sum of $200.00 monthly.*
>
> *When my nephew Jean reaches the age of 25 years, I desire that the residue, if any, be given to him. In the event of his death then the residue shall be distributed equally to my sister Maria and my brother Alberto."*

George read and then re-read the document. Here on the thin carbon copy were Rudy's instructions exactly as he remembered them; with one significant and glaring exception. The only instruction George had no recollection of ever receiving from Rudy, was the bombshell that he never left his estate in a three-way split between his brother, sister and Teresa Werner, but had instead bequeathed everything to his nephew Jean.

Raymond Stewart's legal mind was already in high gear.

"This means," he said, "that the only way Alberto or Maria could ever have any legal share in Rudy's estate, beyond their stipend, would be in the eventuality of Jean's death before he turned twenty-five. Good Lord George, this could present a serious problem for you as far as the cash advances to Alberto, Maria and Teresa Werner are concerned."

George began grasping precisely what the attorney was saying.

"You mean that Alberto and Maria have no future share in the estate as long as Jean is alive?"

"Precisely, George. The money you advanced to them cannot be deducted from their share in the estate because they have none. Except for their weekly stipend checks, you had no authority to advance them a penny or give them any estate items. Past those weekly stipends, it all belongs to Jean."

George's initial elation upon hearing of the document's discovery was fading fast into grave concern. He stared at the document and was not surprised to see that Rudy signed the document the same day he signed his will, September 1st, 1925. But when he read name of the document's sole witness, he was dumbstruck; Luther H. Mahoney.

As Raymond Stewart rambled on with more legal ramifications of the incredible find, George remained fixated on Lou Mahoney's signature. Raymond Stewart droned on with his legal analysis as it dawned on George that Lou had known all along that Rudy had endorsed this sheet of instructions as a valid second page to his will. Why, George thought, while he sought so desperately for any proof of this document's existence for four long years, had Lou not come forward and why had he said absolutely nothing?

George handed the sheet of paper back to Raymond Stewart and mumbled he had an errand to run. Before Raymond Stewart could say another word, George was out the door and headed for his car. With his hands gripping the steering wheel, he sped along the streets of Los Angeles taking the Lord's and handyman Lou's names in vain.

Chapter Nine

A Mineralava Country Mile

Seven years earlier, Brooklyn, New York, January 1923 -

As soon as the holiday decorations were stored away for another year, residents of Brooklyn, New York grew weary of the wintry weather. Even the hardiest of souls entertained thoughts of spring as they wiled away the chilly days stoking parlor coal stoves and hauling out the board games for the bored. In one Brooklyn home, on one particularly frosty day, a red hot coal stove filled a parlor with equatorial heat and a card table was being prepared for the afternoon's entertainment.

This parlor game would be no tedious round of Parcheesi, for the parlor belonged to Cora McGeachy, costume designer, musician, artist, psychic and automatic writing adept. Channeling messages from the ethers by means of a peach wood pencil was an every day pastime for Cora and she often invited her friends to join in her sessions. Cora's guests that afternoon were two of her closest friends, Rudolph Valentino and Natacha Rambova.

While Cora busied herself lowering the parlor blinds, Rudy and Natacha positioned five chairs around the table; one for each of them, one for Cora and two more for the two spirit guides they were about to summon. On the table directly in front of Cora's chair sat a stack of loose sheets of blank paper and three peach wood pencils. Rudy and Natacha were familiar with Cora's ritual as they'd visited her parlor many times that winter.

When Cora was satisfied every detail was in order, she leaned back in her chair, closed her eyes and drifted into contact with Rudy's spirit guides, Black Feather and Mesolope. She summoned first the spirit of Black Feather, the American Indian who guided Rudy through his daily affairs and then spoke directly to the two thousand year old Egyptian, Mesolope, who instructed Rudy on issues of a more arcane nature. With her eyelids quivering and open a mere slit, Cora scrawled rapidly across the first sheet of paper. Rudy and Natacha leaned forward in their chairs waiting for her pause. Cora wrote on in silence for several minutes, line after line, before opening her eyes and sliding the sheet of paper across the table to Natacha.

Despite the lack of punctuation in Cora's cryptic writings, Natacha read easily the latest word from the other side. On this afternoon it was welcome news. Black Feather told of a long and profitable journey in Rudy's near future and assured him help for his troubled career would soon arrive in the form of a businessman who would become his manager.

Rudy and Natacha were elated with the news as they held unconditional faith in Cora's psychic abilities. Neither Cora nor Natacha questioned the increasing seriousness with which Rudy blithely accepted the surrealistic counsel of the long-deceased sages Black Feather and Mesolope. So when Rudy and Natacha left Cora's parlor that afternoon to return to their respective homes in Manhattan, they felt renewed confidence that Rudy would be victorious over Famous Players-Lasky. This was exactly the news they'd hoped to hear from the other side.

When Rudy arrived in New York City from Foxlair estate the previous August, news that "The Sheik" was refusing to honor his contract with Famous Players-Lasky Corporation received front page coverage in newspapers coast to coast. Rudy was adamant he explain to his public how he'd walked off the job only to gain artistic control over his films, and instructed his attorney, Arthur Grahm to convene an immediate press conference. On September second, Rudy, with a prepared statement in hand, appeared before a gathering of New York press. To Arthur Grahm's bewilderment, Rudy never gave the written statement a single glance.

He proceeded instead to expound at length upon his frustration with Famous Players-Lasky, the studio's head of production Jesse Lasky and its president, Adolph Zukor. He then handed the rapt press all the details of the poor treatment he received from the studio and its executives during the filming of both *Blood and Sand* and *The Young Rajah*. While attorney Arthur Grahm made futile gestures to silence his client, Rudy charged Lasky and Zukor with breaking the terms of his contract and accused them of acting with callous disregard towards Natacha. He alleged that at the time he signed his contract with Famous Players-Lasky, the studio assured him he would have artistic input in his films. Rudy added that until such time that he was granted complete artistic control over all of his films, he would not work another day for Famous Players-Lasky.

Knowing he held the attention of every reporter present, Rudy then divulged the details of one of the motion picture industry's worst kept secrets; block-booking. He described the finer points of how movie studios forced these "cheater" films upon the public. Most of the reporters listening to Rudy's tirade were fairly confidant they were witnessing the Sheik's public career suicide. When one reporter inquired what legal action he would take if Lasky and Zukor slapped him with an injunction prohibiting him from working until his contract expired in 1924, Rudy had his answer. He said he would appeal any such injunction as he owed it to his fans to appear only in quality films. By the end of the press conference, Rudy had thrown down the gauntlet and vowed to accept nothing less than total victory.

On September fourteenth, Famous Players-Lasky responded by petitioning the New York State Supreme Court to issue a no-work injunction against Rudy. The court ruled promptly in the studio's favor by prohibiting him from working until his contract with the studio expired two years later. Through his attorney Arthur Grahm, Rudy filed his appeal of the court's decision.

Meanwhile, he moved his belongings into Frank Mennillo's apartment in the Hotel des Artistes on 67th Street. When Rudy became a resident of the Hotel des Artistes, the establishment's management was under intense pressure from the public and the District Attorney for reportedly leasing flats to unmarried couples and young people "pretending to be artists" who were "actually engaging in bohemian lifestyles". The District Attorney asserted that the hotel "cloaked loose living and free lifestyles". The Hotel des Artistes' management soon bowed to the public pressure and began requiring proof of a couple's marriage license in order to prevent any living in sin on the premises.

When Rudy moved into Frank Mennillo's two-story flat in the controversial Hotel des Artistes, Frank was a married man. However Frank and his wife Zelinda had recently separated. He and Zelinda shared custody of their twelve-year old son Arnold who spent a good deal of his time living with his father in the Hotel des Artistes.

During the winter of 1922-1923, Frank was frequently out of town as he was spending a great deal of his time in Washington, D.C. or on the road traveling with President Warren G. Harding. Whenever

Frank was away, his roommate Rudy was often left in charge of the preteen Arnold. In Frank's absence, Rudy became an influential role model for the boy as well as his personal instructor of all the latest dances steps.

After returning to New York from Foxlair, Rudy and Natacha maintained separate residences as they were under constant surveillance by detectives presumably dispatched by either Los Angeles District Attorney Woolwine or Jesse Lasky. Woolwine's stern warning that he could still pursue bigamy charges against Rudy and convene a grand jury was of genuine concern to both Rudy and Natacha. Nevertheless, the skulking detectives' prying eyes forced Natacha and Rudy to become creative in their efforts to enjoy private time together.

Natacha moved into a conveniently located apartment with her aunt Teresa Werner on 67th Street just off Central Park, not far from the Hotel des Artistes. Two years earlier when Rudy and Natacha lived together in their Whitley Heights home in Los Angeles, Rudy used Paul Ivano's residence as a cover for his actual place of residence. In New York during the winter of 1922, he used Frank's Hotel des Artistes' flat as a cover for his primary residence, Natacha's apartment. The detectives trailing Rudy's every move were none the wiser as he perfected his Hotel des Artistes' escape routes. According to Frank Mennillo, late most every night Rudy slipped out of the apartment and headed around the corner to sleep with Natacha.

Both Frank Mennillo and Aunt Teresa assumed their roles as guard dogs against the detective's interfering presence. But Rudy and Natacha had one other key ally in their subterfuge that winter. This third ally was Frances Steloff, owner of the Gotham Book Mart on West 47th Street. Frances Steloff was not only the patron saint of many authors working in New York at the time, but also a loyal friend. She included among these loyal friends both Rudolph Valentino and Natacha Rambova.

Frances Steloff visited Natacha in Los Angeles on several occasions and many of the rare manuscripts and antique books in Natacha and Rudy's collections were purchased from Steloff's Gotham Book Mart. Francis Steloff sympathized with Rudy's stand against Famous Players-Lasky and was aware of both his and Natacha's dire financial straights as a result of his unemployment. With this in mind, she often adjusted the price of their literary purchases accordingly. As payment for one rare volume, Frances accepted a deposit of several of Natacha's bracelets which were slipped off her wrist on the spot.

Rudy and Natacha were grateful to Frances Steloff for more than her generosity and expertise in locating rare books. The stacks of the Gotham Book Mart became a convenient hide-away where they regularly enjoyed private time together. While bored detectives loitered outside the bookstore and fumed that Rudy and Natacha were taking their sweet time browsing for books, the objects of their hunt reveled in a few intimate moments deep within the hinter-stacks.

Meanwhile, Francis Steloff tended to business seated at her desk in the front of the store. She knew exactly what was transpiring amidst her dusty book shelves and was ready to sound the alarm at a moment's notice. Consequently, Rudy and Natacha's book collection grew at an astonishing rate despite the fact they were always short on cash. For as they left their Gotham Book Mart trysts, Frances made sure a few purchases were tucked under their arms. The detectives never caught on and consequently Frances Steloff, Rudy and Natacha all made out in one way or another.

On October 1, 1922, The Supreme Court issued their rejection of Rudy's appeal of Famous Players-Lasky's no-work injunction. The court did slightly alter the injunction by allowing Rudy to seek work as long as his employment did not require his appearance on stage or as an actor. As soon as Lasky and Zukor learned of Rudy's disappointing news, they offered to increase his weekly pay from $1250.00 to $7500.00 if he returned to work at once. Rudy refused their offer saying he intended to remain true to his statement made during his press conference. He reminded them of his public vow to reject any offer that did not include artistic control over his films which this offer clearly did not. He then leveled his public response in an open letter published in the January 1923 issue of *Photoplay.*

"I don't want to be a cog in a machine that grinds pictures out, cuts them to put them in cans like sardines. I am selfish to make good pictures."

Although the public admired Rudy's artistic integrity, his personal reality of living without a paycheck soon had its sorry effect. He was supporting a significant financial overhead while continuing to enjoy a lifestyle that came at a steep price. His attorney Arthur Grahm's weekly fee was nearly $2500.00 and three thousand miles away in Los Angeles, furious bill collectors were referring his long overdue accounts to collection agencies. These agencies were also contacting Rudy's Los Angeles attorney, W.I. Gilbert demanding their payments or else. With meager funds at his disposal, Gilbert did his best to fend off this legion of creditors which included everyone from disgruntled contractors to utility companies. For a while Rudy extended his credit by making a few payments from money borrowed from producer Joe Godsol and Frank Mennillo.

While Rudy endeavored to pay his bills, news of his plight was having an unsettling ripple effect upon the motion picture industry. Actors and actresses held their collective breaths and hoped Rudolph Valentino's potential victory over Famous Players-Lasky might set precedence for improvement in their own careers. Studio management, on the other hand, vowed actors would never gain control over their product. On both sides of the issue there was a general consensus in Hollywood and New York that Rudolph Valentino's movie career was over. Convinced Hollywood producers and studio executives would never again grant him the slightest screen role, the word on everyone's lips was, "Valentino is through!"

In defense of his refusal of Lasky and Zukor's latest offer, Rudy presented his cause directly to the public by issuing several articles and making a few personal appearances. In an effort to improve his public image, he collaborated with *Photoplay* magazine writer Herbert Howe to write a carefully crafted autobiography for serialized publication. He also granted a radio interview which was broadcast from The American Radio Exposition and in the January twenty-third issue of *Photoplay* he published an open letter titled, "The Truth About Myself" in which he wrote,

"I cannot work for this motion picture corporation. I cannot endure the tyranny, the broken promises or the system of production. I cannot forgive the cruelty of the company to Mrs. Valentino."

Rudy's serialized autobiography proved to be successful self-promotion and *Photoplay's* offices were flooded with fan mail supporting his stand. This prompted the magazine's editor, James Quirk, to phone Jesse Lasky requesting that the studio pay for the processing of Rudy's fan letters. Stung by the reminder that his uppity box office star's popularity was soaring, Lasky flatly refused.

While Rudy was doling out minimum payments on his mounting debt, his fans were filling movie theaters to capacity with each showing of his films. At the end of their long days, tired workers dug deep into their pockets to find the coin for admission and watched all of his movies including *The Sheik*, *The Four Horsemen of the Apocalypse*, *The Conquering Power*, *Blood and Sand* and *The Young Rajah*. In doing so they granted all of Rudy's former employers an unheard-of reward in box office receipts.

All of Rudy's previous employers realized his stand against Famous Players-Lasky was a bonanza of free publicity and began cashing in. Every frame of Valentino footage was dusted off and reissued. His early film, *The Married Virgin* was re-released as *Frivolous Wives*, *An Adventuress* was re-titled, *Isle of Love*. One of Rudy's first onscreen dance numbers was re-issued with the brief footage spliced together in order to create a longer dance performance in a continuous sequence. With more movies to attend, Rudy's faithful fans continued to stand patiently in long lines at the corner picture shows to palpitate, swoon, sigh and shriek even louder for their Sheik.

Despite his raging popularity, by January of 1923, Rudy's career was on ice as frozen solid as The Pond in Central Park. He was being stalked by detectives, was unable to work in his chosen profession and lived each day in a perpetual fret over money. As the focus of the press and the public's rabid interest, living his life became a daunting and often dangerous endeavor.

❧

Both Rudy and Frank Mennillo instructed young Arnold Mennillo that he was never to open the door of their Hotel des Artistes apartment without first knowing the prospective visitor's identity. Frank explained to his son how Rudy's fans would do anything to get into the apartment. Arnold was understandably anxious about the situation and obeyed his father and Rudy to the letter. There were a few close calls when women pursued the boy through the hotel's corridors pleading for the big favor. But Arnold was a savvy young man and only once did he slip up and the inevitable occurred.

Rudy was upstairs the day Arnold's twelve-year old mind went blank when he heard the knock at the door. He had barely cracked the door an inch when a young woman screaming, "Rudolph! Rudolph!" burst into the living room. Hearing the woman's hysterical shouting, Rudy appeared quickly on the balcony overlooking the living room and sized up the situation below.

167

As his trembling fan faced the heart-stopping target of her break and enter, Rudy spoke in a calming voice as he graciously escorted her across the living room and towards the door. He asked her name and where she lived, but before she could open her mouth to answer she found herself standing dazed and confused in the hotel corridor. Rudy locked the door and turned to Arnold who was swearing this would never happen again. "Uncle Rudy" gave him a pat on the back saying,

"Non ti preoccupare." (Don't worry about it.)

༄ஐ༄

In the days and weeks following his visit to Foxlair estate, Rudy became convinced his personal correspondence was being compromised. Throughout that winter he surrendered to this advancing paranoia and began encrypting a great deal of his business correspondence in ever-changing, elaborate codes. He grew wary of mailmen and delivery boys and before opening any letters or telegrams, he examined the seal of the envelope with a magnifying glass.

As the public's pursuit of Rudolph Valentino intensified, he was not only preoccupied with devising codes but withdrawing from the fray by delving deeper into the occult. His interest in the supernatural was not unique to his generation, as activities such as consulting psychics, holding seances and murmuring over Ouija boards were gaining popularity that winter. Despite the fact that this behavior was frowned upon by every religious denomination and most social organizations, young people, including Rudy and Natacha, found the lure of such wild belief irresistible.

Rudy was especially enticed and familiarized himself with all aspects of psychic phenomena. Under intense harassment by his fans and the press, he found welcome solace in any altered state that allowed him to feel safe from outside intrusion. But the more familiar he became with these psychic diversions, the more reliant he became upon the advice of his master guides Black Feather and Mesolope. Frank Mennillo, Natacha and Aunt Teresa grew to accept this fact and Rudy's daily communications with these two vaporous advisers became a part of all their daily lives. As Rudy became more proficient at slipping in and out of a trance and writing lengthy directives from his master guides while in a state of semi-consciousness, the barrier

168

between his troubled earthly reality and his peaceful astral plane grew thinner.

On the many occasions when Cora McGeachy's psychic predictions did manifest, Natacha and Rudy referred to these events as "demonstrations." Rudy needed scant initiation into Cora's process of automatic writing and he was soon foretelling, also by means of a pencil, his own "demonstrations". If Cora McGeachy divined more practical directives for Rudy from Black Feather and Mesolope, Rudy utilized his automatic writing skills to channel poetry from deceased, famous poets and comforting messages from his dearly-departed mother.

Natacha encouraged Rudy's psychic activities and believed the poetry he transcribed while in a trance to be worthy of publication. When she presented the idea of publishing his psychic poetry to publisher Bernarr MacFadden, he seized the idea to capitalize upon Rudy's extraordinary popularity. A project was launched and Natacha and MacFadden were soon collaborating on the publication of Rudy's collection of poems titled, "*Day Dreams*".

While Natacha edited through the best and worst of Rudy's mystic verse, across Manhattan a young man just Rudy's age was poring over the accounting ledgers of a national cosmetics firm. George Ullman was troubleshooting the Mineralava Company's flagging profits and after a thorough review of the company's operations, the budding ad man discovered the company was spending more money on advertising than they were grossing in sales. It wasn't long before George Ullman devised an intriguing and innovative solution to the problem.

≈§∞

George Ullman was no different than any other New Yorker that winter and had read plenty about Rudolph Valentino's employment woes. With this in mind, he devised a plan which he felt might solve the problem of his client's vanishing profit margin. George Ullman also knew Natacha Rambova was the stepdaughter of the cosmetics firm's owner and founder, Richard Hudnut. George was confident Richard Hudnut would receive his idea of a celebrity dancing tour starring Rudolph Valentino as spokesman for Mineralava Beauty Clay as a winning proposal.

However, when George presented his brainstorm to a roomful of Mineralava executives, they remained unmoved. They all received his concept of hiring a celebrity as a corporate spokesperson, even Richard Hudnut's future son-in-law Rudolph Valentino, as an innovative concept. But they frankly had no idea how his mere sponsorship of their product could possibly benefit their company. George forged on with his presentation by explaining to the unreceptive executives that he had already related the details of his plan to Valentino's legal representative Arthur Grahm. But he had to admit, he received an initial chilly response.

Sensing this revelation was not advancing his proposal, George assured the executives that upon their approval he would contact Valentino's attorney a second time. He said he would explain to the attorney how a tour could be arranged to accommodate the terms of the injunction currently in place against Valentino. He assured the Mineralava executives he would inform Arthur Grahm how Famous Players-Lasky's injunction only prevented Valentino from appearing on stage as an actor. If the Mineralava Company engaged the movie star as a sales representative and guaranteed he not perform on an actual stage, Valentino would not technically be violating the terms of the injunction.

George did his homework before presenting his lengthy proposal to the Mineralava executives and included all financial projections for the proposed promotional tour. He allocated seven thousand dollars a week plus all expenses paid for Valentino and a stage dancer, presumably Natacha's services. The couple would perform nightly on a road trip of approximately three month's duration. George's plan also provided for a local beauty pageant to be held during each of Valentino's performances. At the culmination of the tour, George told the executives, the Mineralava Company would host a highly-publicized gala beauty pageant in New York City where they would crown the winner of the national competition.

The advertising potential for their product was not lost on Mineralava management and they granted George permission to place a second call to attorney Arthur Grahm. It wasn't long before George received a reply from Grahm; Rudolph Valentino was ready to negotiate. George convened a second meeting with Mineralava where he relayed the good news. As he closed his briefcase, he believed he was set to submit his invoice for services rendered. The executives thought differently. They informed George that he would be overseeing all phases of the tour's organization.

Until that day no single entry in George's disparate resume qualified him to organize a promotional road tour. In 1916, he was mustered into service in the Army Reserve and rode the Texas plains with the cavalry in pursuit of Pancho Villa. After this stint in the Army Reserve, George married his eighteen-year old sweetheart, Beatrice Mallet, "Bee", and attended law school while working for The Federal Reserve Bank. He boxed professionally, studied industrial engineering at New York University and with the birth of his first child, Daniel in 1918, he became a father. But the fact remained; George knew nothing about the business of producing a three month road show.

Nevertheless, over the next few weeks he labored over the tour's many details. When he was confident he had accomplished his next assignment for the Mineralava Company, he filed his final report with the cosmetics company by informing them the tour was set to launch the next evening from Chicago, Illinois. The Mineralava executives again informed George his services were still needed, as he would be traveling to Chicago that night to join the tour as Mineralava's representative and road manager.

With only six hours to pack and board the next train to Chicago, George hurried home to inform his distraught wife that he was leaving that very night. Bee was four months pregnant at the time, caring for their rambunctious four-year old son Danny and not thrilled to learn her husband would be away from home for the next three months. While George tossed his clothes into a suitcase, he assured his wife that whenever possible she would join the traveling show.

Throughout George's negotiations with attorney Arthur Grahm and the organization of the Mineralava tour, he'd never met Rudolph Valentino or Natacha Rambova. With little notice he found himself heading towards Chicago to do just that. As his train left New York that night he realized the success or failure of the entire venture rested squarely upon his shoulders. He just hoped his plan to salvage Mineralava's profit margin would be successful and that the celebrity couple might draw sufficient crowds to sell some Mineralava Beauty Clay along the way.

On March 14, 1923, George arrived in Chicago aboard the Twentieth Century Limited. He hurried across the rail yard to board another train which was parked on a side track awaiting his arrival. Even though he had yet to lay his eyes on the private rail car that had just been connected to the west bound train, George knew every detail of its interior.

From his office in New York City he had personally supervised the conversion of this rail car, once occupied by the King of Belgium, into sumptuous accommodations for Rudolph Valentino and Natacha Rambova. George christened the car, The Colonial and ensured it was furnished with gilt-framed mirrors, Turkish carpets, original oil paintings and period furniture. The customized car was also equipped with two full-sized showers, expansive wardrobes and a coal stove to heat a comfortably appointed parlor. Adjacent to an elegant sitting room were two adjoining bedrooms. Rudy and Natacha's bedroom included their private bathroom and a king-sized, brass bed which was spread with custom-fitted satin sheets.

George planned to occupy the second bedroom adjacent to Rudy and Natacha's bedroom, except on those occasions when Aunt Teresa Werner traveled with the tour. Then George would surrender his bedroom for her use while he slept in a regulation sleeping car berth. The Colonial's private dining room was staffed with a chef and steward and each meal on board would be gourmet fare served on the finest china and table linens. So as George paused for a moment on the railroad tracks, he took a good look at the train car he knew so intimately; day one of the Mineralava tour was about to get underway.

He jumped up onto the rail car's steps and stepped into the Colonial's parlor for the first time. There, leaning against the far wall, smoking a cigarette was Rudolph Valentino. Seated in an armchair warming her hands by the coal stove was an exotically dressed and turbaned Natacha Rambova. George introduced himself as Mineralava's representative and thought Rudy seemed belligerent, even angry. To ease the tension of the moment, George initiated small talk and before long Rudy pushed himself away from his post against the wall to relax into friendly conversation.

Although George noticed Rudy spoke with a noticeable Italian accent, he was impressed with his speaking voice and command of the English language. George was also impressed by Natacha Rambova's beauty and personal style of dress. Before he could open the discussion of the impending tour, Rudy and Natacha were eager to share the details of their marriage ceremony which took place that afternoon in Crown Point, Indiana.

With the long year of their enforced estrangement finally behind them, Rudy and Natacha were at last free to marry. They explained to George they faced further marital complications as they were unable to obtain a marriage license in Illinois. Apparently state law required the bride to maintain residency in order to qualify for marriage within the state. Consequently, they said their marriage took place earlier that day after yet another border crossing; this time into Indiana.

Before the conversation in The Colonial turned to the specifics of the tour, Rudy took George aside to inform him of his troubling financial situation in Los Angeles. He told him it was imperative the tour avoid Los Angeles at all costs, at least until he could settle a few accounts with his angry bill collectors. Rudy went on to say his situation was so grave he feared he would be thrown in jail if he did step foot in Los Angeles. George pressed Rudy for a few details regarding this "grave" situation and assured him it sounded as if none of the judgments held against him were based on any criminal offenses. He said he would look into the matter and then turned the discussion to the logistics of their journey.

He explained how an advance man with a staff of two assistants would be setting up each evening's performance. He outlined more details by saying that any time it was necessary for their private car or any accompanying rail cars used by the Mineralava Company to be connected to another train, he would pay the railroad for twenty-five tickets. And every ten days he would pay the railroad a flat rate of one thousand dollars for food, linens and support personnel.

Rudy and Natacha also learned the tour's six musicians, chef and steward would be traveling in coach accommodations in an accompanying train car. And as Rudy was prevented from performing on stage by Famous Players-Lasky's injunction, George assured him this technicality would be circumvented as none of his performances would take place on a legitimate stage. Instead, he and Natacha would be performing on canvas covered boxing rings and gymnasium and armory floors.

This first encounter between Rudolph Valentino and George Ullman ended with a handshake. Without the advantage of his own spirit master guide advisory board, George did not realize the significance of that handshake. But Rudy and Natacha had known for weeks that someone like George Ullman was about to arrive.

The first performance of the Mineralava tour was scheduled to take place in Omaha, Nebraska. Despite all of George's meticulous planning there was one detail he could not control; the weather. On the first night of the tour, Mother Nature dumped a spring blizzard on Omaha. While the snow piled up in the streets bringing traffic to a standstill, George wrestled with the decision whether to cancel the tour's first performance due to whiteout conditions.

One hour before the show was scheduled to begin, hundreds of shivering citizens of Omaha were abandoning their cars in the streets to tromp through the snow to see the Valentinos' performance. By the time George motioned for the musicians to begin playing, every seat was taken and hundreds of people were being turned away.

As the musicians played the final strains of the overture, George stepped to the microphone to introduce Rudolph Valentino and his new bride, Natacha. His introduction was barely audible over the crowd's thunderous reaction to the start of the show. Rudy and Natacha then stepped arm in arm out from behind a strategically placed screen to make their entrance dressed in full costume for their first number; a tango. Rudy wore the traditional black gaucho bombachas, rastra and boleador and Natacha was radiant in a fitted velvet dress. Most people in the audience were aware of Rudy's stand against Famous Players-Lasky, so it wasn't just the thrill of seeing the Sheik that had the crowd in a frenzy. They hailed him as a hero who was sacrificing his own career for the quality of their movies. Shouts of support rang out over the deafening applause.

"Atta, Boy Rudy! You're all right!"

The first number of the night's performance was the same Argentine tango Rudy performed in the cantina scene in *The Four Horsemen of the Apocalypse*. This piece was followed by a brief, tempestuous dance which Rudy and Natacha choreographed themselves. After a few more numbers, Rudy took the microphone to rail against the evils of Famous Players-Lasky's block-booking system. He concluded his remarks with a short speech extolling the merits of Mineralava Beauty Clay. Proof of the product's excellence, he told the rowdy crowd, was his wife Natacha's flawless complexion. He then announced that the beauty contest portion of the program would begin.

Twenty young women vied for the title of the most beautiful woman in Omaha and after a few elimination rounds, the winner was chosen by audience applause. Rudy presented the beaming beauty queen with a silver-plated trophy engraved with the words, "Winner of the Mineralava Beauty Contest". He also presented the winner with a set of custom made miniature dolls as models of himself and Natacha in the same tango outfit they wore for their opening tango number. George custom-ordered the dolls from Sardieux in New York and paid an extravagant one hundred dollars for each set. Despite Omaha's snow storm, the Mineralava Tour was off to a rousing start and scheduled to perform in eighty-seven cities across the U.S. and Canada.

From the first day of the Mineralava tour, George had his capable hands full. The daily hordes of Rudy's fans were not his only challenge and in every city he was presented with a new set of logistics. As manager he was responsible for all aspects of the complex road show such as the maintenance of the daily accounting ledgers, the overseeing of the payroll and personnel, crowd management and a myriad of other details necessary to ensure the well-being and comfort of the show's stars.

It was also George's responsibility to tally each evening's box office receipts and then walk alone to the nearest telegraph office to wire the cash to Mineralava's bank account in New York City. Most evenings his trek to the telegraph office was delayed as he paced about impatiently waiting for Rudy to transpose his encrypted telegrams to Cora McGeachy into his latest code.

Although George was confidant he was doing everything possible to guarantee the Valentinos enjoyed the utmost comfort, traveling by train was tedious. Rudy and Natacha traveled in opulence befitting royalty, but there was still no avoiding the train's distinct smell of kerosene and smoke and the constant jostling of life on the rails. Their days were divided into destinations and whistle stops and for Rudy and Natacha this meant crowds of eager fans waiting for them whenever they stepped into view. And with each successive engagement, George grew more self-assured; the road show had been one phenomenal idea.

Cheering crowds lined both sides of the railroad tracks whenever the Mineralava train steamed into even the most remote station. Many mayors declared the day of the train's arrival a work and school holiday to guarantee every citizen an opportunity to see Rudolph Valentino and his beautiful wife. As the Mineralava Tour journeyed deeper into the heartland, the press began devoting pages of copy to the every move and slightest whim of Rudolph and Natacha Valentino.

≈≈≈

Not all of these articles were positive and as the tour progressed, some reporters suggested snidely that perhaps Rudolph Valentino was slathering his own face with the beauty clay. Rudy's fans ignored these provocateurs in the press and hurried to purchase their tickets for the next Mineralava show. In a few cities, local police departments issued stern warnings to the city's youth in advance of the tour's arrival, warning that any emulation of the controversial movie star would not be tolerated during his visit.

On the day the Mineralava train pulled into Portland, Oregon local newspapers reported a citywide police sweep of any youth sporting the style of dress stereotypically considered to be under "Sheik" influence; slick-backed, vaselined hair and any fashion deemed "flashy". Headlines in *The Morning Oregonian* told the story, "Sheiks Have Convention in Municipal Jail Cells" with the crimes of Rudy imitators listed as general "hoodlumery". The detainees in the municipal jail were referred to as "sheiks" and "sheiktesses" and one apparently less natty fellow received the dubious honor of being dubbed a "sub-sheik".

Nevertheless, Rudy's appearances in city after city continued to inspire highly charged opinions about his popularity. For as deftly as he had seduced millions of hormonally driven teenagers and bored housewives, he had also inspired the mobilization of anti-Sheik activists intent upon quashing his allegedly nefarious influence. One particular individual intent upon doing some serious quashing was *The Oregonian's* reporter on the beat the day the Mineralava tour arrived in Portland. Prim correspondent Leone Baer was one of the few women who loathed Rudolph Valentino and believed Mr. and Mrs. Valentino were not Hollywood immortals but Hollywood immorals.

Apparently someone tipped Rudy off to Miss Baer's low opinion of him, for at the last minute he refused to grant her scheduled interview. His snub did not bode well with Leone Baer and this was

176

reflected in her article in *The Oregonian* the following day. She mocked his Italian accent, "there isa goin' ta' be a great war soon, a war against the motion picture trusts, in which brains and art will be shed instedda bloodshed." Furthermore, she accused Rudy of "effeminacy" by wondering if he canceled their interview because his face was caked with the beauty clay. She titled her invective, "Cold-Cream Sheik Hides from Caller", with a sub-title, "Valentino, Model for Effeminate Lads, Is Here."

Despite a spate of disparaging articles, the Mineralava tour sparked a national sensation and Jesse Lasky and Adolph Zukor were forced to rethink their hardline position with their wayward star. Their continuing standoff with Rudy only served to publicize the Mineralava tour and every stop along the way, in city after city, week after week, Rudolph Valentino was all the rage, the bees knees and the cat's pajamas.

✑✑

The Children's Orthopedic Hospital in Seattle, Washington held its annual "Pound Party" on the hospital's lawn. During this popular event, the hospital hosted a tea party for the community and opened its doors allowing local entertainers to perform throughout the wards. All that was required of the good citizens of Seattle was that they fill the provided bins with generous donations of "pounds" of anything; cheese, flour, sugar, rice or canned goods.

The Pound Party was always a profitable event, but in 1923 this was especially so as patrons came out in record numbers. For coincidentally, the Pound Party that year was held on the same day Rudolph Valentino's Mineralava tour was scheduled to perform in Seattle. When the Pound Party's organizers realized their fortuitous timing, they contacted the tour's manager George Ullman to request an appearance by the famous movie star and his wife. Without hesitation, Rudy and Natacha agreed to pay a visit to the kiddies' ward. So on the day of the event, the morning edition of *The Seattle Post-Intelligencer* announced the unbelievable news to its subscribers; sometime between 2:30 and 3:30 p.m., Rudolph and Natacha Valentino would be attending the Pound Party.

At two o'clock that afternoon a torrential rain brought a halt to the event's activities on the hospital lawn as tables and folding chairs were carried hastily inside. The police department's band, local

177

songsters, dancers and clowns made the best of the lousy weather and did a noble job entertaining guests and ailing children. But even a lariat performer, his horse Onions and a costumed monkey failed to distract the Pound Party's guests from the true focus of their attention. By 2:30, the hospital's corridors were lined with anxious, trembling women and girls anticipating the moment of Rudolph Valentino's arrival.

Precisely upon the appointed hour, the elegant couple made their entrance to a reception of gasps, applause and scattered swooning. Rudy and Natacha began their tour of the childrens' ward by walking from little hospital bed to little hospital bed greeting the young patients and pausing to speak with the nurses. *The Post's* reporter snapped one photograph of Rudy as he dangled a rattle for a mildly amused baby.

One of the childrens' nurses whispered to the reporter that the Valentinos seemed gracious enough, but Rudolph did not appear to know the slightest thing about infants. She found it hilarious that he asked a few of the babies how they were doing and seemed upset when one baby had no teeth in her mouth. The nurse told the reporter she had to explain to Mr. Valentino that the baby had no teeth because she was only eight days old.

Rudy and Natacha's appearance at the Pound Party drew hundreds of people to the event that would not have otherwise attended. Inspired by the famous couple's endorsement of the worthy cause, the hospital's donation bins were filled to the brim with clothing and food and a few benevolent guests even contributed pounds of money. At precisely 3:30, Rudy and Natacha left the childrens' ward to return to the business of their day. It was back on the Mineralava train to head towards the next city, the next show and the next beauty contest.

In advance of the tour's arrival, George was often contacted by local dignitaries requesting a private meeting with the Valentinos. In Rochester, Minnesota the eminent Dr. Walter Mayo made such a request by inviting Rudy, Natacha and George to tour his clinic including the psychiatric wards housing the most afflicted patients. This seemingly harmless invitation turned out to be a hair-raising experience for Rudy.

As Dr. Mayo escorted his guests down one corridor of the womens' ward, the female patients began shrieking and rattling the metal doors of their cells. When some of them recognized Rudy, they began clawing at him through the door's barred windows. The resulting bedlam became so deafening and terrifying that the stroll through the asylum was cut short. Natacha consoled her visibly shaken husband as she whisked him out the nearest exit, while George diplomatically concluded the visit with Dr. Mayo.

In nearly every city along the tour something unusual or memorable occurred. In Atlanta, Georgia, local segregation laws mandated that George schedule two performances; one in the afternoon for whites and one in the evening for blacks. While Rudy and Natacha danced their way through the final number of the afternoon's performance, a matronly white woman approached George as he stood by the box office watching the show. The woman snapped at him,

"Mr. Ullman, you must immediately cancel the evening's performance!"

George replied he had no intention of doing any such thing and explained he'd already sold every seat. The woman pressed her point further and insisted Rudolph Valentino would not be performing before a black audience.

When George had heard enough, he waved the woman off with the back of his hand. He walked away telling her one more time that the performance would go on as scheduled. But the woman followed him and asked in an ever louder voice,

"George Ullman, have you ever heard of the Ku Klux Klan?"

She continued with her harangue threatening that the Ku Klux Klan had already guaranteed there would be problems during Rudolph Valentino's evening performance.

"If Valentino and his wife do perform this evening, they will regret their actions!"

George recognized the ominous sincerity in the woman's words. Fearing for Rudy and Natacha's safety, he reluctantly canceled the evening's performance, refunded every ticket and within a few hours the Mineralava train was steaming out of Atlanta.

In Montreal, Rudy delivered his usual speech between dance numbers and charmed another enthusiastic crowd. As he took his bow, he realized he'd just delivered his speech to a bilingual audience.

Stepping back to the microphone, he repeated every word in French to cheering and applause.

It was during Rudy and Natacha's last number that night in Montreal, that a woman from the audience approached George and removed a five hundred dollar bill from her purse. She pressed the bill into the palm of his hand and whispered in his ear; the five hundred dollars was his if he would guarantee she would be able to wait in Rudolph Valentino's hotel room after the show. George returned the five hundred dollar bill and reminded the woman that Mrs. Valentino would never hear of such behavior. Attempts to bribe George were a nightly occurrence on the Mineralava tour, but the woman in Montreal was the only person who ever flashed a five hundred dollar bill his way.

In Toronto, Rudy landed in some hot water with his wife, his manager and a family of well-to-do locals. Typically, before and after each show Rudy posed for publicity photographs with the evening's beauty contestants. One contestant in Toronto, who happened to bear an uncanny resemblance to Natacha, made more than a passing impression upon Rudy during the scheduled photo session.

Apparently beauty contestant Norma Niblock spent a bit too much private time with Rudy before the evening show and it was whispered among her fellow contestants that a certain inappropriate exchange was eye-witnessed. News of Rudy and Norma Niblock's indiscretion was blabbed post haste to the young woman's parents who were furious at their daughter's behavior.

The situation deteriorated during the evening's performance when Rudy ignored the audience's selection of their beauty queen by applause and instead planted the crown squarely upon Norma Niblock. The other beauty contestants, Norma's family and Natacha bristled. Those who witnessed the backstage carryings-on snickered, but Norma's parents considered her crown a brazen admission that she earned her award by fooling around with *The Sheik*.

Toronto wasn't the only city in which Rudy broke protocol with the "selection by audience applause" to crown his own beauty contest winner. While dancing with Natacha in Manchester, New Hampshire, he apparently kept one eye on his audience. When it came time to crown the winner from Manchester's competing beauties, Rudy instead reached into the audience and selected his own favorite. Miss Irene Dion of 195 Bell Street was dumbstruck when Rudy plucked her from her front row seat and proclaimed her the most beautiful girl in all of Manchester, New Hampshire.

It was after the nightly performance in Duluth, Minnesota that George became the victim of a robbery. As was his usual routine, that evening he counted the box-office receipts backstage and prepared to wire the money to New York. He sat thumbing through the thousands of dollars in the company of a Mineralava executive, who happened to be traveling with the tour for a few days. As George counted another pile of bills, the room suddenly went dark. Within a few moments the lights flickered back on, but George noticed one of his neatly wrapped stacks of a thousand dollars was missing. As he and the executive were only two people in the room at the time, George knew who filched the cash.

For the next few hours he feigned a search for the missing money as the Mineralava executive did his level best to convince George that the box office cashier was the culprit. Without a thorough frisk of the executive, George could not prove he had taken the money. He agreed reluctantly to go along with a perfunctory search of the cashier's hotel room, but the money was never recovered.

In Atlantic City, New Jersey, Rudy and Natacha ran late for their performance after spending the afternoon in New York City. George was frantic and tried to calm an agitated audience. As the hour grew late, the local sheriff threatened to charge George with fraud if the Valentinos did not arrive in time for the show. Just as he was about to slap George in handcuffs, Rudy arrived with a substitute dance partner George did not recognize. It seemed Natacha was ill and Rudy said he was late because he'd been lining up her replacement. When George announced to the crowd that Rudolph Valentino had finally arrived with a new dance partner, no one accepted his offer to refund their tickets.

In Salt Lake City, Utah, a major traffic jam blocked the arrival of the show's stars and made them late for the performance. The audience began jeering and stomping and by the time Rudy and Natacha arrived at the arena they faced a serious situation. Without pausing to change into his costume, Rudy sprinted directly to the microphone in his street clothes and explained to a suddenly silent audience that surely they could understand his tardiness because after all he had been caught up in their traffic jam. Applause broke out and someone yelled,

"Do your stuff, Rudy! You're all right!"

Before that evening's show commenced, a husky man approached George to introduce his girlfriend as one of the Mineralava beauty queen contestants. George recognized the man as heavyweight boxer Jack Dempsey and his girlfriend as Estelle Taylor. Estelle won the competition that night and Rudy, George and Jack Dempsey would become fast friends.

Throughout the grueling road tour, Rudy and Natacha were impressed with George's managerial abilities and they became convinced he should manage Rudy's career. When they made their official request, George initially rejected their offer by asking Rudy,

"You don't have much to manage now do you?"

Rudy's answer to his question was simply, "You will be my manager someday, George. I'm sure of that."

George felt he had no other option but to decline the offer because he was a family man with a second child on the way. Rudy, on the other hand, was a screen performer, heavily in debt and unable to work in his chosen profession. George also knew how effectively Rudy and Natacha spent large sums of money with incredible ease. He had to wonder; if he did accept Rudy's offer to be his business manager, would he ever be paid on a regular basis?

But George was also witness to Rudy's drawing power and continued to weigh the proposition. As the tour reached San Antonio, Texas he told Rudy and Natacha he would accept their offer. Cora McGeachy's second prediction had come true. Rudy was elated hearing George's decision and told his new manager he always knew his answer would be yes because, "Black Feather told me!"

As the Mineralava tour wended its way through the final weeks of the journey, the on-train entourage grew. By the time the train reached Boston, Massachusetts, Rudy's friend from Hollywood, Robert Florey joined the tour as a publicity and advance man. Along the way, photographer, James Abbe came on board and a pregnant Bee Ullman often traveled to work as her husband's secretary. During the last days of the tour, Rudy and Natacha spent most of their free time planning their impending honeymoon. During the summer they would visit London, Paris and Natacha's parents' chateau on the French Riviera while George negotiated Rudy's return to the silver screen.

The final Mineralava performances took place just as Rudy's book of poetry *Day Dreams* appeared in book stores coast to coast. While many of his detractors were doing their level best to portray him as a thick-headed foreigner who barely spoke pidgin English, *Day*

Dreams proved them wrong. Since many of Rudy's *Day Dreams* happened to be love poems for Natacha and many of these poems were allegedly "written" by deceased famous poets, Rudy's critics perceived his passionate words as just more dubious influence on young people. Many of *Day Dreams'* female readers hid the fact they were reading Valentino's poems and slid their copies under their beds or tucked them into convenient laundry baskets. Nevertheless, the book was an instant bestseller and publisher Bernarr McFadden was hard pressed to keep the small, red volume in print.

For three months, life on the rails had often been an ordeal for Rudy, Natacha and George. But with a best-selling book and a new manager poised to resolve his impasse with Famous Players-Lasky, Rudy was in high spirits by tour's end. He indulged himself in his penchant for expensive caviar and bootleg liquor and many evenings life inside The Colonial became a raucous party.

As the Mineralava tour crossed the U.S. border from Vancouver, Washington into Vancouver, British Columbia, an American customs official boarded the train. He stood in The Colonial's parlor and read George the riot act, more specifically the Volstead Act by informing him that the laws of prohibition were strictly enforced in that district. Rudy and Natacha stood listening only a few steps behind George and were well within earshot as the official explained,

"If any whiskey is found on this train upon its return from Canada, this car and all of Mr. Valentino's party will be detained on a side track until the case can be heard in a Federal Court."

Upon delivering what he felt to be his fair warning, the official disembarked and the train proceeded on to Vancouver, Canada. After the evening show, George tallied his box office receipts and began his walk to the nearest telegraph office. He was gone about one hour. Upon re-entering The Colonial, George could see Rudy and Natacha squelching laughter and knew some chicanery had taken place in his absence.

He quickly spotted the source of their amusement. Stashed under all of the beds, including his own, were wooden cases of Canadian Scotch whiskey. Just as the train began chugging its way towards the U.S. border, George hit the Colonial's roof. His furious tirade did not dampen Rudy's glee in the slightest and he yanked at George's coat sleeve as he pulled him into the car's narrow hallway. As George continued to sputter, Rudy knelt down and with little effort removed a wooden floorboard. There, haphazardly wedged into the small space, was more of Rudy's booty; a few more cases of whiskey.

George was frantic. Why in God's name, he protested to Rudy, would he think of doing something so risky when he could afford whatever liquor he wanted from his own bootleggers? But George had just spent months on the road with Rudy and knew he never resisted any temptation to gamble on his luck. He also knew Natacha went blithely along with her husband's schemes. Facing the specter that they might all be arrested and detained indefinitely with a car full of bootleg whiskey, George read Rudy and Natacha his own riot act. He explained that when the train was boarded by custom officers the following morning, they were to remain in their bedroom and not come out for any reason until he told them to do so.

Just at dawn, the train slowed to permit U.S. customs officials time to board for their inspection. George was wide awake in his bed and waiting for his cue. A few moments after the officials stepped on board, George heard the loud shouting emanating from the cooking galley. Still wearing his pajamas, he stumbled in the direction of the racket. When he spotted a customs official standing in the galley, George pretended to be suffering from a wretched hangover as a result of a night of heavy drinking on the legal side of the border. The customs official was shouting at the top of his voice, waving an empty whiskey bottle in the chef's face and pointing to two more empties which had been tossed on the floor. George joined the official and roared at the chef,

"I warned you! I warned you! This will cost you!"

The poor chef lowered his eyes and accepted his scolding while George assured the customs officer he would deduct the cost of the whiskey from the chef's pay. He then conveniently produced a fast thirty dollars from the shirt pocket of his pajamas, handed it over to the officer, shook his hand and thanked him so very much for his trouble. To the chef and George's relief the shell game worked, the official pocketed the cash, swung off and signaled the train to move on.

As George shuffled towards his bed, he found Rudy and Natacha wide awake. They'd been listening to the entire episode that had just taken place in the galley. With George's successful defense of Rudy's contraband whiskey, they were feeling mighty smug in their choice of business manager. And as George filled them in on every detail of how their loyal chef had done his part in the ruse, Rudy and

Natacha were convulsed with laughter. George was not sure how amusing he found the situation. While he shook his head and caught his breath after the narrow miss, Rudy had only one thought in mind,

"So what is your plan, George, to get the whiskey off the train?"

"My plan?" George threw his hands in the air. "Damn it, Rudy, crack open one of those cases of whiskey and I'll see what I can come up with."

By the time a plan was hatched, a red-eyed Rudolph Valentino and his new business manager George were feeling no pain.

Chapter Ten

A Child's Resemblance

A few months later, New York City, June 1923 -

"In my office now is Mr. George Ullman, the manager of Rudolph Valentino. I suggested that he meet with you to seek a solution to the contractual impasse."

Attorney Max D. Steuer paused in his telephone call to Famous Players-Lasky's' attorney Emil Ludwig to ask George, "Today?"

George glanced at his pocket watch and nodded, "Sure, four o'clock."

George knew he barely had enough time to make that appointment with attorney Emil Ludwig, so he wasted no time leaving Max Steuer's office at forty-two Broadway. In his brand new role as Rudolph Valentino's business manager, George was entertaining no thoughts of professional failure. But with his first critical meeting with Famous Players-Lasky only minutes away, he was feeling a shade less than invincible. During the short ride across Manhattan, he made every effort to bolster his confidence by reveling in his initial managerial victories.

Retaining attorney Max Steuer was one of the first orders of business George transacted on Rudy's behalf. Steuer was a highly-respected New York City attorney and once practiced law with the firm of Prince and Nathan where he represented Blanca DeSaulles when she sued her husband for divorce. George retained Max Steuer within hours of firing Rudy's attorney, Arthur Grahm. He was adamant Grahm had bilked Rudy out of tens of thousands of dollars while doing nothing to negotiate the stalemate with Famous Players-Lasky. Arthur Grahm did not go quietly and upon learning of his termination, he instigated an angry exchange with his replacement, Max Steuer.

This occurred after Steuer requested Grahm surrender Rudy's entire case file. Grahm responded by submitting a bill to Steuer for an additional $27,000.00 for services rendered. He attached an ominous note to his hefty invoice, which stated that if payment was not received in full he would not only retain possession of Rudy's case file, but release every snippet of confidential material in said file to the press. Max Steuer fired back by dispatching a courier to hand-deliver a copy of the law's penalty for blackmail to Grahm's office.

Steuer also attached a personal note to his correspondence warning Grahm that he would not hesitate to report his threat to the District Attorney's office. After several more heated exchanges, it was Grahm who finally conceded when he agreed to exchange his "top secret" Valentino file for a settlement of $10,000.00. When George and Max Steuer sat down to pore over Grahm's, "Valentino file", they found it contained nothing more than newspaper clippings, a few court documents and police records of Rudy's run-ins with the law during his early days in New York.

George and Max Steuer then turned their attention to Rudy's debt. As they made their initial review of his dire financial state of affairs, it was obvious Rudy had not the vaguest clue as to how to manage the business complexities of his success. They found no accounting system for any of his personal transactions or his several bank accounts. The result of Rudy's failure to document his financial situation, was that he had no idea how much money he kept in these accounts. He also did not know the precise amount of money he owed to an army of despairing creditors.

George and Max Steuer found some evidence of Natacha's valiant endeavors to bring order to her husband's chaotic paper trail. But it was also painfully clear that she was almost as devoid of any business acumen as Rudy. Neither Rudy or Natacha maintained consistent records of their transactions and both carried overdue lines of credit. George tackled the bleak situation by organizing some form of effective book keeping system and instructing Steuer to negotiate partial payments on the many accounts in arrears. He then focused upon the resolution of Rudy's dispute with the Famous Players-Lasky Corporation.

It was in the course of this endeavor, George found himself headed for a long overdue and guaranteed contentious confrontation with attorney Emil Ludwig. As George stepped into the attorney's office that afternoon, he knew full well that the future of Rudy's movie career was contingent upon the outcome of that very meeting. After an obligatory handshake, George took the offensive and began presenting the terms of his proposal. Rudy would complete his contractual obligations with the Famous Players-Lasky Corporation by starring in two more films. For his work in these two movies, he would receive an increase in salary from the previous amount of $1250.00 a week to $6500.00 a week and would be granted complete artistic control over both films. With this said, George took a deep breath and prepared to fight for the terms he had just outlined. To his utter amazement and relief, Emil Ludwig agreed to his proposal without hesitation.

The attorney informed George that Rudy's final two films with Famous Players-Lasky would not be filmed in Hollywood but at the studio's lot in nearby Queens, New York. George countered by demanding Rudy receive an additional $500.00 a week for living expenses as he would be required to live in New York during filming. Ludwig agreed to this request but stipulated Rudy's salary would not begin until his first day of filming and would end the day the second picture was completed.

Over the course of the next hour, George and Emil Ludwig got down to the business of negotiating the specifics of the proposed contract. When George was satisfied his business with Ludwig was complete, he slid his notes into his briefcase and prepared to leave. It was then the attorney asked him to please wait just one moment while he placed a telephone call to Famous Players-Lasky's Vice President in charge of production, Jesse Lasky. Ludwig asked Lasky if he could please stop by his office to review the tentative agreement he'd just worked out with Rudolph Valentino's manager. The prospect of an unexpected face-to-face with Lasky took George by surprise. He braced himself for a possible row with the man Rudy had been impugning to his Mineralava tour audiences on a nightly basis for the past three months.

In George's brief career as a professional boxer he'd learned a thing or two about the fine art of absorbing a punch. He drew upon this knowledge as Jesse Lasky entered Emil Ludwig's office a few minutes later. He greeted the executive with an awkward handshake, but Lasky did not say hello, did not look him the eye and said nothing. He just grabbed the proposed contract and began to read. He read in silence for a few minutes, handed the papers back to Emil Ludwig and then turned to address George saying,

"I don't want anything to do with Valentino! You will make these pictures!"

With this reprimand, Lasky abruptly left the office. George was at a loss for words and stared at Emil Ludwig for a long moment before saying with apprehension,

"That was just a figure of speech, I'm sure."

Ludwig gave George a matter-of-fact, "No, he means it."

George replied sheepishly that he knew nothing about the production of motion pictures. Ludwig's response was a nonchalant, "You'll learn." The attorney then concluded the meeting by placing another brief telephone call to the studio manager at the lot in Queens,

"A new producer, George Ullman, is on his way to meet with you."

George was dumbfounded. Only an hour earlier he was feeling his way into a new field of employment about which he knew relatively little; celebrity management. As he left Emil Ludwig's office and headed for the Famous-Players Lasky's studio lot in Queens, he realized he had just become a movie producer.

❧❧

While embarking upon his sudden crash course in motion picture production, George continued to negotiate the terms of Rudy's new contract and devise a plan to reverse his sure spin downwards into financial ruin. Step one of George's strategy was to establish a corporate alter ego for Rudy which would shield him from lawsuits and allow all of his private and professional transactions to be conducted under the protection of a business.

George and Max Steuer established Rudy's corporate alter ego with the purchase of a research laboratory, Cosmic Arts Incorporated. As soon as Rudy affixed his signature to the documents, he became the new owner of Cosmic Arts Incorporated and began funding the research of the laboratory's two scientists, Albert Lambert and Jean Gauthier. Lambert and Gauthier benefited from the arrangement as they were able to continue their experimentation while George was able to assign all of Rudy's future contracts to the ownership of Cosmic Arts, Incorporated. As owner of the laboratory, Rudy also held legal ownership of the scientists' patent on their process called, "The Lambert Process."

Ten shares of Cosmic Arts' stock were issued at the time Rudy purchased the laboratory and all ten shares were immediately signed over to Natacha's ownership. She then assumed her role as the laboratory's sole stockholder and president of Rudy's newly-formed corporation. George acted as secretary and treasurer and was contractually assured a ten percent commission of any profits he might generate from the sale of the Lambert Process patent. By incorporating

Cosmic Arts as a "Delaware Corporation", Rudy joined many other Americans at the time who were taking full advantage of Delaware's lenient incorporation laws.

It was not long after Rudy assumed ownership of Cosmic Arts Incorporated that George began negotiating with enterprising independent motion picture producer, J.D. Williams. Williams made the initial contact with George to inform him that he and several other wealthy New Yorkers wanted to form a production company, Ritz-Carlton Pictures with the sole intention of producing Rudy's independent movies as soon as he was contractually free from Famous Players-Lasky.

After reviewing the offer, George advised Rudy that it would be wise to negotiate some sort of deal with Williams. He assured Rudy that the terms of any contract negotiated with Williams' Ritz-Carlton Pictures would be precisely those he was close to securing from Famous Players Lasky; complete control over all phases of production and final word on the selection of stories, writers, directors, editing and casting. Rudy heeded his new manager's advice and George and J.D. Williams were soon hashing out the details of the deal. After the initial round of discussions, George requested a $25,000.00 retainer for Rudy as a sign of good faith from William's new production company.

When Rudy and George deposited Williams' $25,000.00 retainer in the 42nd Street branch of The National City Bank, Rudy surprised George and the bank teller by depositing only $14,000.00. He then requested eleven crisp one thousand dollar bills as change and told George that they were cabbing directly from the bank to the office of producer Joe Godsol at the Metro-Goldwyn building. George knew that Frank Mennillo advanced Rudy a great deal of money over the years, but until that day he had no idea Godsol also acted as an underwriter. As soon as the debt to Godsol was cleared, George suggested to Rudy that he immediately wire payments to some of his many creditors. Rudy wasn't sold on this idea and said he planned to spend the remainder of William's retainer on his impending European honeymoon.

In the days before Rudy left on his honeymoon, he and George attended to one other pressing order of business. On July sixth they met in Max Steuer's office and signed two contracts. One contract officially hired George as Rudy's business manager and a second contract granted George full "Power of Attorney." About the same time George was signing these contracts, he was also concluding negotiations on Rudy's new contracts with both Famous Players-Lasky and J.D. Williams' Ritz-Carlton Pictures. These contracts guaranteed that upon Rudy's return from his honeymoon, he would begin work in two movies with Famous Players-Lasky and then embark upon the production of his first independent movies with Ritz-Carlton Pictures. The welcome news that Rudy was at last returning to the movies was officially released to the public and Rudy and Natacha were elated with George's efforts. He appeared to be solving all of the troublesome issues that had been plaguing Rudy's career for years.

As the happy couple put the finishing touches on the honeymoon, they were relieved to see George bringing order to their financial affairs in Los Angeles and in New York. They encouraged him to assume complete authority over their professional dealings as well as their personal finances. Unfortunately, as George bore down on the business of policing the couple's personal finances, he grew increasingly unpopular with Natacha. Initially, she embraced the luxury of having George tote the cash and enjoyed the convenience of delegating him with the responsibility of dealing with all of those pesky bill collectors. However, Natacha's satisfaction with her husband's new business manager would be fleeting and as his influence over their finances and Rudy intensified, so would her resentment of George's very presence in their lives.

The Valentino's European honeymoon taught George one important lesson about Rudy and Natacha; never hand them an open line of credit. It was just such a letter of credit George secured for them before their departure. In doing so he granted the happy honeymooners the ability to spend with reckless abandon. On July twenty-third, just as news of Rudy's triumphant return to the movies became front pages news, he and Natacha jostled their way through a crush of reporters and fans swarming the gangplank of the ocean liner, The Aquitania. As official honeymooners they were armed and ready with not only the remainder of J.D. William's retainer but with George's letter of credit directing all charges to his office in New York City.

Ten years had passed since Rudy's first trans-Atlantic crossing. As an eighteen-year old he spent most of that first voyage anxious over his arrival in America and envious of the privileged treatment bestowed upon the ship's most wealthy passengers. He made that journey in the dead of winter and endured rough seas and frigid temperatures. On his return voyage in the summer of 1923, he and his elegant wife luxuriated in first-class accommodations, traveled with unlimited financial resource and enjoyed the company of a small entourage including Aunt Teresa Werner and photographer James Abbe.

The Aquitania's captain and staff pampered the famous movie star and his wife with VIP attention usually reserved for traveling royalty. Towering, fresh floral arrangements and neatly-tied bundles of telegrams were courteously delivered to their stateroom each morning. In addition to George's daily communiques, Rudy and Natacha received numerous invitations requesting their personal appearance upon their arrival in England. When The Aquitania docked in Cherbourg, Aunt Teresa parted company with her niece and Rudy in order to continue on her journey south to the Riviera and the Hudnut chateau.

The Aquitania steamed on towards Southampton with the two famous honeymooners not entirely sure what sort of reception to expect upon their arrival. As soon as they set foot on the British Isle, they realized Rudy's English fans shared the same fanaticism for his movies as their counterparts on the other side of the pond. Despite a torrential rain, over one thousand screaming fans crowded London's train station to greet the Valentinos. Rudy signed autographs for nearly an hour before he and Natacha made their getaway in a waiting limousine. Outside The Carlton Hotel more crowds of fans milled in the street below the Valentino's suite window. And after Rudy mentioned to the British press that he planned to purchase a few new suits while visiting London, a procession of Savile Row tailors wedged their way into the crowds outside The Carlton.

While visiting England, Rudy and Natacha toured abbeys and museums, attended the theatre and were wined and dined by London's elite. They visited Natacha's boarding school, Leatherhead Court and journeyed on to Surrey and the Pekinese kennels of Mrs. Ashton Cross. After a thorough review of Mrs. Cross' newest litter, Natacha purchased three of the Pekes at the steep price of fifteen hundred dollars a pup. She instructed Mrs. Cross to forward her invoice for payment to Mr. George Ullman in New York City.

Rudy surpassed Natacha's extravagance with the purchase of twenty suits and a new wardrobe of shirts, hats and riding boots.

Receipts for these purchases were also forwarded to George's office. George responded by wiring the carefree honeymooners with pleas they exercise fiscal restraint. Rudy and Natacha made a meager effort to oblige by making minimal deposits on some purchases and signing for the balance on credit. Soon it was time to leave London for Paris by boarding an airplane for a turbulent flight to Paris' Le Bourget airport.

Upon their arrival in Paris, they received a cablegram from George reporting the news that Rudy's first film with Famous Players-Lasky would be Booth Tarkington's novel, *Monsieur Beaucaire*. Natacha and Rudy were thrilled with the choice, as Tarkington's popular novel would afford Rudy the opportunity to portray both the roles of the Duke of Chartres and his alias, *Monsieur Beaucaire*. They felt the period costume drama, set in the court of Louis XV, to be a perfect fit for Rudy as he would perform several first-rate sword duels. As Rudy and Natacha checked into Paris' Hotel Plaza Athenee, their honeymoon assumed the added dynamic of research and planning for the production of *Monsieur Beaucaire*.

If Rudy left London's finest tailors sated with his outrageous orders, Natacha exceeded his extravagance in the salon of French couturier, Paul Poiret. She spent days adrift in Poiret's salon where she modeled his latest creations before photographer James Abbe's camera. Natacha and designer Paul Poiret also spent a great deal of time poring over her preliminary sketches for *Monsieur Beaucaire*'s costumes. In very short order Natacha commissioned the designer to create sixty costumes for the film. When George received Natacha's cablegram with news of Poiret's mighty commission, he was off to Famous Players-Lasky's offices to request additional funding to pay Poiret's expert tailors.

During Rudy and Natacha's visit to Paris, the director of the Theatre des Champs Elysees, Jacques Hebertot, assumed the role of tour guide par excellence. Monsieur Hebertot hosted lavish A-list dinner parties in their honor and organized a road trip to his native city of Deauville in the province of Normandy. He timed the drive to Deauville to coincide with the Grand Prix road race. When stormy weather resulted in the cancellation of the annual race, Rudy made the best of the change in plans by gambling in Deauville's casino. The cordial relations between the Valentino's and Monsieur Hebertot cooled when Rudy refused to leave the action at the roulette wheel long enough to accompany his host and Natacha on a tour of a few nearby, muddy battlefields.

Before the honeymooners left Paris for the Riviera and the Hudnut chateau, they placed an order for a luxury custom vehicle for Natacha; an Isotta Fraschini Cabriolet. Natacha's two-seated Cabriolet roadster would be a scale-downed replica of Rudy's full size Isotta Fraschini limousine and shipped directly to New York upon its completion. Rudy then made the purchase of the vehicle of his dreams; a Voisin Avion roadster.

During the summer of 1923, the Voisin Avions were indisputably the world's most coveted automobiles. The custom built roadsters were each personally designed by French aviation engineer, Gabriel Voison and his wealthy clientele paid ten times the price of the average family car for one of his masterpieces of aerodynamic design and art deco artistry. When Rudy placed his order, he discovered he and Gabriel Voison shared a common passion; they were both tinkerers. Consequently, when the two men got down to the discussion of each minute detail of Rudy's new Voison, the negotiations continued for several days.

They debated the use of flush bronze rivets, sketched several designs for custom door latches and weighed the advantages and disadvantages of an automatic jacking system. Gabriel Voisin suggested the installation of an extra foot pedal in order to by-pass the motor's silencer mechanism to allow for more engine power. This prompted Rudy to spend hours under Voisin's personal roadster examining this complicated feature. With a final selection of gun metal gray exterior paint and vermilion Moroccan leather upholstery, Rudy's order was at last a fait accompli.

As the custom automobile could not be completed for months, Gabriel Voisin offered Rudy the use of one of his private vehicles for the remainder of his honeymoon. Rudy's first run at the wheel of the Voisin loaner was the six hundred mile drive from Paris south to Juan les Pins on the French Riviera and the Hudnut chateau. With the powerful vehicle crammed with satchels, trunks and three excitable Pekinese puppies, Rudy and Natacha left Paris to embark upon an exhilarating ride towards the Mediterranean coast.

After spending years repairing leaking, burned-out engines, Rudy reveled in the state-of-the-art automobile. His enjoyment of this occasion was not tempered by his lack of expertise in the handling of such a responsive machine. With a leaden foot he sped along the highway, thrashing the gears, wrenching the huge steering wheel, slamming on the brakes and terrifying his wife. A windblown Natacha and her three puppies were flung left and right and it wasn't long before Rudy's ham-fisted navigation took its toll on all of their nervous systems. Natacha pleaded with her husband to slow down, but the roar of the Voisin's engine was deafening, the road dust suffocating and her protests went unheeded.

A few hours into the journey, Rudy accelerated up another steep incline just as the road before him disappeared suddenly. In an effort to avoid a plunge into the abyss beyond, he stood upright on the brake. With a force challenging even Gabriel Voisin's expert engineering, he spun the steering wheel in a hard right turn. Natacha shrieked as the car rocked to a stop with its left rear wheel spinning over the cliff's edge. Before the smoke and dust cleared Rudy leaned towards his wife, who sat pale, trembling and staring straight ahead.

"Did you see him?" he whispered, "Did you see Black Feather when he helped me turn the wheel?"

Natacha stared straight ahead and said nothing. For the remainder of the drive she resigned herself to her fate and barely uttered another word. It was nearly ten o'clock that evening when Uncle Dickie, mother Muzzie and Aunt Teresa heard the Voisin rumbling up the chateau's driveway. This was Rudy's first visit and despite being filthy with road soot and exhausted from the long drive, he insisted upon a grand tour of the palatial estate.

He learned Uncle Dickie purchased the twenty room chateau in 1914 and Muzzie informed her son-in-law that she personally decorated the chateau's interiors in the style of Louis XVI. She was eager to add that in anticipation of their arrival, she renovated a bedroom especially for them in brilliant colors and modern lacquered furniture. Muzzie also pointed out how she filled their eclectic room with armloads of fragrant tuberoses from the chateau's gardens.

The sun, sea and seclusion of Juan les Pins would provide an idyllic retreat for Rudy and Natacha. The stately environs became the perfect setting for Rudy to begin a smooth transformation into his next screen character; the aristocratic Monsieur Beaucaire. When photographer James Abbe arrived from Paris to visit the Valentinos, he captured some of the immediate effects of how life at the chateau was influencing Rudy. He had retired his Savile Row suits to sport casual white slacks, open shirts and a beret. While he assumed the subtle characteristics of Booth Tarkington's privileged French nobleman on the French Riviera, on the steamy streets of New York City, "producer" George Ullman was preparing to hire his first director.

"What do you think of Rudolph Valentino?" George asked director Sidney Olcott.

"I think he's a very talented young man but very much misunderstood! I like him!" replied Olcott.

George had been waiting a week for Sidney Olcott's arrival in New York and was eager to have the director agree to join the project. When he initially contacted Olcott, the director was working in Hollywood. Olcott wired George saying he would travel to New York immediately to discuss the possibility of directing *Monsieur Beaucaire*. George was impressed by Olcott's direction of Marion Davies' film, *Little Old New York* and felt confidant he was the perfect director to handle Rudy's crucial return performance. Not long after meeting with George, Olcott accepted the position of director and the two men then turned their attentions to the selection of a screenplay writer.

Sidney Olcott suggested George contact a screenwriter he knew in Brooklyn, New York; Forrest Halsey. It took little convincing to bring Halsey on board the project and he was soon hard at work transforming *Monsieur Beaucaire* into a suitable screenplay. Every few days he delivered a few pages of the script to George's office for review.

Despite George's limited knowledge of film production, he was acutely aware that Natacha was assuming an executive role in *Beaucaire's* pre-production and doing so while on her honeymoon. It was with trepidation he read her daily cablegrams as they inevitably included her demands for an increase in his prudent budget. With Famous Player-Lasky's' executives counting the days until they could kiss both of the Valentinos a goodbye forever, each time George presented them with a fresh request for more funding for *Monsieur Beaucaire*, he was greeted by stony resistance.

So he was hardly surprised when he read another lengthy wire from Natacha informing him of her "great discovery". She wrote how through her friend, Jacques Hebertot she met a young newspaper reporter, Andre Daven. Her wire instructed George to secure a role for Monsieur Daven in *Monsieur Beaucaire* as she had already invited him to travel to New York and appear in the film. This particular cablegram from Natacha would not have been as troubling for George had it not been for Natacha's demand that all of Monsieur Daven's expenses for this trip be paid in full by Rudy.

As George surveyed the fresh stack of Rudy and Natacha's incoming unpaid invoices, he was stunned with this development. He dispatched an immediate wire of response, informing Natacha that it would be financially impossible to offer Monsieur Daven an all-expense paid trip. But George's protest arrived too late. Andre Daven was already Natacha's newest protege and any further discussion of the matter was closed.

George let the issue of Monsieur Daven's impending visit slide, as he was preoccupied with more pressing concerns that August. He was not only supervising the writing of *Beaucaire's* screenplay and the construction of the sets in Queens, but organizing the Mineralava Beauty Pageant scheduled to take place in November. And on August thirteenth, his wife Bee gave birth to their second son, Robert Warren, "Bobby". With two children and a wife to support, George was focused upon his job at hand and failure on any level was no option.

Only ten days after Rudy's arrival at the Hudnut chateau, he decided to make the short drive to Italy in the Voison with Natacha and Aunt Teresa. Around noon on the first day of this road trip, Rudy slowed the Voison for the border crossing at Ventimiglia. A customs officer sidled up to the impressive automobile to announce that it was his lunch hour and he was about to go off duty for the next two hours.

The guard shuffled around the car while eyeing the several boxes of imported cigarettes tossed on the back seat. He informed the three travelers they would have to wait for the next two hours as the border was officially closed. Rudy responded with disgust by throwing his cigarette into the dusty road. The guard bristled at Rudy's defiance and this inspired an exchange of hand gestures and Italian expletives between the two men.

For two long hours, Rudy, Natacha and Aunt Teresa could do little else but wait and fume. Around two o'clock, the guard reappeared and Rudy renewed his demands that he be allowed to cross the border. The guard agreed to do so only if a hefty duty was paid on those boxes of cigarettes. This infuriated Rudy and he shouted at the guard; as an Italian citizen he owed exactly nothing! Hearing this, the guard nodded towards Natacha and made a crack how Rudy could well afford to pay the duty on the cigarettes as he was obviously married to an heiress. This insult sent Rudy over his boiling point and he pulled a fistful of cash from his pocket. He slammed the money in the guard's hand, threw the Voisin into gear and roared down the road in a cloud of dust. For ten years he had envisioned his glorious return to Italian soil, but after a two hour wait and an angry encounter with the guard, the actual moment of his return slipped by unnoticed.

He drove for an hour along the Italian Riviera before stopping at a roadside inn. The three weary travelers were seated at a table on the inn's terrace where a melancholy Rudy quickly downed several glasses of wine. Natacha and Aunt Teresa were surprised by his obvious distress upon his much anticipated return to his homeland. Apparently the radiant vista of the Mediterranean Sea was only adding to his despair. Over another glass of wine, he began a soulful narration of the circumstances of his departure from Italy ten years earlier by divulging the details of a contentious Guglielmi family gathering just before he sailed for America.

He recalled how during that meeting his aunts and uncles wagged their fingers in his face and shouted at him for bringing shame upon his dear mother and the family's good name. As Rudy shared the story with Natacha and Aunt Teresa, they could see he was still anguishing over the sorry events of that day long ago. He continued his story by saying his angry relatives came to a quick consensus; he should leave his home town of Taranto and travel as far away as soon as possible.

Aunt Teresa pressed him for specifics of this crime that so shamed his family, but Rudy did not respond. Instead, he explained that his family was adamant he leave immediately even though his abrupt departure meant crossing the Atlantic Ocean during the bitter cold of winter. As he recalled this unhappy occasion, Rudy's gaze fixated upon a distant point in the evening sky and Natacha noticed his eyes brimming with tears.

Rudy concluded the dreary tale by saying his relatives pooled their resources to raise the necessary funds for his passage and sent a cablegram to family friends, Frank and Ciro Mennillo in New York City alerting them to his arrival. Despite Natacha and Aunt Teresa's many questions, Rudy was through reminiscing. He informed them abruptly that he wanted to drive on to Genoa to spend the night and then motor on to Milan the following morning to visit his sister Maria.

It was not long after this tearful reunion with his sister Maria the following day, that evidence of the sibling's ten years of separation became apparent. Maria's world famous brother had done well for himself, while she lived a simple life and seldom ventured more than a few miles from her provincial home. She was critical of her new sister-in-law and informed her that in Italy no respectable woman ever wore a glove over her wedding ring or make-up, perfume and brightly colored clothing during the day. Maria's instructions failed to motivate any alteration in Natacha's fashion or behavior. Instead, Natacha took it upon herself to buy her plain looking sister-in-law a colorful new outfit. Decked out in her fashion upgrade, Maria joined her brother, Natacha and Teresa Werner when they journeyed further south to Rome and on to Campobasso to visit their older brother Alberto.

Somewhere on the road between Siena and Florence, Rudy turned the Voisin into the drive of a farmhouse advertising rooms for the night. The farmhouse was old-world worn and the floor of Natacha and Rudy's bedroom sloped at a precarious angle. The room's only furnishings were a bed and one rickety milking stool. Their double bed was piled so high with feather bedding that a small wooden ladder had to be positioned for the climb.

In the silence of their farmhouse bedroom that night, Natacha lit a few candles and climbed the ladder to sit on the bed with her husband. He had already covered the bedspreads with sheets of blank paper and was preparing to receive his evening's messages from the other side. As he sat with his eyes closed, he wrote long messages from his mother, Mesolope and Black Feather. His three contacts from the other side apparently had a great deal to say and he wrote late into the night, long after Natacha crawled under the feather bedding and fell to sleep.

In remote, rural Italian villages neither Rudy nor his films were known. Consequently, he was not recognized and there were no crowds of shrieking female fans seeking autographs. This was not the case when he arrived in Rome, where he was greeted as an international celebrity and escorted about the city by notable figures of the Italian cinema. He and Natacha were entertained on the set of the film, *Quo Vadis* and dined with the German star of the film, Emil Jannings. And as Maria had never seen any of her brother's films, a private showing of *The Four Horsemen of the Apocalypse* was arranged for her benefit.

When Rudy announced he was leaving Rome and heading south to Campobasso, Natacha stunned her traveling companions by saying she had no intention of continuing on to visit Alberto and his family. Despite what anyone said to convince her otherwise, she could not be dissuaded and she boarded a train bound for Juan les Pins.

Several different explanations for Natacha's abrupt return to France at this juncture have been presented over the years. It has been alleged she became pregnant during her honeymoon and Rudy's wild driving caused her to miscarry their unborn child. It has also been reported she was unable to tolerate the stress of the road trip over Italy's rural roads. But perhaps Natacha left for France because she was well-aware of the dynamic awaiting her in Campobasso and was emotionally unwilling to face that particular reality of Rudy's past.

⊷⊷⊶

When ten-year old Jean Vittorio Gabriele Adalberto Guglielmi first laid his piercing, dark eyes on his famous uncle, he ran straight into his arms and hugged him so tightly around the neck that Rudy wept openly. Everyone witnessing their first encounter could not help but recognize the emotional significance of the moment. Although Jean shared certain facial characteristics with both his grandfather and Alberto, his distinctive, intense eyes and sinewy hands were certainly Rudy's. This was not the only notable likeness to his Uncle Rudy. Jean exhibited the same restive personality and irrepressible interest in all things mechanical. Rudy recognized these traits as his own and tagged Jean with his childhood nickname of "Mercurio" or "quick-silver". Rudy and Jean were inseparable during the visit and the two spent hours tinkering on a bicycle which Rudy purchased and riding around the narrow, stone streets of Campobasso in the Voisin.

At the time, Alberto was employed as a local village clerk and living in a modest home. Although he was pleased initially to reunite with his famous younger brother, he rejected Rudy's invitation to join him on a drive further south to the town of their birth, Castellaneta. It was soon apparent to both Rudy and Aunt Teresa that neither Alberto nor his sister Maria held any interest in returning to Castellaneta. Nevertheless, Rudy made his preparations to leave Campobasso.

Young Jean was stricken at the news of his uncle's departure, but Rudy promised the boy he would soon send passage for him to visit him in America. He also assured Alberto he would forward money to pay for Jean's piano lessons and continued schooling. Affectionate family photos were snapped, tearful goodbyes said and Rudy and Aunt Teresa loaded the Voisin for the drive to Castellaneta.

Castellaneta is situated in the instep of the boot of Italy and during the summer of 1923, few visitors ever ventured to visit the remote outpost. Consequently, when Rudy's great automobile rolled

200

into town, he and Aunt Teresa were the targets of many townsfolk's suspicious glares.

Rudy ignored the sinister welcome and happily pointed out all of the landmarks of his childhood to Aunt Teresa; the great view of the sea and the white-washed stucco home where he was born. He parked the Voison outside the local church of San Michele to pay a visit to the local priest. The priest greeted him with a less than warm reception. He chastised Rudy for ever leaving his homeland and suggested he atone for his actions by making a sizable donation to the church right there on the spot.

Aunt Teresa nudged Rudy towards the Voison, but he insisted upon snapping one more photograph of his boyhood home. By then a group of townsfolk surrounded the vehicle and began shaking their fists in the air and spitting on the ground. Rudy got the message and executed his speedy get-away from the town of his birth.

He drove hard, due north for Campobasso. There, he paused briefly to allow his sister Maria to join him on the return drive to the chateau. Upon his arrival at Juan les Pins, Rudy found Natacha once again upbeat and energized as she shared George's encouraging cablegrams from New York. Aunt Teresa was grateful to see Rudy and Natacha in such high-spirits and said nothing about the depressing return to Castellaneta. She left the details of that trip to Rudy who related a heavily edited version of the actual events. George's many cablegrams urged the honeymooners to return to New York post haste. He explained that under the terms of Rudy's contract with Famous Players-Lasky, he would not receive his next paycheck until he arrived for his first day of work. With the bills pouring in from their honeymoon deluxe, George wired, "Head home! The honeymoon is now over."

Rudy and Natacha heeded his advice and were soon settling into their stateroom on board The Belgenland.

Ten days later George stood on the deck of a tugboat watching The Belgenland steam up the Hudson River. He received permission from New York's harbor master to ride out on the tug in order to board the great ocean liner before it docked. Rudy and Natacha were surprised and overjoyed to see George striding towards them on deck and he found them both to be well rested and excited to be returning to New York.

He shared every detail of the luxurious new suite he had just leased for them at the Ritz-Carlton Hotel and as a proud new father he told them all about the birth of his baby boy, Bobby. Rudy was so elated to hear about little Bobby's arrival, he insisted on becoming the baby's godfather. On a handshake aboard The Belgenland, Rudy's wish was granted. As Rudy, Natacha and George prepared to pass through customs, Rudy handed George a large and unwieldy camera. George toted the camera through customs and all the way back to the hotel suite where Rudy finally relieved him of the heavy load by saying,

"Do you know, George, that you are now a smuggler?"

Before George could answer such an odd question, Rudy unscrewed the lens of the camera and a large, uncut diamond tumbled into his hand. He was elated with the success of his latest gamble and handed the gem to Natacha. She was so blase about the precious stone that George knew immediately she was in on the subterfuge. Realizing his role as smuggler, George insisted they return to customs at once and declare the gem. It was only after Rudy swore he would smuggle no more, that George decided to let the incident slide.

He was more anxious to hear their reaction to a copy of Forrest Halsey's *Monsieur Beaucaire* screenplay which he had tucked in his coat pocket. Rudy was too keyed up to give the script more than a cursory glance and passed the rolled up papers to Natacha. Unlike Rudy, she sat down and read with intense interest, began notating changes on each page and remarked to George that screenwriter Halsey made several critical errors with his entrances and exits.

Rudy was animated and in no mood to discuss work. Instead, he busied himself by summoning room service and placing an order for a can of the hotel's finest Russian caviar. He then informed George they would spend that evening toasting their return to New York in his favorite way; by eating a can of caviar with a large spoon and drinking one of the flasks of whiskey George thoughtfully stashed about the suite. George declined Rudy's invitation saying he was headed home to Bee and the boys. But when he received the first week's invoice from the Valentino's Ritz-Carlton suite, he realized Rudy's toasting of his return to New York continued longer than that one evening. The caviar bill alone for Rudy's first week in New York totaled over one hundred dollars.

It was during this same week George issued daily press releases in an effort to promote Rudy's return to the movies. He deemed this publicity not only critical to *Monsieur Beaucaire*'s success but to the reinventing of Rudy's image. George crafted his press releases with the intention of transforming the public's perception of Rudy from that of marauding, sex-obsessed Sheik to the courtly *Monsieur Beaucaire*. It was imperative he elevate Rudy's image in the eyes of his public and with this in mind George ensured Rudy was photographed with pipe in hand and eyes focused upon the pages of a weighty tome.

Privately, George knew Rudy seldom read anything other than sport magazines and that E.M. Hull's *The Sheik* was the only book he acknowledged he ever read cover to cover. Other than a cursory perusal of a book as a prospective screen project or a scan of an auction catalog, Rudy never read. Nevertheless, George began publicizing him as a tea-toting, studious, professorial intellectual and seized every opportunity to meld Rudy's public persona with his next onscreen character. Instead of being portrayed as a desert chieftain and an irresistible sexual force, Rudy began to resemble a refined, bookish philosopher. With each press release his public image grew more scholarly and as the gap between this new Rudy as advertised and his actual self widened, he felt the pressure to measure up.

He confided in George that he was embarrassed about his lack of formal education and asked him to buy a few college textbooks for his use. George assuaged Rudy's anxiety with the purchase of several textbooks which he noticed were by and large left unread around the Valentino's apartment and Rudy's dressing room on the studio lot in Queens. When George noticed that these textbooks, as well as other personal belongings, were disappearing from Rudy's dressing room, he posted a security guard around the clock outside the door.

While George struggled with these safety issues, Natacha began meeting with *Monsieur Beaucaire's* director Sidney Olcott and screen writer Forrest Halsey. Olcott and Halsey listened patiently as she outlined a litany of instructions regarding all aspects of production. George was less accommodating and most of his meetings with Natacha erupted into heated arguments and ended with considerable door slamming. With one wary eye on the film's hemorrhaging budget, George received Natacha's directives as just more delay and outrageous expenditure. Much to Natacha's distress,

Rudy never intervened in his manager and wife's angry tete-a-tetes and more often than not it was George who acquiesced.

Although George spent most of his days absorbed in *Beaucaire's* pre-production, by the end of November he was also attending to the last details of the Mineralava Beauty Pageant scheduled to be held in Madison Square Garden. The eighty-eight beauty queens were converging upon New York City and preparing to compete for the title of America's Queen of Beauty. By November 27th, the dazzling young women had all safely arrived and were backstage adjusting their banners; it was show time.

The New York City mounted police patrolling Madison Square Garden that chilly night would earn their pay, as they worked feverishly to restrain the crowds from crashing through the barricades. When Rudy's limousine arrived, the police lieutenant on the scene made the executive decision to close the street for the movie star's safety. While Rudy waited in the limousine for the police to clear the street, spotlights swept across the night sky and inside Madison Square Garden every seat was taken.

For the past seven months, George and Bee Ullman worked side by side organizing the beauty pageant. In addition to arranging the details required to hold such an event in Madison Square Garden, they coordinated the contestants' transportation from their hometowns to New York City, arranged their hotel accommodations and assigned each contestant an individual chaperone. During the early phases of planning, George was concerned; by sending the contestants cash or a prepaid rail ticket they might pocket the money and never arrive in New York. He devised a solution to this potential problem by negotiating a deal with the railroad. He prepaid the contestants' tickets and in return the railroad instructed their conductors to accept each contestant's signature en lieu of a ticket. The arrangement went off without a hitch and every contestant arrived on time.

George and Bee also organized a short excursion by train from New York to Washington, D.C. for the eighty-eight American beauties. There, each contestant and her chaperone shook hands with President Calvin Coolidge before returning to New York City. Their busy schedule then required their participation in a parade up 5th Avenue to 59th Street in a fleet of cars George leased from a local automobile agency. Bee Ullman worked diligently with her husband organizing the Mineralava pageant and she was personally in charge of all hotel arrangements, chaperones and discipline.

With the night's festivities only minutes away, a young, aspiring producer, David O. Selznick hurried to position his movie camera and lights in order to film a short documentary of the event. When Rudy finally made his entrance into Madison Square Garden, he walked on stage to remind a cheering audience that he had but a single vote on a panel of judges. He then returned to his seat to view the contestants as they made their first promenade down the runway. After this initial review, Rudy took the microphone again to announce the semi-finalists. From these contestants five finalists were chosen; Miss Los Angeles was an early favorite and Miss New York, in black velvet and pearls, received raucous support from her hometown crowd.

When it came time to crown the winner of America's Queen of Beauty, Rudy bestowed the title upon none other than Miss Norma Niblock from Toronto, Canada. His seemingly random choice generated a wave of response backstage and some wondered about Rudy's alleged single vote on the panel of judges. The uproar was in response to his naming a "foreigner" as "America's" beauty queen, but also due to the fact that his brief relationship with Miss Niblock in Toronto was by then common knowledge among the other eighty-seven contestants. With David O. Selznick's camera and George's eyes rolling, Rudy winked at his Canadian queen of beauty and planted the platinum and diamond tiara upon her pretty head.

The Mineralava Pageant completed Rudy's contractual obligation with the Mineralava Company and he was then free to devote his full attention to the production of *Monsieur Beaucaire*. But no sooner had work begun in earnest on the set in Queens than the announcement was made that Natacha felt the script needed extensive work. It was also announced that while the script was being retooled, the star of the film and his wife would be traveling again to France and Juan les Pins for the Christmas holiday.

On this journey, Rudy and Natacha sailed the Atlantic on separate ocean liners, with Rudy arriving in France ten days before Natacha. His new contracts were about to be assigned ownership to Cosmic Arts Incorporated and as sole stockholder of Cosmic Arts, Natacha was required to remain in New York to affix her signature to the necessary paperwork. Why Rudy refused to remain in New York in order to travel with his wife remains a mystery, but perhaps some tiff inspired him to sail solo. When he arrived in Paris he was greeted by Aunt Teresa and by the time Natacha arrived to join them on the drive south to the Riviera, it was Christmas Eve.

ربی

While Rudy's fans lurked outside his empty dressing room in Queens, while the press debated whether he still had enough box-office drawing power to score a major hit, while Paul Poiret's tailors put the finishing touches on their sixty costumes and while screenwriter Forrest Halsey hunched over his typewriter in Brooklyn, the star of *Monsieur Beaucaire* and his wife Natacha welcomed 1924 by getting plastered at a party in their honor at the Hotel Negresco in Nice.

Muzzie and Uncle Dickie were also guests at the New Year's Eve soiree. Sometime on the 1923 side of midnight, Muzzie passed by the hotel's piano bar where she spotted her son-in-law engaged in some questionable behavior. She informed her daughter she best get in there and do something quickly. When Natacha found Rudy, he was kneeling on the bar room floor and jabbing the air with a cane. To the peels of laughter from his equally tipsy audience, he was re-enacting a bullfighting scene from *Blood and Sand*. When the inebriated bullfighter looked up to see his wife strolling into the bar, he swayed backwards yelling,

"My God! I've killed the bull!"

Fortunately for Rudy, Natacha had already downed sufficient cheer to find his drama on the carpet highly amusing. When she failed to reappear, Muzzie decided to see for herself just what had happened to the "children". She finally found Rudy, seated at the bar with his arms draped around a half-conscious beauty who was not Natacha.

He was whispering in the giggling woman's ear, but Muzzie could clearly hear his every word from across the room. Oh, he was saying, she would be a successful actress if she ever came to Hollywood. Muzzie's face flushed as she scanned the room in search of her daughter. There, seated in the opposite corner of the bar was Natacha. With a cocktail held at arms length she was seated on a divan and holding court before eight handsome, rapt young men.

As the bar's musicians struck up a rendition of "Happy Days are Here Again", Muzzie recruited Uncle Dickie to assist her as she shuffled the children out of the bar and towards a waiting Renault. The Hudnut's chauffeur sat poised behind the wheel of the vehicle, alerted to hit the gas upon Muzzie's nod. Rudy had no intention of leaving the party, was all bluster and thoroughly sloshed. Before anyone realized what had happened, he managed to climb up onto the car's roof. Everyone realized the futility of convincing him that he should not ride atop the Renault with his legs dangling in the chauffeur's face while singing at top volume,

"Yer care n' troubles are gone. Lez' sing a song of cheer again. Happy, happy days are here again!"

Chapter Eleven

Paragraph Fourth

Seven years later, Los Angeles, February 1931 -

It was disorder in the court from the moment attorney Raymond Stewart announced to a packed courtroom that he had located a copy of Rudy's instructions for George. Reporters scribbled on their notepads, spectators buzzed in anticipation and the judge demanded silence. Throughout the court's long holiday recess, Raymond Stewart and George were unable to shake a sense of dread at the prospect of surrendering the document to the court. Both men knew full well that in doing so they would instigate a disastrous chain of events that would impact everyone involved in the case of Guglielmi v. Ullman. The first casualties would be Alberto Valentino and Lou Mahoney, who sparred from the witness stand to disavow any role in the disappearance of the original copy of the document. Tempers flew, accusations were made and before the dust settled one of them would commit perjury.

When the judge handed the fragile sheet of onion skin paper to the court clerk for submission as evidence, Alberto's attorney, James Scarborough rose to object to the document's authenticity. He alleged attorney Stewart's carbon copy was an outright forgery and demanded the original typewriter used to execute the document be located and brought into the courtroom for examination. He then petitioned the court to subpoena the stenographer who typed Rudy's September 1925, "Last Will and Testament" as well as this alleged sheet of instructions. When the judge determined the stenographer to be deceased, Raymond Stewart, as the lawyer who executed Rudy's will, was summoned to testify.

Under oath, he explained how he discovered the carbon copy while reviewing the Valentino's divorce file in search of a copy of their property settlement. He reminded the judge that he subpoenaed a copy of the Valentino's property settlement before court adjourned the previous December. During further questioning, Stewart recalled delivering both the existing page of Rudy's will as well as the sheet of instructions to Falcon Lair. He asserted, that at that time neither page was signed by any witnesses. Stewart concluded his testimony by saying that until he found the copy in his files, he did not know if Rudy ever signed the page of instructions, thereby rendering it a legal document. He added he did not know if George Ullman ever received a copy of the first page of the will or the sheet of instructions.

Teresa Werner's attorney made a rare appearance in the courtroom to petition the court to declare the carbon copy a valid portion of Rudy's will. Throughout the lengthy court proceedings, Teresa Werner never filed a single objection to George's performance as executor and in reference to the carbon copy of instructions she stood by him once again.

Through their respective attorneys, Teresa Werner and George objected to Alberto's request that the typewriter be subpoenaed by arguing that a search for the typewriter would unnecessarily delay the court's proceedings. The judge agreed and set this issue aside. The line of questioning then returned to whether the original instructions were removed from the first page of the will and if this were the case, by whom. For one brief moment everyone in the courtroom was in agreement on one key point. No one disputed Rudy kept his will in Falcon Lair's safe and that the only three people with access to this safe were Rudy, Alberto and handyman Lou Mahoney.

Lou Mahoney was again subpoenaed to testify and trudged back to the witness stand. Under oath he acknowledged he signed the sheet of instructions as a witness but blamed the disappearance of the original copy of that portion of the will upon "Mr. Valentino" himself. In response to a question as to how Mr. Valentino could tamper with his will in the days following his own death, Lou had an answer. He alleged that on the day before Mr. Valentino left Hollywood for the last time in July of 1926, he summoned him to Falcon Lair's office and opened the safe. It was then, Lou said, that Mr. Valentino removed his will and showed him both pages of the document. Under further questioning, Lou could offer no explanation why his boss shared his will with his handyman at that particular time.

Lou went on to recall that it was early the following morning when Mr. Valentino drove to Pola Negri's home to say goodbye before leaving on his trip east. According to Lou, a short while later Mr. Valentino telephoned him requesting he drive to Pola Negri's as he needed a ride home. Again Lou could offer no explanation why Mr. Valentino drove his own vehicle to Pola Negri's and then telephoned his handyman for a ride home. Side-stepping certain deep holes in his testimony, Lou continued. In his gravelly voice he testified that Mr. Valentino returned home that day with ample time to open his office safe and destroy the second page of his will before leaving for New York on the evening train. Lou was also adamant he drove his boss to meet that train.

Lou was then asked if he personally witnessed Mr. Valentino removing the sheet of instructions from the will or if he had any knowledge why Mr. Valentino would destroy a critical portion of his will before leaving on a routine promotional tour. Lou replied no to both questions. With another sidestep, Lou testified that he returned to Falcon Lair's office the day after Mr. Valentino left Los Angeles and attempted to open the safe. He told the court he was unable to do so because the lock had been changed. Lou had no recollection of why he needed to open his boss' safe on that particular day and instead turned an accusatory finger on a more ready target, Alberto Valentino.

Lou alleged it was Mr. Alberto Guglielmi Valentino who was the guilty party and that he changed the safe's combination the very morning Mr. Rudolph Valentino left Los Angeles. Lou had honed his nerve as a cop with one of the toughest precincts in New York City and despite further intense interrogation he did not flinch. In his final version of events, Lou swore his boss Rudolph Valentino shared the contents of his two-page will with him shortly before leaving on a trip from which he never returned. According to Lou, Mr. Valentino then proceeded to secretly destroy the second page of his will before his departure from Los Angeles and the following day Alberto changed the combination of the office safe.

Across the courtroom Alberto suffered through Lou's convoluted testimony and when he took the witness stand he fired back with a contradictory story. He testified his brother Rudolph did not visit Pola Negri's home early on the morning of his final day in Hollywood but instead spent the entire day at home in Falcon Lair. He continued by saying it was late afternoon when he and Rudy drove together to Pola's Ambassador Hotel bungalow where she joined them on the drive to the Southern Pacific train station.

There, he told the court, they met George and Bee Ullman, said their goodbyes and Rudy and George boarded The Southern Pacific's "Lark". Alberto then explained how he drove Pola Negri home in Rudy's car before returning to Falcon Lair. He denied ever opening his brother's safe or ever changing the lock on the safe. He said that at that time he was busy preparing for his and his family's departure for New York and insisted no one opened the office safe the day Rudy left, the day before or the day after. With Lou and Alberto swearing to opposite stories, it was anybody's guess who had just committed perjury.

George's attorney, Leonard Wilson, requested the court subpoena Pola Negri to clarify the issue. Soon after it was determined she was in Europe, he dropped this request. Before Lou could be recalled to the witness stand to respond to Alberto's contradictory testimony, the judge declared the entire line of questioning a waste of the court's time. He ruled that it appeared impossible to determine precisely what happened to the original sheet of instructions and to everyone's astonishment he declared the smudged carbon copy, the legitimate second page of Rudolph Valentino's will. The document was labeled Paragraph Fourth.

For nearly five years Rudolph Valentino's "Last Will and Testament" existed as a one page document in which he specified that the financial assets of his estate be divided between three apparent heirs; his two siblings and Teresa Werner. On February 7, 1931, a second page was added to his will. In the revised will, which included Paragraph Fourth, Rudy named his sole heir and beneficiary of his trust as Jean Valentino and instructed all assets of his estate be held in trust for him alone until his twenty-fifth birthday. The document also designated that not a penny more than specified weekly stipends be distributed from estate funds to Alberto, Maria Strada or Teresa Werner. Only Jean's premature death would elevate Alberto and Maria to the status of Rudy's lawful heirs. Paragraph Fourth also irrefutably granted George Ullman sweeping authority over all of Rudy's postmortem affairs and charged him with the dual role of estate executor and head of Rudolph Valentino Productions. And precisely, as George had always claimed to be the case, Rudy specifically called for the continued existence of his production company.

Although George was obviously relieved to have tangible evidence of the instructions he claimed Rudy once verbally shared with him, Paragraph Fourth complicated his legal situation. Since Rudy's death, George, as executor, had acted solely upon the contents of the existing first page of his will which apparently named Alberto, Maria and Aunt Teresa as Rudy's rightful heirs. Based upon this single page, George advanced these three people nearly $70,000.00 of estate funds. According to Paragraph Fourth, as executor he disbursed these

211

estate funds without authority and he could be held personally responsible to reimburse the estate for the entire amount.

Except for one perjurous individual, everyone in the courtroom was baffled by the legal interpretation of Rudy's elusive instructions. They also wondered why Lou Mahoney, who signed Paragraph Fourth as a witness, failed to come forward to verify the paper's validity as a legal document during the four years of the contentious settlement of Rudy's estate.

Privately, George doubted that Alberto had any involvement in the original document's disappearance. Despite the obvious fact Alberto would have benefited financially from the disappearance of the instructions, George knew that at the time the document vanished, Alberto struggled with even basic conversational English. He also knew that during the few days between Alberto's arrival in Los Angeles and the filing of the single page will on September tenth, Alberto had no legal representation. George not only thought it unlikely that Alberto could comprehend the legal terminology of Paragraph Fourth, but also knew Alberto's testimony regarding Rudy's last forty-eight hours in Los Angeles to be the absolute truth.

George could not as easily eliminate Lou from the list of the two people who had access to Falcon Lair's safe in the days following Rudy's death. For George, the fact Lou signed the document and said nothing about its existence to him, the court or Alberto strained the credulity of Lou's testimony. George also knew that as a veteran cop Lou had substantial experience with the judicial system and had served subpoenas, issued arrest warrants, taken the witness stand on multiple occasions and could easily have understood the terms of Paragraph Fourth.

George wondered if Lou removed the second page of the will in an effort to eliminate his role as head of Rudolph Valentino Productions. If this were the case George was not surprised. Throughout his tenure as Rudy's manager it was his job to supervise Falcon Lair's household staff, including the resentful handyman Lou Mahoney. George could not help but remember that just prior to leaving on that fateful trip east with Rudy, he told Lou to look for another job.

George also theorized Lou might have engaged in a little evidence tampering after reading the clause in Paragraph Fourth stating Alberto would receive a stipend of only one hundred dollars a week. On that meager allowance, barely twice Lou's salary as handyman, Alberto's ability to maintain Falcon Lair would have quickly become a financial impossibility. In that eventuality, Lou, as handyman of the prestigious residence, would have been out of a job.

Despite George's troubling speculations, he was not the only victim of Paragraph Fourth's discovery as the unexpected turn of events dealt a stunning blow to Alberto. News that his brother left him no more than a stipend of one hundred dollars a week was a humiliating loss of face. He was also shocked to learn that Rudy had indeed appointed George head of Rudolph Valentino Productions in addition to naming him executor of his estate. Alberto had been waging a public battle against George Ullman for years claiming the exact opposite was true.

Nevertheless, he refused to surrender to the ignoble situation and continued to assert that Paragraph Fourth was a fraudulent document. When Alberto was summoned to the witness stand, he could offer little driving theory as to why anyone would have forged it the first place. He was questioned by George's attorney Leonard Wilson and asked to explain why he continued to accept George's weekly stipend if he believed his brother's instructions to do so never existed.

≈৵৯≈

Leonard Wilson leaned against the railing of the witness stand and asked Alberto, "Did you believe Paragraph Fourth had been destroyed?"

Alberto hesitated for a moment before answering in his heavy accent, "No, I believed that it never existed."

"It never existed?"

"Yes sir."

"You were taking $100 a week from Mr. Ullman, though, during that time weren't you?"

Alberto's attorney jumped up in protest, "That is objected to as incompetent, irrelevant and immaterial."

Leonard Wilson looked up at the judge, "Your honor, if he did not take it under this instrument, then I want to know where he thought he was getting it from and by what authority he took it."

The judge dispensed his best look of judicial irritation and gave Wilson the nod to proceed.

The attorney cleared his throat and returned to his line of questioning, "Go ahead. Do you understand that question?"

"No. Can you read it?"

Leonard Wilson requested that the question be read once again for Alberto's benefit. The court stenographer took a moment to flip through the rolls of paper on her small desk before reading in a flat monotone, "You were taking $100 a week from Mr. Ullman, though, during that time weren't you?"

Alberto let out a heavy sigh and asked, "What time please? It is not determine the time."

Wilson was growing impatient and began pacing before his witness, "Well, during 1929."

"Yes," Alberto nodded.

"Where did you think that stipend was coming from?"

"From my share."

"For what period of time did you receive this $100 a week?"

"In March 1930."

"You mean to state now that you don't know by what authority Mr. Ullman gave you that $100 a week?"

"Excuse me," Alberto flashed a bewildered look towards his attorney, "Explain to me what means authority; I don't understand."

Wilson paused to repeat the question.

"Don't you know what authority means?"

"No. Will you change the question?"

"I want to know what right Mr. Ullman had to give you $100.00 a week?"

"What means 'what right?' "

"Don't you understand what the word 'right' means?"

"I don't understand the question." Alberto shifted nervously in his seat, "Will you please explain it to me? It is not clear to me."

"Why was Mr. Ullman giving you $100.00 a week, if you know?"

"If I know what?"

Now visibly exasperated, attorney Wilson folded his arms over his chest and turned to face his witness.

"Do you know why Mr. Ullman was giving you $100.00 a week?"

"He was giving me on my share, I told you before."

"My share from what?"

"From the estate."

214

"Did you ever ask him for this money, this $100.00 a week?"

"No. Yes, I did ask him for $100.00 a week."

"Did you name the amount?"

"No. I name not the amount."

"What did you ask for?"

"I ask him to give me a certain amount."

"Well, what did you ask him for, how much?"

"How much he could give me."

"Well did you go in and say 'I want a certain sum?'"

"It was my attorney had arranged that."

"How is that?"

"It was my attorney had arranged that. I did not ask him myself."

"Who was your attorney then?"

"Well, at the time it was Mr. Mann."

"Sir?"

"Mr. William Mann."

"He has always been representing you in this matter?"

"At that time, yes."

"Did you ever register any complaint against George Ullman for giving you the $100.00 a week?"

"No, I did not."

"You took that didn't you?"

"Yes. I did."

"That was satisfactory with you, wasn't it?"

"What means 'satisfactory?' "

❧

Attorney Leonard Wilson delivered a passionate closing statement in which he argued that Paragraph Fourth authorized George to continue in his role as head of Rudolph Valentino Productions after Rudy's death. He clarified that during George's tenure as executor he acted upon the terms of the only document he had access to at the time when he issued cash advances to Alberto Valentino, Maria Strada and Teresa Werner. Wilson explained to the court precisely how George had accommodated the supposed heir's solicitations for these advances and argued it would be ludicrous, in light of the unexpected appearance of Paragraph Fourth, to hold him personally responsible to refund the money to the very people who spent every dime of it.

Wilson pleaded with the court to allow George to retain the total amount of the salary he drew as executor and then detailed once more the finer points of the loans he made to Frank Mennillo and The Pan American Bank. The attorney held up the thick ledger of the court ordered audit's findings as evidence that expert accountant Harry Baskerville had not found a single error in George's books. In closing, the attorney stated that George Ullman was Rudolph Valentino's honest and loyal friend who performed remarkably under difficult and highly unusual circumstances. As evidence of this fact, Wilson pointed to the value of the Valentino estate which had plummeted from $300,000.00 to $130,000.00 in the eight short months since George's removal as executor. With this the judge called an end to the proceedings. It would be one year later on August 18, 1932 when a final verdict was rendered. The judge threw the book at George and he took it straight between the eyes.

Although Paragraph Fourth was declared a valid portion of Rudy's will, the document had no influence upon the judge's decision. He issued his ruling by stating George was never granted the authority to run Rudolph Valentino Productions and in his role as executor he should have obtained the court's permission for every business transactions. The judge ordered George to personally reimburse the estate for all of the money he loaned to Frank Mennillo, both the $40,000.00 for the tomato juice cannery in Merced and another $9100.00 advanced as cash. He also ordered George to reimburse the estate for the total amount of the outstanding debt still owed the estate by the defunct Pan American Bank and every cent he advanced to the Cosmic Arts laboratory. The judge permitted George to retain $15,000.00 as salary for his four year tenure as executor but held him responsible to reimburse the estate the nearly $70,000.00 he advanced to the three people he presumed at the time to be Rudy's heirs.

The entire judgment levied against George in August of 1932, was calculated at 7% interest retroactive to the date of the transactions. The total rang up at a mind-boggling $183,754.00; by today's monetary exchange this would be a judgment of nearly two million dollars. Utterly devastated by the court's decision, George granted not a single interview, accepted no telephone calls from the press and flipped an off switch in his mind where the affairs of Rudolph Valentino were concerned. He was simply done in.

Facing the specter of such a crippling judgment, George filed his immediate appeal of the court's decision and focused upon the success of his S. George Ullman Agency. He tried to ignore the disturbing reports that his replacement as executor of Rudy's estate, A.P. Giannini and his Bank of America, were conducting close-out clearance sales of Rudy's belongings. Particularly painful for George was notice of Giannini's sale of the last of Rudy's antique armor previously appraised at $20,000.00. The Bank of America sold the entire lot for less than $1000.00. Powerless to do a thing about it, George sat by while all of his financial successes as the executor of Rudy's estate faded away.

He was profoundly wounded by the dire turn of events, both emotionally and financially. With funds evaporating, he was forced to move his family once again, this time into another rented home on Canon Drive. He could scarcely contemplate the repercussions to his household if the appeals court did not reverse the judgment. His wife Bee continued to be in fragile health as she battled a persistent case of tuberculosis and this only compounded George's overly anxious state. By 1932, Bee spent a good deal of her time bedridden while she recovered from several subsequent surgeries. Her husband was sick with worry.

The Ullman children were too young at the time to have the slightest inkling that an appeals court judgment loomed over their home like a swinging wrecking ball. But even at their tender ages all three children were aware their father faced some stressful situation. On Sunday afternoons when Dad retreated to his den with his violin under his arm and a tall, green glass of bourbon in hand, Dan, Bobby and Bunny Ullman all knew he was to be left strictly alone.

During the 1930's, San Francisco's Montgomery Street was a bustling commercial hub. On any given hour during the work week the thoroughfare was congested with traffic and pedestrians rushing to and from the street's many brokerage houses. Although attention was usually focused on the afternoon's next appointment, a few Montgomery Street passersbys may have glanced up late one afternoon to gasp at the sight of a portly businessman about to be shoved out of a high-rise office window.

From the crowd's vantage point on the street below, it would have been impossible to recognize the poor fellow struggling to keep from toppling to his death as the President of the Bank of America. But inside that high-rise window, Frank Mennillo was tightening his grip around the leathery neck of banker A. P. Giannini and roaring at full volume,

"Bastardo! Bastardo"

If George Ullman was retreating to his den to cope with the deteriorating situation, Frank Mennillo was taking a more hands-on approach. A. P. Giannini landed in his death defying predicament after Frank and his son Arnold met with one of Giannini's disgruntled employees, George Underhill. Frank spent the afternoon convincing Underhill to jump Giannini's ship and join his organization.

As Frank, Arnold and George Underhill walked the office building's corridor, they made a quick and fateful stop into a mens' room. No sooner had the three men entered the restroom than the door swung open again and A. P. Giannini made the fat mistake of swaggering in. The moment Giannini spotted Frank Mennillo he sensed the imminent threat and whirled around to make his exit. With his hand on the doorknob, he paused to snap back at his mutinous employee, George Underhill,

"Don't you think you should be keeping better company, Underhill?"

Before Arnold Mennillo could make a move to prevent the inevitable, Frank lunged at the suited tycoon. Calling him every foul name he could spit in his direction, Frank grabbed Giannini by the neck, dragged him across the tiled mens' room floor and hefted him up and over the sill of an open window. Arnold was finally able to break his father's grip just long enough to allow Giannini to dash out of the mens' room rubbing his half-broken neck.

It was no secret Frank Mennillo hated A. P. Giannini. The rift between the two men had grown so fierce that no member of the Mennillo family ever stepped foot inside any of Giannini's banks. By 1932, Frank had survived some lean years in California's central valley, but he had somehow managed to keep his California Tomato Juice, Inc. solvent. However, Frank blamed Giannini's continuing vendetta against him for most of his business' difficulties.

Frank terminated his affiliation with the Valentino family upon receipt of George's $40,000.00 loan and then headed north to the San Joaquin Valley to work diligently in his new plant on K Street. But times were tough and as was the case with almost everyone else in the country during the great depression, Frank was usually short on cash. He was often unable to afford dinners at his residence, the Merced Hotel, and fed himself and his son Arnold by buying a loaf of bread and some olive oil and visiting his tomato growers to "taste the crop."

Frank Mennillo was not alone in his dire straits. During the first few years after Rudy's death, the cataclysmic downturn of the nation's economy had its unhappy effect upon all of the once powerful players in his life. With the exception of the attorneys, no one in this disbanding brotherhood benefited financially from Alberto's prolonged lawsuit against George. While Frank was struggling in Merced and George awaiting a decision from the California Court of Appeals, Alberto continued to petition the court for more cash advances from the dwindling estate funds. He was curtly denied on every occasion and consequently at the height of the depression, he was destitute.

Any loyalty A. P. Giannini and Joe Schenck might have held for Rudy's only brother had long since waned. As Giannini's Bank of America eliminated the remnants of Rudy's estate, they did much the same with Alberto. The days of George's generous cash advances were long over and Giannini was unwilling to advance brother Alberto another penny. He did, however, toss him the job of caretaker of Falcon Lair for the unremarkable remuneration of $35.00 a month; about $145.00 less than Lou Mahoney was paid to do the same job many years before.

Alberto's benefactor of yesteryear, Joe Schenck could no longer be bothered with the continuing legal travails of Rudy's estate as he was facing his own great depression challenges. In 1933, he and the former head of production at Warner Brothers Studio, Darryl F. Zanuck founded Twentieth Century Productions with a loan of three million dollars from pal, A. P. Giannini. Schenck and Zanuck then merged their production company with the floundering Fox Films to form Twentieth-Century Fox Films. As Chairman of Twentieth-Century Fox, Joe Schenck still held his powerful seat on A. P. Giannini's Bank of America board of directors. It was about this same time that Schenck began cozying up to an even more powerful Hollywood ally than Giannini; Willie Bioff.

Willie Bioff was a Chicago racketeer and kingpin in the mob's shakedown of Hollywood during the thirties. Not long after his arrival in Hollywood he commanded Joe Schenck's full attention. As Schenck began engaging in some shady dealings with the organized crime boss, he had no idea Federal agents were hot on his movie mogul trail.

❧

While Americans were despairing over the lack of jobs, money and opportunity during the 1930's, such scarcity and privation had no affect upon Rudolph Valentino's popularity. Unlike his estate's disappearing bank account, his popularity thrived. Even though his films had been gathering dust for years, he still commanded an impressive posthumous fan base. Many of the memorial fan clubs George founded in the days immediately following Rudy's death still flourished and every year faithful fans flocked to his crypt in Hollywood to celebrate the precise moment of his tragic demise. The years of controversy surrounding the settlement of his estate kept Rudy's name in the headlines and few silent movie stars, especially those deceased, received such consistent press.

Rudy's open acknowledgment he participated in occult activities and practiced automatic writing only added to his postmortem popularity. His dabbling in the other side inspired mystic leanings in many of his followers who adamantly believed he established his presence among the heavenly hosts long before he ever joined them.

Consequently, many psychics during the 1930's advertised their own private lines of communication with Valentino on high. They chanted his name, intoned his holy spirit and a few even clacked out divine transmissions on their typewriters. From the most serious students of the arcane to ridiculous charlatans, they all attempted in one way or another to bridge the ethers and reach the soul of Rudolph Valentino.

In 1938, psychic Carol McKinstry claimed she typed a screenplay with Rudy's ethereal assistance which she titled, "A Warning From Out the Ages, A Psychic Consignment from Rudolph Valentino". In Pasadena, Miss Marchen Jorgensen alleged she was able to drop into a trance, sit at her typewriter and transcribe psychic grocery lists as dictated by The Great Lover. She said she passed Rudy's laundry lists off to an accomplice who signed for the goods on credit. When it was discovered that Miss Jorgensen's partner was forging a relative's signature on the sales slips for said purchases, both he and Miss Jorgensen were arrested.

220

The continuing intrigues of Rudy's devotees kept his memory alive despite the disturbing appearance of what was fast becoming a legacy of far-fetched, inaccurate versions of his life story. So many disparate accounts of The Great Lover's activities were presented for the public's enjoyment that in the resultant hullabaloo, Rudy's legendary talents for lovemaking reached mythical proportions. Unfortunately, this also left him ripe for a smut peddler's picking. Cheap opportunists sidled onto the scene to make their livings by satisfying the public's craving for a juicy read about "The Sheik". Most notorious of these shysters during the 1930's was Samuel Roth. In 1931, he ghost-wrote and published most of his raunchy, pulp classics under the imprint of "Dollar Books", which included such titles as *Padlocks and Girdles of Chastity* and *Sacred Prostitution and Marriage by Capture*.

That same year Samuel Roth also churned out *The Intimate Journal of Rudolph Valentino*. Roth swore on a stack of bibles that this book was indeed Rudolph Valentino's authentic personal diary and many of his readers believed this to be the case. It was not. A few years after publishing Rudy's fictional, dirty little diary, Samuel Roth was convicted on several charges related to his underhanded publishing tactics and sentenced to a lengthy stay in a Federal penitentiary. Nevertheless, while Roth sat in his prison cell, his readership was held captive by Rudy's torrid, albeit fictional, revelations.

Another writer, a reporter from *The Chicago Daily News*, Hiram Kelly Moderwell also contributed to this increasingly sordid spin on Rudy's life story. Moderwell gained some measure of notoriety after he published what he claimed were interviews conducted after Rudy's death in the town of his birth, Castellaneta. At the time of his alleged interviews, Hiram Moderwell was closely affiliated with two organizations known for voicing strong disapproval of Rudolph Valentino, his films and his influence; the Catholic Church and Italian Dictator Benito Mussolini's Fascista Party.

While Hiram Moderwell was allegedly traveling to Castellaneta to conduct his interviews, he was also working as a reporter at the Vatican and writing in ardent support of Italian dictator Benito Mussolini. Nevertheless, Moderwell reported that he'd traipsed off to southern Italy in the days following the movie star's death and returned with a wealth of disparaging and lewd accounts from his childhood. He alleged that as a child Rudy was molested by a pedophile nanny, that he exposed himself in front of the congregation of his local church and that he had been repeatedly beaten by an abusive father. None of Hiram Moderwell's claims were ever substantiated.

Not all readers of the continuing saga of the beloved Rudolph stooped to thumb through the self-indulgent porn of Samuel Roth and Hiram Moderwell. A few respectable publications such as *The Literary Digest* reported upon the continuing activities of the many Valentino Memorial Guilds. In London, *The Daily Express* reviewed a showing of Rudy's film, *Monsieur Beaucaire*, as hosted by the London Valentino Memorial Guild and commented upon the arrival of one ardent fan's homage to Rudy. The woman arrived at the theater toting an old shirt which she tearfully explained Rudolph Valentino had once worn. She carried her precious item in a custom-made, gold embroidered miniature casket.

By the spring of 1934, one contributor to Rudolph Valentino's legacy, Mrs. Zunilda Mancini had withdrawn her support of the Valentino memorial she funded by filing her own lawsuit against George Ullman. She alleged the Burnham statue titled "Aspirations" cost considerably less than the total of her checks, $6900.00 and demanded a full refund. When George was unable to document his claim that the statue in fact cost considerably more, the court ruled in Mancini's favor and he was ordered to repay the New York widow $5400.00. George hired another attorney, Arthur C. Fisher to handle this case and appeared in court to explain his dire straights. He stated that although his talent agency had twenty clients at the time, few of them were currently working. He then filed an appeal of the new judgment against him with the California Court of Appeals.

When the *Los Angeles Times* reported the news of the court's ruling in Mancini's favor, Alberto Valentino took exception with the article and wrote the newspaper a scathing letter to the editor. He interpreted the paper's reference to Mrs. Mancini's remark about "all Italians being good men" to imply that the Burnham statue had been commissioned by an Italian. In his letter, he erroneously stated that George Ullman commissioned the statue, was not an Italian and had been forced to resign as executor. Alberto went on to accuse the *Los Angeles Times* of issuing a "severe and unwarranted" insult to all Italians. *The Times* responded by issuing a "No Reflection Intended" response but added further injury to Alberto's perceived insult when they referred to him as "Gilbert".

For all of the furtive perusing of news about Rudolph Valentino, whether reverent or lewd, fact or fiction, few of his fans probably caught a tiny fifteen line item which appeared in a few local papers in Los Angeles on April 18, 1934.

"The District Court of Appeals yesterday exonerated S. George Ullman of charges of mismanagement of the estate of Rudolph Valentino, of which he was executor, when it reversed an order of The Los Angeles Probate Court.

Ullman's management had been objected to by Jean Guglielmi, nephew and heir to the estate, who charged that Ullman had made too many cash advances to the other heirs. The Appellate Court praised Ullman for his work."

With no further elaboration upon the Appeals Court's decision, any readers who did spot the insignificant article could scarcely have understood the ramifications of the reversal of the judgment. George had been waiting a long time to read news of his unconditional exoneration and the Appeals Court not only praised his hard work for Rudy's estate, they defended it from criticism.

The Appeals Court chastised the lower court judge who levied the original judgment against George and agreed that it could not be determined who was responsible for the disappearance of the second page of Rudy's will, Paragraph Fourth. The Court of Appeals also reported they found no evidence George ever had any knowledge of the terms of Paragraph Fourth prior to disbursing cash advances to the three people he honestly believed to be Rudy's legitimate heirs.

The Appeals Court's decision criticized Alberto Valentino for having brought his lawsuit against George in the first place and stated that after reviewing the court-ordered audit of George's books and after conducting their own investigation they found "not the slightest scintilla of evidence" that George Ullman ever acted in bad faith. The Appeal Court's decision dismissed George's liability for the $40,000.00 loan made to Frank Mennillo and dismissed his liability for the Cosmic Arts' operational costs as well as any losses incurred from his loan to The Pan American Bank. The Appeals Court held that these transactions were made in the course of running the legitimate business, Rudolph Valentino Productions. However, this was the entire extent of any good news for George from the Appeals Court.

The Appeals' ruling went on to elaborate that as a result of the discovery of Paragraph Fourth, Alberto Valentino, Maria Strada and Teresa Werner were never entitled to any cash advances other than their weekly stipends. Consequently, the court held George legally responsible to reimburse the estate for the total of all cash advances made to those three individuals; nearly $70,000.00.

The revised judgment handed down by the Court of Appeals in August of 1934 declared George innocent on Alberto's charges of fraud and mismanagement but still held him accountable for the $70,000.00 of cash advances plus a portion of his executor's salary not allowed by the court. This entire amount was calculated at seven percent interest and totaled nearly $100,000.00.

The welcome news of his exoneration was still a severe financial blow for George but he held on to one lingering hope; Alberto and Jean Valentino might dismiss the entire judgment based upon a key recommendation issued by the Court of Appeals. The Appeals' decision advised, that in light of the unusual disappearance and discovery of Paragraph Fourth, Alberto and Jean Valentino should waive George's liability for the reimbursement of the cash advances and establish instead an "appropriate fairness lien against the beneficial interest of those who actually participated in the advancement of the property and funds."

In December of 1934, four months after the Appeals Court decision was handed down, all parties involved met once again in a Los Angeles courtroom to sign their signatures and hopefully declare an end to the disputed settlement of Rudy's estate. On this occasion the court addressed the legal quandary of George's liability for the cash advances made to the ersatz heirs and addressed the possible establishment of a lien to recuperate the funds for the estate. Instead of ruling on this troublesome issue, the judge passed the buck by dismissing the entire subject until such time that the final decree of distribution of the estate was issued and Jean Valentino inherited the estate.

This stop-gap measure postponed the final decision on the subject of George's liability for the cash advances, thereby deducting $70,000.00 from the judgment and temporarily reducing his total due the Valentino estate to $25,849.00. George held his breath, took the reprieve and delayed worrying about those aggravating cash advances until the final decree of distribution took place when Jean turned twenty-five. But the reduction of the judgment to $25,000.00 was still an empty victory for George. With the average American family's income in 1934 somewhere between $1300.00 and $1600.00 a year, clearing a debt twenty times this amount from George's modest earnings would be nearly impossible.

For Alberto Valentino, the Appeals Court's decision meant he could finally initiate official collection processes on George. This came at an auspicious time for Alberto as his financial situation was by then so grave that he sat down with gossip columnist, Louella Parsons to bewail his rotten luck story. He told her he had less than $17.00 in his pocket at that very moment and implored her to inform her readers that he was in search of a job. Alberto explained his plight by saying he was downright penniless after years of litigation settling his brother's estate. He neglected to add that this litigation was entirely his doing.

During this interview, Alberto demonstrated little understanding of the recent appeals court's decision, when he informed Ms. Parsons that George Ullman owed him $25,000.00 as his "share" of his brother's estate. He also acknowledged that while his lawsuit against Ullman had been pending, the Bank of America hired him as caretaker of his brother's Falcon Lair. He continued his interview by telling Louella Parsons that when the bank recently sold the property, he had been given fifteen days notice to vacate the premises. Louella pounced upon the shocking news that Rudolph Valentino's brother was about to be tossed to the curb.

She appealed to the public to run, not walk, to Alberto's assistance. Apparently her plea was heard, as the Bank of America permitted him to move into Rudy's Whitley Heights home and he secured several uncredited roles in a few b-movies including *Fatal Lady, One Rainy Afternoon* and *China Slave*. Louella Parsons would soon have more to write about as bad luck continued to stalk Rudy's older brother. While he was moving into the Whitley Heights home, burglars broke through a back window and robbed the place blind.

Meanwhile, George was acutely aware that his every asset, no matter how trivial, had become vulnerable to Alberto and Jean Valentino's seizure. With this in mind, he transferred legal ownership of his personal property to his S. George Ullman Agency, Incorporated. While he endeavored to safeguard his home and business, the 7% interest on the judgment continued to accrue.

By this time the name George Ullman had ceased to make headlines and consequently the public knew next to nothing about the finer points of his complex and unhappy situation. The half-hearted one and a half column inch report of his vindication by the appeals court sounded to the few who read it as if the subject of Valentino's estate was finally a closed book. Indeed George, Alberto and Jean Valentino were the only players left in the melodrama. Even lingering interest from Valentino's old guard had dried up; they were all, one by one, taking their leave.

By 1936, Frank Mennillo had closed his tomato juice plant in Merced and moved south to Los Angeles to work in produce brokerage. It was doubtful A.P. Giannini was unhappy to learn Frank had finally gone out of business. It was not long after Frank's return to Los Angeles from the San Joaquin Valley that Giannini parted ways with one of his longstanding Hollywood compadres, Joe Schenck. The severing of their relationship took place during a Bank of America board of director's meeting in which Giannini expounded upon one Los Angeles Jewish banker's "damnable conspiracy" to take control of his bank. With the Jewish Joe Schenck seated beside him at the board table, Giannini had bellowed,

"That god-damned Jew is in for a fight to the finish!"

Schenck was so deeply offended by the remark he stormed out of the meeting and two days later he submitted his resignation from Giannini's Board of Directors. Schenck had no time for anti-semitic remarks as he was facing a much greater threat to his Hollywood position; he was about to be indicted by the Federal government for his underworld dealings.

Consequently, by the time the Final Decree of Distribution of Rudolph Valentino's estate was handed down, the cast of characters had narrowed considerably. On that occasion there were no lengthy front page articles covering the court's proceedings, no reporters crowding into the courtroom, no mention of any movie executives and barely any mention of the name Rudolph Valentino. On what would be the final decree in probate case number 83678, only George and Jean Valentino appeared before the honorable judge. And if George Ullman left the courtroom in December of 1934, staggering under the weight of the court's reduced judgment of $25,000.00, he nearly collapsed under the impact of the court's final decree of distribution in 1937.

At the time of this Final Decree of Distribution, Jean Valentino informed the court he intended to ignore the appeals court recommendation to dismiss George's liability for the cash advances. He said he found no cause to establish any such "fairness lien" to recuperate the money from the very people who benefited from the funds.

The last notice the public ever read was that George Ullman owed Rudolph Valentino's estate $25,000.00. In fact, at the time of the Final Decree of Distribution, the judge complied with Jean's decision and added the total of all cash advances George made before the discovery of Paragraph Fourth back onto the $25,000.00 judgment. The precise amount was itemized as; Alberto Valentino, $37,411.00, Maria Strada, $12,516.33, Teresa Werner, $7617.00, and the cash amount loaned to Frank Mennillo on behalf of Maria's alleged future share of Rudy's estate, $9100.00. The total of these advances, $66,644.33 did not include years of accrued interest. Eleven years after Rudy's death, George was ordered to surrender a revised total of $92,493.53.

❧

The cover of *Life* magazine's June 20th 1938 issue carried a full page profile of Rudolph Valentino and a headline reading, "The Man That Came Back!" For ten cents, *Life's* subscribers read how three hundred old-fangled silent films were being dusted off that year to be shown in theaters across the country. The article reported that the most popular of all of these films was Rudolph Valentino's, *The Son of the Sheik*. In Chicago *The Son of the Sheik's* box office revenues were even exceeding the year's favorite new features, *Test Pilot* and *Robin Hood* and in New York the movie played to packed theaters on Broadway and grossed $10,000.00 and $11,000.00 a week.

Critics were mystified as to why the public held any remote interest in these cinematic relics and could only attribute the phenomena to the inferior quality of new films being cranked out by Hollywood studios during the depression. Whatever the reason, in 1938 Rudolph Valentino was thrilling a new audience of starry-eyed fans. Women were once again gasping and swooning as *The Son of the Sheik* forced himself on the beautiful dancing girl, Yasmin and as he rode his Arabian stallion across the desert sand dunes at blistering speed. In 1938, there was not a dry eye in the movie house as everyone knew this was Rudolph Valentino's last screen kiss and his final heroic ride into the sunset.

In addition to the public's enthusiastic reception, *Son of the Sheik's* 1938 revival generated sorely needed income for his estate, namely Jean Valentino, as he was poised to at last receive his inheritance. As this auspicious day approached, the cash value of his inheritance was vanishing as surely as his attorney's bank accounts were thriving. With some sources reporting that the estate was actually insolvent, revenue from *The Son of the Sheik's* revival was welcome coin in the coffers.

On August 14th, 1939, Jean celebrated his twenty-fifth birthday and legally inherited Rudy's estate. But during Jean's twenty-five years of life he'd also inherited one other legacy; Alberto's trenchant anger towards George Ullman. While Alberto had been tenaciously demanding his piece of Rudy's estate and George Ullman, young Jean paid close attention. By 1939, he wore this Ullman angst like a family crest.

He ascended into his new role as benefactor of Rudy's estate by declaring a new order. Any further public mention of such embarrassing issues as weekly stipends, collection processes against George Ullman and the very existence of that second page of Rudy's will, Paragraph Fourth were henceforth silenced. With Jean in command of the Valentino estate all reports to the public about such unpleasantries, other than the pointed reminder than George Ullman owed the estate an enormous amount of money, summarily ceased. As far as Jean was concerned, the public need never know that he paid his attorneys a small fortune to enforce a court order which demanded that George reimburse $66,644.33 to the very people, including Alberto, who spent that money many years before.

Publicly, George remained silent on the issue of the judgment. He tried to move on with his life and never commented upon the increase in the final judgment from $25,000.00 to nearly $100,000.00. He just hoped to negotiate a reasonable settlement with the young blood Jean and settle the impossible debt. Whether Jean was about to ease Alberto's hard line or not, only time would tell.

≈✧≈

Jean and Alberto Valentino were not alone as they downplayed the seamier aspects of the settlement of Rudy's estate. Lou Mahoney was also keeping mum. He said nothing about his involvement in the disappearance of Paragraph Fourth nor did he ever extend his apologies regarding his refusal to come forward to acknowledge the critical document's existence.

Nevertheless, Lou received considerable national press coverage in 1930 as he narrowly dodged incriminating evidence on the witness stand. After his high-profile appearance in the courtroom,

Lou's role in Rudolph Valentino's story seemed to grow more influential with each telling. As Valentino's handyman he did have many genuine anecdotes upon which to construct his history of events. After all he fed the falcons, dug the movie star's ditches, fetched his broken-down cars, repaired his masonry, ran errands, built aviaries and checked the oil and changed the tires on his vehicles.

Although "Mr. Valentino", as Lou referred to him, retained many other loyal staff members on Falcon Lair's payroll, including Lou's own brothers, only Lou had been subpoenaed into court where he received national press coverage for his role in Valentino's life. Surpassing the ordinary accomplishments of his fellow members of Falcon Lair's staff, it seemed fate tapped only Lou the handyman to become a part of the story.

Basking in this limelight, Lou embellished and glamorized his role in the events long after they had transpired by issuing reports of his substantial authority in his boss' life. In Lou's post-Valentino world his position as hired hand was transformed into that of power broker and grandfatherly confessor, despite the fact he was only two years older than Rudy at the time of his employment.

While Lou recounted his sentimental yarn of life at Falcon Lair, he had difficulty accurately recollecting several key appearances with Mr. Valentino at various train stations. This rendered many of these scenarios chronologically impossible. He claimed he met Mr. and Mrs. Valentino in New York during the summer of 1924 and drove them to the train station when they left New York City for Hollywood in November of 1924. Lou added that it was upon Rudy's personal invitation he then packed up and moved his family to Los Angeles within the following year. In fact by November 1924, as Rudy and Natacha boarded that train in New York, Lou was already three thousand miles away and had been living in Los Angeles with his family for seven months.

Lou's memory continued to drift as he alleged that neither Mr. Valentino nor Mrs. Valentino ever had the slightest inclination towards spiritualism of any nature nor had they ever participated in seances or automatic writing. And although Lou owned and operated Rudy's dry-cleaning business for years, he emphatically stated he never had a thing to do with that business or any dry-cleaning business. He further alleged he was never employed by Rudolph Valentino as his handyman but as his "personal affairs manager" and that he "was in charge of his house and the domestic help and everything that belonged to him".

George said nothing to dispute Lou's many false impressions. Consequently, the handyman's hazy recollections contributed to Alberto and Jean Valentino's new order of meticulous censorship and the truth about all of their involvements in Rudolph Valentino's life began to veer hopelessly towards outright fiction. It would not be too far in the distant future that this turn of events would rewrite both Rudolph Valentino's and George Ullman's life stories.

Chapter Twelve

Hoping to be Kindly Remembered

New York City, the spring of 1924 -

In 1924, the going rate for a New York City police officer's silence was forty dollars a night. The temptation to refuse bribes from restaurant and club owners was too great for many of New York's finest and they often pocketed the cash to look the other way while bootleg liquor was served with abandon. Although the Volstead Act of 1919 banned the sale and manufacture of alcoholic beverages, by 1924 a devil-may-care attitude about the legislation so permeated mainstream America that even ardent supporters of "The Noble Experiment" admitted Prohibition was a bust. Most club owners simply surrendered to the times, reviewed their accounting ledgers and decided it was better business to slip regular payoffs to the police than to deprive loyal, paying customers their liquor.

A few New York City police precincts became so corrupt during the height of prohibition that Police Commissioner Enright launched a campaign to rout out the worst culprits. In March of 1924, he executed one of his most successful undercover stings in a Queens' nightclub and arrested one incorrigible offender on the police force, Chief Inspector of the Twelfth Division, Thomas J. Kelly.

Chief Kelly was charged with the non-enforcement of prohibition laws and the acceptance of bribes. Every member of his precinct was subpoenaed to testify during his impending trial. The list of officers scheduled to appear on the witness list included one of Chief Kelly's most loyal officers who had worked by his side for the past seven years; Luther H. Mahoney. No officer in the Twelfth Division was comfortable at the thought of incriminating their boss from the witness stand and Lou Mahoney was no exception. As Chief Kelly's trial drew closer, Lou and his two brothers, Charles and George, also New York policemen working in other precincts, made their move; a move out of town. On April 30, 1924, Lou Mahoney surrendered his badge and officially resigned from Chief Kelly's precinct. His brothers followed suit in their respective precincts. Eighteen members of the Mahoney clan then crammed their worldly belongings into four cars in preparation for the long drive west to their parent's home in Los Angeles.

Lou Mahoney did not leave his home at 96 Canal Street quietly and on May sixth, the morning of his departure, he placed a telephone call to the local press. In light of the upcoming trial of Chief Kelly, news of the resignation of three police officers was enough motivation for a few reporters to investigate Lou's story. By the time the press arrived, Lou had built up a head of steam and gave them an earful about the public's shameful treatment of Chief Kelly and his precinct by saying,

"Out west they are friendlier than here. We cops stand a lot of abuse. Being a policeman is a tough job and when we get to California we hope to go into the trucking business. No more policemen's life for us."

The publicity opportunity was not lost on the three Mahoney brothers and their respective families posed for the press in matching khaki safari outfits. A lone cameraman cranked his newsreel camera as the Mahoneys waved goodbye to their neighbors and drove down Canal Street. Despite Lou's brief, public defense of his former superior at the precinct, Chief Thomas Kelly would receive no support from his ex-officer in the courtroom that spring. Lou would ensure there were plenty of miles between himself and that hot seat.

✑✑✑

Just inside Grand Central Station's 42nd Street entrance, an elderly man sat slumped on a folding chair next to his small display of fruit. His handwritten cardboard sign read, "For Sale." It was a nippy spring evening in early May and business was not brisk. So when three well-dressed New Yorkers paused to eye his fruit, he rallied with a pitch.

"Fresh plums, fresh, juicy plums."

The old man's hopes for a sale at that moment were pinned on Rudy, Natacha and George. But at that late hour, the weary vendor did not recognize the handsome movie star bending down to select one of his plums.

"How much?" Rudy asked.

"Ten cents," The man replied.

Rudy raised an eyebrow, set the plum back in the crate and looked the vendor in the eye.

"I won't pay ten cents for a prune!"

Natacha ignored Rudy's rebuke and began filling a small paper bag with the plums while George stepped forward to count out the change for the purchase. Rudy didn't sputter long about the indignity of paying a dime for a plum and before walking another city block he was munching on the fruit.

If Rudy could sign for a purchase on credit he did not hesitate to spend his money extravagantly. He imported his "Abdullah Number Five" black tobacco Turkish cigarettes and expensive English shaving soap, packaged in hand-polished wooden bowls, by the case and had these expensive items shipped directly from the manufacturer. However, if the deal required reaching into his pocket, no matter how grand the acquisition or how juicy the plum it was a different story. Those awkward moments were left to George. Rudy's tight fistedness with his cash on hand was not due to any thriftiness on his behalf. For by time he and Natacha returned from their Hotel Negresco New Year's celebration to settle into their lavishly appointed new apartment at 270 Park Avenue, any fiscal restraint on their behalf was a distant past.

It was George's sole responsibility to fund this lifestyle of unparalleled spending. In this endeavor, he not only struggled to maintain their shaky household budget but the budget of Rudy's next movie *Monsieur Beaucaire* as well. George's original budget for the film was decimated as Natacha hired a scenic artist, a costume director, four wardrobe assistants, an art selector, an interior decorator and assistant, an expert draper, a supervisor of make-up, a fencing master as her husband's coach, a dancing master, a poetry reader, a violinist and two valet assistants. The ever-expanding payroll added considerably to *Monsieur Beaucaire*'s escalating production costs and threatened any amicable working relationship between George and Natacha. Their professional affiliation grew more volatile as Rudy seldom made the slightest move without first consulting his manager. His increasing reliance upon George did not bode well with Natacha.

Nevertheless, George negotiated the occasional detente with Natacha as he continued to secure the necessary funding for her *Monsieur Beaucaire* directives. Her relationship with *Beaucaire's* Director, Sidney Olcott, did not fare as well. Olcott grew exasperated and made several failed attempts to prohibit Natacha from previewing the daily rushes of filming. But as Rudy's contract ensured his complete artistic control over the production, Natacha's wishes were never seriously challenged. The final edit of *Monsieur Beaucaire* was ultimately hers, with the film's final price tag totaling just over a half a million dollars. This figure did not include a few substantial financial outlays incurred during filming by the Valentinos that were not paid for by Famous Players-Lasky.

During the production of *Beaucaire*, both Rudy and Natacha extended themselves personally as well as financially in the promotion of their individual "discoveries". In one instance, Rudy asked George to negotiate a screen contract for the film's leading lady, Doris Kenyon. After a few days of negotiations, George secured a one-year contract with Metro Goldwyn Mayer Studios which guaranteed Miss Kenyon $500.00 a week plus all expenses.

One of Natacha's proteges exacted more of a financial sacrifice. The handsome, young reporter she met in Paris the previous year, Andre Daven accepted her invitation to visit New York. Just as she'd promised, Natacha ensconced him in regal style in her Park Avenue apartment and cast him in *Monsieur Beaucaire*. To George's frustration, Natacha also granted Daven the ability to charge all of his expenses on her various personal accounts around New York.

George soon realized that Monsieur Daven could spend money with as much abandon as his benefactress. The Frenchman rang up enormous tabs despite complaining in letters to his Parisian girlfriend that he was only earning sixty dollars a week for his work in *Beaucaire*. He also borrowed large sums of money from the Valentino's personal friends which he never repaid. While Daven was busy stiffing the Valentino's friends, he was also writing home explaining how he tagged along on a hunting trip with *Beaucaire's* star. He also wrote that Mrs. Valentino set up a little office space for his use, complete with a used typewriter. There, he said, he planned to do some part time clerical work for an extra fifty dollars a week.

By the time Daven completed his few scenes in *Monsieur Beaucaire*, Natacha's interest in her discovery waned and future roles for him in the movies were not forthcoming. He did not return to France and obscurity however before completing a dental makeover with Natacha's dentist. Apparently Daven's teeth were a wreck because the dentist charged a small fortune for the extensive work. The dentist forwarded the substantial bill to George for payment just a few days after Daven quietly left for Paris without the meekest "au revoir" to the generous Madam Valentino.

When George informed Rudy that Daven had skipped town leaving him holding the bill for his dental work, Rudy was so furious he could not be calmed down. He yelled at Natacha, criticized her willingness to extend his line of credit and told George to forward an immediate statement of indebtedness demanding full payment from Monsieur Andre Daven. A few weeks later, George received Daven's reply stating that he had no intention of paying Mr. or Mrs. Valentino one franc. He went on to explain how he felt they owed him money as they had interrupted his newspaper career in Paris. For this, he said, he held them responsible for time lost.

George's daily lectures advising Rudy and Natacha to curb their expenditures were inevitably followed by their earnest assurances they would be more frugal. But by the time work ended on *Beaucaire*, they were spending a reported $1000.00 a night in New York auction houses purchasing choice pieces of antique armor, weaponry, ivory carvings, books and tapestries. One evening Rudy attended the American Art Association's sale where he purchased, again on credit, two 16th century family portraits of the Duke and Duchess of Savoy for $640.00. He then topped this extravagance by signing for a $475.00 purchase of a 15th century carved walnut chest.

With the sets already under construction for Rudy's next and final movie with Famous Players-Lasky, *The Sainted Devil*, the much anticipated end to his hostile relationship with the studio was tantalizingly close. The prospect of his impending ability to earn even more money starring in his own independent movies inspired both Rudy and Natacha to borrow against those future, fatter paychecks with a vengeance.

∾∾

The Sainted Devil was loosely based upon a gruesome story of murder, revolution and misery set in Haiti. The original story was written by Rex Beach and first published in *Cosmopolitan* magazine in May of 1913 under the title of "Rope's End." By the time Famous Players-Lasky converted "Rope's End's" into a screenplay, the plot line had gone south.

Sainted Devil was re-written as the story of a South American "Don" whose wife was kidnapped by bandits. Despite the watered down script, Rudy found his character of a drunk and volatile Latin lover an easy fit and allowed make-up artists to leave the pronounced scar on his cheek exposed to grant his character edge. He would play opposite an impressive line up of beautiful actresses; Helen D'Algy, Louise LaGrange and Natacha's friend, Nita Naldi. Amid rumors Rudy was too smitten with co-star, actress Jetta Goudal, Natacha promptly replaced her by hiring Dagmar Godowsky.

To work by her side designing *The Sainted Devils'* costumes, Natacha hired Adolph "Adrian" Greenburg, a graduate student fresh from the Manhattan branch of Parson's School of Design. Her sponsorship of Andre Daven had fallen flat on his expensively reconstructed teeth, but Adrian would become one of Natacha's most successful proteges. *Monsieur Beaucaire's* screenplay writer Forrest Halsey and photographer Harry Fischbeck were again contracted for work on *The Sainted Devil.* But *Beaucaire's* director, Sidney Olcott, could not be convinced to work another minute with Natacha and was replaced by director Joseph Henabery.

As filming on *The Sainted Devil* got underway, Natacha and Rudy spent their time away from the set attending auctions, browsing through antique shops and sifting through the book shelves at The Gotham Book Mart with Francis Steloff. When Natacha's custom built Isotta Fraschini Cabriolet finally arrived from Paris, she became the envy of all New York as she rode around Manhattan in the one-of-a-kind vehicle. Tucked in the Cabriolet's velvet upholstered single bucket seat, Natacha was protected from the public's prying eyes and her Italian chauffeur by a partition of ornately etched smoked glass.

With New Yorkers clambering for any news about the Valentinos, Rudy and Natacha did all they could to keep their profiles low. Despite their meager security measures consisting of George, studio security guards and the Cabriolet's glass partition, during the summer of 1924 they were vulnerable to fan harassment and often sought safe retreat in the homes of trusted friends.

That summer Rudy assumed his role as Bobby Ullman's proud godfather by spending many afternoons tossing the squealing tyke in the air and rough-housing with Bobby's six-year old brother, Danny. Rudy was also a favorite visitor in Frank Mennillo's home where a fourteen-year old Arnold Mennillo pressed him for more dance instructions. Arnold so emulated his "Uncle Rudy" that he covertly organized his own nightclub act that summer with a considerably older danseuse from the George White Scandals. Arnold performed with the professional dancer for six weeks before his father learned about his son's nightly gigs around New York. Frank put an end to

Arnold's nightclub act and laid down the law; no son of his would pursue a career as a professional dancer.

It was also during the summer of 1924, that Rudy and his friend Oscar Odd McIntyre waged a heated competition to find the loudest tie in New York. Oscar Odd McIntyre wrote the popular column, "New York, Day by Day," and he and his wife Maybelle were close friends of both the Valentinos and the Ullmans. Odd would claim victory in the loudest tie contest after telephoning Rudy with a request that he stop by his apartment to view the winning entry. When Rudy knocked on Odd's door one hot summer day, he was wearing a pair of fur ear-muffs in order "to stifle the din" of Odd's blaring cravat.

During July and August, the Valentinos, the Ullmans and the McIntyres were all frequent guests of New York antique dealer, Victor Miller. Although an invitation to dine with Victor Miller in his Manhattan apartment inevitably meant participation in one of his after dinner seances, the greater enticement to spend an evening with Victor Miller was the prospect of enjoying one of his haute cuisine dinners. Miller bragged to his guests that he prepared the meals entirely by himself, but as no one had ever seen him boil water, none of his friends believed the claim for a minute.

While the Valentino's friends did their best to shield them from the public's fanatical pursuit, Rudy's popularity continued to soar. Despite the fact that he had not released a movie in two years, he was crowned "King of the Movies" at the Theater Owners Ball at New York's Hotel Astor. But as the day of *Monsieur Beaucaire's* premiere grew closer, odds makers placed their bets and deemed the success of the film a long shot. New York columnists joined in the debate and filled their columns with speculation; would *Monsieur Beaucaire* launch Rudolph Valentino's triumphant return to the movies or bomb at the box-office and mark an embarrassing end to his career?

On August 24th, long lines of moviegoers wound through the streets surrounding New York's Mark Strand Theater. The odds makers and nay-sayers in the press did not deter Rudy's fans from turning out en masse to see for themselves whether he still had what it takes. Each showing of *Monsieur Beaucaire* was filled to capacity and initial reviews raved over the gorgeous production. But by the time fan magazines hit the streets with their reviews, it was evident that some viewers were not so swept off their feet.

They weren't sure how much they enjoyed watching Rudolph Valentino in a movie where his only action scene was a brief fencing duel. No one disputed that Natacha's attention to historical detail and her art direction made *Monsieur Beaucaire* a visual masterpiece. But fans preferred their Rudy Valentino a little more wicked and a lot more dashing. It seemed *Monsieur Beaucaire*'s polished, courtly restraint left many audience members on the edge of their seats hoping that the tippy-toed action would cut loose and entertain. After such a long wait for Rudy's next film, audiences were rewarded with meaningful bows and head nods instead of hot desert pursuits and passionate embraces.

Many of Rudy's frustrated fans placed their protests squarely upon Natacha's lithe shoulders and rumors began the predictable swirl alleging "The Sheik" was subject to his wife's controlling will. Men, in particular, found Natacha's influence appalling and vented their displeasure at this dominant woman who seemed to fit no known standard of the ideal, apron-ed wife.

By marrying "The Sheik", "The Great Lover", "The King of the Movies", Natacha had positioned herself as prime target for an onslaught of henpecking insinuations. If her authority over her husband's career challenged mens' perceptions of a wife's place in the home, womens' reactions directed against her were more visceral. For millions of Rudy's female fans she lived the fantasy role they held desperately dear. She shared a bed with their heartthrob, Rudolph Valentino and that alone made her all too easy to hate.

However, Rudy's public was unaware he was quite satisfied with his wife's take charge attitude and as sole stock holder of Cosmic Arts, she held the controlling interest over his studio contracts. In fact by 1924, Rudy was deferring to Natacha so frequently that a frustrated George Ullman believed he was growing mentally lazy in her presence.

With George and Natacha running all aspects of his everyday life as well as his professional career, Rudy was free to occupy his time away from work enjoying his favorite daily diversions. For a short while he demonstrated some interest in those college textbooks George provided for him and he expressed a sincere desire to learn to play the piano. His Park Avenue apartment was strewn with the open textbooks and littered with sheets of his poetry and automatic writing scribblings.

Each day he awaited the delivery of Cora McGeachy's automatic writing missives and weighed her messages from Black Feather and Mesolope with solemn consideration. Based upon his analysis of her communiques, he then scrawled copious notes for the following day. However, during the summer of 1924, it would be Natacha and not Rudy who would write in all seriousness. Assuming the pen name of Justice Layne she began work on a screenplay for Rudy's first independent film to be produced by J.D. William's new production company, Ritz-Carlton Pictures.

Natacha's screenplay would go through several title changes. Her work was initially titled *The Scarlet Power* and then changed to *The Flame of Destiny* before finally becoming *The Hooded Falcon*. Her screenplay was a re-working of the story of El Cid, the legendary Spanish military leader who led his forces against the Moors. Rudy's character in the film was that of the 11th century hero. Natacha planned to have the film shot entirely on location in Spain and estimated the cost of the epic production at one million dollars; twice that of *Monsieur Beaucaire*.

When Natacha pitched her proposal to Ritz-Carlton Pictures' president J.D. Williams, he agreed to produce *The Hooded Falcon* as Rudy's first independent movie. Williams did not agree to film the movie on location in Spain as he was a seasoned veteran in the relatively young motion picture business. He knew only too well that filming a movie abroad added considerable cost to its production. Williams was anxious to move forward with Natacha's *Hooded Falcon* project as he was contractually obligated to pay Rudy a weekly salary whether he was working or not. And so it was upon Williams' approval of *The Hooded Falcon*, that Ritz-Carlton Pictures advanced Rudy and Natacha a $40,000.00 line of credit for props and research materials which they would purchase in Europe before filming commenced.

Williams' handed the advance to the Valentinos along with some stunning news; Rudy's Ritz-Carlton movies, including *The Hooded Falcon*, would not be filmed in New York but in Hollywood. He went on to explain that he planned to publicize his fledgling production company on the west coast where he hoped to sell more stock. This was thoroughly depressing news for Rudy and Natacha as Williams had effectively just ordered them to relocate to Los Angeles immediately upon their return from their *Hooded Falcon* shopping trip abroad.

With great resignation, they instructed George to set plans in motion for their return to California. Natacha's friend and Rudy's co-star, Nita Naldi accepted their request to star in a leading role in *Hooded Falcon*, and agreed to join them on their European shopping excursion. While Nita Naldi, Rudy and Natacha were abroad, George would begin the laborious process of orchestrating the Valentino's move. He would also be closing his own home in New York as he, Bee and the boys would be moving to Los Angeles as well. Before Rudy left for Europe, he confided in George that had no intention of ever setting foot in Los Angeles before his outstanding debts were paid and all of the legal collection actions against him were settled. As soon as Rudy, Natacha and Nita sailed out of New York, George headed in the opposite direction on a train bound for California.

When he arrived in Los Angeles, he opened the Valentino's Whitley Heights' home, hired a domestic couple and leased an office and a home for his family. In his new role as production manager of Ritz-Carlton Pictures, he negotiated the lease of studio space in Hollywood where Rudy would film his independent movies. George narrowed his choice of studio space to three studios, United Studios on Melrose Avenue, Pickford-Fairbanks Studios and Selig Studios. He made his final decision to lease lot space from United Studios. In mid-September, he and J.D. Williams sat down with United Studios President, M.C. Levee and signed a contract making the largest and best equipped leasing studio in Hollywood the new home of Ritz-Carton Pictures.

Meanwhile set designer William Cameron Menzies had just begun his work drafting Natacha's preliminary set designs for *The Hooded Falcon*. That September "Bill" Menzies would spend a great deal of time in his new office on the United Studios lot and one morning his work was interrupted by a telephone call from his wife. After learning her car had just broken down he said he would send someone right over.

Bill Menzies left his drafting table and walked across the studio yard in search of the nearest lot mechanic. Spotting a pair of coverall covered legs stretching out from under a truck chassis, he asked the half-hidden worker if he could take a look at his wife's stalled car. The grease-covered mechanic slid out from under the vehicle, wiped his hands on a dirty rag and nodded. When Menzies returned to his desk he telephoned his wife with news that he'd taken care of her problem.

"A mechanic is on his way, dear, his name is Lou Mahoney."

Six thousand miles away in Paris, Rudy was raving over his new Voisin roadster. The coveted automobile he ordered the previous year was polished, primed and ready for his first road test; the drive south to Juan les Pins with Natacha. Traveling companion Nita Naldi opted to remain in Paris, but promised to join her friends on the Riviera as soon as they returned from a scheduled *Hooded Falcon* shopping foray to Spain. Rudy and Natacha then drove out of Paris in the shiny new Voisin with their sole passenger on this voyage a gift from their friend, Jacques Hebertot; a magnificent Doberman Pincher named Kabar.

The sole purpose of this trip abroad for Rudy and Natacha was the purchase of artifacts for *The Hooded Falcon* and consequently their visit to the Hudnut chateau was brief. They left for Spain with Aunt Teresa Werner and Muzzie almost immediately after their arrival in Juan les Pins. In Madrid and Granada, Natacha researched costume design in local libraries and she and Rudy purchased antique cloaks, Spanish shawls, masks, armor and weaponry. One memorable Sunday afternoon Rudy, Natacha and Muzzie attended a bullfight in Seville which was sponsored by the local Red Cross.

Seville's Red Cross charity event was a huge success that day as the entire city, from royalty to humble workers, turned out to cheer as several unlucky bulls were released into the ring for sacrifice. When the afternoon's final kill snorted before the matador, the roaring crowd was on its feet, hurling hats, jewelry and scarves into the ring. In one spectator box, Natacha and Muzzie tugged frantically on Rudy's coat tails as he stood teetering on the box's railing yelling himself hoarse.

When Rudy entered the Seville arena earlier that afternoon he arrived lugging a movie camera and a cumbersome still camera all in the hopes of capturing some of the very scenes he portrayed two years earlier in *Blood and Sand*. But he found the action in the ring so riveting that he never snapped a single photograph. Instead, he joined the cheering crowd and when hats were flung into the sand, he spun his beret in with the rest, jumped up onto the box's railing and shouted over the din to Natacha and Muzzie,

"I'm through with the movies! I'm going to be a matador!"

He was convinced that somewhere in that bloody arena he saw his future. Natacha and Muzzie dismissed his enthusiasm as a passing whim but he vowed one day to return to live in Spain and study the art of bullfighting. On the return trip to Juan les Pins he did little else but plead his case for his bright future as a bullfighter in Seville.

Upon their arrival at the chateau, Rudy and Natacha found that Nita had just arrived from Paris and a tour of the chateaus of the Loire Valley was quickly organized for her benefit. It was during this spontaneous excursion that Rudy, Natacha, Nita and Muzzie toured the 15th century fortress at Loches. This infamous fortress had once been used as a military prison by King Louis XI and in 1924 his dungeons were a popular tourist attraction.

The exploration of the King's dungeons required the precarious navigation of winding corridors and steep, stone stairways. Muzzie and Nita refused to venture into the dungeons and thought the idea of touring any site where confessions were routinely tortured from political prisoners just ghastly. But Rudy and Natacha found the lure irresistible and they began picking their way through the dark passageways while balancing themselves with one hand on the damp stone walls.

The two adventurers were so unfazed by their expedition they soon separated to explore on their own. Within a few minutes, Rudy heard a bone chilling scream echoing through the maze of tunnels. Convinced some tourist had tumbled down one of the dungeons' long staircases, he sprinted along the stone corridors in the hopes of offering assistance. Unable to see where he was going, he stumbled into a wide chamber two stories high. Just at that moment the awful screaming ceased and on the dimly lit far wall of the dungeon a skeleton hung suspended in wrist and ankle manacles, its bony feet dangling a few inches from the stone floor.

As Rudy later related the spine-tingling tale, at that moment the skeleton vanished into thin air leaving only iron chains swinging against the wall. This experience ended Rudy's fascination with dungeons and he, Natacha, Muzzie and Nita made a speedy retreat to the Hudnut chateau. There they initiated preparations for an immediate return to the less supernatural streets of New York City.

❧

While they were sailing across the Atlantic, a postcard from Spain arrived at the Manhattan address of Oscar Odd McIntyre. The image on the postcard made its arrival a noteworthy event. Rudy, standing next to a goat, had written the following inscription across the card.

"The one with the beard is the goat."

Odd McIntyre was the first to know. In anticipation of his impending role as El Cid in *The Hooded Falcon*, Rudy had grown a beard.

The Master Barbers Association of America reacted to this development during their 1924 annual convention in a ballroom in Chicago's Hotel Sherman. On the agenda that year was a proposed boycott of Rudolph Valentino's films. When the issue was put to a vote, the barbers unanimously passed a motion stating that if Rudolph Valentino did not immediately shave off his beard they would boycott his movies.

A few days earlier on November eleventh, Rudy returned from Europe with Natacha and Nita Naldi, sporting the neatly-trimmed goatee. With his awesome sway over young men's fashions, this was truly a horrifying development for the men who made their livings shaving whiskers from chins across the land. From the floor of their convention the master barber's alleged Valentino's beard threatened their very livelihood and argued that if American men dared follow his lead they could scarcely be distinguished from Russian men. Although their anxiety may have had merit, the truth was the motion to boycott Rudy's films at the annual convention was prompted by none other than Famous Players-Lasky's publicity genius Harry Reichenbach. What better way to promote the opening of *The Sainted Devil* than to instigate a furor at the barber's convention over Valentino's goatee?

While America read about the barber's protest of Rudolph Valentino's facial adornment, George was working day and night putting the finishing touches on the grand move to California. He returned to New York well in advance of Rudy, Natacha and Nita Naldi's arrival from Europe, but by the time he met the three weary travelers he was reeling from an ugly, heated exchange with J.D. Williams.

Williams had just informed George that Rudy and Natacha exceeded his $40,000.00 advance by charging, on his line of credit, an additional $60,000.00 worth of artifacts. He then proceeded to say that he had changed his mind and now found Natacha's *Hooded Falcon* a dreadful choice for Rudy's first film. Neither of these two problems seemed surprising or insurmountable to George. But Williams' next tidbit of information certainly was. He informed George he had just sold the distributing rights to Rudy's independent films made with Ritz-Carlton back to Famous Players-Lasky and their distributing company, Paramount. He added he had also accepted funding for Rudy's independent films from the Famous Players-Lasky Corporation. George could hardly believe what William's was saying, as Rudy's contract had apparently been sold to the very people he swore he would never work for another day in his life.

George tore into Williams and made it clear he had broken the terms of his contract with Rudy. Williams replied it was already a done deal, to which George replied something to the order of, "You Son of a Bitch", "bastard" and "double-crossing bastard". The two men came close to fisticuffs before George managed to calm down long enough to conclude the conversation. He told Williams in no uncertain terms that if Rudy ever learned of his double-cross he would go on strike again and this, George said emphatically, must be avoided at all cost.

Despite his profound distress over this development, George assured Williams he would not pursue legal charges against him for his obvious breech of contract if he agreed to keep any news of Famous Players-Lasky and Paramount's involvement from Rudy. Williams agreed to say nothing as long as Rudy complied with his contract with Ritz-Carlton Pictures. Privately, at that moment George considered Rudy's contract with Ritz-Carlton null and void and decided he would do something about the situation as soon as possible. Saying nothing to Williams about his intentions, he resolved Rudy would never spend another day unemployed and immediately sought a new contract for Rudy with another production company. Before George left that contentious meeting, Williams handed him a final bit of bad news.

He said that Rudy's first independent film would be a film based upon the Broadway play, *The Cobra* and not Natacha's *Hooded Falcon*. George knew the play and told Williams it was a ludicrous choice for Rudy. He reminded Williams that *The Cobra* bombed on Broadway and despite producer L. Lawrence Weber's best attempts to keep the show running, the show closed after sixty-three performances at the Hudson Theater. Furthermore, George said, as Rudy contractually had the final say about his choice of screenplays, he would advise him to reject the project and continue with his plans to produce *Hooded Falcon*. Williams responded with a blank stare.

J.D. Williams kept his word to George and did not reveal the identity of those "wealthy New Yorkers" funding Rudy's films to either Rudy or Natacha. But before the Valentinos made their exodus for the west coast one more meeting with Williams was convened. Williams seized the occasion to reiterate to Rudy and Natacha that the unauthorized $60,000.00 they spent in Europe added considerably to the overhead of *Hooded Falcon* and explained that screenwriter June Mathis had been working on the film's script and found it a difficult task. Williams continued with his litany of snags by reporting that *Hooded Falcon*'s budget was being cut in half from one million dollars to $500,000.00 and nary a single frame of footage would be shot in Spain.

It was then he reopened the discussion of *The Cobra* as Rudy's first film with Ritz-Carlton. *The Cobra* was a contemporary drama and Natacha did not hesitate to tell J.D. Williams she had no interest in having anything to do with such films. Rudy added that he knew the popular play and felt it was all wrong for him. No decision was made on William's proposal to produce *The Cobra* and George, Natacha and Rudy abruptly left the meeting.

George and Natacha were adamant Rudy refuse Williams' offer to produce *The Cobra*. A few days later Rudy stunned them both when he calmly made the announcement he had decided to comply with Williams' wishes and begin work on *The Cobra* as soon as they arrived in Los Angeles. Once again George repeated that the film was a dreadful selection. Before he could elaborate further, Rudy said his decision was final as he had just received instructions from Black Feather through Cora McGeachy to accept the role. This ended the conversation as both George and Natacha knew better than to argue with Black Feather.

During the Valentino's final days in New York, George sold Natacha's Isotta Cabriolet for $7000.00, the same price Rudy originally paid for the luxury vehicle. He also shipped Rudy's larger Isotta limousine, purchased for an outrageous $12,000.00, to California. In order to oversee the advance publicity in Hollywood for the Valentino's return, George boarded an earlier train west with his family. When Rudolph Valentino returned to California with his beautiful wife Natacha, their friend, Nita Naldi, designer Adrian Greenberg and an assorted entourage and menagerie, George had already been hard at work for days ensuring the press was out in full force.

As reporters snapped their photographs of Mr. and Mrs. Valentino's smiling faces, they failed to capture a certain malaise obscured from the public's view. The move to California was generating substantial conflict between Rudy and Natacha. After a two year absence from Los Angeles, Rudy was eager to be home, but it was no secret Natacha hated Hollywood. The previous year she published a tirade against the evils of the motion picture industry and "the yellow shadow of graft brooding over Hollywood." As she smiled for the cameras at the train station in Los Angeles, she was poised to confront the industry she considered so despicable. Rudy gave a great impression to the crowd at the train station that he was on top of the world. The fact was otherwise; his wife's misery was already having its melancholic effect upon their uprooted household.

Returning to their Wedgwood Place home was no light undertaking and with renovations underway and rooms jammed with boxes, trunks and antiques, life was anything but restful. Crews of workmen rushed about polishing the black marble floors and setting up towering metal scaffolding. The long abandoned home was freshened with noxious coats of canary yellow, silver, Chinese red and black paint. While the Valentino's hillside home was being refurbished and repainted, new furniture was delivered and the yard uprooted for landscaping. Surveying the chaos before her, Natacha suggested to her husband and George that perhaps what they really needed was a larger home.

As renovations on the property grew more extensive, the household staff expanded with the hiring of a groomsman and a full-time gardener. Whenever the construction projects required additional man power, muscle was borrowed from the United Studios' lot. Such was the case when Natacha's plans for an aviary required the excavation of a trench to facilitate the installation of a fountain. The task of digging this trench was assigned to a studio lot mechanic, Luther Mahoney. He arrived at the Valentino household upon glowing recommendation from Bill Menzies.

The new day laborer, Lou arrived early every morning, worked late every night and befriended the downhearted "Mrs. Valentino" as he referred to her. Meanwhile, Rudy avoided the turmoil of the renovations and his wife by spending most of his time out of the house. Early every morning he drove to nearby Griffith Park to ride horses before returning home for his breakfast. After breakfast he either drove to the United Studios lot on Melrose Avenue to work on the set of *The Cobra*, retreated to his garage or engaged in a lengthy sparring session with his trainer or George. Despite George's busy schedule, he never refused an opportunity to lace on a pair of boxing gloves and go a few rounds with Rudy.

Rudy and George shared a passionate interest in boxing and they were not only active participants in the sport but avid fans. One of George's first orders of business upon his arrival in Los Angeles was the purchase of a block of eight seats in the American Legion Arena. There, without exception, every Friday night the Valentinos and the Ullmans were seated ringside. Usually decked out in a beret, a pair of knickers and a tweed sport-coat, Rudy cheered in Italian if an Italian pugilist was in the ring and in English if the boxer was American. On a few occasions he cheered in Spanish along with actress Lupe Velez for the American Legion's Mexican boxers. The crowd always knew when Rudy was in the stadium; he was loud, especially after he had a few drinks.

It became one of the most demanding aspects of George's job during the fall of 1924 to prevent the press from reporting any news of Rudy's increasingly rowdier public indiscretions. George continued to issue his stock press releases and censor all copy written about Rudy before it was released to fan magazines. He did so in a calculated effort to portray Rudy as having no more than a glass of wine with dinner and behaving at home and in public as a veritable boy scout.

In fact a loyal fleet of bootleggers provided Rudy with cases of top-shelf liquor and after his return to Los Angeles he was often inebriated. He drank quantities of liquor far more often than he had in New York and to make matters worse he was becoming a disagreeable drinker. This disturbing trend presented such problems for George, he retained three public relations men with powerful connections with the press and police. He placed these men permanently on the payroll. Rudy's fans knew nothing of his drunken behavior or the efforts of the whitewash team keeping the distressing facts from the public.

One of these harrowing incidents occurred after Rudy announced to George, Bee and Natacha that he was driving them all to San Diego for dinner at the beachside resort, the Coronado Hotel. The four friends left Los Angeles on the three hour road trip traveling south along the Pacific Coast Highway in Rudy's Voison roadster. Once inside the Coronado Hotel's restaurant, Rudy was recognized and women began swarming around him. George diplomatically tried to move the women along. Rudy was not in a magnanimous mood, waved his arm in the air in defiance and demanded loudly that he be left to his dinner.

It was not long before the situation became intolerable and Rudy began elbowing his way through his persistent fans, storming out of the restaurant and heading for the Voison. With George, Bee and Natacha barely seated in the car, Rudy hit the accelerator and careened onto the highway to drive further south to Tijuana, Mexico. Ignoring George's protests, he bore down on the road and insisted they spend the night gambling in the casino. George demanded to take the wheel, as he knew Rudy had already had far too many shots of whiskey from the flask he kept in his coat pocket. Rudy would hear none of it.

A short while later, Rudy stood before a grand roulette wheel in a Tijuana casino where he ordered round after round of scotch whiskey. He quickly gambled away a small fortune and with each loss he increased his next bet and became more belligerent. Natacha and George's shushing only incited him to bark louder at everyone. When the casino's security demanded he shut up or they would summon the local police, Rudy staggered a few steps and bellowed,

"To hell with the Mexican police!"

A Mexican police officer just happened to be in the casino at the time but was thankfully out of earshot. However, a casino security guard heard Rudy's rant and waved the police officer over to the gaming table. When the officer heard how Rudy had just damned him to hell, he sidled close to Rudy and asked him in broken English,

"What deed joo say?"

By then George had a tight grip on Rudy's arm and leaned in to whisper in his ear, "For God's sake, Rudy, say 'Viva the Mexican Police!'"

Rudy flashed a withering look of disgust at the security guard, wrenched his arm from George's grasp and took another staggering step of defiance in the police officer's direction. Recognizing the impending fisticuffs, George grabbed Rudy, spun him around and slugged him full-force in the jaw. His fist delivered enough of a blast to end Rudy's drunken rant and prevented the police officer from arresting him on the spot. Before Rudy knew what had hit him, George was shuffling him to a nearby table while Natacha rushed to retrieve a cup of coffee for her dazed husband. Within the next few minutes, Rudy gulped downed a cup of coffee and was scuttled out of the casino towards the Voison. Unfortunately, before George managed to shove him out the nearest exit, Rudy was squarely recognized.

He put up no further fight when George refused to allow him to drive the return trip to Los Angeles. During the wee hours of that night, George and his three publicity men made their calls and managed to prevent any mention of the hubbub in Tijuana from appearing in the morning papers. By the following morning, Rudy had once again sobered up, was wracked with remorse and making his apologies to anyone who would listen. Thankfully for George, generating positive press for Rudy was always an easier feat.

Just before Christmas that year, he staged an elaborately coordinated press event in honor of barber Ellis G. Bond's public shaving of Rudy's infamous goatee. Soon after this highly publicized shave, Rudy was seized by more than his usual near paralyzing paranoia and he became convinced his hair was falling out. He could not be persuaded to the contrary and steadfastly believed the Master Barbers of America had zapped his famous head with a curse. In an effort to ward off the barber's bad mojo, he began carrying amulets and ordered a toupee.

❧

On December 21, 1924, soon after his public shaving, *Los Angeles Times'* reporter, Alma Whitaker interviewed Rudy on the set of *The Cobra*. Stroking his pale, bare chin, Rudy lamented to Miss Whitaker how the whiskers had itched and that he was actually relieved they were finally gone. He then expounded upon his work on *The Cobra* and praised his wife's editing abilities for the box-office success of *Monsieur Beaucaire*.

"I made *Monsieur Beaucaire* without interference and was allowed my own way in everything under my contract with Famous Players-Lasky. But I did not cut or edit the picture myself, my wife did that. I do not think the actor can bring his best judgment to bear in cutting a picture himself."

In response to a question Miss Whitaker posed about his childhood, Rudy replied he was a "very troublesome boy who occasioned his mother much sorrow." He then explained to Miss Whitaker that she could "never, never know the sorrow" that he caused his poor, dear mother in the days before he left Italy. This piqued the reporter's interest and as she pressed on Rudy was in no mood to hold back.

"I fell in love with a woman as old as my mama," He lamented.

Alma Whitaker asked, "You don't mean that women fell in love with you that young, do you?"

"No, ladies do not fall in love with me," Rudy sighed.

"What about all those piles of fan letters?" Alma asked him.

"Oh, they are in love with the characters I play, not with me, the man. That is why I disapprove of personal appearances. I fall so short of their ideals of the characters I play when they see me in an ordinary modern suit."

He then abruptly changed the subject.

"Isn't it dreadful to see those fine trees being cut down in the street outside the studio there? Just to make a street wider…and they take fifty years to grow to such beauty."

Sensing her interview had come to an end, Alma Whitaker requested an autograph and handed Rudy a pen and one of his publicity photos. He held the pen and the glossy photograph for a moment before obliging her request by scrawling across the bottom of the print,

"Hoping to be kindly remembered, Rudolph Valentino."

On Christmas day, 1924, Natacha's gift to her husband was a solid platinum slave bracelet which he had permanently welded onto his wrist. His gift to his wife was a diamond encrusted wrist watch. With an affectionate kiss, Mr. and Mrs. Rudolph Valentino exchanged their gifts that Christmas morning in the presence of Bee and George Ullman and their two little boys.

Despite the exchange of these cherished gifts, Rudy and Natacha had been up all night fighting and by dawn they were barely speaking. Nevertheless, early Christmas morning Natacha telephoned George with the news that Rudy had a great surprise planned for the Ullman boys. "Come over at once!" she said. By the time the sleepy headed Ullman boys arrived at Wedgwood Place with Mom and Dad, Uncle Rudy and Auntie Natacha had apparently made up and were all smiles. Since Uncle Rudy's surprise was not quite ready, the Ullman family stood in the foyer with Natacha waiting for the "OK" to be sounded.

While George and Bee restrained their fidgety boys, Natacha filled them in on the night's quarreling. She said that a number of things sparked the rough night; Rudy's recent purchase of six vicious falcons he planned to keep as pets, his long hours away from home and her anxiety over the future of *Hooded Falcon*.

George listened to Natacha and swallowed his fear that she or Rudy would learn of J.D. Williams double-cross before he could negotiate a new contract for Rudy. He did not tell Natacha that at that moment he knew her *Hooded Falcon* was a doomed project nor did he tell her he was already in negotiations with another production company. By the time *The Cobra* wrapped, he hoped to have a brand new contract ready for Rudy to sign with Joe Schenck's United Artists Studios.

On that Christmas morning, Rudy and Natacha believed the future of Rudy's independent film career was still rosy and the truth was no one doubted he reigned unchallenged as "King of the Movies". American women were completely under his spell and no movie star was more dreamed upon that Christmas Eve than Rudolph Valentino. But unknown to his adoring public, he had just spent that night catching a terrible cold, arguing for hours with his wife and sniffling his way across his living room floor with an oil can and a screw driver.

He had labored until dawn constructing an expensive toy train by linking the intricate fastenings of the metal track and wiring several transformers. Natacha fumed over her husband's extreme effort but at last the entire living room floor was covered with several tiny villages and two trains steaming around miniature bends whoo-whooing right on cue.

By the time the sun rose on that Christmas morning, an exhausted Uncle Rudy had blown his nose beet red as he stood like some great giant surveying his impeccable countryside on the living room floor. He gave a call to the Ullmans and Natacha that everything was finally ready. Santa Claus really came through for the Ullman boys that year. Baby Bobby was too young to remember the sight of the magnificent train, but Danny never forgot it.

Chapter Thirteen

The Kestral Feed

Peregrine falcons eat song birds that chirp on swaying branches. As raptors they neither flit nor warble from treetops but swoop down upon their fellow birds to exact a not-so-neat kill. Master falconers devote long hours to training these predators to resist a natural instinct to slash at their prey with their razor sharp talons. If these wary handlers are successful in their efforts, falcons learn to return their lifeless quarry intact.

In January of 1925, the arrival of six Peregrine falcons at 6774 Wedgwood Place had every resident of the neighborhood on edge. This was not due to any negligence on behalf of their trainer. The six birds were accustomed to being blinded by a leather hood while perching on their master's gauntlet until the moment of their release. The residents of Wedgwood Place jittered because the falcons' new owner, Rudolph Valentino had yet to be instructed in the art of handling the no nonsense birds.

In anticipation of the falcon's appearance in *The Hooded Falcon*, a master falconer was summoned to the Valentino residence to bring Rudy up to speed. But as Rudy was spending most of his time on the set of *The Cobra*, the grisly chore of feeding his falcons was delegated to his nervous household staff. They signed for L.B. Nolte Poultry's deliveries of one hundred pound lots of sacrificial feeder chickens and gasped in horror as the poor birds were shredded the moment they were heaved into the hungry falcons' aviary.

While the falcons awaited their introduction to their new master, he was doing his level best to ensure his first independently produced film, *The Cobra* be worthy of his top billing. He was also preoccupied with the purchase of a larger home for himself, his wife Natacha and their ever-expanding menagerie. Only two months after their return to Los Angeles, Rudy and George were closing a deal on a two year old Mediterranean home situated high above Los Angeles on a five and a half acre hillside lot at 2 Bella Drive in Beverly Hills. As soon as Rudy assumed ownership of the property, he initiated such extensive renovations that it would be months before the new home could be readied for occupancy. The six peregrine falcons inspired him to name his future residence, Falcon Lair.

Despite George's insistence that the renovations were far too ambitious, Rudy embarked upon the creation of an estate rivaling the Hudnut's Foxlair. As the heavy machinery began wending its way up the steep road to the property, residents along Bella Drive surmised correctly their future neighbors were spending a fortune on the reconstruction. In fact by January of 1925, the renovation of Falcon Lair was not the only outrageous expenditure contributing to Rudy's soaring financial overhead.

George's accounting ledgers recorded each payment made to the growing Valentino household staff which included a domestic couple, a handyman, a chauffeur, a groomsman, a gardener, three publicity men, a secretary, a clerk-typist, several lawyers and two bootleggers. In addition to paying the new monthly mortgage payment on Falcon Lair, George also issued checks for mortgage payments on the Valentino's home on Wedgwood Place and Aunt Teresa Werner's Los Angeles home on Sycamore Street.

He dispatched regular bank drafts to Alberto Valentino in response to his frequent letters requesting money and more bank drafts were issued to finance Rudy's latest investment; a dry-cleaning plant, Ritz Cleaners. The cleaning business rarely turned a profit and required monthly subsidy. George also dispatched monthly checks to scientists Albert Lambert and Jean Gautier to fund their Cosmic Arts laboratory.

While endeavoring to keep all Valentino household accounts in perfect order, George issued more checks to Griffith Park to pay the boarding fees for Rudy's horses, to the Italian Store for weekly groceries, to Western Hay and Grain, the Union Ice Company, Chris Schirch's Meat Market and a range of other miscellaneous accounts. He did his best to chip away at the exorbitant credit charges made by both Rudy and Natacha for their purchases of antiques, clothing, furniture, artwork and expensive foreign automobiles. Consequently, George was understandably nervous to learn of Rudy's plans to excavate an underground tunnel passageway between Falcon Lair's main house and its servant's quarters. After hearing how Rudy was also installing a steel reinforcement wall to shore up the property's hillside in the event of heavy rains, George had no lingering doubt that Rudy's Ritz-Carlton Pictures paychecks were being stretched perilously thin.

While George worried over his bottom line, Rudy and Natacha were busy planning a vacation to Palm Springs as soon as filming on *The Cobra* was completed. Throughout *The Cobra*'s production, George and Natacha never wavered in their original opinion that J.D. Williams' choice of this particular screenplay was a lousy one for Rudy. Despite this, they were heartened by the fact that William Cameron Menzies' set designs and Harry Fischbeck's innovative photographic techniques ensured the film would at least be an esthetic gem. Although they were pleased with the soft visual effects created by Fischbeck's recently patented camera device, both George and Natacha felt the contemporary settings and Rudy's modern wardrobe were an unsettling contrast to his previous costumed roles.

In *The Cobra*, Rudy played the role of an Italian Count and antique dealer who immigrates to America where he engages in a torrid love affair with his friend and sponsor's wife. The unfaithful wife was played by Nita Naldi who reprised her role as the moral downfall of her leading man. Unfortunately, the film's script never rose above uneventful parlor yarn and despite Fischbeck's slick visuals, the plot line and the direction of the film bordered on rigor mortis. Wide, wooden tableaux shots captured Rudy seated awkwardly behind an office desk. Only in the film's one brief historical flashback was Rudy granted the opportunity to sport his infamous goatee and revive a few moments of his familiar gallant yet menacing screen persona.

In a valiant attempt to animate the stilted screenplay, Rudy arrived on *The Cobra*'s set each morning toting sheets of paper covered with his handwriting. Apparently the film was receiving directorial assistance from master guide, Black Feather. Rudy alleged he had been psychically transcribing the reams of suggestions the previous evening.

By early March, filming on *The Cobra* was at last complete and Natacha and Rudy drove to Palm Springs and the home of their friend Dr. Florilla White. Before they could unpack their bags, Rudy received an urgent phone call from George in Los Angeles. He informed Rudy that J.D. Williams had officially closed Ritz-Carlton Pictures. George quickly added that he was about to finalize negotiations on a new contract for him with Joe Schenck's United Artists Studios.

Rudy was undoubtedly aware George had been negotiating with United Artists long before he and Natacha left for Palm Springs.

For when he passed the breaking news along to his wife, he appeared visibly calm. By contrast, Natacha reacted with disbelief and left immediately to drive back to Los Angeles, alone. While she grew angrier at J.D. Williams, George and Rudy with each passing mile, Rudy was saddling up one of Dr. White's horses and preparing for a long ride into the canyons.

❧❧

Only a few hours after hearing the news of the dissolution of Ritz-Carlton Pictures, Natacha was standing face to face with George in his office. She would later spin the details of this meeting to the press as having been a civil exchange in which she told George she understood why he initiated negotiations with Schenck without her knowledge. In fact, the meeting was an angry showdown.

When she demanded to know precisely why J.D. Williams folded Ritz-Carlton Pictures, she received what she considered to be evasive and vague answers. As George tried to distract her by laying out the terms of Rudy's prospective contract with Joe Schenck, Natacha suspected her husband had been aware of these negotiations all along. She became even more infuriated when George revealed that all production on *Hooded Falcon* had been suspended. Despite this bitter and devastating disappointment, Natacha could not dispute George's argument that any interruption in her husband's income would be calamitous.

If Rudy signed the contract with Schenck's production company, she knew he would join a prestigious lineup of stars and his future films would benefit from the studio's superior production standards. But as George itemized each term of Joe Schenck's prospective contract, Natacha became even more irate learning she was not included in any executive capacity in the production of Rudy's projected films with United Artists. She railed at George for what she perceived as an oversight and insisted he inform Schenck at once that Rudy would never sign such a contract without acknowledgment of her executive role. George assured her he would speak to Schenck about amending the contract and with this Natacha stormed out of George's office to drive straight back to Palm Springs.

In the spring of 1925, it was relatively unheard of for a movie star to receive a percentage of their film's profits. If Rudy did sign the contract George was finalizing with Schenck, he would not only receive his stipulated salary, but nearly fifty percent of the profits from two films produced within the next year.

After George's fiery meeting with Natacha, he met once again with Schenck to finalize the contract which contained several groundbreaking terms. Rudy would appear in two movies of not less than five reels, no more than ten reels and be guaranteed he would be consulted regarding the choice of both screenplays. In addition to Rudy's impressive fifty percent of the profits, he would receive a salary of $100,000.00 per film. He would receive this $100,000.00 as follows; for the first of these two films he would receive $50,000.00 cash upon signing the contract and another $50,000.00 upon completion of the film. For his work in the second film, he would receive a weekly paycheck of $10,000.00 which would be deposited in his bank account every Saturday morning. Upon the completion of the second film, if Rudy's salary totaled less than $100,000.00, the balance would be paid in full. Rudy would also receive an additional $50,000.00 if production costs for each of these films totaled less than $400,000.00.

According to the stipulations of the contract, Rudy's promotional appearances with his co-stars would be optional and he would have approval of the film's publicity and promotional materials. Joe Schenck's mighty contract hinged upon one clause; if Rudy suffered any physical disfigurement the contract was considered null and void. Other than this unthinkable occurrence there were two troublesome omissions in the contract's final draft.

Even though Joe Schenck was essentially offering Rudy the potential of becoming a millionaire within the next calendar year, the contract did not provide for Rudy's artistic control over either film made with United Artists. Schenck reserved ultimate authority over any production disputes and refused to cede control to Rudy. Schenck would not budge on these points saying he would not tolerate excessive production expenditures or delays in shooting schedules. Despite Natacha's insistence that George negotiate a revised contract which included her role in Rudy's films, her name was not mentioned within the text of the final document.

However, if Rudy signed with United Artists, his contract would be assigned ownership to his corporate alter ego, Cosmic Arts laboratory. Joe Schenck may have eliminated Natacha's direct hands-on involvement in her husband's United Artists' films, but as sole stock holder of Cosmic Arts, Inc. she would still technically own his contract.

Any artistic input on her behalf would have to be tactfully executed behind the scenes.

After returning to Palm Springs, Natacha began to fully grasp the terms of the United Artists' contract and consequently her vacation with her husband became anything but restful. The more she seethed, the more Rudy paced. The reality that he was about to sign a contract which essentially eliminated his beautiful and talented wife from any executive role in his films began to take a toll on both of them. Their vacation became one of long, deadly silences and tense exchanges as they dreaded George's notice that the final draft of the contract was ready for Rudy's signature. While they awaited his telephone call, Rudy avoided his furious wife by saddling up another horse and disappearing on the trails behind Dr. White's residence. Even in the solitude of the rocky mountain paths, he could not escape the nagging thoughts of his spiking overhead. He knew that despite Natacha's protests, he had no other option but to sign on the dotted line.

On March thirtieth, the Valentinos drove home to Los Angeles so Rudy could sign his new contract with United Artists Studios as well as a separate distributing contract with United Artists Corporation. He and Natacha then returned to Palm Springs leaving George to transact the receipt of Rudy's first paycheck of $50,000.00 and prepare the contract for assignment of ownership to Cosmic Arts.

A few days later, George was hard at work in his office when he received a desperate telephone call from Rudy. He told George that Natacha was so angry at him for signing the United Artists' contract that she was barely speaking to him. He added that Natacha had requested he drive to Palm Springs immediately to speak with her. It was then George's turn to make the two hour drive across the desert and on this occasion it was in the midst of a torrential rainstorm. After the treacherous drive along a flooded highway, George arrived to find Natacha curled up on a divan nursing a sprained knee. He noticed Rudy appeared unusually exhausted and depressed.

Within minutes of George's arrival, Natacha launched into a lengthy explanation of her plans to produce her own independent movie. She told George she could finance this film in part from Rudy's $50,000.00 from United Artists, in part by securing a loan using the new contract as collateral and in part by hiring her friends in the movie business to work at cost. Her new project would be titled *What Price Beauty* as a spoof of the cosmetics industry and the extreme measures women go to in their quest to look beautiful.

For a few moments George was speechless by the whole idea. He had barely deposited Joe Schenck's first check and he could not help but perceive Rudy's complete resignation to fund such a project as nothing more than a last ditch attempt to contain Natacha's fury. George took a deep breath and explained to Natacha that he did not see how he could raise more than $30,000.00 for such a film. She assured him that she would be thrifty and $30,000.00 would be more than sufficient. While George continued to explain how securing a distribution agreement for the film should be her first and primary order of business, Natacha gathered up a stack of her notes and sketches for his perusal. With her story outline and a list of prospective cast members in hand, George then left to drive home to Los Angeles.

He managed to fund Natacha's new brainchild and secured the start-up capital for *What Price Beauty* by investing some of his own money and signing for several loans in his name. With Nita Naldi cast in the film's lead role and another of Natacha's protegees, aspiring actress, Myrna Loy, cast in a minor role, filming began on *What Price Beauty* only a few weeks after the Valentino's return from Palm Springs.

On April twenty-first, Rudy's new contract was assigned to Cosmic Arts' ownership, just as he was preparing to begin work in his first film with United Artists, *The Eagle*. *The Eagle* was the screen version of Alexander Pushkin's novel, *Dubrovsky* and the story of a Russian Robin Hood. It was an exceptional vehicle for Rudy and in his role as Lieutenant Dubrovsky he appeared in full Cossack costume and rode in thrilling pursuit of a fair damsel played by blonde Hungarian beauty, Vilma Banky. George signed Clarence Brown as *The Eagle's* director after negotiating with Brown's wife and business manager, Ona.

Rudy's arrival on the set of *The Eagle* was highly anticipated by everyone working on the United Artists' Studio lot. Even though movie star's on-site private bungalows were a rarity at the time, Joe Schenck ordered the construction of luxurious accommodations for the star of *The Eagle*. Conveniently for Rudy, just as his home fires began flaring a bit too hot, he was able to retreat to his brand new studio bungalow hideaway.

As Natacha's hours on the set of *What Price Beauty* grew longer, her husband took to brooding in her absence. The conspicuous tension between the two erupted frequently into loud quarreling which was inevitably followed by days of bitter silence. Natacha grew weary of her husband's wandering eye and late nights in his bungalow and she began to distance herself from the painful situation. If Rudy hoped that funding *What Price Beauty* might ease his escalating marital rift, his plan was about to fail miserably.

❦

In the aftermath of one particularly angry spat, George watched a visibly trembling Natacha marking her script on the set of *What Price Beauty*.

"Why, Natacha?" he lamented, "When almost every woman in the world would like to have Rudy, yet you..."

Natacha cut George off mid-sentence to deliver a tirade he had heard too many times before. She demanded to know why he and Rudy negotiated the contract with Joe Schenck behind her back and why she was not included in some executive capacity. George explained one more time how his negotiations with Schenck had been difficult and pointed out it was because of her and Rudy's extravagant lifestyles that the contract had been a necessity. Quite frankly, he told her, Rudy had to work. George outlined Schenck's reasons for her exclusion, but his conversation with Natacha flared into more argument. Despite George's appreciation of Natacha's "very pretty mouth", he was always taken aback when she let loose with a barrage of expletives.

It took a while for Natacha to come to terms with the full extent of her excommunication from her husband's career. When several United Artists' writers met with Rudy at Wedgwood Place to work on *The Eagle*'s screenplay, Natacha sat in on their meetings. Her many suggestions exasperated the writers, who marched straight back to Joe Schenck with their protests. This prompted Schenck to issue his final ultimatum; this time in writing. His note was addressed to George and reiterated that in light of United Artists' substantial investment in *The Eagle* no costly delays or interference in the work of the studio's writers would be tolerated. Schenck added that Natacha was to have nothing to do with the film's production and from that day forward she would not be allowed to step foot on the United Artists' lot.

Natacha's unconditional banishment from her husband's workplace only exacerbated the stress of her daily life as production costs on her film *What Price Beauty* began to soar. More battles raged in the Valentino household and this prompted Natacha to work even

259

later on the set of *What Price Beauty* and Rudy to spend more time in his new United Artists' bungalow. Chafing at each others prolonged absences and lack of attention, they were never in much of a hurry to return home.

It was about this time, Spanish portrait artist Federico Beltran-Masses arrived in Los Angeles. Rudy and Natacha met Senor Beltran-Masses in Seville during happier times and they had extended an invitation to visit them in California. Unaware of the bad timing of his visit, Beltran-Masses moved into Wedgwood Place to join George and Aunt Teresa as one more ineffectual peace broker. In spite of Southern California's unusually warm temperatures that summer, by the time filming began on *The Eagle* on June sixth, there was a chill in the Valentino household which no amount of tactful diplomacy could thaw.

Rudy was focused on his work in *The Eagle* and despite Joe Schenck and George's protests he insisted upon performing his own stunt riding. The film's opening scene called for his scrambling over a team of run-away horses in an attempt to grab hold of the reins. This reckless stunt resulted in such a thrashing, that Rudy limped about sore and bruised for weeks. According to his co-workers, he was focused on more than stunt riding on the set of *The Eagle*. As Natacha grew more aloof by the day, Rudy turned a wandering eye upon his vivacious co-star Vilma Banky.

While Rudy and Vilma Banky were clicking on the set of *The Eagle*, Natacha confided in Aunt Teresa saying she felt her marriage was in serious trouble. She told her doting auntie that since she was barred from visiting *The Eagle*'s set, she had resorted to dispatching handyman Lou Mahoney to keep an eye on her husband. Indeed Natacha's devoted handyman arrived at Rudy's bungalow on a range of excuses and random errands and had no trouble listening in on "Mr. Ullman" and "Mr. Valentino's" private conversations. After witnessing Rudy's flourishing social life on the set, Lou quickly took sides in the Valentino's deteriorating domestic state of affairs.

It was not long before Lou developed a fierce loyalty to the beguiling mistress of the household. Unable to find the meekest fault with "Mrs. Valentino", he blamed the couple's intensifying marital distress squarely upon his famous boss Mr. Valentino and his manager, George Ullman. In George's role as overlord of the Valentino's staff, he was often subjected to the insubordinate handyman's protests. Lou grew to harbor resentment towards "Mr. Ullman" and perceived him as the infuriating comptroller of the household. But Lou was unaware that in the actual chain of command it was Rudy who gave George his orders. It was in this manner that Rudy's gracious rapport was maintained with not only Lou, but the entire household staff.

Nevertheless, Lou was soon returning from his errands to Rudy's United Artists' bungalow with earfuls of fresh gossip for Natacha. While he kept her well informed of her husband's activities, he also exploited her growing resentment of George's influence over her husband. Reinforcing this reliable wedge, Lou informed Natacha that Mr. Ullman was trying to break up her marriage. As Natacha grew increasingly dependent upon her handyman for information, his inflated perception of his role in the household grew. Under less emotionally raw circumstances she might have recognized Lou's ire towards George as having been rooted in a volatile management and labor dispute. But Natacha was vulnerable in her depreciating situation, desperate for information from the set of *The Eagle* and listening carefully to anything Lou had to say. In a familiar good cop, bad cop routine, Lou relayed his bounty of hearsay between a grateful Mrs. Valentino and an unsuspecting Mr. Valentino.

As filming on *What Price Beauty* neared completion, Natacha toyed with the idea that perhaps a yacht might be the solution to her melancholy. Rudy was still optimistic he could smooth things over with his distant wife and purchased, on credit, a thirty-two foot Fellowcraft cabin cruiser. The luxury craft, christened "The Phoenix", provided no peace of mind for Natacha and the $330.00 monthly payment to the Seaboard National Bank and the steep California Yacht Club's slip fee just became more drain on the straining bank account. It would be Rudy and not Natacha who spent time at sea aboard the Phoenix.

With renovations on Falcon Lair still weeks away from completion and tensions at home becoming unbearable, Rudy moved into his imperial bungalow on the set of *The Eagle*. He appointed his home away from home with comfortable easy chairs, velvet rugs and bookcases laden with armor, swords and autographed pictures of his movie star friends.

His tasteful bungalow became such a popular haunt, that lunch with Valentino, as prepared by his private cook, became a highly coveted invitation. Lou's colorful accounts to Natacha of Rudy's bungalow lunches only aggravated the Valentino's precarious home life. Nevertheless, Lou dutifully passed along news of Vilma Banky's revelation that filming on *The Eagle* had to be halted several times a day to remove Rudy's female fans from the set. Natacha was aware of this rash of Rudy's emotionally charged female stalkers. These women had become such a persistent threat on the set of *The Eagle* that George expanded his role as manager to that of personal bodyguard and began carrying a loaded handgun. An unnerved Rudy purchased a few handguns himself. Instead of the antique weapons he typically collected, these were modern, efficient and deadly firearms.

Some of Rudy's love-struck fans went to great lengths to maneuver him into compromising situations. One of the more intrepid stalkers on the set of *The Eagle* was a pretty, young woman whom George first discovered hiding in Rudy's bungalow. He delivered his sternest warning to the woman and threatened to have her arrested on the spot if she ever trespassed again. He then summoned the studio's security guards and identified the woman as a dangerous trespasser. Despite the threat of arrest, over the next few days the woman was removed repeatedly from the premises. One evening as George and Rudy entered the bungalow, the same woman bolted out from behind a rack of costumes.

She shrieked at Rudy and claimed if he didn't give her a role in *The Eagle* she would tell the local newspapers he raped her in his bungalow that very night. Before the woman could finish her harangue, George grabbed her by the arm, dragged her out the door and handed her over to studio security. One hour later, George answered the bungalow's telephone to hear the editor of *The Los Angeles Times* on the line. Apparently Rudy's stalker followed through on her threat by going directly to the newspaper with every detail of her alleged humiliating sexual assault that evening at the hands of Rudolph Valentino. The editor knew well enough to place a call to George who explained the situation and killed the woman's story.

During the first weeks of July, Natacha's nocturnal absences from home became so frequent that house guest Federico Beltran-Masses suggested his friend Rudy hire a private detective to follow her. In Spain, he said, that is exactly what any man in his situation would do. When George heard Beltran-Masses' suggestion, he told Rudy in no uncertain terms that hiring a detective to trail Natacha would only result in disaster. But Rudy's mind was made up and George was dispatched to hire a detective. When Rudy received the detective agency's first report of his wife's covert activities, George's worst fears realized.

On that fateful night of July 17th, 1925, most women would have gone berserk to hear Rudolph Valentino's voice on the telephone at two o'clock in the morning. Bee Ullman just yawned and mumbled to her sleeping husband,

"Rudy's on the phone."

Telephone calls from Rudy in the dead of night were not an uncommon occurrence in the Ullman household but this was more than the usual rude awakening.

"She isn't home yet, George!" Rudy spit out his words, "And when she gets here I'm going to kill her!"

George mumbled a few words of reassurance and hung up the telephone. He pulled on a pair of golf knickers, an old sweater and some tennis shoes and hurried out of the house. As he backed his car down the driveway and onto Foothill Road, he just hoped he would arrive in time.

As he sped down Sunset Boulevard, he regretted ever agreeing to hire the detective agency. Rudy shared the agency's first report with him that afternoon; a lengthy account reporting how Natacha spent the afternoon alone with a cameraman in a private bungalow. Just as George feared, Rudy became so enraged by the contents of the report that he began drinking heavily and working himself into a full-blown homicidal rage. Rudy knew the cameraman mentioned in the detective's report and also knew he was a married man with four children.

When George turned his car into the Wedgwood Place driveway, he spotted Rudy pacing in the driveway. He caught the glint of a revolver in his hand and slammed on the brakes, his car screeching to a halt in a spray of gravel. Without pausing to shut the car door he headed straight for Rudy.

"Give me that gun! God damn it! Don't be an idiot!"

Rudy put up a fight and continued yelling, "I'll kill her, George. I swear I'll kill her!"

The two men grappled for the weapon, but George being the stronger of the two quickly gained control of the thirty-eight caliber Smith and Wesson. After shoving Rudy inside the house, George cocked the barrel of the gun to find that it was indeed fully loaded. As he slid the six bullets from the spinning chamber and slipped them into the pocket of his knickers, Rudy began lugging a large armchair across the darkened living room. He positioned the chair to face out the front window and for the next hour he did nothing but sit staring straight ahead, half-listening to George's calculated small talk. It was around three a.m. when the long beams of headlights swept across the living room wall. Natacha's car was pulling into the driveway. George ceased his banter and careful not to set off the hair trigger seated in the easy chair, he said in low voice,

"Don't move, Rudy. You stay right here."

Rudy did not flinch.

When George appeared in the driveway to greet Natacha in the middle of the night, she acted as if nothing was amiss and commented on his sporty knickers and tennis shoes.

"Aren't you the country gentleman, George," she purred.

Without saying a word, George escorted her into the foyer. But before he could warn Natacha about the imminent threat awaiting her inside, Rudy made his entrance, tearing down the stairs from a second floor bedroom with another revolver in his hand. A scuffle ensued before Rudy surrendered his second loaded gun of the night. Facing his wife unarmed did nothing to diminish Rudy's rage and when she strolled calmly past him to enter the living room he stormed after her demanding, "Where have you been? Tell me! Where have you been?"

Natacha dismissed her husband with a light excuse by explaining she had only been matching frames at the studio. Before she could finish her sentence, Rudy raised his fist in the air and bellowed,

"You dirty liar! You god damned dirty liar!"

Before George could make a move, Rudy leveled his clenched fist in a furious crack across Natacha's face. She absorbed the blow with a forced lack of reaction and continued with the explanation of her whereabouts in her silkiest voice. This only further infuriated Rudy and he continued shouting,

"I'll divorce you! I'll divorce you!"

By then George had hurried off to the kitchen to retrieve ice and a towel for Natacha's bleeding and swelling mouth. When he returned to the living room, he found Rudy had turned his attention from beating his wife to a frantic and irrational discussion of a property settlement and immediate divorce. He ignored George's advice that neither of them were in any condition to sign a thing that night. As Natacha pressed the ice pack against her reddened face, she assured George she was in complete agreement with Rudy. A property settlement was indeed the next order of business. She said she was through fighting and insisted he draw up some draft of a settlement immediately.

With the promise of a property settlement temporarily defusing the situation, George drove home to execute a rough document. Before he left he took Rudy aside and advised him to sleep downstairs on the sofa and not get into bed with Natacha until things cooled down. Rudy nodded in agreement and George headed home where he spent the remainder of the night laboring over a preliminary property settlement. Early the next morning, with the papers in hand, he drove back to Wedgwood Place.

The alarmingly sunny sight that greeted him when he entered the Valentino's home that morning caused his exhaustion to hit him full force. Rudy and Natacha were cooing affectionately over a cozy breakfast. They demonstrated little interest in George's sketchy property settlement and instead invited him to join them for coffee. After the baffling breakfast, Rudy took George aside to explain that soon after he left the previous night, he and Natacha reconciled and spent the night in bed together "making up."

George was dumbfounded, listening to what he perceived as evidence of Rudy's sheer gullibility. As Rudy went on and on claiming how Natacha explained to him that she had just been advising the married, father of four on his marital problems, George knew it would not be long before he would see through his wife's obvious bluff. Just as he expected, it wasn't long before Rudy and Natacha's tumble-down marriage returned to its volatile worst.

On August thirteenth, less than one month after Rudy's assault and battery on his wife, George and Natacha met at Wedgwood Place at precisely two o'clock in the afternoon. George arrived directly from his son Bobby's second birthday party and came armed with a briefcase crammed with papers ready for Natacha's signature. The documents were in essence her pink slip and outlined the incorporation of Rudy's new corporate alter ego, Rudolph Valentino Productions.

Upon Natacha's signature, ownership of Rudy's United Artists' contract would then be transferred from Cosmic Arts, Inc. to his new production company. As George laid the papers before Natacha one by one, she signed her ownership of Cosmic Arts' stock over to Rudolph Valentino Productions. One document read that as owner of Cosmic Arts, Incorporated, Rudolph Valentino had become "dissatisfied with the management" of his laboratory, namely his wife Natacha, and that her signature signified her "voluntary surrender of her stock holdings and any future interest in Rudolph Valentino Productions." From that day forward, Rudy and George would conduct all of their business, without Natacha, under the corporate umbrella of Rudolph Valentino Productions.

The agenda for the remainder of that day included a carefully choreographed appearance by Rudy and Natacha at the train station where they would announce their marital vacation. Natacha would deliver a statement, as prepared by George, stating she was traveling to New York with her Aunt Teresa to seek a distributor for her film, *What Price Beauty* and then on to France to visit her mother. She would also announce that as George Ullman had business to attend to in New York, he would be accompanying her and Aunt Teresa on the journey east.

The entire plan would be carried out without a hitch. Early in the evening of August thirteenth, the Valentinos' were chauffeured from their Whitley Heights home to the train station in their Isotta Fraschini town car. Before press and photographers they behaved as a couple embarking on a brief and amicable separation as they affectionately kissed each other goodbye. What was not known to the press or anyone present that day; this would be Rudy and Natacha's last kiss and they would never see each other again. The crowd at the station that evening was also unaware that only a few hours earlier Rudy had already divorced his wife from his business affairs by stripping her of any legal involvement in his career.

They issued their separate statements; Rudy stated his plans for an amicable marital vacation and Natacha showed less restraint when she informed the press,

"...When a husband and wife are both possessors of temperaments, I think they should have a vacation from each other. Since I've begun making my own pictures, we have been drawn more or less apart, and I can't find the time to devote to the home that I used to. My husband is a great lover of home life...With butlers and super-butlers, maids and the rest, what work is there for a housewife? I won't be a parasite. I won't sit and twiddle my fingers, waiting for a husband who goes to the lot at 5:00 a.m., and gets home at midnight and receives mail from girls in Oshkosh and Kalamazoo..."

Whatever the public believed to be the actual circumstances contributing to the Valentino's separation, only George, Rudy and Natacha knew the facts; a cuckolded Rudy separated from his wife because he caught her in the act and then attempted to kill her for a betrayal he considered unforgivable. As the train carrying Natacha, Aunt Teresa and George made its way towards New York, angry telegrams between Rudy and Natacha continued to be dispatched and received in every city along the way.

It was not long after Natacha left Los Angeles that Rudy finally moved into Falcon Lair. Natacha would never spend a single night in the home in which Rudy hoped to raise his brood of children and live happily ever after with his adoring wife at his side. Instead, his extensively renovated new home became an opulent tomb. He consoled himself by taking a few painting lessons from house guest Federico Beltran-Masses and initiating more renovations on the property.

Three thousand miles away, Natacha changed her plans to travel directly on to France and asked George to secure work for her in New York. Before George returned to the west coast, he turned the matter of Natacha's possible employment over to a friend who found a role for her in a movie scheduled to begin production later that fall. Natacha's stage debut would be in the aptly titled production of *When Love Grows Cold*.

Instead of waiting in New York for her work in *When Love Grows Cold* to begin, Natacha then sailed for France. When she arrived at the chateau in Juan les Pins, she related the depressing tale of Rudy's physical abuse to her mother Muzzie, but made no mention of her affair with the married cameraman. This prompted Muzzie to wire furious telegrams to her son-in-law in Los Angeles. Muzzie's invectives stung Rudy, but he could not bring himself to reveal the truth about her daughter's infidelity. His mother-in-law was not the only person with scant information about the truth of his separation from Natacha.

Fan magazines and the press were busy second guessing the Valentinos' split. Did Mrs. Valentino refuse to stay at home and bear her husband's children? Was the Sheik unfaithful to his wife with one of his beautiful leading ladies? In every account one theme was consistently reported; without his wife, Rudolph Valentino was sad, depressed and rattling about his new home. This was not exactly the case.

On the night of August 22, only nine days after Natacha's departure from Los Angeles, Rudy was cited for his excessive speeding along Santa Monica Boulevard in his Voison roadster. According to the police officer who pulled him off the road that night, Rudy's lady friend was visibly intoxicated and leaning on his shoulder while another tipsy couple occupied the back seat. The officer noted on his citation that Rudolph Valentino and everyone in his party were "noticeably under the influence of alcohol." It seemed Rudy was not particularly as housebound with grief over his "marital vacation" as the public was being led to believe. Only a week and a half into his new found bachelorhood, Rudy was already sowing some wild oats.

On one sultry August afternoon, the engines of his yacht, the Phoenix churned through the waters of the Pacific Ocean just off the shore of Catalina Island. At the helm of the vessel was make-up artist, Mont Westmore. Below the craft's polished deck "The Great Lover" was engaged in precisely the avocation his international reputation was founded upon; some great loving. Mont Westmore shifted in his seat, tried to ignore the sounds of love making and kept his eyes focused on the horizon. With Rudy in his stateroom's master bed was his voluptuous co-star, Nita Naldi.

After sharing many on-screen steamy embraces and back breaking kisses as co-stars, Nita and Rudy tumbled into a ready heap when the big moment finally arrived. Unfortunately for Nita, she misinterpreted Rudy's spontaneous love making as a more meaningful act than his own sexual gratification. For no sooner did the Phoenix dock that afternoon than Rudy dropped Nita Naldi like yesterday's vamp. Hell hath no fury like a co-star scorned, and Nita responded to Rudy's rejection by delivering a fatal blow to the Valentino's marriage. She blurted out to Rudy that during his marriage to Natacha, his wife aborted three of his children. In fact, Nita said, she even accompanied Natacha to one of the procedures. This tragic allegation flat-lined any lingering hope of reconciliation between Rudy and Natacha.

The alleged abortions sparked another furious exchange of telegrams between Rudy and Natacha and she seized the highly charged moment to announce to the press that she was about to write a tell-all book about her life with Rudy. Publicity photos were snapped as she sat poised before a typewriter preparing to spill her guts to the world. By the end of August as final retakes of *The Eagle* were being filmed, Rudy was spiraling out of control and indulging himself in more wine, women and wee hours speeding along the highway.

He crashed one vehicle into a tree and ran another into a telephone pole on Western Avenue. Joe Schenck grew anxious about the emotional state of his box office star and George grew red-eyed and sleep deprived struggling to prevent news of Rudy's run-ins with the law from appearing in newspapers. By then Rudy had lost all interest in Cora McGeachy's telegrams relaying sage advice from Black Feather and Mesolope and her many, many telegrams remained unopened. In an attempt to vent his anger and frustration over his failed marriage and his wife's possible abortions, Rudy spent hours every day lifting weights and slamming his fists into a swinging punching bag. His biceps and forearms grew at an alarming rate and he no longer held the slightest interest in maintaining his public image as Natacha's faithful husband. Bee Ullman noticed that "Rudy always had a girl on his arm" and when she and George met him one Friday night for the regular boxing match at the American Legion Arena, Rudy arrived with a date; his *Eagle* co-star, Vilma Banky.

Despite attorney Raymond Stewart's and George's heartfelt advice that hurried, drastic legal actions were inevitably short-lived, Rudy's mind was made up. He demanded that a new "Last Will and Testament" be executed. Raymond Stewart had the various documents delivered to Rudy's office where they remained for a few days before he finally affixed his signature and summoned a few witnesses. When he signed his new will and the list of itemized instructions for George on September 1st, Rudy bequeathed his entire estate to his sole heir, a twelve year old boy a half a world away in Italy. He left his lawfully wedded wife Natacha, one thin dollar bill.

As soon as the documents were signed by witnesses, Rudy tossed them in his office safe and retreated to his library. There he spent the remainder of the day nursing a flask of scotch whiskey and contemplating suicide. Sometime just before midnight, as he slouched on a red Genovese velvet fifteenth century chair, he began threading six shiny bullets into the revolving barrel of his Smith and Wesson. George and house guest Federico Beltran-Masses were acutely aware of Rudy's deteriorating mental state and his heavy drinking and meticulously swept the premises clean of any firearms. They missed one.

As Rudy loaded the handgun, Beltran-Masses had already gone to bed and George had left for the night. Alone in his library, a disheveled Rudy clicked the barrel of the revolver into place and pressed the weapon to his right temple. It was at that moment Beltran-Masses, unable to sleep, headed towards the kitchen for a bite to eat. Just as he passed the library, he caught a glimpse of the back of the great chair and Rudy's arm holding the revolver to his head. Federico took a few silent steps before lunging from behind to grab Rudy's arm. The gun was surrendered as Rudy collapsed into anguished sobs.

Ten days later, Rudy was scheduled to appear in court on his August twenty-second speeding citation. In the company of one of his publicity men, he arrived in the courtroom directly from shooting retakes on the set of *The Eagle*. He was still wearing his black velvet Russian Cossack costume and limping on a cane after another fall from a horse. News that Rudolph Valentino was scheduled in court that day prompted a bank of cameramen to set up their cameras for the snap away and a gallery of woozy flappers trying their best to grab Rudy's attention. After Rudy was summoned to approach the judge, he was asked whether he had been drinking on the night in question. He answered an emphatic,

"Certainly not!"

The arresting officer disputed this claim, but was countered by Rudy's publicity man who attempted to spin the situation by suggesting that perhaps it had been garlic and not alcohol that the officer smelled on Rudy's breath. That idea had everyone in the courtroom howling with laughter as Rudy began pleading his case.

"I have a French car, your honor, a Voisin. It has on its dashboard a speedometer reading in "kilometres a l'heure" not miles per hour. I was going between forty and fifty kilometers. Was that too fast? I don't know. I was in a hurry to get home."

"So your foot was pretty heavy then?" The judge asked.

Rudy and the judge proceeded to carry on a brief discussion as to the conversion of kilometers into miles per hour and Rudy admitted he "wasn't much of a mathematician." The judge suggested that from now on he might affix a conversion table to his Voisin's dashboard.

When Rudy received his sentence, the galley of wound-up women collectively exhaled. The game, but nevertheless dashing Cossack was ordered to pay the court fifty dollars or spend five nights in jail. Rudy's publicity man paid the fine and the show was over.

Rudy did not exactly hurry home to calculate that conversion table for the Voisin. His self-destructive behavior continued and his increasingly botched attempts at being covert with his female companions thrilled Hollywood gossip columnists. Although he was still a married man, it was reported he was seen about town in the company of his *Eagle* co-star, Vilma Banky. Whether Rudy was having an affair with the Hungarian beauty or not, within the Falcon Lair household George, Beltran-Masses and Aunt Teresa knew that Vilma Banky was a frequent late night dinner guest.

It was about this same time that Beltran-Masses returned to Seville and Rudy began dating not only Vilma Banky, but Polish movie siren, Pola Negri. It was no secret around Hollywood that Pola Negri had designs on Rudolph Valentino. After several attempts to arrange an introduction, she finally met him at a costume party hosted by their mutual friend, actress Marion Davies. That night Pola wore a costume from her starring role in *Catherine the Great* and Rudy, arriving with his date Vilma Banky, was decked out in the same toreador suit of lights he wore in *Blood and Sand*. A few weeks after this initial meeting, Pola and Rudy met once again, this time on the dance floor of the Biltmore Hotel. They returned to her home where they spent the night together. From that night on, Pola became a serious contender for Rudy's attention. Despite Pola's attempts to publicly legitimize her relationship with Rudolph Valentino, behind the scenes they were on less solid ground.

Although Pola Negri hoped to become Mrs. Valentino number three, when she began dating Rudy he was still married to Natacha. George knew Rudy had no intentions of committing to a serious relationship with any one woman at that point in his life. He formed this opinion after observing Rudy's concurrent affairs with Pola Negri and with actress Mae Murray. George was not only eyewitness to Rudy's volatile relationship with Pola Negri but to a few of his intimate exchanges with Mae Murray.

One of these occasions took place on a Friday night, as George and Rudy left an American Legion boxing match where they met Mae Murray in the parking lot. Mae Murray was still married to director, Robert Leonard at the time but their marriage was on the rocks. That night in the American Legion parking lot, Rudy greeted Mae by wrapping his arms around her in a passionate embrace. While George resigned himself to the awkward moment, Rudy and Mae engaged in a heated and prolonged kiss. They became so physically engrossed in each other they forgot about George, slipped into Rudy's car and drove off. George was left standing alone in the parking lot wondering how he would get home.

Despite Rudy's continuing love affair with Mae Murray, the tenacious Pola Negri spent many nights sharing Rudy's bed at Falcon Lair. It was not long before she packed a bag of her personal belongings, including several negligees and hung them neatly in his master bedroom closet. George never said a word to Rudy about Pola's part-time residency at Falcon Lair, but her increasing presence about the house infuriated Lou Mahoney.

His bitter contempt directed at George was soon extended to Rudy's Polish mistress Pola Negri. Lou was not comfortable with the many changes in the post-Natacha household and still believed Mrs. Valentino would soon return home, reconcile with her husband and restore order.

Meanwhile, George and Rudy did their best to keep Natacha's infidelity a top secret. That October they faced a crisis when the press learned detectives stalked her before she left Los Angeles. Rumors about the Valentino's "marital vacation" were still rife and when the press was mysteriously alerted to the detective agency's involvement in the Valentino's separation, they descended upon Rudy's United Artists' bungalow. He and George dodged every question, gave no straight answers and the frustrated press could only glean that the purpose for hiring the detectives was some "closely guarded secret."

They reported how Rudy reacted angrily and "indignantly" to their questions about why detectives followed his wife and that he evaded answering their questions as to who actually hired them. When Rudy was asked if George Ullman hired the detective agency he replied,

"I know nothing of detectives and as for Mr. Ullman...what interest could he possibly have in the matter? Besides he wouldn't hire detectives without letting me know."

With this statement Rudy abruptly stormed out of his bungalow. The reporters were still not satisfied and headed for George's office where they badgered him with more questions. In a successful maneuver to deflect the heat from Rudy, George admitted he had hired the detectives.

"What for?" one reporter asked.

"I decline to go into the particulars about that," George said as he leaned back in his chair, sighed in exasperation and threw his hands up in the air. The following day, October third, the breaking news that Mrs. Rudolph Valentino had been followed by detectives was broadcast to the public. As George read about this "new mystery" in the Valentino's separation, he realized he and Rudy had dodged another bullet.

It was also in October that Rudy began spending a great deal of time at the Ullman's Foothill Road home. He visited there so often the little Ullman boys began thinking of him as just another member of the family and George wondered if Rudy was becoming more popular than he was with his sons. "Uncle Rudy" jogged around the back yard with seven year old Danny on his shoulders and little Bobby toddling along behind with his arms in the air squealing,

"Swing me up too, Uncle Rudy!"

While Uncle Rudy romped with Danny and Bobby, George was busy making travel arrangements for Rudy's impending trip east to New York and London for *The Eagle* premieres. He was also scheduling Rudy's trip to Paris where he would file for a divorce from Natacha. George was delving into another serious matter on Rudy's behalf that fall; the legal adoption of his nephew Jean. When Rudy first mentioned the adoption, George advised him that international law would reject any such application. He also told him that by law, in order to adopt Jean, Alberto would be required to surrender all parental rights to the child. George knew this would never happen. But Rudy remained determined and George was soon filing a formal petition to the Italian courts requesting Rudy be permitted to adopt Jean and bring him home to America as his own son.

Chapter Fourteen

Warning: Read This...You Could Be Sent To Prison!

Sixteen years later -

By 1941, Joe Schenck was wearing prison stripes and cracking rocks in the yard of a federal penitentiary in Danbury, Connecticut. The once powerful Hollywood mogul was serving a five year sentence on a conviction of three counts of tax evasion and one count of committing perjury to a grand jury. Joe Schenck landed behind bars after a federal investigation revealed he pocketed millions of dollars from a lucrative arrangement with the Hollywood mob.

Prior to his conviction, Joe Schenck and Chicago crime boss, Frank Nitti's Hollywood front man, Willie Bioff engaged in a profitable partnership for several years. After Nitti sent Bioff to Hollywood, Bioff assumed control over the 125,000 member union of the International Alliance of Theater Stage Employees. Recognizing Bioff as a valuable ally, Joe Schenck began contributing to his crooked operation.

Schenck's regular payoffs assured there would be no interference from the powerful union while he hired and fired at will and forced his studio employees to work long overtime hours during the height of the depression for no extra compensation. Schenck made his payments to Willie Bioff by passing cash, wrapped in brown paper packages, through a series of middlemen. While Schenck saved millions by cheating union workers out of their hard earned overtime pay, Willie Bioff enjoyed a ten-carat lifestyle. The gig was up when Schenck mistakenly made one of his payments to Bioff in the form of a personal check.

As Schenck's $100,000.00 check changed hands, someone put the two and two together. The check was forwarded to the Screen Actors Guild's President, actor Robert Montgomery and he wasted no time telephoning the Internal Revenue Service. After a thorough scouring of Schenck's books, the Feds handed down an indictment. Facing what promised to be a lengthy prison sentence, Schenck cut a deal with the Federal government and divulged every detail of the scam as he sang his heart out to a grand jury.

As a result of Schenck's testimony, every studio head in Hollywood was subpoenaed to testify in the unfolding scandal. When the dust settled, the most notorious Chicago and Hollywood mob bosses, as well as Joe Schenck were all sent off to prison. Only Frank Nitti evaded a lengthy stint in jail by putting a loaded gun to his head and blowing his brains out.

While Schenck served his hard time in a federal penitentiary, out in Hollywood his old nemesis George Ullman was facing his own brush with the law; the L.A. County Sheriff. Nearly two decades after Rudy's death, a twenty-seven year old Jean Valentino was still trying to collect on the judgment he held against George. Jean diligently ensured his collection orders never expired by instructing his attorneys to regularly file the necessary paperwork with the court and the L.A. County Sheriff's office. By Christmas time of 1941, Jean's collection orders were once again in place and the amount George owed, plus interest, totaled just over $100,000.00.

Jean steadfastly ignored the California Appeals Court's recommendation that the entire judgment against George be dismissed in light of the unusual disappearance and discovery of Paragraph Fourth. Bound and determined to collect the entire amount due, he instructed his attorneys to have at Mr. Ullman by offering them a percentage of any money they were able to collect.

Jean's legal actions resulted in years of uninterrupted property seizure and wage garnishment orders being filed against George. These court orders, declaring all of George's assets and his talent agency's profits subject to Jean's confiscation, were served on George at his agency and at his home by deputies from the L.A. County Sheriff's office. Sixteen years after Rudy's death, George was far from being a wealthy man and earning a modest income as a talent agent. The probability that Jean would ever reap his handsome windfall was slim to none. Jean remained undeterred and by 1941, he was not only intently focused upon the enforcement of his collection orders but also upon the compilation of a list of items he believed George had removed, without permission, from Falcon Lair many, many years ago.

His lengthy list, however, did not include those items that George, as executor, permitted Alberto Valentino and Maria Strada to remove from Falcon Lair after Rudy's death. These items included among other things Rudy's platinum wrist watch, a pair of platinum cuff links, a white gold cigarette case, emerald and sapphire rings and an automobile. Whether Jean was aware of the technical loophole or not, a portion of the judgment he was seeking to collect from George included the cash value for these very items George once disbursed as "unauthorized property advances". Nevertheless, Jean kept this list of items close at hand and devoted himself to the reclamation of each and every one.

With Jean's property seizure and wage garnishment orders again under full enforcement by the end of 1941, George's economic survival depended upon the vigilant defense of his personal property and agency. He incorporated his business, maintained meticulous accounting ledgers and extensive inventories of his property, while recording every household and business transaction. He was ordered by the court to regularly submit these ledgers to Jean's attorneys for review and complied upon every occasion. Completely unaware of Jean's list of missing items, George stored his remaining keepsakes from his days as Rudy's manager in two large, unremarkable wicker hampers in his garage. He paid little attention to the contents of the crates other than an occasional Sunday afternoon sentimental perusal.

Under intense scrutiny from Jean's attorneys and the L.A. County Sheriff's office, George worked every day in his Sunset Boulevard office and supported his family by securing work for the actors he represented including John Carradine, Frank Orth and Francis Lederer. The Ullman boys were by then teenagers and contributed to the family's income by working part-time jobs after school. And as soon as daughter Bunny could type, she went to work in her father's office.

On December 11, 1942, George made his first payment to Jean Valentino of just less than $6000.00. He received the funds for this payment from the final settlement of the $100,000.00 insurance bond he posted in October of 1926, as a guarantee of his performance as executor. The issuer of the bond, the Indemnity Insurance Company would have paid the entire judgment held against George had the company not gone bankrupt during the first years of the depression. Jean deposited George's check from the defunct Indemnity Insurance Company and then promptly renewed all of his collection orders on the remainder of the judgment.

By some uncharitable twist of fate, Jean's reinstatement of the collection orders cycled a few days before Christmas. This generated considerable yuletide bitterness in the Ullman household towards both Alberto and Jean Valentino. As George's steep legal fees continued to accrue, Jean's holiday collection orders eventually exacted their financial toll. In February of 1943, George filed a voluntary bankruptcy petition. When he filed for bankruptcy, the court assessed his personal liabilities at $106,000.00 and reported that he held zero assets other than his personal insurance policies and household goods which were itemized in a lengthy inventory and declared exempt from Jean's seizure.

Meanwhile, George's wicker hampers of souvenirs from his life with Rudy sat in the corner of his garage, neglected, shrouded in cobwebs and gathering dust. The crates contained a hodgepodge collection of miscellaneous artifacts including a few bundles of molding documents, envelopes crammed with photographs and letters, Rudy's several address books and other musty mementos. In 1943, the contents of these wicker hampers were of such material insignificance they did not merit the slightest mention in the extensive inventory conducted by the court at the time of George's bankruptcy petition. But this was all about to change, as George's hampers were on the verge of becoming hot property. A stranger had just arrived in Los Angeles who was about to inflate the value of those dusty containers to crown jewel status.

༺༻

One slow afternoon at the S. George Ullman Agency, George looked up from his work to see a lanky young man standing before him. He introduced himself as William Pelf and informed George he was seeking work as an actor. George motioned for him to take a seat and began asking a few stock questions.

When the young man said he had no experience in front of a camera, George replied he couldn't do a thing for him. Any other aspiring actor might have been thwarted by the agent's rejection, but William Pelf had more than a passing interest in the man behind the desk at the S. George Ullman Agency that day. He knew George Ullman was once Rudolph Valentino's business manager and closest friend and when it came to the subject of Rudolph Valentino, William Pelf was nothing if not zealous.

After arriving in Los Angeles from his home town in Ohio, Pelf quickly and quietly tracked down any of Rudolph Valentino's friends, family members, lovers and wives who might still be living in Hollywood. So when George Ullman sent Pelf on his way, the actor was hardly dismayed. He soon began stopping by the S. George

277

Ullman Agency on Sunset Boulevard for some friendly small talk with George about his old pal, Rudolph Valentino.

William Pelf would secure work in only a string of minor screen roles, but in his role as soft-spoken, affable Midwestern good guy he could have taken an Oscar home year after year. He handily charmed his way to the top in record time and found ample opportunity to hobnob with Valentino's peers of the silent movie era. He hit the golf courses and tennis courts and attended celebrity funerals just "to see who might show up". Before long he was being invited to the Ullman home and including Rudolph Valentino's manager on his growing list of new best friends.

Rudy's old guard believed they'd found a sincere friend in William Pelf. Alberto and Jean Valentino, Rudy's first wife Jean Acker, Rudy's friends Paul Ivano and Robert Florey and George and Bee Ullman all held complete faith in Pelf's genuine interest in Rudy and supported him wholeheartedly when he began collecting Valentino memorabilia. Only Pola Negri refused Pelf's overtures by bristling that he "only wanted to talk to her about Rudy."

The one missing trophy in Pelf's collection of "Valentino friends" was Natacha Rambova. He grew frustrated with his inability to connect with the elusive Rambova, as she had yet to return to the west coast. In case he did meet her, Pelf petitioned the aging Paul Ivano for a letter of introduction which might convince Rambova that he was a "good guy." Ivano obliged and Pelf carried this letter with him at all times.

William Pelf was acutely aware that when it came to befriending Alberto and Jean Valentino and George Ullman he "walked a fine line." Consequently, Pelf maintained a precarious balance between the three men. Jean's continued efforts to collect the $100,000.00 judgment from George complicated Pelf's efforts to become friendly with the warring parties. As Pelf would soon learn, he had his work cut out for him as Jean was relentless in his pursuit of the hundred grand.

In November of 1947, he petitioned the court to revoke the S. George Ullman Agency's status as a corporation and requested a complete court audit of the agency's records. Jean informed the court he believed the S. George Ullman Agency's profits "truly belonged to him." If the court ruled in Jean's favor, he could seize George's agency and its assets. The court complied and subpoenaed all of George's business records including his payroll accounts, bank statements, canceled checks and all contracts with the artists he represented. As the Christmas lights were being untangled and strung up one more time that year, George was again being served with a series of legal documents by the L.A. County Sheriff. His desk was buried under another incoming wave of notices of wage garnishment, summons to appear in court, subpoenas for documents, notices of complaints on the judgment and stipulations on the judgment.

When Jean Valentino made his Christmas 1947 raid on George's agency, the total of the judgment, including interest, had increased to nearly $120,000.00. As George gathered the subpoenaed records, he realized that in doing so many of his client's confidential contracts were about to become public record. After spending an afternoon sorting through his office files, he arrived home lugging a few heavy cardboard boxes full of paperwork. While his family wondered what he was doing, George chucked the cartons in his backyard and began tossing fistfuls of the papers into a rusty incinerator can. With the strike of a match he sent it all up in flames. The court would rule against Jean Valentino and for the time being the S. George Ullman Agency was safe from seizure.

In an effort to trim his business expenses during those leanest of years, George leased half of his Sunset Boulevard office to a fellow talent agent. Only a few days after this agent assumed occupancy of the space, George discovered that Rudy and Natacha's letters, kept in his desk drawer, had been replaced with some shoddy forgeries. George eyed his new coworker as the perpetrator of the switcheroo and showed him the door. For over twenty years George had paid little attention to his Valentino mementos, but he suddenly realized they were accruing in value. With this in mind he headed for his garage to take a closer look at the contents of those wicker hampers.

He knew that if this property did indeed have any monetary value Jean Valentino could seize and liquidate the lot into cash. Adamant Rudy's archives deserved safer guardianship, George began giving gifts of his Valentino artifacts to his friend and avid collector William Pelf. It was then George and Pelf initiated an annual tradition that would continue for many years. Every year on Pelf's birthday, June twenty-first, George arrived at Pelf's home to present him with another Valentino treasure for his collection.

Over the years, Pelf changed the direction of his Hollywood career from bit actor to successful television producer and George believed his interest in owning Rudy's possessions went well beyond any cash value. George had no idea that Jean regularly shared his "missing items list" with Pelf or that Jean claimed legal ownership of every snippet of Rudolph Valentino whether it had been in George's personal possession for decades or not. George also had no idea William Pelf was forging a solid friendship with both Jean and Alberto Valentino or that they were also handing him tidbits of Rudy.

It was only a matter of time before Jean spotted a few of the items on his list being proudly displayed in Pelf's burgeoning collection. When he confronted Pelf about the situation, Pelf informed Jean that since these items were given to him as birthday gifts from George Ullman, he would keep them for the time being. Pelf appeased Jean's ire by agreeing to bequeath the items to him when he "kicked the bucket." One of these disputed items was George's birthday gift of the last photo ever taken of Rudy which he inscribed to Pola Negri.

Pelf's private Rudy reserve continued to grow, and he deftly assumed ownership of a cache of archives including letters Rudy wrote pleading with his first wife Jean Acker to be his wife in every sense of the word, Rudy's original United Artists contract, the files of Rudy's attorney, W. I. Gilbert and Rudy's personal copy of *The Sheik* inscribed to him by the book's author, E.M. Hull.

George remained confident he was safeguarding Rudy treasures and during increasingly dark financial times he continued to deliver his remaining Valentino mementos to Pelf as birthday gifts. Collector Pelf was elated with each fresh acquisition and George believed his friendship with Pelf grew stronger and Rudy's earthly legacy secured. But even though George had worked with actors his entire career, when it came to William Pelf he failed to recognize a stellar performance.

෴

On April 15, 1952, Her Majesty Queen Juliana of the Netherlands and His Royal Highness Prince Bernhard arrived in Los Angeles for a state visit. A parade was organized for the royal couple and they rode down Broadway to City Hall in an open touring car waving to the cheering crowds lining the streets. After a visit with the mayor of Los Angeles, Queen Juliana and Prince Bernhard were given a grand tour of Metro-Goldwyn-Mayer studios by studio chief Louis B. Mayer.

Later that afternoon, the Queen and her Prince returned by motorcade to the Beverly Hills Hotel on Sunset Boulevard. Every newspaper in Los Angeles published the royal couple's itinerary days in advance of their arrival and this guaranteed crowds of Los Angelinos following their every move. By 4:15, as Queen Juliana's motorcade inched its way down Sunset Boulevard towards the Beverly Hills Hotel, the crowds of onlookers brought traffic to a standstill. In an effort to get the traffic moving again on the busy thoroughfare, the Beverly Hills Police Department dispatched a few more officers to the scene.

These reserve police officers rushed to the line of duty, waving their arms and blowing their whistles. Few people in the crowd that afternoon probably recognized two of these uniformed Beverly Hills police officers as Rudolph Valentino's manager George Ullman and his son Bob. George and Bob usually worked the night shift downtown in the city's business district, but on that afternoon they were called into emergency service as traffic cops.

The streets were a lot tamer back in 1923 when Officer George Ullman first arrived in Los Angeles. In those days signs were posted on the back of the city's streetcars warning, "Don't shoot rabbits from the rear of the platform!" and Hollywood's only traffic cop worked the corner of Hollywood and Vine. But on April 15, 1952, on the very Sunset Boulevard where he once rushed between his luxurious home on Foothill Drive and Rudy's Falcon Lair on Bella Drive, Officer Ullman waved to the stalled traffic and yelled a perfunctory, "Move it along!"

On December 2, of that same year one headline simply read, "From Bad to Worse" and apparently the reporter filing the article grasped the gist of it all. Twenty-six years after Rudolph Valentino's death, his business manager was still chin deep in hot water as a result of his tenure as the late star's executor. Jean Valentino had just renewed all of his property seizure and wage garnishment orders. Jean's attorney, Morton Feiler explained his client's recent legal action to the press by saying that the interest alone on the judgment against Ullman had reached a "tidy sum of $41,000.00".

He then reported that the total amount his client Jean Valentino was demanding from Ullman had reached $160,000.00. The attorney added that over the years George Ullman faithfully complied with every court order and had kept "his client abreast of his financial situation." He also acknowledged it was quite obvious Ullman was "unable to make good on the judgment." When one reporter asked why Jean Valentino would continue to pursue this fruitless collection process, attorney Feiler answered,

"Well, who knows, maybe Ullman will strike it rich some day!"

There was no doubt it had been a litigious year for Jean Valentino. In October of 1952, he settled out of court on another widely publicized lawsuit which he filed against independent movie producer Edward Small. Jean objected to nearly every aspect of Small's film titled, *Valentino,* by claiming he alone held exclusive publicity rights to Rudolph Valentino. The precise amount the court awarded to Jean was not disclosed but it was rumored among the press to have been nearly a half a million dollars.

While Ed Small was losing his battle in court with Jean Valentino, collector William Pelf began production on a television show for CBS titled The Schlitz Playhouse of Stars. As the show's producer, Pelf hired many of his Valentino acquaintances as well as other silent movie stars including Francis X. Bushman and Doris Kenyon. Jean Valentino was hired as a sound engineer, Rudy's one-time press agent Robert Florey hired as a director and Rudy's friend Paul Ivano as a cameraman. Rudy's first wife Jean Acker was cast as an extra in several episodes and many of the show's actors were represented by the S. George Ullman Agency. Over the next few years William Pelf produced two hundred and eight episodes of The Playhouse of Stars for "The beer that made Milwaukee famous" and the credits often read like a who's who of Rudolph Valentino's life.

Producer Pelf was acutely aware of the bitter contempt between Jean Valentino and George Ullman, and on and off the set of The Schlitz Playhouse he continued to play both sides of the contentious dispute which by then had dragged on for thirty-two long years.

ৡয়৸

In 1956, Dwight David Eisenhower sat in the Oval Office, Elvis Presley hit the record charts for the first time with "Heartbreak Hotel", *My Fair Lady* opened on Broadway and Grace Kelly married Prince Rainier of Monaco. That same year a sixty-three year old George

Ullman was finally released from any further legal entanglements with Rudolph Valentino's estate.

After working his entire career under the threat of Jean's court orders, George was about to retire. On July 17, 1956, Jean accepted a payment from George for $2500.00 and agreed to file a "Satisfaction of Judgment" with the court. George made this $2500.00 payment from funds collected from the sale of his home. With all three of the Ullman children married, George and Bee were moving into an apartment on DeLongpre Avenue in Hollywood. Upon receipt of the $2500.00, Jean and his lawyer Morton Feiler signed the document labeled "The Satisfaction of Judgment."

Although Jean told William Pelf that he "never got a thing from George Ullman," George had managed to reimburse the estate for the portion of his executor's salary which was not allowed by the court. He was not able to reimburse Jean for the cash advances he made to Alberto, Maria Strada and Teresa Werner. After decades of collection processes, Jean was at last legally free to move on and have no further interest in George Ullman. This would not be the case.

According to William Pelf, George "never shared an unkind word" with him about Alberto or Jean while they continued to speak "terribly" about him. Pelf alleged that following the 1956 settlement of the estate, Jean clung to his list of missing items and chided him every June when another item on this list seemed to appear in his collection. For over the years, George continued to arrive with another birthday gift for Pelf and each year he told the collector that he would soon have "nothing left to give."

George parted with Rudy's personal address books, his secretary's address book and more photographs and legal papers. Although Jean and Alberto were convinced George was financially benefiting from William Pelf, he was not. In fact George's family lamented his generosity with Pelf as he eventually handed the collector nearly every item he had to give. If this property had been solely of material interest to George, he would have sold it decades earlier for desperately needed cash.

Each June twenty-first, as George shared a birthday cocktail with Pelf, he had no idea that he was drinking with the enemy. For the collector had long since become a double agent vowing his primary allegiance to the Valentino family. For when it came to the subject of George Ullman, Pelf's loyalty to Alberto and Jean Valentino was steadfast and unconditional. While George believed Pelf was his heartfelt friend, he was unaware that behind his back Pelf was passing along the Valentino's disparaging reports about him. Anyone listening to Jean, Alberto or William Pelf would readily assume that the Court of Appeals never issued a complete exoneration of George's performance as Rudy's executor.

Fueled by a decades old vendetta against George, Jean signed the final Satisfaction of Judgment and then launched a retaliatory act of revenge against George Ullman. For even though court records and logic proved otherwise, Jean believed George was solely responsible for the loss of the financial worth of his inheritance. In the wake of the final settlement of the judgment, Jean continued to exact his vengeance; no longer by legal means or by waging a bare-knuckled vendetta against George but by instigating a vendetta "a viva voce"; by word of mouth. To their families, Rudy's biographers, the press and William Pelf, the name George Ullman became synonymous with nefarious bogeyman upon which all of Jean and Alberto's financial woes, past, present and future could be summarily blamed.

On the other hand, George said so little about his role as Rudy's executor and his legal involvement with the Valentino estate that his children knew next to nothing about the entire subject. He seldom mentioned the issue in the Ullman household other than an occasional "that damn Alberto". But Jean and Alberto Valentino were after all Rudolph Valentino's kin and their lineage carried weight in Hollywood. As they imparted their story of the "disreputable" and "sinister" Mr. Ullman, each publication on Valentino strayed farther and farther from the truth.

When they were interviewed by biographers, they again reported Rudy left his estate in an equitable three way split between his brother Alberto, his sister Maria and Teresa Werner. No mention was made that George was ordered to reimburse the estate an enormous amount of money that these three people personally spent, no mention was made of any embarrassing weekly stipends, of the fact that Rudy left his siblings no legal share in his estate unless Jean died before reaching the age of twenty-five and no mention was made of George's complete exoneration on the charges of fraud and mismanagement. In regards to the subject of Rudy's "Last Will and Testament", Jean and Alberto made no mention that Paragraph Fourth ever existed. They divulged nothing about this critical document which by then, for all intents and purposes, had disappeared from public access for a second time. Meanwhile, George maintained his

284

silence on the entire subject and his refusal to defend his reputation severely frustrated his family and everyone who knew him.

On yet another June twenty-first, as George rummaged in his garage for a remaining relic for his pal William Pelf's birthday gift, he made a sickening discovery. His wicker hampers had vanished without a trace and with them his few effects of his days with Rudy. But George's wicker hampers and Paragraph Fourth were not the only particulars of Rudy's legacy that were about to turn up missing.

Despite Alberto and Jean Valentino's ardent outward appearance that they were protecting Rudy's legacy through frequent litigation, in fact little about Rudolph Valentino was safe from the pilfering and no single aspect of his legacy would find safe sanctuary. Jean and Alberto's unshakable vendetta, a vengeful voice from the past, greed and rampant literary license were about to rewrite Rudolph Valentino's entire story. The real Rudolph Valentino and the real George Ullman were about to be buried deep in a bedrock of wild fabrication.

❧

On February 27, 1961, the French magazine, *La Presse* carried an anonymously written article which purported to be Rudolph Valentino's personal diary. The article expanded upon the successful diary format of ex-convict Samuel Roth's pulp fiction work, *The Intimate Journal of Rudolph Valentino*. Convinced there was more money to be made from the fictionalization of Rudy's sex life, the *La Presse* article's author expanded upon the theme by transforming Samuel Roth's heterosexual Rudy into a homosexual Rudy.

The *La Presse* author wrote Rudy into a string of exclusively homosexual scenarios. Despite the anonymous author's claims that Rudy and a male lover "made love like tigers", the alleged personal diary was never authenticated. It was difficult for anyone to believe the journal had any credibility as the inaccurate dates, locations and specifics of all of the events read as muddled fiction.

A French biographer of Valentino, Jeanne DeRecqueville issued a public challenge to the author of the *La Presse* article requesting that a single line of this alleged diary be publicly reproduced for handwriting authentication. In her Valentino biography, DeRecqueville published an authenticated letter, in Rudy's handwriting, to allow for an easy comparison. The *La Presse* article's author never came forward

285

and never produced a single line of the diary. Despite the *La Presse* article's lack of historical accuracy and the author's steadfast anonymity, the article's episodes were accepted as fact and soon quoted and referenced in future publications on Rudolph Valentino.

Five years after the publication of the *La Presse* article, a man named Chaw Mank would make a name for himself by writing undocumented fan fiction about Rudy. During the 1920's, Chaw Mank lived in Hollywood where he founded some fifty unofficial fan clubs while working as publisher and sole employee of his *Movie Fan Newsletter*. Mank boasted he mailed 25,000 letters a year to movie stars, including Rudolph Valentino, in which he requested memorabilia and answers to his questionnaires. Regarding his correspondence with Valentino, Mank would claim the star divulged confidential secrets of a graphically sexual nature to him. In light of Mank's ability to relay anything a star shared with his fan clubs via his newsletter, it is unlikely any of the movie stars did so. Nevertheless, Mank asserted Rudolph Valentino did just that.

After Mank left Hollywood, he retired to southern Illinois and a modest suburban home where he worked amidst towering stacks of papers. He accumulated his tumbling archives not only from years of organizing fan clubs, but from composing country western songs. During his career, Chaw Mank scored one country western hit titled, *"I Don't Want a Bracelet of Diamonds, I Just Want Elvis,"* and one hit book, *The Intimate and Shocking Expose of Rudolph Valentino*.

In 1965, Mank collaborated on *The Intimate and Shocking Expose of Rudolph Valentino* with self-proclaimed authority on unidentified flying objects and alien abductions, Brad Steiger. Although Brad Steiger authored books titled, *The Flying Saucer Menace* and *Flying Saucer Invasion-Target Earth* and asserted aliens attended his lectures disguised as human beings, his interest in writing about Rudolph Valentino was based upon one more down to earth fact. He believed his father-in-law was Valentino's illegitimate son.

The cover of Mank and Steiger's sensational novel screamed, *"The Shocking Expose of the Fiery Love God, Rudolph Valentino!"* The subtitle read, *"Was he Sheik or Sham?"* Mank and Steiger portrayed Rudy as a confused homosexual who lived his life as a promiscuous frequenter of gay bath houses in Hollywood where he only "resorted" to homosexuality after failing to satisfy women.

They elaborated upon one of his "humiliating failures" by portraying Rudy shedding tears of "embarrassment" and "spraying vomit in disgust" while his frustrated female sexual partner refers to him as a "god-damned queer." It was because of scenes such as these, claimed Mank and Steiger, that Rudy was "motivated into" becoming gay. They expounded at length upon Rudy's "silly" interviews before his death and implied his interest in the sport of boxing at this time in his life was only feigned as a "pathetic attempt to prove his manliness." They claimed Rudy was so emotionally weak, that he trembled in fear in Natacha Rambova's presence and that the Valentino's marriage was loveless, platonic and "arranged."

Since Chaw Mank did have a correspondence with Rudy decades earlier, as he had with fifty other movie stars, he and Steiger had some authentic material to exploit. But Rudolph Valentino could never have imagined that Chaw Mank would later splice his gracious comments, forwarded for use in *The Movie Fans Newsletter*, into an X-rated and homophobic narrative as if to imply he was personally commenting upon the text.

In the forward of their book Steiger and Mank wrote, "One never knows when a harmless bit of exaggeration may someday return to require the substantiation of an outright lie." When Brad Steiger was asked to substantiate some of these "exaggerations," he claimed the book was based solely upon Mank's own memories as "he did have extensive contacts among the Hollywood gay community at the time." Despite this, in their *Shocking Expose*, Mank and Steiger refer to homosexuals attending a tribute to Rudy as "deviates." Their book is littered with references to Rudy's "ludicrous love life" and his "unresolved sexuality," and is so sexual in content that in many libraries it is not cataloged under "Biography" but under the heading of "Human Sexuality."

Mank and Steiger's book enjoyed tremendous play, was made into a movie and became a prime reference source for further biographies published in subsequent years. Other authors expanded upon Mank's book by claiming Valentino had sexual relationships with nearly every man he met. These books also demonstrated a lack of solid documentation for any of these reports. As these books were most often presented by their authors as non-fiction, readers began believing that perhaps they were true.

Despite this, every member of Rudy's family and his personal acquaintances were frustrated with the inaccurate books. They protested the efforts of the literary opportunists who were creating an increasingly popular assertion that Rudy led his brief life as a closeted gay man.

They lived their lives in his daily presence, knew him intimately and adamantly claimed this was not Rudy's truth. Paul Ivano and Jean Acker criticized everything from the outrageously fictional books, to the anonymous articles and even the annual reveling at Rudy's mausoleum on the day of his death. Nevertheless, the smut and soft-porn about Rudy issued by Steiger, Mank and other authors continued to generate enough prurient interest to sell books and turn a profit.

Rudy's sexual orientation was not the only aspect of his life undergoing major reconstruction. By the end of the 1960's, both he and George Ullman could scarcely have undergone more thorough makeovers if they'd enrolled in witness protection plans. And with the sexploitation of Rudolph Valentino moving into high gear, Jean and Alberto's defamatory version of George's performance as the executor of Rudy's estate was about to receive a mighty assist from none other than Luther H. Mahoney.

While Jean Valentino had been pursuing his collection processes on George, Lou worked as a mechanic for the Lockheed Martin Corporation in Burbank, California. He slipped into relative obscurity after his appearance in the courtroom in 1930, and did not receive the slightest mention in any books written about Rudolph Valentino, even those published by George Ullman and Natacha Rambova.

In 1973, this would all change. It was then writer Raymond Lee conducted an interview with Lou regarding his employment with Rudolph Valentino. Lou seized the opportunity to grab the spotlight once again and handed Raymond Lee his own version of the tale; one that would warm the hearts of Jean and Alberto Valentino. Lou taped a few hours of rambling thoughts and it was from the content of these tapes that Lee wrote his article, "The Legend of Valentino" for *Movie Classics* magazine.

In his article, Raymond Lee made no reference to nearly half of Mahoney's lengthy reminiscence which was nothing more than a furious tirade directed at George Ullman. Lou's trenchant animosity towards George apparently festered during his years on the Lockheed assembly line in Burbank. For when he sat down with writer Raymond Lee to record his memories of working on Valentino's cars, feeding the falcons and digging ditches at Falcon Lair, he did little else but roast George Ullman.

Although many of Lou's recollections were foggy inaccuracies, he exhibited superhuman powers of memory while relating certain conversations verbatim which he claimed took place forty years earlier. These selected conversations cast him in the role of power broker, peacemaker and fatherly confidant to his employers, "Mr. and Mrs. Valentino". He made no mention of the settlement of the estate or of his role in the court proceedings. He also blamed "Mr. Ullman" for everything from the Valentino's divorce to Natacha's exclusion from Rudy's United Artists' contract and for outright embezzling every cent of Rudy's fortune. He also erroneously took full credit for negotiating a loan for Rudy from the Cinema Finance Company and timed this loan a full year before its actual transaction.

Lou's fractured fairytale of life in the Valentino household, where he, as the venerable handyman, appeared to hold the seat of power at the head of the dinner table, became more of the questionable, undocumented fabrication that was soon believed to be fact. For even though Raymond Lee chose to omit Lou Mahoney's screed about George Ullman in his article, Lou's taped reminiscences were soon in circulation and future publications on Valentino were taking a fresh look at the handyman's role in the movie star's life.

With Lou Mahoney bolstering Jean and Alberto Valentino's thirty year vilification of George Ullman, the truth about Rudy's manager faded not-so-slowly from the public domain. And as George continued to say nothing, the resulting new version of the story became a patchwork artifice of inaccuracies with Lou Mahoney the hero, George Ullman a thug and Rudolph Valentino a gay icon.

∽≈∾

"No! Of course not! I was not even married yet!" This was Alberto Valentino's reply to a question posed by a reporter from the Italian-American newspaper, *L'Italo Americano*. The reporter sensed he'd hit a nerve after commenting upon how Alberto's son Jean physically resembled his famous uncle Rudolph.

"When did Rudolph know your son?" The reporter continued to pry. "When he left Italy naturally your son had not been born yet."

Alberto reiterated his point by saying he was still a single man when his brother left Italy in December of 1913. He then abruptly changed the subject by informing the reporter how lawyers were making off with the little money that remained of his brother's estate. He went on to explain that he recently retired from his position as an accountant with Twentieth Century Fox. To the reporter's surprise, he then proceeded to divulge the shocking news that his brother Rudolph once filed a petition to legally adopt Jean. The reporter had to wonder; why would Rudolph Valentino attempt to adopt his brother's son?

At the time Alberto made this startling revelation to the *L'Italo Americano* reporter, Jean Valentino was living in Los Angeles, working as a television sound technician and operating a stereo installation business. Among his famous clientele were Bing Crosby, Frank Sinatra and Danny Kaye. Jean was busy filing several more lawsuits over the years, including a suit against the Disney Corporation after their showing of a clip of *The Son of the Sheik* without his permission. Another suit was filed against Spelling and Goldberg Productions protesting their television production, *The Legend of Valentino: A Romantic Fiction*. In the latter case the judge ruled that the "right to exploit Rudolph Valentino was not exclusively Jean Valentino's".

Jean not only owed some of his success as a Hollywood sound engineer to his famous last name, but also to William Pelf. As an influential television producer, Pelf granted Jean steady work in a string of successful television shows in the early 1960's. By then Pelf had become a wealthy man and lived in a Bel Air hilltop home a stone's throw from Falcon Lair. It was just at that last bend in the road, where visitors to his residence could climb no higher above the City of Angels, that Pelf called home.

On the right side of his elegant home's foyer, a spiral staircase swept up to a second floor landing. About half way up this staircase, anyone of moderate height could spot the toes of a pair of polished black riding boots jutting out eye-level through the landing's wrought iron railing. Rudy's riding boots were positioned as gatekeepers to Pelf's inner sanctum; his Valentino collection. These very boots were once inverted in the stirrups of Rudy's favorite horse, Firefly, during the memorial service held in his honor by the Hollywood Breakfast Club.

Decades later these infamous boots sat frozen in time on William Pelf's landing where they collected dust along with several glass curio cabinets chocked full of Rudy's ruins; his personal shaving case with the letters R.G.V. embossed on the leather cover, a circular leather box of shirt collars imprinted by Rudy's laundry, a cigarette holder used as a prop in *The Sheik*, a heavy crescent dagger worn by Rudy in *The Son of the Sheik* and random photographs and movie stills which were strewn about. Hanging on the walls of this narrow landing were framed photographs of Pelf with his Valentino friends; including one snapshot of Jean Valentino resembling Rudy if he had lived to be sixty years old. "Yes," Pelf would proudly say, "He looked exactly like him!" In an ante room adjoining this landing were boxes of more Rudy archives; the detective agency's reports of Natacha's affair, Rudy and Natacha's love letters and Rudy's clothes still draped on their hangers.

Rudy shared his niche in William Pelf's home with other valuable collections; shelves of leather-bound first edition books, various gifts from Pelf's famous friends in show business including Fred Astaire, Spencer Tracy and Katherine Hepburn and choice memorabilia once owned by the author of The Wizard of Oz, L. Frank Baum. Pelf displayed L. Frank Baum's sundial on the wall of his den. His fascination with the historian of Oz was understandable, for when it came to the subject of collecting memorabilia, Pelf was a bonafide wizard. Whether Jean, Alberto and George visited Pelf over the years for his assurances their Rudy treasures were safe for posterity or whether they courted him to secure work in one of his television shows, they had all paid close attention to the man behind the curtain.

It was inevitable Pelf would eventually acquire competition as he collected Rudy's earthly baggage and one particular collector in the Chicago suburb of Evanston, Illinois gave Pelf a serious run for his position as Valentino collector nonpareil. But to Pelf's dismay, the Evanston collector revered Chaw Mank and was an outspoken and leading proponent of the belief that Rudy led his life as a closeted homosexual. His conviction that Rudolph Valentino led a secret sex life extended well beyond his collection of artifacts and to the purchase of a crypt near Rudy's in Hollywood where he planned to cozy up to his favorite screen icon during the afterlife. Any attempts by William Pelf and those who knew Rudy personally to convince the Evanston collector his assessment was incorrect went unheeded. Despite whispered warnings about the Evanston collector's alleged underhanded business practices, few dared to confront his self-proclaimed authority on the subject of Rudolph Valentino. No one stepped forward to dispute his assertion that Rudy had an army of secret gay lovers. Anyone daring to protest, whether in person or online were called "bigots" and "homophobes" and promptly rebuffed.

The Evanston collector soon found devoted kindred spirits, as his purporting that Valentino was gay, gained popularity. Accepting the contents of the two undocumented books on this subject as fact, he and his followers expounded upon the fan fictional accounts at the annual crypt ceremony at Rudy's grave site. As an influential owner of Rudy memorabilia, the Evanston collector often delivered the keynote address at this highly publicized mausoleum tribute to Rudy. There he and his cadre promoted their various books on Rudy's alleged secret life, forged their alliances and transacted the business of pricing and selling their Rudy wares.

Meanwhile, William Pelf grew suspicious, even fearful, of his competition and wholeheartedly disagreed with the Evanston collector's fundamentalist conviction that Rudy had a secret gay life. After Pelf witnessed the collector's ruthless campaigns to destroy the reputations of several fellow collectors, he assumed a wary stance and gave the collector a chilly shoulder. However, where Pelf was concerned, business was still business and with more deals to be negotiated, many of his Rudy holdings were soon whipping back and forth between his Bel Air mansion and Evanston, Illinois. It seemed some of those personal treasures that Alberto, Jean and George dedicated to Pelf for his safe keeping were slipping right out his back door.

On the fiftieth anniversary of Rudolph Valentino's death, William Pelf organized a showing of Rudy's film, *The Four Horsemen of the Apocalypse* with the Screen Actors Guild and CBS television at the Academy of Arts and Sciences on Wilshire Boulevard. It was after this gala event, that Alberto and Jean Valentino presented Pelf with a special gift; Rudy's favorite platinum wristwatch. Pelf was thrilled with his latest bauble, for even after his decades of serious collecting there were pieces of Rudy he still coveted. He lamented Rudy's toupee had "slipped by him" and hoped one day he might get his hands on any photographs of Rudy's body as it was being embalmed.

≈≈≈

George's resolute silence regarding his legal travails with Alberto and Jean eventually inspired his curious adult children to seek the truth regarding their father's affiliation with the settlement of

Rudolph Valentino's estate. Decades after the fact, they believed that reading the actual court documentation of their father's tenure as executor would be the logical place to launch their investigation. By reading the publicly archived court records, anyone would be able to review the facts of the settlement of the estate, the details of George's performance as executor and the text of Rudy's will. All of this documentation would, by law, be held for public access in The Los Angeles County Hall of Records.

The Ullman children dispatched a private investigator on their behalf to recover this documentation. After a lengthy search, only a few documents in case #83678 - Rudolph Guglielmi Valentino, were recovered. These records were only notices of Jean Valentino's collection processes on George and were all dated well after 1939. Some thirteen years of Rudolph Valentino's estate records appeared to be mysteriously missing from the Los Angeles County Hall of Records.

The Ullman's private investigator then conducted an exasperating year long search for Rudy's missing records. This case file would, by law, contain all of the court's records from the settlement of his estate and span a time frame from Rudy's death in 1926 to those few existing records still on file in the Hall of Records dating after 1939. When the Hall of Records was alerted to their missing case file, they completed their own internal search. They then forwarded a notarized letter to the Ullmans issued by the Executive Officer of the Superior Court of Los Angeles which was labeled as "Certificate of Clerk". It read that in regards to Rudolph Valentino's pre-1939 records,

"The subject case was not readily available for inspection by the public due to the case file being missing."

The law in Los Angeles County clearly states that all requests for access to documents archived in the County Hall of Records be accompanied by the completion of a small form. Printed across the top of this form in bold letters are the words, "Warning-Read This-You Could Go to Prison!" The form's fine print explains how the removal of a single sheet of documentation represents the theft of government property and thereby constitutes a felony in the eyes of the law. When not a scrap of documentation, prior to 1939, could be found in the Hall of Records, it became apparent this threat of imprisonment was no deterrent for some brazen thief or thieves who made off with the entire case file of Rudy's public records.

The Ullman's private investigator persevered in the search for any existing copies of Rudy's missing documents. It was at this point

William Pelf was questioned about his knowledge of Rudy's purloined case file. Pelf made a stunning admission when he acknowledged cagily that at one time he'd actually had all of those "stolen" records in his personal possession.

With no hesitation, he proceeded to point his finger east and incriminate his troublesome adversary, the Evanston collector. It was he, Pelf alleged, who currently had possession of the entire file of Rudy's stolen records. Pelf added that the collector would never admit to having the documents in his possession and proceeded to divulge how the Evanston collector once loaned him the file for his perusal. "I read them and then shipped them directly back to him," Pelf swore. As he reiterated that anyone citing the contents of the stolen records would be incriminating themselves as having had them in their possession, Pelf proceeded to do just that.

He recalled how he read that Jean and Alberto once accused George Ullman in court of spending estate money on baby food, pork chops and even peanut butter. Pelf was quick to point out he only read the stolen file of documents before promptly returning them all to their un-rightful owner in Evanston, Illinois. Pelf then agreed to telephone the collector to see whether he would allow the ill-gotten public documents to be read one more time.

Perhaps Pelf believed confession to be good for the soul, for he then blurted out to the Ullman's investigator one more unsolicited tidbit of information. He said that he "didn't know what happened to those cartons that were stolen from George Ullman's garage" some thirty years earlier. It was not long after this cryptic admission, that Pelf relayed a message to the investigator, via e-mail, from the Evanston collector. Pelf said the collector denied any access to the stolen case file and reported he had just that very week shipped all of the Hall of Record's missing stolen documents to the spokesperson for the Valentino family, Jean Valentino's granddaughter by saying, " Unfortunately, the Valentino collector who has all the legal records regarding the dispute between the Valentino family and George Ullman has decided to turn them all over to the Valentino family." This is "where they belong" he added. Pelf closed his e-mail by saying that since Jean Valentino's grand-daughter was working on a book herself he, "doubted that she would share them with....anyone." The Evanston collector neglected to pass along the news to William Pelf that in exchange for handing the stolen file over to the Valentino family, he accepted one of Rudy's dress shirts as compensation.

This was distressing news for George Ullman's children, as they realized the very documents they had been searching for had been in the possession of the Evanston collector; a man whose platform they disagreed with wholeheartedly. For the collector not only purported that nearly every male Rudy ever encountered was one of his secret gay lovers, he also claimed their father George Ullman was also Rudy's gay lover. The Ullman's disappointment was further compounded, when they realized the Evanston collector had just returned the stolen court records to the very people who were still nursing a decades old and bitter vendetta against their father.

The next logical step for their private investigator was to schedule an interview with Jean Valentino's granddaughter. This request was denied due to what she referred to in her written response as the "personal nature of our documentation." Fortunately for the Ullman children, at this juncture there were no further frustrating dead ends in their search for the truth about their father's role in the settlement of Rudolph Valentino's estate. For their investigator had just uncovered a duplicate set of Rudy's missing records. Unknown to the Evanston collector, William Pelf and the Valentino family, when George filed his appeal of the judgment against him in 1932, most of those very court records were copied and filed with the Court of Appeals library in San Francisco.

This enormous case file of over one thousand pages, included not only the Court of Appeals decision but a wealth of other supporting documentation including transcripts of court testimony, details of Rudy's business holdings and transactions, documented proof of George's performance as Rudy's executor, Falcon Lair's household records and payroll accounts and the court ordered Baskerville audit schedules. After months of anticipation, George Ullman's children finally sat down to read.

They found that the court records contained some startling revelations. Contrary to the commonly held version of the story, as related in every book and article published about Rudolph Valentino to date, they discovered Jean was Rudy's sole heir and that the Valentino estate was never divided in a three way split between Alberto, his sister Maria and Natacha's Aunt Teresa Werner. As the Ullman family read through the records, they discovered a copy of the elusive Paragraph Fourth tucked within the stack of documents before them. They had read the widely publicized single page of Rudy's will, but knew nothing of the second page's existence.

After disappearing for decades, Paragraph Fourth surfaced once again to prove Rudy named Jean his sole heir and left his brother nothing more than an inheritance of a weekly allowance which terminated the moment Jean turned twenty-five. And contrary to Alberto and Jean Valentino's version of events, the court records definitively proved George Ullman was exonerated on all charges of fraud and mismanagement and a court ordered audit found his executor's ledgers to be in perfect order. The Ullman's also learned Alberto and Jean Valentino's pursuit of the judgment against their father was not to collect money he had allegedly embezzled from the estate, but an attempt to force him to reimburse them for the very money they spent decades earlier.

The court records revealed other information directly at odds with Alberto and Jean's public accounts. Over the years Alberto claimed he was still a single man with no children when his younger brother Rudolph left Italy in December of 1913. According to court records, he was married on December 19, 1912, one year earlier. Upon further analysis of the court documents, a possible reason why Alberto may have been confused about this critical date came to light. A simple mathematical calculation and a wealth of accompanying circumstantial evidence created a compelling, possible scenario.

Jean Valentino was born on August 14, 1914, in Santeramo en Colle, a small town located a few miles north of Rudy's last home in Taranto, Italy. Jean's birth took place nearly two years after Alberto's marriage and just less than eight months after Rudy's confrontation with his outraged family members and subsequent hasty departure for America. What could have prompted Alberto to swear publicly that he did not marry until well after his brother left Italy? If this were the case, then this would have been tacit admission that his son was conceived out of wedlock. Perhaps Rudy was not the only Guglielmi brother whose life was forever changed during that infamous and contentious family meeting.

Had both Alberto and Rudy dutifully obeyed the mandate of the family elders issued on that fateful day? Had the Guglielmi family's solution to a lamentable but common predicament resulted in a lifetime of resentment and anger between the two brothers? Were the court records stolen from the Hall of Records and the story purposely skewed over the years by the Valentino family to prevent the public from ever discovering a dark family secret?

Had the older, employed, married yet still childless Alberto been informed that he would save the family's face by signing the birth certificate of his teenage brother Rudolfo's love child? Was Alberto told that he and his wife would raise this child, conceived sometime during the end of October and the first of November in 1913, as their own son? Were Rudy's regular cash payments made to Alberto over the years sent as child support? And during the final months of Rudy's life did he attempt to gain legal custody of his only son as his sole heir? Did Jean consequently spend his life attempting to reclaim, in any possible way, his true heritage which he was denied at birth?

And by mere happenstance, had George Ullman simply stepped into the line of fire and become an unsuspecting target for a family willing to go to any lengths to prevent the answers to these and more questions from ever being known? George's children wondered; could their father's silence over the years and his refusal to ever publicly criticize Jean Valentino, in word or in print, be explained by his own knowledge of this well kept secret and his respect for Rudy's profound love for the son he had been forced to surrender as a teenager?

The daring and effective heist of all of Rudy's public records preceding the date Jean inherited the estate in 1939, ensured that the only documents filed under Rudolph Valentino's name in the L.A. County Hall of Records pertained solely to the collection processes on the judgment held against George Ullman. Consequently, by absconding with not only critical pieces of the puzzle but the entire puzzle, none of this documentation, including the contents of Paragraph Fourth, could ever be referenced by the public.

For George Ullman's family this unfortunate situation meant that any evidence that might have vindicated his tarnished reputation as Rudy's executor was also unavailable to the public for decades. The even more shocking revelation, was the realization that for many years the Valentino family, the Evanston collector and William Pelf all had possession of and access to, the entire body of missing court records. Despite having full knowledge of the contents of these remarkable documents, they'd all conspired to suppress the facts about George Ullman's role as executor, the terms of Rudy's will and the circumstances of Jean's inheritance.

෴

In the wake of William Pelf's request that the Evanston collector allow the stolen records to be read one more time, the collector severed all ties with Pelf. The two collectors would share no more cordial luncheons in Hollywood and conduct no further business dealings. Nevertheless, the Evanston collector and his fellow Valentino collectors continued to collaborate and produce shinier Valentino documentaries, convene in Hollywood on the anniversary of Valentino's tragic death, purchase more Valentino memorabilia and publish their own books on their favorite subject. Over time, they closed ranks as they enforced a fanatical and ruthless control over the legacy of Rudolph Valentino and their valuable collections. Fierce alliances were formed and for decades they have portrayed their false and undocumented versions of both Valentino's and George Ullman's lives as gospel truth. Anyone challenging their status quo, is promptly cut from the herd by means of a range of well-known, under-handed tactics including online defamation, harassment and even litigation.

During the initial days of the Ullman private investigator's search for Rudy's court records, a collector of celebrity archives was contacted. This collector's professional reputation was founded upon his expert ability to conduct extensive searches for celebrity documents within the L.A. County Hall of Records. He offered the following commentary upon the subject of Rudolph Valentino's missing records.

"We have requested dozens of very obscure yet high profile probate cases that can date back nearly a hundred years, and the only two that never surfaced were Valentino's and that of L. Frank Baum, the author of the Wizard of Oz books."

❧❧

Under a freeway overpass on the seamier side of Los Angeles, a bronze and copper casket was hauled out of a mortuary warehouse for the first time in seventy-seven years. Like a great vessel run aground, the metal case was so cumbersome it took the efforts of three brawny workers to heft the unwieldy bark onto a mortuary gurney. It was oppressively hot that summer morning and no day to be working up such a sweat. But the men had their orders; they were to have the neglected relic on display in one of the mortuary's private chapels by nine o'clock sharp. Just before the hour they wheeled the casket into the small sanctuary, lifted off the heavy cover and propped it against the wall.

It was the responsibility of the floor mortician to oversee the arrangements in each of the mortuary's chapels and it was during his inspection he noticed what appeared to be an inscription on the casket's tarnished lid. He returned to his office where he rummaged about for a rag and a can of brass polish to wipe away the years of neglect.

Returning to the chapel, he marveled at the case's extraordinary condition and its masterful construction. He knew that during the 1920's this type of case was actually a sarcophagus, a shipping case which was legally required whenever a coffin was transported across state lines. The mortician continued his buffing, ran his hands over the delicate beads of solder and tried to remove a few scratch marks still evident from the transport of the interior coffin. When he'd restored the copper to a brilliant shine, he read the inscription.

Rudolph Guglielmi

Rudolph Valentino

Born May 6, 1895

Died August 23, 1926

It was then he realized the significance of this sarcophagus. In this case, Rudolph Valentino's lifeless body had jostled along the rails on its long and final ride home to California. Just as his last film, *The Son of the Sheik* was opening in theaters across the country, this very case was being shoved aside in a warehouse where it would sit in the shadows for the next seventy-seven years.

When news reached William Pelf that Rudolph Valentino's sarcophagus had just been discovered in the dark recesses of a Los Angeles mortuary, the race was on. He swooped down from his Bel Air aerie to open negotiations with assorted morticians and shady middlemen. In hushed voices of funereal condolence they got right down to business and began crunching the numbers for their deal of a lifetime. The cross and double-crossing soon had the bidding soaring into the tens of thousands of dollars as any last regard for the sanctity of Rudolph Guglielmi Valentino's final resting place twisted like chaff in the dry Santa Ana winds. Hovering over the great sarcophagus, the men scrutinized every detail of their prize and pondered that one gaping detail missing from the scenario; the corpse.

Chapter Fifteen

The Son of the Sheik Says Goodbye

London, December, 1925 -

As two more delivery trucks pulled up to the Italian Hospital's kitchen door, the mother superior shook her head and muttered in Italian. She had no idea who ordered this quantity of goods, but she was doing her best to accommodate the stacks of crates and boxes in her tiny, cramped kitchen. The perplexing deliveries continued to arrive at the small Catholic hospital on London's Queens Square throughout that chilly December afternoon; boxes of Seville oranges, colorful tins of candy, toys of every description and enough freshly baked Italian Panattone to feed a hundred people. While the flustered nun wedged the heavy crates into every available space, she had yet to make the connection between the bounty of Christmas cheer and a handsome young man who stopped by the hospital earlier that day.

In his tailored suit, he'd stood hat in hand in the hospital's foyer as he explained to the Mother Superior how he was searching for an address on Queens Square when he came across the Italian Hospital. Was there anything, he asked, that he could do for the childrens' ward? The mother superior thanked the stranger and informed him the hospital was too poor to maintain a separate ward for children. She added they were simply cared for in the adult wards. Hearing this, the passerby wished the nun a "Buon Natale!" and left.

She hadn't given their exchange a second thought. As she and several other curious nuns sorted through the crates stacked about the kitchen, they noticed a taxi cab pulling up to the kitchen door. Out stepped the same young man the mother superior spoke with earlier in the day. The sisters paused in their work to watch him bound into the kitchen with a great gold box under his arm. Surveying the crowded room, he confessed he had ordered the oranges, the toys and the towers of fruitcakes. As the nuns stood dumbfounded, their visitor opened his golden box and shook out a brand new Santa suit.

With no further explanation, he slipped the bright red suit over his own and strung the ends of the long white beard over his ears.

They found him believable, despite a curious slave bracelet on his wrist and a profound scar creasing one cheek. After gathering up an armful of toy boats, soldiers, dolls and candy, he headed down the hospital corridor towards the nearest ward. An entourage of excited nuns traipsed behind him bringing up his rear with even more gifts.

Santa's sudden appearance in the hospital ward triggered pandemonium. Adults who were not too ill to do so, sat up and waved, children jumped up and down on their beds and shrieked at pitch volume and a few younger charges wailed in terror. For the next hour, Santa patted heads and ho-hoed his way through each ward. After returning to the hospital's kitchen, he stepped out of his crimson suit and stood in his street clothes to say his goodbye. By this time the nuns were frantic to know who he was, but he shook his head explaining,

"I should like to do this all without name."

The sisters insisted he identify himself.

"But we want to pray for you."

It was then that one of the younger nurses made the connection between the mysterious Santa and the movie posters advertising the opening of the movie, *The Eagle*.

"It's Rudolph Valentino!" she gasped loudly enough for everyone in the kitchen to hear.

Rudy flashed a look of concern her way and began pleading with the sisters to keep news of his visit a secret.

"I am able to do so little as a private person and I would enjoy the memory of this all so much more if it could remain a private thing."

The nuns were in no position to refuse Rudy any request and they kept their promise made to him that day. News of his merry sweep through the Italian Hospital could have been choice publicity for *The Eagle*, but instead was kept confidential for the next thirty years. That Christmas, Rudy was confident he was on the verge of becoming more than just a Santa Claus, Babbo Natale. If his petition to adopt his sole heir was approved, he would at last become Jean's father, his Padre, his Papa.

While he was secretly playing Santa for a ward of infirm kiddies, on the other side of the Atlantic the editor of *Photoplay* magazine, James Quirk, was writing an article about movie star Rudolph Valentino for an upcoming issue. The Sheik's trip to London and his impending divorce in Paris had the media debating whether the Valentino's split resulted from Rudy's desire for children and Natacha's refusal to bear his offspring. Editor Quirk found it ridiculous that Rudy Valentino was somehow frustrated over his childless state.

"I have never heard of Mr. Valentino hanging around an orphan asylum and I can not quite visualize the picture of the Sheik walking the floor on a cold California night crooning the junior to sleep...Divorce is no joking matter, but I cannot hold back a little snicker at Rudy's crying on the shoulders of the public and yearning for kiddies."

James Quirk was not alone in the dark about Rudolph Valentino, as there was a great deal the public did not know about their screen idol. Behind his public scenes, Rudy and George waged a continual battle to hold the line between his public image and private life. Fortunately for Rudy, with George as guard dog of that porous divide, success was more often the case. But George's efforts in this capacity were always daunting feats of long distance management whenever Rudy traveled abroad.

In these instances, it was necessary for George to dispatch daily cablegrams and frequent international money transfers from Rudy's account in the Wilshire National Bank in Los Angeles to his account in the Morgan-Harjes Bank in Paris. George's efforts were further complicated by Rudy's paranoia that their private business correspondence might be compromised. This required that their communiques be composed in Rudy's system of rotating codes. In November of 1925, Rudy's trip to New York and London to attend the premieres of *The Eagle* stretched George's transatlantic managerial skills to the limit.

He did not accompany Rudy on this journey in order to remain in Los Angeles and receive the Italian court's imminent decision on Jean's adoption. In his stead, Rudy traveled with his and George's friend, the commercial attache of the Los Angeles and San Francisco Mexican consulates, S. Manuel Reachi. It was George's idea to dispatch Manuel Reachi as he believed his diplomatic expertise would serve Rudy well on the road. Reachi was the husband of Rudy's co-star in *The Sheik*, Agnes Ayres and at the time of *The Eagle* promotional tour she was six months pregnant with the Reachi's first child.

On the day of Rudy and Manuel Reachi's scheduled departure from Los Angeles, Agnes Ayres, George and Rudy's anxious girlfriend, Pola Negri waved good-bye from the Pasadena train station platform. They had no idea Rudy and Manuel were about to be away considerably longer than the scheduled few weeks. They would in fact be gone for so long, Agnes Ayres later cited her husband's European trip with Rudolph Valentino in November of 1925 as proof of his desertion.

Agnes Ayres would divulge a few other intimate details of Rudy's traveling companion when she divorced Manuel Reachi. She revealed to the court her husband possessed such a violent temper, on several occasions he attempted to strangle her leaving finger marks on her neck. She testified he "once threw her on the bed causing her great physical and mental anguish" and when her maid attempted to intervene, he told her to "shut up." Mrs. Reachi also lamented how the press referred to her handsome husband as a "Latin Lover" and revealed his adulterous affairs with women were too well known to comment upon. But in November of 1925, George knew none of this and had every reason to believe Senor Reachi was a solid citizen and businessman. He briefed Reachi for the journey and passed along detailed instructions regarding his role as Rudy's front line attache.

While Rudy and Manuel Reachi were en route to New York, Natacha was returning from France. Rudy arrived in New York only a few days before his estranged wife and just in time for the opening of *The Eagle* at the Mark Strand Theater. The film's New York debut became a logistical nightmare when thousands of his fans converged upon the theater in the hopes of catching a glimpse of The Great Lover. The morning papers referred to the melee outside the Mark Strand as a "stampede of Rudy fans", but critics declared *The Eagle* a hit and lauded the return of Rudolph Valentino as an action hero.

Rudy wasted no time handing the New York press more fodder for gossip when he arrived at a matinee showing of *The Eagle* with actress Mae Murray on his arm. New Yorkers whispered "fling" and wondered if Rudy might wed Mae when his divorce from Natacha was declared final. Rudy insisted he and Mae were only friends, but in Hollywood his pining sweetheart Pola Negri, kept one green eye glued on all reports of her wandering lover's activities.

Natacha's ship docked in New York the day after *The Eagle* premiere and the press pursued both Mr. and Mrs. Valentino with questions about a possible reconciliation. During the next few days, Rudy and Natacha's paths nearly crossed by a few city blocks but neither made the slightest effort to contact each other.

On November 10th, Rudy made a brief appearance in the Federal Building where he applied for U.S. Citizenship and a few days later he boarded the ocean liner The Leviathan with Manuel Reachi to sail for London. In the first of what Rudy would brush off as mere coincidences, Mae Murray also left New York for Europe on the same day, on another ocean liner only a few slips away.

As The Leviathan steamed down the Hudson River and Rudy settled into his stateroom for the crossing, news of his application for American citizenship wended its way towards Italian dictator, Benito Mussolini. Il Duce was about to be molto infelice to learn of Signor Valentino's expatriating activities and would level a swift response usually bestowed upon enemies of the state.

❦

On November twenty-third, *The Eagle* premiered at London's Marble Arch Pavilion and a battalion of bobbies locked arms to restrain Rudy's faithful chanting the familiar refrain, "Rudy! Rudy! Rudy! " When the object of their hysteria stepped from his limousine, the faltering police line ruptured. In the surge of screaming women, flying handbags, high heels and cloche hats, Rudy abandoned any pretense of a poised debut and sprinted for the safety of the theater lobby.

The London press gave *The Eagle* rave reviews and greeted the Sheik with columns of sympathetic coverage concerning his marital woes. In Rudy's first public statement in London he admitted that perhaps the rift with his wife had been because he was just an old-fashioned husband who wanted children.

"Should I try again to find me a wife," he explained, "let me find one who wishes to have children and who when she has had them, wishes to take care of them."

During his week long stay in London, Rudy wired his brother Alberto in Italy to tell him he had just purchased passage to London for him, his wife Ada, young Jean and their sister Maria. Rudy explained he would be in Paris for the next few weeks but would return to London in plenty of time to join them there for the holidays. He then boarded the boat train with Manuel Reachi and headed for France.

After checking into the Hotel Plaza Athenee in Paris, Rudy filed for his divorce and then boarded another train bound for Berlin where he happened to run into Mae Murray. Although Mae and Rudy continued to toy with the press by claiming they were just old friends,

304

they made no effort to conceal the fact they both registered at Berlin's Hotel Adlon near the Brandenburg Gate. Rudy and Mae's low profile get-away to Berlin was not to be, as Rudy's presence in Germany stirred up more than his female fans. Members of the National Socialist Party held city wide demonstrations upon his arrival, protesting the denigrating portrayal of German officers in his film, *The Four Horsemen of the Apocalypse.*

To avoid this political furor, Rudy and Mae left Berlin and secluded themselves in a first class stateroom on a train traveling south to the French Riviera. Upon their arrival on the Cote d'Azur, Rudy paid a brief visit to the Hudnut chateau. There, Muzzie consoled her soon to be ex-son-in-law, as he reportedly broke down and sobbed in her arms. While Rudy paid his respects to the Hudnuts, Mae Murray bided her time down the road in Nice. She and Rudy were soon on the train again traveling north to Paris. Rudy then hurried on to London for the holidays and arrived in time to play Santa one afternoon at the Italian Hospital on Queens Square.

While Rudy was crisscrossing the English Channel, a half a world away Joe Schenck and George Ullman were monitoring a troubling situation in Italy. Mussolini had just declared Rudolph Valentino's application for U.S. citizenship an act of treason and issued an official boycott of his movies.

With Rudy fast becoming a bulls eye for the militant Italian Fascista, George dispatched an urgent wire to London. He informed Rudy that as his divorce was already filed, it was time to curtail his trip and return to Los Angeles. George had another reason for demanding Rudy's immediate return. After sorting through Rudy's bills, he realized this jaunt was no longer a publicity tour for *The Eagle*, but Manuel Reachi's toot royale entirely funded by Rudy. Frustrated, George continued to wire Rudy with news of the developing situation in Italy and admonishments to be more frugal.

In London, Rudy steamed at Mussolini's reaction to his bid for U.S. citizenship and attempted to appease the irate dictator by sending him a lengthy personal letter. Despite Rudy's impassioned declaration of fidelity to his country of birth, Mussolini remained unmoved and dispatched his Fascista minions throughout Italy to confiscate all of Rudolph Valentino's films. The name Rudolfo Valentino was removed from every theater marquis and all periodicals with any reference to the movie star were heaved into boxes. Any image of the previous

Signor Valentino, now Mister Valentino, vanished from his homeland overnight.

While Rudy celebrated Christmas in London with Alberto, Ada, Maria and Jean, in Milan on the Piazza San Pietro a paperback book titled, *Rodolfo Valentino, A Passionate Expose Against the Renouncer of Our Country* appeared on newsstands. The Fascista publication referred to Rudy as a miserable renegade, an indignant citizen who had revoked his origins and itemized in detail his "atrocious offenses to all Italians".

Despite this mounting political uproar and George's many cablegrams imploring him to sail home immediately after Christmas, Rudy left London with Manuel Reachi and instead returned to Paris. To George's consternation, Reachi hardly turned out to be a sobering influence on Rudy and the invoices from their nightly escapades proved this fact. The two men were regular attendees of "La Revue Negra" at the Theatre Champs-Elysees where they cheered and whistled at the show's opening number; a bottomless Josephine Baker being carried onstage while performing an upside down split on the shoulders of her partner Joe Alex. It was nightly revelry in exclusive clubs and restaurants, where Rudy rang up outrageous charges hosting private dinner parties all capably organized by Manuel Reachi.

While George opened the invoices for these exorbitant fetes, a portrait of Rudy dressed as The Sheik was removed from the lobby of Milan's largest theater. Word of this anti-Valentino uprising prompted Joe Schenck to remind George of United Artists' investment in Rudy's next film, *The Son of the Sheik* which was scheduled to begin production upon his safe return. Nevertheless, Rudy and Manuel arrived in Paris after the holidays and began charging more liquor tabs and signing for more restaurant charges, haberdashery services and the purchase of antique armor, silver and jewelry. In Hollywood, George Ullman was having conniptions.

❧

The threat to Rudy's personal safety posed by the Fascista boycott was further compounded in Paris by his fanatical female fans. Unlike their semi-restrained English counterparts, les femmes de Paris were so obsessed with Rudy, he could seldom venture forth during daylight hours. It was during this time he initiated a routine of sleeping through the day in order to slip past his fans and the Parisian press late at night. He knew if word leaked out that he was on the move, the encampments in the Hotel Athenee's lobby would mobilize in pursuit of their quarry. His female fans were persistent as they grasped at him to wrest any souvenir, with the press equally as unrelenting as they shouted questions his way. Most of these questions concerned his plans with Miss Mae Murray.

Mae was not the only beauty draped on Rudy's arm in Paris that January. He was spotted in the company of several Parisian showgirls and one notable companion; a tall, blonde British royal, Lady Shelia Loughborogh. It didn't take long for the reportage of Rudy's nocturnal dalliances to reach Pola Negri's burning ears. If she was almost sure Mae and Rudy were just friends, she was not as convinced when it came to Lady Loughborogh.

Along with George and a very pregnant Agnes Ayres, Pola Negri urgently wanted Rudy and Manuel Reachi to return home to Los Angeles. This was emphatically the case after she read all the details of how Rudy and Lady Loughborogh danced until dawn in a Parisian jazz club, downed quantities of expensive champagne and beer and won first prize in the club's dance contest.

Undaunted by this news, Pola upped her ante by informing her friends that she was, in fact, engaged to marry Rudy. In Paris he was doing his best to prove otherwise. It was night after night of easy conquests and Mae Murray, comely British royalty and a backlog of fawning show girls all waiting for their turn on his arm. No matter how adamantly Pola Negri claimed to be Rudy's fiancee, he had just filed for his divorce from Natacha and was bearing down on bachelorhood with all the restraint of a recently released convict.

On January 18, 1926, the Tribunal of the Seine heard arguments in the Valentino's divorce and although neither Natacha nor Rudy attended the hearing, their divorce was granted without objection. By then Rudy and Manuel Reachi had returned to London where Rudy informed his brother that young Jean would be traveling home with him to California. As soon as George received the urgent wire from Rudy, he booked passage for not only for Jean but for Alberto and his wife Ada as well. The entire Guglielmi family then sailed for America and on January twenty-seventh, they greeted the New York City press.

In photos snapped upon their arrival, Rudy appeared uncharacteristically exhausted as he told the reporters he was enjoying his "restoration to bachelorhood." At his side, tucked protectively under his arm was his spitting image, eleven-year old Jean.

Pola Negri welcomed her "fiancé" home to Falcon Lair with a swift slap across his face. She guessed he had it coming for his time not well spent with Lady Loughborogh. But within minutes of Pola's strike, she and Rudy picked up right where they left off the previous November; in Falcon Lair's master bedroom. To house guests Alberto and his devoutly Catholic wife's horror, Rudy's Polish mistress practically moved in.

In a move that would have raised every eyebrow in their provincial hometown in southern Italy, Pola placed a framed photo of herself on Rudy's dresser, tossed her delicates in his dresser drawers and hung more negligees in his bedroom closet. Her brazen sleepovers triggered morning wars between the brothers Valentino and their thunderous voices rocked the house from one end to the other. Rudy did little to accommodate his brother's objections and continued to do exactly as he pleased. This not only included sleeping with Pola Negri but devoting a great deal of his time to ensuring Jean be the most pampered eleven-year old in Beverly Hills.

He outfitted the boy in full riding gear and ordered him a pair of custom made black leather riding boots to match his own favorite pair. If Rudy and Jean were not horseback riding along the firebreak roads behind Falcon Lair, they could be found covered in grease in Rudy's fully equipped garage. There, Rudy delivered lengthy instructions to the attentive child on the complex maintenance of the Voisin roadster.

Fan magazines devoted full coverage to Rudy's return to the states with his family, to his upcoming film *The Son of the Sheik* and to his love affair with Pola Negri. Any news of Rudy and Pola made for spicy copy, but behind the scenes Rudy was competing for Pola's affections with Serge Mdivani. Serge Mdivani and his brother David were recent arrivals in Los Angeles and alleged to be displaced Russian princes. Unknown to Pola Negri and rest of Hollywood at the time, the brothers Mdivani had not recently abandoned some musty, romantic castle on the Baltic Sea but a couple of unglorious positions as roustabouts on a Sinclair oil field in Oklahoma.

Nevertheless, "Princes" Serge and David cleaned up remarkably well and deftly seduced their way into Hollywood's elite social circles by wielding their thick Russian accents and newly minted family seal with a vengeance. While Pola Negri was being seen with Rudolph Valentino, she was also seeing a great deal of the dashing Prince Serge. Her clumsy efforts to juggle her two suitors, her flash temper and Rudy's incorrigible unfaithfulness made the future of the Valentino-Negri relationship as vague as it was volatile. In between photo-ops at such glamorous settings as Marion Davies' beach house and The Sixty Club, Pola and Rudy floundered through a classic love/hate.

At home, Rudy's relationship with his brother wasn't faring much better. Life under the same red tile roof as Alberto became so contentious, Rudy counted the days until he and George could leave for Arizona to begin filming *The Son of the Sheik*. While he anticipated their departure, Rudy avoided his heady home fires by continuing to imbibe excessively in bootleg whiskey and spin out of Falcon Lair's driveway on a series of spontaneous road trips which resulted in more vehicular disasters than George could keep under wraps.

His spectacular wreck of his Isotta Fraschini limousine on the railroad tracks south of San Francisco sparked a rash of reprimand from the press in Los Angeles. This public outrage in response to his reckless behavior provoked Joe Schenck to draw up an addendum to Rudy's contract. The document stated that until production of *The Son of the Sheik* terminated, Rudolph Valentino was not permitted to drive himself anywhere. If he did get behind the wheel, Schenck contractually forbid him to drive over fifty miles per hour. Rudy could have cared less and continued crumpling his cars and racking up more speeding tickets.

His enjoyment of his "restoration to bachelorhood" was apparently not solely a European activity. During the days before Rudy began work in *Son of the Sheik*, George recorded weekly payments in Falcon Lair's expense ledgers to the local police for a string of Rudy's traffic citations. The ledgers also revealed business was booming for Falcon Lair's bootleggers, as Rudy's liquor tab skyrocketed from hundreds of dollars a month prior to his recent trip abroad to thousands of dollars a month after his return to Los Angeles. It appeared that when he wasn't intoxicated and speeding along California's highways, Rudy was at home locking horns with his brother Alberto. On many occasions these arguments were fueled with top shelf liquors and vintage wines and instigated by Alberto's demands for money. Alberto found Rudy's lavish Hollywood lifestyle a sweet fit and upon his arrival in February of 1926, he cashed weekly checks of $500.00 drawn upon Rudy's personal Wilshire National Bank account.

George issued the checks to Alberto while overseeing Rudy's other daily expenditures with the wild eyed desperation of a captain of a sinking ship. He held absolute authority over the management of Falcon Lair's finances and staff but had no control over the spending habits and rash behavior of the often absent and increasingly inebriated young master at the helm.

While George did his best to curb expenses, Manuel Reachi was doing his best to convince Rudy that George Ullman was far too conservative with his cash. It was true that Rudy was often drinking heavily and resenting his manager's attempts to tighten the purse strings. As tempers flared, Reachi sensed opportunity and pressed Rudy saying he was sure he could do a better job as his business manager. But Rudy and George knew one fact that Manuel Reachi was not aware of at the time; by the spring of 1926, Rudy was over $200,000.00 in debt.

The private world of Rudolph Valentino, which his public envisioned to be as professionally groomed and manicured as his studio photographs and slick fan magazine copy, was fraying under the strain of his enormous debt, reckless alcoholism and the escalating conflicts within his household. Rudy was increasingly delegating the care of his horses and dogs to his groomsman and the maintenance of his fleet of cars to Lou Mahoney and his two brothers, Charles and George. His interest in renovating Falcon Lair waned and his yacht, which he previously maintained in peak mechanical condition suffered breakdowns. On one evening jaunt to Catalina with Bee and George, the boat's engines sputtered and died leaving the craft and its passengers drifting until daylight before they were finally spotted and towed into port.

There was, however, one subject which held Rudy's full attention; *The Son of the Sheik*. It was a tough sale for George to convince Rudy to have another go at Sheikdom. Rudy abhorred the moniker "Sheik" especially when the word was used to imply "wolfing" and lecherous behavior. Just before leaving for *The Eagle* premiere in London the previous fall, he vowed to one reporter he would never again play that loathsome character. On the eve of what would become an epic three month European bender of champagne, beer, showgirls and luxurious hotel rooms, Rudy told a reporter,

"Heaven knows, I'm no sheik...all the time I was a farmer at heart and I still am. When I am working I go to bed at nine thirty and get up at five...I am through with sheiking...If any producer comes to me with a sheik part I am going to murder him!"

The visage of Rudolph Valentino as an early to bed farmer rising at the crack of dawn to till his five acre spread in Beverly Hills made for great press. But two compelling factors brought Rudy to his senses; the stack of unpaid bills on his manager's desk and news that Joe Schenck signed George Fitzmaurice as *Son of the Sheik*'s director. Jesse Lasky's rejection of George Fitzmaurice as director of *Blood and Sand* contributed in great measure to Rudy's rift with Famous Players-Lasky in 1922. *The Son of the Sheik* would prove Rudy correct in his belief that he would work well with the French speaking director.

Son of the Sheik promised to be a challenging role for Rudy as he would play the dual role of the young Sheik and his aging father. Audiences were about to witness Rudy's onscreen brush with old age in his convincing portrayal of the bearded, gray-haired elder Sheik. And in contrast to Famous Players-Lasky's penny pinching on the production of original film, *The Sheik*, United Artists spared no expense producing *The Son of the Sheik*. All of Rudy's extravagant purchases of gilt edged sheik accoutrement were approved, including a $4000.00 antique sword and a $3000.00 sapphire ring.

Rudy's love interest in *The Son of the Sheik* would again be played by his *Eagle* co-star, Vilma Banky and the role of the aging Sheik's wife was reprised by Agnes Ayres. Ayres had just given birth to a daughter a few weeks before her scenes were filmed and her husband Manuel had abandoned his career as a diplomat to accept a position as personal assistant to *Son of the Sheik*'s Director George Fitzmaurice.

On location in Yuma, Arizona, director Fitzmaurice and Rudy collaborated on every detail of production. The same Arabian stallion, Jadaan, used in *The Sheik* was transported from Pomona, California for a second performance in *Son of the Sheik* and desert sand dunes were whipped into violent sandstorms with strategically placed airplane engines. The infernal sand blasting and one hundred degree Arizona heat resulted in a grueling work experience for everyone on location; everyone except the star of the movie. For Rudy the searing inconvenience was balmy relief in comparison to his Beverly Hills home front.

For word finally arrived from Italy with the long awaited news of Jean's adoption, and just as George anticipated the Italian courts summarily rejected Rudy's petition. Rudy was devastated when he heard the news. From the moment he learned his sole heir would never be his legal son, any lingering civility towards his brother Alberto hardened into contempt. Bitterly disappointed, Rudy turned the focus of his days from fight to flight and to George's dismay he weighed radical options for his future.

During Rudy's final days in Arizona on the set of *The Son of the Sheik*, he confided in George that he was sick of playing the romantic lover. He swore he would soon work only behind the camera as a director. He lamented to George at length how he had lost all interest in acting and wanted to set plans in motion to purchase a home in Spain where he would study the art of bullfighting. George listened patiently and reminded Rudy he still had many obligations in Los Angeles.

As soon as the final location scenes in Arizona were filmed, Rudy and George returned to Los Angeles, only to discover that in their absence Alberto had been waging war with Falcon Lair's staff. He had just ordered the installation of padlocks on all of the refrigerators in order to prevent the hired hands from eating his food. Appeasing the disgruntled staff was not George and Rudy's only immediate concern upon their return.

With *The Son of the Sheik* headed into post-production, Rudy had fulfilled his contractual obligations with United Artists and his paychecks ceased. His legions of creditors from Los Angeles to New York, London and Paris were well aware of this inevitable day and with this in mind George turned his attentions to securing Rudy's future income. As a band-aid on the hemorrhaging financial situation, George negotiated a stop gap $150,000.00, one year loan at 7% interest from the Cinema Finance Corporation. In order to secure the loan, George was required to post nearly all of Rudy's real property and assets as collateral.

With the Cinema Finance Company's check in hand, George paid off Rudy's loudest creditors. However, the loan's monthly payment of $13,375.00 only increased the pressure on George. In addition to this steep monthly payment, Rudy was also responsible to pay the monthly premium on a $125,000.00 life insurance policy purchased on his valuable self by the Cinema Finance Company. Rudy was no different than any other thirty-one year old, and perceived the life insurance policy required to secure the loan as nothing more than annoying paperwork. But George was about to make only three payments on the life insurance policy before it would have to be cashed in.

≪≥≫

George delayed contacting Joe Schenck to pitch a new contract for Rudy in the hopes Schenck would make the first move. During this standoff, George met with William Fox, the President of Fox Films and Carl Laemmle of Universal Pictures to discuss a possible deal for Rudy. Fox told George he could ill afford to produce Rudy's pictures as the cost of producing a movie at Fox Films was seldom more than $35,000.00 a picture. At Universal, Carl Laemmle gave George the same response. But George would not waiver; he was adamant Rudy receive no less than $150,000.00 a film, in addition to a percentage of the profits.

A few days after meeting with Fox and Laemmle, George received a telephone call from Joe Schenck's assistant, John Considine. Considine set up a meeting between Schenck and George in which Schenck explained he had no intention of offering Rudy a second contract under the generous terms of the last. He claimed box office receipts from *The Eagle* did not merit such a large payment to Rudy. George knew those box office numbers and argued to the contrary. He presented Schenck with his final offer; $6500.00 a week for two more pictures plus 25% of their profits. He then stormed out of Schenck's office on a bluff after warning him not to sit too long on his decision because Rudy had several other offers on the table.

George knew Rudy was visiting Pola Negri at the time and drove directly from his meeting with Schenck to her home. There he explained to Rudy that under no circumstance was he to speak with Schenck or Considine if they tried to contact him that evening. George then drove home and just as he sat down to dinner, his telephone rang. It was John Considine with Schenck's counter offer; $3500.00 a week and 10% of the profits. George snapped at Considine saying Rudy would be insulted by those terms. Nevertheless, he said he would relay the offer to him anyway.

George then drove back to Pola Negri's to explain the details of Schenck's offer to Rudy and advise that he reject it. Pola overheard their exchange and told George she thought Rudy had no other option

313

but to accept the offer because he might be out of work for a long time. Rudy cut her off mid-sentence.

"It is entirely up to George and he will decide what to do!"

George reiterated to Rudy that he not communicate with Schenck or Considine and drove home once again. He then placed a telephone call to Considine to tell him Rudy would not budge from his original numbers and in fact he had been deeply offended by Schenck's offer. With a heavy heart, George sat down to his cold dinner wondering if he'd ruined any possible deal for Rudy with United Artists. About ten o'clock that night the Ullman's telephone rang again. It was John Considine.

"I think he's crazy but Mr. Schenck said that we would accept your terms for the new contract."

Before George hung up the telephone, he confirmed with Considine that Rudy's $6500.00 a week salary would commence immediately upon his signing the contract. George then made one more trek to Pola Negri's home. When he entered Pola's foyer on this occasion he witnessed a scene he would never forget. With her head thrown back in high indignation, Pola was stomping up her front stairs while a furious Rudy seethed at her from the living room below. As George began relating the terms of the new contract, he sensed the volatile situation and gave Rudy a quick pat on the back saying,

"It's time to get out of here."

George had witnessed the repercussions of Rudy's boiling point many times and repeated,

"Rudy, let's get the hell out of here."

As George began edging him towards the front door, Rudy turned around to lean against the stair railing and yell up at top volume,

"You bitch!"

❧

Rudy signed his second contract with United Artists on May twenty-second and his first movie under this contract was scheduled to be, *The Firebrand*, a screenplay based on the life of the Italian sculptor, Benvenuto Cellini. Production on *Firebrand* was not scheduled to begin until October. As soon as Rudy signed the contract, his United Artists' paychecks resumed and George was able to keep his creditors and the Cinema Finance Company at bay. While Rudy returned to work by meeting with *Firebrand*'s writers and preparing for *The Son of the Sheik*'s impending premieres, Pola Negri turned up the volume on her campaign to become Mrs. Valentino number three.

By the end of June she was immersed in wedding planning; not her own nuptials but those of her other beau, Prince Serge Mdivani's brother David to Mae Murray. Despite the fact that Mae was fourteen years older than David Mdivani, the recent marriage of her ex-husband, director Robert Leonard as well as Pola Negri's insistence that she was Rudy's fiancee, sent Mae scurrying to the altar. Whether Pola was blind to Rudy and Mae's love affair or calculating that by rushing Mae down the aisle she would have her out of the picture forever, was anyone's guess. George knew the truth of Rudy's simultaneous involvement with both women and wisely kept mum on the uncomfortable subject.

He also knew Rudy resented his Russian competition as Pola's continental beau ideal. For this reason, he was stunned to learn Rudy complied with Pola and Mae's wishes on the sunny afternoon of June twenty-ninth. On that day, Rudy acted as best man when his two lovers, bride Mae and maid-of-honor Pola convened for the holy Mdivani matrimony. When George saw the first copies of the Mdivani's wedding photos, with Rudy wedged between Mae and Pola, he could only cringe at the awkward predicament.

On July eighth, one week after Mae's wedding, *The Son of the Sheik* opened at Grauman's Million Dollar Theater in Hollywood. Rudy and Pola attended the gala opening in the company of Hollywood luminaries including columnist Louella Parsons, Charlie Chaplin, June Mathis, Mae Murray and her new husband Prince David. Although *The Son of the Sheik* was soundly hailed by critics and fans as Rudy's most solid performance to date, by sharp contrast his private life was in a state of turmoil.

It was around the time of the Grauman's opening when Rudy evicted his brother from Falcon Lair. While George was making plans for his and Rudy's scheduled trip east for *The Son of the Sheik*'s premieres, Rudy asked him to book passage for Alberto and his family's return trip to Italy. Rudy specifically requested George time Alberto's departure for Italy with his own stay in New York City. The terminal strife between the Valentino brothers was not the only disruptive force contributing to the growing malaise in Rudy' household that summer.

When Lou Mahoney heard the scuttlebutt that Manuel Reachi was aspiring to unseat George as Rudy's business manager, the handyman made his move. He approached Rudy and put a word in for Reachi's ascendancy. He informed "Mr. Valentino" that he felt the household was continually short on cash because "Mr. Ullman" was stealing it. As a result of Lou Mahoney's sore underestimation of Rudy's faith in his stalwart manager, he would end up with the ax instead of George. Despite pressure from Reachi and Mahoney to fire George, Rudy stood by his friend and manager. He listened calmly to Lou and then went straight to George with instructions that he fire Lou Mahoney as well as his brothers George and Charles. It was just prior to leaving Los Angeles with Rudy that George faced off with the Irish ex-cop and spelled it out for him; while he and Rudy were in New York he was to seek other employment.

It was shortly before leaving for the east coast that Rudy's *Son of the Sheik* co-star Vilma Banky convinced him to accompany her for a consultation with a psychic reader in Santa Monica. The reader's name was Dr. George Dareos and he was well known for his ability to recognize a person's previous lives by the way they walked. Rudy was anxious to hear what the noted psychic had to say and expected nothing but glowing encouragement from the other side. But he and Vilma would abruptly leave the reading after only a few minutes, when Dr. Dareos predicted Rudy's imminent death.

July fourteenth was Rudy's last day at home in Falcon Lair. He puttered around the house, worked on his cars and late that afternoon he loaded his luggage into one of those vehicles and asked Alberto to drive him to Pola Negri's home. There Pola joined the two brothers and they all continued on to the train station where they met Bee and George Ullman. On this occasion George would be accompanying Rudy on the trip east.

They said their goodbyes and George and Rudy boarded the evening train north along the California coast. The following morning they were welcomed to San Francisco by the city's Mayor Rolph who presented Rudy with the gift of a pedigreed black water spaniel. Realizing the July heat would make the journey to New York unbearable for the dog, Rudy arranged for the animal to be driven back to Falcon Lair's kennels. Before parting with his newest pet, he posed for a few photographs and named the affectionate pup, Mission Rudy.

In the days before air conditioning, midsummer train travel was not for the faint hearted, and like most other passengers Rudy survived the heat of the journey by sleeping. But any similarities between Rudy and his fellow passengers went no further than his long naps. While his public perspired in cramped coach cars only a few feet away, Rudy was shielded from any undue discomfort in luxury accommodation.

George ensured that all of his favorites were stocked in sufficient supply for the cross country trek; bottled Vichy water, flasks of Canadian scotch whiskey, cartons of Abdullah cigarettes, cans of Russian caviar and to quell his chronic indigestion, boxes of bicarbonate of soda. If Rudy wasn't passing the time sound asleep, he rambled on about a subject George had long since learned to be one of his favorite topics; himself. In the privacy of his sleeper compartment, Rudy fretted over his thinning hair and his new toupee and mused to George that he believed he was finally ready to apply himself and get that formal education. As the train rocked along the rails, he wiled away the miles of countryside expressing his profound guilt over his mother. He lamented how she died before he became a star and how he had shamed her and his family as a teenager before he left Italy.

Although Rudy could fret with the best, he did not worry long about psychic Dr. Dareos' doom saying. George, on the other hand, did. With growing concern, he noticed Rudy was sleeping far too much. He found it unusual Rudy could barely be coaxed into making more than a few whistle stop appearances on local platforms to greet his fans and press. George was also increasingly alarmed by Rudy's propensity to down an entire flask of scotch whiskey before he could fall off to sleep.

One warm evening during the train's lay over in St. Louis, Missouri, George arranged for a private dinner for Rudy and himself in a local restaurant. In a ballroom below their private dining room, a group of factory workers were holding a banquet. When word spread Rudolph Valentino was having his dinner upstairs, an emissary was appointed to request that the movie star make an appearance. The nervous messenger was greeted by an unusually magnanimous Rudy who said he'd been enjoying the music from the ballroom during his meal and would be happy to come downstairs and even dance for them.

The messenger rushed downstairs to alert the musicians who rustled up a tango just as Rudy made his entrance. To the crowd's cheers, whistles and wilting, Rudy strolled into the ballroom. He gave the crowd a nod as he selected his dancing partner, the most plainly dressed woman in the room. As he bowed low and took her hand, her face shot crimson and before she could close her mouth or straighten her dress she was twirling across the dance floor.

It was an all too brief spin in Rudolph Valentino's arms and before the starry eyed woman knew what had happened, Rudy glided across the dance floor to return her to her seat. Rudy and George were soon boarding the train once again to head north to Chicago. As they fought to stay cool in the oppressive heat of their private car, neither of them realized they were steaming directly into the cross hairs of an enemy in wait.

Over their morning coffee at the Hotel Blackstone in Chicago, George read an anonymous editorial in *The Chicago Tribune* and then tossed the paper across the table to Rudy. For the rest of his life George would regret ever having done so. Rudy suffered through his share of denigrating tirades directed at him over the years, but this particular piece was about to devastate his day, his next week and each and every one of his few remaining days on earth. Like a soldier working his way through a "Dear John" letter from home, Rudy stiffened as his eyes moved down the page. The anonymous author of the editorial was in an uproar over the appearance of pink powder dispensing machines in a few mens' rooms around Chicago. It read in part,

"A powder vending machine: in a mens' washroom! Homo Americanus! Why didn't someone quietly drown Rudolfo Guglielmi, alias Valentino, years ago?.... It is time for a matriarchy if the male of the species allows such things to persist... Better a rule by masculine women than by effeminate men."

The writer went on to lay all blame for these powder machines on Rudy.

"How does one reconcile masculine cosmetics, sheiks, floppy pants and slave bracelets with a disregard for the law and aptitude for crime?...

Chicago may have its powder puffs; London has its dancing men and Paris its gigolos...Hollywood is the national school of masculinity. Rudy, the beautiful gardener's boy, is the prototype of the American male."

By the time Rudy set the newspaper down on the table, George could see his reaction and sought to downplay the situation. He insisted Rudy not give the despicable article a second thought. But he could see the words cut deep and that being referred to as an effeminate role model and having his father's name raked through the mud was more than Rudy could bear. Within minutes, Rudy instructed George to telephone *The Chicago Tribune's* arch rival *The Chicago Herald Examiner* to inform the paper that his response would be ready for publication in their next day's edition. It read as follows:

"To the man(?) who wrote the editorial entitled "Pink Powder Puffs" in The Chicago Tribune:

The above-mentioned editorial is at least the second scurrilous personal attack you have made upon me, my race, and my Father's name. You slur my Italian ancestry; you cast ridicule upon my Italian name; you cast doubt upon my manhood.

I call you in return a contemptible coward, and to prove which of us is the better man I challenge you to a personal contest. This is not a challenge but a duel in the generally accepted sense-that would be illegal. But in Illinois boxing is legal; so is wrestling. I, therefore, defy you to meet me in the boxing or wrestling arena to prove, in typically American fashion (for I am an American citizen) which of us is more of a man.

I prefer this test of honor to be private, so I may give you the beating you deserve, and because I want to make it absolutely plain this challenge is not for the purposes of publicity, I am handing copies of this to the newspapers simply because I doubt that anyone so cowardly as to write about me as you have done would respond to a challenge unless forced by the press to do so.

I do not know who you are or how big you are, but this challenging stands if you are as big as Jack Dempsey.

I will meet you immediately, or give you a reasonable time in which to prepare, for I assume that your muscles must be flabby and weak, judging by your cowardly mentality, and that you will have to replace the vitriol in your veins with red blood-if there be a place in such a body as yours for red blood and manly muscle.

319

I welcome the criticism of my work as an actor-but I will resent with every muscle in my body attacks upon my manhood and ancestry.

Hoping that I will have an opportunity to demonstrate to you that the wrist under a slave bracelet may slap a real fist into your sagging jaw, and that I may teach you respect of a man even though he prefers to keep his face clean. I remain with utter contempt,

Rudolph Valentino

P.S. I will return to Chicago within 10 days. You may send your answer to me in New York, care of the United Artists Corporation."

When the author of the editorial offered no immediate response to this public challenge, Rudy became unhinged. On the final leg of the trip east to New York, he drank more than his usual excess and was wracked with persistent bouts of indigestion. He was inconsolable and told George he worried that to those who did not know him personally the label of effeminate just might stick. When George asked him what he would do if the author of the editorial turned out to seven feet tall and weigh twice his weight, Rudy snapped back,

"...If I am licked by a more powerful man that will be no disgrace and at any rate I'll show him that I am no pink powder puff!"

By the time Rudy and George checked into their suite in New York's Ambassador Hotel, the mercury was inching into the triple digits and news of Rudolph Valentino's challenge to the author of *The Chicago Tribune* editorial was reaching pitch media hysteria. George tried valiantly to talk Rudy down off his ledge by arguing he was in no physical condition to enter a boxing ring with an unknown opponent. Unable to convince Rudy to let the issue slide, George turned to Frank Mennillo. As Rudy's oldest and closest friend in New York, George hoped he would be able to prevent the hell-bent Rudy from pounding the life out of his opponent in Chicago or having the life pounded out of him. Frank assured George he would see what he could do and sat down to dinner with Rudy.

Fourteen years Rudy's senior, Frank Mennillo felt fatherly solicitude for the friend he'd helped out so many times over the years. So when Rudy persisted in a furious rant about his impending fight with the *Tribune* writer, Frank made every effort to change the subject. He told Rudy about his recent purchase of five acres in the San Joaquin

320

Valley in California and his plans to build a tomato juice cannery on the property. He also boasted how his son Arnold would be returning to California with him to operate the plant. But Frank could see Rudy was distracted and suffering considerably in New York's humidity. He told him to get some rest and warned that if he planned any serious fisticuffs, he'd better lay off the whiskey for at least a day or two.

Rudy followed through on his promise to return to Chicago to accept his unnamed opponent's reply. While he made the one day trip back to the windy city, George remained in New York to bear the brunt of the added publicity from the *Tribune* flap. From his Rudolph Valentino Productions office at 1440 Broadway and from the sitting room of the Ambassador Hotel's suite, George worked into the wee hours of every morning.

In addition to his usual workload of poring over invoices, paying bills and dictating correspondence, he scheduled Rudy's *Son of the Sheik* appearances and fielded a barrage of press requests. He also juggled a myriad of more mundane, but nevertheless critical tasks. He paid Rudy's New York bootlegger for a fresh supply of whiskey and with Rudy then smoking almost one hundred cigarettes a day, George stockpiled cases of Abdullahs around the suite. Other than his New York secretary, Estelle Dick, George was running the show as a harried army of one.

He was so overwhelmed by the added stress of Rudy's challenge to *The Chicago Tribune* writer, he telephoned Bee in Los Angeles to ask her to leave the children with a nurse and board the next train east. He told her that in addition to Rudy's scheduled appearances for *The Son of the Sheik* premieres, he had just accepted an invitation from *The New York Evening Journal's* boxing expert, Buck O'Neill to spar a few exhibition rounds on the Ambassador's roof. George was calling in his troops.

When Bee Ullman arrived in New York, she moved into the suite to assist her husband in bringing some order to the chaos. By then the Ambassador's switchboard was connecting so many calls to Rudolph Valentino's suite that an extra telephone operator was hired. That busy Ambassador Hotel suite consisted of two bedrooms, the Ullman's and Rudy's which were located on opposite ends of an elegantly appointed sitting room. From the day George and Rudy arrived in New York, Rudy would spend few nights in his bedroom. Continuing in the routine he'd instigated in Paris, he caroused through most nights arriving just before dawn to sleep through the heat of the day.

For Gotham was deep in the throes of *Son of the Sheik* mania during the summer of 1926, and the breaking news that the star of the film was in town and spoiling for a fight was as welcome a distraction from Manhattan's dog days as an unexpected cool breeze. It was hard to miss all the hullabaloo, as Rudy's well meaning fans goaded him on to victory. Despite his public saber rattling, behind the scenes Rudy was exhausted and yielding to a meltdown of deadly proportion.

Nevertheless, *The Son of the Sheik* kept up his very public appearances and as rakish as ever he fooled everyone. His image graced the covers of every fan magazine and looking invincible as ever in his desert finery, news of *The Son of the Sheik* filled the front pages of every newspaper. His name received top billing on the guest lists of all uptown parties, Ziegfeld Follies clambered for a moment of his time, Park Avenue playboys jockeyed for position next to him in speakeasies and the city's cultural illuminati devised chic soirees in his company.

George and Bee Ullman on the other hand were worried. They knew there were too many "mornings after" and "afternoons after" when the star of the show felt considerably less than a million bucks. From their bedroom in the Ambassador Hotel suite, they were witnessing the personal toll of Sheik madness and kept their wary eyes on the comings and goings of "Rudy, Rudy, Rudy."

On the day Alberto, Ada and Jean left on their journey home to Italy, Rudy, George and Bee accompanied them to the docks along the Hudson River. It was the day after the overly publicized bout on the Ambassador's roof with Buck O'Neill and Rudy's face bore the evidence. Buck fared worse after taking several solid jabs from Rudy before a panicky George called a halt to the exhibition match. *The Chicago Tribune* writer was still cowering in silence behind his scathing editorial, but Rudy was confident he'd succeeded in showing him that he packed a mean punch. Even if his opponent never surfaced, Rudy felt his exhibition match demonstrated to the world that anyone else daring to refer to him as a pink powder puff might soon feel his fist on their jaw as well.

It was a brief but visibly emotional farewell between Rudy and Jean. The boy said his tearful goodbye after a long hug from Rudy. As

Alberto was about to follow his wife and Jean up the ocean liner's gangplank, he paused and pulled George aside to ask him for money. He said he'd just asked Rudy for cash but his brother told him he wouldn't give him another "damn dime". George shoved his hand deep in his pocket and told Alberto that he was tapped out. Bee Ullman overheard this exchange and before Rudy knew any transaction had taken place, she handed Alberto one hundred dollars in small bills. With this coin in his pocket, Alberto was up the gangplank and headed home to Italy. George was surprised by Rudy's lackluster goodbyes to his family, but thought this was probably due to his eagerness to head out of the crowd and back to his bed in the Ambassador suite.

With sirens blaring and banners fluttering, the great ship began its slow ease out into the Hudson River just as Rudy spotted his brother standing on deck. Alberto stood alone and gave a wave in his brother and the Ullmans' direction. With a halfhearted shrug Rudy said to George,

"There he goes. I hope I never see the bastard again."

Chapter Sixteen

Lost in the Woods

New York City, August 1926 -

During the summer of 1926, Egyptian Fakir Rahman Bey was getting under magician Harry Houdini's skin. This was not due to the fact that Fakir Bey's popular stage act included such feats as snoozing on the business edge of a steel sword, being buried alive in a coffin and threading foot long steel needles through his skin. Houdini was miffed because each of Bey's performances concluded with a public taunting as he mouthed the word, "Houdini".

Bey accomplished his wizardry while exhibiting not a twinge of pain and without shedding a single drop of his fakir blood. He claimed he was able to do the impossible because of his ability to slip into a cataleptic trance and slow his heart and breathing to a near death rate. Harry Houdini denounced Bey's claims as pure bunk and began staging his own rebuttal performances to prove he was a fraud. Rahman Bey and Houdini took each others bait and the rivalry was on.

During the heated competition, Fakir Bey acquired a devoted following and by August he was a popular performer in several Manhattan speakeasies including the 300 Club on 54th Street. Discreetly billed as "The World's Most Famous Rendezvous of Stage, Screen, Society and Finance," the 300 Club was owned and operated by Mary Louise Cecilia Guinan, a.k.a., "Tex" Guinan from Waco, Texas. Knowing Fakir Rahman Bey to be a guaranteed showstopper, Tex Guinan hired him to amaze her famous clientele.

On one August evening, Tex Guinan told her forty fan dancers to give their ostrich feathers a rest and motioned for Fakir Bey to take the floor. Seated in Bey's audience in that jam-packed, smoky room were Rudolph Valentino and George Ullman. Along with everyone else in the crowd they were throwing back way too many drinks and by the time Tex wedged her way over to their table with Fakir Bey, they were lit. Tex gave a holler to her patrons to pipe down, because the Fakir was about to astound them all. With Rudy's help he did.

While Rudy and George stared in amazement, Bey slipped a steel needle into his cheek and out through his mouth. As he held the needle high and took his bow, the audience applauded and shouted for an encore. It was then Tex Guinan challenged the Fakir to perform the same trick on Rudy. With the patrons of the 300 Club shouting in approval, Rudy nodded that he was game. George's resounding voice of dissent was barely audible over the din. He was not so inebriated that he failed to recognize the real threat to Rudy's most valuable asset and yelled across the table at Rudy, "If Fakir Bey is piercing anything for God's sake make it your arm!"

Rudy savored the moment and lit another cigarette. To the crowd's whoops and whistles he stood, removed his jacket and rolled up one sleeve. So the Sheik's forearm came to be pierced clean through with a steel needle wielded by a man in Sheik's clothing. Amazingly, the trick worked like a charm and Rudy felt nothing, did not bleed and laughed the performance off by shaking Bey's hand.

George missed the entire demonstration as he was searching for rubbing alcohol in order to disinfect the two small puncture wounds on Rudy's arm. Before Rudy could roll down his sleeve, George was slopping his forearm with the alcohol and grateful it hadn't been his face. Fakir Bey offered no explanation to his cheering audience as to how his cataleptic trance prevented Rudy's arm from bleeding and fortunately this was one trick Harry Houdini passed on replicating.

Rudy and George arrived in New York City that July to attend the east coast premieres of *The Son of the Sheik*. After seeing his brother Alberto and family off on their return journey to Italy, Rudy resumed his dolce vita often with Ziegfeld Folly, Marian Benda along for the ride. Whether it was Marian Benda or whomever else he chose as his escort for the night, the opportunity to share in Rudy's limelight was jealousy guarded. The press was hot on his high profile and New Yorkers eagerly read coverage of his nightly appearances around town. As a result of this unrelenting publicity, lines outside theaters showing *The Son of the Sheik* were long and box office takes nothing short of titanic.

While Joe Schenck savored the revenue for United Artists, George Ullman was the busiest man in Manhattan. With Rudy commanding such intense media attention, even the news clipping bureaus George retained to track the publicity struggled to stay abreast of the press. With all of his personal and business affairs being handled by George, Rudy had ample time to instigate even more uproar. He accepted more invitations to the theater, sporting events and private parties than he could possibly attend and hosted his own A-list dinner parties. He even met with Paramount Picture's Adolph Zukor in an apparent effort to make amends and granted an interview to writer and journalist H.L. Mencken.

With George tracking invoices and remitting payments for this imperial Manhattan lifestyle, Rudy continued to sign on the bottom line and no one disputed he was a guaranteed high time that summer. But whether beauty Marian Benda was aware of it or not, she had competition for his company. Gossip columnists buzzed that eligible bachelor Rudy was seen with several different women on his arm. One late night he was spotted dining with his first ex-wife, Jean Acker. According to the report, Jean Acker was on her way to Europe with her mother but decided to spend a few days in New York to make amends with her ex.

In between Rudy's social spinning, he and George met their obligations with United Artists by attending the east coast openings of *The Son of the Sheik*. By the time they made a quick trip back to Chicago for the movie's premiere at the Roosevelt Theater, Rudy had yet to receive a response from the author of the pink powder puff editorial. The Chicago press seized upon the publicity opportunity of the unrequited challenge and Rudy obliged by lacing on a pair of boxing gloves and staging another exhibition sparring match in a local gym. He then proclaimed victory over his unidentified opponent by publishing his statement of final defiance. The piece appeared in every newspaper in Chicago except *The Chicago Tribune* and read in part,

"It is evident you cannot make a coward fight any more than you can draw blood out of a turnip. The heroic silence of the writer who chose to attack me without any provocation in The Chicago Tribune leaves no doubt as to the total absence of manliness in his whole make-up... I feel I have been vindicated because I consider his silence as a tacit retractio, and an admission which I am forced to accept even though it is not entirely to my liking..."

After *The Son of the Sheik*'s showing at the Roosevelt Theater, Rudy walked on stage to a thunderous ovation and delivered a heartfelt speech to the standing room only crowd. He praised his friend Agnes Ayres for her commitment to perform in *Son of the Sheik* after she had just given birth to her first child. Opening night in Chicago went smoothly, but this would not be the case when the film debuted in New York.

There, the streets around the Mark Strand Theater became so congested with crowds straining for a glimpse of Rudy that George requested a police motorcycle escort for his safe arrival. But fans arrived early, and as Rudy and George's limousine pulled up to the theater every entrance was blocked. When the police failed to clear a path from the limousine to the theater door, George took matters into his own hands. He threw his suit jacket over Rudy's head and with the forward rush of a football linebacker he cut his way through the mob.

Despite George's body guarding, every button and both cuffs were torn from Rudy's shirt, the pockets ripped from his suit coat and hair yanked from his head. His return sprint to the limousine after the film's opening was an even more perilous mission. When Rudy and George did reach the safety of the limousine, fans clawed through the car's open windows and surrounded the vehicle making it impossible to move the car in any direction.

In the thick of this melee, someone in the crowd was struck by the limousine. Rudy, George and the driver heard the awful thud but could see no one who appeared to have been hurt or injured. Knowing Rudy would be mauled if the car doors were opened, George waved the driver to move on. In the Ambassador Hotel suite Rudy fretted over his missing tufts of hair and peeled off one more ruined suit, while George put a call through to the police. He inquired if anyone had just reported an incident outside the Mark Strand. The police said no and the subject was closed.

Rudy's final *Son of the Sheik* appearance was scheduled for August sixteenth in Philadelphia. He would then head home to Los Angeles with George and Bee to begin filming the first movie under his new contract with United Artists, *The Firebrand*. During the week prior to this appearance in Philadelphia, George scheduled a radio interview for Rudy to be broadcast from the Steel Pier on the Atlantic City boardwalk in New Jersey.

On the drive to Atlantic City, Rudy took the wheel of the car and reached his usual breakneck speed. George was all too familiar with Rudy's lead foot but that day he was less concerned over his rough ride to the Jersey Shore than he was with Rudy's haggard appearance. It was obvious the sweltering August heat was only aggravating Rudy's condition and his past week of late night revelry and imbibing in quantities of bootleg whiskey was taking a severe toll.

The crowds swarming along the boardwalk that afternoon proved to be unusually stressful for both Rudy and George. During Rudy's radio interview, hordes of his fans pressed against the radio station's windows with such force that George kept a nervous eye on the plate-glass as he watched it bow under the pressure.

Exhausted from the afternoon's efforts, George hoped he and Rudy would return to Manhattan immediately after the broadcast for some sorely needed rest. Instead, Rudy gulped down a tall glass of bicarbonate of soda and water and informed his weary manager that he wanted to stay in Atlantic City that evening to attend a performance of, "Gus Edwards' All-Star Revue". Against his better judgment, George telephoned the nightclub where the show was headlining to make the usual arrangements for Rudy's safety; entry through a side door and seating at a private table obscured from public view.

Gus Edwards was a showman well known for dragging anyone, especially a celebrity, on stage to be a part of his show. And as soon as he spotted Rudy and George, he made a show stopping announcement, "Ladies and Gentlemen! The Sheik will now dance a tango!" Rudy emerged from the shadows to the chants of "Rudy! Rudy! Rudy!" and stepped reluctantly into the full glare of the spotlight. He sauntered onto the dance floor leaving a trail of swooning women in his path and there selected the most ravishing stage dancer in the show to be his dance partner.

Unaware of his deteriorating physical condition, the audience roared in approval as Rudy swept the chorus girl into a brief but dramatically executed tango. When news of his performance reached nearby strollers on the boardwalk, crowds rushed to the nightclub's entrances and pressed in closer for a glimpse of the show. The club's kitchen staff craned their necks over their hot grills and waiters stopped in their tracks. By the time Rudy took his few perfunctory bows he was sweating profusely and as he attempted a return to his table he faced an impasse of grasping fans. George wasted no time and within a few minutes he was muscling his way through the sea of flailing arms and safely escorting Rudy away from the melee and out the nearest exit.

Gus Edwards' audience that night was unaware they had just enjoyed an historic floor show. They may not have seen Rudy's most polished tango performance, but they were all witness to his final one. It was only a few days later while he visited his friend columnist, Adela Rogers St. John that she discovered Rudy rummaging through her medicine cabinet in search of bicarbonate of soda. He complained of acute indigestion and attributed his malaise to having eaten too many snails the night before. Adela St. John thought differently as she was of the opinion that Rudy was ailing because he missed his ex-wife Natacha.

She wondered if his divorce might have been the inspiration for his increasingly liquid diet of whiskey. Rudy boasted to her and his other friends that he was following his whiskey regime to shed a few pounds and claimed he could go days without a bite to eat. Whether the source of his indigestion was his divorce from Natacha or the effects of too much questionable bootleg whiskey, Rudy was hardly pining for anyone. Natacha had recently returned to her parent's chateau on the French Riviera and Rudy's girlfriend Pola Negri was a neat three thousand miles away in Hollywood. Bottom line was, he was being faithful to no one.

George knew this to be the case especially concerning Pola Negri. He shared the Ambassador suite with Rudy and overheard his many heated phone calls with Pola. On what would be their last conversation, George caught the end of the spat as Rudy bellowed into the phone,

"Well, you can go to hell!"

With these words he slammed down the receiver and turned to George.

"Well, she can go out with her so-called Prince if she wants to, but not with me!"

Rudy's late hours and exhausting social schedule were taxing even George's stamina. Some mornings he woke when he heard Rudy enter the hotel suite, but more often he slept soundly through his arrivals. When George didn't stir, he was often roused from his sleep by a tap on the shoulder. Rudy, still in his evening clothes, would be standing over him. It was early on the morning of August fourteenth when George opened one eye to again see Rudy standing by his bed. On this occasion he was holding a glass of iced mineral water.

"George, " Rudy nudged," Would you like some water?"

"Why the C.P.R. service?" George rubbed his face in an attempt to rally.

"Oh, I thought you might be thirsty," Rudy handed him the ice water.

"You mean," George said as he sat up in bed and took a drink, "that you are bringing me this peace offering, hoping that I will not scold you for getting home at five o'clock in the morning!"

"Well," Rudy made his point, "Actually I intended to ask you to see that I am not disturbed until noon."

Late that afternoon Rudy showered, shaved and dressed for yet another round of parties and guest appearances. His date for the evening would again be Marian Benda. They shared a late dinner at Lido's Restaurant and then stopped by Tex Guinan's before cabbing back to Marian's place just after midnight. After a two hour tryst in her apartment, elevator operator Frank Gross ferried Rudy and Marian down to the lobby and noticed it was around three a.m., when he witnessed Rudy hailing a cab.

The driver of that taxi cab, Mike Li Calzi, then drove the couple to East 80th Street and Park Avenue; the apartment of playboy Barclay Warburton. Upon arriving at the address, Rudy left Marion waiting in the cab while he rang the door bell of the prestigious residence. When no one answered, he yelled up towards the apartment windows and whistled through his teeth a few times in an attempt to rouse Warburton's attention. Receiving no response, Rudy decided to head around the corner where he entered the building through a side door. Before long he reappeared from the building's main entrance, paid cabbie Li Calzi a dollar for the sixty cent fare and escorted Marion up to Warburton's apartment.

That Saturday night, Barclay Warburton was entertaining a few of his friends in celebration of the news that his Parisian divorce was declared final that day. According to Marion's account, Rudy downed many drinks at the wee hour's gathering, ate a ham and egg sandwich and complained he felt rotten. The party at Warburton's continued until dawn and by the time Rudy dragged himself home to the Ambassador Hotel, he was in the throes of what he believed to be just another bout of indigestion.

❧

When he walked into the suite that Sunday morning, George and Bee were eating their breakfast in the sitting room. George looked up, quickly accessed Rudy's appearance and told him he looked like

330

hell. Rudy replied he would join them for breakfast in a few minutes and then disappeared into his bedroom. He was in his room only a minute before George and Bee heard him curse loudly and groan. George was up from the breakfast table and through the door of Rudy's bedroom.

He found him sitting on the edge of his bed holding a tall glass tumbler. George said he was calling the hotel desk requesting they summon a doctor, but Rudy waved him off saying, "No, George, I'll be fine." He then began filling the empty glass with straight bourbon from a flask on his night table saying he didn't want to be disturbed until late that afternoon because he had a big date that night. In one long gulp, Rudy swallowed the entire glass of bourbon, then stretched out on the bed and said to George, "See? I feel better already." Since this scene had been repeated for days, George shook his head and returned to his breakfast. On their way out for the day, George and Bee stopped by the hotel's front desk with a request that all calls to Mr. Valentino's suite be held until their return.

About four o'clock that afternoon, the Ullmans returned to the Ambassador Hotel and immediately upon entering the suite they heard a loud groaning emanating from Rudy's bedroom. George was through the bedroom door for the second time that day and found Rudy doubled up on his bed, clutching his stomach. Before Rudy could say a word, George grabbed the telephone and called the hotel desk demanding a doctor be sent up to the suite as fast as possible. The desk clerk knew that a Dr. Paul Durham lived nearby and placed the call.

Within five minutes, Dr. Durham was making a quick assessment of Rudy's condition. He diagnosed Rudy's severe abdominal pain as a perforated ulcer and suggested he be transported to a hospital at once. Rudy balked at the idea and maintained more whiskey would bring him around. Dr. Durham and George denied this request and instead placed a telephone call to another nearby physician, Dr. Manning. Dr. Manning arrived within a few minutes and after he confirmed Dr. Durham's diagnosis, George called for an ambulance.

At five-fifteen that Sunday afternoon, Rudy walked from the ambulance into the Polyclinic Hospital's emergency room. Despite his excruciating pain, he refused to be carried in on a stretcher. Upon his admittance, he was examined by Dr. William Rawls, the hospital's Chief Resident Surgeon. When Rudy explained to the physician he'd been suffering from his symptoms for nearly ten hours, Dr. Rawls feared the worst; Rudolph Valentino was probably a dead man. Dr. Rawls and his attending surgeon, Dr. Howard Meeker both knew that anyone experiencing Rudy's exact symptoms for more than eight hours had little chance of ever recovering.

They found Rudy was running a high fever and his pulse was racing. More alarmingly, they discovered his abdominal muscles were manifesting a board-like rigidity; all symptoms of advancing peritonitis. In the days before antibiotics this type of aggressive infection was seldom reversed after reaching this stage. Knowing time to be of the essence, Dr. Meeker instructed the attending nurse to prepare his patient for surgery.

While Rudy was wheeled away on a gurney, word was spreading on the street that the Sheik had just been admitted to the hospital. Reporters descended upon the Polyclinic's front desk and so many curious people were filtering into the hospital's lobby that a nearby office space was designated as a press room. Recognizing the obvious urgency to protect Rudy's privacy, George asked Dr. Durham to assist him in the selection of two trustworthy nurses and two security guards.

One of these guards would be stationed outside the door of Rudy's room and the other would patrol the hospital corridor. It was sometime around six o'clock, only forty-five minutes after Drs. Rawls and Meeker made their initial examination, when Rudy was placed on the operating table. While George chain smoked and paced a fast groove in the carpet of a nearby waiting room, the ether mask was lowered over Rudy's face and Dr. Meeker reached for his scalpel.

Instead of making his rounds as the toast of Manhattan that Sunday evening, *The Son of the Sheik* checked his Savile Row suit for a mantle of crisp hospital linens. The face that had women all over the world dizzy with love was inhaling ether through a black rubber mask and the muscular body which Rudy proudly flexed for his swooning public over the past few weeks was being swabbed with iodine. When Dr. Meeker determined his patient to be under the effects of the anesthesia, he made his first incision, a vertical slice through the right rectus muscle.

What Dr. Meeker and the attending physician then discovered defied even their grimmest expectations. The body cavity of the apparently robust, thirty-one year old was ravaged. Rudy's entire intestinal tract was coated in a greenish gray mucous and a lesion one centimeter in diameter gaped on the anterior wall of his stomach. Dr. Meeker would later notate the precise location of this profound ulcer as being three centimeters from the pylorus valve and two centimeters from the lesser curvature of the stomach.

With no natural walling off of the stomach fluid and food particles, Rudy's intestinal tract was thick with debris. While the surgical nurse began suctioning this fluid, Dr. Meeker excised the area of tissue immediately surrounding the ulcer. The surgeon could see that this ulcer had not developed overnight, but had obviously been festering for some time. He came to this conclusion after discovering an area of about one and one half centimeters around the opening of the ulcer that was already in the advance stages of gangrene.

Meeker cut away the necrotic, gangrenous tissue and began stitching with mattress sutures to repair the hole in Rudy's stomach. As he threaded the fine linen sutures through the wound, he stitched a rubber drainage tube into Rudy's side. The surgical nurse continued her suctioning, while flushing the entire body cavity with a saline wash to ensure the drainage tube was properly positioned. Meeker then made his decision to remove Rudy's appendix.

As a surgeon he realized any further surgery at that juncture might jeopardize Rudy's recovery, but he had no other option. The appendix was so inflamed as a result of the acute abdominal infection that it was constricting a portion of Rudy's intestinal tract called the terminal illeum. Meeker snipped away at the appendix and implanted a second drainage tube in the right illiac fossa pelvic area. He then began his final suturing of the abdominal wound. During the operation Rudy came close to death when he slipped into profound shock. His pulse rate soared to 140 and his fever reached 104.5 degrees. With his heart racing and still under the effects of the ether, he was wheeled back to his heavily guarded room on the Polyclinic's eighth floor.

Dr. Meeker entered the waiting room to give George his report. After hearing the medical details of Rudy's operation, George asked the surgeon exactly what were Rudy's chances of survival. Meeker's two ton words leveled him,

"Fifty-fifty."

George was speechless and immediately left Dr. Meeker to see Rudy. He found him already in his room, still unconscious and suspended in leather shoulder harnesses on a bed slanted in a vertical position to facilitate proper drainage from his wound. George stumbled forward, staring in shock at the sight of Rudy hanging on his iron crucifix of a bed. He knew he had only a little time before Rudy woke from the effects of the ether and he turned his attention to the pressing details of Rudy's stay in the hospital.

He barred any visitors from the sick room except himself and Frank Mennillo and forbid any medical staff from relaying a word to Rudy about the true gravity of his illness. He also warned the two nurses on duty, Pearl Frank and Jean Littlefield, that they were not to allow a single newspaper in the room. Knowing more reporters were gathering in the hospital's press room, George then walked down to the hospital's first floor to hand them the blow by blow developments.

By the time George returned from his first press conference, Rudy was regaining consciousness. When he saw George enter the room, he asked in a frail but resolute voice,

"Well, George, did I behave like a pink powder puff or like a man?"

❧❧

New Yorkers awoke that Monday morning to the sound of newsboys screaming the bad news about Rudolph Valentino's surgery. While the world read of Rudy's medical plight, he woke that Monday morning on the eighth floor of The Polyclinic Hospital strapped to his vertical bed with a nurse flushing his body with saline injections. With his fever spiking, he told George that he felt "so tired."

All day Monday and Tuesday, Rudy slept fitfully in this upright position and there was little change in his condition. By Wednesday morning the drainage from his abdomen ceased and his temperature dropped to nearly normal. But despite his feeling better and being allowed to sip a cup of broth, Rudy was reaching his limit with the shoulder harnesses. He demanded George light a cigarette for him and barked at his nurses to allow him to sit upright. His ill temper was a relief to George and a sure sign of his recovery. But Rudy's doctors were not as encouraged and continued to meet in closed door conferences.

They knew that the next twenty-four hours would be critical and monitored Rudy for any signs of post-surgical infection. On Wednesday, Rudy's temperature was almost normal and his pulse rate slowing as he and George discussed a few possible locations for what promised to be a lengthy recovery.

But on the streets below the eighth floor hospital room and George and Rudy's encouraging bedside conversations, there were rumblings and Rudy's sudden illness came under suspicion. Many people believed someone might have tried to kill Rudolph Valentino. His fans perceived him as a veritable man of muscle and indomitable action hero and were adamant he'd been in perfect health. The news he fell gravely ill so quickly was not easily accepted and along Broadway rumors ran rampant that he might have been poisoned at Barclay Warburton's late night party the previous Sunday.

By Wednesday, the rumors of Rudy's possible poisoning, perhaps even by arsenic, were making national headlines. This situation prompted New York Assistant District Attorney Pecora to telephone George and assure him he would open an investigation if any credible evidence was brought to his attention. But Rudy's doctors and George knew Rudy's illness was no mystery. His condition had not manifested unexpectedly at any one party but had been developing over a period of many weeks. For George the troublesome poisoning rumors became just more disturbing information to keep from Rudy.

The rumors of foul play and arsenic poisoning caused Joe Schenck to be concerned about their possible negative impact on his hefty *Son of the Sheik* revenues. He was in New York at the time and issued his own statement to the press in which he requested that out of respect for Rudy the unsettling insinuations must cease at once. Everyone from George to Drs. Meeker and Rawls to Barclay Warburton, Marian Benda and even Rudy's nurse, Pearl Frank, who was accosted by reporters in her home, all swore there was no evidence to support the poisoning theory.

By Thursday, crowds milled in the streets below Rudy's hospital room and a few permanent vigils claimed strategic locations directly under his window. Through George, Rudy issued a message of gratitude to his fans and well wishers who showered him with so many floral arrangements the surplus had to be donated to the hospital's free wards. He graciously thanked them for their kind letters, their thoughtful gifts and their hundreds of religious medals. As the diehards tended to their camps below Rudy's window, they hung on every detail of his progress as issued by his doctors and George.

Recognizing the public's intense interest in Rudy's hospitalization, newspapers devoted pages of copy to the movie star's childhood in southern Italy, to his struggle to become a success in the motion picture industry, to his marital woes and to in-depth analysis of his revolutionary lovemaking techniques. By midweek, Rudy's illness and recovery had taken on an air of riveting suspense rivaling any of his movies. It seemed the world was waiting on baited breath for the Sheik to rise from his hospital bed, dash to his own nick-of-time rescue and ride along the ridge of some distant sand dune towards another thrilling ending.

By Thursday afternoon it appeared this just might happen. Rudy took care of a little business and asked George to dispatch wires to Natacha and Alberto. He was able to sit up in his bed for a while and listen as George read some of the hundreds of telegrams from his fans and his friends in Hollywood. He chipperly told Dr. Meeker that he looked forward to taking him on a fishing trip after his full recovery. Despite Rudy's upbeat mood, George still eyed his doctor's concern and wondered why their long faces.

On Friday, George placed his regular morning phone call to Lou Mahoney at Falcon Lair and spoke with Frank Mennillo to give him an update on Rudy's condition. Frank visited Rudy every day during the previous week and that Friday he informed George of his plans to leave for Tom's River on the Jersey shore the following Monday to vacation with his son Arnold. He told George that he'd put these plans on hold if Rudy did not continue to improve over the weekend.

George assured Frank that Rudy felt well enough that afternoon to ask him for a hand mirror. He went on to relate how he'd hesitated because the fact was Rudy looked horrible; his face was ashen, his cheeks hollow and his eyes blood red. But George explained to Frank that he'd handed him the mirror anyway because Rudy wanted to see what he looked like in case he ever played the part of an ailing character. By studying the effects of his illness on his face, he said he would know exactly what to do with his make-up.

That Friday afternoon, just as George was dispatching another round of encouraging telegrams, Rudy's fever began an ominous climb. When he complained of a sharp pain in his upper left chest and side, George summoned Dr. Meeker. Meeker made his examination and diagnosed pleurisy in Rudy's left lung; an inflammation of the membrane surrounding the lung and symptomatic of the onset of pneumonia. George felt the immediate impact when Dr. Meeker said the word "pneumonia". He knew Rudy had been smoking one hundred cigarettes a day and feared his lungs would be in no condition to survive the dreaded disease.

During this examination, Dr. Meeker also listened to Rudy's heart and quickly summoned a consultant to verify his next diagnosis; the valves of Rudy's heart were malfunctioning. Both the heart failure and pneumonia were evidence of an aggressive infection spreading through the abdominal cavity. Meeker ordered Rudy back into the shoulder harnesses, his bed elevated once again and the regular saline injections resumed. He scrawled his diagnosis of septic endocarditis on Rudy's chart hanging on the end of his bed. To any physician of the day, this meant imminent death.

The inflammation in Rudy's left lung caused his every breath to be excruciatingly painful. With his fever again rising past 103 degrees, his doctors ordered injections of morphine around the clock. Unfortunately for Rudy, this merciful drug not only rendered him pain free and unconscious for a few hours but also flat-lined any lingering ounce of strength he might have had to fight the advancing infection.

Despite the morphine being administered every three hours, much of the time Rudy writhed in agony. His acute suffering caused George to panic and he convened another conference with the medical team. On Saturday, he and the physicians brainstormed two last resorts for Rudy; blood transfusions and the possible use of Metaphen. Metaphen was a mercury based antiseptic not widely available at the time and its intravenous applications were still considered to be in the experimental stages. The fact that the only laboratory producing Metaphen was located in Detroit, Michigan made this treatment even more of a long shot. But by Saturday the discussion was no longer on expediting the delivery of the drug but whether its use would save or kill Rudy.

Desperate for any solution, George explored every option to ferry the drug from Detroit to New York as fast as possible. With Rudy's condition deteriorating rapidly the only feasible solution

George could think of was to send an airplane to Detroit. But even this drastic and expensive measure guaranteed nothing.

The possibility of performing blood transfusions on Rudy seemed to be a more practical solution. A donor with Rudy's blood type was located and the volunteer was stationed on the hospital's eighth floor. The blood transfusions were postponed and then canceled as the medical consensus was unanimous that Rudy would not survive the procedure. At George's request, Dr. Rawls and Dr. Meeker canceled all of their private practice appointments in order to remain at Rudy's bedside and issue hourly bulletins to the press. By Saturday evening, the possible arrival of any Metaphen looked bleak and the mood on the eighth floor of The Polyclinic Hospital took on an air of defeat.

It was on that Saturday evening, George had a disturbing run-in with Dr. Paul Durham. As he entered what he presumed to be a vacant hospital room next to Rudy's in the hopes of resting for a while, he heard Dr. Durham calling out to him. George discovered the physician prone on a hospital bed holding a stethoscope on his own chest.

"Ullman," Durham ordered, "get in here and let me check your heart! It's in bad shape."

With Rudy clinging to life a few doors down, George made his disgust with Durham's antics known. He stormed out throwing his hands in the air saying,

"I think you're crazy!"

It was also on Saturday, that a Catholic priest talked his way past the eighth floor security guard to approach George saying he wished to hear Rudy's confession. Fearing that the sight of a priest standing at his bedside might frighten Rudy, George refused the priest's request. Before leaving the priest admonished George saying,

"If he should die without the last rites, it will be on your head, George Ullman!"

Late that afternoon, George lifted his ban on admittance to Rudy's room by allowing two visitors to come to his bedside. Joe Schenck arrived to speak with the fallen star of his new blockbuster movie and on his way out of the hospital he paused to speak with reporters. He told them Rudy said he planned to fool his doctors and get well. And after George telephoned Jean Acker, she arrived to spend a moment with Rudy before rushing out of his room in tears.

By Sunday, George thought better of his refusal to grant the priest's request to hear Rudy's confession and he placed a call to St. Malachy's Church on 47th Street. He later felt he'd made the right decision in summoning the priest as Rudy rested more peacefully after the visit.

Sometime after the priest left, the nurse administered Rudy's scheduled injection of morphine. As soon as he fell to sleep, George hurried back to the Ambassador for a quick shower and a shave. Knowing the medication was having less effect on Rudy with each dose, within the hour George was trudging down the hospital's eighth floor corridor. After a glance at the medical chart hanging on the end of Rudy's bed, he turned to the nurse on duty and told her to call his wife at the Ambassador Hotel as well as Frank Mennillo and request that they both come to the hospital at once.

That Sunday evening, Frank's son Arnold was already on the New Jersey shore where he planned to meet his father the following morning. But when Frank took the call from the hospital nurse he didn't pause to phone his son with his change of plans. He grabbed his hat and within a half an hour he was standing in Rudy's hospital room. George and Frank would share the vigil at Rudy's bedside that long Sunday night, pacing the room as his fever remained consistently above 104 and as nurses fought to bring it under control with alcohol sponge baths. The acrid alcohol vapors made it nearly impossible to breathe in the stifling room and George and Frank could do little for Rudy. Other than adjust the electric fans, they could only sit for hours on the chair next to his bed and be there whenever he opened his eyes.

Throughout the night, Rudy faded in and out of consciousness and George and Frank watched him struggle to comprehend his dismal situation with his waning sensibilities. It seemed to them that he wasn't sure if minutes, hours or days were passing by or whether he was even awake or dreaming. The activity in his hospital room competed for his dwindling attention with the confusing dreams of his morphine haze. In one moment he could hear George speaking with someone by the door and in another he watched Frank dozing in the chair next to his bed. In the next moment Rudy was again sinking into another treacherous dream; a dream in which he was a little boy peering over a window sill of his childhood home, a dream in which he could clearly see the long view of the Ionian Sea.

In this particular dream, he stood before the familiar window, clutching his father's steel razor in his little hand. With his other hand he fingered a deep, bloody gash across his cheek. At this distant memory of his first, tragic shave, Rudy struggled for just one more deep breath to regain consciousness. With leaden steps he was running from his nightmare's landscape, through an olive orchard, thick with brambles and into a dense forest.

It was dawn on Monday morning when he opened his eyes. George was stroking his head. Hoping Rudy might return to a more restful sleep, George turned to lower the blinds on the window. Rudy raised his hand from the bed saying,

"Leave the blinds, George. I feel fine. I want the light to greet me."

George hesitated, knowing the sunlight would soon streak across Rudy's bed. In a voice stronger than George had heard in days, Rudy asked,

"Wasn't it an awful thing that we were lost in the woods last night?"

George was too shocked to reply and returned to stroking Rudy's head.

"On the one hand, George," Rudy went on," you don't appreciate the humor of that do you?"

George tried to smile,

"Sure I do, Rudy, sure I do."

With a distant look in his eyes, Rudy added,

"On the other hand you don't seem to appreciate the seriousness of it either."

Monday morning, August twenty-third, promised to be another scorcher and George and Frank had been awake all night rotating their watch at Rudy's bedside. From their vantage point high on the hospital's eighth floor, they could see the encampments of Rudy's faithful milling on the street below with their flickering candles and bouquets of flowers already fading in the morning heat. While vendors hawked their hot dogs and shaved ice to Rudy's crowd, horns honked, cars slammed on their brakes and those New Yorkers not praying upwards in the direction of Rudolph Valentino's hospital window, headed off into their work week.

340

As George and Frank hovered and made small efforts to assist in the business of Rudy's terrible morning, down on the Jersey shore Arnold Mennillo wondered what had happened to his father. While his phone calls to his father's apartment rang unanswered, Frank and George were leaning in over Rudy. Sometime around eight o'clock he opened his eyes for a brief moment and uttered only one word which he spoke in Italian.

"Madre."

After this faint declaration he closed his eyes. George and Frank stood by in silence hoping he would awaken and say more, but Rudy did not regain another flicker of consciousness. After an hour passed, Frank left the room to phone Father Joseph Congedo from St. Malachy's to request that last rites be given to Rudy. Within a half an hour Father Joseph and a second priest made their entrance into Rudy's hospital room.

Processing in a robe and white stole, Father Joseph sprinkled holy water on Rudy and blessed the room. Frank explained to George that if he planned to remain in the room for the rite of extreme unction, he would be required to do so on his knees. After the nurse spread a clean sheet over Rudy, she reluctantly left her patient's side. With his face drawn from the fight, Rudy was comatose, sweating profusely, his lungs rapidly filling with fluid and his heart faltering. Father Joseph then conducted a brief absolution of Frank and George's sins as they knelt before him. Meanwhile a second priest spread a white linen cloth on a small table by the bed and arranged an altar of two candles, a crucifix, a pyx containing communion wafers and a vessel of consecrated oil.

Father Joseph assessed Rudy's unconscious state and whispered to his assistant that the rite of communion would be omitted from the sacrament as Rudy was unable to swallow. The two priest's methodical movements irritated George and he shifted from knee to knee. After all Frank was the devout Catholic and he had insisted on these last rites. For George it seemed that everything should be done as quickly as possible at that point. He felt physically sick with panic at the horrifying development; for the first time in a week no one was medically attending to Rudy.

While the assisting priest lit the two candles and arranged the crucifix on the table, Father Joseph removed his white stole and replaced it with a violet one. He then processed once more around

Rudy's bed to bless the room and in a monotone chant he delivered his first prayer,

"In the name of the father, and of the son, and of the Holy Spirit, may any power that the devil has over you be utterly destroyed as I place my hands on you and call upon the help of the glorious and holy mother of God, the Virgin Mary. Amen."

With Rudy's fever gaining strength by the minute, his hollow breathing grew louder and rattled Frank and George's nerves. Father Joseph calmly went about the business of the last rites by placing his thumb into the container of consecrated oil. He then leaned over Rudy to anoint each of his eyes saying,

"May the Lord forgive you by this holy anointing and his most loving mercy whatever sins you have committed by the use of your sight. Amen."

This prayer was repeated again and again as Father Joseph anointed Rudy's forehead, his ears, his nostrils, his lips, the palms of his hands and his feet.

"May the Lord forgive you by this holy anointing and his most loving mercy whatever sins you have committed..."

"May the Lord forgive you by this holy anointing and his most loving mercy whatever sins you have committed..."

When Father Congedo folded the sheet to anoint Rudy's feet and hands, George eyed the open blinds. The sun was streaking across the bed and he could not shake his feeling of dread that this might be increasing Rudy's fever. George's anxiety mounted during the twenty minutes it took to administer the sacrament. As soon as Father Joseph delivered his final prayer and left the room, George was off his knees and closing the blinds. Rudy's nurse had already rushed into the room to resume her bedside tending.

Frank did not return to his usual post on the chair but instead sat next to Rudy on the bed. When the nurse informed him this was strictly against hospital policy, he waved her off duty. Sliding one arm under Rudy's shoulders, Frank lifted him up from the pillow and held him close to his chest. With the blinds clicked shut and Rudy at last safe from the morning sun, George was overcome with emotion. Leaning his weight against the wall, he finally broke down and cried.

As the two men waited on, they were unaware Rudy was already walking in Black Feather's shadow. In the Moon of the Black Cherries and to the solemn beat of a skin drum, the ancient American Indian had just spirited Rudy away; far from the pain of the hospital room, far from the echo of his death rattle and far from his losing battle with the fever. While Frank held him in his arms and while George wept, Rudy and Black Feather were breaking through the clouds and heading towards the Sacred Mountain.

⋘⋙

George stood just outside the Polyclinic Hospital's press room and paused for a moment under the stairwell to catch his breath. He stared in at the reporters slouching on their metal folding chairs; their hats plopped down over their faces as they lounged in the noon heat awaiting his next bulletin. It was slowly dawning on him that he'd been so focused upon Rudy throughout the past week, he had not allowed himself a single thought of life without him. Disoriented at that looming prospect, he swore silently to himself that he would just do whatever was required of him for Rudy. He stood there gathering his thoughts. What would he say to the press and how would he say it?

With a deliberate breath of thick hospital air, he stepped forward into the press room. At George's sudden arrival the reporters shuffled to attention, their chairs clunked down against the floor. While they opened their notebooks to record Rudy's latest vitals, George raised his arms straight out to his sides and gave it to them.

"He's dead."

George stood there motionless and offered no further explanation as the press room ruptured upon the impact of his two words. The metal folding chairs flew as reporters fell upon the door in a race for the nearest telephone. Before George turned to leave, he could already hear a newspaper boy in the street wailing the unbelievable.

"Valentino's Dead! Valentino's Dead!"

On the march back along the familiar path from the press room up to Rudy's room, George could hear shrieking out in the street and women along the hallway bursting into tears. Passing the hospital switchboard he heard the operators frantically answering one call after another.

"Yes, He died…died! Yes, he's dead!"

George knew the news was hitting hard and this had him picking up his pace. As he walked for the last time down the eighth floor corridor he caught a glance at his pocket watch and made the quick calculation. It was almost nine thirty in the morning in Los Angeles.

"Damn," he mumbled, "I've got to call Lou."

Epilogue

Rudolph Valentino's records are still on file within the archives of Campbell's Funeral Home. The faded, fragile documents survive as an operating blueprint of the chaotic ten days between his death on August twenty-third and his final departure from New York City on September second. In 1926, a typical entry in Campbell's accounting ledgers reflected their "polite tradition" and consisted of two pages; one page of commentary and a second page serving as an invoice of services rendered. The entry titled, "Rudolph Guglielmi (Valentino)", is a notable exception to Campbell's clerical restraint. In contrast to the ledger's measured penmanship, these eight pages are a muddle of scrawled entries, misspellings, scribbled billing references and George Ullman's signature here, there and everywhere.

Within a few hours of Rudy's death, George met with Frank E. Campbell and listened to the funeral director's sales pitch for a top of the line $30,000.00 silver coffin. George selected a silver and bronze casket at a more modest but still extravagant $6000.00.

According to Campbell's records, George then agreed to pay for the services of house organist, Mr. H.E. Hull and any extra telephone operators hired at a flat rate of four dollars a day. He also agreed to reimburse Campbell's for the cost of all refreshments served to the additional staff. Before George left this meeting with Frank Campbell, he handed him a check for $10,000.00 and on a handshake assured him any balance due would be paid within ten days. Rudy's final invoice at Campbell's totaled $11,087.10 with additional charges totaling $1,677.00 later forwarded to George's office in Los Angeles. It was also during this initial meeting with Frank Campbell that George delivered one of Rudy's formal suits. With the suit and George's check in hand, Frank Campbell got down to the grim business at hand.

He supervised the installation of Rudy's embalmed body in the funeral home's prestigious Gold Room and insisted the room be illuminated only by candle light. He signed for floral arrangements from nearby Roseland Florists and had them carefully positioned around the bier. A receipt for one delivery of $575.00 of palms and roses is still tucked in Campbell's ledger along with the written request by George Ullman that all surplus floral arrangements be delivered to neighboring hospitals.

As local radio stations broke the news of Rudolph Valentino's death, several announcers broadcast the erroneous news flash that the movie star's dying wish had been that his fans view his lifeless body. Despite George's frantic calls to these radio stations alleging the opposite, the broadcasts continued to air. Both George and Frank Campbell realized this call for pilgrimage would draw huge crowds in the morning when the funeral home opened its doors. In anticipation of a sure onslaught, the two men held a second meeting to discuss additional security measures.

As their first order of business, they placed a telephone call to the local police precinct requesting that a dozen foot policemen and several officers on horseback be stationed outside Campbell's by dawn on Tuesday, the following morning. Frank Campbell then informed George he would be hiring twenty additional men as, "watchers," to work in continuous eight hour shifts for ten dollars a day. These "watchers" would patrol the street outside Campbell's, supervise the establishment's main lobby and stand guard beside Rudy's bier in the Gold Room. George then hired several more men to work exclusively with him as assistant managers.

While the call for pilgrimage continued to crackle through radio sets urging New Yorkers to head straight for Campbell's at 1970 Broadway, George avoided the gathering crowds by slipping into the funeral home through a rear entrance. As he ducked into Campbell's just before dawn on Tuesday morning, he noticed trinket and hot dog vendors already setting up their wares in the street. Despite the morning's oppressive humidity, by noon ten thousand people, believing they were honoring Rudy's dying wish, had made their way to Campbell's Funeral Home. Within the next hour, the crowd swelled to twenty thousand mourners anticipating the opening of the establishment's doors. As the crowd continued to grow, Frank Campbell and George placed another telephone call to the police station demanding that more police officers be dispatched to the scene before the funeral home opened.

At 2 p.m., the mounted police informed the crowd that Campbell's would not be open to the public until six in the evening in order to allow ample time for private viewing. This news was met by boisterous outrage and chants of protest from the tens of thousands of New Yorkers who had just endured the peak hours of the day expiring in the heat. Within minutes of this announcement, nearly thirty thousand people surged forward, crashed through police barricades and slammed full force into Campbell's plate glass display windows. In the ensuing panic, shards of glass rained down on the stampeding crowd and those closest to Campbell's doors were shoved into the finely appointed foyer.

While mourners in the street continued to be crushed underfoot, the mounted police fought to gain control of the escalating riot. Their frightened horses reared and added to the frenzy by trampling the victims already wounded on the ground. Inside Campbell's, the rush towards the Gold Room was on and those mourners not wounded in the melee hurled potted ferns to the floor, cast furniture aside and even waged hand-to-hand combat with the "watchers" in the Gold Room.

The sacking of Campbell's Funeral Home raged for the next hour before any order was restored. One hundred New York City police officers were finally successful in clearing an area in front of Campbell's doors just wide enough to allow ambulances to remove some one hundred wounded people. Frank Campbell shouted over the din to the police sergeant in command saying he should announce to the crowd that the funeral home would be closing its doors until 4 o'clock to repair the devastated interior. As the police sergeant barked this unwelcome news, the tens of thousands of people still straining at the repositioned barricades became even more determined to fulfill what they assumed to be Rudy's dying wish. While Campbell's rushed to reclaim the funeral homes' devastated interior, the police and the "watchers" maintained a tenuous hold on law and order.

Ambulances headed for nearby hospitals with the injured and broken glass was swept away, while inside Campbell's, Rudy's casket was scuttled to a smaller viewing room on the second floor. There his body was transferred to a glass covered coffin which was then nailed securely to the wall. Meanwhile, George and Frank Campbell discussed the possibility of prohibiting the public from paying their respects to Rudy. They were soon reminded that tens of thousands of emotionally charged people milled in the streets and they decided to reopen the funeral home and proceed with the public viewing. George positioned police officers strategically throughout the funeral home and gave them instructions to allow each mourner only a second at Rudy's bier before being prodded along.

At 3:15 that afternoon, another skirmish broke out in the street when a rogue mob smashed the display window of the Brown "Drive-it Yourself" Automobile Co., and overturned a car in the showroom.

Fearing any further uprisings, Campbell's reopened their doors precisely at four o'clock. By then the two hundred and fifty police on the scene had managed the impossible; the formation of a line of thirty thousand people, eight abreast, stretching five city blocks north of Campbell's. When this mighty line finally began filing into Campbell's, a tight formation of police officers lined a path through the lobby, upstairs to Rudy's bier and out a back entrance. For the remainder of the day and evening Rudolph Valentino's public paid their respects at a swift clip of one hundred and fifty people a minute.

At midnight Campbell's closed its doors but the crowd in the street did not leave. Nervous neighboring businesses spent the remainder of the night boarding up their windows and nailing wooden barricades into place. Around midnight, George met with staff in Frank Campbell's office and two uniformed men were allowed entrance through Campbell's back door.

They identified themselves as members of the Fascista League and claimed Benito Mussolini had personally dispatched them to act as an honor guard by Valentino's casket. Surprised by the Italian government's apparent reversal in policy towards Rudy, George agreed to allow the men to assume their posts in the morning.

On Wednesday, the weather cooperated with the police and a heavy rain forced crowds under umbrellas and into well formed lines. That same morning, George met with a priest in St. Patrick's Cathedral and listened in disbelief to his official refusal to grant a mass for Rudy. The priest explained the church believed Rudy failed to lead an exemplary life, had been divorced twice, admitted to dabbling in the occult and openly lived in sin. As George reminded the priest Rudy received last rites by two Catholic priests, he was well aware the papal publication, *L'Osservatore Romano* had just issued a statement on Rudy's death and labeled him a symbol of wanton worldliness.

The publication declared, "his popularity as a sign of the decadence of the times..." and added that the rioting at Campbell's, "...would make us laugh if they did not cause the most profound pity. It is a collective madness, incarnating the tragic comedy of a new fetishism, the last logical consequences of a materialist civilization which has given man dominion over everything but himself."

Undeterred by St. Patrick's refusal, George headed for St. Malachy's on West 49th Street to speak with the priest who performed Rudy's last rites. With little arm twisting, he agreed to conduct the funeral, with a mass, on the following Monday, August thirtieth.

348

George realized Alberto would not arrive in time to attend a Monday funeral and knew he was perilously close to having no mass for Rudy, so he agreed to the date. Pola Negri would arrive in time for the Monday funeral as she was due in New York over the weekend. Paramount Studios suspended production on her film *Hotel Imperial* to allow her time to travel to New York with a nurse and her secretary Florence Hein.

During the two days of the public's viewing of Rudy's body, the circus like atmosphere outside Campbell's was depressing for George. For this reason on Wednesday afternoon he made the executive decision to terminate any further access to Rudy's casket except by his personal approval. That day he also filed papers with the New York City Health Department requesting that Rudy's body remain uninterred until his brother Alberto arrived the following week.

Campbell's records itemize three possible final resting places for Rudolph Valentino; New York, Los Angeles and Italy. George deferred this final decision to Alberto but nevertheless proceeded with plans to transport Rudy's body home to California. In the days before Alberto arrived in New York, George negotiated the legal complexities of transporting a casket across the county by train. The railroad agreed to honor Rudy's return ticket to California, but informed George the law stated that transporting a body across state lines required the coffin be sealed inside a shipping case or sarcophagus. Realizing such a sarcophagus would have to be custom-made, George placed an order for a $900.00 bronze case.

He had one other motivation for moving this process along. The New York Police Department demanded George remove Rudolph Valentino's body from their fair city as soon as possible. George reiterated he was awaiting Alberto's arrival to allow him time to view his brother before he was sealed in his coffin. Over the weekend, Pola Negri arrived in New York to begin her public wilting on George's arm. In Frank Campbell's office she spent only a few minutes with Rudy's body before staging the first of many dramatic faints for the press. She then secluded herself in an Ambassador Hotel suite with her secretary and a Dr. Sterling Wyman. The chivalrous Dr. Wyman arrived at the Ambassador Hotel assuring Pola Negri he'd been sent to assist her by Frank E. Campbell.

Even though George terminated public access to Rudy's casket, the situation at 1970 Broadway continued to be volatile. Urban legends whipped through the lingering crowd including one rumor claiming

Rudy's body had never been on display at Campbell's but had in fact been replaced by a wax counterfeit. Adding to the macabre atmosphere, reports surfaced that some of Rudy's fans were following him into the afterlife. One distraught fan, claiming she'd worn a picture of Rudy pinned inside her dress for years, surrounded herself with his photographs, downed a vial of poison and died on the spot. Another twenty-year old mother attempted to do the same. Before she could terminate her own life by shooting herself in the head, she was admitted to Bellevue Hospital for psychiatric evaluation.

While one hundred police officers continued to patrol the streets outside Campbell's over the weekend, Alberto steamed towards New York on *The Homeric* and Pola Negri issued regular, emotionally wrought statements to the press via Dr. Wyman. In Frank Campbell's office accusations were flying between the mortician and George Ullman over just who was responsible for the Fascista honor guard. Their presence ignited immediate protest from anti-Fascista organizations and prompted George to abruptly order their removal. When the Fascista and Mussolini denied any responsibility for the gesture, George accused Frank Campbell of having masterminded the charade as a publicity tactic.

Five hundred tickets were issued for Rudy's funeral and on Monday morning, August thirtieth, all five hundred guests gathered at St. Malachy's Church. Rudy's funeral procession wended its way from Campbell's under an escort of twelve motorcycle policemen and on this somber occasion the crowds lining the streets behaved. By order of the Motion Picture Producers Association, at that same moment in Hollywood all work in every studio came to a halt in observance of a moment of silence in honor of Rudolph Valentino.

During Rudy's funeral, an ambulance ordered by Dr. Wyman was parked outside the church in case Pola Negri needed to be rushed to the hospital. Inside, Jean Acker fainted and Pola Negri became hysterical as she hobbled in on George's arm. Speakeasy owner Tex Guinan had to be shushed for her loud sobbing and two tabloid photographers were routed out a side entrance by George's assistants. Among Rudy's pallbearers was one tall, impeccably dressed Italian, Frank Mennillo. And as the priests from St. Malachy's conducted their mass over Rudy's casket, a few lawsuits were being filed against Campbell's Funeral Home for injuries incurred in the stampede the previous Tuesday.

On September first, *The Homeric* finally docked in New York and George obtained permission from the harbor master to ride a tugboat out to board the ocean liner. Alberto greeted him on deck by saying,

"I am sorry. But I will take his place."

This audacious remark jolted George, but not as profoundly as Alberto's next question.

"How big is the estate?"

Utterly offended, George replied, "I haven't any idea."

The two men then rode by taxicab to Campbell's where Alberto took a quick look at his brother in his coffin before leaving for his hotel. There, through a translator, he made a statement to the press expressing his dismay at his brother's sudden death and announced he would be taking his body back to California for burial. George was already aware of Alberto's final decision to bury Rudy in Los Angeles and had hurried off to spend the remainder of that day attending to last minute preparations for the trip west. According to Campbell's records he personally supervised the installation of the shipping case on the funeral train by hiring a welder to solder the bronze case onto custom-made braces which were bolted to the train's floor. The following day at 6:30 in the evening, two private rail cars were hooked up to the Lake Shore Limited in Grand Central Station and Rudolph Valentino and his grieving entourage were at last on their way home to California.

One car carried Rudy's polished bronze sarcophagus surrounded by a bank of flowers and the other, George and Bee Ullman, Pola Negri, her nurse and secretary Florence Hein, Alberto and James Quirk, the editor of *Photoplay* magazine. George denied Pola's request to include Dr. Sterling Wyman on the passenger list. Just prior to leaving New York, George learned Frank Campbell had no connection with Dr. Wyman and that he'd never sent him to assist Pola Negri. Upon hearing this, George dispatched a friend of his, a reporter in New York, to investigate the solicitous doctor's background.

On the train ride west, George noticed the grief-stricken Pola Negri ate her way across the county "like a starved animal". She told George "emotion always made her hungry". In advance of every whistle stop she dispatched James Quirk to check and see if crowds were large enough at the train station to merit another one of her public faintings.

"Not enough people to faint for," Quirk would call out to Pola, "you might as well stay here!"

When the train reached El Paso, Texas, George received the telegram he had been waiting for from his reporter friend in New York. The lengthy telegram informed George that Dr. Wyman was no doctor. In fact he had done a stint at a hospital for the criminally insane. George also read that it was Dr. Wyman who recruited the Fascista honor guard at Campbell's. Under questioning, the uniformed recruits admitted to being professional actors hired for their appearance at Rudy's bier by Dr. Sterling Wyman. The sorry story of Pola's con artist doctor immediately went public and George issued his statement saying Wyman never had his authority to act on his or Pola Negri's behalf. He added that Sterling Wyman's claims he was acting on their behalf were obvious that the man was 'laboring under some derangement."

With no Guglielmi family burial plot awaiting Rudy in Los Angeles, Alberto accepted June Mathis' offer to bury his brother in her family crypt in the Hollywood Park Cemetery. On September 7th, 1926, Rudy was finally laid to rest after his Los Angeles funeral service at The Church of the Good Shepherd in Beverly Hills.

Within the next two months, George and Natacha published short books on Rudy; George's titled, *Valentino as I Knew Him* and Natacha's, *Rudy: an Intimate Portrait of Rudolph Valentino*. The second half of Natacha's book would inspire a frenzy of paranormal activity surrounding Rudy's sudden death. In a section she titled, "Revelations", she related Rudy's eloquent descriptions of heaven, his visions of heavenly architecture and his attempts to contact the living as revealed to her through seances.

Natacha's transcripts of Rudy's ethereal discourses were auspiciously timed. By the fall of 1926, many Americans were fascinated with the supernatural and the subject was gaining widespread popular support. The alleged ability to contact the deceased was not without its opposition. Magician Harry Houdini led a fierce campaign to debunk the trend but was powerless to quell the public's growing obsession with the occult. The ghost of Rudolph Valentino was ripe for the conjuring.

A few weeks before Natacha returned to New York in November of 1926, the Hindu Theosophist, Jiddu Krishnamurti added to the furor after he was besieged by reporters in Chicago. When asked if it could indeed be possible to still contact Rudolph Valentino, he gave a surprising response.

"Yes, of course, Rudolph Valentino, cinema sheik, is not dead. His soul is alive and can be reached by those on the proper spiritual plane. Valentino will come back to this earth in another physical cast. If he was beautiful, it was his soul and it lives, so why all this mourning? Next to the chase for money, the western world magnifies its sex life far out of proportion and thinks of these things when thoughts should be of the spirit."

With Krishnamurti's comment bolstering Natacha's reams of testimony from Rudy as he basked in a heavenly limelight, it was assumed by many of his grieving fans that he was readily accessible in any darkened room. This titillating prospect was seized upon by credible and non-credible psychics as a veritable gold mine.

While the faithful murmured over their Ouija Boards and convened for seances, enterprising psychics, mediums, tarot readers and crystal ball gazers began peddling their own direct line of communication with the dearly departed Rudolph. Many were convinced George Ullman's presence at their eerie fetes might inspire Rudy to materialize and included George's name on their seance guest lists. Although never true believers in the occult, George and Bee Ullman did attend a few seances in Rudy's honor.

The attempts to contact Rudolph Valentino were so widespread that the minister of St. Paul's Presbyterian Church in Hollywood delivered a sermon titled, "Valentino's Spirit Returns" and pamphlets were circulated with titles such as, "Is Valentino Communicating with Mortals?" The February 1927 issue of *Photoplay* got into the act by publishing Natacha's direct questions made to Rudy during one of her seances. Hollywood did its best to defuse the disturbing trend by publishing an article, "Exposing the Hocus Pocus" and *Collier's* magazine issued their spin on the phenomena with a piece titled, "The Actor Who Won't Stay Dead."

Even actress Mae West announced she had successfully contacted Rudy's soul during one of her seances held in a Manhattan loft. She claimed Rudy spoke to her in the company of speakeasy owner Tex Guinan and her brother, gangster Tommy "Killer" Owney. This psychic interest in Rudy did not diminish over the years and some twenty years after his death, thirty noted psychics organized a commemorative seance at Falcon Lair. They gathered in the room that had once been Rudy's den and warbled to the tune of My Darling Clementine, "Valentino, Valentino, we *desire* to contact you...". But other than an alleged sighting of Kabar loping through the room any verifiable paranormal activities or Rudy sightings failed to manifest.

The list of Rudy seers would be long and colorful and include Las Vegas astrologer, Mohawk Princess Springwater who alleged Rudy gave her a ring both literally and figuratively. Mme. Fourie of Johannesburg, South Africa reported a vision of Rudy in which he told her of "a lady with a hat of mine inside of which are the names of seven most important movie stars." There were many notable psychics claiming contact with Rudy's ghost over the years and many of them sought out George Ullman. In the 1970's, one psychic wrote him a letter relaying the news that Rudy was still alive and well and living in Paris. This infatuation with all things Rudy was not, however, exclusive to psychics.

In Italy, a brisk black market circulated his alleged cufflinks, shoelaces, handkerchiefs and spare teeth and an effort to canonize him flopped as quickly as it was suggested. Many of the Valentino Memorial Guilds, which George originally organized to promote *The Eagle* and *The Son of the Sheik*, flourished and some became Rudy cults. In Hungary, the police investigated the head of one of these Valentino Guilds who was allegedly pocketing dues from its unsuspecting members.

And in Hollywood, visitors to Rudy's crypt continued to chip away at his vault, mysterious characters lurked about the cemetery and a parade of keening women became regular fixtures in his mausoleum. The events at Rudy's crypt were so bizarre, cemetery caretaker Roger Peterson published his account of these events in *The New Movie Magazine*. He reported he kept a diary of the anguished women who made pilgrimages to wail at the wall of the Great Lover. He went on to relate one tale of a very pregnant young woman he discovered in the mausoleum early one morning who asked him to place a bed by the famous crypt so she could give birth then and there to Rudy's child.

Alberto and Jean Valentino pursued legal avenues attempting to halt the maudlin crypt demonstrations held annually on the day of Rudy's death. They referred to them to the press as "disgraceful displays" and "degrading carnivals" and vowed to do all they could to end the tradition of the ceremony. Over the years, the focus of these ceremonies was increasingly upon the appearance of mysterious women, dressed in widow's weeds and veiled from recognition, placing roses at Rudy's crypt. These "Ladies in Black" became such a colorful aspect of the annual crypt events that speculation over their identities became the subject of passionate debate. Pola Negri's name was bandied about and one woman, claiming she was the original Marian Benda, held the title for a few years before she committed suicide. Over the years a few of these women did remove their veil and enjoy the spotlight for a while as the "reigning" Lady in Black.

There were tangible efforts to immortalize Rudy. Immediately after his death the townsfolk in his home town in Castellaneta, Italy appeared to have forgotten their famous citizen. But they would eventually commemorate his life with the installation of a statue in the town square. In the U.S. another statue to Rudy titled, "Aspirations" was commissioned and placed in DeLongpre Park in Hollywood. George's own attempts to organize a fund for Rudy's memorial with Joe Schenck fizzled within a few months. One of the more lasting tributes to Rudy would be the dedication in his honor of a new childrens' ward in the same London Hospital where he once paid a surprise visit as Santa Claus.

In the forefront of this effort to immortalize Rudolph Valentino; a cadre of actors George referred to as, "The Applicants." As studio heads sought to replace Rudy on screen, a few worthy pretenders to his throne emerged; Ramon Novarro, Antonio Moreno, Ricardo Cortez and Warner Baxter. A slew of minor players included movie producer Edward Small's favorite candidate Tony Dexter as well as Klayton Kirby, Jack Dunn and Rossano Brazzi who was discovered in Italy by David Selznick. One winner of a Rudolph Valentino lookalike contest in Italy, Alberto Rabagliatti also made the rounds in Hollywood with his convincing Sheik impression.

It was not unusual for George to be contacted by psychics, aspiring actors, writers with screenplays in hand and fringe elements of Rudy's fan base. On one occasion the front door of his apartment was pelted with raw eggs by a furious "applicant". When George opened his front door and failed to recognize this Rudy reincarnate, the frustrated man bellowed in his face. "George, It's me, Rudy!" George abruptly shut the door, whereupon "Rudy" reached for his eggs.

Movie producer Ed Small contacted George to inform him his movie, *Valentino* would be based upon his book, *Valentino as I Knew Him*. On several occasions George informed Ed Small that the "brief outline" of Valentino's life contained within his short book was by no means sufficient material upon which to write a decent screenplay. He also impressed upon Small that there was a spiritual aspect to Rudolph Valentino that should be an important aspect of any movie on his life.

Small ignored George's advice and forged ahead with plans for his movie. Together with his friend, screenwriter George Bruce, Ed Small retreated to Palm Springs where the two men wrote their screenplay. When George read their final product, he told Small he thought it was dreadful and that he would have nothing to do with the film. In 1951, the amateurish and highly-fictionalized production was released starring Small's discovery, actor Tony Dexter, in the role of Rudy.

One of the more notorious Rudy "applicants" was discovered in Los Angeles in 1953, when police responded to a call on Hollywood Boulevard. When the door of the apartment opened, a man in full desert robes gave his name as Rudolph Florentino. He informed the police he'd devoted his life to Rudolph Valentino's memory. The policemen then discovered the floor of the apartment was covered in sand and an enormous tent had been erected where several women lolled about in harem costumes. With Rudy memorabilia cramming every nook and cranny of his Hollywood desert hideaway, Florentino made the logical decision to share his fabulous obsession and opened his home to the public as a museum.

Over the years Rudy's homes, Whitley Heights and Falcon Lair were ransacked by souvenir hunters. Falcon Lair became such a bull's eye that the property's many owners soon grew weary of the curious peering over the walls. This nuisance, along with the persistent rumors Rudy's ghost haunted his last home, had real estate agents despairing. In 1949, one valiant attempt was made by a San Francisco syndicate to convert Falcon Lair into a shrine to Valentino. The syndicate promised nightly red, white and blue fireworks displays, vesper services, a wishing well and the donation of The Great Lover's bed to The Smithsonian Institute. These plans never materialized due to lack of funds.

In the continuing confabulation over Rudolph Valentino, even his cause of death was not exempt from speculation. Many of his fans were unwilling to accept the fact that a man as exceptional as

Valentino had suffered such an unremarkable demise. Their attempts to invest his death with more meaning gave rise to a range of conspiracy theories. It was reported Rudy died of arsenic poisoning and that an emotionally unstable Barclay Warburton tried to assassinate him before committing himself to a sanitarium. Many years after Rudy's death, a story was circulated that he'd been caught in an affair with the wife of a motion picture mogul who shot him in the stomach. Pola Negri claimed he died from ingesting an experimental hair tonic. And in 1972, Rudy's friend from his earliest days in Hollywood, Paul Ivano, gave an interview in which he claimed Rudy had been stabbed at Warburton's party. Leading the rumor mill for a time was chemist Howard J. Force. After publishing a few pamphlets, "Poisons Formed by Aluminum Cooking Utensils" and "Are You Heading for Your Last Round-Up?', he asserted Rudolph Valentino died from eating food cooked in the deadly cookware.

When it came to the subject of Rudolph Valentino, even the most outlandish assertions went unchecked and his ever-evolving legacy became a claim staker's free-for-all. Restaurateurs marketed his patronage, tango dancers recognized the cash reward of claiming some blood lineage to Rudy Valentino and a small army of Italian men alleged they'd once worked as his double. Before very long, hucksters claimed Valentino slept here, ate there, haunted this and once owned that. Quests to recover and own his many cars, his fabulous jewelry and his slave bracelets have been executed with the religious fervor of crusades for some holy grail. And the list of Rudy's relatives from distant cousins, aunts and uncles twice and thrice removed now stands at a record number of individuals. Rudy, it seemed, had been related to thousands of people and as a ghost was tripping about the globe as omnipresent as a god.

Throughout the years, a mythical Rudolph Valentino evolved as a man capable in death of traversing dimensional barriers to not only deliver lengthy discourses from beyond and transcribe screenplays through psychic's typewriters, but to continue to have his postmortem way with women. George was notified of no less than thirty-five alleged love children who were all conceived long after Rudy's death. No legal claim of paternity was ever presented in a court of law but reports of this miraculous conception by the spectral Rudolph Valentino continued for years. Ironically, it may have been one love child from his real life that ultimately defined his destiny.

Just before dawn on the raw and blustery morning of December 23, 1913, a teenage Rudolph Valentino stood on the deck of the ocean liner, The S.S. Cleveland to catch his first glimpse of New York City. He joined his fellow weary passengers to welcome the first sight of land as the lights of Manhattan appeared on the horizon. Wrapped in their woolen blankets, everyone on board that morning swore they would never make that trip again. They had just crossed the North Atlantic in the dead of winter and endured foul weather, bitter cold and turbulent seas.

As the Statue of Liberty and Ellis Island finally came into view, Rudy leaned against the ship's railing and wound his blanket tighter across his chest. The shivering teenager was a long, long way from the warmth of his home in southern Italy. Mercifully, he was also a long way from a band of outraged relatives, his disappointed mother, a pregnant woman and an older brother who might or might not do what was required of him to save a family's reputation.

But two days before Christmas in 1913, the twinkling lights of New York City had Rudy only facing forward. It would be another seven months before the child bearing a disturbing resemblance to him would be born. And it would be another ten years before "Uncle" Rudolph would begin paying close attention to this child, initiate legal processes to adopt him and appoint him his sole heir.

On that frosty morning, Rudy was just fixated upon a fleet of tugboats maneuvering The S.S. Cleveland towards a pier at Ellis Island and like most teenagers he was living passionately from minute to minute. As the blasts from the great ship's horns reverberated across the mouth of the Hudson River and echoed through the streets of lower Manhattan; his life in America was about to begin.

What Ever Happened To...

Jean Acker-

After Rudy's death, Jean Acker Valentino wrote a song dedicated to her ex-husband titled, "*We Will Meet at the End of the Trail*". The ditty caught on and for a while Jean's name continued to be in the news. When the popularity of her plaintive song waned, Jean accepted bit parts and uncredited roles in movies and television. As Jean Acker legally changed her name to Jean Valentino, in the episodes of the *Schlitz Playhouse of Players* in which she appeared, two Jean Valentino's were listed in the show's credits. Jean Guglielmi Valentino also worked as a sound engineer.

Jean Acker Valentino spent the remaining years of her life in Beverly Hills with her companion, Chloe Carter. Both Jean and Chloe Carter worked as extras throughout the 1940's with Jean landing uncredited roles in *It's a Wonderful Life, Spellbound* and *My Favorite Wife*. Jean Acker reported her entire collection of Rudy memorabilia was stolen from her Los Angeles home some time during the 1950's. Rudy's first and fleeting wife appeared in her last movie in 1952 and died in 1978 at 85 years old.

Marion Benda -

After Rudy's death, Marion continued to be one of the most famous Ziegfeld Follies Girls and in 1927, New York City Mayor James Walker named her "Miss New York". That year she was also among the official party that greeted aviator Charles Lindbergh upon his return from Paris. Marion later married William Wise, a Los Angeles sportswriter and after their divorce she married Baron Rupprecht von Boecklin from whom she reportedly received a $200,000.00 settlement when they divorced. Her third husband was a leading doctor in Santa Monica, Dr. Blake H. Watson.

In 1945, as Marion Watson, she downed the first of several overdoses of sleeping pills and at that time alleged she and Rudolph

Valentino were married shortly before his death. Alleging she was Rudy's third wife and true widow, she told reporters she and Rudy had two children together. These children, she claimed, were being raised in seclusion in Europe. It was also surmised at this time that Marion was the reigning "Lady in Black." In March of 1949, Marion again attempted suicide and was ordered to a mental institution as her fortune had vanished as well as her sanity. In November of 1951, she was found dead of an apparent overdose of sleeping pills.

Dr. Paul Durham -

A few weeks after Rudy's death, the physician who hurried across the street to the Ambassador Hotel to make the first examination of the stricken movie star was declared legally insane and confined in a home for the mentally ill in Texas.

Blanca DeSaulles -

After a jury declared Blanca Errazuriz DeSaulles innocent of murdering her ex-husband, she headed west to California. By January of 1918, it was reported she and Jack, Jr. traveled to San Francisco and also to the Los Angeles area. Whether she and Rudolph Valentino reconnected in either of these destinations, it is not known.

Eventually Blanca returned to her native Chile with her young son, John Longer DeSaulles Junior where she married wealthy Chilean businessman, Fernando Santa Cruz Wilson. Blanca's acquittal was not the end of scandalous international headlines plaguing her well-to-do family in Valpariso, Chile. Blanca's brother, William "Billy" Errazuriz brought more sorrow and shame upon the household.

As a Chilean diplomat in Paris in 1922, Billy fell head over heels in love with tall, blonde showgirl, Peggy Joyce Hopkins. Billy planned to wed Peggy Hopkins and then sail home to Valpariso with his new bride by his side. But Peggy Joyce Hopkins was no demure senorita. She soon earned a reputation for being such an unabashed gold-digger, she became the inspiration for Chaplin's film *A Woman of Paris*, as well as the Anita Loos character Lorelei Lee in her play, *Gentleman Prefer Blondes*.

It was after a night of heavy drinking and clubbing that Peggy Joyce Hopkins informed the Chilean playboy, Billy Errazuriz she loved another. Hearing this, Billy retreated to a room adjoining Peggy Joyce's boudoir and shot himself in the head. The headlines reporting this tragic incident were so sensational that the Ohio Film Board censored David Selznicks' newsreel footage of Peggy Joyce Hopkins when she returned to America. Blanca and Billy's mother, who once rushed to New York to be at her daughter's side during her murder trial, traveled to Paris to retrieve her only son's body.

Blanca's marriage to Fernando Santa Cruz Wilson ended in divorce and in 1940 she died at 47 years of age in her home in Valpariso, Chile.

Foxlair -

After Richard Hudnut's death in 1928, the Foxlair estate became property of the Police Athletic League of New York City. For many years the hillside residence was used as a summer camp for inner city boys. By 1966, the police abandoned the summer camp and the entire estate was assimilated into the Adirondack Mountain State Park. It was then park rangers discovered vandals destroying the "Big House," where Rudy Valentino and Natacha Rambova spent a few idyllic weeks in the summer of 1922. The decision was made to torch the once luxurious mountain retreat and the "Big House" and every other remaining building on the property were burned to the ground.

Falcon Lair -

Falcon Lair had several owners before being purchased by heiress Doris Duke, who died in the residence in 1993. After a lengthy estate battle the home was once again sold in 1998 for less than three million dollars. A renovation was planned but not completed, with the home being partially destroyed in 2006. Today only a portion of the original residence remains along with the gates and stable.

Douglas Gerrard -

Rudy and Natacha's friend Doug Gerrard spent most of his career in Hollywood working as a director. The handsome Irishman can be seen today in one of the many surviving movies in which he appeared as an actor. The Warner Brothers' 1927 silent movie, *The First Auto,* is probably his meatiest role. In this film, Doug Gerrard is cast as the flamboyant Squire Rufus Stebbins. Doug Gerrard's long career in show business began in 1913 and ended in 1950 when he suffered a stroke while walking along the streets of Los Angeles. The massive stroke caused him to fall on the sidewalk with such force that he fractured his skull.

Paul Ivano -

Throughout the 1940's and 1950's, Paul Ivano worked as a cinematographer on mostly "B" movies including *The Spider Woman Strikes Back* and a string of television programs including *The Texan, The Loretta Young Show, The Man From Uncle, Daniel Boone, Family Affair* and *Daktari.* He married in 1935, retired from show business in 1970 and died at 84 in 1984 in Woodland Hills, California.

Jadaan -

After his two infamous appearances in *The Sheik* and *The Son of the Sheik,* the Arabian Stallion, Jadaan, made three more public appearances in the Tournament of Roses Parade. In his third Rose Bowl Parade, the celebrated horse garnered press coverage after he reared for the crowd and galloped through the streets of Pasadena with a frantic rider clinging to his neck. There were a few more screen roles for Jadaan before he was finally "put down" in 1945. The stallion's skeleton is still used as a classroom display at University of California College of Agriculture at Davis, California and Jadaan's original saddle and tack used in *The Son of the Sheik* is currently the property of Cal Poly in Pomona, California.

Norman Kerry -

Rudy's friend, Norman Kerry, is best remembered as the leading man in several of Lon Chaney's films, *The Hunchback of Notre Dame*, *The Phantom of the Opera*, and the grisly horror movie, *The Unknown*. Often compared to action heroes such as Douglas Fairbanks and John Gilbert, Kerry has been largely forgotten today. After enjoying a thirty-five year career in Hollywood, he retired in 1941. He died in 1956.

June Mathis -

After leaving Famous Players-Lasky, Mathis signed with MGM as an editorial director. Her first major projects were *Greed* and *Ben-Hur*. Both projects were disastrous for Mathis. She salvaged her career by signing with First National Pictures in 1924 where she wrote and edited comedies, including several of Colleen Moore's films.

After terminating her contact with the Valentinos, she eloped with Italian cameraman Silvano Balboni. By 1926, she had parted ways with First National and was working as a freelance writer.

The legendary screenwriter who gave Rudolph Valentino his first big break in *The Four Horsemen of the Apocalypse*, died on July 27, 1927 while attending the theater in New York with her grandmother. She is buried in a crypt next to Valentino.

Arnold Mennillo -

Arnold Mennillo enjoyed a long and profitable career as a certified public accountant in Los Angeles. In 1986, he suffered a stroke which left him unable to speak. Rudy's young dance protege never forgot his tango lessons and although impaired by the effects of the stroke, at a spring event held by the Italian community in Los Angeles, Arnold performed his last dance with his wife. He was a prominent citizen in the Italian community in Los Angeles and recognized by many Italian organizations for his community activism. He died in 1992.

Frank Mennillo -

During the leanest years of the depression, Frank struggled to keep his cannery in Merced solvent. In the spring of 1936, he closed his California Tomato Juice Company and returned to Los Angeles to work in the produce brokerage business. Only six months after returning to Southern California, he was diagnosed with cancer. A major surgical procedure was performed to stave off the advancing disease, but Frank's post-surgical condition deteriorated rapidly. Less than one week later, a fifty-four year old Frank Mennillo passed away with his brother Ciro and son Arnold by his bedside. Frank's many obituaries in Los Angeles, San Francisco and Merced made no mention of his affiliation with Rudolph Valentino but instead praised "The Olive King's" contributions to the canning business and "his improvements in canning procedure and the development of new processes."

Frank never divorced his wife Zelinda. She worked as the principal of the Sullivan Street School in Greenwich Village and was a well-known activist and advocate for the underprivileged children of New York. She founded the Mother's Club, organized a boycott of Tammany Hall politicians and holds the distinction of being the first honorary police woman in New York City.

Lou Mahoney -

Lou Mahoney's obituary in his hometown paper read, "Aide to Valentino, Succumbs," and reported erroneously that he was Rudolph Valentino's manager. The article also alleges that in the years following Valentino's death, Lou acted as custodian of Rudy's memorabilia and classic automobiles.

In his taped memoirs, Lou recalls he met Rudolph Valentino when he was summoned to Paramount's New York studio lot shortly before the movie star moved to Los Angeles the end of 1925. Lou claimed he was dispatched as a police officer to protect Valentino after the movie star received a threatening letter from a criminal organization known as the Black Hand. When Lou asserts this event transpired, he had already resigned from the New York Police Department, was living in Los Angeles and the much feared Black Hand had ceased to be. As the forerunner of the mafia, the Black

Hand's hey-day occurred years earlier around the turn of the century. With the advent of prohibition in 1921, the business of selling bootleg liquor was seized upon by the underworld as a far more profitable means of extorting money than the delivery of letters bearing the mark of a black hand.

Lou may have at least in part based his yarn upon actual police activities. For along with every other cop in New York at the time, Lou knew the details of an infamous sting involving the Black Hand and Mr. Valentino. But this sting took place several years before Lou alleged it did and he played no role in the episode. The police had not been summoned to protect movie star Rudolph Valentino from the Black Hand's threats but instead the owner of a pool hall in New York's Washington Square whose name was Giovanni Valentino.

For a few years, Lou ran the dry-cleaning business which George sold to him for $250.00 after Rudy's death. Just after the second World War he went to work for Lockheed Aircraft in Burbank where he worked for twenty years before retiring to Newport Beach, California to operate a post office sub-station and greeting card shop. While living in Newport Beach, Lou volunteered to serve on the Orange County Grand Jury and in his later years was well-known in the community as an "inveterate" writer of letters to the editor of the local paper. Lou Mahoney died in 1968.

Mae Murray -

Mae Murray's marriage to Prince David Mdivani in 1926, had a disastrous effect upon her movie career. Mdivani assumed total control of his new wife's business affairs and encouraged her to terminate her professional relationship with the studio that made her a star, MGM. By the time Mae divorced Prince Mdivani, her mismanaged career had been destroyed and she'd lost custody of her son. Mae worked with Jane Ardmore Kesner to publish her biography, *The Self-Enchanted* in 1959. After struggling financially for the remainder of her life, she died in 1965.

Nita Naldi -

Nita Naldi finished work on Natacha's film *"What Price Beauty?"* and this marked the end of her U.S. film career. She traveled to Europe where she appeared in a few films, the last being Alfred Hitchcock's *"The Mountain Eagle"* in 1926. Naldi married J. Searle Barclay in 1930, and at that time she announced her retirement from films.

The Barclay's finances soon drained and Naldi declared bankruptcy in 1931. Naldi then returned to acting on stage. She performed in 1933, in *The Firebird* as well as *Queer People*. When Naldi's husband died in 1945, she was left destitute. She granted several interviews and made a few TV appearances, speaking of her silent film days and occasionally mentioning Valentino.

By 1959, Naldi was diagnosed with a heart condition. She succumbed to the effects of the disease in 1961 and was found dead in a small room in the Wentworth Hotel in New York. Naldi's funeral was paid for by the Actor's Fund.

Pola Negri -

George Ullman was not the only person affiliated with Rudolph Valentino who was ordered by the court to reimburse Alberto Valentino funds he once spent. In 1929, Pola loaned Alberto $7000.00 and some years later when he repaid her only $500.00 on the loan, she sold the unpaid note to the Bank of America. Pola Negri then co-signed Alberto's refinanced loan. When Alberto again failed to make good on that loan, as co-signer, Pola Negri was sued by the Bank of America for the entire amount, plus interest.

In July of 1927, Pola married Rudy's competition for her heart, Prince Serge Mdivani. The marriage ended in divorce and after the stock market crash of 1929, Pola was virtually bankrupt. Her financial situation worsened with the advent of talkies as her thick Polish accent left her unemployable. In an attempt to regain her lost fortune, she sailed for Europe in search of stage and screen roles. She made several movies in Germany with UFA during the 1930's before returning to the U.S. in 1941. Collector William Pelf made several attempts to contact Pola Negri, but she refused to meet with him believing his only interest in her was to ply her for information about Rudy. Pola retired to San Antonio, Texas, made one last film appearance in *The Moonspinners* in 1964 and died in 1987.

Natacha Rambova -

After Rudy's death, Natacha pursued a brief stage career in New York, wrote a play as a satirical parody of her life in Hollywood titled, *All That Glitters* and opened a dress salon on 5th Avenue. In 1928, Richard Hudnut died and left a sizable inheritance to his beloved step-daughter.

This made it financially possible for Natacha to relocate to the island of Mallorca, Spain in 1931, where she invested her inheritance in the restoration of Mediterranean villas. There she met and married a Basque count, Alvaro Ursaiz, who bore a striking resemblance to Rudolph Valentino. During the 1930's, Natacha and Alvaro Ursaiz toured the Middle East and Egypt and when the Spanish civil war broke out Natacha returned to France and the safety of the chateau at Juan Les Pins. Marital bliss was not to be for Natacha and Alvaro Ursaiz and they eventually divorced.

In 1939, Natacha was single once again and she returned to the U.S. and her homes in Connecticut and Phoenix, Arizona. She devoted the remainder of her life to her writing and the study of Egyptian art, dream analysis, symbolism, myth and the theories of the lost civilization of Atlantis.

In 1965, Natacha Rambova was discovered collapsed on the floor of an elevator in The Gotham Hotel in New York. Suffering from the advance stages of scleroderma and nearly unable to swallow, Natacha's family in California brought her to Los Angeles where she lived until her death on June 5, 1966. During the final days of her life, Natacha ate a diet of eggs and caviar, enjoyed the company of her Pekinese dogs and according to her relatives seldom spoke of her life with Rudolph Valentino.

Today three galleries display her private art collections; The Natacha Rambova Collection of Egyptian Antiquities in The Utah Museum of Fine Arts in Salt Lake City, Utah and The Natacha Rambova Gallery of Nepali and Lamaistic Art in The Philadelphia Museum of Art in Philadelphia, Pennsylvania. A 10,000 piece Egyptology collection of Rambova's was gifted to Yale University in

2010. Pieces of the collection have been displayed at the Yale Egyptological Institute in Egypt.

Vilma Banky -

After Vilma's affiliation with Valentino, her name was linked to many Hollywood playboys before she married actor, Rod la Rocque.

The coming of sound proved treacherous for Banky and her Hungarian accent. After making three talkies, she retired from the screen in 1932, though she continued to act on stage with her husband. Banky and La Rocque enjoyed a long and happy marriage, ending with his death in 1969. She became a recluse, rarely granting appearances. She died in 1991 at the age of 90.

Agnes Ayres -

Agnes Ayres' troubled film career began long before filming her second role as Lady Diana. After a disastrous affair with Jesse Lasky, she married Manuel Reachi and left Paramount for the independent studio PDC. Ayes sued PDC in 1925, as she felt they were not fulfilling her contract.

After her appearance in the *Son of the Sheik,* Ayres divorced her husband and returned to film full time. Several of these films included talking sequences. Ayres professional and personal life went adrift in 1929, when she lost her fortune in the stock market crash. Ayres began touring in vaudeville and sought to obtain roles in talking films. In 1937, she suffered a nervous breakdown and in 1939, she relinquished custody of her daughter. Ayres died on Christmas Day 1940, after suffering a cerebral hemorrhage. She was 42.

Joe Schenck -

After serving only four months of his sentence in a Connecticut State Federal Penitentiary, Joe Schenck was pardoned by President Harry Truman. The deposed mogul then returned to Hollywood and accepted a position as head of production at Fox Studios. By the early

1950's, Joe Schenck was still wielding his executive might and convinced Harry Cohen, the head of Columbia Pictures, to grant a screen contract to a young starlet named Marilyn Monroe. In 1950, the man who once granted Rudolph Valentino a lucrative contract, interviewed a new heartthrob candidate, Marlon Brando. Joe Schenck retired in 1957, after suffering a stroke and died in 1961.

Dr. Wyman -

In the course of Dr. Sterling Wyman's career as arch-imposter, Ethan Allan Weinberg, or "Dr. Wyman", posed as a doctor, an attorney, a uniformed police officer and an array of diplomatic officials. As the United States Consul to Monaco, a special representative in the U.S. for the Republic of Salvador, the Consul General for Romania and Lieut. Royale St. Cyr, Weinberg, a.k.a., "Dr. Wyman" accumulated a lengthy albeit bogus resume.

In addition to posing as Pola Negri's physician in New York at the time of Rudy's death and boasting to the press that he authored a prestigious publication titled, "*Wyman on Medical Jurisprudence*", the ersatz Dr. Wyman also crashed through police lines in full uniform to greet the Bremen aviators as they passed through New York on their way to Washington. Undetected, the con man extraordinaire then personally escorted the Bremen flyers to their train under the alias of "Captain Stanley Wyman".

Weinberg/Wyman did not always escape incarceration for his outrageous flim-flammery. In 1922, he was sentenced to two years in an Atlanta penitentiary for arranging a reception for President Harding as, "Lieutenant Commander Stanley Wyman". Weinberg assumed his alias of Dr. Wyman while working in a "diploma factory" in Washington where he purchased his medical degree for $25.00. Shortly after Wyman left for New York with his new identity in hand, the Dean and President of the shady diploma factory were convicted of using the mail to defraud and locked in a Federal Penitentiary.

Wyman/Weinberg 's life came to an end as he bled to death on the floor of a small hotel in New York City where he was employed as a night clerk. Robbers burst in late one night while he was on duty and in the course of the stick-up, Lieutenant Commander, Captain, Dr. Stanley Sterling, Weinberg, Wyman was shot and killed.

George Ullman -

During the first few weeks after Rudy's death, George and Bee Ullman traveled to San Francisco to return Rudy's pedigreed pup, Mission Rudy, to its previous owner, Mayor Rolph. When the Mayor and his wife greeted the Ullmans' at their door and saw the dog they'd given to Rudy only a few weeks earlier, they both broke down in tears.

It was also during this same time that George endeavored to distribute Natacha's film, *What Price Beauty,* as the movie was an asset of Rudolph Valentino Production Company. He first sought its distribution with United Artists' President, Joe Schenck, but after a few test showings, Schenck informed George he had no interest in the film. George then went to the Pathé Company where he negotiated a contract for their worldwide distribution of the film. George hoped Natacha's movie would generate income for the estate, but this was not to be. Pathé dropped the project and George fought unsuccessfully for Pathé's return of the film's original negative. George and Natacha never spoke another word to each other after Rudy's death and although George debated calling her many times, he never did.

According to his memoir, George was most proud that in October of 1931, he was able to have $61,432.00 of federal tax liens against the Rudolph Valentino Production Company abated for over assessment of income taxes and interest. This may be verified by tax records and was recorded in the L.A. County Library card index number 1-9-4 on October 11, 1931.

Many years after Rudy's death, George and Bee Ullman enjoyed a Sunday afternoon at the Los Angeles Farmer's Market and heard a voice calling, "Mr. Ullman! Mr. Ullman." George was surprised to see Norma Niblock, the Canadian beauty Rudy once crowned as the winner of the Mineralava beauty contest. Norma told the Ullman's that after the beauty contest she moved to Los Angeles from Toronto to pursue a career in the movies. Unable to secure work in the movies, she married and settled in Pasadena.

In 1950, George was asked by author Norman Mackenzie to write the introduction for his biography of Rudolph Valentino. Norman Mackenzie wrote George a letter of appreciation in which he stated that he considered him the "absolute authority on Rudolph

Valentino," and added that he was honored to have had, "Rudy's closest friend," write the introduction to his book.

In 1975, upon his childrens' encouragement, an aging George Ullman penned his memoirs about his life behind the scenes with Rudy. He began the project as a rewrite of his original book, *Valentino As I Knew Him*, published in 1926, but abandoned this direction to write a rambling tale of anecdotal material relating to the personal and business affairs of Rudolph Valentino. As George completed his handwritten pages, his children ferried the manuscript to a typist. Soon after he completed his memoir, George passed away.

The Ullman Family -

George and Bee Ullman lived the last years of their fifty-nine year marriage in their DeLongpre Avenue apartment in Hollywood. After George's death, Bee Ullman moved to Northern California to live with daughter Bunny and her husband. Despite Bee's long battle with tuberculosis and many devastating surgeries during the 1930's, she lived to be 89 years old.

The Ullman's eldest son Dan, became a successful screenplay writer during the 1950's for both television and movies. His work included *A Good Day for a Hanging*, *The Oklahoman*, *An Annapolis Story* and *Seven Angry Men*. Dan Ullman died in 1979.

Today, Bunny Ullman and her husband are both retired professionals living in Northern California. They have four children and nine grandchildren.

After Rudy's godson, Bob Ullman attended Stanford University, he completed a distinguished career as a U.S. Naval Officer and settled in Southern California. He worked as a mortgage banker, fathered two children and was an accomplished tennis player. Due to his father's experiences, Bob harbored a deep resentment of Hollywood and the motion picture industry. A few weeks after completing work on this book and after assisting with the editing of his father's memoir, Bob Ullman passed away at home in August of 2005.

Alberto Guglielmi Valentino -

In August of 1934, Alberto, his wife Ada and Jean re-entered U.S. territory in Ensenada, Mexico to officially file their petitions to become U.S. citizens and sign their required renouncements of allegiance to the Italian King, Victor Emmanuel III. On the various documents they signed that day, Alberto listed his occupation as writer, accountant and doctor. He would also state he was a lawyer in his previous homeland, Italy.

In addition to writing foreign dialogue for MGM and FOX studios, Alberto secured work as an actor in a few minor roles in *Fatal Lady, One Rainy Afternoon, China Slaver* and *Tropic Madness*. For twenty-seven years he was employed by Fox studios as an accountant before he retired in 1965. Alberto Valentino and his wife had no other children. Alberto died in Los Angeles in 1981 and his eulogy was delivered by William Pelf.

Jean Valentino -

Jean Valentino kept his word to never pursue a career in front of the cameras. Instead, he worked as a Hollywood sound engineer and owned and operated his own business, Valentino Electronics. Jean was employed as sound technician on many television shows in the 1950's including; *Twilight Zone, Rawhide, Bewitched, Father Knows Best* and *Petticoat Junction*. He died in Los Angeles in September 1996 and is survived by his two daughters.

Rudy's Voice -

Rudolph Valentino died before the advent of the "talkies" and consequently no record of his speaking voice exists on film. Two recordings of him singing, "Kashmiri Song" and "El Relicario" have survived as the only record of his voice. The recordings, made in 1923, were thought lost in the libraries of the Brunswick-Balke-Collender Company until they were found and released by the Platt Music Company in 1930.

Zela -

Zela's fate is unknown. The lion lived for a while in Azusa, California at Doc Graf's ranch until the owner of Doc's menagerie, Nell Shipman moved to Idaho to establish her own movie studio in the north woods. She and Doc caged and transported many of her pets to the woods of Idaho but Zela was not among those that made the arduous trek. At that same time many of Shipman's animals were donated to the San Diego Zoo and it is more probable that this became Zela's final home.

Thank-You

As the author of this book, I wish to extend profound gratitude to Bunny Ullman and Bob Ullman for their enthusiasm for this project and patience as they granted many interviews and opened their family archives and homes to me. I owe an enormous debt of thanks for their hard work throughout the long process of bringing this book to publication. Bob Ullman read the final chapter of the manuscript a few weeks before he passed away in August of 2005. His insistence I not report about his father's tenure as Valentino's executor without accurate documentation directed me to delve deeper into this subject than I would have otherwise. In this respect, this story belongs to him.

I sincerely thank the Mennillo family for their continued support and kind assistance as they also opened their family archives for my use. They shared a wealth of new information, as passed down from Frank and Arnold Mennillo, which added immeasurably to my work and Valentino's revised story.

I am also grateful to the following people who assisted me at various times throughout the creation of this book: to Armando Zumaya for his research, support and discoveries and to Father Michael Morris for his years of analysis and support and for the Convegno Valentino.

I also wish to acknowledge the assistance of Sally McManus and Jeri Vogelsang at the Palm Springs Historical Society, Julianne Gick and David G. Badertscher, Principal Law Librarians at the New York Supreme Court, Andreas Brown for information regarding Frances Steloff and The Gotham Book Mart, Kathy Kirkpatrick at Gensearch for her genealogical searches, Chris Aprato at The Los Angeles Public Library, Ted James at www.celebritycollectibles.com, Cesare Mannino and Kevin Mack at Frank E. Campbell's Funeral Chapel, Rudy Urrea at Funeraria Los Angeles, a Pierce Brothers Mortuary, Francesco Labrile in Santeramo en Colle, Provincia di Bari, Italy, Sid Moormeister for her early consultations on the chemistry of internment and the embalming process, Janet Lorenez at The Fairbanks Center for Motion Picture Study, Linda Weir, Public Services Librarian at The Hastings Law Library, Barbara Hall and Doug Bell at the Margaret Herrick Library, David Hall at the Tyneside Gay Hall of Fame, Stephen Salmons of The San Francisco Silent Film Festival,

Wendy Watts of *The Toronto Star*, Lytton Smith, Chief Librarian at *The Seattle Post-Intelligencer*, Barbara Quinn and Sue Swisher at the Sierra Research Center, Shannon Bowen, Assistant Archivist at The University of Wyoming, Lyle Wiley and Vicki Schuster of the American Heritage Center at The University of Wyoming, Hugh Munro Neely at The Pickford Foundation, Claude B. Zachary, University Archivist at the University of Southern California, Valerie Verneuille for her translations of Robert Florey's works, Suzanne Harman and Dennis DeCuir of The Beverly Hills Police Department, Maureen A. Hemler, Senior Court Manager and Don Cameron at The Los Angeles County Hall of Records, Michael C. Cronin, curator and Kerri Brockner of The New York City Police Museum, David M. Carroll, Collections Manager-Chief Registrar at The Utah Museum of Fine Arts, the supportive staff at NARA, National Archives and Records Administration, Pacific Region, Karen S. Frank, Attorney at Law, Peter Keane and the memory of Bill McGuire.

I wish to also express my gratitude to Valentino expert Dominic Caruso for his enthusiastic support and encouragement, to Aurelio Miccoli for sharing his scholarly expertise on Castellaneta and Valentino's early years, to Antonio Miredi for his kind commentary included in this publication and a special thank-you to Ms. Chicca Guglielmi for writing the introduction to *Affairs Valentino*, for her editing of the Italian version, *L'Affare Valentino* and for permitting the first time publication of many of her family photographs.

I also wish to thank literary agent Sam Fleishman for his wise counsel, professional insights and direction on this project.

Notes and References

Key:

- GU ms - denotes the manuscript of the George Ullman memoir
- GU- denotes George Ullman
- RV – denotes Rudolph Valentino
- *LAT* – Los Angeles Times
- *NYT* – New York Times
- All court record references and citations refer to California Appellate Court records on file in the case of Ullman v. Guglielmi
- The Registry of Actions and other documents relating to the collection processes on George Ullman are on file in the Los Angeles County Hall of Records.

Prologue: A Vanishing Act

Details of Hudnut Chateau and George Wehner's visit in August of 1926: M. Morris, *Madam Valentino* and N. Rambova, *Rudy: An Intimate Portrait of Rudolph Valentino.*

News of Rudy's condition dispatched by telegram: GU ms.

Details of Falcon Lair and Lou being left in charge in RV and GU's absence: L. Mahoney's taped interview. Court testimony.

Lou resented taking orders from George: L. Mahoney taped interview. Court testimony.

George Ullman tells Lou to look for another job: Ibid.

Pola Negri's secretary: GU ms.

Pola Negri and her work on *Hotel Imperial*: P. Negri, *Memoirs of a Star.*

George does not telephone Negri with updates: GU ms.

Ullman family nurse and children in Los Angeles: Ullman family interviews, 2003-2005.

Details of Metaphen treatment and procurement: J. DeRecqueville, *Rudolph Valentino.*

Friday night seance at the Hudnut Chateau: M. Morris, *Madam Valentino.* N. Rambova, *Rudy.*

Natacha Rambova chain smokes: M. Morris interviews, 2003.

Telegrams from George to Natacha: GU ms. M. Morris, *Madam Valentino.*

George has Rudy's nurse telephone Bee Ullman and Frank Mennillo: GU ms.

Continuing discord between Valentino brothers: GU ms. Court transcripts . W. Pelf interviews, 2003.

George's telegrams to Natacha and Alberto: GU ms.

Alberto loses weight on return voyage to New York: I. Schulman, *Valentino,* "Alberto..lost twenty pounds.."

Kabar's howling at time of Valentino's death as heard by Beatrice Lillie: I. Schulman, *Valentino.* Louella Parsons column, *LAT* - 8/26/26.

Rudy's body being removed in basket: GU ms.

George's telegram arrives at chateau day after Rudy's death: M. Morris interviews, 2003.

Details of Rudy's master bedroom: GU ms.

Lou removes Pola Negri's lingerie from master bedroom: As related to M. Morris by L. Mahoney's daughter, Madeleine Reid Mahoney.

Box of jewelry kept under stairs at Falcon Lair: L. Mahoney's oral account of his sweep of Falcon Lair in the hours following RV's death. GU ms., account of tin box of Rudy's jewelry.

Lou's access to Falcon Lair's safe and being alone at Falcon Lair at the time: *LAT*-11/8/30, "Valentino Safe Raid Asserted."

Details of Valentino's Last Will and Testament: Text of actual document.

Second page of will missing: *NYT*-11/8/30, "Valentino Paper Missing." Appeals Court records and Court testimony.

1. Skeletons in the Closet

"Then there is nothing left for me to do..." *NYT* - 8/4/1917, "John L. DeSaulles Slain in His Home by Former Wife."

Cabbie James Donner and the James Hamilton garage: *New York Herald* – 8/6/1917, "Mrs. DeSaulles Arm Nerved to Kill Husband."

Details of DeSaulles' murder: *NYT* – 8/10/191, "DeSaulles Killing Re-enacted by Maid". *NYT*- 8/6/1917, "Mrs. DeSaulles Tells Her Story of the Tragedy". *NY Herald* – 8/6/1917, "Mrs. DeSaulles Arm Nerved to Kill Husband."

Blanca's arrest and confession: *NYT* – 8/9/1917, "Little Son Sees Mrs. DeSaulles", also, "Where is boy? Only Thought of Mrs. DeSaulles."

Blanca confesses to Henry Uterhart: *NY Journal* – 8/7/1917, "Mrs. DeSaulles in Cell."

"Little Jacky" playing with toy boats: L. Larrain, *Blanca Elena-Memoria Indiscreta De La Quinta Vergara.*

Tango references: *NYT* uncited - "Afternoon Dances Develop a New Kind of Parasite" and "New Villains on Broadway."

District Attorney on subject of cabaret dancers, cocaine and tango as threat to health: *NYT* – 4/26/14, "Ferraro On The Dance Craze." uncited article - "Expert Points Out Harm in Tango". *NYT* – 5/30/15, "Women Aroused by Dance Evils". *NYT* – 1/14/14, "All New York Now Madly Whirling in the Tango" and uncited article - "Tango Pirates Infest Broadway."

Reporters question Henry Uterhart about Rudolfo Guglielmi at time of DeSaulles' murder: *NY Herald* – 8/6/17, "Stung By Litigation and Depressed By Loneliness Says Counsel". *NY World* – 8/12/17, "... asked at Mineola jail." *NY World* – 8/12/17, "DeSaulles Divorce Secrets Now Bared."

Details of Rudolfo meeting Blanca at war benefit: L. Larrain, *Blanca Elena.*

Blanca's personal tastes: Ibid.

Information on Jack DeSaulles: *NYT* – 8/4/1917, "John L. DeSaulles Slain in His Home by Former Wife."

Blanca frequenting Club Maxim's and her love of dancing: L. Larrain, *Blanca Elena.*

Details of Jack's infidelities and involvement with Joan Sawyer: *NY World* - 8/12/16. L. Larrain, *Blanca Elena.* *NYT* – 8/11/16, "DeSaulles Friends Divorce Accusers."

Frank Mennillo business, family information and his involvement with Rudy's arrival: Mennillo family interviews, 2003-2004. *LAT* – 12/30/1917, "New Truck and Tractor Handled by New Firm." *LAT* - 11/23/1917, "The Little Tractor that 'Walks' Across the Fields."

RV's arrival at Ellis Island in NYC: Commentary by I. Shulman as contained within his archives, "...Fear was a cold hand constricting around his (RV's) heart at the prospect of interrogation, for it was Alberto, by right, who should have been on that ship and immigration officials would ask why he, rather than Alberto, had come to the US..."

Blanca checks into Majestic Hotel as Mrs. John Smythe: *NY Herald* - 8/4/17, "DeSaulles Shot and Killed."

RV's testimony at divorce hearing: *NYT* – 8/11/16. *NY World* - 8/12/17.

RV's incarceration in the Tombs: *NYT* – 9/6/16, "Vice Squad in Raid Near Carnegie Hall."

RV's childhood stories: GU, *Valentino as I Knew Him* - As cited account of RV's father as doctor of veterinary medicine dying of malaria as a result of his laboratory experiments with this disease. RV's second sister, Beatrice, who died in infancy. Ibid.

Blanca's custody battle: L. Larrain, *Blanca Elena.*

RV meets Norman Kerry and takes flying lessons five miles from Blanca DeSaulles summer home at The Crossways in Roslyn, New York: GU, *Valentino as I Knew Him. NYT* – 12/1/1917, "Mrs. DeSaulles Not Guilty of Murder."

Henry Uterhart communicates with RV: *NYT* – 8/11/17, "DeSaulles Friend's Divorce Accusers". *NYT* – 8/5/17, "Insanity Pled". *NY World* – 8/12/17, "Divorce Secrets in the DeSaulles Case Now Bared."

Blanca found innocent and courtroom details: *NYT* – 12/1/17, "Mrs. DeSaulles is Not Guilty of Murder."

The Little Princess Information: The Margaret Herrick Library, Special Collections, Mary Pickford Scrapbooks - Article dated – 11/11/1917, also articles titled - "Uses San Francisco Atmosphere" and "'The Little Princess' to Open Engagement This Morning". Also interviews with The Pickford Foundation.

RV meets with Norman Kerry and travels to Los Angeles: GU ms and *Valentino as I Knew Him.* J. DeRecqueville, *Rudolph Valentino* - "Vers la Californie."

Frank Mennillo's business in San Francisco area at the time: Mennillo family interviews, 2003-2004.

Frank Mennillo offers employment to RV: Ibid.

A.P. Giannini denies RV's request for business loan: Ibid.

RV's poor eyesight: Alberto Valentino's revelation to William Pelf that RV's poor eyesight was the result of his contracting syphilis from a prostitute as a teenager. William Pelf interviews, 2003-2004.

The Passing Show: GU ms. Also GU, *Valentino as I Knew Him.* I. Schulman, *Valentino.*

2. Opportunity Knocks on Room A4

Hollywood Hotel scenario: GU ms. And GU, *Valentino as I Knew Him.* I. Schulman, *Valentino.* Jean Acker's testimony at divorce hearing, *LAT* – 11/14/1921, "Stars to Battle in Court."

Christmas with Viola Dana: *Hollywood* - The miniseries by K. Brownlow and D. Gill.

Mercer info: Mercer Raceabout @carfolio.com and Chandler Wheels.

RV drives "one hundred miles an hour" : R. Florey, *La Lanterne Magique* and *Hollywood Yesterday and Today.*

Rudy lives on La Cienaga: W. Pelf interviews, 2003-2004.

Records found in Jean's lawyers archives after RV's death: GU ms.

Jean Acker tells friends RV told her on their wedding night he had gonorrhea: W. Pelf interviews, 2003-2004.

Jean rumored to be lesbian: Ibid.

Anti-Italian sentiment in US: F. Allen, *Only Yesterday*. Time-Life, *The Fabulous Century*. R. Lynd and H. Lynd, *Middletown-A Study in American Culture*. R. Sklar, *Movie-Made America* and *The Plastic Age*. B. Marinacci, *They Came from Italy*.

Frank Mennillo ruined by Giannini: Mennillo family interviews and archives.

Jean Acker's telegram: Uncited article – *LAT*, "Telegrams in Case" and "Pled in Letter." "...Please Jean, Darling, come to your senses and give me an opportunity to prove to you...." I. Schulman, *Valentino* and *LAT* – 11/14/1921, "Stars to Battle in Court."

Lone Pine set/*Round-Up* details: Acker and Valentino divorce court testimony.

Scenario @ Grace Darmond's and separation details: Attorney Neil McCarthy questions Jean Acker on the witness stand.

RV meets Paul Ivano: M. Morris, *Madam Valentino*.

Eyes of Youth synopsis and Rowland embarrassed by Rudy's reaction: *The Eyes of Youth* and GU, *Valentino As I Knew Him*.

Archainbaud told: Ibid.

RV's clothing tastes: P. Negri, *Memoirs of a Star*.

Information on mens' clothing/gender and bright clothing in Italy: Kidwell and Steele, *Men and Women-Dressing the Part*. B. Marinacci, *They Came from Italy*.

3. Calling the Shots

Natacha and George Wehner's arrival in New York: *LAT* – 11/26/26, "Sheik Shade Waits Cue." Uncited article – 11/25/26, "Rambova Says Dead Star has Talked to Her."

Terms of Will and controversy: Actual document and Court records of proceedings.

GU posts personal bond: GU ms. Court records.

GU continues business as if RV was alive: Ibid.

Notice to RV's creditors published: Registry of Actions.

Itemization of Rudy's postmortem debts: Ibid.

Alberto's request that estate fund Ambassador Hotel bungalow: GU ms.

Alberto's attorney being Milton Cohen: GU ms. Court records and P. Negri, *Memoirs of Star*.

Pola Negri's bungalow 'La Reposa': Ibid.

Pola Negri and Alberto's relationship: GU ms.

Persistent calls from Alberto and his attorneys: Ibid.

Pola's spending of Guglielmi brother's money: Ibid.

GU summons Teresa Werner and her arrival: *LAT* – 11/8/1926, "Ready to Guard Interest, Mrs. Teresa Werner, One of Beneficiaries Under Will of Actor, Heeds Ullman's Call".

George issues regular checks to Alberto: Falcon Lair ledgers labeled "Grey Books". Rudolph Valentino Production Company ledgers.

Alberto removes property from Falcon Lair: GU ms. *LAT* – 11/13/26, "Rudy's Brother Loses Car, Dog."

Alberto in possession of Kabar at this time: *LAT* – 11/13/26, "Rudy's Brother Loses Car, Dog."

Home Valentino Shrine and GU reads fan letters: I. Schulman, *Valentino* and GU ms.

Letters from England: "Are They Making Valentino a Saint?"- August 1928, Uncited article in USC, I. Schulman archives.

Letters reporting Rudy's alleged offspring: GU ms.

Alessandro Gabelleri considered: Uncited article - "Files Suit Over Memorial to Valentino" - 4/10/1928. Gabelleri sues estate for payment of work completed, i.e. sketches and trip to Italy to select marble for memorial and also suit dismissed information – L.A. County Library Card Index Reference.

Hollywood Jack's: Currently known as The Formosa Café located at 7156 Santa Monica Boulevard, Los Angeles, California.

"Forty suits ordered from London and bills..." GU ms.

Milton Cohen moves to strike the will as being vague: GU ms. Court transcripts.

Alberto smoking RV's Abdullah's: Ibid.

GU organizes memorial guilds: Court testimony of G. Ullman and W.I. Gilbert from Objection to 1st acct., p.36-37 lines #108-109.

Alberto requests advance of $5000.00, estate funding for bungalow and details of his objections: GU ms. Court transcripts. Falcon Lair Gray books expense ledgers. William Pelf Interviews, 2003-2004 - "...Most of Alberto's letters to Rudy that I read were just petitions for money..."

Alberto's total annual income: Court records. Baskerville Audit Schedules. Falcon Lair expense ledgers.

Alberto requests he be appointed executor of the estate: *NYT* – 10/5/1926, "Argue Valentino Will." Court records.

Leonard Wilson requests continuances: Court records.

Pola Negri's beach house: P. Negri, *Memoirs of a Star.*

Pola Negri informs press she gave Alberto $15,000.00 to bring his family to US: Ibid.

Pola Negri submits fifteen thousand dollar claim against Rudy's estate: Registry of Actions.

Jean does not arrive in US until July of 1929: *LAT* – 7/24/19, "Valentino Nephew Shuns Actor's Life."

Alberto explains nose surgery to Pola: P. Negri, *Memoirs of a Star.*

Alberto speaks about nose surgery: *The Literary Digest* – 9/21/29, "The Tragedy of Valentino's Brother's Nose." *LAT* – 10/19/27, "Valentino II Sports New Face."

Pola upset about nose surgery: P. Negri, *Memoirs of a Star.*

"Jean is in Turin": *LAT* – 7/24/29, "Valentino Nephew Shuns Actor's Life." Alberto speaks with press in advance of his arrival - *LAT*- 7/17/1929.

Auction returns below expected amount: GU ms.

Lou retained on Rudolph Valentino Productions' payroll to organize auctions: L. Mahoney taped interview. Court testimony.

The *Phoenix* is placed in dry dock and books are stamped with Rudy's signature: L. Mahoney and GU's court testimony.

GU's total sales for auction: Court records. Baskerville Audit Schedules. Failure to close sale on Falcon Lair - I. Shulman archives - Unidentified article citing specifics of sale.

Date of Maria's arrival: M. Strada's court testimony and Uncited article in Margaret Herrick Library – 2/19/1927, "Sister Arrives to Pray Beside Valentino Tomb."

Everyone removes estate property: As itemized in court records and Baskerville Audit Schedules.

Maria's items removed from Falcon Lair: Baskerville Audit report itemized as "Items advanced to Maria Guglielmi Strada by the executor" and also Objection To 1st Acct., p.196 line #587, "... Yes, I received...some jewels and some pajamas.." Also as itemized in Baskerville Audit Schedules - Detail #9 under "Items Advanced to Maria Guglielmi Strada by the Executor."

GU motivated by sentiment for Rudy's sister: GU ms.

GU witnesses Alberto removing jewelry box: Ibid.

Alberto charges the cash value of Rudy's Franklin Coupe against his future share of the estate: Objection to 1st acct., p.172 lines #516-517. "..was that a part of the property advanced to Alberto Guglielmi..?"

GU removes Rudy's address books and papers: W. Pelf interviews, 2003-2004.

Maria living in The Hollywood Plaza Hotel: Court records - Supplement to Executor's 1st acct., p.69, line #205.

RV relates Colona and Guglielmi feud story to GU: GU ms.

4. Babykins

Details of poaching activity in Hollywood Hills: N. Rambova, *Rudy* and M. Morris, *Madam Valentino*.

"Natacha was always Rudy's girl": Paul Ivano's interview notes - M. Morris archive.

RV and Natacha meet: N. Rambova, *Rudy - An Intimate Portrait of Rudolph Valentino by His Wife Natacha Rambova*.

RV shares Sunset Boulevard bungalow with Natacha: Catholic Church refuses mass after Valentino's death as he lived in sin with Natacha Rambova - GU ms and *Osservatore Romano* as quoted in *NYT* - 8/29/16 and also revealed in W. Pelf interviews.

Nazimova remarks about RV being responsible for Jack DeSaulles' murder: G. Lambert, *Nazimova*..

Home life at the bungalow and various business ventures: N. Rambova, *Rudy* and M. Morris, *Madam Valentino*.

RV and Natacha's bootleg liquor consumption: GU ms.

Walter Wanger information: Hollywood Renegades Archive, SIMPP Research Database. M. Bernstein, *Walter Wanger- Hollywood Independent*.

Sheik effect on society information: GU, *Valentino as I Knew Him*. GU ms. L. Allen, *Only Yesterday, Middletown Notes*, "Using Leisure", "What the Movies Taught". A. Walker, *Rudolph Valentino*. R. Sklar, *Movie Made America. Collier's National Weekly* – 1/16/1926, "Are the Movies a Mess or a Menace?"

Legislation pending in Utah: L. Allen, *Only Yesterday*.

RV kept inscribed copy of *The Sheik* on his nightstand: Alberto Valentino relates this to William Pelf. W. Pelf interviews - 2003-2004.

Renovation of the 1914 Cadillac: M. Morris, *Madam Valentino* and N. Rambova, *Rudy*.

Sheik opening at Grauman's Million Dollar Theater: *LAT* - 10/30/1921, "Desert Lure at Grauman's Rialto". *Lifestyle* magazine - "Temple to Cinema", November/December 2006.

Zela pursues detective: N. Rambova, *Rudy*

RV signs one picture deal with Famous Players-Lasky Corporation: *LAT* - 7/11/39, "Rubbish Yields Valentino Contract."

Natacha and RV in San Francisco and Helen McGregor photographs: M. Morris, *Madam Valentino*. N. Rambova, *Rudy*. Paul Ivano interview notes.

Acker divorce proceedings: *LAT* – 11/14/1921, "Stars to Battle in Court". GU ms. GU, *Valentino as I Knew Him*. I. Schulman, *Valentino* and J. DeRecqueville, *Rudolph Valentino*.

Nell Shipman private zoo information: SVP Productions. J. Zemel, *Nell Shipman*. N. Shipman, *The Silent Screen and My Talking Heart*.

Zela taken to Felix "Doc" Graff's ranch and RV and Natacha perch atop runway watching East Indian honey bear: N. Rambova, *Rudy* and N. Shipman, *The Silent Screen and My Talking Heart*.

Christmas Eve details: N. Rambova, *Rudy*

Poem Titled, "You" : As published in M. Morris, *Madam Valentino*, GU, *Valentino as I Knew Him*, R. Oberfirst, *Rudolph Valentino, The Man Behind the Myth*.

5. Best Friend and Manager

Harry Carey's return from Africa: *LAT* – 3/31/30, "Ghost of Valentino Laid. Spooky House Puzzle Solved."

Wiring removed from Falcon Lair and seance information: GU ms.

GU holds lease on Falcon Lair: GU ms. Executor's 1st Current Account - p.58 line #174. "....cash deposits not large enough to satisfy court..." I. Schulman archives - USC.

Falcon Lair leased for 150$/month: Executor's 1st Current Account, p. 8 line #24.

Tunnel construction at Falcon Lair: GU ms.

Evidence of George's success raising money for the Valentino estate and Cosmic Arts, Inc.: Executor's Opening Brief, p.73 line #217 and also p. 238 Executor's Exhibit #2. Cosmic Arts' contracts included in Court records.

Richard Ingalls as sales rep: Objection to 1st Account- p. 58 line #174 and Ingalls position promoting patent - Obj. to 1st acct., p.58 line #174.

Details of Estelle Dick's services: Obj. To 1st Account - p.55 line #164.

Valentino purchases Lambert Process patent: Obj. To 1st Account- p.57 line #170.

Laboratory as Valentino's corporate identity and reassigning of his contracts to Cosmic Arts: Obj. to 1st Account – p. 72 line #216.

All Cosmic Arts stock signed over to Natacha during initial meeting: Obj. to 1st Acct. - p. 73 line #219.

GU nearly sells patent for quarter of a million but deal falls through: Obj. To 1st Account – p. 57 line #170.

George's checks issued to Cosmic Arts: Obj. To 1st Account. Baskerville Audit Extracts – p. 247 line #740 and Cosmic Arts' book keeping ledger entries.

Cosmic Arts expenditures come under Alberto's scrutiny: Court records. Obj. to 1st Acct - p.72.

Alberto's list of objections: Registry of Actions.

Objections to George's book-keeping form: GU ms.

George's executor's accounts rejected by Alberto over forty times: Registry of Actions .

Valentino estate assets @ $300,000 by 1930: Obj. To 1st Account. Baskerville Audit – p. 244 line #732. Supplement to First Account, Schedule C, "...property of said estate now remaining...@ $287,462.50." Also details of GU's efforts to reward estate taken from testimony of W.I. Gilbert as itemized in Obj. to 1st Account – p. 178 line #533.

Surplus of money in estate account: Valentino's individual bank accounts. Executor's Supplement – p. 48 line #143 also Baskerville Audit – p. 11 Schedule "B". Testimony of Harry H. Baskerville – p. 70 line #236. *LAT* – 3/3/28, "Valentino's Estate Now Totals..."

"Alberto did not deny that George Ullman had done an admirable job spinning...": *LAT* – 3/3/28, "Valentino's Estate Now Totals..."

Dispute over GU's authority to operate Rudolph Valentino Productions: Court records.

All excerpts from both pages of Valentino's will: Court records.

George refers to his memory of missing paper: *NYT* – 10/5/1926, "Argue Valentino Will." *NYT* – 11/8/1930, "Valentino Paper is Missing". *LAT* – 2/5/1931, "Lawyer Backs Valentino Will." *LAT* – 11-8-1930, "Valentino Safe Raid Asserted". Court testimony.

"Alberto continued to maintain...": Alberto's court testimony. Obj. to 1st Acct. - p.188 lines #564-572.

Alberto requests liquidation of Rudolph Valentino Productions: Court records.

Alberto charges George with fraud and mismanagement: *LAT* – 5/16/1930, "Management is Charged." Court records.

Charges against GU as itemized in Alberto's lawsuit: Ibid.

"The filing of the suit against me is ill-advised.." *LAT* – 5/20/30, "Executor of Valentino Raises Veil on 'Tricks'".

Formation of S. George Ullman Agency: Ullman family interviews, 2003-2004.

GU's final paycheck from Rudolph Valentino Productions: Obj. To 1st Acct. - p. 20 lines #58-60. W. I. Gilbert approves George's salary as executor - Obj. To 1st Acct. - line #173 and #519, "...I told him the court would allow.."

GU believes Joe Schenck funds Alberto's legal team: GU ms.

Buster Keaton and sale of his production company: Buster Keaton.com.

Schenck information and details of RV's contract: Court records and Text of actual contract.

***Firebrand* contract details**: GU ms. Court records. Respondent Brief – p. 62 lines #184-189. *Firebrand* costs - Supplement to Executor's 1st account – p. 62 line #185.

Schenck visits RV: GU ms. *Daily Mirror* – 8/25/1926, "Schenck Denounces Poison Story about Rudy." *San Jose Mercury* – 8/17/1926, "Report Condition of Valentino is Still Unchanged."

Schenck offers George a job with United Artists: GU ms.

Schenck offers to buy out RV's contract and Schenck Details: GU ms. Appellant's Opening Brief – p. 29 itemizing Schenck's royalty paid as totaling @ $321,326.60. Obj. to 1st Account – p.251. Baskerville Audit Schedules under "Income Derived from Various Estate Assets" - p. 251 lines #751-753.

Information on Cinema Finance Co. insurance rebate and George's successful effort collecting $19,000.00 for the Valentino estate: Supplement to First Account - p.60 line #178 also p. 33 line #99 of Obj. to 1st Acct.

RV's debt to Schenck paid in full by April 1927: Obj. To 1st Account – p. 32-33 lines #95-96.

Information on *Firebrand* life insurance policy and pre-production costs: Obj. to 1st Account – p. 56 lines #168-169.

George pressures Schenck for weeks: GU ms. Obj. 1st Account - p.61 lines #181-183. Supplement to Executor's account – p. 56 line #167.

George travels to NYC and Schenck refuses to give him a job with UA: GU ms.

Giannini grants Schenck seat on board of Bank of America: F. Bonadio, *A.P. Giannini*, p.230.

Alberto's attorneys and Schenck connections: GU ms. Milton Cohen represents Schenck's wife - Milton Cohen obit – *NYT* - 7/2/50, also *NYT* - 11/22/30, *NYT* – Uncited Article - 7/27/24 and 1/6/29. James C. Scarborough and United Artists connection - Earp/Hart Letters from The Tombstone History Archives and *NYT* – 1/20/25, "Mrs. Hart Wins Right.." Morton E. Feiler's connections to United Artists – *NYT* – 12/31/28, "Mr. Feiler is executive with United Artists…"

Alberto works at MGM: Obits in *Variety* – 6/17/81 and *LAT* - 6/8/81 also *LAT* – 6/15/81, "Filmland Tried to make what Valentino's Brother Lacked".

Alberto and GU's lawyers identified: Registry of Actions. Court testimony.

Alberto's lawsuit as threat to Ullman household: Ullman family interviews - 2003-2004.

Alberto's new face: *LAT* -10/19/27, "Valentino II Sports New Face"

Quote taken from Alberto's interview: *Literary Digest* – 9/21/29, "The Tragedy of Valentino's Brother's Nose."

Alberto appears in, *Tropic Madness*: *LAT* – 9/6/28, "Guglielmi Gets in Film at Last…"

Alberto says he "never intended to go into pictures" and claims he did so in order to keep Rudy's name alive: "…I would not dream of imitating him…etc." Article contained within I. Schulman archives dated 8/1928 and titled, "Are they Making Valentino a Saint?"

Alberto sues Dr. Balsinger: I. Schulman, *Valentino*.

Alberto in car accident: *LAT* – 6/29/29, "Valentino's Brother to Collect $9…" also *LAT* -7/19/29, "Guglielmi Gets $9 in Damages."

Alberto borrows $6880.00 from Pola Negri: *L.A. Herald* – 3/7/41, "Pola Negri, Valentino Kin Suit Renewed." *Citizen-News* – 3/7/1941, "Judgment Dogs A. Valentino."

As executor George pays Alberto's bills: GU ms.

Alberto's efforts to discredit Ullman: Court records. GU ms and quote from GU memoir "….No one can possibly understand the persistent attacks upon my integrity and judgment in the handling of Rudy's estate brought by Rudy's brother, Alberto".

Initiation of the dispensation of stipends in lieu of cash advances in December of 1928: "…It was then that George made a very unpopular…" - Obj. To 1st Account – p. 188 line #564. Also Alberto's testimony.

Alberto's objections delay settlement: Registry of Actions.

Teresa Werner and Maria Strada file no objections to George's accounting: Obj. to 1st Acct. - p.131 line #391. Court records.

Alberto's lifestyle information: GU ms. Falcon Lair household ledgers.

Alberto resides in both of Rudy's homes: *LAT* – 11/22/32, "Youth Injured in Crash with Valentino Kin." *LAT* – 4/26/35, "Burglars Rob Valentino Kin."

GU issues checks to Alberto for amounts stated: Obj. To 1st Account - p.194 line #581. Alberto's testimony. Appellant Opening Brief – p.134. Falcon Lair Household expense records.

Pola Negri money given to Alberto: P. Negri, *Memoirs of a Star*.

RV advances Alberto $7000.00: Falcon Lair household ledgers. Exhibit #9 - Gray Books as itemized under weekly cash advances made to Alberto from April to July 1926 – p. 268.

GU's performance as executor: "…Still turning a profit for the estate" - Brief of Respondent - p.15. "…Having accumulated a surplus of funds…"

Details of Jean's arrival in U.S.: *LAT* – 7/24/29, "Valentino Nephew Shuns Actor's Life." Uncited articles – 7/17/29, "Nephew May Be New Valentino." 7/9/29, "Nephew On Way To Visit Tomb." Also - 7/13/29, "Valentino Kin is Here."

Alberto speaks to reporters upon Jean's arrival: *LAT* – 7/ 17/29.

Request from Alberto's attorneys for court audit: Baskerville Audit Schedules.

Itemized materials GU surrenders to court: Ibid.

GU's defense that "work would have come to a standstill": GU ms.

Roger Noble Burnham and Mancini information: *LAT* – 2/10/34, "Woman Held Too Generous". *LAT* – 4/18/35, "Judgment in Valentino Row Upheld for Woman". LAT – 4/10/34, "Valentino Action Has Court Echo". "Mancini v. Ullman"- Court records dated 4/1935 and *LAT* – 8/2/1936, "Our Artists in Person: Roger Noble Burnham."

Money in estate @ $125,000.00 in cash when George makes investments: Baskerville audit schedules - "...Showing a substantial profit..." Obj. to 1st Account - "...Having accumulated a surplus of funds in his administration of the estate..." Respondent's Brief - p.15.

Mae Murray loan: Obj. to 1st Acct. - p. 44 line #130 - "...did you not, on or about the 2nd day of September 1927 loan Mae Murray some $20,000.00" and "....Is it not a fact that the loan was repaid..."

Information on Frank Mennillo's life and business: Mennillo family interviews - 2003-2004.

Frank's duel: *LAT* – 3/18/27, "Valentino's Friend Wroth," and "Unable to Fight Duel with Count de Clairmont in Elopement Row, Mennillo Files Suit."

Frank meets with Maria Strada in NYC: Maria's testimony - Supplemental to Executor's account – p. 71 line #211. Maria grants Frank power of attorney - Executor's Supplement to 1st Account. Maria's testimony – p. 70 lines #208-213.

Details of the meeting @ The Jonathan Club between GU and Frank: Court testimony and Obj. To 1st Acct. - p. 125 line #373.

Mennillo as The Olive King: Frank's obit *LAT* – 11/7/36, "Illness Fatal to Olive King."

Vab and Mennillo loan information: Executor's Opening Brief - p.86-87 line #257. "...George knew that Frank financially supported Rudy, etc..." Executor's Opening Brief - p.122 line #366.

Text of Maria's letter of guarantee: Obj. to Executor's 1st Account – p. 242 line #726. Also Executor's Exhibit #4.

Details of the Mennillo loan and GU acting upon Maria's request: Executor's Opening Brief - p.122 line #366. Text of M. Strada's note to GU as submitted to the court as Executor's Exhibit #4 – p. 242 line #726.

Executor's Supplement – p. 73 line #218. George's position on Vab board – p. 126 line #378.

Signed copy of loan contract between Ullman and Mennillo: Appellant's Opening Brief - p. 84 lines #251-256. "….In March of 1928, GU loaned $50,000 to the Pan American Bank…" - Executor's Opening Brief - p. 60 lines #178-170 and other Court records.

Pan Am stock worth $68,000.00: Executor's Opening Brief, Re-Direct Examination of George Ullman – p. 69 line #207, also p.18 of Respondent's Brief.

Pan Am advertisement: *LAT* – 12/26.

Blue Monday information: F. Bonadio, *A.P. Giannini.* p.136.

Mennillo's business falters: Mennillo family interviews - 2003-2004.

Refinancing of Vab loan and partial payment received from Pan Am: Appellant's Opening Brief – p. 76.

S. George Ullman Agency information and Ullman family information: Ullman family interviews. Court records.

Charge against Ullman as itemized in Alberto's lawsuit: Court records.

George's biographical information: Ullman family interviews.

6. The Third Degree

Detectives Winn and King: *LAT* – 5/19/22, "Valentino's Case to Test Laws" and "Valentino in Trap, Is Claim."

"…ordered to go south to El Centro." *LAT* – 5/19/22, "Inquiry Begun By Woolwine."

Interlocutory decree of divorce: *LAT* – 5/19/22, "Valentino Case to Test Laws."

Details of Mexicali wedding: N. Rambova, *Rudy.* M. Morris, *Madam Valentino. LAT* – 5/16/22, "Valentino's Chum Tells of Wedding."

Wedding night in Palm Springs: *LAT* – 5/19/22, "Valentino Case to Test Laws"

D.A. Woolwine's problems: *LAT* – 5/27/22, "Investigation Ordered on Woolwine Charges," also "Valentino Case To Test Laws", "Valentino Marriage Invalid, Judges Say." *NYT* – 5/17/22, "Valentino Case Pushed."

Woolwine's studio snitches: I. Schulman, *Valentino.*

Two detectives armed with cameras: *LAT* – 5/22/22, "Accuse Cinema Men of Bigamy."

The Valentino's horseback riding: M. Morris, *Madam Valentino.*

RV's thinning hair: GU ms.

Information on Dr. Florilla White: *The Palm Springs Limelight News* - 3/19/43, "Death Comes to Dr. White, Loved Palm Springs Pioneer". Information also contributed by The Palm Springs Historical Society and The Palm Springs Desert Museum.

Valentinos return to Los Angeles: M. Morris, *Madam Valentino*. N. Rambova, *Rudy*.

In the privacy of the car: Ibid.

Details of scene @ train station: *LAT* – 5/18/22, "Valentino and Bride Separate."

Decision that Natacha leave Los Angeles: M. Morris, *Madam Valentino. LAT* – 5/22/22, "Valentino's Bride Seeks Seclusion."

Natacha resigns herself to her situation: N. Rambova, *Rudy-An Intimate Portrait of Rudolph Valentino by his Wife.*

The Eastbound Train pursuit by press: *LAT* – 5/20/22, "Pledges Love to Valentino."

Natacha's quote, "Forever..." *LAT* – 5/20/22, "Pledges Love to Valentino."

RV turns himself in to District Attorney: *NYT* – 5/20/22, "Arrest Valentino on Bigamy Charge." *LAT* – 5/19/22, "Investigation of Valentino's Wedding Opens", "Valentino In Trap, is Claim" and "Valentino and Bride Separated."

RV's night in jail and friends bail him out: *LAT* – 5/21/22, "Valentino Gives Bond."

Godowsky and Mayo marriage: *LAT* – Undated Article -"Valentino Case to Test Laws."

RV's statement outside county jail: *LAT* – 5/21/22, "Valentino Gives Bond." *LAT* – 5/20/22, "Arrest Valentino on Bigamy Charge." *LAT* - 5/19/22, "Now He's Wondering Which One is His Wife".

Blood and Sand controversy: Text of the Famous Players-Lasky vs. Rudolph Valentino injunction, Affidavit of Rudolph Valentino.

Sequences edited out from Blood and Sand: Ibid.

Backlash against RV and campaign to clean up Hollywood in spring of 1922: M. Viera, *Sin in Soft Focus; Pre-Code Hollywood.*

Wedgwood Place details: M. Morris, *Madam Valentino.* R. Florey interview notes - M. Morris Archives.

RV's Fairfield Ave. address: William Pelf interviews - 2003.

Whitley Heights household staff: GU ms.

Natacha arrives in NYC: Foxlair family history - M. Morris archives.

Foxlair estate information: Ibid.

Bigamy hearing courtroom scenes: M. Morris, *Madam Valentino.*

Ivano and Nazimova testimony as being false: Paul Ivano interview notes - M. Morris archives.

Elderly Cahuilla Indian: F. M. Bogert, *"Palm Springs History, The First One Hundred Years"* .

"What better way to keep Rudy in line...": Analysis by M. Morris.

RV's spending habits: GU ms.

Request for RV's signature on Famous Players' waiver: Ibid.

Rosa Rosanova information and quote by RV: "...How shall I answer you? I am happy, etc." - Interview with R. Rosanova - *NYT* – 8/25/1926, "Screen Mother Recalls Movie Life of Valentino." *LAT* – 8/25/26, "Sheik Declared Lovelorn".

7. About Face

Information on Foxlair: Excerpts from family history by Elizabeth Hudnut Clarkson. Further information from the New York State Department of Land and Forestry, Warrensburg, New York.

Dick Dorgan's "I hate Valentino!" : *Photoplay magazine* - July 1922.

Problems between RV and Lasky: Famous Players-Lasky vs. Rudolph Valentino Injunction, Affidavit of Rudolph Valentino.

Impact of the Sheik: Sklar, *Movies Made America.*

Natacha Rambova and Theodore Kosloff information: M. Morris, *Madam Valentino.*

Rudy's double bed and bedspread: Photograph of Rudy's room in Foxlair family history as included in the Foxlair family history.

8. The Whole Truth

Psychic disrupts court proceedings: *LAT* – 3/26/30, "Medium Breaks Up Trial". *LAT* – 7/6/32, "Judge Ends Trial Over Baby's Death".

Frank Mennillo's problems with A. P. Giannini: Mennillo family interviews - 2003-2004.

Parcel of land accepted as partial payment by Pan American Bank: Appellant's Opening Brief – p. 107.

GU's testimony- Obj. To 1st Account – p. 31 line #93.

GU's reply to..."What did you do in connection with..": Obj. To Executor's First Acct. - p. 40 lines #119-122.

"I was Mr. Valentino's personal..." GU testimony.

George's clients: Ullman family interviews - 2003-2004.

Love letters in George's desk drawer: Bob Ullman interview - 2003.

George sees value in Rudy's address books and letters: W. Pelf interview.

Alberto keeps Rudy's jewelry and clothes: Ibid.

GU's testimony about prop house meeting: Obj. To 1st Acct. - p.118 line #353.

Maria's testimony @ her arrival in US: Supplemental to 1st Account – p. 71 line #211.

Quote from Executor's Exhibit #4, Maria's letter addressed to George: Obj. to 1st account – p. 242 line #726.

Frank Mennillo subpoenaed: Obj. to 1st Acct. - p. 95 line #283.

GU testimony: "...There were several elements.." Obj. To 1st acct. - p. 123 line #369. George petitions court for reimbursement of personal funds he spent on vet bills for Rudy's dogs and spent tipping police in New York at time of funeral - Ibid.

Maria's testimony: Supplemental to Executor's 1st Account – p. 68-72 also p.195 line #583 and p. 196 line #587.

James C. Scarborough: "You state at page six of your account..." Obj. to 1st Acct. - p. 136 line #407.

GU testifies "....When I first took over the estate..": Obj. to 1st Acct. - p. 147 lines #440-441.

GU's salary as executor disputed: W. I. Gilbert testimony. Obj. to 1st Account – p. 138 line #412 also p.140 line #420 and p.135 line #404.

As executor GU not paid for two years: Baskerville Audit, Also Obj. To 1st Acct. - p. 29 lines #58-60.

W.I. Gilbert testimony: Obj. To 1st Acct.- p. 173 lines #518-521.

W.I. Gilbert testifies, "...I don't know whether I should make this statement...": Obj. to 1st Acct. - p. 177 lines #531-533.

GU resigns as executor..."That discord might not cloud...": *LAT* – 7/8/1930, "Valentino's Friend Out of Estate."

GU's testimony, "....When did you start west with...": Obj. to 1st Acct. - p. 35 lines #103-112.

GU Testifies, "...I wanted to give him the finest funeral I knew how to give..." : Obj. to 1st Acct. - p.38 line #112.

GU gives Lou business: L. Mahoney taped interview. Court records.

GU pays Ritz Cleaners debt before giving business to Lou Mahoney: Court records.

GU testifies he sold Ritz Cleaners to Lou for $250.00 : Obj. to 1st Acct. - p. 53 line #157.

Lou denies affiliation with dry-cleaning business: L. Mahoney's memoirs as reported in J. Scagnetti, *The Intimate Life of Valentino.*

Lou reports occupation as dry-cleaner in 1930: US Census Forms on file @ New York Supreme Court Civil Term Library.

Dates of Lou's tenure on New York City police force: The New York City Police Museum archives.

Lou serves on Inspector Kelly's staff: *NYT* – 4/20/1924, "The Mahoney's are Off."

Inspector Kelly "....could not be touched": *NYT* – 12/10/1931, "Queens Police Head Unable to Explain $35,596 in Deposits". *NYT* – 12/29/31, "Inspector Kelly Finally Quits Force."

"Not first time Kelly..": *NYT* – 3/26/24, "Policewomen Used in Drive on Liquor". *NYT* – 10/18/24, "Policemen Indicted in Liquor Plot".

Tin Box Brigades: H. Mitgang, *Once Upon a Time in New York.*

Judge Seabury launches investigations: K. C. Murphy, *Lost Warrior: Al Smith and the Fall of Tammany Hall.* H. Mitgang, *Once Upon a Time in New York.*

Lou reads news of NY investigation: *NYT* - 12/10/1930 and 12/4/1930, "New York Vice Trap Explained" and "Twenty-Eight Policemen in Vice Graft Net". *NYT* – 12/29/31, "Queens Police Head Unable to Explain $35,596.00 in Deposits". *NYT* – 12/11/1931, "Policemen Bares League Protecting Speakeasy Owners". *LAT* – 12/4/1930, "New York Vice Trap Explained".

Lou's testimony: Obj. to 1st Acct. - p. 165 line #491.

Lou tells court that as executor George Ullman kept everyone fed and paid and that Alberto did nothing during that time: *LAT* -11/11/30, "Valentino Case Gets Surprise."

Lou testifies he met Valentino in 11/25: *LAT* – 11/11/30, "Valentino Case Gets Surprise." *LAT* – 11/11/1930, L. Mahoney testifies -"...Ullman was busy trying to get money so Valentino's employees could eat."

GU presents RV's blank checks to the court: *LAT* – 11/13/30, "Two Notes Offered" and "Film Star's Executor Shows Unused Signatures" also "Court Declares No Proof of Integrity Required". GU ms.

Judge refuses to admit blank checks: *LAT* - 11/13/30 -"Two Valentino Notes Offered."

Judge praises GU's performance as executor: Obj. To 1st – p. 107 line #321. Impact/conversion of judgment relating to today's exchange - American Institute for Economic Research.

Total of possible judgment against GU: Respondent Opening Brief - p.#21 line #134. Appellant's Opening Brief - p.16.

GU requests that judge subpoena the will's missing page: *NYT* – 11/8/1930, "Valentino Paper Missing". *LAT* – 11/8/1930, "Valentino Safe Raid Asserted".

All relevant Cosmic Arts testimony: Obj. to 1st Acct. - p. 73-78.

Raymond Stewart finds ragged carbon copy in the file of RV's property settlement papers: *LAT* – 2/5/31, "Lawyer Backs Valentino's Will". *LAT* – 2/5/31, "Torn Evidence in Valentino Court Case". Court records and testimony.

Text of Paragraph Fourth: Appellants' Opening Brief – p. 6-7 and actual document.

Alberto and Maria have share in Rudy's estate only in the event of Jean's death: Appeals Decision - "...that the brother (Alberto) and sister (Maria) were entitled to a distributive share in the estate only in the event of the death of the nephew, Jean."

9. A Mineralava Country Mile

Cora McGeachy and her Brooklyn séances: GU ms.

RV and Natacha receive news of impending road trip and manager's arrival from Cora: Ibid.

RV moves in with Frank and Arnold: Mennillo family interviews.

RV uses Hotel des Artistes as address and skips out at night: Ibid.

Hotel des Artistes controversy: *NYT* – 9/17/22, "Raid Fake Studios, Is Plea of Artists."

Arnold and Frank information: Mennillo family interviews.

Quote by RV from *Photoplay* - "Open Letter to his public": January 1923. Adela Rogers St. John, *"Love, Laughter and Tears, My Hollywood Story."*

Injunction altered and RV appeal denied: *NYT* – 11/1/22, "Famous Players Wins Valentino Injunction".

Issues of RV's debt in Los Angeles: GU ms.

Arthur Grahm threatens to release information about RV to press: Ibid.

Frank Mennillo loans RV money: Court records.

Joe Godsol loan: GU ms.

"Valentino is Through!": O.O. McIntyre's introduction to *Valentino as I Knew Him.*

Quote from Valentino's, "The Truth About Myself": *NYT* – 12/23/22, "Radio World Sits in at Double Wedding".

Arnold Mennillo and the desperate fan story: Arnold Mennillo's first hand account.

RV's obsession with codes and increasing paranoia: GU ms.

George Ullman and negotiations of the tour: Ibid.

RV fears arrest in L.A. because of debts: Ibid.

Mineralava Tour details: GU ms. GU, *Valentino as I Knew Him. The Oregonian* – 6/2/23, "Cold Cream Sheik Hides From Caller". *The Oregonian* – 6/3/23, "Valentino Leaves City" and "Sheiks Have Convention in Municipal Jail Cells". *Chicago Tribune* – 3/14/23, "Winifred and Sheik Re-wed at Crowne Point" and "Sheik to Wed Winifred Here First of Week".

Pound Party Details: *The Seattle-Post Intelligencer* – 6/1/23, "Valentino Charmed" and "Pound Party Has Novel Program" and "Actors to Aid Child Hospital Today".

Robert Florey information: William Pelf's revelation.... "Florey was bitter in later years as he was the only person Rudy ever personally fired." Florey came on board tour as publicity man - R. Florey, *La Lanterne Magique*.

10. A Child's Resemblance

Conversation in Max Steuer's office: GU ms.

Negotiations with Arthur Grahm: Ibid.

Max Steuer represents Blanca DeSaulles for Prince & Nathan: *NYT* – 8/11/1916, "...Max D. Steuer appearing for Prince & Nathan..."

Negotiations with Paramount attorney Emil Ludwig and Jesse Lasky: GU ms.

All references to incorporating Cosmic Arts, Inc.: Obj. to First Acct.- p. 53-54 line #159-160 and p. 260 line #219.

Cosmic Arts incorporated on May 23, 1923: Court records.

Joe Godsol repayment @ Metro-Goldwyn Building: GU ms.

Terms of GU's contract and GU granted power of attorney: GU ms. Also Alberto Valentino reports in *L'Italo Americano* interview, "...(Ullman)to whom Rodolfo had given power of attorney to manage all his affairs....."

Negotiations with J.D. Williams and Famous Players-Lasky Corporation: GU ms.

Information on RV's New York bank: Robert Florey's contract inside address listed as, " Rudolph Valentino, c/o National City Bank, 42nd Street Branch, New York, New York."

Information on GU and Florey's contracts: Actual documents.

GU has power of attorney: GU ms. Alberto's interview with *L'Italo Americano*, Argentina Brunetti - 10/1/1977.

On board *Aquitania* and honeymoon events: GU ms. N. Rambova, *Rudy*. M. Morris, *Madam Valentino*.

Information on Hebertot trip to Deauville and Rudy's refusal to visit battlegrounds: Jeanne DeRecqueville, *Rudolph Valentino*.

Cost of RV's cars: GU ms.

Gabriel Voisin and custom ordering of Voison Avions: carfolio.com and ukcar.com

Story of the near plunge and terrifying ride, "Did you see him...": N. Rambova, *Rudy*.

Information about the chateau at Juan les Pins: GU ms.

Negotiations with Sidney Olcott: Ibid.

Natacha brings Andre Daven on board: Ibid.

Border crossing episode: N. Rambova, *Rudy.*

On stopping for dinner, RV melancholy with tears in his eyes: Ibid.

Story of angry uncles and aunts and RV's departure from Italy: Ibid.

Milan and Maria: Ibid.

RV's automatic writing "by means of the pencil" at inn: Ibid.

Events in Rome: GU ms.

Jean "spitting image of Rudy," as Rudy's "reincarnation": E. Leider, *Dark Lover.* W. Pelf interviews and photographs.

Jean Valentino's birth information: Citizenship papers. Court records and birth certificate as filed in Santeremo en Colle, Italy.

Account of Valentino's return to Castellaneta: GU ms.

George greets the Valentino's ship by tugboat: Ibid.

Incident of the smuggled diamond, the caviar order and subsequent bill: Ibid.

RV's new contract: *NYT* – 7/19/23, "Valentino to have His Artistic Liberty".

RV showed no interest in reading script but Natacha reads: GU ms.

RV could not finish reading and seldom read a book: GU ms. W. Pelf reporting Alberto's revelation that the only book Rudy ever read was *The Sheik.*

RV as "..bookish intellectual...": *The Bookman* - 1/8/1923.

Clashes between George and Natacha: GU ms.

Mineralava Pageant details: GU ms. D. Selznick, *Memo From David O. Selznick. NYT* - 11/27/23, "Beauties Dazzle Hulbert".

Natacha's signature required to assign ownership of new contracts to Cosmic Arts: Cosmic Arts' documents and contracts.

Account of New Year's Eve party at The Negresco Hotel: N. Rambova, *Rudy.*

11. Paragraph Fourth

Carbon copy of Second Page of Will discovered by Raymond Stewart and his testimony regarding: *LAT* – 2/5/31, "Lawyer Backs Valentino's Will." Appeals Court decision. Raymond Stewart testifies GU never had copy of will - *LAT*- 2/5/31, "Lawyer Back Valentino's Will".

Lou and Alberto spar: *LAT* – 2/6/31, "Rudy's Goodbye Scene Disputed". Uncited article - "Valentino's Last Visit with Pola Disputed".

Lou alleges he drove Valentino to train station in July 1926: R. Lee, "The Legend of Valentino"- *Movie Classics* 8/73.

Information regarding the admitting of Paragraph Fourth: *LAT* – 2/7/31, "Valentino Case Given to Judge". *LAT* – 2/6/31, "Rudy's Goodbye Scene Disputed". *LAT* – 2/5/31, "Lawyer Backs Valentino's Will". *LAT* – 2/5/31, "Torn Evidence in Valentino Court Case".

Information regarding the admittance, contents, impact and analysis of Paragraph Fourth: Appeals Court decision - Obj. to 1st Account and Appellants' Brief.

Teresa Werner allies with GU: Court testimony and records.

Only three people had access to Falcon Lair's safe: *LAT* – 11/8/30, "Valentino Safe Raid Asserted". Court records.

Alberto's version of events: "Valentino's Last Visit with Pola Features Trial" - Uncited article filed in Margaret Herrick Library.

Pola Negri in Europe and unable to testify: *LAT* – 2/9/193, "Rudy's Good-by Scene Disputed".

Paragraph Fourth Admitted as legitimate portion of Rudy's will on Feb.7, 1931: Court records.

Terms of Paragraph Fourth: Paragraph Fourth document.

GU knew RV's instructions existed: *NYT* – 11/8/1930, "Valentino Paper is Missing". "...The attorney said Mr. Ullman...failed to find the original..." *NYT* – 9/11/26, "Valentino Heirs Move to Speed Settlement"

Only in the case of Jean's death before age twenty-five: Appeals Court decision.

Alberto's command of English: Campbell's Funeral Home records reporting Alberto used a translator in 1926.

Lou earns $45.00 a week as handyman: Exhibit #9 - 1926 Falcon Lair "Gray Book" Household Expenses - line #801 entered as payroll itemization.

Alberto alleges Paragraph Fourth is a fraudulent document: "...Did you believe Paragraph Fourth had been destroyed?" Court transcripts.

Judgment levied against GU: *LAT* – 8/18/32, "Ullman Loses Valentino Suit". Also Court records.

Value of Valentino estate @ $130,000.00: *LAT* – 2/21/32, "Valentino Estate Nigh Insolvency". *LAT* – 12/11/1934, "Late Valentino Home Sale Approved by Court.

Terms of judgment: *LAT* – 8/18/32, "Ullman Loses Suit". *LAT*- 1/7/33, "Appeal Papers in Valentino Action Filed". Court records.

Sale of Valentino's armor for less than a thousand dollars: GU ms.

Alberto petitions Bank of America for partial distribution: Registry of Actions.

GU retreats to den with violin and effects of judgment upon Ullman household: Bob and Bunny Ullman interviews - "...a tall, green glass full of bourbon...", Bob Ullman interview - 2004.

Frank Mennillo and A. P. Giannini mens' room brawl and reports regarding business in Merced with Arnold: Mennillo family interviews

Mennillo's California Tomato Juice, Inc. plant and travails: Mennillo archives, Merced yellow pages. *Merced Bee* – 11/6/1936, "Mennillo Dies in Los Angeles".

Alberto continues to object to Bank of America tenure and petition for distribution of funds: Registry of Actions

Alberto destitute: Louella Parson's article - *L.A. Herald Examiner-* 2/6/35, "He Wants a Job!". *LAT-* 4/26/1935, "Burglars Rob Valentino Kin". *LAT* photo - 2/7/1935 titled, "Valentino's Brother in Dire Straits" courtesy of the Film Study Center, Museum of Modern Art.

Schenck and the mob: Americanmafia.com also Noircity.com/dark city. *NYT* – 10/28/41, "I Did It For Joe, Bioff Testifies". *NYT* – 11/7/41, "Bioff, Browne Guilty!"

Carol McKinstry: *LAT* – 2/13/39, "Medium Tells of Contact with Valentino Spirit" and *"A Warning Throughout the Ages, A Psychic Consignment From Rudolph Valentino in 1938"* by Carol McKinstry.

Miss Jorgensen's grocery lists: *LAT* – 6/1/35, "So-Called Spirit Letters Hold Couple in Forgeries".

Samuel Roth and his work: Text of his *The Intimate Journal* and Samuel Roth's Imprints, 1920-1940. Also various imprints including Big Dollar Book Company and William Faro.

***The Literary Digest* and *The Daily Express* reports:** *The Literary Digest* - 8/29/27. *The Literary Digest* – 8/20/27, "Remembering Valentino".

Zunilda Mancini information: *LAT* – 4/10/34, "Valentino Action Has Court Echo". *LAT* – 10/24/33, "Valentino Memorial Donor Sues Ullman". *LAT* – 2/17/34, "No Reflection Intended, Gilbert Valentino". *LAT* – 2/10/34, "Woman Held Too Generous". *LAT* – 4/18/35, "Judgment in Valentino Row Upheld for Woman". Appeals Court records for Mancini v. Ullman- 4/35.

Ullman Exoneration: *The Hollywood Reporter* – 4/18/34, "Ullman Exonerated in Estate Row". Court recommends the establishment of fairness lien - Appeals Court decision. Temporary reduction of judgment to $25,849.20 - Court documents.

Appeals Court defends Ullman's performance as executor: Appeals Decision - Mancini decision upheld but ruling issued found no intent of fraud on Ullman's behalf.

GU had no prior knowledge of Paragraph Fourth and court could not determine who was responsible for loss of document: *NYT* – 9/11/26, "Valentino Heirs Move to Speed Settlement."

Appeals Court chastises Alberto's suit against George demonstrating, "...Not a scintilla of evidence..." also stating the lawsuit, "....does such violence to any reasonable interpretation of Valentino's will and his instructions that it is entirely without merit...": Appeals Court decision.

Final judgment amount and the Appeals Court fairness lien recommendation: *LAT*- 8/18/32 -"Ullman Loses Suit".

Appeals Court decision: Appeals Court records.

Subject of cash advances dismissed until final decree of distribution: *LAT* – 12/11/34, "Late Valentino's Home Sale Approved by Court". *Illustrated Daily News* – 12/1//34, "Valentino Estate Settled after Long Fight".

Alberto hired by Bank of America as Falcon Lair's caretaker: Louella Parsons' article - *L.A. Examiner* – 2/6/35, "He Wants a Job!"

Alberto lives in Whitley Heights in 1931: *LAT* – 4/26/1935, "Burglars Rob Valentino Kin" . L.A. County LIbrary Card Index.

Wage garnishments and property seizures on GU: Actual documents on file in the L.A. County Hall of Records.

Mennillo in produce brokerage business: *Merced Bee* – 11/6/1936, "Mennillo Dies in Los Angeles".

Giannini's anti-Semitic remarks inspires Schenck's resignation: F. Bonadio, *A. P. Giannini, Banker of America.* p.261.

Decree of Final Distribution of estate adds $66,644.33 to total of judgment against George on November 2, 1937: L.A. County Hall of Records document on file stating, "...the sum of $25,849.20, with interest at 7% from December 7, 1934, the date of said decree, upon which said interest had been credited in the sum of $2,880.62 in accordance with the Final Decree of Distribution entered November 2, 1937, together with the addition sum of $66,644.33 added by said Decree of Distribution in said proceeding to said judgment."

"The Man that Came Back": *Life* magazine - 6/20/38. *LAT* – 1/10/38, "Yesterday's Stars of Screen Firmament are Now Glimmering in New Orbits". *LAT* – 5/27/38, "*The Sheik* Revived at Four Star".

Jean's citizenship information, marriage and addresses: *San Diego Sun* – 6/23/36, "Vital News". *Evening Tribune* – 6/23/36, "Marriage License Listings".

Jean takes over estate: Registry of Actions, various documents on file at Los Angeles County Hall of Records. Appeals Court decision.

Jean's date of birth: Jean's birth certificate as filed in Santeramo in Colle.

Value of estate diminishes and is reported as insolvent by 1938: Alberto Valentino's interview with Brunetti, for *L'Italo-Americano* 10/1/77. *LAT* - 2/21/32, "Valentino estate Nigh to Insolvency".

Lack of subsequent public knowledge of Paragraph Fourth and the lack of reportage of the Appeals Court's recommendation that Jean establish fairness lien to recover funds and any information regarding the weekly stipends: Evident as being untold in publications, books and articles about Valentino.

Lou's erroneous version of his life, i.e. train station details, time of departure from New York City, Valentino's lack of interest in spiritualism and involvement in dry-cleaning business after Valentino's death: R. Lee's - "The Legend of Valentino"- *Movie Classics*, 8/73. M. Morris, *Madam Valentino*. Census records. Obit reporting his position as "Valentino's manager...." L. Mahoney's obituary in *The Daily Pilot*-Newport Beach, California, 4/27/68. Also as quoted by Lou in his taped interview and in J. Scagnetti's, *The Intimate Life of Valentino*. "...I slipped out of the picture in so far as the dry cleaning operation was concerned." Court testimony.

Lou claims he had nothing to do with dry-cleaning business: *LAT* – 11/11/30, "Valentino Case Gets Surprise".

12. Hoping to be Kindly Remembered

March/April 1924 - Commissioner Enright's investigation of Lou Mahoney's precinct and Inspector Kelly: H. Mitgang, *Once Upon a Time in New York*. Files of the New York Supreme Court Civil Term Library archives. New York City Corruption Investigation Commissions - 1894-1994. *NYT* – 7/14/24, "Oust 2 Inspectors, Fines 7 For Laxity". *NYT* – 3/26/24, "Policewomen Used in Drive on Liquor".

Lou turns in badge #5779 on April 30, 1924: Records of his original appointment to police department on 1/19/17 and retirement on file in New York City Police Museum.

Mahoney clan leaves NYC and Lou's quote: *LAT* – 5/7/24, "Clan Mahoney Hits the Trail". Departure from NYC – *NYT* – 4/30/24, "The Mahoney's are Off".

The refusal to buy the plum story, including RV's quote: GU ms.

RV's cigarettes and shaving soap: Ibid.

Natacha's hiring of staff: M. Morris, *Madam Valentino*.

Natacha and George on verge of battle: GU ms.

Sidney Olcott/Natacha, tensions between: Ibid.

Cost of *Beaucaire* and Doris Kenyon contract: Ibid.

Details of Andre Daven salary and stay in NYC and also Daven's letters as quoted by: J. DeRecqueville, *Rudolph Valentino* - "...a son amie parisienne, Daven ecrit..." and "....Je n'ai que deux scenes..." Also GU ms.

Daven's dental charges and rude departure, etc.: GU ms.

RV's purchases at American Art Auction: *TIME* magazine - May 5, 1924.

Rex Beach's story "Rope's End": R. Beach, *The Crimson Gardenia and Other Tales of Adventure.*

Nita Naldi information: "The Reminiscences of Nita Naldi" - Columbia University Oral History Research Office as interviewed by Joan and Robert Franklin in 1959.

Jetta Goudal rumors: M. Morris, *Madam Valentino.*

Natacha hires Adrian Greenberg: M. Morris, *Madam Valentino.*

Isotta Cariolet details: GU ms.

Arnold Mennillo's nightclub act: Mennillo family interviews.

Loud tie contest with Odd McIntyre: As recounted in the introduction to Ullman's, *Valentino As I Knew Him.*

Victor Miller, Odd and Maybelle McIntyre and seances: GU ms.

"Odd's makers doubting...": O.O. McIntyre's introduction to *Valentino As I Knew Him* by George Ullman.

Reviews of *Beaucaire*: I. Schulman, *Valentino.*

Fans unhappiness with Natacha: M. Morris, *Madam Valentino.*

Natacha sole stockholder of Cosmic Arts and her ownership of RV's contract: Court records and testimony.

RV mentally "lazy" in his wife's presence: GU ms.

RV attempting to read textbooks, researching auction purchases and waiting for Cora McGeachy's missives: GU ms.

Hooded Falcon info: GU ms.

Naldi's role in *Hooded Falcon*: *LAT* – 9/7/1924, "Rudy to Return to Work Soon."

Williams selling stock on west coast and George makes trip to L.A. to settle debts: GU ms.

GU leases studio space in Los Angeles from M.C. Levee: *LAT* – 9/2/1924, "Studios Here to Spend Millions". *LAT*- 9/7/1924, "Rudolph to Return to Work Soon". *LAT* – 10/13/1924, "Eastern Film Boom is Over". Blue Book of the Screen (1923).

Bill Menzies and Lou's work on his wife's car: J. Scagnetti, *The Intimate Life of Rudolph Valentino.*

Red Cross bullfighting details and all details of trip to France in 1924: N. Rambova, *Rudy.*

Fortress Loches: Ibid.

Odd McIntyre receives postcard: GU, *Valentino As I Knew Him*, McIntyre's introduction.

Master Barbers vote and Reichenbach's involvement: I. Schulman, *Valentino*.

GU's fight with J.D. Williams: GU ms and as quoted from memoir. "....I will not go into the things I said to Williams! "

RV accepts *Cobra* role upon Black Feather's advice: GU ms.

GU sells the Valentino's cars: Ibid.

Natacha's quote about Hollywood: *L.A. Herald Examiner* – 3/6/1978, reprint from *Movie Weekly* - 7/7/23.

Renovations on Valentino L.A. home: GU ms.

Natacha's fountain, aviary and Lou's arrival: L. Mahoney taped interview.

RV's activities away from home: GU ms.

All boxing details and Coronado Hotel story, Tijuana fracas and press men activities, all quotes verbatim: Ibid.

RV's bootleggers: Falcon Lair household ledger's liquor entries and Baskerville audit, Obj. to 1st Account – p. 282-283 lines #846-847 as itemized under "Liquor Accounts."

Shaving of the goatee and amulet carrying: GU ms.

Interview with Alma Whitaker: *LAT* – 12/21/24, "Secrets of Valentino's Life".

Christmas 1924: GU ms. Ullman family interviews and GU, *Valentino As I Knew Him.*

13. The Kestral Feed

Peregrine falcons and trainer: GU ms. L. Mahoney taped interview.

6774 Wedgwood Place property: Appellant's Opening Brief – p. 20 -"Lot #6, Tract 6774, etc."

L.B. Nolte Poultry and other household accounts: Registry of Actions. Falcon Lair household ledgers.

Purchase of Falcon Lair: GU ms.

RV financially supports Aunt Teresa Werner and RV receives "nearly weekly letters from Alberto requesting money...", resulting in payments as issued to Alberto: GU ms. Itemized entries in Falcon Lair household records. William Pelf quote...." Most of the letters from Alberto to Rudy that I read were just requests for money."

Renovations on Falcon Lair: GU ms.

Ritz-Cleaners: Obj. to 1st Account – p. 52 line #154.

GU left in charge of Falcon Lair restoration and staff: P. Negri, *Memoirs of a Star.* GU ms.

Fischbeck camera invention: *LAT* – 11/2/1924, "Camera Device to Give Picture Softer Effect".

RV and Natacha arrive on set of *Cobra* with automatic writing notes: As told by Colleen Moore. M. Morris, *Madam Valentino.*

Details of the closing of Ritz-Carlton and signing of the United Artists' contract: GU ms. United Artist's contract. Also Valentino signs separate distributing contract as stipulated in UA contract. Both documents submitted as court's evidence and held on file within court records.

All details of the United Artists' contract: Text of the contract as admitted as, "Executor's Exhibit #1- United Artists' Contract.

RV's percentage calculated after deductions at 43¾ percent of the profits: Appellant's Opening Brief - p. 11- personal property listings.

Natacha's name not mentioned in contract: Text of UA contract.

Joe Schenck's verbal edict Natacha had no executive role: GU ms.

Natacha as sole stockholder of Cosmic Arts: Obj. To First Acct. - p. 73 line #219.

Details of Palm Springs meeting: GU ms. "...Rudy returned then. He looked haggard and depressed. I am certain that he had heard, even in greater detail, Natacha's plans and her inflexibility."

United Artists' contract signed on March 30th: Obj. to 1st Acct. - p.156 line #467.

United Artists' contract reassigned to Cosmic Arts on April 21st: Appellant's Opening Brief, p. 99. Executor's Exhibit #1, detailing assignments of contract to Cosmic Arts as signed by Rudolph Valentino on April 21, 1925.

Natacha's presentation of *What Price Beauty* proposal: GU ms.

GU invests his own money in *What Price Beauty*: RV's quote, "Ullman signed most of the notes for the production of the picture. I had only a little money in it myself but will pay Ullman whatever his loss is." *LAT* – 10/25/25, "Breach Widens for Valentinos".

Myrna Loy in *What Price Beauty*: M. Morris, *Madam Valentino.*

GU negotiates with Ona Brown: GU ms.

RV's strained marital relations: Ibid.

GU asks Natacha,"....Why? Almost every woman, etc.... and ensuing argument and expletives: GU ms.

***Eagle* writers work at Wedgwood Place, Schenck's reaction and ultimatum**: GU ms.

Beltran-Masses visit and RV's social life on the set of *The Eagle* with Vilma Banky: GU ms.

Lou's role as spy for Natacha: L. Mahoney taped interview.

Lou's angst and resentment of George Ullman: L. Mahoney taped interview. Natacha Rambova Research Foundation. M. Morris, *Madam Valentino*.

Details of the yacht Phoenix and monthly payment: Falcon Lair household ledgers.

Details of Rudy's United Artists' bungalow: GU, *Valentino As I Knew Him*.

Women stalkers on the set: GU ms.

GU carries a loaded gun: Bob Ullman interviews.

Beltran-Masses encourages RV to hire detective: GU ms.

RV threatens to kill, hits Natacha and then sleeps with her: GU ms.

Details of the Cosmic Arts meeting and Natacha's surrender of stock and controlling interest in Valentino's contracts: Obj. to 1st Acct, p.155 lines #464-467. Appellant's Opening Brief, p.99. "...Natacha voluntarily surrendered interest in Rudolph Valentino Productions...."

RV and Natacha's press statements: I. Schulman, *Valentino*.

RV wounded by Muzzie's telegrams: GU ms.

RV arrested and limps into court on August 22: Uncited Article – 9/10/25, "Valentino Run Over By Horse" .

Mont Westmore and *The Phoenix* tryst between Rudy and Nita Naldi below deck: M. Morris, *Madam Valentino* and as recounted by Mont Westmore's brother Frank Westmore - " ..while Mont stood on the bridge with his eyes peeled for the treacherous reefs off Catalina, he could hear Nita's melodious voice extolling Rudy's capabilities.." Also Westmore's affiliation with Valentino - *The Smithsonian Magazine*, May 2000.

Naldi tells RV about Natacha's three alleged abortions: M. Morris, *Madam Valentino*. Tony Altimoreno notes in M. Morris archive.

RV and Vilma Banky to Friday night fights: GU ms. P. Negri, *Memoirs of a Star*. ".....Rudy's life of easy conquests, etc."

"Rudy always had a girl on his arm." William Pelf and Bob Ullman interviews 2003.

RV's "September 1" will as executed by Raymond Stewart: Court testimony and text of will.

RV's suicide attempt: Beltran-Masses,*"Guillot de Saix, Comoedia*, 9/25/26.

RV appears in court: Uncited Article -9/11/25, "Trouble All with Rudy's French Car" and "Valentino Fined $50 on Speeding Charges".

RV about town with women and Vilma Banky's late night dinners at Falcon Lair: GU ms and Bee Ullman tells William Pelf and children that "Rudy always had a girl on his arm." Also GU, *Valentino as I Knew Him*.

Pola simultaneously dates Mdivani: GU ms.

RV and Mae's kissing in The American Legion Stadium parking lot: Ibid.

Lou dislikes Pola Negri, loyalty to Natacha and returns falcons to zoo: L. Mahoney taped interview.

Pola's negligees in Rudy's bedroom closet: L. Mahoney, as related to M. Morris by Lou's daughter.

Press learns detectives followed Natacha: *LAT* -10/3/1925, "Cinema Sheik's Wife Shadowed" also Rudy alleges, "...a woman's place is in the home.."

GU home and back yard playing with Uncle Rudy: Bob Ullman interviews.

RV initiates legal action to adopt Jean: Alberto Valentino laments to reporter from *L'Italo-Americano* on 10/1/77.

14. Warning-Read This-You Could Go To Prison!

Joe Schenck and the mob: Americanmafia.com and noircity.com also *NYT* – 10/28/41, "Did it for Joe, Bioff Testifies" and *NYT* – 11/7/41, "Bioff, Browne Guilty".

Jean Valentino and his attorney James M. Sheridan: Complaint on Judgment No. 481480, Superior Court of California and County of Los Angeles.

Jean files Property Seizure, Wage Garnishment and Complaints against George Ullman: Sheriff's office documents filed in The L.A. County Hall of Records, interest on judgment taken from same documentation @ $4,677.20 a year.

Court of Appeals recommends Jean dismiss collection process on judgment against GU en lieu of fairness lien: Appeals Decision 4/17/34. quoted... "In said proceeding, where said trust instructions, which the executor trustee claimed were lost, directed monthly payments to be made until decedent's nephew should reach the age of twenty-five years, but if he were dead the residue was to go to two of said named persons, if the advances were made in good faith and at the solicitation of the beneficiaries, and defendant is held to be accountable to the estate therefore, he should be given an appropriate fairness lien against the beneficial interest of those who participated in the advancement of the property and funds of the estate." And "..he (George Ullman) should not be charged to account to the estate in full for those advances or for interest as if he had defaulted or misapplied the funds to his own use."

Jean offers attorney percentage of money collected from Ullman and Jean sued by James Sheridan: *LAT* – 6/7/47, "Valentino Kin Sued by Lawyer". *Citizen News* – 9/15/47, "Valentino Claim Settlement Reached".

Summons served on GU: Text of Summons as filed in The L.A. County Hall of Records, dated November 4, 1942.

Court orders: As filed in The L.A. County Hall of Records and "Affidavit for Subpoena Duces Tecum," ...."affiant alleges that S. George Ullman..."

Jean compiles list of missing items and shows to Pelf: William Pelf interviews.

Property removed from Falcon Lair before auction: Baskerville audit itemization of "items advanced to Maria Guglielmi Strada" also as itemized in Detail #9 of the Baskerville Audit report and also listed as "cash and property advances" in the Appeals Court decision.

Alberto removes box of Rudy's jewelry and Rudy's Franklin Coupe against his future share of estate: GU ms.

GU keeps items in wicker basket in garage: Ullman family interviews and verified by William Pelf interviews.

GU's payment to Jean: The Partial Satisfaction of Judgment document and GU complies with court order on December of 1947. *LAT* – 12/22/47, "Valentino's Estate Hangs Fire Twenty Years".

GU posts bond in 1926 and the failure of insurance company holding this bond to compensate: Court document filed in Probate case #83678, untitled and cited as "page 2" as front page is missing.

Jean renews all court actions against GU in 1942: Court records as filed.

GU files for bankruptcy: *L.A. Examiner* – 2/25/43, "Insolvency Plea Made by Ullman".

Average income in 1941: Historical Text Archive.com -"1941-42 - Cost of Living Indicators" and also current exchange from 1943 to present @ x12, this would make the judgment over one million dollars today.

Pelf asks GU for work and is refused: W. Pelf interviews.

William Pelf meets and befriends Valentino's friends and family: Ibid.

Pelf attends celebrity funerals to "see who might show up": Ibid.

One of Pelf's "missing trophy" being Rambova: Ibid.

Pelf carries Ivano's letter reporting he was "good guy": Ibid.

Pelf "walked a fine line" between Ullman and Jean Valentino: William Pelf quote.

Jean renews collection orders in December of 1947: *LAT* – 12/22/47, "Valentino's Estate Hangs Fire Twenty Years". *L.A. Examiner* – 12/22/47, "Big Sum Due Valentino Kin".

Itemization of 1947 orders filed against GU: Actual documents as filed in The L.A. County Hall of Records as Affidavit for Subpoena Duces Tecum - "Affiant (Jean Valentino) alleges that S. George Ullman Agency ... truly belongs to him".

GU burns papers in backyard of home and story of the forgeries of the love letters stolen by agent in George's office: Bob and Bunny Ullman.

GU gives Valentino items to Pelf on his birthday: William Pelf, Bob and Bunny Ullman interviews.

Pelf also receives items from Alberto and Jean: William Pelf interviews.

Pelf tells Jean Valentino he may take possession of George Ullman's gifts to him when he "kicks the bucket" and pressure from Valentino family in this matter: William Pelf interviews.

Items in Pelf collection: As shown to author.

Details of the Queen of the Netherlands visit: *LAT* – 4/15/52, "Welcome Mat Out for Queen Juliana". Bob Ullman account.

"Don't Shoot rabbits": K. Brownlow, *Hollywood, The Pioneers*.

Morton Feiler tells the press, "Maybe he'll strike it rich.....": *Citizen-News* – 12/2/52, "From Bad to Worse" and "Ex-Agent for Valentino Sued by Kin of Actor".

Guglielmi's settle lawsuit against Ed Small: *LAT*- 10/15/52, "Kin of Valentino Settle Film Suit out of Court". *Examiner* – 10/15/52, "Substantial amount to Kin in $500,000.00 Valentino Suit". *Mirror* – 10/15/52, "Valentino's Kin Settle Suit Over Film Production".

Edward Small appeals to GU: GU ms.

Schlitz Playhouse of Stars info: William Pelf and The University of Wyoming, The American Heritage Center.

GU's final pay-off: Stipulation of Judgment document.

Morton Feiler and Jean sign Satisfaction of Judgment in 1956: Actual document

Jean tells Pelf he "never got a thing from Ullman.....": William Pelf.

Items Pelf received from Ullman: As itemized by William Pelf

Jean tells Pelf that George "owed him" and that Jean and Alberto were "both awful about George": William Pelf.

"George never had an unkind word....": Ibid.

Pelf passes along denigrating and inaccurate remarks about GU: Pelf speaks with M. Morris.

Erroneous reports on the final decree of against GU judgment and his performance as executor go unchecked by Valentino family as evident in: E. Leider, *Dark Lover*, "....A final settlement was reached two years later, reducing Ullman's debt to the estate to about $26,000.00..."

also Alberto reports in *L'Italo Americano* interview…"Ullman immediately profited by the situation and made a pile of investments…" also as William Pelf reports to M. Morris.

Wicker basket stolen and Pelf's admission to knowledge of: Bob and Bunny Ullman and W. Pelf interviews.

William Pelf's, Alberto and Jean's "version" of events as inaccurate: Alberto speaks with Louella Parsons, William Pelf interviews and Alberto reports in *L'Italo Americano* interview…"Ullman immediately profited by the situation and made a pile of investments.." Also GU ms. Ullman says, "….No one can possibly understand the persistent attacks upon my integrity and judgment in the handling of Rudy's estate brought (against me) by Rudy's brother, Alberto."

Information on the *La Presse* article, challenge of authenticity and vetting of article: J. DeRecqueville, *Valentino*.

Evidence of anonymous, fictional *La Presse* article repeated as fact: E. Leider, *Dark Lover*. Kenneth Anger, *Hollywood Babylon*. Raymond Murray, *Images in the Dark* and others.

Information on Mank: *The Chaw Mank Estate, The Autograph Collector*, October 1980.

Brad Steiger web site: http://www.bradandsherry.com/ and interview with author 2003.

Steiger states that his book was …"based on Mank's memories" and "reason why marriage was one of convenience…": Author's interview and direct quote from Brad Steiger

Mank and Steiger's book filed under Human Sexuality: Cornell University's Kroch Library.

RV's friends protest: DeRecqueville letter and quotes from Rene Clair and Robert Florey. GU ms. William Pelf.

Lou Mahoney works for Lockheed: Lou's obit in The *Daily Pilot*-Newport Beach, California, 4/27/68.

Lou Mahoney interview with Raymond Lee: *Movie Classics* - August 1973. Jack Scagnetti's, *The Intimate Life of Valentino*.

Alberto interviewed for *L'Italo Americano* - October 1977: "…he tried to adopt Gianni (Jean) legally. Naturally our laws did not permit this so he made him his sole heir."

Jean Valentino installs stereo systems and Alberto retires: Respective obits, Jean in *LAT* - 9/26/96 and Alberto in *Variety* - 6/17/81.

Jean sues Disney and Spelling-Goldwyn: *LAT* – 9/1/77, "Valentino's Heir's Suit Tossed Out on Appeal" and Uncited Article - "Disney Firm Sued by Kin of Valentino".

Details of Pelf's home and collection: Author's interviews in his home and viewing of collection.

Info on Chicago collector and their "deals": W. Pelf

Alberto gives Pelf RV's platinum watch after SAG event: W. Pelf interviews and admission Jean once tried to sell RV's platinum watch for $5000.00.

Pelf seeks photo of RV's body as it is being embalmed: W. Pelf requests this of author.

Info on records search: The L.A. County Hall of Records

Request form and letter from County Clerk as The Certificate of Clerk: Actual document.

Pelf "knowing nothing about the theft of Ullman's case" : W. Pelf interviews.

Pelf admits in writing to the possession of and whereabouts of the stolen records and also the negotiations with Chicago collector and return of records to Jean Valentino's granddaughter: W. Pelf writes to author, as preserved on e-mail server, on 9/1/2003. Also verified by secondary/independent report of the exchange of the stolen records for a shirt, etc. by Donna Hill in 11/2005.

Duplicate set of the missing records discovered: Authors collection.

Alberto's wedding date: Declaration of Intention #77378 National Archives and Records Administration/Pacific Region, Laguna Niguel, Ca. Also Naples City Records.

Only other case file missing that of L. Frank Baum: Celebrity Collectibles, Ted James

All info on sarcophagus: W. Pelf, Dick Cunningham and Cesare Mannino @ Campbell's Funeral Home.

15. The Son of the Sheik Says Goodbye

Rudy's Christmas at The Italian Hospital from article included in GU ms, undated article titled: "Valentino's Memory, The Valentino Association is Evidence that his Art and Kindness Still Survive".

Rudy's petition to adopt Jean: Alberto relates in interview given to *L'Italo Americano*" in 1977.

James Quirk quote: *Photoplay*- 2/26, "Speaking of Pictures".

Details of RV's banking and his codes: GU ms. Baskerville Audit Extracts, p. 243-244 lines #728-732. Falcon Lair Household Ledgers.

Information on S. Manuel Reachi and Agnes Ayres: *LAT* – 6/25/27, "Agnes Ayres Tells Her Woes". *LAT* – 6/8/27, "International Romance Ends". *LAT* – 3/14/26, "Diplomat Quits Post For Films". *LAT* – 9/11/24, "Latin Lover Wins Actress". *LAT* – 11/3/25, "Stork Bearing Little Bundle for Agnes Ayres".

The Eagle's **opening in New York**: *LAT* – 11/15/25, "Stampede of Rudy Fans".

Natacha's arrival in New York: M. Morris, *Madam Valentino*.

Mussolini's reaction to RV's petition for U.S. Citizenship: J. DeRecqueville, *Rudolph Valentino* – p.113, "Mussolini Bannit Rudy". Also RV applies for citizenship - NYT – 11/11/25, "Valentino Seeks Citizenship Here" and NYT – 8/25/26, "Says Actor Rebuffed Fascists".

General information on European trip: GU, *Valentino As I Knew Him*. GU ms.

Murray trains from Juan les Pins Mae to Paris with RV: *LAT* – 1/2/1926, "Film Sheik Back from Trip Abroad" cited, "...from Southern France to Paris and then to Berlin..."

Mae Murray separated from Robert Leonard and he is engaged to Gertrude Olmstead: *LAT* – 2/17/1926, "Film Couple Announce Troth".

Mussolini and Fascista campaign against RV: J. DeRecqueville, *Rudolph Valentino*, p.113 - "Mussolini Bannit Rudy".

Fascista publication on RV: Ibid. "*Una Fiera Rampogna Contro Il Rinnegatore Della Patria*"

Reachi organizes trip events and steep charges: GU ms.

Portrait removed from Milan theatre: J. DeRecqueville childhood memory.

RV in Paris with Lady Lougborough: *Time* magazine, January 11, 1926.

Josephine Baker night club act details: redhotjazz.com

RV's divorce: 1/20/26, "Movie Sheik Sails for U.S. as Mate is Granted Decree" , Uncited article archived in The Margaret Herrick Library.

RV looks bloated: GU ms."....Rudy looked haggard and exhausted..."

Pola slaps RV: *Photoplay* - July 1926, p. 78 - "He Who Gets Slapped and Why".

Pola moves into RV's bedroom and leaves negligees: P. Negri, *Memoirs of a Star* and L. Mahoney's daughter.

RV and Pola sleep together upon his return to Los Angeles: P. Negri's, *Memoirs of a Star*.

RV and Jean Valentino's activities: Ibid.

Mdivani brothers as "reputed princes from the Republic of Georgia" and they work as roustabouts for Sinclair Oil Company: *LAT* – 2/6/26, "David Mdivani on Stand Denies Oil Deal Embezzling Charge, Early Struggle Described". RV's competition and resentment of Mdivani brothers: GU ms.

Fights between Pola and RV and their relationship in general: GU ms.

Continual strife between RV and brother Alberto: GU ms quote, "....There were numerous quarrels between Rudy and Alberto during the family visit and I know that these quarrels definitely ruined Rudy's last few weeks at Falcon Lair....."

Falcon Lair expenses, including all payments made to Alberto: Falcon Lair's household ledgers.

Reachi plans to be RV's manager: L. Mahoney and GU ms.

RV's debt @ over $200,000.00: Registry of Actions and as itemized in estate settlement records.

Problems with staff at Falcon Lair and RV delegates oversight to GU: GU ms. Falcon Lair household records and payroll accounts.

RV's yacht breaks down at sea: GU ms.

Mahoney's brothers hired: Falcon Lair payroll accounts.

Tough sale for George and RV's interview: *Collier's The National Weekly* - January 1926, "I'm Tired of being a Sheik".

RV hates the moniker "The Sheik" as relating to "wolfing": *L.A. Herald Express* – 7/12/1944, "Dead Valentino Still Hero to His Agent" by George Ullman as included in the Irving Schulman archives @ USC.

Reachi as Fitzmaurice's assistant: *LAT* – 3/14/1926, "Diplomat Quits Post For Films".

RV's request to adopt Jean is rejected: Alberto tells interviewer, "....Unfortunately Italian law did not permit..." in *L'Italo Americano*.

RV relates revised future plans: GU ms.

Alberto installs padlocks on refrigerators: Ibid.

Details of The Cinema Finance loan and "only three payments made": Objection to 1st Acct., p.153 lines #458-460 also GU under oath in Supplement to First Current Executor Acct. p. 60 lines #178-182 "....A few months before his death...." Also premiums paid on life insurance policy @ $13,375.00 from Supplement to First Current Account p.157 line #471.

Details of RV's new contract with UA: GU ms and contract.

GU knew of RV's simultaneous involvement with both Mae Murray and Pola Negri: GU ms.

L. Mahoney is fired and accuses GU of stealing: L. Mahoney's taped interview.

Dr. Dareos: Badartcafe.com

Details of RV's last day in L.A. and Alberto is evicted: Alberto's testimony. GU ms.

RV and Mission Rudy: Text of letter from Mayor Rolph to GU.

Personal info @ RV's favorites being Vichy water, bicarbonate of soda and topics of conversations: GU ms.

Ballroom story in St. Louis: O.O. McIntyre's foreword to GU, *Valentino As I Knew Him.*

Powder Puff info: GU, *Valentino As I Knew Him*. GU ms

All information on Frank Mennillo: Mennillo family interviews.

GU and his work in The Ambassador suite in 8/1926 with Bee and Estelle Dick: GU ms.

GU and Bee observe Rudy's health deteriorating: Ibid.

Bee loans Alberto one hundred dollars: Ibid.

RV says, "There he goes. I hope I never see him again.": GU ms. "There he goes. I hope I never see the *bastard* again." The word "bastard" added by W. Pelf as related to him by GU. Court records. GU's sworn testimony, "....And I shall *never* forget those words...." and Alberto's attorney petitions to have this testimony stricken from records.

16. Lost in the Woods

Rahman Bey and Harry Houdini: C. Milbourne, *Houdini-The Untold Story*.

RV's love of burlesque shows and fan dancers: Falcon Lair household financial ledgers, counter tabs and bills as itemized in Objection to 1st Acct. p.257 line #771.

Texas Guinan information: jazzbabies.com also Tommy Guinan's Playground with Tex Guinan's 'Mob' and playground review.

RV's arm being pierced: GU ms. GU, *Valentino As I Knew Him*.

Press clipping bureaus subscriptions: GU ms.

Jean Acker in NYC: Ibid.

Trip to Chicago, Roosevelt Theater and NYC opening: GU ms and GU, *Valentino As I Knew Him*.

RV's final defiance of *Tribune* writer : Ibid.

Agnes Ayres delivers baby: *LAT* – 11/3/1925, "Stork Bearing Little Bundle to Agnes Ayres".

Atlantic City information: GU ms and GU, *Valentino As I Knew Him*.

Adela Rogers St. John and RV: A. Rogers St. John, *"Love, Laughter and Tears, My Hollywood Story."*

RV's liquid diet: *Daily Mirror*- 8/25/26, "Friend Says Rudy Lived on Liquids." Uncited article included in Irving Schulman archives titled, "Poison Rum Killed Rudy, New Report on Broadway".

GU and RV's conversations: GU ms.

RV wakes GU at dawn with ice water: GU ms and GU, *Valentino As I Knew Him*.

Cabbie Mike Li Calzi recounts the ride from Marion Benda's apartment to Warburton's party: *The Graphic* - article and photos included in private archives of Irving Schulman - "Saw Rudy in Best Health But 15 Minutes Before Stricken".

Warburton Divorce: *NYT* – 8/14/26, "Divorce Granted Wife of B.H. Warbuton, Jr."

Marian Benda relates details of final date with RV: *Daily Mirror*-8/27/26, "Follies Girl Says Rudy Asked Her to Marry Him".

RV is taken to hospital and account of his illness: GU ms.

Dr. Rawls knew RV was "a dead man" and "victims of peritonitis seldom survived after six hours of symptoms" and RV "....walked into the hospital": W. Pelf interviews with Dr. Rawls.

All medical references and surgical details: Dr. Howard Meeker's report sent to GU, "...Dear Mr. Ullman, I examined Rudolph Valentino for the first time at 5:15 p.m..."

GU recruits Polyclinic nurses and guards: GU ms.

Meeker tells GU that RV's chances are 50-50: Ibid.

"Did I behave like a pink powder puff or like a man?": Ibid.

RV's nurses: *NYT* – 8/26/1926, "Associates Pay Tribute".

Frank Mennillo only other visitor allowed in RV's room: GU ms and Mennillo family interviews.

RV "so tired, demands a smoke and wants to sit up": GU ms.

Details of recovery: Dr. Meeker's report. GU ms and various articles in *NYT* and *San Jose Mercury* – 8/17/26, "Report Condition of Valentino is Still Unchanged".

RV Poisoning Rumors: *Chicago Tribune* – 8/23/26, "Hint Valentino Poisoned". *Daily Mirror* – 8/24/26, "Story Rudy Was Poisoned Branded False by Friend".

D.A. Pecora and Alberto behind poisoning rumors: GU ms.

Joe Schenck's statement: *NY Daily Mirror* – 8/25/26, "Joe Schenck Denounces Poison Story about Rudy".

RV thanks his fans: *NYT* – 8/24/26, "Associates Pay Tributes".

RV tells Meeker about fishing trip: *NYT*- 8/26/1926, "Associates Pay Tribute".

Frank Mennillo's vacation plans to New Jersey: Mennillo family interviews.

RV requests mirror: GU ms and GU, *Valentino As I Knew Him*.

Weekend relapse: *Chicago Tribune* coverage, 8/26/26. GU ms.

Metaphen and blood transfusions: J. DeRecqueville, *Rudolph Valentino*. GU ms.

Doctors cancel appointments: GU ms.

Dr. Durham calls out to GU: Ibid.

GU refuses first priest's visit: Ibid.

Details of last hours in RV's hospital room: GU ms. Mennillo family interviews.

RV relates dreams to GU: GU ms and GU, *Valentino As I Knew Him.*

RV's last word "Madre": GU ms.

Last rites: Father Bartholomew de la Torre consultation.

RV dies in Frank Mennillo's arms: Mennillo family interviews.

GU tells press: GU ms.

Epilogue

Campbell's records: Campbell's Funeral Home Archives.

Frank Campbell tries to sell GU coffin priced at $30,000.00: GU ms.

Details of riots: Campbell's scrapbook of newspaper clippings.

St. Patrick's refuses mass: GU ms and quote from "Article 5 - No Title – NYT-8/29/26, *Osservatore Romano*, "....The described scenes at Rudolph Valentino's bier in New York, says *Osservatore Romano...*"

Priests from St. Malachy's agree to mass: GU ms.

GU files request with Health Department: Ibid.

Furor over Fascista Honor guard: *NYT* – 8/25/1926, "Says Actor Rebuffed Fascista" "....When Valentino took out citizenship papers in America last winter...his films were boycotted throughout Italy at the order of Mussolini. Feeling ran so high among Fascista in Rome, who said he was a traitor to his native country, that they shot at the screen when his films were shown..."

Details of shipping case: Campbell's Funeral Home and viewing of actual case.

Police pressure GU: GU ms.

Furor surrounding Campbell's and suicides: *NYT* – 8/28/26, "Lays Death to Valentino's". *NYT* – 10/6/26, "Denies Girl Suicide Had Known Valentino." *NYT* – 12/30/26, "Valentino Admirer Held".

Lawsuits filed: *NYT* – 2/18/27, "Hurt in Rudy, Sue".

GU meets Alberto on board Homeric: As quoted from the GU ms, "...Alberto rushed to me. He said, 'I am so very sorry. I will take his place.' This jolted me, of course for several reasons...I was so affronted by his egotism...for his next question to me there on the deck of the Homeric was, 'How big is the estate?'..I turned away saying, 'I haven't any idea.'"

Details of trip west, Pola and James Quirk and follow-up: GU ms and funeral in L.A., *NYT* – uncited - 8/28/26.

Dr. Wyman an imposter: GU ms. *LAT* – 5/13/28, "Arch-Imposter Squelched" and GU's quote – *NYT*- 9/6/26, "Repudiated by Ullman" and *NYT* – 9/24/1926, "Wyman on Medical Jurisprudence".

Natacha Rambova's *"Revelations"*: N. Rambova, *Rudy*

Jiddu Krisnamurti information and quote: *TIME* magazine - 9/13/26.

George and Bee Ullman attend séances: GU ms.

Mae West seance: walkingwiththespirit.com

Seance at Falcon Lair in 1948: *NYT* – 5/16/48, "Sorry, Rudolph, Wrong Number".

Princess Springwater: Uncited article in Margaret Herrick Library, 6/17/47 -"Word awaited From Valentino by Astrologer".

Mme. Fourie: Uncited article in Margaret Herrick Library – 11/13/30, "Medium Talks with Valentino".

RV alive and well in Paris: GU ms.

Italian Black market info: J. DeRecqueville, *Rudolph Valentino*.

Hungarian cult: *NYT* – 2/17/29, "Valentino Cult Formed".

Events at Crypt: Roger Peterson, Uncited article in Margaret Herrick Library- 2/16/32, "Guard of Tomb of Valentino's in Weird Visits". *New Movie Magazine* – 4/32, "My Strange Experiences at Valentino's Grave".

Alberto and Jean try to legally halt crypt ceremonies: *LA Examiner* – 8/29/51, "Valentino's Hit Tomb Display, Kin of Movie Star Move to End Annual Antics at Ceremony".

Ladies in Black: GU ms.

Home town forgets Valentino: *NYT*- 8/26/26, "Native Town Forgets Actor". *NYT* – 10/8/61, "Town's Statue of Valentino Stirs Critics of Italy". *NYT*- 10/16/76, "Hometown Acting to Shape Virile Defense of Valentino".

LA statue: GU ms. Court records of GU's settlement regarding- "Mancini vs. Ullman". Appeals decision, p.222-223. *Citizen-News* - 4/17/35, "Valentino Memorial Fund Backed". *LAT* – 4/18/35, "Judgment in Valentino Row Upheld for Woman".

GU and Joe Schenck early efforts to memorialize RV: GU ms. Uncited article in Margaret Herrick Library – 3/3/27, "Valentino Fund Grows".

London Hospital names ward: Uncited article in GU ms.

"The Applicants": GU ms. *LAT*- 6/21/27, "Resemblance to Valentino Seen in Café Dancer". *Motion Picture Magazine* – 6/15/28, Jack Dunn and Leroy Mason and Rossano Brazzi. Louella Parsons - 11/48. *NYT* -7/11/40, "Valentino Double Jailed".

Rudolph Florentino: *LA Examiner* – 5/21/53, "Police Crash Valentino Shrine on Tip-Off of Suicide Attempt".

Falcon Lair proposed shrine: *SF Chronicle* – 2/11/49, "A Valentine for Valentino; Sunset Rockets, Starlit Vespers and A Wishing Well".

Death theories: P. Negri, *Memoirs of a Star*. Paul Ivano and from J. DeRecqueville, *Rudolph Valentino*. Howard J. Force @ snopes.com

RV's love children: GU ms. Author's interview with Brad Steiger.

Jean's birth certificate information and Alberto tells of RV's petition for adoption of Jean: *Italo-Americano* interview, 10/1/77.

What Ever Happened To...

Jean Acker changes name: *NYT* – 11/11/22, "Ex-Wife Would Use Valentino's Name".

Jean Acker lives with Chloe Carter: W. Pelf interviews

Marion Benda: I. Schulman, *Valentino*. *LAT*- 11/11/45, "Valentino's Wife? 'Lady in Black' Great Puzzles Still Unanswered". *LAT*- 3/30/49, " 'Lady in Black' Ordered to Mental Institution".

Blanca DeSaulles: *NYT* – 5/2/22, "Blanca DeSaulles' Brother, A Suicide in Paris Over Peggy Joyce". *NYT* – 12/23/21, "Mrs. DeSaulles' Weds Again in Chile". Obit – *NYT* – 3/22/40, "Heiress, Once Wife of J.L. DeSaulles". *Oakland Tribune* -1/13/18, "Is Coming Here" and "DeSaulles Widow Goes to Pasadena".

Dr. Durham: GU ms.

Foxlair: Foxlair Family History.

Jadaan: www.csupomona.edu/, Cal Poly Arabian Horse Center, "Jadaan, The Sheik and the Cereal Baron" and *Daily News* -11/7/49, "Bones of Jadaan, Famed Valentino Stallion, Acquired". *LAT* – 10/20/30, uncited article "...memories of Rudolph Valentino arise...."

Kabar: I. Schulman, *Valentino*.

Frank Mennillo: Mennillo Family interviews and Frank Mennillo obits - *LAT* – 11/7/36, "Illness Fatal to Olive King" and *Merced Bee* obit.

Lou Mahoney: Lou Mahoney's obit - Newport Beach -*The Daily Pilot* - 4/27/68. Black Hand info @ *NYT* – 12/28/06, "Black Hand Agent Caught, Sleuths Get Man Who Took Cash from Threatened Italian". Also "Rudolph Valentino's Borrowed Tomb" by Steve Gibson included I. Schulman archives.

Nita Naldi: "The Reminiscences of Nita Naldi," Columbia University Oral History Research Office as interviewed by Joan and Robert Franklin in 1959.

Pola Negri sells note she held on Alberto's loan back to Bank of America and is sued: *L.A. Herald* – 3/7/41, "Pola Negri, Valentino Kin Suit Renewed".

Natacha Rambova: M. Morris, *Madam Valentino*. Natacha marries again - *L.A. Examiner* – 8/16/34, "Rambova Seals Civil Marriage".

Dr. Wyman: GU ms. *NYT* – 9/24/26, "Meeker's Explanation". *LAT* – 5/13/28, "Arch-Imposter Squelched". *NYT* – 9/24/26, "Wyman Medical

Jurisprudence." *LAT* – 4/29/28, "Flyer Trio in Gotham". *LAT* – 4/30/28, "NYC Acclaims Bremen Flyers Today".

George Ullman: Ullman family. Norman Mackenzie letter from Ullman collection. Ullman's involvement in *What Price Beauty* - Uncited 1/5/27, "Schenck Passes to Pathé." Zunilda Mancini information - Appeals Court records and Uncited article dated 2/10/34 and *LAT*- 2/17/34, "No Reflection Intended", published as letter to the editor by Alberto Valentino. Tax Abatement negotiated by GU for $61, 432 - Court Records and L.A. County Car Index 1-9-4 and dated 10/11/1931, also GU ms.

Alberto Valentino: NARA citizenship records. LAT – 7/11/34, "Valentino's Kin Seek to be Citizen's" on file at the Film Study Center, Museum of Modern Art. Obits @ *Variety* - 6/17/81, *LAT* - 6/8/81 and *LAT* – 6/15/81, "Filmland Tried to make what Valentino's Brother Lacked" and also *LAT* – 9/6/28, "Guglielmi Gets in Film at Last!" W. Pelf interviews.

Jean Valentino: Obits *LAT* - 9/26/96 and *Variety* - 9/27/96 and W. Self interviews.

Zela: J. Zemel, *Nell Shipman* at SVP Productions and N. Shipman, *The Silent Screen and My Talking Heart*.

The Search for the Missing Documents

The initial search for Rudolph Valentino's probate records, case file #83678 was conducted at the Los Angeles County Hall of Records. Various searches were conducted under the name of Rudolph Valentino and George Ullman with the assistance of Don Cameron and Maureen Hemler, Senior Court Manager. This search resulted in the recovery of the "Probate Register of Actions", dating from September 10, 1926 – October 8, 1959, the first page of Valentino's will as "Last Will and Testament of Rudolph Guglielmi" and the following individual documents:

-Seven pages of unidentified documents, first page missing, signed by Judge of the Superior Court, E.P. Shortall, filed on January 10, 1935.
-"Complaint on Judgment" #606767, December 1, 1952 signed by attorney Morton E. Feiler.
-"Stipulation for Judgment" #606767, filed January 22, 1954, signed by George Ullman and Jean Guglielmi, a.k.a. Jean Valentino.
-"Stipulation on Judgment" #606767, filed on January 4, 1955, signed by Judge of the Superior Court Richards.
-"Return on Garnishment, filed by the Office of the Sheriff of the County of Los Angeles, November 21, 1947, signed by Deputy Sheriff F.E. Mooney.
-"Counter Affidavit" of James M. Sheridan, sections #481-480, filed May 7, 1947.
-"Partial Satisfaction of Judgment", sections #481- 480, filed November 6, 1947 with attached "Substitution" filed on November 13, 1947, signed by Jean Guglielmi a.k.a. Jean Valentino, Philbrick McCoy and Morton E. Feiler.
-"Affadavit and Order for Appearance of Judgment Debtor", filed November 26, 1947, signed by Morton E. Feiler.
- "Affadavit for Subpoena Duces Tecum #481480," filed November 28, 1947.
-"Complaint on Judgment" #537845, signed by Morton Feiler, filed on December 3, 1947.
-"Stipulation on Judgment" #537845 filed on December 13, 1947, signed by George Ullman, Jean Guglielmi, a.k.a. Jean Valentino and Morton Feiler.

-"Judgment" #537845 filed on December 18, 1947 signed by S. George Ullman and Jean Guglielmi a.k.a. Jean Valentino.

-"Writ of Execution" #481480, filed on January 12, 1948.

-"Complaint on Judgment #481480", filed on October 30, 1942.

-"Affadavit of Military Service" #481480, and "Memorandum of Costs and Disbursements", filed on December 3, 1942 signed by James E. Sheridan.

-"Affadavit of Service by Mail", #481480, (date of filing obscured)

-"Summons" #481480, filed on November 4, 1942.

-"Judgment by Court after Default", #481480, filed on December 11, 1942 and signed by Judge Wilson.

-"Satisfaction of Judgment" #606767 filed on July 17, 1956, signed by Jean Guglielmi a.k.a. Jean Valentino and Morton E. Feiler.

-"Receipt for Papers Re: Change of Venue to Orange County" #709137 re: Jean Valentino lawsuit v. Disney Corporation, filed December 17, 1958.

The file of copied court records of the original missing probate documents was located in the San Francisco Hastings Law Library, Appeals Division with the assistance of Ms. Linda Weir, Public Services Librarian. These documents are authenticated by the imprint of the various case file numbers. The Appeals Case is filed under First Civil #9321, Supreme Court of the State of California, S. George Ullman as Appellant vs. Alberto Guglielmi, Maria Guglielmi Strada, Bank of America National Trust and Savings Association, as administrator of the estate of Rudolph Guglielmi with the will annexed Teresa Werner and Ray L. Riley, State Controller as Respondents.

The existence of these copies, housed in the California Court of Appeals Library, verifies that the original documents were once housed in the Los Angeles County Hall of Records. The last known public access to the original records, precedes 1965 and Irving Schulman's biography on Valentino. He cites the lack of reference as evidence revealing they were not available at that time. The Valentino one page will, was the only probate document included in Schulman's archive housed in the rare book room of the University of Southern California, Los Angeles, California.

Album One

Courtesy of Author's Collection

Courtesy of Author's Collection

Blanca DeSaulles

Courtesy of the Mennillo Estate

Frank Mennillo

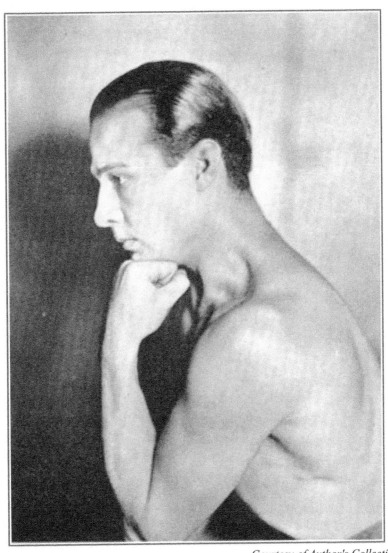

Courtesy of Author's Collection

Rudolph Valentino

Courtesy of Author's Collection

Blanca DeSaulles and Son "Jacky"

Courtesy of Author's Collection

John DeSaulles

Courtesy of Author's Collection

Blanca DeSaulles

Courtesy of the Mennillo Estate

Frank Mennillo on the Lawn of the White House with President Coolidge and Members of the Italian-American League

Frank Mennillo – Center, Fourth from the Left
President Coolidge – Second from the Right

Jean Acker

Courtesy of a Private Collection – All Rights Reserved

Rudolph Valentino - 1917

"The Big House" at Foxlair

Rudolph Valentino's Room at Foxlair

Courtesy of the Ullman Family

George Ullman, Teresa Werner, R. Valentino and N. Rambova

Courtesy of the Ullman Family

Bee & George Ullman   George Ullman, Bee Ullman, Rudy

Courtesy of Ullman Family   *Courtesy of Michael Morris*

George Ullman and Sons-1924   Rudy & Natacha @ 1923

Rudy, Jack Dempsey and Sparring Partner

Rudolph Valentino at Home and in Character

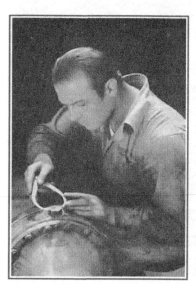

Courtesy of the Mennillo Family

L-R, New York City Mayor LaGuardia, Rudy, Frank Mennillo at The
Columbus Day Parade

Courtesy of Michael Morris

Natacha Rambova

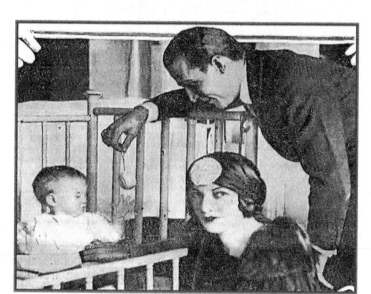

Courtesy of The Seattle Post-Intelligencer-June 2, 1923. All Rights Reserved

Rudy and Natacha Attend the Pound Party

Courtesy of the Ullman Family

George Ullman @ 1923

Courtesy of the Author's Collection

Rudy and George on the set of The Eagle -1925

Courtesy of the Ullman Family

Uncle Rudy, Bob and Dan Ullman – Foothill Road - 1924

Rudy and Norma Niblock

Norma Niblock

EIGHTY-ONE YEARS OF FAITHFUL SERVICE

GIMBEL BROTHERS

32ND STREET — BROADWAY — 33RD STREET — NEW YORK CITY

GIMBEL MONTH IN NEW YORK

Sale of Mineralava Beauty Clay

—*The Lowest Verified Price
Elsewhere is $1.50*

On Sale
Saturday   **$1**.00   *A
Bottle*

*   *   *   *

Scotts   Scotts
Mineralava Beauty Clay   Face Finish Tonic
Regular 50c tube 25c   Regular $1.30 bottle 75c

GIMBELS DRUG SHOP—Street Floor

Rudy and Natacha

MAX D. STEUER
42 BROADWAY
NEW YORK

TO WHOM IT MAY CONCERN:-

MR. S. GEORGE ULLMANN is my sole business manager. I have none other, and any one other than Mr. Ullmann representing that he is my business manager does so entirely without my sanction and authority. The production of this letter by Mr. Ullmann will evidence his authority from me to act as my said agent.

Dated, New York, July 6, 1923.

Rudolph Valentino (L.S.)

City, County & State of New York, SS:

On this 6th day of July, 1923, before me personally came RUDOLPH VALENTINO, to me known and known to me to be the individual described in and who executed the foregoing authority and he duly acknowledged to me that he executed the same.

[signature] Notary Public N.Y. County #493 Comm. Expires Mch 30/1925

Courtesy of the Ullman Family

Contract Signed Between George Ullman and Rudolph Valentino

Rudolph Valentino in The Young Rajah

Courtesy of The Palm Springs Historical Society -All Rights Reserved.

Dr. Florilla White

Courtesy of The Palm Springs Historical Society

Rudolph Valentino and Dr. White Ready to Ride in Palm Springs

The Equestrian Valentino

Rudolph Valentino in His Voison

The Phoenix

Courtesy of Donna Hill

Alberto, Jean and Ada Guglielmi

N. Rambova, Nita Naldi & Rudy

Rudolph Valentino, Manuel Reachi and Pola Negri

Courtesy of the Ullman Family

Rudy and Dan Ullman @ 1925   Rudy as The Young Rajah

Courtesy of the Author's Collection

Jean, Rudy, Kabar, Ada and Alberto arriving in New York City - 1925

Courtesy of the Filomarino Family - All Rights Reserved

Alberto, Jean and Rudy - Falcon Lair, the Spring of 1926

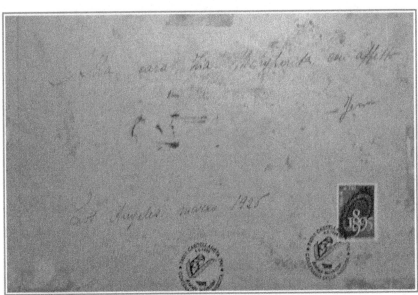

Seal Posted on the 100ᵗʰ Year Celebration of Valentino's birth – All Rights Reserved.
Courtesy of the Filomarino Family

The Back of the Above Photo - "To Dear Aunt Margherita with Affection – Jean" - Los Angeles, March 1926

RODOLFO VALENTINO

UNA FIERA RAMPOGNA CONTRO
IL RINNEGATORE DELLA PATRIA

Friend Says Rudy Lived on Liquids

It was learned yesterday that Rudolph Valentino had been dieting for sometime before he went to the hospital, living on whiskey and soda, and little else.

"He told me he was worried about his weight," said a friend, "and that he decided the best thing he could do was to drink whiskey and soda. He assured me he hadn't eaten a thing in days, but that he had taken a considerable quantity of whiskey."

Gen. Lincoln C. Andrews, apprised of this, said that, if it was true that the star was drinking the sort of whiskey that is to be obtained in New York today, "it was no wonder he developed gastric ulcers."

Mussolini's Publication-1926   Daily Mirror -8/25/1926

Courtesy of the Ullman Family

Checks Admitted as Evidence by George Ullman

Courtesy of Donna Hill

L-R, C. Levee, J.D. Williams, G. Ullman Signing United Studios Contract

Back Row Second and Third from Left, A.P. Giannini and Joe Schenck,
Cecille B. DeMille, Center Front
"The Bank of Italy's Hollywood Connection"

Pola Negri, Mae Murray, Prince David Mdivani, Rudy-1926

Courtesy of the Ullman family

Rudy and Mission Rudy -1926

Rudolph Valentino and Kabar

Courtesy of the Mennillo Family

Center L-R. Frank Mennillo, Rudy and Mae Murray

Alberto, Ada and Jean Guglielmi Valentino @ 1929

Courtesy of Irving Schulman Archives

Cabbie LiCalzi, Marion Benda & Rudy   Pola Negri & George Ullman

Pola Negri @ her Santa Monica Beach Home

Courtesy of Author's Collection

Rudolph Valentino's Bier

Courtesy of the Ullman Family

Bee Ullman and Secretary Read Condolences

Courtesy of Author's Collection

Rudolph Valentino's Shipping Case

Courtesy of the Author's Collection

Campbell's Funeral Church Scrapbook

Courtesy of Author's Collection

Interior of Shipping Case

Courtesy of the Author's Collection

Shipping Case - 2003
with
Orb of Light Over Shipping Case

Courtesy of Author's Collection

Interior View and Hardware Detail of Shipping Case

Courtesy of Author's Collection

Pages from Campbell's Funeral Home Scrapbook

Courtesy of Author's Collection

Courtesy of Author's Collection

Pages from Campbell's Funeral Home Scrapbook – 2

Courtesy of Author's Collection

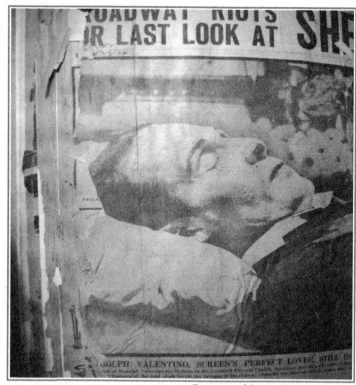

Courtesy of the Author's Collection

Pages from Campbell's Funeral Home Scrapbook – 3

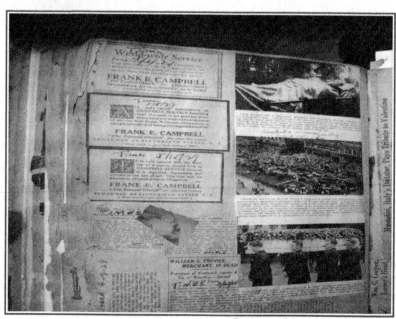

Courtesy of the Author's Collection

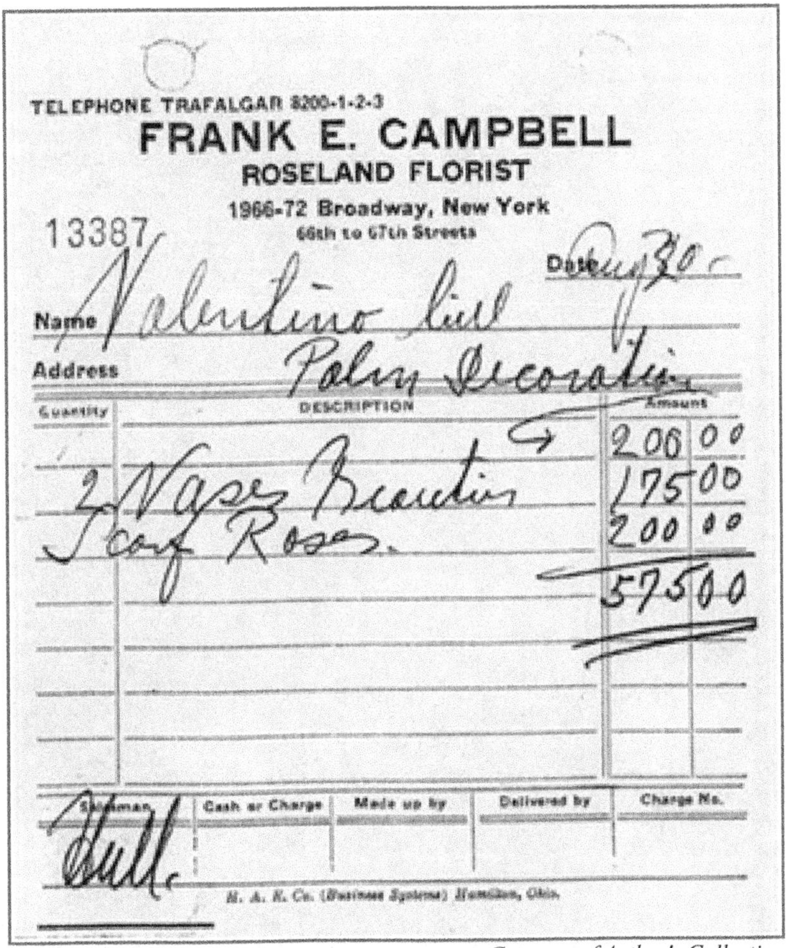

TELEPHONE TRAFALGAR 8200-1-2-3

FRANK E. CAMPBELL
ROSELAND FLORIST
1966-72 Broadway, New York
66th to 67th Streets

13387

Name *Valentino bill*

Date *Aug 30*

Address *Palm Decoration*

Quantity	DESCRIPTION	Amount
		200 00
3	*Vases Beauties*	175 00
	Scarf Roses	200 00
		575 00

Salesman	Cash or Charge	Made up by	Delivered by	Charge No.
Bill				

H. A. K. Co. (Business Systems) Hamilton, Ohio.

Courtesy of Author's Collection

Invoice for "Palm Decoration" of Palms and Roses
Delivered to Campbell's Funeral Home

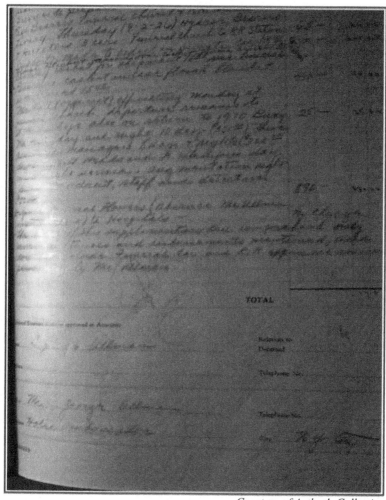

Courtesy of Author's Collection

Invoice of Rudolph Valentino's Funeral Expenses
Signed by George Ullman

Name GUGLIELINI (VALENTINO)   File No. **27598**

Date *Aug. 29* 19 2_

	AMOUNT	Sales	Auditor	Dist

CASKET, Stock No. *Silver Bronze oakes* — 6000 —

Plate inscription *Eng. by* — 25 —

Handles *as is*

Solid Copper Inner Lining   Half   Full Glass   Solid Top

OUTSIDE CASE   Pine   1½ Chestnut   Steel   Copper   [Bronze] — 900 —

CAMPBELLS CAST STONE VAULT

Zinc lining for outside case — 15 —

Tufted Mattress for outside case — 25 —

FACE VEIL — 730 —

Clothes   Suit   Dress   Underwear   Shirt   Collar   Tie   Stockings   Studs

Robe No. *None*   Slippers

SLUMBER ROBE — {300

EMBALMING — 50 —

CASKETING and DRESSING — 2 —

GRAVE OPENING   NEW GRAVE   CRYPT OPENING

EVERGREEN GRAVE LINING   Chairs-Tent-Lowering Device

RECEIVING VAULT —

CREMATION

HEARSE   Motor   Horse — 25 —

LIMOUSINES 4 — 1200 —

— 28 —

REFRESHMENTS — 280 00

GENTLEMEN PALL BEARERS   House   Church   Station   Cemetery — 120 —

Bearers' Limousine — 40 —

REMOVING BODY Motor and Men — 54 —

DELIVERING OUTSIDE CASE TO CEMETERY STATION — 27 —

USE OF REPOSING ROOM NO. — 350 —

WATCHER   Female   Male   days   nights   per   meals

DEATH NOTICES — 105 00

CASH ADVANCED — 150

CORPSE TICKET $ and   fares to   EXPRESSAGE

PULLMAN   chairs to   Berths Upper Lower   Car

   Compartment   Car   drawing room   Car

FLORAL DOOR PIECE

FUNERAL CHURCH

CLERGY FEE — 200 —

PALM DECORATION — 6000 —

ORGAN —

VOCAL MUSIC   Soloist   Duo   Trio   Quartette — 75 —

FUNERAL DIRECTOR and —

FLOWERS 4 Vase of Red roses — 175 —

TRANSCRIPT OF DEATH CERTIFICATE — 50 —

Inscription   Date of Death

CHAIRS AT HOME   CANDELABRA — 50 00

— 200

TOTAL — 15

12 —

Campbell's Funeral Home Invoice

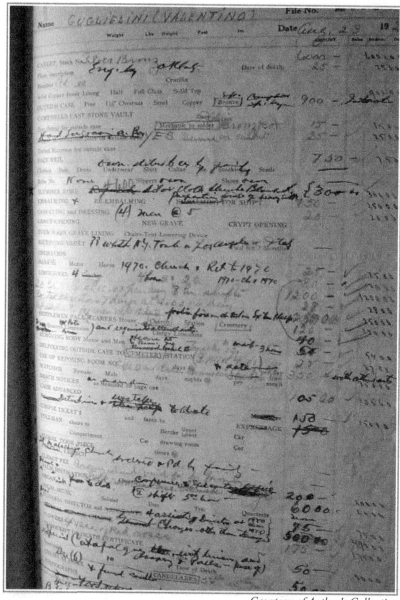

Courtesy of Author's Collection

Itemization of Funeral Expenses in Campbell's Funeral Home Ledger

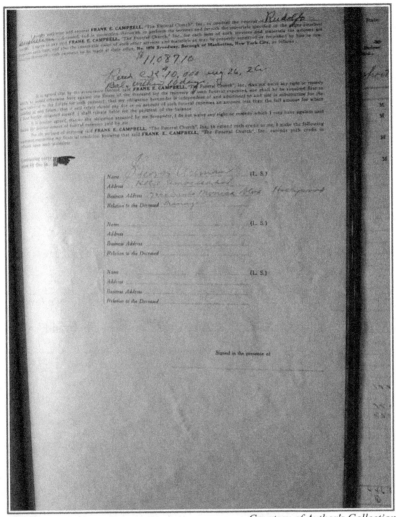

Courtesy of Author's Collection

Receipt from Campbell's Funeral Home of Payment
Made by George Ullman

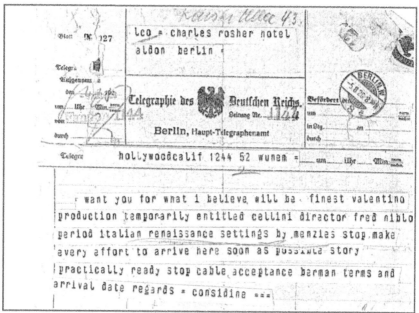

Courtesy of Kevin Brownlow

J. Considine Contacts C. Rosher @ Movie "The Firebrand"

Courtesy of Kevin Brownlow

L-R, E. Carewe, Leroy Mason and G. Ullman Negotiate Movie on Valentino

Courtesy of the Mennillo Family

Ciro and Frank Mennillo- Merced, Cal.

Lou Mahoney

grind house.

James M. Cain Buys His MGM Contract

James M. Cain has returned $3,330 to MGM and begged out of wr'ting the screen play for "Duchess of Del-monico," on the ground that he had no desire to go through with the as-signment and preferred to work on a novel he had already started.

The William Morris office returned its commission on the deal, having set a contract for $10,000 for the writer, one-third of which was paid down.

Sol Rosenblatt Turns Down Vaude Labor Bd.

New York.—Sol Rosenblatt has re-fused to take any action at this time on the recommendations of the Vaudeville Actors' Labor Committee.

He says that action now would mean the re-opening of the entire code and require open hearings at which all sections of the code would be discussed. This he is unwilling to see happen.

Loretta Young Figures In Double Loan Deal

Due to the postponement of the starting date on "Professional Corres-pondent," MGM yesterday loaned Lor-etta Young to Fox. The arrangement

---

week. The list comprises:
"I Like It That Way" at the May-fair Monday; "Modern Hero" at the Strand today; "Stand Up and Cheer" at the Music Hall tomorrow; "Wharf Angel," with Gloria Swanson on the stage, at the Paramount; "I'll Tell the World" at the Roxy, and "Tarzan and His Mate," with radio stars on the stage, at the Capitol on Friday.

Ullman Exonerated in Valentino Estate Row

San Francisco.—The District Court of Appeals yesterday exonerated S. George Ullman of charges of misman-agement of the estate of Rudolph Valentino, of which he was executor, when it reversed an order of the Los Angeles Probate Court.

Ullman's management had been objected to by Jean Guglielmi, nephew and heir to the estate, who charged Ullman had made too many cash ad-vances to the other heirs. The Appel-late Court praised Ullman for his work.

Twelvetrees Wins Suit

Rebecca and Silton lost their suit for $236 against Helen Twelvetrees yesterday in Superior Court when Judge Thomas C. Gould sustained a demurrer claiming the court had no jurisdiction because of the amount of the suit.

New Universal Title

---

much so, ma
to take him o
run around a
Austrian Tyrol
the boy to ta
fast and follo
and that, if h
all right. So
and everyth
smoothly whe
instructor fre
and evident!
Thinking the
vise him of so
he should kn
up and finally
structor. No
very little En
rushed up ex
what he want
just grinned a
"Who's afraic

Add to the
the torture of
a half hours
other evening
collapse from
big brawny ou
to the usher
manager, and
ger asked hir
He claimed t
the place, t
that the stag
a few minut
been two hou

Courtesy of the Ullman Family

George Ullman's Personal Copy of *The Hollywood Reporter*
Announcement of His Exoneration and Praise – 4/18/1934

September 29, 1926.

Mr. S. George Ullman,
Rudolph Valentino Productions, Inc.
7200 Santa Monica Boulevard,
Los Angeles, California.

Dear Mr. Ullman:

    I greatly appreciate your thoughtful courtesy
in sending me the pedigree of "Mission Rudy", following
your kindness in returning the dog to me.

    I was very much pleased to greet you and Mrs.
Ullman in my office when you visited San Francisco, and
I too hope that you may both return soon.

    With kindest personal regards and again thanking
you for your courtesy, I am

Very sincerely yours,

James Rolph

Mayor.

Courtesy of the Ullman Family

Letter from San Francisco Mayor Rolph to George Ullman, thanking him
for returning Rudy's dog "Mission Rudy."

The Chateau

Courtesy of the Ullman Family

Hand-written Page From George Ullman's Memoir

The Author of *The Sheik*, E. M. Hull

Mr. S. George Ullman,

Hotel Ambassador,

New York.

Dear Mr. Ullman:

I examined Rudolph Valentino for the first time at 5:15 P.M.
August 22nd, 1926 at the Polyclinic Hospital. He was suffering great pain,
had a moderate rise of temperature, a very rapid pulse, a board like rigidity
of the entire abdominal wall and presented the picture of a rapidly spreading
vicious peritonitis. A diagnosis of probably perforated gastric ulcer was
made although other possibilities could not be excluded at this advanced stage.
I urged immediate operation as his only chance for life.

Operation Findings:

The abdominal cavity contained a large amount of fluid and food
particles. All the viscera were coated with a greenish gray film. A round
hole 1 cm. in diameter was seen in the anterior wall of the stomach, 3 cm. from
the pylorus and 2 cm. below the lesser curvature. There was no walling off by
natural processes and fluid was still coming through the opening. The tissue
of the stomach for 1 1/2 cm. immediately surrounding the perforation was necroti
The appendix was acutely inflamed from a secondary infection, turned on itself
and so fixed by a plastic exudate at its tip and by an old band at its mid
point as to constrict the terminal illeum.

Courtesy of the Ullman Estate

Page One - Medical Report Sent to George Ullman
from
Valentino's Surgeon, Dr. Harold D. Meeker

Median vertical incision over right rectus   All possible fluid
and foreign particles removed by suction apparatus. Necrotic tissue around
mar of ulcer excised, the edges of the opening were approximated by mattress
sustures through all coats except the mucosa. A portion of the lesser omentum
was stitched with fine linen over this suture line, this was in turn reinforced
by a portion of greater omentum over it. A rubber drainage tube was stitched in
place with fine catgut. The appendix was removed because it was constricting
the gut otherwise it would not have been touched at this time. A second drainage
tube was placed in the right illiac fossa and the abdominal wound closed. The
patient was placed in bed in position most favorable to gravity drainage. He
was in profound shock when put on the operating table with a pulse of 140.
This condition did not change appreciably during the operation.

Progress:

    There was a steady improvement up to the 5th day. Abdominal
drainage ceased on the 3rd day, pulse and temperature normal on the 5th day. On
the morning of the 6th day the patient had a slight chill, complained of severe
pain in upper left abdomen and left chest. An area of pleurisy was detected,
this rapidly extended, scattered areas of pneumonia developed in the left lung.
On the 6th day there was a marked involvment of the valves of the heart. The
patient died about noon on the 8th day overwhelmed by the sepsis. The above is
a true account of the last illness of Rudolph Valentino as observed by me.

    August 28th, 1926.   (Signed) Harold D. Meeker

Courtesy of the Ullman Estate

Page Two – Medical Report from Dr. Harold D. Meeker

LAST FOUR DAYS

By Order of Court
THE ESTATE
of

Rudolph Valentino
AUCTION

Commencing Today at 1:30 p. m. and continuing each afternoon 1:30 p. m. and evenings 7:30 p. m., the most important of Mr. Valentino's possessions will be sold at public auction.

Silverware, Luggage, Swords, Guns, Books, Costumes, Paintings, Jewelry and Valuable Art Objects Still Available.

HALL OF ARTS STUDIO
1753 North Highland Avenue
HOLLYWOOD

S. GEORGE ULLMAN
Executor.

A. H. WEIL
Auctioneer.

resumed the stand for further

[Rep. Tr. p. 54, lines 21 to 26.]

Cross-Examination

164 By Mr. Scarborough:

Q. My understanding from your testimony, Mr. Ullman, was that those are the only two pictures that were produced under that contract; that is correct, isn't it, "The Eagle" and "The

[Rep. Tr. p. 55, lines 1 to 4.]

Son of the Sheik"? A. Yes, that is correct.

* * * * * * * *

Q. Those are the pictures that you described 165 in the inventory, are they not? A. Yes.

[Rep. Tr. p. 83, lines 19 to 26.]

Direct Examination (continued)

By Mr. Wilson:

Q. Mr. Ullman, you knew Joseph Schenck, did you not? A. Yes, sir.

Q. What negotiations did you have with Mr. Schenck in connection with the recovery and ultimate receipt of the sum of $40,000.00 in this Valentino matter? A. When Mr. Valentino died, I found that there has been an insurance

Sample Court Records – Court Testimony & Estate Itemized

	Account	Reference Schedule No.	Items
	Expense Chargeable to Income	2i	$133,291.65
	Total Credits		$442,764.65

3. As to Executor's Inventory as of date January 31, 1930

"A" Items remaining from Inventory and Appraisement and at original appraised values, and Cash

731	Cash		
	Real Estate	$125,000.00	
	Personal Property	11,270.95	
	43.75% Interest in ture "The Eagle"	75,000.00	
	43.75% interest in picture "Son of the Sheik"	100,000.00	
	"What Price Beauty"	5,000.00	
	10 Shares capital stock Cosmic Arts, Inc. (Lambert		
732	Process)	5,000.00	
	20 Shares capital stock Hollywood Music Box Review	No value	
	Balance due on Contract of sale of Rex, Inc.	640.36	
	Trust Deed—Lot 6	3,500.00	
	Cash — Pan American Bank	121.64	
	Cash — Wilshire Natl. Bank	246.41	$325,779.36

This visit to Madrid was very costly, because, while Rudy was buying swords and old guns daggers and other arms, Natacha was purchasing a great many pieces of ivory and her mother was buying jade. All of this accounts for the constant shortage of funds here because these purchases were all charged to our production company.

On several occasions Rudy told me of the tremendous thrill he experienced while watching the bull fights in Seville. He demonstrated the toreador's art and his grace and enthusiasm were a sight to behold. I don't believe that he seriously meant it, but he did say to me that he would like to get out of motion pictures and begin to seriously take up the art of bull fighting!

(new page)

After we were more or less settled in Hollywood about 6 months, I felt the need of a larger house for my little family and talked to Rudy about this & he was all for the idea of my building a house in Beverly Hills but I knew that I didn't have the time or money to start such a project at that time. Nothing would deter him from going with me to inspect the various houses referred to me by the agents and we finally found one that pleased him immensely. It was a modern house but the builder had gone in for the ornamental like beams and there was much beautiful marble and black marble fireplaces and beautiful tile in the bathrooms.

The house had its faults somewhat out of ...

8/ 5/26	Commerce Dis-count & Accept.	78 33	44
8/ 5/26	Best Universal Lock Co.	6 75	45
8/ 4/26	Seaboard Nat'l Bank	330 00	46
8/ 4/26	J. M. Hale	750 29	47
8/ 4/26	S. Geo. Ullman	200 00	48*
8/ 4/26	Raymond Fager	75 00	49
8/ 4/26	Cash	110 00	50
8/ 4/26	Rothacker Aller Lab.	28 91	51
8/ 4/26	Lee C. Balch	600 00	52
8/ 4/26	Dr. Edwin Moffitt	100 00	53
8/ 4/26	Eugene O. Walser	45 00	54
8/ 4/26	Dr. W. Carl Wright	490 00	55
8/ 4/26	J. B. Avian Co.	35 35	56
8/ 4/26	Duncan Vail Co.	5 70	57
8/ 4/26	Barker Bros.	133 60	58
8/ 4/26	J. W. Robinson Co.	147 91	59
8/ 4/26	Sun Lumber Co.	22 51	60
8/ 4/26	S. George Ullman	500 00	61*
8/ 4/26	Cash	85 00	62
8/ 4/26	Rudy Rauly	69 19	63
8/ 5/26	James McClure	30 00	64
8/ 5/26	Melcher Luchsinger	40 00	65
8/ 5/26	Young's Market	29 05	66
8/ 5/26	Italian Stores	185 45	67
8/ 5/26	Beverly Hills Hotel	242 50	68
8/ 5/26	R. Frazzis Co.	12 95	69

Sample Page from Court Records – Falcon Lair Household Accounts
Titled
"Grey Books"

```
                    Publicity
1926
May    5   Egyptian Theatre              20.—
       8   Elite Catering Co.            16.25
       8   L. A. Biltmore               66.05
       8   Cash                          15.—
      13   Exc· 'ior Electric Co.        41.61
      13   McF    Jen Pub.               36.
      19   Cash                          30.
      28       "                         15.
      28   L. A. Biltmore               13.20
June   4   Cash                          15.
      15   El Capitan                    93.50
      18   R. K. Ballroom Party         225.—
      18   A. E. Bradstater             200.—
      24 · Cash—3 weeks                  45.
July   6   Elite Catering Co.            50.
       "   Beverly Hills Hotel          247.25
Aug    5       "      "      "          242.50
      12       "      "      "          266.43
      12   Ambassador                   100.—
      14   Old Colony Restaurant        372.25
```

Sample Court Records – Evidence Entered as Publicity Expenses
and Letter to George Ullman from Maria Guglielmi Strada

```
              [Executor's Exhibit 4]

      Maria Strada-Guglielmi
                          December 1st. 1927
      Dear Mr. Ullman,
726     Our friend, Mr. Frank Mennillo, is coming in
      Los Angeles and I am sure that his intervention
      will take out many difficulties.
        As it is natural that his expenses shall not
      be supported from him, I would be very grate to
      you if you would give him directly on account
      of me, how much he will ask you for.
        Thanking you in anticipation will you agree
      my best regards.
                      MARIA GUGLIELMI STRADA
```

(SEAL)

Judge of the Superior Court,
Attest: L. E. LAMPTON, County Clerk,
By G. W. McDonald, Deputy.

FILED: NOV 10 1926,
L. E. LAMPTON, County Clerk,
By G. W. McDonald, Deputy.

ENTERED: DEC 4 1926,
By D. Keene,
Compared _____ Deputy

.No. 83678

LAST WILL AND TESTAMENT OF RUDOLPH GUGLIELMI.

- - - o - - -

IN THE NAME OF GOD, AMEN: I, RUDOLPH GUGLIELMI, of the city of Los Angeles, County of Los Angeles, State of California, being of sound and disposing mind and memory and not acting under the duress, fraud or undue influence of any person or persons whatsoever, do hereby make and publish this my LAST WILL AND TESTAMENT in the manner following, that is to say:

FIRST: I hereby revoke all former Wills by me made and I hereby nominate and appoint S. George Ullman of the city of Los Angeles, County of Los Angeles, State of California, the executor of this my LAST WILL AND TESTAMENT, without bonds, either upon qualifying or in any stage of the settlement of my said estate.

SECOND: I direct that my Executor pay all of my just debts and funeral expenses, as soon as may be practicable after my death.

THIRD: I give, devise and bequeath unto my wife, Natacha Rambova, also known as Natacha Guglielmi, the sum of One Dollar ($1.00), it being my intention, desire and will that she receive this sum and no more.

FOURTH: All the residue and remainder of my estate, both real and personal, I give, devise and bequeath unto S. George Ullman, of the city of Los Angeles, County of Los Angeles, State of California, to have and to hold the same in trust and for the use of Alberto Guglielmi, Maria Guglielmi and Teresa Werner, the purposes of the aforesaid trust are as follows: to hold, manage, and control the said trust property and estate; to keep the same invested and productive as far as possible; to receive the rents and profits therefrom, and to pay over the net income derived therefrom to the said Alberto Guglielmi, Maria Guglielmi and Teresa Werner, as I have this day instructed him; to finally distribute the said trust estate according to my wish and will, as I have this day instructed him.

—1—

FIFTH: Should any other person after my death be able to establish in any Court of competent jurisdiction by proper judgment and decree therein, that he or she is entitled as an heir-in-law, or otherwise, to any share or portion of my estate, I give, devise and bequeath to such person, and each of them, the sum of $1.00 and such person shall take no other or further share in my estate.

SIXTH: In case any person or persons, to whom any legacy, gift, devise or benefit out of, from or by reason of this my Will, shall come, shall commence suit in any Court whatsoever, or by any ways or means sue and disturb or cause to be sued or disturbed by Administrator, my Executor, Administratrix or Executrix, or any other person or persons whatsoever, to whom anything is by me given in this my Will, from the recovery, quiet-enjoying and possession of what is by me herein given as aforesaid, and in such manner as is therein mentioned, then my Will and meaning is that all and every, the legacy and legacies, gift and gifts, benefit or benefits herein by me given to any such person or persons whatsoever, who shall so sue and disturb, as aforesaid, shall cease, determine and be utterly void, and to such person or persons, so suing or disturbing I hereby give, devise and bequeath in the place and stead of such legacy, gift, devise or benefit, the sum of $1.00 each, and no more.

IN WITNESS WHEREOF, I have hereunto set my hand and seal this 1st day of September, 1925.

Rudolph Guglielmi

The foregoing Instrument, consisting of three pages, including the page signed by the Testator, was at the date hereof by the said Rudolph Guglielmi, signed, sealed and published and declared to be his last Will and Testament in the presence of us, who at his request and in his presence, and the presence of each other

—2—

have subscribed our names as witness thereto.

Raymond A. Fager

Residing at   38 St. James Park, Los Angeles, Cal.

Margaret Neff Waters

Residing at   835 McCadden Place
Los Angeles, Calif.

—3—

The Last Will and Testament of Rudolph Valentino – Page 1

"To

S. George Ullman.

I have this day named you as executor in my last will and testament; it is my desire that you perpetuate my name in the picture industry by continuing the Rudolph Valentino Productions, Inc., until my nephew Jean shall have reached the age of 25 years; in the meantime to make motion pictures, using your own judgment as to numbers and kind, keeping control of any pictures made, if possible.

Whenever there are profits from pictures made by the Rudolph Valentino Productions, Inc., it is my wish that you will pay to my brother Alberto the sum of $400.00 monthly, to my sister Maria the sum of $200.00 monthly, and to my dear friend Mrs. Werner the sum of $200.00 monthly.

When my nephew Jean reaches the age of 25 years, I desire that the residue, if any, be given to him. In the event of his death then the residue shall be distributed equally to my sister Maria and my brother Alberto.

Sept. 1, 1925

RUDOLPHO GUGLIELMI

Witness:

Leo Mahoney   RUDOLPH VALENTINO."

Court Transcript of The Last Will and Testament of Rudolph Valentino
Witnessed by Leo (sic) Lou Mahoney
Page 2

"Paragraph Fourth" – As Filed in California Appeals Library

ENDORSED: 83675
FILED: SEP 10 1926,
L. E. LAMPTON, County Clerk,
By H. H. Doyle, Deputy.

IN THE SUPERIOR COURT OF THE STATE OF CALIFORNIA
IN AND FOR THE COUNTY OF LOS ANGELES.

IN THE MATTER OF THE ESTATE
OF
RODOLPHO GUGLIELMI, also known
AS RUDOLPH VALENTINO,
           Deceased.

(WITNESS)
CERTIFICATE OF PROOF OF WILL AND
FACTS FOUND.

STATE OF CALIFORNIA, } ss.
County of Los Angeles,

    I, Frank R. Willis, Judge of said Superior Court, do hereby certify that on the 11th day of October, 1926, the annexed instrument was admitted to Probate, as the last Will and Testament of Rodolpho Guglielmi, also known as Rudolph Valentino, deceased, and from the proofs taken and the examination had therein, the said Court finds as follows:
    That said Rodolpho Guglielmi died on or about the 23rd day of August, 1926, in the County of New York, State of New York, that at the time of his death he was a resident of the County of Los Angeles, State of California, that the said annexed Will was duly executed by the said decedent, in his lifetime, in the County of Los Angeles, State of California, and signed by the said testator in the presence of Raymond A. Fager and Margaret Neff Waters, the subscribing witnesses thereto; also that he acknowledged the execution of the same in their presence, and declared the same to be his last Will and Testament, and the said witnesses attested the same at his request in his presence and in the presence of each other; that the said decedent, at the time of executing said Will, was of the age of eighteen years and upwards, was of sound and disposing mind, and not under duress, menace, fraud or undue influence, nor in any respect incompetent to devise and bequeath his estate.
    IN WITNESS WHEREOF, I have signed this Certificate, and caused the same to be attested by the Clerk of said Court under the seal thereof, this 12th day of November, 1926.

(SEAL)

Frank R. Willis,
Judge of said Superior Court,
Attest: L. E. LAMPTON, County Clerk,
By F. A. Hudson, Deputy.

FILED: NOV 12 1926,
L. E. LAMPTON, County Clerk,
By F. A. Hudson, Deputy.

ENTERED: DEC 7 1926,
By D. Keene,
Compared _____Deputy.

Certification of Will Filed with Probate Court -1926

Standard Register®

DATE:_____ CASE
                      NUMBER:_____

CASE NAME: _____

NAME:_____

STREET ADDRESS:_____

CITY/ZIP:_____ TELEPHONE NUMBER: (   )_____

( ) PUBLIC ( ) COURT STAFF ( ) ATTORNEY ( ) ATTORNEY SERVICE #:_____

WHERE FILE WILL BE USED:_____

CHARGED OUT TO:_____ BOX LOC:_____

( ) DL#:_____ ( ) BAR#:_____ ( ) OTHER ID#:_____

( ) FILE/VOL #'S:_____ ( ) MICROFILM ( ) MICROFICHE#:_____

"WARNING! - READ THIS - YOU COULD BE SENT TO PRISON!"

DO NOT REMOVE, DAMAGE OR CONCEAL A COURT FILE OR CHANGE OR TAKE ANYTHING OUT OF IT OR TAKE IT APART FOR ANY REASON. IF YOU DO, YOU ARE GUILTY OF A SERIOUS CRIME, AND COULD BE SENT TO STATE PRISON. (SECTIONS 6200 AND 6201 OF THE CALIFORNIA GOVERNMENT CODE).

ADM 022 8/02
REPLACES 760870

Los Angeles County Hall of Records Warning on File Request Form

SUPERIOR COURT OF THE STATE OF CALIFORNIA

FOR THE COUNTY OF LOS ANGELES

IN THE MATTER OF THE ESTATE OF,   )   Case No. P083678
)
      RUDOLPH VALENTINO,   )   AFFIDAVIT OF CUSTODIAN OF
)   RECORDS RE CASE FILE
               Decedent.   )   UNAVAILABLE FOR PUBLIC
)   INSPECTION
)
_____)

   I, JOHN A. CLARKE, Executive Officer/Clerk of the Superior Court of California, County

of Los Angeles declare:

   That I am the duly authorized custodian of the records of the above court;

   That the case file for the above subject case should normally be stored in the County

Records Center, 222 North Hill Street, Los Angeles, California 90012;

   That on April 4, 2004   made a request to inspect the case file for the

above subject case;

   That upon written request of a missing case file search was initiated on April 4, 2004.

   That based upon the preceding information, the case file for the above subject case was

not readily available for inspection by the public since , due to the case file being missing.

   IN WITNESS WHEREOF, and under penalty of perjury under the laws of the State of

California, I declare the foregoing is true and correct and hereto affix the seal of this court.

Executed on the 3rd day of May 2004, at Los Angeles, California.

JOHN   A.   CLARKE,   Executive
O f f i c e r \ C l e r k   o f
the Superior Court of California, County of Los
Angeles.

By:_____Deputy.
           J. HERRERA

Certificate of Clerk Attesting to Case File Being Missing

Jean Guglielmi, Rudolph Valentino and Alberto Guglielmi

Postscript

An Analysis by the Author

I

Mare Adriatico

Castellaneta, Province of Taranto, Italy – June 2014

It was hot, unbearably hot. Yet oddly, the wind outside my hotel room was howling. There was something unsettling about that ninety degree wind but I was doing my best to ignore it. I sat on the bed in my overly appointed, cavernous hotel room in the Casa Isabella, remote in hand, clicking through the few available television channels. I hoped to find something to drone on as background noise while I sorted through my day's research notes. Alas, Italian television can be disappointing. There are far too many dated travel documentaries and contentious political debates. However, that evening I was lucky. How perfect I thought, an episode of *Ai Confini della Realtà*; The Twilight Zone.

I turned to the work at hand as I was eager to make sense out of all that transpired during my day in Rudolph Valentino's birthplace, Castellaneta. I jotted down my initial impressions; from the long journey south from my home in Turin in northern Italy to the contrasting geography and shifting cultural nuances of the southern Italian coast some six hundred and fifty miles away.

I recalled my departure three days earlier and my anxiety over the two day drive looming before me. I say loomed, because traffic in Italy can strain even nerves of solid steel. Policing of the highways is relatively unheard of, lane demarcation lines are seen as mere "suggestions" and the speed limit is eighty-five miles per hour. Most drivers bear down on the road at a speed of at least ninety miles per hour. I was traveling with my publisher and fortunately he, an Italian, would do all the driving. Nevertheless, it would be fair to say I was in a state of pitch anxiety over the prospect of the road trip to Castellaneta.

For two days we sped along the Italian Autostrada, pausing briefly to eat the surprisingly delicious fare offered at the Autogrills.

For two days, we traveled south along the Adriatic Sea. Those were radiant, sunny days with a cloudless, azure sky and the "Mare Adriatico", the deepest shade of turquoise. Colorful beach communities popped up here and there along the shoreline with their festive coral stucco walls and red tile roofs. As we progressed further south, the air grew drier, windier and olive orchards appeared along the roadsides, often spreading on for miles. Here and there small herds of goats grazed lazily in the June heat.

The point of this journey was not to observe the landscape or jitter over Italian drivers, but to search for answers to the supposition I posed in this book alleging the possibility that Rudolph Valentino's nephew Jean could have been his love child. Of all the new material I presented in *Affairs Valentino*, I knew this would be the most controversial.

I felt I developed and documented my arguments thoroughly before presenting this premise; the timing of Valentino's sudden departure from his homeland, his bequeathing his estate to Jean and his brother Alberto admitting Rudolph once tried to adopt Jean. Perhaps the most compelling argument has always been the orchestrated cover-up of this information. If there was nothing to hide, then why hide and why the decades of subterfuge?

Thankfully, the campaign to remove publicly archived documents in order to prevent this story from ever being told, has not been a complete success. I have discovered critical documents that have been missed, archives still in existence and enough evidence to further support my theory about this mysterious aspect of Rudolph Valentino's life.

I knew from the onset of my research into the love child theory, that it might be impossible to ever prove as fact. Many decades have passed and too many publicly archived documents, which would have greatly assisted my research, are not-so-mysteriously missing. Consequently, the best I have always hoped for was to strengthen my case with new documentation.

In regards to the response to my presentation of the love child theory, I acknowledge here that the resulting fierce attacks upon me and my work by a determined few only served to strengthened my resolve to delve deeper. My first publication of the love child theory in 2011, also prompted several websites and Valentino fan forums to post wildly inaccurate accounts of my research discoveries.

Contrary to these fictional reports and lengthy, inaccurate

articles plagiarizing my work, I never stated, as fact, that Jean was Valentino's love child. I did instead leave readers to wonder and see this as an enigma. I always intended to travel south to Castellaneta; to search for more evidence and hopefully a documented resolution to this issue. As I headed to southern Italy to do so, I had no idea just how involved this new phase of my research would become.

As the sun set on my day one in Castellaneta, I sat upon the grand bed in my Casa Isabella suite, revising my schedule for day two. There was no doubt it had been an eventful day and I was anxious to get on with my research.

That day, my publisher and I were honored to have as our tour guide, the authority on Valentino's life in Castellaneta, Professor Aurelio Miccoli. He greeted us upon our arrival and escorted us on a visit to the home where Valentino was born. We then strolled the narrow streets of Castellaneta's historical district and walked along the city's main promenade to absorb the breathtaking, panoramic view of the Ionian Sea. Professor Miccoli is a native of Castellaneta and the author of the definitive book about Valentino's years in the city titled, *The Infancy of the Myth.* As he conducted his tour, I listened attentively to his running narrative as I was eager for any morsel of new information which might resolve even one of my many questions.

Although I first published *Affairs Valentino* in 2011, I never ceased in my quest to determine if Jean was Valentino's love child. In this effort, I planned to visit not only Castellaneta, but also the neighboring town of Santeramo In Colle where Jean Guglielmi Valentino's birth certificate was filed. In 2004, while living in Los Angeles, I requested a copy of Jean's birth certificate from a local researcher in Santeramo. For a fee of ten Euros, I received a hand-written transcript of the information verifying Jean's registered birth date as August 14th, 1914. This form also verified that Alberto and Ada were registered as mother and father. [1]

I knew that in Italy, at the time of Jean's birth, the process of documenting a child's birth involved registering the information with the City Clerk, or "Segretario Comunale", in the presence of two

1 Comune Di Santeramo In Colle, Provincia di Bari, Estratto dell'Atto di Nascita, transcript signed on July 28, 2004.

witnesses; most often friends or relatives. It was the duty of the City Clerk to then register this information on a separate document called a "Family Form". In Italian this is called a "Foglio di Famiglia". This document was kept on file in the city of the child's birth for posterity. I knew the basic information from Jean's birth record in 2004, but I still hoped to examine the original register. I also hoped to verify that Alberto and his wife Ada resided in Santeramo at the time of Jean's birth. Although a decade had passed since I first requested the transcript of Jean's birth information, I still had many unanswered questions.

If Jean was Valentino's love child, then who was the boy's mother? Was Alberto's wife Ada, Jean's birth mother? I also wondered why Jean was given the French version of his grandfather Giovanni's name and not the Italian version. In Italy it is tradition to name the first grandson after the paternal grandfather. Why was he named "Jean" and not Giovanni? And why did Alberto Guglielmi state in an interview he granted in 1977, that he was "not even married yet" when his brother Rudolph left for America? [2]

If this last statement was correct, then the marriage date of December 19th, 1912, which Alberto entered on his and Ada's "Petitions for Naturalization" and "Declarations of Intention", filed when they officially entered the United States and applied for citizenship, would be in error. [3] If he was not married to Ada Del Mazzone by December of 1913, when Rudolph left for America, then Jean would have been conceived out of wedlock. Why would Alberto admit this?

I also wondered why Rudolph Valentino's mother Gabrielle, a devoted, intelligent and loving woman, left her home in Taranto in 1915 to move to Besançon, France. Did she abandon her infant grandson Jean within a few months of his birth, her eldest son Alberto, daughter-in-law Ada and sister, Marie Leonie [4] in Taranto to move to Besançon? I found this to be one of the most inexplicable aspects of this mystery.

The currently held explanations for Gabrielle's departure from Taranto in 1915, with her daughter Maria, are vague, contradictory and vary from her seeking health treatment to serving the war wounded.

---

2   Alberto interviewed by *L'Italo Americano* in October 1977.
3   Ada and Alberto's "Petitions for Naturalization" and "Declarations of Intention" on file with the National Archives and Records Administration, referred to hereafter as NARA.
4   *The Infancy of the Myth*, by Aurelio Miccoli.

There is also a report she left Taranto to avoid the war. This last explanation is false as she would have been, at that time leaving an area of no military conflict to head directly towards the war with her daughter.

Besançon was not located in the area of France experiencing the most intense fighting along World War One's western front. It was, however, frightfully close and situated a mere one hundred miles from the fighting along the German and Swiss boarders. The arena of conflict in the First World War in Italy was contained well within the north and northeastern areas of the country. No direct threat was ever posed to the citizens of southern Italy, such as Castellaneta and Taranto.

Gabrielle's departure in 1915, meant that she moved to Besançon with her daughter Maria to travel to the region directly abutting the bloody western front along the French and German border. For the outbreak of the First World War occurred when the German army first attacked France through neutral Belgium on August 4th, 1914. Clearly, I needed an explanation as to why a rational and loving mother would make such a seemingly reckless move. On my day one in Castellaneta I would hear many disparate urban legends about this and nearly every aspect of Rudolph Valentino's life.

The townsfolk in Castellaneta were indeed eager to speak with me about their famous son Rudolph. Everyone I met had some story to share and all claimed a distant affiliation with their city's famous son. Some of the most conflicting reports I heard referred to the reason why Rudolph left for America. One story claimed the Guglielmi family pooled their resources to assist the eighteen-year-old "Rodolfo" in the purchase of a local farm. This allegedly transpired after his graduation from an agricultural school in Genoa in 1912. It was then he returned home to Taranto with his diploma in hand as certification of his status as a "rural agent" capable of managing a "small farm." [5] According to this Castellaneta legend, the Guglielmi relatives invested their money in the purchase of a farm for young Rodolfo, but he instead took their investment and left for America.

A second story shared with me as to why Rudolph left for America was that he possessed a great, "sense of adventure." Knowing the story as well as I did, I found this difficult to accept. I could not reconcile the thought of an eighteen year old leaving his homeland, a

---

5 *The Infancy of the Myth*, by Aurelio Miccoli

family he relied upon both emotionally and financially, a mother he adored and just before Christmas to journey impossibly far away, in the middle of winter to a destination so removed from Taranto that it would be nearly impossible for him to ever return.

A final account reported that Rudolph asked to have his inheritance from his father so he could travel to America. His mother complied and this enraged his brother Alberto. Despite these varied stories, Professor Miccoli pointed out that many in Castellaneta allege knowledge of Valentino's life there, speaking of him as if he was an adult at the time. They sometimes fail to recollect that he left Castellaneta to move to Taranto when he was nine-years-old.

Nevertheless, I kept these fresh tales in mind as Professor Miccoli continued to explain the significant landmarks on our tour of Castellaneta. When he noticed that the life-sized blue commemorative statue of Valentino was under restoration and barricaded by plastic netting, he pulled back the netting to allow my publisher and I to snap a few photographs. That day we also visited the grave of Valentino's sister Bice, who died in infancy. When I noticed the date of her death on her tombstone as being August 14th, I realized this was also the birth date of Jean. Could this be just a remarkable coincidence? Was Jean born on the very same day of the year that his Aunt Bice died?

Professor Miccoli then escorted us to a precariously narrow stone balcony atop the Castellaneta Cathedral to view the Gravina Grande, or Great Ravine. After our visit to the cathedral, we paused in a small cafe on a side street in the city's historical district. It was there Professor Miccoli finally shared a few intriguing details about the Guglielmi family.

I will not hesitate to admit that after years of research into this subject, I was rendered speechless when the Professor related that on April 19th, 1914, a few months before the registry of Jean's birth, Alberto was appointed as the "Segretario Comunale", or City Clerk of the city of Santeramo In Colle. He added that at that time, Alberto had just turned twenty-two-years-old.

I knew Jean's birth was registered in Santeramo, yet I was surprised to learn that Alberto possessed the authority to personally register Jean's birth. In his role as City Clerk, Alberto was in charge of registering all the information of the town's population including births, marriages and deaths. He was also in charge of maintaining the important documents; those Family Forms.

Italian law requires that this form stand as a family's composite history and must by law be held on file in every city or town where a family resides. A copy of this document of utmost importance is transferred from town to town as a family or individual relocates. The Family Form was and is still legally required to be on file in any city where one claims residence. This form also designates the "Capofamiglia" or "Head of the Family."

A discussion with my publisher revealed a puzzling aspect of Alberto's appointment to the position of City Clerk of Santeramo just prior to the registration of Jean's birth. He found it nearly impossible to believe that a twenty two year old would ever be appointed to such a prestigious government position. He said this would have been, and still is, a position held by an older, experienced civil worker and typically held by a lawyer with years of experience. He could not fathom that a twenty two year old would ever have been considered for such a position as they would barely have been old enough to have earned their law degree; a prerequisite for the position.

When Professor Miccoli was asked about this, he said that in regards to Alberto's qualifying law degree, he found only a record attesting that Alberto entered a third year of law school in Naples. This, we agreed, would imply his completion of the first two years. Although Professor Miccoli has conducted extensive research in all local archives, he found no publication of Alberto's completion of a law degree.

After saying good-bye to Professor Miccoli, we returned to the hotel to telephone the City Clerk's office in Santeramo and schedule an appointment for the following day. We told the City Clerk we wished to see the registration of Jean Guglielmi's birth, any documentation of Alberto, Ada and Jean's residency in the city and the Guglielmi "Family Form" which would be, by law, still on file in Santeramo's Historical City Archives.

On that first evening back in the Hotel Casa Isabella, I wrote feverishly recording my initial impressions, not wanting to forget a single detail of the day. As the Italian dubbed episode of "The Twilight Zone" played on in my background, I pondered the fate of the Guglielmi family and a little boy named, Jean.

I reminded myself that I was not there to enjoy a guided tour, not there to view artifacts and statues, but to uncover all I could about Jean Guglielmi Valentino; a young boy who, as the result of Rudolph Valentino's death would come to live, work and die in Hollywood, California. A Jean Valentino who would enjoy a long and successful career as a sound engineer in television in the 1960's. How fortuitous for the Guglielmi family, I thought, that Rudolph would become so famous in America. How his great success and his sudden death changed all their lives. His fame surely rescued the family from the obscurity of such a rural and provincial destiny.

As I sat analyzing the new information I learned that day, the familiar, eerie music of the closing of "The Twilight Zone" played and I gazed up to watch the credits rolling by. There on the screen, the "Sound Engineer" was listed as one, "Jean Valentino."

Yes, I knew the subject of my research and the purpose of my trip south, once worked on this very television show. And yes, I knew he was hired by the producer of "The Twilight Zone", his close friend and Valentino collector, William Pelf.

Another gust of hot wind rattled the ancient windows of the Casa Isabella as Rod Serling's iconic voice warned, "You're traveling to another dimension, a dimension not only of sight and sound, but also of mind; a journey into a wondrous land whose boundaries are that of the imagination." All well and good Mr. Serling; but my imagination was not enough; I needed facts. I needed documentation.

II

Someone Knew the Mayor

The following morning it was another terrifying merge back onto the Autostrada for the twenty mile ride to Santeramo In Colle. I told no one about my trek to Santeramo with my publisher; no one. I had learned some difficult lessons over the decade I had been researching Rudolph Valentino. I guess referring to those lessons simply as "difficult" could be construed as a gross understatement. Suffice to say that the opposition to my work has been so aggressive that any hint that I was about to retrieve another document, almost always guaranteed it would turn up missing. This happened so frequently that I came to refer to this as the "missing document" phenomenon. Consequently, it was "mums the word" as I headed for the Historical City Archives of Santeramo In Colle.

There was an air of definite secrecy and anticipation during the drive to Santeramo that morning. I was anxious because I requested that transcript of Jean's birth certificate in 2004. Perhaps because I did so, any documents relating to Rudolph Valentino and Jean Guglielmi would be gone. Although it took me far too long to take my opposition seriously, I eventually learned one lesson well; do not announce research destinations. So I told no one about my trip to Santeramo and hoped for the best.

Santeramo In Colle is located twenty miles northeast of Castellaneta in the Murge Highlands. By comparison to the hot winds of parched Castellaneta, the air in Santeramo was markedly fresher and cool. Our hotel, located just on the outskirts of Santeramo, was shaded by towering pine trees which were not blowing in the relentless hot winds of Castellaneta. We appeared to be the only guests registered in the hotel that morning, judging by the lack of cars in the hotel parking lot and the sleepy desk clerk. Despite the absence of fellow guests, the hotel restaurant's breakfast buffet was set graciously

435

in an empty dining room and spread to feed at least a hundred people. We checked in, perused the sumptuous buffet and then headed down the hill to the Santeramo City Hall.

The City Clerk was at attention and awaiting our arrival in his office. He rose from behind his grand desk to shake our hands and then pointed to a large, old ledger placed upon a small table. The ledger was typical of the "protocollo" Italian legal format; hardcover bound and published around the turn of the twentieth century. The City Clerk seemed eager to be of assistance and opened his precious archive to a page marked with a strip of white paper.

Although we requested to see Jean's birth registry, proof of residency and the Guglielmi Family Form, we had not yet informed the City Clerk that Alberto Guglielmi was employed as the City Clerk in Santeramo in 1914 and twenty-two-years-old at the time. When we did share this information with Santeramo's current City Clerk, he looked visibly taken aback and reiterated my publisher's sentiment expressed the previous day.

He said it would have been highly unusual for someone that young to receive such an appointment. [6]As the City Clerk mused, he repositioned the great ledger for our viewing. He then paused for a moment and turned to say with a sly smile and an air of quiet authority, "Qualcuno conosceva il sindaco"; "Someone knew the mayor."

The pages of the ledger, called the "Civil Registry" or "Registro dell'Anagrafe", were yellowed and fragile but we could easily read Alberto Guglielmi's signature on the registrations of births, death and marriages occurring during his brief tenure as Santeramo's City Clerk. There was one exception. The entry dated August 14th, 1914, Jean's birth registry, was signed by the mayor himself and witnessed by two of Alberto's employees in his City Clerk's office. The birth was registered on August 18, 1914, with the address of Alberto and his wife Ada's, Santeramo residence entered as 56 San Eligio Street.

Upon seeing the Guglielmi family's local address, the City Clerk said he would search the files to verify the Guglielmi's residency. He left his office and returned a few minutes later with a look of confusion on his face. He said he could not understand why he found no record of any registered residence in Santeramo for Alberto, Ada or Jean Guglielmi. He explained that they might have kept a legal

---

6 *The Infancy of the Myth*, Aurelio Miccoli, p. 215.

residence elsewhere, but decided this discrepancy would certainly be explained on the Guglielmi Family Form. He added that he had never encountered this situation before and found it troubling. I had seen his expression many times before throughout the research of this story. Bureaucrats charged with the safe-guarding of public archives are not happy when records are found to be missing. In somewhat of a huff, the City Clerk turned and left us again, determined to solve the mystery as to why a City Clerk would have no official record that he or his family ever lived in the city.

In this search, the dedicated bureaucrat took his sweet time. Our long wait became mounting evidence of his inability to locate the Guglielmi Family Form; a document which would certainly have once been on file for a City Clerk. When he finally reappeared, he was shaking his head saying, "Niente, Niente!" He'd found nothing. He reiterated that during his tenure he never found a single instance where a Family's Form was entirely missing. I was not so surprised. While the City Clerk scratched his head, my publisher and I returned to examining the one piece of evidence we had found; the registry of Jean's birth.

As we read the entry again, we noticed an address, apparently written in pencil in Alberto's handwriting, entered just below Jean's full name and next to the location of his birth. We leaned in for a closer look. There, incredibly, was the child's full name with the words, "Resident of Via Nizza 9 in Turin" written below.

The Santeramo City Clerk could offer no explanation why the child's address and residency would not be the same as the parents. Was this a second place of birth noted in the registry? Indeed, as we turned through the pages of the ledger just previous and after Jean's registry, there was not another similar entry.

We left Santeramo's City Clerk that day, after writing down the mysterious address of the newborn "resident" of Turin, Jean Guglielmi, as well as the address Alberto entered as his Santeramo residence on San Eligio Street. Upon leaving the Santeramo City Hall, we set our trusty Italian GPS and drove directly to the Santeramo address wondering what this "unregistered" Guglielmi home might look like.

When I first laid eyes on the San Eligio property, I could scarcely believe this edifice ever served as a Guglielmi family home. I could only blame the passing of time and had to hope that in 1914, this building's ominous entrance was then not quite as foreboding. Perhaps at that time it was a more livable and charming domicile. For we found a block of a building with but one small barred window and a barred door set inches from the curb. There were no terraces adorned with the typical Italian flower pots, no garden, no entry way and in all appearances this building appeared to serve as some sort of utility or storage facility.

I had just spent over a decade tracking down Guglielmi family records from one continent to another and of course I was not surprised to find more critical, publicly archived documents missing. This said, I was always frustrated and suspicious whenever I found them to be missing. Too many documents had been removed and despite this making my research nearly impossible, I became all the more convinced there was something of great importance that was being hidden and at all cost.

Even more surprising to me than the discovery of more missing Guglielmi public records, was learning that Alberto worked as the Santeramo City Clerk. In this position he held the ability to file Jean's birth as he wished, the authority to do so, held access to all city records and possessed every opportunity to alter a document or remove any document he felt might need to be "missing". Although Alberto was appointed to the position of City Clerk of Santeramo in 1914, by the mayor himself and with certain fanfare, I learned that day he left this position within a few months to move to the nearby city of Putignano.

There was little doubt that the next target of my research and investigation would be that cryptic, penciled-in address of the newborn Jean; Via Nizza 9 in Turin. I could not get there soon enough.

III

Via Nizza 9

At the time of this writing in 2015, some things have changed along the broad boulevard in Turin called, Via Nizza. The first three blocks of the boulevard are located just to the side of the city's main train station, Porta Nuova. The sidewalks of these three city blocks are covered with arched porches just as they have been for almost two hundred years. Via Nizza's proximity to the central train station in Turin has always made the boulevard the first landing place for immigrants. At the turn of the twentieth century the immigrants arriving in Turin were primarily from southern Italy; Naples, Taranto, Sicily. In those days, Via Nizza was populated by the city's newest residents who could only afford the cheap hotels catering to the arriving populace. The neighborhood was then known for its many red light theaters and dance halls and notorious for those women referred to as the "walking" prostitutes.

Today Via Nizza looks much the same, except the many hotels are of a certain higher quality than they were at the turn of the twentieth century and the red light establishments have closed. However, one does not have to walk along the boulevard for too long before seeing the "walking" prostitutes. Today, the side streets along Via Nizza are well known haunts for local drug dealers. And today, the immigrants pouring out of the Porta Nuova train station are not from southern Italy but from North Africa and Eastern Europe.

Immediately upon my return from Castellaneta and Santeramo, I paid a visit to Via Nizza 9. The only person I could find to speak with was the manager of a hotel next door and he offered nothing in the way of enlightenment as to the history of Via Nizza 9, the building's previous owners or residents. The only information he shared was to say that over the years the building had been divided into many apartments. I had to agree as I counted fifty-three buzzers to different apartments at that one address.

I was stymied as to how to proceed in my quest to find out why Alberto wrote this particular address as Jean's official residence in the Civil Registry in Santeramo. I decided the only logical thing to do would be to search for residency records for Alberto, Ada and Jean in the Turin Historical City Archives. I knew that on their United States immigration documents, which I retrieved many years prior, all three cited Turin as their last place of residence in Italy. [7] So I was off in search of information about Alberto Guglielmi, Ada "Delmazzone" Guglielmi and Jean Guglielmi.

The Turin City Historical Archives are still preserved on microfiche which makes the searching process laborious and the reading of the faded records extremely difficult. This facility houses the records of Turin's residents dating back as far as the eighteenth century. It is important to understand that even today, the registering of one's residence in Italy is taken most seriously. For example, after someone moves to a new address, the police visit to ensure they actually live there. The Italian Civil Code requires citizens to file one's residency information in the local Civil Registry. I lamented the fact that the addresses were filed by resident's names and that no archives existed where I could search residential records by an address. Nevertheless, I hoped to find the significance of Via Nizza 9, by researching the Guglielmi family.

My initial search revealed that only Jean was ever registered as a resident of Turin. [8] I found no evidence that any Alberto or Ada Guglielmi were registered residents. [9] I also discovered there was no Guglielmi Family Form on file and that Jean's Turin residence was entered as, "Via San Francesco da Paola, 27". As I soon discovered, this was the address of a still active and well-known private school, "Istituto San Giuseppe dei Fratelli delle Scuole Cristiane". Jean's Turin Historical City Archives residency record also noted that he lived in a "residential community"; this meant he was a boarded student living at the school. His father, Alberto Guglielmi's occupation was registered as "lawyer" and mother's name was noted as "Ada Daimazzini" with her surname circled in pencil and above this written "Del Mazzone". [10]

I then paid a visit to Jean's school, the Istituto San Giuseppe on

---

7   "Petition for Naturalizations" on file in NARA for Alberto, Ada and Jean. "Declaration of Intentions" on file in NARA for Alberto and Ada.
8   "Anagrafe della Citta di Torino", Turin Historical City Archives, Jean Guglielmi.
9   Ibid.
10 Alberto's various occupations: On his marriage record in 1912, "publicist", on NARA records first as "Writer" in 1934, as "Doctor" on Ada's "Declaration of Intention", as "Accountant" in 1940 and "Lawyer" on Jean's school registration in 1926.

Via San Franceso da Paola, where incredibly, Jean's school registration card was still on file. [11] The information on his card reported he attended the Istituto San Giuseppe for one school year, 1926-1927. He transferred into the school from the Mamiani School in Rome at twelve years old entering the American equivalency of the sixth or seventh grade. This was not surprising to me, as I knew Alberto returned to New York upon hearing of Rudolph's sudden death in 1926. Jean was registered that year to enter the Mamiani School in Rome yet enrolled in the Istituto San Giuseppe in Turin. I wondered why Turin?

Despite his boarding at the school, Jean's home address was entered on his school registration card as Corso Vittorio Emanuele II 115 in Turin. Why did Jean live at the school despite having a home address in the city? My subsequent research into the possible residents of his home address of Corso Vittorio Emmanuele II 115 turned out to be a dead end as this residence now houses several offices and apartments.

I then returned to the Turin City Historical Archives to take a second look at Jean's residency registration where I learned that he maintained his official residence at the school, Istituto San Giuseppe in Turin until 1935. It was then he changed his official residence to Hollywood, California. On my second visit to the Turin Historical City Archives, I noticed one important detail I previously missed on Jean's residency registration card. It was then I noticed Ada's last name was spelled as Del Mazzone; two words. In my initial search for Ada, I searched her name as one word, Delmazzone.

My immediate search for Del Mazzone was rewarded with the discovery of two women, Ole Del Mazzone, who married a Mr. Imperatrice and her sister Ebe Del Mazzone, who married a Mr. Baldassarri. I found nothing else on their files except the name of these womens' mother, Erminia Filomarino. Initially, I found no record of Ada Del Mazzone and wondered if this could be her family.

I then conducted a search of the mother's family name of Filomarino and discovered she was married to Vittorio "Dalmazzone". The confusion over the spelling of this unique last name was finally resolved when I located the Del Mazzone Family Form, filed under a misspelling of the father's name, "Dalmazzone". From this document I discovered that Vittorio Del Mazzone was married to Erminia Filomarino.

---

11 All Istituto San Giuseppe School Information, on file in school archives.

I also noticed a common date for all four of the Del Mazzone's official registrations in Turin; August 4th, 1914. For this reason, I assumed they were members of one family. According to their Family Form, they arrived in Turin about ten days before registering and all moved to Turin from Sampierdarena, a neighborhood in Genoa.

At that point I still had no proof these four people were related to Ada Del Mazzone Guglielmi. It was then, upon further scrutiny of the faded records, I noticed a faint notation of the Turin address of the Del Mazzone parents Vittorio and Ermina Filomarino; Via Nizza 9, the very same address Alberto penciled in as the residence for the newborn Jean.

Within days of this discovery, I sent a mailing to a list of Del Mazzone and Filomarino families as well as several families with the surname of Imperatrice and Baldassarri. I hoped there might be a distant relative eager to share the family's history. Within a week, I received a call from Mr. Vincenzo Filomarino of Taranto. He confirmed he was a relative of Ada Guglielmi and that I had indeed located her family in Turin and yes, they lived at Via Nizza 9. [12]

Mr. Filomarino's grandfather was the brother of Ada's mother Erminia and Ada's uncle. He said that Ada's mother, Erminia was one of fifteen children, including his grandfather. He added that one of the fifteen children was Ernesto, who went to live in America and knew Rudolph Valentino when he lived in New York. He verified that Ada was a sister of Ole and Ebe and that there were four other Del Mazzone siblings; sister Ida and brothers Ugo, Emo and Igo. He also related that the Del Mazzone family once lived across the street from the Guglielmi family in Taranto and this was how they knew each other.

He forwarded a photograph of Ada as well as a photograph of Jean, taken in 1926, with Rudolph and Alberto on horseback in the yard of the Falcon Lair stables. He also forwarded a copy of Alberto and Ada's hand-written marriage certificate. [13]

Despite the fact that Alberto told a reporter in 1977, he and Ada were not married when Rudolph left for America in 1913, the

_____

12 All Ada Del Mazzone family information from interviews with Mr. Vincenzo Filomarino.

13 Date of Alberto and Ada marriage also confirmed by Marriage Certificate retrieved as officially certified document from the City Historical Archives of Naples. Noted on Marriage Certificate, Ada received permission to marry at home by "justification" as reason of illness.

marriage certificate reveals that they were indeed married on December 19th, 1912. There was one other curious piece of information included in this document; Alberto married Ada in her home, then in Naples. As she was too ill that day to leave her bed, the city officials, the "Assessore", a justice of the peace and his secretary accompanied Alberto to her sickbed where the marriage was performed.

I had finally verified the address Alberto posted in Jean's Santeramo birth registry as that of Ada's parents in Turin. But as I discovered over my years researching this story, I was once again left with more questions. Why would Alberto include the address of his mother and father-in-law as a place of birth for his son, Jean? Why was Jean a resident of Turin at the time of his birth? And why did Ada's parents move there with two of her sisters from Genoa just a few weeks or days before Jean's birth?

Clearly, by end of July 1914, two families were in motion. The Guglielmi family in Taranto had somehow managed to have their twenty-two-year-old law student appointed as City Clerk in Santeramo and the Del Mazzones of Genoa were moving to Turin and an apartment at Via Nizza 9.

IV

The Pizzeria Barbin

I began researching Rudolph Valentino some time in the year 2000. During the past fifteen years, I have turned over many stones and covered this story for longer than I ever envisioned doing so. I have come to know the rocky territory and the characters in the "Valentino World" as it is often referred to. I never felt as though I was one of those characters or that I ever belonged to the Valentino World. I was a writer who investigated an incredible story and tried my best to do it justice. It was never my goal or intent to be a fan or a collector of all things Rudolph Valentino. I was not a member of the closely-knit "Rudy World" when I began my research and have remained an outsider for reasons which are too well known to mention.

In hindsight, I am able to say that the common theme in my decade of Valentino research would be a glaring headline reading "Missing Documents!" I understand things do occasionally turn up missing for one reason or another; the passage of time and unscrupulous people recognizing the cash value of a celebrity's document. However, in my case, the missing documents were revealingly selective and specific in subject and content. Consequently, many of my most significant research discoveries were made by understanding why those certain documents were missing. Major elements of this story have been told by what was not being said, by the documents which were gone; removed from their rightful locations as publicly housed archives.

I found the documents relating to Jean Guglielmi, the residency of Alberto, Ada and Jean and the court records regarding George Ullman's performance as estate executor to be those most frequently missing from public archives. [14] Despite this regrettable situation, the pieces of this mystery I was able to verify with documentation, although scant, have consistently supported the love child theory. The story holds up to the scrutiny of the evidence I was

---

14 Residency records and Family Forms missing for Alberto, Ada and Jean in Santeramo City Archives, also no evidence of residency in Campobasso City Archives, also no listings in Putignano Historical City Archives.

able to uncover.

As stated, when I began to formulate the love child theory over a decade ago, I realized this would be nearly impossible to verify with documents. For in reality, the very nature of such profound family secrets cause them to be well-guarded within a family for generations and are seldom, if ever shared.

The love child theory developed only after I discovered the George Ullman memoir. This was not Ullman's doing as he made no mention of Jean in his memoir. It was during the fact-checking process of his memoir that I discovered some one thousand pages of Rudolph Valentino's lost, or previously "missing" court documents. Only during the vetting of Ullman's memoir and these documents, did I realize the importance of such vital information as the missing second page of Valentino's will labeled as Paragraph Fourth and Alberto's claims that Rudolph tried to adopt Jean.

I wish to elaborate here upon the subject of Valentino's adoption of Jean as I first reported in *Affairs Valentino*. I reported this as it was stated emphatically by Alberto himself and there was little doubt as to the meaning of his words spoken to the *L'Italo-Americano* reporter. [15] Personally, I now doubt Valentino ever filed this adoption petition. If he did so, Alberto sharing this news with a reporter stands as a shocking revelation. In Italy, if someone petitions the court to legally adopt your child, it is required by law that you and your spouse surrender all paternal rights.

Perhaps Valentino desired to adopt Jean or threatened to do so after he and Natacha separated in the fall of 1925. Perhaps this took place at the time he made out his revised *Last Will and Testament* bequeathing his estate to Jean. If he did, in fact, file a petition in Italy to adopt Jean, then Alberto admitted to the reporter that he had once agreed to sign away his paternal rights to Jean.

Alberto stated that the adoption was denied as the "Italian courts refused" Rudolph's request. If this were the case, both Alberto and Ada would have been prepared, upon the Italian court's approval of Rudolph's adoption petition, to surrender all rights to Jean. The death of Rudolph Valentino made the subject a moot point and other than Alberto's own testimony and admission, I found no documents to support an actual filing.

Despite specific pieces of this mysterious puzzle being missing,

---

15 Alberto interviewed by *L'Italo Americano*, October 1977.

the existing evidence is sufficient to create a scenario which, in my opinion, accounts for every last piece of documentation I have uncovered. I present the following analysis based upon my research in two continents, over fifteen years and after having exhausted countless archives, in three languages. I share some of these relevant documents in the section following this Postscript titled, "Album Two".

୶୰ঌ

In 1924, Rudolph Valentino told a reporter for the *Los Angeles Times* he was, *"....a very troublesome boy who occasioned his mother much sorrow."* He added that no one could, *"...ever, ever know the sorrow..."* as he claimed he, *"...fell in love with a woman as old as my mama..."* [16]

At the turn of the twentieth century, there was a popular joke being told in Genoa about one of the city's toughest neighborhoods; Sampierdarena. The joke is about a man pausing in the main square of Genoa to ask which is the shortest way to the neighborhood of Sampierdarena. He is told to walk west along the sea and stop to check his watch every few minutes. The man then asks, "But how will I know when I have reached Sampierdarena?" The answer; "When you can't find your watch!" [17]

In 1913, Vittorio Del Mazzone and his wife Erminia lived in the rough Sampierdarena neighborhood of Genoa. It is not certain whether Vittorio, his son-in-law, or both men, were employed by the Italian National Railroad. However one fact has been documented; that year, at least two of Vittorio's seven children lived at home; daughter Ebe and daughter Ole. [18] His daughter Ada, married Alberto Guglielmi the previous year.

Over the years prior to moving to Sampierdarena in Genoa, Vittorio Del Mazzone moved his family frequently. The previous year, they lived in Naples and before this, in Taranto. In Taranto, the Del Mazzone family lived across the street from the widow Gabrielle Barbin Guglielmi, her two sons, Alberto and Rodolfo and daughter

---

16 *The Los Angeles Times* - 12/21/24, article titled, *"Secrets of Valentino's Life."*
17 Joke about Sampierdarena, Renato Floris.
18 Anagrafe della Citta di Torino, Del Mazone Family Form and residency registration cards.

446

Maria. [19] And in 1912, when Ada and Alberto were married, Vittorio Del Mazzone and his family were living in Naples.

The urgency of Ada and Alberto's wedding might have had something to do with the Del Mazzone parent's impending move in 1913. For by that time, father Vittorio was again preparing to relocate and this time to Sampierdarena in Genoa.

As the Del Mazzones moved from Naples to Genoa, Rudolph Valentino had just completed his schooling in Genoa where he attended the technical school; the Royal School of Agriculture Bernardo Marsano in the neighborhood of Sant'Ilario. He was enrolled in this school in 1910, at fifteen years of age and boarded there for two years. By 1912, he returned to Taranto.

With his qualification as a "rural agent", it is said he traveled to Paris to visit his mother's relatives before returning home from Genoa. Other reports claim he then stopped to gamble at the casinos in Monte Carlo and lost a great deal or all of his money. This has been disputed as he would have had to prove his age as twenty-one to enter a casino in Monte Carlo at the time. He was seventeen. One account is widely reported and generally accepted as true, during the summer of 1913, Rudolph gained a reputation locally as a Casanova.

While he was dallying with the women of Taranto, a twenty-five-year-old Ada and her husband, twenty-one-year-old Alberto moved back to Taranto from Naples and the Del Mazzone family moved north to Sampierdarena in Genoa. From that fateful summer of 1913 on, the stories of the Guglielmi and Del Mazzone families forever merged.

∾♥♥∾

..." I am happy but my heart is heavy with regret. I am a success, but beyond there is something that I dare never speak of..."[20]
Rudolph Valentino speaks with his *Blood and Sand* co-star,
Rosa Rosanova

I found it logical to deduce that the Guglielmi family was forced to deal with some devastating event which occurred by the end of the summer of 1913 and early fall. I allege this event was so

---

19 Interview with Mr. Vincenzo Filomarino.
20 Interview with Rosa Rosanova, *New York Times*, 8/25/1926, "Screen Mother Recalls Movie Life of Valentino. Also, *Los Angeles Times*, 8/25/1926, "Sheik Declared Lovelorn".

grievous as to prompt the drastic banishment of Rudolph Valentino by his mother Gabrielle in December of that year. What could have prompted such an action and at a time of year when the Atlantic winter seas were rough and families in Italy traditionally celebrate the holidays for two weeks? Why would Rudolph be exiled and alone, so hopelessly far from home at such a young age? Why then?

Some insight into possible answers to these questions was provided to me in 2009. It was then I traveled to Turin to deliver a lecture at an international conference on Rudolph Valentino hosted by The University of Turin. Upon delivering my speech, a member of the audience rose to speak, introducing himself as being from Castellaneta. [21] He spoke for about ten minutes as to why Valentino left Taranto for America. He was an elderly gentleman, alleging he was born in 1930 and claiming his parents knew people in Taranto who knew Rudolph Valentino. The gist of his colorful tale was that young "Rodolfo" was shipped to far away friends and relatives in New York, because that summer he made a local man "… three times cornuto" or "…the most cornuto in Taranto"; "cornuto" meaning a man whose wife is making love to another man. In this case, the gentleman claimed that Rudolph was not only having an affair with this man's wife, but his daughter and also his son's wife.

In closing, the speaker raised his voice to pronounce with all authority; "… many men in Taranto hated Valentino because he made them cornuti." He continued by saying that many mens' wives went with young Valentino with, "great pleasure" and it was, "enough for women to just know him to want to have sex with him." Now if Rudolph Valentino left for America simply to avoid being confronted by an irate father, husband and father-in-law and to quell a dubious playboy reputation, the story and subterfuge would have ended there. As I discovered, it did not.

Could the "sorrow" so apparently tormenting Valentino that he lamented about it openly to a *Los Angeles Times* reporter years after the fact, refer only to his being an incorrigible rogue with a mighty reputation in Taranto that summer? I do not believe this to be the case. Dispatching a teen-age son to the other side of the world, alone in the dead of winter would have been far too drastic a response for just this behavior.

In Italy, then and now, such a reputation is something most

---

21 Transcript taken from online video of this speaker as provided by the University of Turin.

men admire; overtly or secretly. It is not uncommon. It is the women who bear the weight of the shame of sexual promiscuity; the man is perceived as a sexually gifted hero in the estimation of Italian men. I also believe that Gabrielle, a mother who loved her son Rudolph dearly; would never have acted rashly on his behalf, taken a family meeting lightly or made the heart breaking decision to send her dearest offspring impossibly far away without serious provocation and reason to do so. A reputation of Lothario is not considered a serious provocation in Italy. There also exists a distinct element of emergency and a sense of finality in not only the sudden departure of Rudolph in December of 1913, but in the subsequent and documented actions of everyone involved.

I believe a more probable provocation, or "shame", was the common complication resulting from promiscuous behavior. In light of the events that were about to transpire, it is not illogical to deduce that Rudolph impregnated one of those "many" women in Taranto. In the staunchly Catholic Italy of 1913, there was absolutely no birth control, no abortions and even the merest dalliance could result in a pregnancy. There was also absolutely no sex education. Unexpected pregnancies, as the result of a complete lack of knowledge on the subject of sex, were certainly not an uncommon occurrence. However, they did require that families go to extreme lengths to save the family and the mother's reputation and social status. It was also critical the family do all that was possible to establish the child's registered history and official documentation.

In a culture where women were sharply and ruthlessly defined as either "haloed Madonnas" or "debased prostitutes", an Italian family facing an unexpected pregnancy would go to extremes to prevent the mother from being known as a "fallen woman". There was no integration between the rigid classifications of women as either temptress or Madonna and an unwanted pregnancy was a call for swift action.

Such a complication could have been resolved by marriage. If this had happened, then the story would have ended there. In Rudolph Valentino's case it did not. There was no marriage yet there was a child conceived sometime around mid-October 1913; a child whose birth would be registered as having taken place during the first part of August 1914. I conclude that the timing of Rudolph's banishment was the onset of a plan which was intelligently devised and executed to prevent a family's secret from ever becoming public knowledge; the effort to protect the woman's reputation.

If this were the case, then the question remains; why did Rudolph not marry the woman? I do not believe he would have willfully abandoned a pregnant woman and he would have taken the honorable route in such a situation. Perhaps he could not do so, because she was already married.

At that time there was no possibility of divorce in Italy; couples might live separately but no one divorced. If the woman Rudolph impregnated was married, she would have to pass the child off as her and her husband's own or disown the child by placing it in an orphanage or with other family members. Such a child was often raised as a brother, sister or cousin.

The prevailing cultural attitude in Italy towards this situation at the time was to bestow some sympathies for such a pregnancy upon the husband as the "cornuto" and address all blame for the predicament upon the woman's moral weakness. However, a married woman's lover was silently admired by all for his sexual prowess. The elaborate cover-ups of an unexpected pregnancy as the result of a wife's infidelity, were not set into motion to protect the woman's lover or the betrayed husband. They were enacted to rescue the woman and the child's reputation from the stigma of illegitimacy and promiscuity.

Yet, in examining all of the evidence surrounding the timing and suddenness of Rudolph's winter departure, I found there to be an added element of profound shame. There seems to be an undeniably heavy twist on this particular story which sent two desperate families into action. If this pregnant woman was just one of Rudolph Valentino's flings in Taranto during the summer and fall of 1913, even a married woman, then this story would have ended there. It did not.

With Rudolph ensconced on the other side of the world, in New York City, by the beginning of 1914, Mother Gabrielle and the other Guglielmi family members who met at that infamous meeting which decided his fate, apparently continued developing their plan in advance of the baby's arrival that summer. Certain unique events occurred. On April 19, 1914, Alberto received the implausible appointment by the mayor of Santeramo In Colle and became a City

Clerk. For the next few months he held this position; although he either did not officially register his residency in Santeramo or hid proof of this by removing the Guglielmi Family Form from the city archives.

And some time towards the end of that July, Vittorio and Erminia Del Mazzone and their two daughters Ole and Ebe left their Sampierdarena home in Genoa to move to Via Nizza 9 in Turin. By the fourth of August, ten days before Jean's birth was registered in Santeramo, they registered their official information in the Civil Registry in Turin.

Santeramo's twenty-two-year-old City Clerk then registered Jean's information in the ledger of birth records. What prompted him to notate that the child was a resident of Turin? Was Santeramo's Mayor aware of the family's predicament and did he suggest that Alberto do so? Why was it written in pencil? Did Alberto intend to erase this at some point in the future? Was Ada living with her family in Genoa and then in Turin where she delivered the baby with her mother and sisters? Or was Jean born to one of Ada's sisters?

It was at this point in my investigation, that I turned the focus of my attention upon Rudolph Valentino's mother Gabrielle's French nationality. For Jean's first name was, as is the tradition in Italy, that of his paternal grandfather. But why was he given the French version of his grandfather's name? Why was he simply not named, "Giovanni"? Italian culture is steeped in such tradition and this was certainly an anomaly.

With Alberto's access to Santeramo's official civil registries and Family Forms, I began to question the very integrity of the records themselves. I even doubted the veracity of the actual date of Jean's birth. Had the French born Gabrielle, still mourning the deaths of her husband and her first child, determined Jean's name and even his birth date? And had Alberto acted dutifully upon his mother and the family's instructions? For "Jean's" birth date was registered as the same date, August 14th, as his Aunt Bice's death.

Had Jean, in actuality, been born in Turin and his mother, a Del Mazzone, given birth surrounded by her family who would care for her and the child? And if Ada was Jean's mother, it is worth considering in this analysis the many reports of her grave health problems during those years. Not only was she married while bedridden, but as late as 1936, when she was weighed and her height measured for her "Declaration of Intention", upon her official entry to the United States, at five feet six she weighed a mere one hundred and five pounds. Was she too ill or frail to care for the baby? Was the birth of the child physically devastating for her? In 1926, George Ullman commented upon her health when he wrote in his memoir that Ada's "illness" prevented any construction on Falcon Lair from taking place during her visit.

This said, the fact remains; with Alberto employed as Santeramo's City Clerk that summer, mother Gabrielle had ready access to a copy of her grandson's birth registry. With this in hand, she could then have documented the child and perhaps included him legitimately on her passport. I have often been asked why I thought Gabrielle, a devoted mother and woman in her sixties, would travel to France, to Besançon, near the then erupting western front of World War One. Why would she leave her new grandson Jean and son Alberto in Taranto and move so far away and to such a dangerous place? Perhaps this was not the case at all; perhaps she did no such thing.

≈⁖∾

Many records in the Besançon City Archives were destroyed in a great fire during the war and the staff in the city offices share the same story offering similar apologies for the scant available records as a result of this tragic event. Only one record remains intact concerning Gabrielle Barbin Guglielmi's life there for three years during the war; her death certificate dated January 1918.

It was upon reading this death certificate that I experienced a jolt of understanding as to the "sorrow" that haunted Rudolph Valentino, the tears he shed upon his return to Italy in 1923, and the "something that he dared never speak of." For mother Gabrielle registered herself in Besançon as the widow of "Jean Guglielmi". [22]

When she filed for her residency in Besançon, she did not use her deceased husband's Italian name, "Giovanni". Instead, she registered her husband as "Jean". Had she instructed Alberto to also register Rudolph's baby as "Jean" instead of "Giovanni" as she intended to raise the child in France? For it was within a few months after Jean's birth when Gabrielle did leave Taranto. Did she take with her a copy of the baby's birth registry making it possible for her to

---

22 Besançon Historical Archives, Ville de Besançon, (Doubs), France.

452

have the authority to cross the Italian-French border with a child, with a French name, who was registered on her passport?

On her way to Besançon, did she pass by Via Nizza 9 in Turin, to claim her grandson? Did Gabrielle's death in 1918, result in Jean being brought back to Taranto as a three-year-old where he would be raised as Alberto and Ada's son? And in 1923, did he meet his real father Rudolph for the first time and sit with him for his first known photographs?

❧

" ....Should I try again to find me a wife, let me find one who wishes to have children and who when she has had them, wishes to take care of them". [23]

Rudolph Valentino speaks with reporters in London

It is usually presumed that a wife who bears her husband's children will "wish" to care for them. What would have prompted this bitter qualification from Rudolph Valentino? Was he already painfully familiar with the harsh reality that a child's birth mother might not care for them? I wondered which Del Mazzone daughter gave birth to Jean and which one was not able to care for or did not "wish" to care for him. As I reviewed the new evidence I uncovered, I was presented with the inevitable, indelicate question; did the beautiful Ada succumb to the eighteen-year-old Rudolph's charm and good looks in 1913 as had many other women, single and married, that summer?

Did she engage in some fleeting, reckless moment or could it have been a genuine love affair she experienced with Rudolph? She would certainly know, being an "older woman", that in Italy there was no divorce, that the "sorrow" and shame of such a love would ruin two respectable families and that Rudolph had no way to support a family. If this did occur, did they have no choice but to act precisely as both families deemed necessary? As I reviewed all the evidence, I personally believe both families did exactly what was required of them and did so with grace and courage. Yet, the mystery remains; how could the family have learned that Rudolph might possibly have fathered the child? Was this discovery or perhaps a direct admittance of the fact, the source of notorious bad blood between the Guglielmi

---

23 London press interview Rudolph Valentino as he promotes *The Eagle* in the fall of 1925.

brothers? [24]

In presenting this analysis, I do so with the utmost respect for the participants of this story, realizing that life presents its challenges and families do what they must at the time, convinced this to be the best option. It would be easy in hindsight to judge, but I, for one, do not.

The possibility that Rudolph Valentino was Jean's father and Ada his mother became a further intriguing prospect for me while reading a letter Rudolph Valentino wrote to his sister-in-law, Ada in November of 1918, ten months after his mother Gabrielle passed away in Besançon, France. The letter was written in a tender and intimate tone with Rudolph speaking candidly with his sister-in-law about lovers, love, women, wives and life in America. Most notably, Rudolph wrote Ada a curious and revealing comment about the then four-year-old, Jean.

In a letter written by Rudolph Valentino to Ada dated November 17th, 1918, [25] I excerpt his Italian, "....*Vedevo Jean già diventato grande, con una bella divisa da ufficiale di Cavalleria, realizzando ciò che è sempre stato un sogno per me; poiché se ha il mio carattere deve certamente amare i cavalli e l'uniforme militare.*"

Rudolph Valentino's words as translated:

"*.....I envision Jean as having grown, wearing a beautiful Calvary officer's uniform, manifesting something that has always been my own dream; if he truly possesses my own character and grows to be like me, he will certainly love horses and military uniforms....*"

Brothers do not typically nurture visions or dream that their brother's sons will develop in their likeness, possessing their "uncles" uniquely, specific mannerisms and physical characteristics. Rudolph Valentino's "dream" for Jean to grow in his image was not a comment made as an observation as to the boy's own predilections at the time or his emulating an "uncle" he had yet to even meet. The letter was written when Jean was of an age when children are focused intently

24 Interviews with William Pelf.
25 Excerpted from passage included in the Kaplan Edizioni, Compendium of Convegno Valentino speeches, p. 78.

upon their immediate and childlike needs. Rudolph's plaintive passage, phrased as a "dream", is revealingly poignant in its obvious sincerity and longing.

⚚⚜

Today there is a single tribute in Taranto to Rudolph Valentino's mother Gabrielle; the building she once called home on Via Massari is now the Pizzeria Barbin. Those making the pizzas in the pizzeria named in her honor share some history with customers and a few photographs of Gabrielle and Rudolph decorate the humble walls of this local establishment.

Few of the hungry patrons of the Pizzeria Barbin realize this location was once the site of a mother's drama and heartache. As they enter to the enticing aroma of the pizzas being shuffled from the ovens into the waiting boxes on the counter, they may not realize that this front door was once locked by a mother, with her bag packed, her daughter Maria by her side, as she left her home in Italy and forever.

By that fateful day long ago, the Pizzeria Barbin's namesake, Gabrielle Barbin had suffered more than her fair share of profound losses; the death of her husband Giovanni, the death of her baby girl Bice, the departure of her son Rudolph for far away America. There is little doubt that upon her husband's death in 1906, Gabrielle did struggle to make ends meet and hold her family together. In the days following the death of her husband, she received a one time "social allowance" equal to four months of her husband's salary as granted to her by the Taranto City Council. [26] Times had been tough for this widow and devoted mother.

Her efforts to control and manage her son Rudolph's notorious promiscuity were in the end, a failed mission. His beauty, his flirtatiousness and irrepressible personality made him not only Gabrielle's source of great pride but also the cause of her further heartache.

I believe it is relevant at this point in my analysis to point out that Gabrielle's father, Pierre Philibert Barbin, was an engineer who designed state-of-the-art railway bridges constructed over the great ravines of the Castellaneta and Taranto area. He was a fine draftsman, a visionary designer and expert in the technical complexities of the

---

26 *The Infancy of the Myth*, Aurelio Miccoli, p. 212

construction of such magnificent structures.

It is my opinion his daughter Gabrielle inherited his ability to calculate, devise and execute complex plans. She possessed her father's scientific sense of precision and his ability to understand and incorporate into her planning even the most minute detail. Consequently, it was in some measure due to her fortuitous inheritance that Gabrielle plotted so successfully her course of action for her family. Without a doubt, the designs of both father and daughter demanded perfection as lives depended upon their wisdom and careful planning.

Today, business is swift for the Pizzeria Barbin as the images of Gabrielle Barbin and her son, Rudolph Valentino have certainly sold some freshly spun pizza pies. But in 1915, this bustling eatery was the very location where Gabrielle Barbin Guglielmi devised and launched her detailed plan; where she first began calling in favors, pulling every last string before leaving on her long and arduous journey for France.

It is my opinion that the timing of her exodus stands as evidence she made the ultimate sacrifice for the love of a newborn grandson, her son Rudolph, her son Alberto and his wife Ada. In my opinion, the evidence discovered to date reveals that it was Gabrielle who acted as architect of the salvation plan for two families. It was Gabrielle, who from her home on Via Massari, organized and executed a complex strategic effort to save the family's name, create a standing documented history for Jean and ensure that Rudolph would some day be free to know and share in Jean's life.

When the day of Gabrielle's final departure from Taranto arrived, it would be with a final twist of the heavy key, that she would have taken one last look at her home before heading for the train station. On that morning she would have assuredly taken a deep sigh before turning away from the only home she knew and her life in Taranto. In 1915, she had no inkling that her son Rudolph would become an internationally known movie star. And at that precipitous moment she had no idea that her home would one day be the Pizzeria Barbin, or that her own image would guarantee the legendary history of this particular Taranto business. On that day in 1915, as the heroine of this story took her seat on the train out of Taranto and as the train crossed the Great Ravine on the trestle designed by her father, she was not dwelling upon the future of her beloved home on Via Massari.

As Gabrielle gazed out the windows of the train wending its way north, past the olive orchards and the small herds of goats grazing in the fields, along the Adriatic Sea, she would have been saying her goodbyes. The strategy of her perfect departure would create a pristine history for her beautiful son Rudolph as he flourished into his iconic position as ultimate motif of classical beauty and elegance. While he worked his way towards a place called Hollywood, she, as devoted mother was bound for France determined to ensure his untarnished image.

A Call for Action

In the section titled, "The Search for Missing Documents" in this publication, I itemized the documents I was able to retrieve from the Los Angeles County Hall of Records. Here, I wish to call upon those who have joined forces to obscure this story, by removing records from public archives to prevent the truth from being told, to return all missing documents to their rightful locations. Only then will future researchers have access to all of the facts of this story.

I call specifically for the following currently missing documents to be returned with the hope future researchers will verify that some, if not all records are again publicly available.

Partial Listing - US

- The original and entire file of the California Supreme Court case of Guglielmi v. Ullman
- The entire Baskerville Audit report
- All evidence, as numbered and admitted, in the case of Guglielmi v. Ullman
- The original copy of Paragraph Fourth appointing Jean Guglielmi as Rudolph Valentino's sole heir as submitted to the court by Attorney Raymond Stewart
- The complete transcripts of court testimony delivered in Guglielmi v. Ullman
- Natacha Rambova and Rudolph Valentino's divorce and property settlement as entered as evidence
- The Cinema Finance loan records
-Itemization and accounting of estate assets and Ullman's book keeping ledgers as admitted as court's evidence
- Falcon Lair Grey Book original extracts.
-The original Rudolph Valentino Production Company ledgers including the Pan American Bank loan records, VAB records and all tax assessment records and payments.
-The Cosmic Arts by-laws

- The assignation of Cosmic Arts to Rudolph Valentino Productions documents and contracts
- The original United Artists contracts as filed as court's evidence
- Cosmic Arts contracts and book keeping ledgers
-Jean Guglielmi's, "Declaration of Intention", first page with photograph, which is missing from the National Archives of Registered Aliens.

Missing Documents from Italian archives:

-Proof of Alberto and Ada's Turin residency from the Turin Historical City archives
-Guglielmi Family Forms or "Foglios di Famiglia" in Turin Historical Archives
-Guglielmi Family Form missing from Campobasso
-Guglielmi Family Form missing from Filadelfia
-Guglielmi Family Form missing from Putignano
-Guglielmi Family Form missing from Santeramo In Colle
-Proof of Jean Guglielmi's Santeramo In Colle residency
-Proof of residency in Santeramo In Colle for Ada and Alberto Guglielmi
-Proof of Alberto's Guglielmi's residency and employment in Campobasso
-Proof of residency for Alberto, Ada and Jean Guglielmi in Putignano
-Proof of Ada Guglielmi's residency in Campobasso

Album Two

Courtesy of Private Collection

Valentino's Mother – Gabrielle

Courtesy of Private Collection

Valentino's Father – Giovanni

Courtesy of a Private Collection

Alberto and Rudolph – Inscription Written by Sister Maria in Her Later Years

Courtesy of the Filomarino Family – All Rights Reserved

Ada Del Mazzone Guglielmi

56 Via San Eligio, Santeramo Guglielmi Address on Jean Guglielmi's Birth
Register

Numero _476_

Guglielmi Jean Vittorio,
Gabriele Adalberto di

Alberto

(circled notation)

(1) S'indicherà la professione o la condizione.

L'anno millenovecento _quattordici_ addì _diciotto_ di _Agosto_
a ore _undici_ e minuti _cinquantacinque_
nella Casa Comunale.

Avanti di me _Alfonso Avvocato Simeone, Sindaco_

Ufficiale dello Stato Civile del Comune di _Santeramo in Colle_
Guglielmi Alberto, di anni _ventitre_
Comunale, domiciliato in _Santeramo_, il quale mi ha dichiarato
alle ore _ventuno_ e minuti _dodici_ del dì _quel_
del _corrente_ mese, nella casa posta in _Via Sant'Eligio_
cinquantasei da la Signora _Ada Del Me..._
sua moglie, gentildonna, seco lui convivente

è nato un bambino di sesso _maschile_, che egli mi presenta e a cui
nomi di _Jean, Vittorio, Gabriele, Adalberto_

quanto sopra e a quest'atto sono stati presenti quali testimoni _Bellomo Paolo_
di _Paolo_ di anni _cinquantasette_, Impiegato
Porfido Giuseppe di anni _trentatre_
Impiegato entrambi residenti in questo Comune.
Letto il presente atto agl'intervenuti, l'hanno
con me nato sottoscritto

Alberto Guglielmi
Francesco Paolo Bellomo teste
Giuseppe Porfido teste
Simeone d'Acqua

MUNE DI SANTERAMO IN COLLE
Ufficio dello Stato Civile
...a conforme all'atto originale rilasciata
uso...   Guglielmi Mario
...eramo in Colle, li _26 FEB. 2015_
L'UFFICIALE DELLO STATO CIVILE
ISTRUTTORE AMMINISTRATIVO
(Sig.ra Chiara Strippoli)

Santeramo In Colle Historical Archives

Birth Registry of Jean Guglielmi
with
Notation,
"Residente Torino, Via Nizza 9"

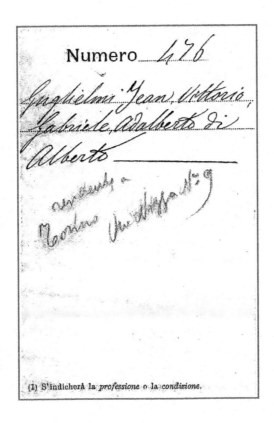

Birth Registry Detail
of
Jean Guglielmi

Jean Guglielmi Residency Register – Turin Historical City Archives

Jean Guglielmi Residency Register – Turin Historical City Archives
Reverse Side of Card

Cognome Nome	*Guglielmi Jean*		Anno scolastico	Classe frequentata	Conv. Semic. Esterno	Promosso I o II sess.	Organizz. Fantute	Varie
Figlio di	*avv. Alberto* Professione							
e di	*Delmazzone Ada*		*26-27*	*1ª Gin.*				
nato a	*Santerone in Colle* Prov. *Bari*							
il giorno	*14-8-1914* Nazionalità							
proveniente da	*5ª el. Mamiani - Roma*							
fornito di								
Inscritto il	*27-9*							
Abitazione	*c.so Vitt. Em. le 115* Telef.							
"								
"								
Osservazioni								
Documenti	Trasmessi a il							
	Archiviati il il							

Jean Guglielmi's School Registration Form

Istituto "Collegio San Giuseppe" Via San Francesco da Paola - Torino

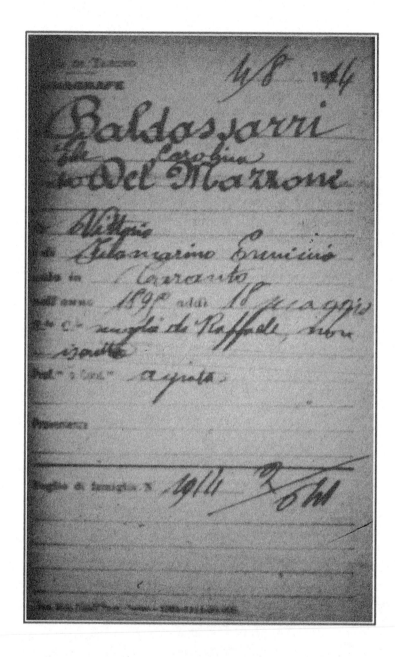

Turin Historical City Archives Residency Register for Ebe Del Mazzone
Citing "Erminia Filomarino" as mother and "Vittorio"
as Father.

Erminia Filomarino Residency Registration – Turin Historical City Archives
Citing Address as "Via Nizza 9"

Vittorio Del Mazzone Residency Registration – Turin Historical City Archives
Citing Address as "Via Nizza 9"

The Del Mazzone Family Form or "Foglio Di Famiglia"
as Registered in the Turin Historical City Archives

Via Nizza 9

Via Nizza

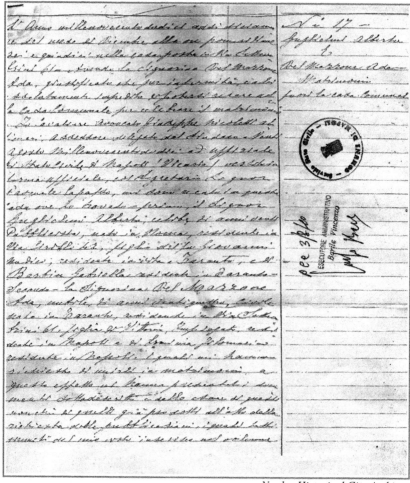

Naples Historical City Archives

Alberto and Ada Guglielmi's Marriage Record
Page One – Excerpt Translation:

..."*This year,1912, on December the 19th at 6:15 p.m., in this house being Ms. Ada Del Mazzone as justified because illness which does not permit her to go to the City Hall to celebrate her marriage, I, Sir Giuseppe Nicoletti, lawyer, Town Councilor in Naples, come to celebrate the marriage between her and Mr. Alberto Guglielmi....*"

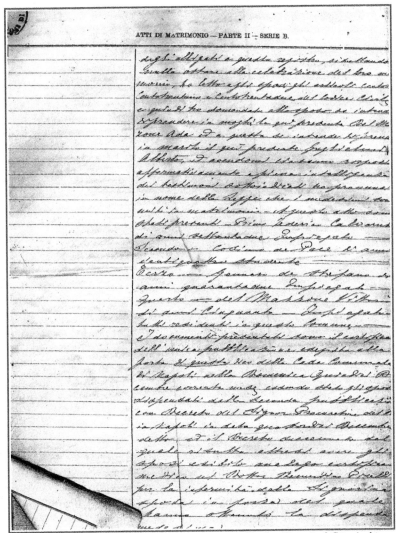

Naples Historical City Archives

Ada and Alberto Guglielmi's Marriage Certificate
Page Two

Città di Campobasso
Ufficio Anagrafe
P.zza Vittorio Emanuele II, 29
86100 CAMPOBASSO

Alla cortese attenzione del Dirigente Ufficio.

Buongiorno, sto facendo alcune ricerche genealogiche riguardo a persone che hanno vissuto in Campobasso; sarebbe utile per le mie ricerche avere le documentazioni relative alla loro presenza in Campobasso, dove risedevano, quale attività svolgessero e, se possibile, avere anche copia del foglio di famiglia.

Le persone oggetto della mia ricerca sono le seguenti: Alberto Guglielmi, Ada del Mazzone in Guglielmi e il loro figlio Jean Guglielmi ed erano certamente presenti in Campobasso nel 1923.

Vi sarei davvero grato poteste inviarmi la maggior quantità di informazioni possibile e vostra disposizione.

Nel caso ci fossero dei diritti da pagare sarò lieto di corrisponderii a seguito di vostra richiesta che potete anche farmi pervenire tramite posta elettronica, a tale scopo inserisco il mio indirizzo email: r·

Allego busta affrancata per la risposta e nel caso l'affrancatura non fosse sufficiente vi invierò, a seguito di vostra richiesta tramite email, quanto necessario per l'adeguamento del costo.

Contando sulla vostra fattiva collaborazione, porgo cordiali saluti.

N.B. Dopo accurate ricerche nel nostro Archivio Anagrafico, non è stato trovato alcun documento dal quale possiamo evincere il certificato da lei richiesto.

2 4 OTT. 2014

Campobasso Municipality City Archives

Response from City of Campobasso to Request for Residency Information for Alberto, Ada and Jean Guglielmi

..."*After careful research in our Muncipal City Archives, we did not find any documentation relating to the employment or residency for the individuals you specified...*"

Buongiorno, sto facendo una ricerca storica riguardo a una persona che, secondo dati a me disponibili, è stato segretario comunale in Putignano nel periodo tra il 1916 il 1917, il suo nome è Alberto Guglielmi, penso anche abbia risieduto in Putignano on la moglie, Ada Del Mazzone e il figliolo Jean Guglielmi.

Qualsiasi informazione a vostra disposizione e relativa a queste persone sarà utile e gradita.

Vi ringrazio anticipatamente per le informazioni che vorrete farmi avere.

Cordiali saluti

COMUNE DI PUTIGNANO
Provincia di Bari

A NOME DI GUGLIELMI ALBERTO - DE. MAZZONE ADA - GUGLIELMI JEAN NON ABBIAMO TROVATO NIENTE - MI DISPIACE - CORDIALI SALUTI -

26 FEB. 2015

L'UFFICIALE D'ANAGRAFE E LEGATO
ISTRUTTORE AMMINIST ATIVO
(LOGLISCI MICHELE)

Comune Di Putignano

Statement From Putignano Archives Attesting to No Residency or Records on File in City Archives

…." Under the name of Guglielmi, Alberto – Del Mazzone, Ada – Guglielmi, Jean – We found nothing. I am sorry – My Distinguished Salutations.

Reproduced from the holdings of the National Archives and Records Administration
Pacific Region (Laguna Niguel)

TRIPLICATE
(To be given to declarant)

No. 77377

UNITED STATES OF AMERICA

DECLARATION OF INTENTION
(Invalid for all purposes seven years after the date hereof)

DISTRICT

UNITED STATES OF AMERICA
SOUTHERN DISTRICT OF CALIFORNIA   } ss: In the ......THE UNITED STATES...... ....LOS ANGELES...... Court
COUNTY OF LOS ANGELES   of .... at ....

I, ...Ada Del Mazzone Guglielmi Valentino......
now residing at ......6776 Wedgewood Pl., Hollywood, Los Angeles, Calif....... (State)
occupation ......housewife......, aged ...47... years, do declare on oath that my personal description is:
Sex ...female..., color ...white..., complexion ...dark..., color of eyes ...brown...
color of hair ...brown..., height ...5... feet ...6... inches; weight ...105... pounds; visible distinctive marks
......none......
race ...Italian (South)...; nationality ...Italian...
I was born in ......Taranto, Italy......, on ......Sept. 28, 1888...... (Year)
I am married. The name of my wife or husband is ...Dr. Alberto Guglielmi Valentino...
we were married on ...Dec. 19, 1916..., at ...Rome, Italy..., she or he was
born at ...Rome, Italy..., on ...April 5, 1882..., entered the United States
at ...San Isidro, Calif..., on ...July 7, 1934..., for permanent residence therein, and now
resides at ...with me... I have ...one... children, and the name, date and place of birth,
and place of residence of each of said children are as follows:
...Jean, 9/14/14, Santerams, Colle, Italy, Hollywood, Calif....

I have ...not... heretofore made a declaration of intention: Number .... on .... (Date)
at .... (City or town) .... (State) .... (Name of court)
my last foreign residence was ......Turin, Italy...... (City or town) (Country)
I emigrated to the United States of America from ......Ensenada, Mexico...... (Country)
my lawful entry for permanent residence in the United States was at ...San Isidro, Calif.... (State)
under the name of ...Ada Del Mazzone Guglielmi..., on ...July 7, 1934... (Day) (Year)
on the vessel ...auto... (If other than by vessel, state manner of arrival)

I will, before being admitted to citizenship, renounce forever all allegiance and fidelity to any foreign prince, potentate, state, or sovereignty, and particularly, by name, to the prince, potentate, state, or sovereignty of which I may be at the time of admission a citizen or subject; I am not an anarchist; I am not a polygamist nor a believer in the practice of polygamy; and it is my intention in good faith to become a citizen of the United States of America and to reside permanently therein; and I certify that the photograph affixed to the duplicate and triplicate hereof is a likeness of me; SO HELP ME GOD.

Ada Del Mazzone Guglielmi
(Original signature of declarant without abbreviation, also alias, if used)

Subscribed and sworn to before me in the office of the Clerk of said Court,
at ...Los Angeles, Cal.... this ...22... day of .... anno Domini 19...36... Certification No. ...23-43589... from the Commissioner of Immigration and Naturalization showing the lawful entry of the declarant for permanent residence on the date stated above, has been received by me. The photograph affixed to the duplicate and triplicate hereof is a likeness of the declarant.

[SEAL]

R. S. Zimmerman, Clerk U. S. District Court.
Clerk of the .... Court.
By .... Deputy Clerk.

Form 2202-L-A
U. S. DEPARTMENT OF LABOR
IMMIGRATION AND NATURALIZATION SERVICE

Declaration of Intention – Ada Del Mazzone Guglielmi

Declaration of Intention, # 77377; "Guglielmi, Ada, Del Mazzone;" 1936; United States District Court for the Central District of California; Records of District Courts of the United States, Record Group 21; National Archives at Riverside.

Reproduced from the holdings of the

116

ORIGINAL
(To be retained by clerk)

UNITED STATES OF AMERICA

No. 79698

PETITION FOR NATURALIZATION

To the Honorable the __District__ *Court of* __the United States__ *at* __Los Angeles, Calif.__

This petition for naturalization hereby made and filed, respectfully shows:

(1) My full name is __ADA DEL MAZZONE GUGLIELMI__

(2) My place of residence is __2645 Bedford St. Los Angeles, Calif.__ (3) My occupation is __Housewife__

(4) I was born at __Taranto, Italy__ on __September 28, 1888.__ (5) My nationality is __Italy__

(6) My race is __So. Italian__ (7) I declared my intention to become a citizen of the United States on __August 22, 1936.__ District

Court of __the United States__, at __Los Angeles, Calif.__

(8) I am __married__. The name of my ~~wife~~husband is __Alberto Guglielmi__, (s)he now resides at __with me.__

_____ we were married on __December 19, 1912__ at __Naples, Italy__

(s)he was born at __Rome, Italy__ on __April 5, 1892__; entered the United States at __San Ysidro, Calif.__

on __July 7, 1954__ for permanent residence therein; was __not__ naturalized on _____

at _____ certificate No. _____ (9) I have __1__ children, and the name, date, and place of birth

and place of residence of each of said children are as follows:

__Jean; 8/14/14; Italy; Los Angeles, Calif.__

(10) My last foreign residence was __Ensenada, B.C., Mexico__ I emigrated to the United States of America from _____

__Tijuana, B.C., Mexico__. My lawful entry (arrival) for permanent residence in the United States was at __San Ysidro, Calif.__

under the name of __Ada Del Mazzone Guglielmi__

on __July 7, 1954__, on the vessel __Auto__

as shown by the certificate of my arrival attached hereto.
(11) I am not a disbeliever in or opposed to organized government or a member of or affiliated with any organization or body of persons teaching disbelief in or opposed to organized government. I am not a polygamist nor a believer in the practice of polygamy. I am, and have been during all the periods required by law, attached to the principles of the Constitution of the United States and well disposed to the good order and happiness of the same. It is my intention to become a citizen of the United States and to renounce absolutely and forever all allegiance and fidelity to any foreign prince, potentate, state, or sovereignty, of whom (which) at this time I am a subject (or citizen), and it is my intention to reside permanently in the United States. (12) I am able to speak the English language. (13) I have resided continuously in the United States of America for the term of 5 years at least immediately preceding the date of this petition, to wit, since __July 7, 1954__

and have resided continuously in and have had a continuous residence within the County of __Los Angeles__ State of __July 7, 1954__

for the term of 6 months at least immediately preceding the date of this petition, to wit, since __July 7, 1954__

(14) I have __not__ heretofore made petition for naturalization: No. _____ on _____ in the _____ Court

at _____ and such petition was denied by that Court for the following reasons and causes, to wit:

and the cause of such denial has since been cured or removed.
(15) Attached hereto and made a part of this, my petition for naturalization, are my declaration of intention to become a citizen of the United States, certificate from the Department of Labor of my said arrival, and the affidavits of the verifying witnesses, required by law.
(16) Wherefore, I, your petitioner, pray that I may be admitted a citizen of the United States of America, and that my name be changed to _____

__ADA GUGLIELMI VALENTINO__

I, do swear (affirm) that I know the contents of this petition for naturalization subscribed by me, that the same are true to the best of my own knowledge, except as to matters therein stated to be alleged upon information and belief, and that as to those matters I believe them to be true, and that this petition was signed by me with my full, true name; SO HELP ME GOD.

X *Ada Del Mazzone Guglielmi*
(Complete and true signature of petitioner)

AFFIDAVITS OF WITNESSES

I, __Attilio di Girolamo__, occupation __Ass't. U.S. Attorney__

residing at __900 Maltman Ave. Los Angeles, Calif.__, and

I, __Rosanita R. Evans__, occupation __Housewife__

residing at __9150 W. 25th St. Los Angeles, Calif.__

each being severally, duly, and respectively sworn, depose and say: I am a citizen of the United States of America; I have personally known and have been acquainted in the United States with __Ada Del Mazzone Guglielmi__, the petitioner above mentioned

since __September 1, 1935__, and that to my personal knowledge the petitioner has resided in the United States continuously preceding

the date of filing this petition, of which this affidavit is a part, to wit, since the date last mentioned and at _____

in the County of __Los Angeles__ State of __California__ continuously since __September 1,__ 1955

and that I have personal knowledge that the petitioner is and during all such periods has been a person of good moral character, attached to the principles of the Constitution of the United States, and well disposed to the good order and happiness of the same, and in my opinion the petitioner is in every way qualified to be admitted a citizen of the United States.
I do swear (affirm) that the statements of fact I have made in this affidavit of this petition for naturalization subscribed by me are true to the best of my knowledge and belief.

Attilio di Girolamo   *Rosanita R. Evans*
(Signature of witness)   (Signature of witness)

Subscribed and sworn to before me by the above-named petitioner and witnesses in the respective forms of oath shown above in the office of Clerk of said Court at

__Los Angeles__ this __3rd__ day of __September__, Anno Domini 19_40_. I hereby certify that Certificate of Arrival No. _____

from the Department of Labor, showing the lawful entry for permanent residence of the petitioner above named, together with Declaration of Intention No. __77877__ of such petitioner, has been by me filed with, attached to, and made a part of this petition on this date.

sj

By _____ Clerk.

_____ Deputy Clerk.

SOUTHERN DISTRICT OF CALIFORNIA [SEAL]

GPO 16—6242

Petition for Naturalization – Ada Del Mazzone Guglielmi

Petition for Naturalization, # 79698; "Guglielmi, Ada, Del Mazzone;" 1940; United States District Court for the Central District of California; Records of District Courts of the United States, Record Group 21; National Archives at Riverside.

U. S. DEPARTMENT OF LABOR
IMMIGRATION AND NATURALIZATION SERVICE

No. 23   43589

CERTIFICATE OF ARRIVAL

I HEREBY CERTIFY that the immigration records show that the alien named below arrived at the port, on the date, and in the manner shown, and was lawfully admitted to the United States of America for permanent residence.

Name: Ada Del Mazzone Guglielmi
Port of entry: San Ysidro, Calif.
Date: July 7, 1934
Manner of arrival: Auto

I FURTHER CERTIFY that this certificate of arrival is issued under authority of, and in conformity with, the provisions of the Act of June 29, 1906, as amended, solely for the use of the alien herein named and only for naturalization purposes.

IN WITNESS WHEREOF, this Certificate of Arrival is issued

Nov. 26, 1935

hls

D. W. MACCORMACK,
Commissioner.

IMMIGRANT IDENTIFICATION CARD ISSUED

Form 161   U. S. GOVERNMENT PRINTING OFFICE: 1934   14—2001

OATH OF ALLEGIANCE

I hereby declare, on oath, that I absolutely and entirely renounce and abjure all allegiance and fidelity to any foreign prince, potentate, state, or sovereignty, of whom (which) I have heretofore been a subject (or citizen); that I will support and defend the Constitution and laws of the United States of America against all enemies, foreign and domestic; that I will bear true faith and allegiance to the same; and that I take this obligation freely without any mental reservation or purpose of evasion: SO HELP ME GOD. In acknowledgment whereof I have hereunto affixed my signature.

Ada Del Mazzone Guglielmi
(Signature of petitioner)

Sworn to in open court, this .... day of ...., A. D. 19 ......

...., Clerk.

By ...., Deputy Clerk.

NOTE.—In renunciation of title of nobility, add the following to the oath of allegiance before it is signed: "I further renounce the title of (give title or titles) an order of nobility, which I have heretofore held."

Petition granted: Line No. .... of List No. .... and Certificate No. 5/86881 .... issued.

DEC 27 1940

Petition denied: List No. ....

Petition continued from .... to .... Reason ....

16—9242

Oath of Allegiance & Certificate of Arrival – Ada Guglielmi

Oath of Allegiance, #5/86881; Certificate of Arrival, # 23/43589;"Guglielmi, Ada, Del Mazzone;" 1940 & 1935; United States District Court for the Central District of California; Records of District Courts of the United States, Record Group 21; National Archives at Riverside.

Reproduced from the holdings of the National Archives and Records Administration
Pacific Region (Laguna Niguel)

No. 77378

TRIPLICATE
(To be given to declarant)

UNITED STATES OF AMERICA

DECLARATION OF INTENTION
(Invalid for all purposes seven years after the date hereof)

UNITED STATES OF AMERICA } ss: In the .... Court
SOUTHERN DISTRICT OF CALIFORNIA   of ...... THE UNITED STATES ...... at ...... LOS ANGELES
COUNTY OF LOS ANGELES

I, ... Alberto Filiberto Guglielmi (known as Valentino)
now residing at ...... 6776 Wedgewood Pl. Hollywood, Calif. ...... (Country) ...... (State)
occupation ...... Writer ......, aged 45 years, do declare on oath that my personal description is:
Sex male, color white, complexion dark, color of eyes brown
color of hair brown, height 5 feet 10 inches; weight 150 pounds; visible distinctive marks
...... scar under the nasal septum
race So. Italian; nationality Italian
I was born in ...... Rome, Italy ...... (Country) ......, on ...... 4-5-92 ...... (Day) ...... (Year)
I am married. The name of my wife or husband is ...... Ada
we were married on ...... 12-19-12 ...... at ...... Naples, Italy ...... (State or country); she or he was
born at ...... Taranto, Italy ......, on ...... 9-15-88 ......, entered the United States
at ...... San Ysidro, Cal. ......, on ...... 7-7-54 ......, for permanent residence therein, and now
resides at ...... with me ...... I have one children, and the name, date and place of birth,
and place of residence of each of said children are as follows: ...... Jean 8-14-14 Italy, resides
...... with me

I have not heretofore made a declaration of intention: Number .... on .... (Date)
at .... (City or town) .... (State) .... (Name of court)
my last foreign residence was ...... Turin, Italy .... (Country)
I emigrated to the United States of America from ...... Ensenada, Mex. .... (Country)
my lawful entry for permanent residence in the United States was at ...... San Ysidro, Cal. .... (State)
under the name of ...... Alberto Filiberto Guglielmi ......, on ...... 7-7-54 ...... (Day) ...... (Year)
on the vessel ...... auto ...... (If other than by vessel, state manner of arrival)

I will, before being admitted to citizenship, renounce forever all allegiance and fidelity to any foreign prince, potentate, state, or sovereignty, and particularly, by name, to the prince, potentate, state, or sovereignty of which I may be at the time of admission a citizen or subject; I am not an anarchist; I am not a polygamist nor a believer in the practice of polygamy; and it is my intention in good faith to become a citizen of the United States of America and to reside permanently therein; and I certify that the photograph affixed to the duplicate and triplicate hereof is a likeness of me: So HELP ME GOD.

Alberto Filiberto Guglielmi
(Original signature of declarant without abbreviation, also alias, if used)

Subscribed and sworn to before me in the office of the Clerk of said Court,
at Los Angeles, Cal. this 22 day of July
anno Domini 19...... Certification No. .... from the Commissioner of Immigration and Naturalization showing the lawful entry of the declarant for permanent residence on the date stated above, has been received by me. The photograph affixed to the duplicate and triplicate hereof is a likeness of the declarant.

[SEAL]

R. S. Zimmerman, Clerk U. S. District Court,
Clerk of the Southern District of California Court.

By .... Deputy Clerk.

Form 2202-L-A.
U. S. DEPARTMENT OF LABOR
IMMIGRATION AND NATURALIZATION SERVICE

Declaration of Intention – Alberto Guglielmi

Declaration of Intention, # 77378; "Guglielmi, Alberto, Filiberto;" 1936; United States District Court for the Central District of California; Records of District Courts of the United States, Record Group 21; National Archives at Riverside.

Reproduced from the holdings of the National Archives and Records Administration
Pacific Region (Laguna Niguel)

119

ORIGINAL
(To be retained by
clerk)

UNITED STATES OF AMERICA
PETITION FOR NATURALIZATION

No. ~~78699~~

To the Honorable the ..District.. Court of ..the United States.. at Los Angeles, Calif.

This petition for naturalization hereby made and filed, respectfully shows:

(1) My full name is ..ALBERTO FILIBERTO GUGLIELMI..

(2) My place of residence is 2645 Bedford St., Los Angeles, Calif (3) My occupation is ..Accountant..

(4) I was born at ..Rome, Italy.. on ..April 5, 1892.. (5) My nationality is § Italy

(6) My race is ..So. Italian.. (7) I declared my intention to become a citizen of the United States on ..August 22, 1936.. District

Court of ..the United States.. at ..Los Angeles, Calif..

(8) I am ....married. The name of my wife ~~or husband~~ is ..Ada.. (8)he now resides at ..with me..

..............; we were married on ..December 19, 1912.. at ..Naples, Italy..

(8)he was born at ..Taranto, Italy.. on ..September 28, 1888.. entered the United States at San Ysidro, Calif.

on ..July 7, 1934.. for permanent residence therein; was ..not.. naturalized on ....

at .... for .... certificate No. .... (9) I have ..1.. children, and the name, date, and place of birth
and place of residence of each of said children are as follows:

Jean; 8/14/14; Italy; Los Angeles, Calif/

(10) My last foreign residence was ..Ensenada, B.C., Mexico.. I emigrated to the United States of America from..

..Tijuana, B.C., Mexica.. My lawful entry (arrival) for permanent residence in the United States was at ..San Ysidro, Calif..

under the name of ..Alberto Filiberto Guglielmi..

on ..July 7, 1934.. on the vessel ..Auto..

as shown by the certificate of my arrival attached hereto.

(11) I am not a disbeliever in or opposed to organized government or a member of or affiliated with any organization or body of persons teaching disbelief in or opposed to organized government. I am not a polygamist or a believer in the practice of polygamy. I am, and have been during all the periods required by law, attached to the principles of the Constitution of the United States and well disposed to the good order and happiness of the same. It is my intention to become a citizen of the United States and to renounce absolutely and forever all allegiance and fidelity to any foreign prince, potentate, state, or sovereignty, of whom (which) at this time I am a subject (or citizen), and it is my intention to reside permanently in the United States. (12) I am able to speak the English language. (13) I have resided continuously in the United States of America for the term of 5 years at least immediately preceding the date of this petition, to wit, since ..July 7, 1934..

and have resided continuously in and have had a continuous residence within the County of ..Los Angeles.. State of ..California..

for the term of 6 months at least immediately preceding the date of this petition, to wit, since ..July 7, 1934..

(14) I have ..not.. heretofore made petition for naturalization: No. .... on .... in the .... Court

at .... and such petition was denied by that Court for the following reasons and causes, to wit:

and the cause of such denial has since been cured or removed.
(15) Attached hereto and made a part of this, my petition for naturalization, are my declaration of intention to become a citizen of the United States, certificate from the Department of Labor of my said arrival, and the affidavits of the verifying witnesses, required by law.
(16) Wherefore, I, your petitioner, pray that I may be admitted a citizen of the United States of America, and that my name be changed to ..

ALBERTO GUGLIELMI VALENTINO

I, do swear (affirm) that I know the contents of this petition for naturalization subscribed by me, that the same are true to the best of my own knowledge, except as to matters therein stated to be alleged upon information and belief, and that as to those matters I believe them to be true, and that this petition was signed by me with my full, true name; SO HELP ME GOD.

Alberto Filiberto Guglielmi
(Complete and true signature of petitioner)

AFFIDAVITS OF WITNESSES

I, ..Attilio di Girolamo.. occupation ..Ass't. U.S. Attorney..
residing at ..900 Maltman Ave., Los Angeles, Calif.. and

I, ..Rosanita R. Evans.. occupation ..Housewife..
residing at ..9130 W. 25th St., Los Angeles, Calif..

each being severally, duly, and respectively sworn, depose and say: I am a citizen of the United States of America; I have personally known and have been acquainted
in the United States with ..Alberto Filiberto Guglielmi.. the petitioner above mentioned
since ..September 1, 1935.. and that to my personal knowledge the petitioner has resided in the United States continuously preceding
the date of filing this affidavit, of which this affidavit is a part, to wit, since the date last mentioned and at ..

in the County of ..Los Angeles.. State of ..California.. continuously since ..September 1, 193..
and that I have personal knowledge that the petitioner is and during all such periods has been a person of good moral character, attached to the principles of the Constitution of the United States, and well disposed to the good order and happiness of the same, and in my opinion the petitioner in every way qualified to be admitted a citizen of the United States.
I do swear (affirm) that the statements of fact I have made in this affidavit to this petition for naturalization subscribed by me are true to the best of my knowledge and belief.

Attilio di Girolamo   *Rosanita R. Evans*
(Signature of witness)   (Signature of witness)

Subscribed and sworn to before me by the above-named petitioner and witnesses in the respective forms of oath shown above at
Los Angeles, this ..3rd.. day of ..September.., Anno Domini 19 ..40.. I hereby certify that Certificate of Arrival No. ..77878..

from the Department of Labor, showing the lawful entry for permanent residence of the petitioner above named, together with Declaration of Intention No. 77878
of such petitioner, has been by me filed with, attached to, and made a part of this petition on this date.

[signature]   Clerk.

By *[signature]*
Deputy Clerk.

ej

gpo 16—9242

No. 23 43588

CERTIFICATE OF ARRIVAL

I HEREBY CERTIFY that the immigration records show that the alien named below arrived at the port, on the date, and in the manner shown, and was lawfully admitted to the United States of America for permanent residence.

Name: Alberto Filiberto Guglielmi
Port of entry: San Ysidro, Calif.
Date: July 7, 1934
Manner of arrival: Auto

I FURTHER CERTIFY that this certificate of arrival is issued under authority of, and in conformity with, the provisions of the Act of June 29, 1906, as amended, solely for the use of the alien herein named and only for naturalization purposes.

IN WITNESS WHEREOF, this Certificate of Arrival is issued

Nov. 26, 1935

hls

D. W. MacCormack,
Commissioner.

IMMIGRANT IDENTIFICATION CARD ISSUED

Form 161 — U. S. GOVERNMENT PRINTING OFFICE: 1934 14—2601

OATH OF ALLEGIANCE

I hereby declare, on oath, that I absolutely and entirely renounce and abjure all allegiance and fidelity to any foreign prince, potentate, state, or sovereignty, of whom (which) I have heretofore been a subject (or citizen); that I will support and defend the Constitution and laws of the United States of America against all enemies, foreign and domestic; that I will bear true faith and allegiance to the same; and that I take this obligation freely without any mental reservation or purpose of evasion: SO HELP ME GOD. In acknowledgment whereof I have hereunto affixed my signature.

Alberto Filiberto Guglielmi
(Signature of petitioner)

Sworn to in open court, this _____ day of _____, A. D. 19 ____

_____, Clerk.

By _____, Deputy Clerk.

NOTE.—In renunciation of title of nobility, add the following to the oath of allegiance before it is signed: "I further renounce the title of (give title or titles) an order of nobility, which I have heretofore held."

Petition granted: Line No. _____ of List No. _____ and Certificate No. 5186834 _____ issued.
DEC 2 7 1940

Petition denied: List No. _____

Petition continued from _____ to _____ Reason _____
16—9242

Certificate of Arrival & Oath of Allegiance – Alberto Guglielmi

Certificate of Arrival, # 23/43588 & Oath of Allegiance # 5/86834; "Guglielmi, Alberto, Filiberto;" 1935 & 1940; United States District Court for the Central District of California; Records of District Courts of the United States, Record Group 21; National Archives at Riverside.

ORIGINAL
(To be retained by clerk)

UNITED STATES OF AMERICA

10?
57683

PETITION FOR NATURALIZATION

No.

To the Honorable the __District__ Court of __United States__ at __Los Angeles, Calif.__

The petition of __JEAN GABRIEL GUGLIELMI (Chariton St.)__ hereby filed, respectfully shows:

(1) My place of residence is __1960 Chariton St., Los Angeles, Calif.__ occupation is __Sound Engineer__

(3) I was born in __Santeramo, Italy__ on __August 14, 1914__ My race is __So. Italian__

(4) I declare ~~~~~ in the ~~~~

Court of ~~~~ at ~~~~

(5) I am ~~~~ married. The name of my wife or husband is __Yolanda__ we were married on __June 26, 1936__ at __San Diego, Calif.__ she was born at __Los Angeles, Calif.__ on __Jan. 22, 1913__; entered the United States at ~~~~ on ~~~~ for permanent residence therein, and now resides at __with me__. I have __no__ children, and the name, date, and place of birth, and place of residence of each of said children are as follows:

(6) My last foreign residence was __Turin, Italy / Ensenado, Mexico__. I emigrated to the United States of America from __San Isidro, Calif.__ My lawful entry for permanent residence in the United States was at __San Isidro, Calif.__, under the name of __Jean Gabriel Guglielmi__ on __July 7, 1934__, on the ~~~~ __highway (auto__ as shown by the certificate of my arrival attached hereto.

(7) I am not a disbeliever in or opposed to organized government or a member of or affiliated with any organization or body of persons teaching disbelief in or opposed to organized government. I am not a polygamist nor a believer in the practice of polygamy. I am attached to the principles of the Constitution of the United States and well disposed to the good order and happiness of the United States. It is my intention to become a citizen of the United States and to renounce absolutely and forever all allegiance and fidelity to any foreign prince, potentate, state, or sovereignty, and particularly to __VICTOR EMMANUEL III, KING OF ITALY__

of whom (which) at this time I am a subject (or citizen), and it is my intention to reside permanently in the United States. (8) I am able to speak the English language. (9) I have resided continuously in the United States of America for the term of five years at least immediately preceding the date of this petition, to wit, since __July 7, 1934__ and in the County of __Los Angeles__ this State, continuously next preceding the date of this petition, since __July 7, 1934__, being ~~~~ least six months next preceding the date of this petition.

Petition filed under Sec. 2, act of 9/22/22, as amended

No. 69628

at ~~~~ and such petition was denied by that Court for the following reasons and causes, to wit: ~~~~ and the cause of such denial has since been cured or removed.

Attached hereto and made a part of this, my petition for citizenship, are ~~~~ certificate from the Department of Labor of my said arrival, and the affidavits of the two verifying witnesses required by law.

Wherefore I, your petitioner, pray that I may be admitted a citizen of the United States of America, and that my name be changed to __JEAN GUGLIELMI VALENTINO__

I, your aforesaid petitioner being duly sworn, depose and say that I have { read / heard read } this petition and know the contents thereof; that the same is true of my own knowledge except as to matters herein stated to be alleged upon information and belief, and as to those matters I believe it to be true; and that this petition is signed by me with my full, true name.

Jean Gabriel Guglielmi
(Complete and true signature of petitioner)

AFFIDAVITS OF WITNESSES

__Rosanita Ruggiero__ occupation __Tutor__ residing at __716 Griswold Ave., San Fernando, Calif.__, and

__Eloise de Renne__ occupation ~~~~ residing at __1120½ Hyperion, Los Angeles, Calif.__ each being severally, duly, and respectively sworn, deposes and says that he is a citizen of the United States of America; that he has personally known and has been acquainted in the United States with __JEAN GABRIEL GUGLIELMI__ the petitioner above mentioned, since __October 1, 1934__ and that to his personal knowledge the petitioner has resided in the United States continuously preceding the date of filing this petition, of which this affidavit is a part, to wit, since the date last mentioned, and at __Los Angeles County__ in the County of ~~~~ this State, in which the above-entitled petition is made, continuously since __October 1, 1934__ and that he has personal knowledge that the petitioner is and during all such periods has been a person of good moral character, attached to the principles of the Constitution of the United States, and well disposed to the good order and happiness of the United States, and that in his opinion the petitioner is in every way qualified to be admitted a citizen of the United States.

Rosanita Ruggiero
(Signature of witness)

Eloise de Renne
(Signature of witness)

Subscribed and sworn to before me by the above-named petitioner and witnesses in the office of the Clerk of said Court at __Los Angeles, Calif.__ this __29th__ day of __Dec.__, Anno Domini 19__37__. I hereby certify that certificate of arrival No. __23-43587__ from the Department of Labor, showing the lawful entry for permanent residence of the petitioner above named, ~~~~ of such petitioner, has been by me filed with, attached to, and made a part of this petition on this date.

~~~~ Clerk U. S. District Court,
Southern District of California
Clerk.

By ~~~~ By ~~~~

Form 2204—LA
U. S. DEPARTMENT OF LABOR
IMMIGRATION AND NATURALIZATION SERVICE
14—8491

Petition for Naturalization – Jean Guglielmi

Petition for Naturalization, # 57683; "Guglielmi, Jean, Gabriel;" 1937; United States District Court for the Central District of California; Records of District Courts of the United States, Record Group 21; National Archives at Riverside.

U. S. DEPARTMENT OF LABOR
IMMIGRATION AND NATURALIZATION SERVICE

No. 23 43587

CERTIFICATE OF ARRIVAL

I HEREBY CERTIFY that the immigration records show that the alien named below arrived at the port, on the date, and in the manner shown, and was lawfully admitted to the United States of America for permanent residence.

Name: Jean Gabriel Guglielmi
Port of entry: San Ysidro, Calif.
Date: July 7, 1934
Manner of arrival: Auto

I FURTHER CERTIFY that this certificate of arrival is issued under authority of, and in conformity with, the provisions of the Act of June 29, 1906, as amended, solely for the use of the alien herein named and only for naturalization purposes.

IN WITNESS WHEREOF, this Certificate of Arrival is issued

Nov. 26, 1935

hls

IMMIGRANT IDENTIFICATION CARD ISSUED

D. W. MacCORMACK,

OATH OF ALLEGIANCE

I hereby declare, on oath, that I absolutely and entirely renounce and abjure all allegiance and fidelity to any foreign prince, potentate, state, or sovereignty, and particularly to ....
VICTOR EMMANUEL III, KING OF ITALY
of whom (which) I have heretofore been a subject (or citizen); that I will support and defend the Constitution and laws of the United States of America against all enemies, foreign and domestic; that I will bear true faith and allegiance to the same; and that I take this obligation freely without any mental reservation or purpose of evasion: SO HELP ME GOD. In acknowledgment whereof I have hereunto affixed my signature.

(Signature of petitioner)

Sworn to in open court, this .... day of .... A. D. 19......

........................, Clerk.

By ...., Deputy Clerk.

NOTE.—In renunciation of title of nobility, add the following to the oath of allegiance before it is signed: "I further renounce the title of (give title or titles) an order of nobility, which I have heretofore held."

Petition granted: Line No. .... of List No. .... and Certificate No. 4418000 issued.

Petition denied: List No. ....

APR 22 1938

Petition continued from .... to .... Reason ....

14-2618

Certificate of Arrival & Oath of Allegiance – Jean Guglielmi

Certificate of Arrival, # 23/43587 & Oath of Allegience, # 4418000; "Guglielmi, Jean, Gabriel;" 1935 & 1938; United States District Court for the Central District of California; Records of District Courts of the United States, Record Group 21; National Archives at Riverside.

Courtesy of Aurelio Miccoli

The Pizzeria Barbin
Via Massari, Taranto

No 58

Le dix janvier mil neuf cent dix-huit, dix heures
Gabrielle Barbin
née à Vure (Haute-Saône) âgée de soixante-un ans
sans profession fille de Pierre Philibert Barbin
et de Marie Billien décédés veuve de Jean
Guglielmi domiciliée à Besançon rue de la
République
est décédée à l'hospice civil rue Girod de Chantrans
Dressé le dix janvier mil neuf cent dix-huit, seize heures,
sur la déclaration de Hyppolyte Richard soixante ans employé
domicilié à Besançon rue Girod de Chantrans et de Sidné Machelas
soixante-cinq ans, vaguemestre domicilié à la dite ville rue des Villas
qui, lecture faite, ont signé avec Nous, Alfred Sancey Adjoint au Maire
de BESANÇON, Officier de l'État-Civil, par délégation.

No 59

Ville De Besançon (Doubs) City Historical Archives

The Death Certificate of Gabrielle Barbin Guglielmi

VILLE DE BESANÇON (Doubs)
Copie certifiée conforme
le 10 OCT. 2014
POUR LE MAIRE,
Le Fonctionnaire Municipal
Délégué

Bibliography

Archival Sources:

Margaret Herrick Library

Personal Archives of Irving Schulman, Special Collections @ University
of Southern California.

George Ullman Archives

Frank Mennillo Archives

Michael Morris Archives

Proquest Historical Newspapers

San Francisco Hastings Law Library

The Los Angeles County Hall of Records

NARA, U.S. National Archives and Records Administration, Laguna
Nigel, California and Riverside, California

Los Angeles County Sheriff's Department-Records Division-Case #481-
480 Garnishment 1947.

Los Angeles County Records Center-Archives Limited Civil-Marriage
Records 1925-1940.

Stanford's Green Library Microfiche Archives

Santeramo en Colle, Italy- City Historical Archives

Los Angeles Public Library- History and Genealogy Departments

U.S. District Court, Central Division Los Angeles

New York Public Library

New York City Historical Society

Palm Springs Historical Society Archives

New York City Police Museum Archives

The Utah Museum of Fine Arts

The University of Wyoming, American Heritage Center

Historical City Archives of Torino

Campobasso State Archive, Citta di Campobasso, Ufficio Anagrafe

Putignano City Archives, Comune Di Putignano

Besancon, France Archives, Ville de Besançon (Doubs), Le
Fonctionnaire Municipal Délégué.

Archives of the Istituto San Giuseppe, Torino

Secondary Sources:

1. Allen, Frederick Lewis. Only Yesterday, An Informal History of the 1920's, Harper & Row Publishers. 1931.
2. The Editors of American Heritage/Bonanza Books. The American Heritage History of the 1920's & 1930's. Crown Publishers, 1987.
3. The readers of Reminisce magazine. From Flappers to Flivvers. Reiman Publications.
4. Mercer, Jane. Great Lovers of the Movies. Crescent Books, 1975
5. The Editors of Time-Life Books. This Fabulous Century, 1920-1930, Volume III. New York. 1969.
6. Stuart, Ray. Immortals of the Screen. Bonanza Books, MCMLXV.
7. Schulman, Irving. Valentino. Pocket Books a division of Simon & Schuster, Inc., 1965.
8. Ellenberger, Allen R. Ramon Novarro. McFarland & Company Inc. Publishers, 1999.
9. Lambert, Gavin. Nazimova. Alfred A Knopf, Inc. 1997.
10. Walker, Alexander. Rudolph Valentino. Penguin Books, 1976.
11. Morris, Michael. Madam Valentino. Abbeville Press, 1991.
12. Lynd, Robert S. and Lynd, Helen Merrell. Middletown, A Study in American Culture. Harcourt Brace Jovanovich. 1957.
13. Finch, Christopher and Rosenkrantz, Linda, Gone Hollywood, Doubleday & Company, Inc., 1979.
14. Anger, Kenneth, Hollywood Babylon II. Dutton, Inc., 1984.
15. Hull, E. M., The Sheik, Small, Maynard & Co., 1921.
16. Encyclopedia of Women in the United States, Scholastic Inc, 1996. Produced by Shelia Keenan.
17. Scagnetti, Jack. The Intimate Life of Rudolph Valentino. Jonathan David Publishers, Inc. 1975.
18. Botham, Noel and Donnelly, Peter. Valentino, The Love-God. Ace Books, 1976.
19. Lockwood, Charles. Dream Palaces, Hollywood at Home. The Viking Press, 1981.
20. Eyman, Scott. Mary Pickford, America's Sweetheart. Donald I. Fine, Inc, 1990.
21. Kidwell, Claudia Brush and Steele, Valerie. Men and Women, Dressing The Part. Smithsonian Institution Press, 1989.
22. Negri, Pola. Memoirs of a Star. Doubleday & Company, Inc., 1970.
23. Edited by Keylin, Arleen. Hollywood Album 2. Arno Press, 1979.
24. Kobal, John. People Will Talk. Knopf, 1985.

25. Card, James. <u>Seductive Cinema: The Art of Silent Film</u>. Alfred A. Knopf, Inc., 1995.

26. Morton, H.V. <u>A Traveler in Southern Italy.</u> Dodd, Mead & Company, 1969.

27. Chaplin, Charles. <u>My Autobiography.</u> Simon and Schuster, Inc., 1964.

28. Sklar, Robert. <u>Movie-Made America.</u> Random House, 1975

29. Franklin, Joe. <u>Classics of the Silent Screen, A Pictorial Treasury</u>. Bramhall House, MCMLIX, Research Assistant William K. Everson by arrangement with Citadel Press.

30. Edwards, John. <u>One Last Time: A psychic medium speaks to those we have loved and lost.</u> Berkeley Books, 1998.

31. Edited by Sklar, Robert. <u>The Plastic Age</u>. Doubleday Canada, Limited, 1970.

32. Zierold, Norman. <u>The Moguls</u>. Coward-McCann, Inc., 1969.

33. St. John, Adela Rogers. <u>Love, Laughter and Tears, My Hollywood Story</u>, Doubleday & Company, Inc., 1978.

34. Selected and Edited by Behlmer, Rudy. <u>Memo From: David O. Selznick</u>. Grove Press, Inc., 1972.

35. Marinacci, Barbara. <u>They Came From Italy, the stories of famous Italian-Americans.</u> Dodd,Mead & Company, 1967.

36. Ullman, George. <u>Valentino As I Knew Him </u>. New York: Macy-Masius Publishers, 1926

37. Milbourne, Christopher. <u>Houdini: The Untold Story</u>. Thomas Y. Crowell Company, 1969.

38. Covina, Gina. <u>The Ouija Book</u>, Simon & Schuster,1970.

39. Swanson, Gloria. <u>Swanson on Swanson</u>. Random House, Inc., 1980.

40. Boller, Paul F. Jr. and Davis, Ronald L., <u>Hollywood Anecdotes </u>. Ballantine Books, 1987.

41. Finler, Joel W., <u>Silent Cinema,</u> B. T. Batsford Ltd., 1997.

42. Tarkington, Booth, <u>Monsieur Beaucaire,</u> Doubleday, Page & Co. 1900, Paramount commemorative edition published by Grosset & Dunlap.

43. Steiger, Brad, Mank, Chaw. <u>Valentino, An Intimate and Shocking Expose</u>. MacFadden Bartell, 1966.

44. Glyn, Elinor. <u>Beyond the Rocks</u>. The Macaulay Company, 1906.

45. French, Philip. <u>The Movie Moguls</u>. Henry Regnery Company, 1969. Published in England by Weidenfeld and Nicolson.

46. Sova, Dawn B., <u>Forbidden Films</u>. Checkmark Books, 2001.

47. Parker, Tyler, A.S., <u>The Three Faces of Film</u>. Barnes and Co., 1960 and 1967.

48. Gardner, Gerald. The Censorship Papers. Dodd, Mead & Company, 1987.

49. Leff, Leonard J. and Simmons, Jerold L., Dame in the Kimono. Grove Weidenfeld, 1990.

50. Brownlow, Kevin and Kobal, John. Hollywood, The Pioneer., Alfred A. Knopf, 1979.

51. Murray, Raymond. Images in the Dark, An Encyclopedia of Gay and Lesbian Film and Video. Plume, 1996.

52. De Recqueville, Jeanne. Rudolph Valentino. Editions France-Empire, 1978.

53. Soares, Andre. Beyond Paradise. St. Martin's Press, 2002.

54. Viera, Mark, Sin in Soft Focus: Pre-Code Hollywood, Harry N. Abrams, Inc. Publishers, 2003.

55. Basinger, Jeanine. Silent Stars. Alfred A. Knopf, 1999.

56. Larrain, Luz. Blanca Elena: Memoria Indiscreta De La Quinta Vergara. Editoral Sudamericana. 1993.

57. Bonadio, Felice.P., Giannini, Banker of America, University of California Press, 1994.

58. Leider, Emily. Dark Lover. Farrar-Strauss, 2003.

59. Mitgang, Herbert, Once Upon a Time in New York. Simon and Schuster, 2000.

60. Balio, Tino. United Artists, The Company that Changed the Film Industry. University of Wisconsin Press, 1987.

61. MacKenzie, Norman A., The Magic of Rudolph Valentino. The Research Publishing Company, 1974.

62. Shipman, Nell. The Silent Screen and My Talking Heart. Hemingway Western Studies Series, Boise State University, Boise, Idaho. @1987 by Barry Shipman.

63. Berstein, Matthew. Walter Wanger, Hollywood Independent. University of California Press, 1994.

64. Kanin, Garson. Hollywood. Viking Press, 1967.

65. Lawton, Richard. A World of Movies. Crown Publishers, 1974.

66. Mitchell, J.A., Amos Judd. Charles Scribner's Sons, 1895.

67. Beach, Rex. The Crimson Gardenia and Other Tales of Adventure. A.L. Burt Company, 1911.

68. Valentino, Rudolph. Day Dreams. MacFadden Publications, Inc., 1923.

69. Quirk, Lawrence J.. The Great War Films. Citadel Press, 1994.

70. Rogers, W.G., Wise Men Fish Here, The Story of Frances Steloff and The Gotham Book Mart. Harcourt, Brace and World, Inc., 1965.

71. Tajiri, Vincent. Valentino, The True Life Story. A Bantam Book, 1977.

72. Lawton, Richard. Grand Illusions. Charles Scribner's Sons, 1973.

73. Jarvis, Everett G., Final Curtain. Carol Publishing Group, 1992.

74. Gordon, Ruth. Myself Among Others. Atheneum, 1971.

75. Loos, Anita. Cast of Thousands. Grosset and Dunlap, 1977.

76. Golden, Eve. Vamp, The Rise and Fall of Theda Bara. Emprise Publishing, 1996.

77. Solomon, Aubre., Twentieth Century Fox, A Corporate and Financial History. The Scarecrow Press, Inc., 2002.

78. Oberfirst, Robert. Rudolph Valentino, The Man Behind the Myth. The Citadel Press, 1962.

79. Peary, Danny. Close-ups. Workman Publishing, 1978.

80. Earley, Mary Dawn, Stars of the Twenties, Observed by James Abbe. Viking Press, 1975.

81. Valerio, Anthony. Valentino and The Great Italians. Guernica, 1994

82. The editors of Entertainment Weekly. The 100 Greatest Stars of All Time. Entertainment Weekly Books, 1997.

83. Anger, Kenneth. Hollywood Babylon. Simon and Schuster, 1975.

84. Ellenberger, Allan R., The Valentino Mystique: The Death and Afterlife of the Silent Film Idol, McFarland. 2005.

85. Rambova, Natacha. Rudolph Valentino: A Wife's Memories of an Icon. 1921 PVG Publishing, original content 1926. Additional Content @ Pickford, Hala, 2009

86. Brownlow, Kevin. The Parade's Gone By, University of California Press, 1968. Behind the Mask of Innocence, University of California Press, 1992. With Bengtson, John., Silent Traces, Discovering Early Hollywood Through the Films of Charlie Chaplin, Santa Monica Press, 2006.

87. Ramsaye, Terry. A Million and One Nights, A History of the Motion Picture through 1925. paperback, Touchstone, 1986 and hardcover, 1926.

88. Belletti, Valeria. Adventures of a Hollywood Secretary, Her Private Letters from Inside the Studios of the 1920's. University of California, 2006.

89. Feretti, Fred, Café des Artistes: An Insider's Look at the Famed Restaurant and its Cuisine, Lebhar-Friedman Books, 2000.

90. Schulman, Irving, personal notes and loose manuscript pages of: The Tragedy of Valentino, An Opera Bouffe in Five Acts, The Square Trap, The Short End of the Stick and Your Hands Entrap My Quivering Heart. On file in the USC Rare Books Library, Los Angeles, California. circa 1965.

91. Chin, Gabriel, editor. <u>Seabury Investigation Report</u>, Vol.3., New York Corruption Investigation Commissions-1894-1994, William S. Hein Co., 1997.

92. Florey, Robert. <u>Hollywood d'Hier et d'Aujourd'hui</u>, Editions Prisma, Paris, 1948.

93. Florey, Robert. <u>La Lanterne Magique</u>, La Cinematheque Suiss, Lausanne, 1966.

94. Ben-Allah, <u>Rudolph Valentino, His Romantic Life and Death</u>, Gem Publishing Co., 1926.

95. Roth, Samuel. <u>The Intimate Journal of Rudolph Valentino</u>. W. Faro. 1931.

96. Valentino, Rudolph. <u>My Private Diary</u>. Occult Publishing Company. 1929.

97. Schildgen, Rachel A., <u>More Than A Dream: Rediscovering the Life and Films of Vilma Banky.</u> 1921 PVG Publishing, 2010.

98. Miccoli, Aurelio. <u>The Infancy of the Myth</u>. Viale Industria Pubblicazioni, Torino. 2015.

99. Guglielmi, Chicca. <u>Rodolfo Valentino, Una Mitologia Per Immagini</u>, Libreria Petrini, Torino, 1995.

100. Miredi, Antonio. <u>Rodolfo Valentino, Sogni ad Occhi Aperti</u>, Libreria Petrini, Torino, 1995.

101. Alovisio, Silvio. Carluccio, Giulia. <u>Rodolfo Valentino, Cinema, Cultura, Societa tra Italia e Stati Uniti anni Venti</u>, Edizioni Kaplan, 2010.

102. Ulllman, S. George. <u>The S. George Ullman Memoir</u>, Viale Industria Pubblicazioni, Torino, 2015.

103. Zumaya, Evelyn. <u>Affairs Valentino, Companion Guide, The Lost Court Documents of Rudolph Valentino</u>, Viale Industria Pubblicazioni, Torino, 2014.

Periodical Articles Referenced and Cited: (Partial Listing)

1. <u>The Literary Digest</u>, August 20, 1927

2. <u>The Literary Digest</u>, September 11, 1926

3. <u>The Literary Digest</u>, January 14, 1922

4. "Foreign News" <u>Time Magazine</u>, January 11, 1926

5. "National Affairs Section" <u>Time Magazine</u>, August 30, 1926

6. <u>The Bookman</u>, January 8, 1923.

7. "The Chaw Mank Estate, The Inside Story" <u>The Autograph Collector</u>, October 1992.

8. Huff, Theodore. "The Career of Rudolph Valentino", Films in Review, Volume III Number 4, April 1952.

9. "Early Hollywood Star Pola Negri Dies", San Francisco Chronicle, August 3rd, 1987

10. Valentino, Rudolph, "Woman and Love," Photoplay Magazine, March 1922

11. Koszarski, Richard, "The Un-Sheiking of Rudolph Valentino," The New York Times. October 27th, 1991

12. Herzog, Dorothy, "Syncopated Heart," Photoplay Magazine, May 1926, p.28

13. "We Suggest New Coiffures for the Stars," Photoplay Magazine, June 1926, p.78

14. "Turbans: Why not roll your own?" Photoplay Magazine, August 1926, p.78

15. Smith, Frederick James, "Does Rudy Speak From the Beyond?" Photoplay Magazine, February 1927, p.38

16. "Natacha Valentino inspired Paul Poiret..." Photoplay Magazine, January 1924, p.42, 43 and 44

17. "At Home After January First 1923," Photoplay Magazine, 1922 p.26, 27

18. Valentino, Rudolph, "An Open Letter from Valentino to the American Public," Photoplay Magazine, January 1923, p.34

19. Valentino, Rudolph, "When I come Back - A Promise," p.22 Photoplay Magazine.

20 Quirk, James R, "Speaking of Pictures," Photoplay Magazine, February, 1926.

21. Madden, Elsie, "Are They Making Valentino A Saint?" article contained within Schulman archives and dated 8/1928.

Index

365, 382